WHELDON'S
COST ACCOUNTING AND COSTING METHODS

WHELDON'S
COST ACCOUNTING
AND COSTING METHODS

TWELFTH EDITION

L. W. J. OWLER, F.C.I.S., A.C.W.A., F.S.S.

and

J. L. BROWN, A.C.W.A., F.Comm.A., A.M.B.I.M.

MACDONALD & EVANS
8 John Street, London W.C.1
1970

First published August, 1932
Second edition May, 1934
Third edition March, 1936
Fourth edition August, 1937
Fifth edition September, 1938
Sixth edition August, 1940
Seventh edition January, 1942
Reprinted February, 1943
Eighth edition January, 1944
Reprinted April, 1945
Reprinted September, 1945
Reprinted February, 1946
Reprinted July, 1946
Reprinted January, 1947
Ninth edition April, 1948
Reprinted July, 1949
Reprinted September, 1951
Reprinted October, 1952
Reprinted September, 1953
Reprinted May, 1955
Reprinted April, 1956
Reprinted August, 1957
Reprinted July, 1958
Reprinted January, 1959
Tenth edition August, 1960
Reprinted September, 1960
Reprinted July, 1962
Reprinted July, 1963
Reprinted April, 1965
Eleventh edition September, 1965
Reprinted (with amendments) August, 1966
Reprinted August, 1967
Reprinted December, 1968
Reprinted September, 1969
Reprinted January, 1970
Twelfth edition June, 1970
Reprinted May, 1971

©

MACDONALD & EVANS LTD.
1970

S.B.N. 7121 0324 4

Printed in Great Britain by Richard Clay (The Chaucer Press), Ltd.,
Bungay, Suffolk

PREFACE TO TWELFTH EDITION

THE ready acceptance of the eleventh edition by professional bodies and students was very gratifying. This new edition has been necessitated by the continuing developments in cost and management accountancy as a tool of management. The opportunity has been taken to convert all the examples involving £ *s. d.* to the decimal currency system, which should be of benefit to students both in the United Kingdom and overseas.

The chapters on standard costing have been updated so as to bring the variance definitions and calculations in line with the I.C.W.A. *Terminology* of 1966. The increasing importance to accountants of a knowledge of electronic data processing has necessitated a complete revision of the chapters on punched-card accounting. They have been replaced by an informative description of computers, their use in industry and the procedures required in the setting-up of a program. In this latter section of the text, the authors have had the assistance of Mr. Roy Newall, M.A., who is a member of the British Computer Society, and to whom gratitude is extended.

Profitability techniques are being adopted in business to an increasing degree and examination candidates now need a detailed knowledge of these techniques, which has required a considerable extension to the chapter on profitability. Present value factor tables and logarithm tables have been included in appendixes to facilitate profitability calculations.

In general, additional material has been added in order to extend the text to meet the increasing demands of modern examinations and efficient business management. Readers may observe that mathematical and statistical techniques have been used to a considerable extent in this edition. The authors believe that these techniques will become much more evident in examinations and in business; in fact, at least one professional accountancy body is including an examination paper on quantitative methods.

The authors are grateful to those lecturers and students who have provided constructive criticism and suggestions, some of which have been incorporated in this edition, and to the accountancy bodies for giving their permission to include examination questions. Many new examination questions have been added, and the following initials will indicate the sources from which the questions have been taken:

I.C.W.A.   The Institute of Cost and Works Accountants.
I.C.A.   The Institute of Chartered Accountants in England and Wales.

C.A.	The Institute of Chartered Accountants of Scotland.
C.A.A.	The Cost Accountants' Association.
A.C.C.A.	The Association of Certified and Corporate Accountants.
C.I.S.	The Chartered Institute of Secretaries.
C.C.S.	The Corporation of Secretaries.
A.I.A.	The Association of International Accountants.
Comm.A.	The Society of Commercial Accountants.
R.S.A.	The Royal Society of Arts.

Some examinations are no longer divided into intermediate and final but are classified in Parts, for example I.C.W.A. Parts I to V. In an attempt to establish uniformity of standards, and to give students a general idea of the level of the question, the questions have been divided into Intermediate and Final.

Acknowledgments are also due to the following companies:

Kalamazoo Ltd.
National Cash Register Co. Ltd.
Copeland Chatterson Co. Ltd.
Burroughs Adding Machine Ltd.
I.B.M. (United Kingdom) Ltd.
Remington Rand Ltd.
Shannon Ltd.
International Computers Ltd.

Use has again been made of the *Terminology of Cost Accountancy*, which is reprinted in full. Thanks are extended to the Institute of Cost and Works Accountants for permission to refer to and quote from their publications.

L. W. J. O.
J. L. B.

March, 1970

CONTENTS

vii

LIST OF ILLUSTRATIONS

CHAPTER 1

INTRODUCTION

DEFINITION OF COSTING

The *Terminology of Cost Accountancy* published by the Institute of Cost and Works Accountants gives the following definitions:

Cost accountancy

The application of costing and cost accounting principles, methods and techniques to the science, art and practice of cost control and the ascertainment of profitability. It includes the presentation of information derived therefrom for the purpose of managerial decision-making.

Costing

The techniques and processes of ascertaining costs.

Expanding the ideas contained in these definitions, it may be said that costing is:

"The classifying, recording, and appropriate allocation of expenditure for the determination of the costs of products or services; the relation of these costs to sales values; and the ascertainment of profitability."

These costs may be ascertained:

(*a*) historically, *i.e.* after they have been incurred;

(*b*) by predetermined standards, combined with subsequent analysis of variances between those standards, and the actual cost incurred; and

(*c*) by the use of marginal methods of presentation for either (*a*) or (*b*), involving the differentiation between "fixed" and "variable" costs.

COSTING AS AN AID TO MANAGEMENT

Although manufacturers are now willing to accept as a principle that costing is of value, there is still a considerable lack of appreciation by many of them as to where its value lies.

Costing enables a business not only to find out what various jobs or processes have cost but also what they should have cost: it indicates where losses and waste are occurring before the work is finished, and therefore immediate action may be taken, if possible, to avoid such loss or waste.

Business policy may require the consideration of alternative methods and procedures, and this is facilitated by cost information correctly

1

presented. For example, by the aid of cost reports management can decide whether the manufacture of certain products increases overhead expenditure disproportionately; whether to treat by-products, even if at a loss, to make possible a more important trade in another product; whether the plant and machinery could be used more advantageously by concentrating on particular products to the exclusion of less profitable ones; or whether prices could or should be adjusted.

It was stated in *Target* that:

"Probably the greatest scope for increasing efficiency and cutting costs is at the design stage. The cost accountant and the design staff should work in close collaboration, not only on new products but on old lines as well, seeking ways and means of reducing the material costs by simplification of design, the elimination of unnecessary parts or features, and by the use, where possible, of cheaper but equally suitable materials. It is the designers who are concerned with the technical points—the cost accountant supplies the figures which measure the value of each idea and the estimates of costs of new products. One of the Productivity Teams which visited the U.S.A. found a system called 'Value Analysis' in use, which reviews the design of component and assembly items by asking a series of questions, for example, of any component:

(*a*) does its use contribute value?
(*b*) is its cost proportionate to its usefulness?
(*c*) does it need all of its features?
(*d*) is there anything better?
(*e*) can it be made by a better method?
(*f*) can a standard part replace it?
(*g*) will another supplier provide it for less?
(*h*) is anyone buying it for less?"

COSTING ESSENTIAL TO INDUSTRIAL CONTROL

An efficient system of costing is an essential factor for industrial control under modern conditions of business, and as such may be regarded as an important part in the efforts of any management to secure business stability. The organisation of an undertaking has to be so controlled that the desired volume of production is secured at the least possible cost in relation to the scheduled quantity of the product. Cost accounting provides the measurement of the degree to which this objective is attained, and thus has a definite place in the organisation of the business. All expense is localised, and thereby controlled, in the light of information provided by the cost records.

COSTING IN PERIODS OF TRADE COMPETITION

When business is not difficult to secure, many manufacturers are able to show a profit notwithstanding the leakages which pass unchecked, but in periods of trade competition concealed inefficiencies have to be tracked down, and rigorous control must be exercised to ensure even modest margins of profit.

Failure to maintain normal output results in overhead expenses not being recovered in full. The value of a costing system is thus seen, since by indicating where economies may be sought, waste eliminated, and efficiency increased, some of the loss occasioned by reduced turn-over and falling prices may be avoided. Further, knowing the real cost of production, a manufacturer, when tendering, can fix the lowest possible price on the reduced output so that he may continue to enjoy a share of the market; and the importance of making use of idle capacity is pressed upon him. The probable effects of reducing prices with the object of increasing turnover can also be presented to him; and in many other ways the cost accounts provide essential data for management decisions.

ESTIMATES

Estimates, it should be observed, are not costs, from which they differ in several ways. Usually, estimates are based on present or pro-spective market prices of materials and labour and, while previously ascertained costs may be used as a guide in fixing prices, it is sometimes necessary to prepare estimates on a competitive basis, making quota-tions even below cost to avoid greater loss where there is a costly plant and fixed overhead expense is heavy.

Cost accounts, however, record the actual or maybe standard costs of materials, wages and overhead. It has been said, very aptly, that "an estimate is an opinion, price is a policy, and cost is a fact."

The ascertained costs, whether actual or standard, provide a measure for estimates, a guide to policy, and a control over current production.

DESIRABLE CONDITIONS FOR A COSTING SYSTEM

The following general conditions should be observed as far as possible when installing a costing system:

(a) The arrangement of the system should be adapted to suit the general organisation of the particular business, subject to such alterations as may be unavoidable. Usually, any scheme to alter the plan of the business to adapt it to a costing system will be unsatis-factory, and, owing to resentment of officials, there is the probability that the fullest co-operation will not be forthcoming.

(b) The technical aspects of the business should be carefully studied and an effort made to secure the sympathetic assistance and support of the principal members of the works staff and of the workers generally.

(c) The minimum amount of detail in which records are to be

compiled should be arranged. Complete analyses are desirable, but over-elaboration must be avoided. The compilation of schedules and analyses with unnecessary details involving undue clerical work will make the system costly, and disproportionate to the benefits received. Nevertheless, the costing system should, without exception, cover the whole work of production and services.

(*d*) The records to be made by foremen and workers should involve as little clerical work as possible. Printed forms should be provided, and all instructions written or printed. It is advantageous to provide written or printed instructions as to the origin, use and disposition of each form.

(*e*) To ensure reliable statistics, every original entry on factory forms should be supported by an examiner's signature, or by counter-checks.

(*f*) Promptitude, frequency and regularity in the presentation of costs and statistics must be arranged for.

(*g*) The cost accounts and the financial accounts should either be interlocked in one integral accounting scheme or be so arranged that the results of the two sets of accounts are reconciled by means of control accounts.

SUMMARY OF PURPOSES OF COST ACCOUNTS

The following summary may be useful to the student:

(*a*) To analyse and classify with reference to the cost of products and operations the same expenditure which, in the Financial Accounts, has been recorded and summarised under Nominal Account headings.

(*b*) To arrive at the cost of production of every unit, job, operation, process, department or service, and to develop cost standards.

(*c*) To indicate to the management any inefficiencies, and the extent of various forms of waste, whether of materials, time, expense, or in the use of machinery, equipment and tools. Analysis of the causes of unsatisfactory results may indicate remedial action.

(*d*) To provide data for periodical Profit and Loss Accounts and Balance Sheets at such intervals, *e.g.* weekly, monthly or quarterly, as may be desired during the financial year, not only for the whole business but also by departments or individual products.

(*e*) To reveal sources of economies in production, having regard to methods, types of equipment, design, output and layout. Daily, weekly, monthly or quarterly information may be necessary to ensure prompt constructive action.

(*f*) To provide actual figures of cost for comparison with estimates, and to serve as a guide for future estimates, or quotations, and to assist the management in their price-fixing policy.

(*g*) To show, where standard costs are prepared, what the cost of production is to be, and with which the actual costs that are eventually recorded may be compared.

(*h*) To present comparative cost data for different periods and various volumes of production output, and to provide guidance in the development of the business. This is valuable in connection with budgetary control.

(*i*) To indicate whether the cost of certain articles or components made in the factory is such that it would be more economical to buy from outside sources.

(*j*) To record the relative production results of each unit of plant and machinery in use as a basis for examining its efficiency. A comparison with the performance of other types of machines may suggest the necessity for replacement.

(*k*) To provide a perpetual inventory of stores and other materials, so that:

(*i*) interim Profit and Loss Accounts and Balance Sheets can be prepared without stock-taking and

(*ii*) checks on stores and adjustments are made at frequent intervals.

(*l*) To explain in detail the sources of profit or loss revealed in total in the Profit and Loss Account.

PRACTICAL EXAMPLE OF THE VALUE OF COST ACCOUNTS

In order that it may be clearly seen how valuable the presentation of cost accounting information may be, the following illustration is given, showing final accounts drawn up both on ordinary accounting lines and also by costing methods.

The financial accountant has prepared a simple account for the year as follows:

	£		£
Materials consumed	15,000	Sales	30,000
Wages	7,000		
Production expenses	2,000		
Gross profit (20%)	6,000		
	£30,000		£30,000
Administration expenses	2,000	Gross profit	6,000
Selling and distribution expenses	1,000		
Net profit (10%)	3,000		
	£6,000		£6,000

This reveals an apparently satisfactory net profit of £3,000, which represents 10% of turnover. However, the information is too general to be of great use to management, who need to know the profit or loss on each product, so that policy decisions can be made.

The allocation of costs to each product is one of the main functions of a cost accounting system, so that reasonably reliable production costs can be ascertained. The cost accountant may produce a simple cost statement, which may look like this:

	A	B	C	Total
	£	£	£	£
Materials consumed	4,800	3,700	6,500	15,000
Wages	1,500	2,500	3,000	7,000
Production overhead	500	600	900	2,000
	6,800	6,800	10,400	24,000
Administration overhead	700	800	500	2,000
Selling and distribution overhead	300	400	300	1,000
Total cost	£7,800	£8,000	£11,200	£27,000
Sales	10,240	10,800	8,960	30,000
Profit	2,440	2,800	—	3,000
Loss	—	—	2,240	—
Profit (%)	24	26	—	10

This statement clearly reveals to management that Products A and B are obtaining approximately 25% profit, but that Product C is pulling down the total profit to 10%. Ignoring such items as plant capacity, plant utilisation, volume of sales, etc., there are four possible courses which management may follow:

    (a) Investigate thoroughly Product C to find possible economies.
    (b) Stop production of C.
    (c) Increase selling price of C.
    (d) Produce C as a "loss-leader," i.e. produce and sell C in the hope of encouraging consumers also to buy A or B.

The cost accountant points out the facts and, where possible, suggests remedies; management must make the final decision on policy.

Examination questions on Chapters 1–4 are given at the end of Chapter 4.

CHAPTER 2

THE ELEMENTS OF COST

THE ANALYSIS AND CLASSIFICATION OF COST

If management is to be provided with the data required for cost control it is necessary to analyse and classify costs.

A classification has to be made to arrive at the detailed costs of departments, processes, production orders, jobs or other cost units. The total cost of production can be found without such analysis, and in most instances an average unit cost could be obtained, but none of the advantages of an analysed cost would be available.

Generally speaking, all expenditure may be divided into groups corresponding to the activities of a manufacturing concern, as follows:

(a) Producing departments or shops. ⎫ Expenditure of
(b) Service departments. ⎬ manufacturing.
(c) Works expenses. ⎭
(d) Administration expenses.
(e) Selling expenses.
(f) Distribution expenses.

Again, total cost can be separated under three broad headings, namely, Materials, Labour and Overhead, and these three groups of expenditure are known as the elements of cost.

THE ANALYSIS OF TOTAL COST

The total expenditure incidental to production, administration, selling and distribution may be analysed by the cost accountant as follows:

(a) Direct material.
(b) Direct labour.
(c) Direct expenses (if any).
(d) Overhead

   (i) Production   ⎫ Production or
                   Factory cost.

       1. Departmental.
       2. General. ⎬ Total costs of
       3. Services.   sales.

  (ii) Administration.
  (iii) Selling and distribution.

7

The first three items constitute prime cost, so that the elements of cost may be said to comprise prime cost and overhead. Each item is defined and explained below.

DIRECT MATERIAL

Direct material is all material that becomes a part of the product, the costs of which are directly charged as part of the prime cost. In other words, it is the material which can be measured and charged directly to the cost of the product. The following groups of materials fall within the definition:

(a) All material specially purchased for a particular job, order or process.

(b) All materials (including primary materials and raw materials) acquired and subsequently requisitioned from the stores for particular production orders.

(c) Components purchased or produced, and similarly requisitioned from the finished parts store.

(d) Material passing from one operation or process to another, e.g. produced, converted or part-manufactured material which is intended for further treatment or operations.

(e) Primary packing materials (e.g. cartons, wrappings, cardboard boxes, etc.).

The following descriptions are used in the same sense as direct materials: process material; prime cost material; production material; stores material; constructional material.

Items such as import duties, dock charges, transport of materials, storing of materials, cost of purchasing and receiving materials and cost of rectifying materials are proper additions to their invoiced price, and when this course is followed the materials are charged out at this augmented initial cost. Indirect material is covered on page 11.

Raw material. Reference may be usefully made here to the term "raw material." In the majority of instances the finished product of one industry is the raw material of another. Thus sheet steel may be the finished product of the steel rolling mill, but the raw material of a metal-cutting works. The finished product of a wool-spinning mill becomes the raw material of the weaving mill. Pulp board is the finished product of mills which pulp timber, but this is part of the raw material of the paper mill.

Circumstances arise when some direct materials are used in comparatively small quantities, and it would be a futile elaboration to make an analysis of them for the purpose of a direct charge. In the manufacture of hats or sewn boots it would be absurd to measure the value of the thread; or, in making cardboard boxes, to determine the glue cost for fixing strips of linen used for binding the corners. Such direct material as this should be treated as a production expense item.

DIRECT LABOUR

Direct labour is all labour expended in altering the construction, composition, conformation, or condition of the product. The wages paid to skilled and unskilled workers for this labour can be allocated specifically to the particular cost accounts concerned—hence the term "direct wages," which may be defined as the measure of direct labour in terms of money.

Other descriptions sometimes used are: process labour; productive labour; operating labour. Indirect labour is dealt with on page 11.

In practice there are often circumstances which permit of wages of certain classes of labour being included under the heading of direct wages which are more commonly regarded as indirect wages. This could be the case when labour, while not directly expended in altering the material or condition of the product, is specifically connected with such activity and can be accurately so identified for costing purposes. In such circumstances the wages of those directly involved in handling a particular product to the finished store or despatch may be regarded as direct. The particular circumstances within certain industries make this practicable.

In a few exceptional circumstances wages in respect of the following may be treated as direct wages: general labour, foremen, charge hands, inspection, shop clerks, internal transport, and trainees; they are, however, normally indirect wages.

DIRECT EXPENSES

Direct expense includes any expenditure other than direct material or direct labour directly incurred on a specific cost unit. Such special necessary expense is charged directly to the particular cost account concerned, as part of the prime cost. Examples of direct expenses (sometimes also known as "chargeable expenses") are as follows:

(*a*) Hire of special- or single-purpose tools or equipment for a particular production order or product.

(*b*) Costs of special layout, designs or drawings.

(*c*) Maintenance costs of such equipment.

OVERHEAD

The three elements of cost just described constitute prime cost, and all expense over and above prime cost is overhead. Prime cost plus production overhead represents production, or factory, cost.

"Overhead" may be defined as the cost of indirect material, indirect labour and such other expenses, including services, as cannot conveniently be charged direct to specific cost units. Alternatively, overheads are all expenses other than direct expenses.

In general terms overhead comprises all expenses incurred for, or in connection with, the general organisation of the whole or part of the undertaking: in other words, the general costs of operating supplies and services used by the undertaking, and including the maintenance of capital assets.

The main groups into which overhead may be subdivided are the following:

1. Production overhead, including services.
2. Administration overhead.
3. Selling overhead. ⎫
4. Distribution overhead. ⎭ Sometimes combined.

Overhead may also be classified as fixed overhead and variable overhead and this aspect of expense analysis is discussed on pages 413 and 435.

PRODUCTION OVERHEAD

This category covers all indirect expenditure incurred by the undertaking from the receipt of the order until its completion ready for despatch, either to the customer or to the Finished Goods Store. Any expenses not taken to account as a direct expense are known as overhead. Other terms used are factory overhead and works overhead.

Examples of production overhead are as follows:

(a) Rent, rates, and insurance chargeable against the works, excluding any which can be apportioned to the general administration offices, selling departments, warehouse and distribution.

(b) Indirect labour, e.g. supervision, such as salary of works managers, wages of foremen, etc.; shop clerical work; testing, gauging and examining; indirect labour in connection with production shops.

(c) Power (steam, gas, electric, hydraulic, compressed air) and other services in aid of production; process fuel; internal transport; canteens, etc.

(d) Consumable stores, and all forms of indirect material, i.e. material which cannot be traced as part of the finished product, such as cotton waste, grease and oil, small tools, etc.

(e) Depreciation, maintenance, and repairs of buildings, plant, machinery, tools, etc.

(f) Sundry expenses re personnel, such as employment office, works police, rewards for suggestions and all forms of welfare, such as canteens, recreation, first aid, works entertainments, works news-papers, radio music and safety first.

Indirect material. In its strict sense, indirect material is material that cannot be traced as part of the product. It usually comprises materials required for operating and maintaining the plant and equip-ment, commonly called "consumable stores" (*e.g.* lubricants, cotton waste, belt fasteners) and items like hand tools and works stationery. Sometimes minor items of material which enter into production are treated as indirect material because of the futility of attempting minute analysis, as mentioned above in the last paragraph of the section dealing with direct materials (page 9).

Indirect labour. This may be defined as labour expended that does not alter the construction, conformation, composition or condition of the product, but which contributes generally to such work and to the completion of the product and its progressive movement and handling up to the point of despatch. It is sometimes referred to as "non-productive" labour, but this is an inaccurate description, and one which has fallen into disuse as being contrary to modern conceptions.

Indirect wages. This term may be defined as the measure of indirect labour expressed in terms of remuneration paid. Under this heading are included the following:

> Supervisors, foremen and chargehands.
> Inspection.
> Labourers and general handling of work and materials.
> Storekeepers.
> Work checkers and recorders.
> Maintenance services, oilers, cleaners and repairers.
> Instructors.
> Transport.
> Drawing office.
> Tool room.
> Works clerical staff.
> Idle time of operatives.
> Works police, gatemen, etc.
> Welfare services.
> Any wages which cannot be identified as directly chargeable to prime cost as direct wages.

Whether materials or labour are indirect or otherwise largely depends on circumstances obtaining in particular businesses.

ADMINISTRATION OVERHEAD

This consists of all expense incurred in the direction, control and administration (including secretarial, accounting and financial control) of an undertaking.

Examples are the expenses in running the general offices, *e.g.* office rent, light, heat, salaries and wages of clerks, secretaries and accountants, credit approval, cash collection and treasurer's department, general managers, directors, executives; legal and accounting machine services; investigations and experiments; and miscellaneous fixed charges.

SELLING AND DISTRIBUTION OVERHEAD

Selling overhead

This portion of the overhead comprises the cost to producers or distributors of soliciting and securing orders for the articles or commodities dealt in, and of efforts to find and retain customers. It includes advertising; salaries and commission of sales manager, travellers, and agents; training of salesmen and sales correspondents; the cost of preparing tenders and estimates for special selling projects; sales stock shortages; rent of salerooms and offices; consumer service and service after sales, etc.; demonstrators and technical advisers to customers or prospective customers.

Distribution overhead

This comprises all expenditure incurred from the time the product is completed in the works until it reaches its destination. Under this heading would be included warehouse or finished-stock-store charges, and the cost of transporting goods thereto, packing-cases, loading, carriage outwards, and of goods on sale or return, upkeep and running of delivery vehicles, despatch clerks and labourers, and other items of like nature.

Selling and distribution overheads are collected and analysed as follows:

(*a*) According to the nature of the expense, and also by function, *e.g.* advertising, salesmen, showrooms, storage, etc.

(*b*) By location, *e.g.* representatives' territories, agents, markets, counties, countries, etc.; by departments, depots, etc.; or by type or grade of products. For the distribution of such costs various factors may be used, according to which is most suitable as regards incidence. Suggested factors are units of product, weights, values by selling turnover, time, distance, cubic capacity, invoices and so on. The object is to show the relationship of sales turnover to costs, and the relationship of sales turnover to the potential market. Hence the analysis of sales turnover and of these costs must be on the same basis. The effectiveness of these expenses towards profit earnings can then be measured.

THE METHODS OF COST ACCOUNTING

The general fundamental principles of cost ascertainment are the same in every system of cost accounting, but the methods of collating and presenting the costs vary with the type of production to be costed.

Seven methods of costing for the ascertainment of *actual* costs may be identified, although basically there are two major groupings: (*a*) job costing, (*b*) unit or process costing. The names given to the seven methods are used as a convenient means of referring to the variations of procedure for different types of production.

The methods are as follows:

(*a*) *Unit costing*, formerly known as "output" or "single output" costing; originally the term referred to the costing of goods.

(*b*) *Operating costing*. Actually this is unit costing as applied to the costing of services. Unit costs may be presented in a variety of aspects in respect of the same expenditure.

(*c*) *Job costing*, sometimes referred to as "terminal" costing. It also includes "contract" costing.

(*d*) *Batch costing*, which is a form of job costing, a convenient batch of production being treated as a "job." The batch cost is then used to determine the unit cost of the articles produced.

(*e*) *Process costing*, sometimes referred to as "average" costing.

(*f*) *Operation costing*, a method of unit costing by operation connected with mass production and repetitive production.

(*g*) *Multiple or composite costing*, used when there are a variety of components separately produced, and subsequently assembled in a complex production (*e.g.* motor cars, aeroplanes).

In addition to costs found by the above methods, mention should be made of two other kinds of cost determined for special purposes of control and policy, namely:

(*a*) standard or predetermined costs;
(*b*) marginal costs.

Any of the above-mentioned methods may be the basis of a uniform system of costing.

Examination questions on Chapters 1–4 *are given at the end of Chapter* 4.

CHAPTER 3

FACTORY ORGANISATION IN CONJUNCTION WITH THE COSTING SYSTEM

PRODUCTION EFFICIENCY

The organisation of a factory or workshop has for its aim efficient production—this efficiency being measured by the number of articles produced, the quality and price of the production, and the quickness of delivery. The requirements for successful competition are that production must be expeditious, correct and at a minimum cost.

The attainment of these objectives demands careful organisation, good management and the fullest use of plant and the other agents of production. The inclusion of a system of costing provides a reliable means of measuring the extent to which the management succeeds in achieving these objectives.

THE NEED FOR CO-OPERATION

It is essential that the works system and routine should include arrangements for providing the cost accountant with the figures and information necessary for preparing the cost data. A costing system, however good, cannot function properly if the works organisation is unsatisfactory, and, therefore, it is desirable that the system should be drawn up in collaboration with the works manager, and, probably, departmental heads, so that the full co-operation of all concerned may be secured. Every effort should be made to eliminate friction and departmental jealousy, and to adopt all suggestions which will tend to make the arrangements run smoothly with the least possible trouble in the workshops.

THE SCHEME OF ADMINISTRATION AND MANAGEMENT

Particular and varying conditions in different industries and works make it impracticable to describe a standard system of works organisation which would be universally suitable, but the principles of works management and organisation can be outlined. For present purposes it will be sufficient to describe the functions of the various departments and officials in a representative works. Others are referred to in later chapters dealing with systems in specific industries. In large works the duties and responsibilities are shared by more officials than in a small factory; hence, when studying the functions outlined below, it should

14

be noted that in a smaller organisation one individual may combine several such functions within his sphere of responsibility. The main principle to observe is that each person should have his authority and responsibility well defined, so that overlapping of duties does not occur. Provision has to be made for the fullest co-ordination and liaison.

THE MAIN DIVISIONS OF MANAGEMENT

The administration of a manufacturing business is usually controlled by a managing director, or general manager, and the main division of managerial responsibility can be identified as follows:

(a) Secretarial and financial.
(b) Sales and distribution of the products.
(c) Production and production services.
(d) Design and research, in large concerns.

The secretarial and financial management is usually the responsibility of the secretary, or a director of a company, or, in many instances, of the chief accountant, or chief clerk. The functions usually include the following:

(a) Secretarial work, and control of the general office staff.
(b) The control of financing operations and the ordinary financial books of account.
(c) Collaboration with the works manager in regard to the financing aspect of equipment and production.

The sales manager is responsible for sales promotion in its various forms. He devises selling and advertising campaigns, controls the salesmen, submits estimates and tenders, and is responsible for all statistics relating to sales. He must collaborate with the works manager, or planning department, as to types and quantities of various goods likely to be required. For estimates and tenders he will consult the cost accountant, or, in some cases, the ratefixer, who often functions as an estimator.

The third division—that of production management—is the most important from the point of view of this book, and will be considered in greater detail, using for purposes of illustration a large engineering works.

PRODUCTION MANAGEMENT

The organisation or production management is co-ordinated by the works manager, and the technical control is exercised by the chief engineer or chemist.

WORKS MANAGER

The works manager supervises all who are in the chain of control of production, the main sections of which are as follows:

1. Production control.
2. The production departments, including stores, labour engagement and welfare.
3. The purchasing department.
4. The service departments.

Much of his time is spent in smoothing out the difficulties of his subordinates, and giving decisions when special matters arise in respect of production. He must keep himself well informed of all that takes place in the works, and act as general controller in all matters relating to production.

1. Production control

Production control is responsible for the following:

(a) Planning—arranging how and where the work is to be done and the issue of instructions.

(b) Control—which regulates the work in accordance with the timetable set by the planning section. Sometimes that department determines the sequence of operations, the control section being responsible for the detailed arrangements.

(c) The tool-drawing office.

(d) The ratefixing and time-study department.

(e) The tool-room, and, sometimes

(f) The tool stores. The tool-room and store sometimes come under the control of the production department.

These will now be dealt with in more detail.

The planning section. This relieves the foremen of many responsibilities, and co-ordinates production by providing the plan of procedure and timetable for the whole works. Arrangements are made for the passing of each order through the shops. Not only the route but also the types of machines to be used are specified, and the supply of requisite materials is ensured. Attention has to be paid to machining and handling methods, and to the volume of production which can be coped with by each department or shop. In matters of cost, the cost accountant has to be consulted, particularly in regard to alterations in procedure.

The control section. This is responsible for the details of manufacture which have been arranged by the planning section. The planning section specifies the sequence of operations, and the control section details the particular machines to be used, regulates the work and "progresses" its movement to time through every stage of manufacture. The control section makes sure that materials required are in stock, or that specially purchased material is delivered to time. It obtains the specifications of materials and drawings from the drawing office, and sees that any necessary jigs or tools are available. Where special tools are required, drawings will be made and orders given for the making of the tools. Schedules are prepared for every movement of the work, so that the progress man knows what work is on each machine, and can be making preparations for the next job to follow. Graphic charts are often used, the Gantt charts being particularly appropriate.

The tool-drawing office. This is another part of production control, which is generally separated from the main drawing office. The jigs, gauges and tools required by the planning section are designed in the tool-drawing office.

The ratefixer. In some works this official may perform some of his functions under supervision of production control. He may decide whether day- or piece-work is to be used, indicate the time allowed, and is responsible for fixing time or piece rates for each piece or operation not produced or paid by ordinary time-work rates. A careful investigation is made in detail for every operation; timing is made with the aid of a stop-watch, and a reliable average time fixed, and, finally, the piece-work or premium-bonus rate. All factors which affect the work are considered, including the type of machine, its speed and the kind of material to be worked upon. It is apparent that the ratefixer must have a practical working knowledge of every machine, and thoroughly understand tool design. Careful enquiry into motion-study methods, advised by industrial psychologists, may lead to better results.

The tool-room. This produces the jigs, gauges and tools required by production control. It examines tools returned from the shops, and reconditions them if this is necessary. The foreman in charge is usually a highly skilled man, and he is provided with machine tools, special furnaces for hardening, etc., and various instruments for measuring accurately. All tools made or returned from the shops are passed to the tool store, from which they are issued only on presentation of formal requisitions.

2. The production department

This department, like that of production control, also comes directly under the jurisdiction of the works manager. It controls the following:

    (a) Shop superintendents, and through them the foremen and chargehands.

    (b) Stores departments,* *e.g.*:

---

* The stores are sometimes under the control of the cost accountant, or financial officer. The control is twofold: (a) financial, (b) physical.

    (*i*) main stores of materials;
    (*ii*) part-finished stores;
    (*iii*) finished stores;
    (*iv*) tool stores, if not supervised by the planning department;
    (*v*) consumable stores.

  (*c*) Despatch packing.
  (*d*) Transport.
  (*e*) Labour engagements and records, and welfare.

Immediately responsible to the works manager are the following:

Works or shop superintendents. Each has one or more producing shops under his supervision and control.

Where there is a personnel department, the works superintendent may be responsible for authorising the engagement of workers requisitioned by foremen. His chief duties are representing the works manager, attending to matters delegated to him and supervising the conduct of the shops for which he is responsible.

The foreman. He is mainly concerned with supervision of the men and work in his shop. Through him all instructions and works orders pass to the workers, and his duty is to see these are duly and correctly carried out.

The foreman will see that proper shop records are kept of orders handed to the workers, and that time spent on each is correctly booked. The modern practice is to have this work done by a clerk assisting the foreman.

The work done in his shop will generally be inspected by him or his assistant, and he will see that machines are kept running, reporting defects to the repair department. In large shops chargehands may assist the foreman.

The storekeeper. He is responsible for the care and custody of materials, and sometimes of finished stock. He must see that all materials are kept in an orderly manner, and that quantities are maintained in accordance with the maxima and minima which have been fixed by the management. Proper records of receipts and issues must be kept by him. He must see that nothing is issued, except on presentation of a duly authorised requisition. He is responsible for these requisitions being sent daily to the cost office.

If departmental stores are kept, in addition to the main stores, an assistant storekeeper will be in charge of each. Stores procedure and organisation will be dealt with in a separate chapter.

Stores audit. It is usual to have a continuous check on the records and physical stock, a portion being done each day or week in a large works.

The despatch department. This department is responsible for the packing and despatch of goods; for the checking of the quantity and weight of packages; and for the careful execution of delivery instructions given by customers.

Transport. This is dealt with later in more detail (*see* Chapter 19).

3. The purchasing department

This department also may be under the direct control of the works manager. It is responsible for dealing with replenishment requisitions from the stores; and for the securing of special direct material.

The buyer purchases materials for all purposes. Generally, materials have to be bought to specification. The requisitions upon which the buyer acts emanate from the storekeeper for replenishment of standard materials, and from the engineer's office or drawing office for special materials for a particular job or order.

The department must see that delivery is made within the time required for use. The most suitable markets must be known, quotations secured and orders placed. Good indexes should be kept, and constantly revised, showing: (*a*) the goods used by the factory; (*b*) suppliers, with their latest prices for such goods, time required for delivery, and other useful particulars. Purchasing procedure is detailed in the next chapter.

4. The service department

"Production department" is the term used to connote the department in which the actual product for sale is manufactured or produced, in contradistinction to the service departments, which are ancillary.

A production service is a facility available to a production department. Examples are: repair and maintenance, and power services: electricity, gas, water, hydraulic pressure, compressed air, vacuum and steam. Some pharmaceutical factories have a service of distilled water to all departments.

Preventive maintenance includes routine inspection of plant, tools and equipment at regular intervals for avoidance of breakdown by prompt replacement and repairs at convenient times instead of when emergencies arise.

CHIEF ENGINEER

The chief engineer supervises the technical side of the works, and acts as technical consultant to almost every section. He designs the articles to be made and any variations arising out of special specifications. It is his duty to study the latest technical information, and to propose improvement in design and materials, after proper research and experiment, if necessary in conjunction with the works chemist.

The departments for which he is responsible are the following:

The drawing office

Under the instructions of the engineer, working drawings are prepared, and the necessary blue-prints for use in the shops. A carefully indexed file of drawings and blue-prints is kept. The tracers and blue-print room are supervised by the chief draughtsman.

Specifications of material (sometimes called bills of material) suggested by the engineer are prepared, and orders pass from the engineer's department to the drawing office and planning department for the issue of instructions.

Experiment and research department

New designs, improvements and new methods are tried out in this department. It is also responsible for testing materials and examining them to ascertain whether they conform to specification. Various physical and chemical tests may be necessary, especially where metals and chemicals are used in the process of manufacture.

INSPECTION DEPARTMENT

The chief inspector must of necessity be a technical man who understands all manufacturing operations to enable him to trace reasons for defective work. Inspection duties can be divided into four sections:

(*a*) Inspection of purchased raw materials. Examination is made as to dimensions, tensile strength, chemical composition, finish or other factors mentioned in the purchase specification. It should be noticed that the finished product of one industry, or department, may be the raw material of another.

(*b*) Inspection of goods purchased in a partly finished or machined condition. The examination is made to see that the article agrees with the specification. Where gauges have been supplied, copies will be used to test the articles, in addition to inspection of the general finish.

(*c*) Inspection of finished parts, or components, made in the factory. This may be conducted after every operation or process; but, if this cannot be done without unduly large expense, it is done by "random sampling" methods. Each person examining will stamp or otherwise impress the articles with his own identification mark.

(*d*) Inspection of finished products for stock or despatch. Each part assembled is examined, *e.g.* the painting, polish and general appearance, the fit if applicable, and the correct components or accessories. Quantities are also usually certified by the inspection department, showing the number of rejects.

THE COSTING DEPARTMENT

The cost and management accountant should be directly responsible to the general manager, but must work in close collaboration with the engineer and the planning and production departments. The department is responsible for the preparation of the cost accounts, returns for the guidance of the management, and particularly for indicating where loss, waste, inefficiency and possibility of saving occur.

Particulars of expenditure of all kinds must be transmitted to it from the general office, and, as both the cost and financial accounts are based on the same original data, the scheme of accounts must be made to reconcile with those of the financial accountant's department. No attempt should be made to effect agreement in details, so long as the final results and main sectional totals are reconciled. Over-elaboration makes the department unnecessarily costly, and may even obscure rather than elucidate results. Whatever cost reports are prepared, they should be in a form readily understood by those managers for whom they are prepared.

The cost office is responsible for recording particulars of requisitions and prices for materials. These requisitions received from the storekeeper must be checked against the shop requisition book counterfoils or duplicates to ensure none is missing. Prices and variations thereof are dealt with.

The wages and timekeeper's offices are usually under the control of the cost accountant, at least in so far as the calculation of times and amounts payable are concerned and the form in which records are entered up. The timekeeper is directly responsible for the recording of the times of workers, computing time and overtime, and the operation of attendance-time recording devices. The wages office, from details supplied by the timekeeper, or from work tickets, makes up the payroll from which the cashier pays. The detailed procedure of these departments is described later.

The organisation in other types of industry will naturally vary, particularly as regards production management. Thus, in the chemical and certain food-manufacturing factories the works manager is a chemist, while inspection assumes the form of laboratory analysis and various kinds of testing at successive stages of production, and of the final product. Research for new chemicals, drugs and combinations of ingredients; for new processes and methods; or for improvement of existing lines or of plant is a continuous and costly part of the organisation. There are also special features as regards the control of stores materials, particularly when costly, and sometimes dangerous, chemicals and drugs are concerned.

Examination questions on Chapters 1–4 are given at the end of Chapter 4.

PURCHASING PROCEDURE

In each industry, and in different works within an industry, the detailed organisation will vary according to particular conditions and ideas, but the general procedure and principles outlined in this chapter may be regarded as typical, although particularly suitable for an engineering or similar factory. The forms used as illustrations are based on some actually in use, but again will vary in ruling and wording to suit particular needs.

A large engineering firm will require an efficient purchasing department, while, on the other hand, a small concern may have all functions, including purchasing, carried out by the owner. However, it is essential that in any firm, whether large or small, only one person or one department should be authorised to place orders with suppliers, or otherwise purchase orders may be duplicated.

ORGANISATION OF THE PURCHASING DEPARTMENT

The buyer in a manufacturing business has considerable responsibility, and in a large concern much money can be lost or saved by his department. He requires a good technical knowledge of the industry, and a large measure of administrative and organising ability; he must keep in constant touch with market prices, reports and market tendencies, and have a working knowledge of contract law and procedure, together with a practical understanding of the principles of economic laws.

The buyer should be provided with a schedule of technical specifications of the materials usually employed, each item having a code number which will be quoted by those issuing purchase requisitions.

The department should keep files suitably indexed, under the names both of suppliers and of materials. Records of prices and quotations for all materials should be kept in schedule form, arranged to show the seasonal and other movements of prices (*see* Fig. 1).

No purchases should be permitted except on receipt of duly authorised purchase requisitions but, in the case of materials largely and regularly used, forward contracts may be made after consultation with the management. Where purchase contracts are placed, a record of orders issued against them and deliveries made should be kept (Fig. 2).

SCHEDULE OF QUOTATIONS

Material: 1″ Copper Tube   **Date:** 20 June. 19...   **File No:** 32

	Rate £	Amount £	Time of Delivery	Terms	Delivery	Remarks
Estimated cost or part price.	760	15,200				
1. Hall & Co.	750	15,000	7 days	Net monthly	Free	
2. Tube Mfg. Co.	720	14,400	14 days	,,	,,	Accepted
3. Copper & Co. Ltd.	760	15,200	4 weeks	,,	,,	
4. F. White & Co.	800	16,000	10 days	,,	,,	
5.						

FIG. 1.—*Schedule of quotations*

These schedules are filed under type of material and form a valuable guide to the prices to be expected.

PURCHASE CONTRACT RECORD

File No.: 87

Material: 1″ Copper Tubes.
Suppliers: Tube Mfg. Co.
Contract No.: 261/22 June, 19...
Completed: 25 Sept., 19...

Quantity: 20 tons.
Price: £720 per ton.
Free delivered.
Net monthly.
Total Cost: £14,400

Ordered			Delivered				
Date	Quantity (tons)	Balance to Order (tons)	Date	Quantity (tons)	Current Price (per ton) £	Value £	Balance to Deliver (tons)
19...			19...				
June 22	5	15	July 7	5	730	3,650	15
July 10	4	11	,, 12	2	730	1,460	13
Aug. 20	11	—	,, 30	2	740	1,480	11
			Aug. 14	5	730	3,650	6
			,, 21	2	750	1,500	4
			Sept. 8	4	740	2,960	—
	20			20		£14,700	

FIG. 2.—*Purchase contract record*

This record gives a continuous check on the position of an order, the delivery of which is spread over a period.

PROCEDURE IN THE PURCHASING DEPARTMENT

On receipt of purchase requisitions the buyer will obtain quotations or, for important requirements, may invite tenders for the supply of the materials required. Consideration has to be given to factors other than price—namely, to specifications, conditions of delivery, various charges, times of delivery, terms of payment and discount (*see also* Fig. 1).

After the buyer has decided which quotation is most acceptable, a purchase order (Fig. 3) is prepared, which is evidence of the contract

---

ORDER

No. 4721

To Messrs. Smith, Jones & Co.,
Birmingham.

From A. Maker & Co., Ltd., Star Works, London, N.W.

Our ref.: Req. 284.   **Date:** 28/2/19...

Please supply, in accordance with the instructions herein, the following:

Particulars	Price	per	Delivery
2 tons ⅞" Mild Steel Bars, round.	£x	ton	At once

Delivery free at our Works.
Mark Order No. on invoice and advice note.
Terms: 5% Monthly Account.

For A. Maker & Co., Ltd.
C. Davis.

FIG. 3.—*Purchase order*

Care should be taken to see that the purchase order specifies the date and terms of delivery, the price, and the cash discount available if payment is made within the stipulated period.

between the buyer and the supplier. The number of copies of the purchase order depends on the organisation of the business: a small firm may require three copies, while a large concern may require five copies.

A possible routing of purchase-order copies is as follows:

(*a*) To the supplier.
(*b*) To the receiving department.
(*c*) To the accounting department.

(*d*) To the department which initiated the purchase requisition.
(*e*) Retained in the purchasing department.

The following up of deliveries on or before due date is important and necessitates the prompt marking off of deliveries from the goods received note. If deliveries are not made on the expected day, and no advice of despatch has been received from the supplier, the receiving clerk must inform the buyer, who will urge delivery.

USE OF EDGE-PUNCHED CARDS

A simple follow-up system may be devised by the use of edge-punched cards, illustrated in Fig. 39 on page 110. Among the particulars coded round the card is the date of delivery expected, and every day the outstanding orders can easily be sorted out, and chased up. In the centre of the card space can be provided for recording the action taken to date, *e.g.* 12th March 'phoned—delivery promised by 17th, 17th March written—strong protest made.

PURCHASE REQUISITIONING

The purchasing department places all orders for materials and supplies in accordance with requisitions received from the following:

(*a*) The storekeeper for all standard materials, the stocks of which require replenishment (*see* Fig. 4).
(*b*) The production control department for all special materials which are required for direct delivery to work in progress.
(*c*) The plant engineer for materials required for capital expenditure or special maintenance projects.
(*d*) The head of the department requiring special indirect material: for example, the accountant may require a new filing basket.

The procedure would then be for the department concerned to prepare each purchase requisition (*see* Fig. 4) in triplicate; these are then routed:

(*a*) to the buyer;
(*b*) to the production control department;
(*c*) retained in the department.

Requisitions received from the production control department and the plant engineer may be based on the specification of material prepared by the drawing office.

A SPECIFICATION OF MATERIAL

Such a specification is a complete schedule of parts and materials required for a particular order, prepared by the drawing office, and issued by it, together with the necessary blue-prints of drawings. For standard products, printed copies of the specification of material may be kept in stock, with blank spaces for any special details of modifications for a particular job. The schedule details everything required, even to nuts, bolts and screws, as well as weights and sizes.

PURCHASE REQUISITION FOR STOCK

Date: 16 June, 19...   **No.** 86

Quantity	Description	Stock Code No.	Purchase Order No.	Supplier
1 cwt.	1½" Copper Nails, Sq.	B. 36	M.S. 681	C. Hall & Co.

Signed
  Storekeeper: J. Stockwell.   **Approved:** T. S. Shaw.

FIG. 4.—*Purchase requisition for stock*

Requisitions for materials kept in regular stock might be initiated by the storekeeper; others by the department concerned.

NOTE: Sometimes an additional column is included for the storekeeper to state the balance of material in stock, for the guidance of the manager and buyer. The last two columns are filled in by the buyer.

A suggested routing is as follows:

(a) To the purchasing department.
(b) To the planning department.
(c) To the foreman of the department concerned.
(d) To the drawing office—copy retained.

An example of a specification of materials is shown in Fig. 5.

Classification code for materials

The use of material specification code numbers is an advantage, not only to the purchasing department and drawing office but also to the pricing clerk in the cost department, in that ambiguity is eliminated. The code may consist of symbols and numbers, the symbol indicating a material or an item, and the number, size, pattern, etc.

SPECIFICATION OF MATERIAL

For Order No. PO. 296. **Electric Motor No.** 7. **Assembly Drawing No.** 39. **Date:** 26 February, 19... **No.** 268

Symbol No. of parts	Description	No. per set	Total No.	Materials: Code No.	Materials: Description	Materials: Quantity	Remarks	For Purchase Department: Reqn. No.	For Purchase Department: Date	For Purchase Department: Deliveries specified	For Purchase Department: Order No.
E.M. 3 C.	Iron casing	2	2	M. 16	Standard	2	Stock				
E.M. 3 B.	Core plates	10		P. 14	Slotted open type	20	Japanned wrought iron				
E.M. 3 F.	Frame	1		M. 15	Cast Iron	1	Stock				
	End rings	4		S. 27	Standard	4	,,				
F.C. 7	Iron cylinder, etc.	1			Parkinson	1	Ref. 276	72	28/2	5/3	273
	Ring bolts	4		B. 9	Standard	8	Stock				
	Nuts. $\frac{1}{2}''$	4		S.N. 4	,,	16	,,				
	Nuts. $\frac{5}{8}''$	2		S.N. 5	,,	2	,,				
	Brass cups	2		B.O. 2	,,	2	,,				
P.M. 81	Brush holders, etc.	3	12	—	Thompson	12	St. 243	72	28/2	5/3	274

Drawing Office Copy. **Date Order:** Feb. 24, 19... **Delivery:** Mar. 19, ... **No. of Sheets:** 4

Prepared by: J. H. Ross. **Checked by:** C. F. Davis.

Dated to stores: Feb. 26, 19...
,, **from stores:** ,, 28, 19...
,, **to shops:** Mar. 7, 19...

FIG. 5.—*Specification of material*

This schedule is often referred to as a bill of material, and shows the complete requirements of raw material and component parts to complete a particular job.

A simple example will make this clear. Screws, brass and steel, could be given the symbols B.S. and S.S. respectively, a number being added for each size, the first in sixteenths, the next two being length in eighths:

B.S. 403 = Brass screw $\frac{1}{4}$ in. × $\frac{3}{8}$ in.   S.S. 403 ⎤
B.S. 504 =   „ $\frac{5}{16}$ in. × $\frac{1}{2}$ in.   S.S. 504 ⎟ Steel screws of the
B.S. 707 =   „ $\frac{7}{16}$ in. × $\frac{7}{8}$ in.   S.S. 707 ⎬ same sizes as stated
B.S. 414 =   „ $\frac{1}{4}$ in. × $1\frac{3}{4}$ in.   S.S. 414 ⎟ for brass.
B.S. 418 =   „ $\frac{1}{4}$ in. × $2\frac{1}{4}$ in.   S.S. 418 ⎦

(In due course, these measurements will give way to metric figures.)

All standard articles will have identifying symbols and numbers, and, although the system may appear complicated, it will be found in practice that storemen, clerks and draughtsmen find these codes easy to work with, since the code numbers of the more frequently used materials are readily memorised. In the cost department the pricing of issued material is facilitated and uncertainty as to size and kind of material is avoided. In the bills of material, stock materials will be indicated by the appropriate code number, but full details will have to be specified for special parts and materials which have to be manufactured or purchased outside.

PURCHASE PRICE

The purchase price per unit of quantity of the material to be ordered will be agreed between the buyer and the supplier. Frequently, however, calculations may be required in respect of the following items:

1. QUANTITY DISCOUNT

Quantity discount is an allowance made by the supplier to the purchaser, to encourage large orders. The larger the quantity ordered, the lower becomes the price per unit—within fixed limits. The producer hopes to enjoy larger production runs, thus reducing production costs, while the expense of delivering one or two large orders is much less than that of innumerable small orders, so packing and distribution costs are reduced. Part of the savings enjoyed by the supplier is passed on to the purchaser by means of this quantity discount. The buyer will try to take advantage of this discount where production requirements, storage and financial facilities permit.

2. TRADE DISCOUNT

Trade discount is an allowance made by the supplier to a purchaser who has to re-sell the article; for example, a manufacturer may allow a wholesaler 20% trade discount. This allowance is to compensate the purchaser for his costs of storage, breaking bulk, re-packing articles, and selling and delivering small quantities.

3. CASH DISCOUNT

Cash discount is an allowance made by the supplier to a purchaser to encourage prompt payments of invoices; for example, a 5% discount may be allowed if payment is received within seven days of the date of the invoice.

NOTE: This discount is allowed only if payment is received in the stipulated time, so it is a question of managerial policy whether or not the buyer takes advantage of the offer. It is thus a financial item, and should not appear in the cost accounts.

4. TRANSPORT AND STORAGE CHARGES

Sometimes the purchase price quoted by the supplier includes the cost of transporting the commodities to the purchaser and any storage charges incurred. Where, however, the price does not include these charges and the purchaser has to bear the cost, the charges should if possible be added to the purchase price. Frequently it is impracticable to add these charges to the purchase price, in which case the charges should be absorbed in factory overhead.

5. CONTAINERS

Containers may or may not be charged by the supplier. If they are not charged, then no accounting entry will be necessary in the books of the purchaser. However, if containers are separately charged, the treatment may be as follows:

Non-returnable containers

The cost of the container will be added to the purchase price of materials.

Returnable containers credited at full value on return

The cost of the container will not be included in the purchase price, assuming the container is returned to the supplier.

Returnable containers credited at reduced value on return

The difference between the cost of the container and the amount credited by the supplier will be added to the purchase price of the material, assuming the container is returned to the supplier.

EXAMPLE

A supplier quotes for material A as follows:

Lot Price   100 units   £0·25 each.
             500   ,,   £0·24 ,,
           1,000   ,,   £0·22½ ,,

Trade discount 20%. Cash discount 5% in seven days.
Containers charged at £0·5 each; £0·37½ credited on return.
1 container required for every 100 units.
The purchaser decides to buy 600 units.
Transport charges amounting to £3·37½ and Storage £0·62½, were charged by the supplier.

Calculation of Purchase Price

		Amount £	Cost per unit £
Material A: 600 units at £0·24		144·00	0·2400
Less Trade discount at 20%		28·80	0·0480
		115·20	0·1920
Returnable containers:			
6 containers at £0·50	3·00		
Less Credited on return at £0·37½	2·25		
		0·75	0·0012
		115·95	0·1932
Transport	3·37½		
Storage	0·62½		
		4·00	0·0067
		119·95	0·1999

NOTE: Cash discount of £5·76 would be received if payment made within 7 days, but would not affect cost accounts.

PROCEDURE ON RECEIPT OF MATERIALS

Suppliers usually send a delivery note, or an advice of despatch, which is passed to the receiving clerk. Invoices received are passed direct to the accounts department.

Materials entering the factory should be unloaded at special receiving centres. These should be situated as near to the road, railway siding, canal or wharf as possible, yet at the same time be accessible from any part of the factory, so as to reduce handling charges to a minimum.

The receiving department should have a copy of the purchase order so that, if necessary, arrangements can be made to unload the materials—special apparatus may be necessary to handle heavy or bulky materials. The goods received can be checked with the details on the purchase order and entered on a goods received note (*see* Fig. 6).

THE GOODS RECEIVED NOTE

The goods received note will have additional copies, the number depending on the organisation of the firm; a suggested routing is as follows:

(*a*) To the purchasing department.

(*b*) To the accounting department.

(*c*) To the department which initiated the purchase requisition.

(*d*) To the stores department.

(*e*) One copy held in the receiving department for reference purposes.

GOODS RECEIVED NOTE

From: Smith, Jones & Co.,
      Birmingham.

G.R. No. 59
Date: 5 Mar, 19...

Goods	Quantity	Packages	Order No.	For Office Use	
				Rate	£
			4721		

Carrier BR	Received by A. Jones	Goods Inspection Report Correct. B. Hall			
Purchase Requisition No. 284	Noted on Progress Chart 5/621	Bin No. 72	Stores Ledger 212	Invoice No. 360	A/cs. Ref. P.J. 84

Fig. 6.—*Goods received note*

This is made out by the receiving department when materials are received and is priced by the cost department from copy orders. It forms the basis of entries to the Stores Ledger made in advance of invoices, with which they are later agreed.

The advantage of goods received notes is that, after being filled in with particulars as to quantities and other information, they can be passed to the official responsible for approving the goods, who signs the notes, and sends them with the goods to the storekeeper. The receiving and approving of goods is sometimes the duty of the storekeeper himself, in which case he will prepare the goods received notes.

Another advantage of the use of goods received notes is that they may be used, in advance of the receipt of the invoices, to keep the Stores

Ledger posted daily, in conformity with the perpetual inventory system (*see* page 52).

Furthermore, since the goods received notes, checked and priced out by the cost department from the copy orders, are brought into agreement with the invoices, checked by the buying department and the accounts department, the whole system becomes a valuable example of "Internal check."

When the purchasing department receive their copy of the goods received note, together with the receiving clerk's copy of the purchase order, the order can be marked off in the order book.

Goods should be inspected for quality to ensure that they comply with any specification which may have been stated on the purchase order. In many large firms an inspection staff is attached to the receiving department, while in small firms the storekeeper is responsible for inspection. If any goods are rejected, the inspector will enter the reason for rejection on a special rejection report, so that the buyer is immediately informed and can contact the supplier.

CHECKING INWARD INVOICES

When invoices are received it is useful to impress each with a rubber stamp, as shown in Fig. 7.

Invoices are numbered consecutively on entry into the invoice register. The purchasing department clerk enters the order number, goods-received-note number, and signs for the correctness of the particulars, which he is able to check with the order and the certified goods received note. The order book should be marked with the invoice number to preclude the passing of a duplicate invoice.

If the invoice is in order the buyer will sign and pass it to the accounts department for payment. There it will be checked by a clerk or preferably a calculating-machine operator, to ensure that the calculations are correct. The invoice is entered in the Purchase Journal, from which the supplier's account is credited in the Purchase Ledger. The total of the Purchase Journal is debited to Purchases Account in the General

Regist. No. 360	Goods Correct A. Buyer	Checked	Noted Works Office	Bought Jrl. Fo. 84	Passed for Payment
Order No. 472	G.R. No. 59	With order: A.B. Prices: A.B. Extens.: R.S.	Charged to: Stores Initials: R.C.	Charged to: Stores A/c	C. Davis

FIG. 7.—*Invoice stamp*

Usually a rubber stamp is used on the bottom corner of the invoice so that the signatures authorising its payment are found in a convenient position.

Ledger and credited to Total Creditors. The detailed procedure for cost accounting and specimen entries are given in Chapter 14.

RECONCILIATION OF COST AND FINANCIAL ACCOUNTS

The goods received note is priced from the copy purchase order, and then the appropriate Material Account is debited in the Stores Ledger, except in the case of material purchased for a specific job, when the debit is made to the cost account for that job. Thus entries in the cost accounts are entered in the first place from the goods received notes, while, as mentioned above, the financial accounts are entered from the invoices.

It is essential to reconcile the cost accounts with the financial accounts; this will be discussed in greater detail in Chapter 15.

EXAMINATION QUESTIONS
Also includes questions on Chapters 1–3

1. Do you consider that the storekeeper should see and pass invoices for material received? What alternative method is suggested for checking the quantities and prices?

(I.C.W.A. Inter.)

2. Describe a system that would definitely link up the purchasing department, goods receiving department and cost department; giving all information for passing invoices, checking goods received and posting to costs.

(I.C.W.A. Inter.)

3. A company has a finished goods warehouse at its factory in Bristol and a sales depot in Glasgow. List each stage in the routine procedure for quantity control, from the time when Glasgow realises the need for a quantity of an article until the quantity is received.

(I.C.W.A. Inter.)

4. Describe what you consider to be an adequate system of checking the receipt of goods and payment for them.

(I.C.W.A. Inter.)

5. Describe fully the routine for control of the purchase and receipt of material from outside suppliers.

(I.C.W.A. Inter.)

6. Describe fully a system by which orders for materials are initiated and placed on outside suppliers, and list the essential information to be included in such orders. What sections of the organisation should be kept informed and why?

(I.C.W.A. Inter.)

7. What factors should be taken into account in determining whether or not to buy increased quantities of materials for stock with discounts given for large quantities?

(Comm. A. Inter.)

8. List the steps whereby:

(a) a supplier's invoice is passed for payment;

(b) an invoice to a customer follows an instruction to the despatch department to send goods.

(*I.C.W.A. Inter.*)

9. (a) Describe briefly the steps to be taken by the purchasing department of an engineering company in connection with the purchase of a new component. It may be assumed that the component will be purchased for about £50 each and that delivery will be taken in quantities of 1,000 frequently.

(b) In connection with the procedure described above, design the following forms:

(i) Schedule of quotations.

(ii) Purchase contract record.

(*I.C.W.A. Inter.*)

10. Discuss briefly the following items and their treatment in the cost accounts:

(a) Carriage inwards.

(b) Storage losses.

(c) Cash discount received.

(d) Trade discount received.

(e) Quantity discount received.

(f) Containers inwards.

(*I.C.W.A. Inter.*)

11. Record the entries for the following invoices for one item of raw material in an analysed purchase book:

Invoice	November 15		November 22		November 29	
		£		£		£
Quantity and cost	100 lb	100	80 lb	67	70 lb	60
Trade discount		15				
		85				
Container	(returnable)	2			(non-returnable)	1
		87				61
Carriage		paid		2	per own ⎱	1
				—	transport ⎰	
				69		
Cash discount		2½%		3⅓%		net
if paid by due date						—
(thereafter net)		December 31	November 29			
Standard price					£0·87½ per lb	

All accounts are paid on the 30th of the month following invoice date. Briefly list the reasons explaining your analysis.

(*I.C.W.A. Inter.*)

CHAPTER 5

STORES ROUTINE

THE stores department in many small firms is often neglected, and it is not realised that materials represent an equivalent amount of cash. Material pilferage, deterioration of materials and careless handling of stores lead to reduced profits, or even losses, so it is essential that to obtain the maximum advantage of a cost-accounting system an efficient, well-equipped stores department be maintained.

ORGANISATION OF STORES

TYPE OF ORGANISATION

In large manufacturing concerns the problem often arises as to the type of organisation which should be adopted in the storage department. There are three main types:

(*a*) Central stores: centralised buying and handling of stores.

(*b*) Central stores with sub-stores: centralised buying, but handling of stores is undertaken by the sub-storekeeper.

(*c*) Independent stores situated in various departments: buying and handling of stores are undertaken by the buyer and storekeeper in each department.

Consideration must, of course, be given to the particular circumstances prevailing in the factory, but in general the first or second course will be adopted.

CENTRALISED BUYING

The advantages of centralised buying are four, as follows:

(*a*) A firm policy can be initiated with regard to conditions of purchasing, *e.g.* terms of payment.

(*b*) Standardisation of articles is facilitated.

(*c*) Expert buying staff is concentrated in one department.

(*d*) Combined purchasing power may result in reduced prices of commodities.

These must be set against the disadvantage that the creation of a special department may lead to high administration costs. Nevertheless, it would appear from the above points that centralised buying is normally to be preferred to de-centralised buying.

CENTRALISED STORAGE

On the question of centralised handling of stores, it is much more difficult to generalise, because even though central stores may be preferred, it is very much a matter of circumstance whether or not sub-stores will be maintained (*see below*). The advantages and disadvantages of purely central storage may be set out as follows:

Advantages

    (*a*) Economy in staff and concentration of experts in one department.
    (*b*) Reduced clerical costs and economy in records and stationery.
    (*c*) Better supervision is possible.
    (*d*) Staff become acquainted with different types of stores, which is very useful if anyone is absent from work.
    (*e*) Better layout of stores.
    (*f*) Inventory checks facilitated.
    (*g*) Stocks are kept to a minimum, thus reducing storage space.
    (*h*) Fewer obsolete articles.
    (*i*) The amount of capital invested in stock is minimised.
    (*j*) Better security arrangements can be made.

Disadvantages

    (*a*) Increased transportation costs.
    (*b*) Stores may be situated at some distance from many departments which draw from them, thus causing inconvenience and delay.
    (*c*) Breakdowns in transport or hold-ups in central store may cause production stoppages in departments.
    (*d*) Greater risk of loss by fire.

IMPREST STORES

The imprest system of stores control operates in rather a similar way to a petty cash system. For each item of stock, a quantity will be ascertained which represents the number of units which is required to be in stock at the beginning of an accounting period. Consequently, at the end of a period, the storekeeper will requisition for the number of units required to bring the physical stock up to the predetermined quantity.

Thus, for example, if the normal consumption of Material 662 is 1,000 units per week, the storekeeper will arrange to have 1,000 units on hand at the beginning of the period. If, at the end of the week, there are 57 articles in stock, the storekeeper will issue a requisition note for 943 units so as to bring the stock level up to the required amount.

Normally, this system is used in an organisation which operates a central store and a number of sub-stores which are situated in various departments. In this way, the organisation can enjoy some of the benefits of central storage and, at the same time, enjoy the benefits of having a small supply of stores near to the production processes. The sub-storekeeper can requisition from the central stores any material required to reimburse his imprest quantity.

STORES LOCATION AND LAYOUT

The location of the stores department should be carefully planned so as to ensure maximum efficiency. It should be as near to the receiving department as possible so that handling charges are at a minimum. There should be easy access to all departments, especially to those in which heavy or bulky materials are to be delivered.

In large factories, where there are many departments, the stores department could not be situated where it is convenient to deliver to all departments and at the same time be near the receiving department, so it is often necessary to set up sub-stores conveniently situated to serve a particular part of the organisation. The central stores department will then issue to the sub-stores the materials specially required for the department or departments serviced by the sub-store. It is strongly recommended that the storekeeper of each sub-store should be responsible to the chief storekeeper. This will ensure that a uniform policy of buying, storing and issuing is followed.

The layout of the department requires careful thought. Shelves, racks, bins, etc., should be situated in clearly defined lanes, so that easy access is provided. In many cases it may be necessary to allow enough room for the passage of trucks, so that white lines should be painted on the floor, determining the position of storage containers.

Special attention must be paid to storage of materials which are affected by atmospheric conditions, because substantial losses may be incurred owing to evaporation, deterioration, etc.

THE STOREKEEPER

The department should be under the control of one person, who may be known as the storekeeper, chief storekeeper or stores superintendent. He should be a man of wide experience in stores routine, able to organise the operation of the stores, of undoubted integrity and capable of controlling the men under his charge.

His duties and responsibilities may be as follows:

(a) Maintaining the stores in a tidy manner.
(b) Accepting materials into the stores, after having ascertained that the delivery complies with instructions detailed on the purchase order and goods received note.

(c) Correct positioning of all materials in store.
(d) Checking the bin card balances with the physical quantities in the bins.
(e) Requisitioning further supplies from the purchasing department when the re-order level is reached on any material (*see below*).
(f) Preventing unauthorised persons entering the stores.

RECEIPT AND ISSUE OF MATERIALS

REQUISITION FOR STOCK

The storekeeper is guided, when requisitioning for stock as outlined on page 25, by the maximum and minimum quantity which he is authorised to store in respect of each kind of material, and the re-order level. These items are shown on the bin card (*see* Fig. 12).

Maximum stock level

The maximum stock level is that above which stocks should not normally be allowed to rise. It is fixed by taking into account such aspects as the following:

(a) Rate of consumption of the material.
(b) Time necessary to obtain new deliveries.
(c) Amount of capital necessitated and available.
(d) Keeping qualities, *e.g.* risk of deterioration, evaporation.
(e) Storage space available.
(f) Cost of storage, particularly if cold storage is necessary.
(g) Extent to which price fluctuations may be important.
(h) Risks of changing specifications or of obsolescence.
(i) Seasonal considerations as to both price and availability of supplies, *e.g.* market shortage.
(j) Economic ordering quantities.
(k) The incidence of insurance costs, which may be important for some materials.
(l) Any restrictions imposed by local or national authority in regard to materials in which there are inherent risks, *e.g.* fire and explosion.

Minimum stock level

The minimum stock level is that below which stocks should not normally be allowed to fall. If stocks go below this level there is the very real danger of shortage of supplies, which may necessitate a stoppage in production. The minimum stock is fixed by taking into account the following:

(*a*) Rate of consumption of the material.

(*b*) Time necessary to obtain delivery of the new materials.

Re-order level

This is the point fixed between maximum and minimum stock figures, at which time it is essential to initiate purchase requisitions for fresh supplies of the material. This point will be higher than the minimum stock, to cover such emergencies as abnormal usage of the material or unexpected delay in delivery of fresh supplies.

Calculations of stock level

The levels of stock to be held may be determined by a policy decision or by the use of formulae. A policy decision may be taken in connection with a change in working capital available when it is decided to increase or reduce stocks. However, mathematical formulae are increasingly being used to calculate these stock levels. Before formulae can be applied to this problem it is necessary to ascertain the consumption of materials, the period taken to obtain new supplies and the usual quantity to be ordered.

Re-order quantity

This represents the quantity which is normally ordered each time fresh supplies are required. It takes into consideration such factors as the following:

(*a*) Cost of storage, *e.g.* interest on capital locked up in materials, deterioration and obsolescence.

(*b*) Cost of purchasing, *e.g.* cost of preparing purchase order, cost of inspecting raw materials.

EXAMPLE SHOWING STOCK LEVELS

The following information is available in respect of material C.G.7:

$$\text{Re-order quantity} = 1,800 \text{ units}$$
$$\text{Re-order period} = 3\text{–}5 \text{ weeks}$$
$$\text{Maximum consumption} = 450 \text{ units per week}$$
$$\text{Normal consumption} = 300 \text{ units per week}$$
$$\text{Minimum consumption} = 150 \text{ units per week}$$

Re-order level

$$\text{Max. C} \times \text{Max. R.P.}$$
$$450 \times 5 \qquad\qquad = \underline{2{,}250 \text{ units}}$$

KEY

Max. R.P. = Maximum re-order period.

Max. C   = Maximum consumption during period.

Minimum stock level

$$R.L. - (N.C. \times N.R.P.)$$
$$2,250 - (300 \times 4) \qquad = 1,050 \text{ units}$$

KEY
R.L.   = Re-order level.
N.C.   = Normal consumption.
N.R.P. = Normal re-order period.

Maximum stock level

$$R.L. + R.Q. - (\text{Min. C.} \times \text{Min. R.P.})$$
$$2,250 + 1,800 - (150 \times 3) \qquad = 3,600 \text{ units}$$

KEY
R.Q.   = Re-order quantity.
Min. C.   = Minimum consumption during period.
Min. R.P. = Minimum re-order period.

FIXING STOCK LEVELS BY STATISTICAL METHODS

If the information is available, it is thought that the levels, especially the maximum level, can be fixed more closely by the use of statistics. For example, suppose the figures shown above were based on the following experience:

Week No.	Demand x	$d = (x - \bar{x})$	$d^2 = (x - \bar{x})^2$	Received	Balance
					1,700
1	360	60	3,600		1,340
2	380	80	6,400		960
3	360	60	3,600		600
4	450	150	22,500	1,000	1,150
5	370	70	4,900		780
6	350	50	2,500		430
7	330	30	900	1,000	1,100
8	210	− 90	8,100		890
9	160	−140	19,600		730
10	150	−150	22,500		580
11	160	−140	19,600	1,000	1,420
12	260	− 40	1,600		1,160
13	360	60	3,600		800
	3,900	0	119,400		

The mean, $\bar{x}$, = 3,900/13 = 300 units.
The range of demand is:

$$\text{Highest} \quad 450$$
$$\text{Lowest} \quad 150$$

The standard deviation is $\sqrt{(1/N \, \Sigma(x - \bar{x})^2)}$

$$= \sqrt{(119,400/13)} = \sqrt{9,184} = 96.$$

The upper limit might be taken as three standard deviations from the mean, *i.e.*:

$$300 + 3(96) = 588$$

that is to say, we are 99% confident that the maximum demand will not exceed 588 in any week.

Now, as we have to wait three weeks on average for a new supply, we could fix our *maximum stock level* at:

$$3(588) = 1,764 \text{ units} \quad . \quad . \quad . \quad . \quad . \quad (1)$$

If we now fix our *re-order level* at:

$$2(588) = 1,176 \text{ units} \quad . \quad . \quad . \quad . \quad . \quad (2)$$

we still have four weeks' supply at average demand before stock run-out is reached.

Our *minimum stock level* might now be taken as:

$$1(588) = 588 \text{ units} \quad . \quad . \quad . \quad . \quad . \quad (3)$$

which gives us nearly two weeks' supply at average demand, and about ten days' supply at the highest demand rate experienced.

The results may be depicted graphically (Fig. 8), and it will be seen that we keep well within our maximum level, and this allows the re-order quantity to be reduced to 1,000 units.

On two occasions we have dropped below our minimum level, but even if the new supply received at week 10 had been delayed until week 11 or 12, we should not have run out of stock.

Considerable savings of capital investment in stocks can be achieved if the stock levels can be lowered in this way. However, the demand has to be fairly steady for this to be done successfully.

FIXING THE RE-ORDER QUANTITY

From the calculations made above, it might be supposed that the maximum and minimum levels are fixed regardless of the economic re-order quantity.

This is far from the case. The re-order quantity, as stated above, has to take into account the monthly demand, the cost of placing orders, the cost of storage of the material after purchase, the prices obtainable by buying in larger quantities and the interest on capital investment.

In fact, the same formula as will be developed later on and shown on page 323 may be made use of, subject to making certain changes in the meanings assigned to the letters of the formula.

Thus we may imagine that the re-order quantity of 1,000 was arrived at in the following way.

Let:

D = Demand per month, say 300
S = Share of cost of placing orders
    Cost of buying department per annum = £5,000
    Number of orders placed by buying department per annum
        = 8,000
    Cost of placing each order £5,000 ÷ 8,000 = £0·62½
    Cost of 20 orders placed for this material = £12·50
I = Rate of interest on capital investment, say 6%
C = Cost per unit of material, say £1·50

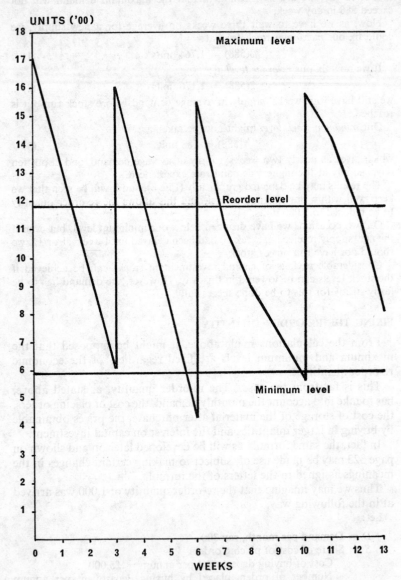

FIG. 8.—*Graph to record stock changes*

Then economic order quantity formula is frequently shown as:

$$\sqrt{(24\ DS/IC)} = \sqrt{\frac{(24)\ (300)\ (12\cdot50)}{(0\cdot06)\ (1\cdot50)}}$$

$$\sqrt{\frac{90,000}{0\cdot09}}$$

$$\sqrt{1,000,000} = \underline{1,000}$$

RECEIPT OF MATERIALS

Purchased materials are passed into the custody of the storekeeper when they have been examined and approved. Some articles or parts for stock are not purchased from outside suppliers but made in the works. These will be inspected in the usual course, and then passed into the stores. In order to keep the accounting uniform, it is desirable that a goods received note be prepared for these articles. The necessary debits and credits, as between production and stores, will be dealt with by the cost office.

ISSUE OF MATERIALS

It is essential that all stores issued should be promptly recorded, so that accurate material costs may be obtained. Materials should be issued by the storekeeper only on presentation of an authorised document—usually called a stores requisition note.

Material requisition

This form (Fig. 9) is an authorisation to the storekeeper to issue raw material, finished parts or other stores. It is usually signed by the foreman, but in some cases when a greater authority is required, for example when extra large quantities are needed for production, the manager's signature may be necessary. Frequently the planning or progress department issue these requisitions to the foreman, who presents them to the storekeeper as and when required.

Any materials ordered for a specific job will be marked with the job number, and kept apart ready for issue. The foreman will be informed that the material is available.

The storekeeper will enter the details of the material requisition on to the bin cards, and adjust the balances in the stock column. The note will then be routed to the cost department, where it will be evaluated, the Stores Ledger credited, and an entry made on the Materials Abstract for posting to the debit of the Cost Ledger.

THE RECEIPT AND ISSUE OF SPECIAL MATERIALS

Materials ordered for a specific job will be marked with the job number, and kept apart ready for issue. The foreman will be informed that the material is available. A good plan for this is for the production department to prepare a stores requisition, and send it to the foreman, who can sign it, and present it at the stores when he is ready to use the material.

MATERIAL REQUISITION

No. 76

Material Required for: Job. E513
  (Job or Process)

Department: Engines

Shop: E3

Date: 20 July, 19...

Quantity	Description	Code No.	Weight	Rate	£	Notes
10 ft.	½″ Brass X.E.D.	B102	12 lb	£0·50 lb	6·00	

Workman: F. Simpson	**Stores Ledger Fo.:** 218 **Bin No:** 975	**Cost Office ref.:** MA364
Foreman: E. Barry	**Storekeeper:** A.S.	**Priced by:** G.B.

FIG. 9.—*Material requisition*

This illustrates the request for materials from stores for a job about to be commenced. It is priced by the cost office according to one of the agreed methods, and posted to the credit of the Stores Ledger Account.

STORES RECORDS

Two records are usually kept of materials received, issued or transferred—namely on the bin cards and in the Stores Ledger. The bin cards are written up in the stores, but the Stores Ledger is sometimes kept by the cost department or stores office.

There is considerable advantage in this procedure, as it leaves the storekeeper with the minimum amount of clerical work, and the stores accounting records are kept cleaner and more accurately by an experienced stores clerk.

Stores appropriation record

A stores appropriation record is often kept when it is not convenient to work to definite maxima and minima of certain types of materials which may be required to meet orders. It may be used in connection with stores materials, or components which are made in the works or ordered from outside, and is of great value to the planning department, in that it shows the quantity in stock and on order. The record may be combined in the ordinary bin card by providing a special column for the purpose, or a separate Stores Appropriation Ledger may be used. When the latter is adopted the procedure is to debit each account with the quantities in stock and ordered. As a quantity is appropriated it is credited, and the balance represents the quantity in stock and on order.

FINISHED PARTS OR COMPONENTS STORE

Items or sub-assemblies awaiting final assembly or sale as spares are sometimes kept in a separate store, under the control of the progress or planning department. It is usual to keep a finished-parts stock record indicating the quantity and also in some cases the value of each class of finished part and its location in the stores. Stock orders for quantities of standard parts will be issued in batches convenient for economical manufacture. A stores appropriation record is useful for the control. The cost, ascertained from the works order for the production of these stock orders, will ordinarily be the charging-out price, when components are issued on requisition for assembly on various works orders.

TRANSFER OF MATERIALS

Transfers of materials from one departmental store to another should be recorded by means of a stores requisition signed by the storekeeper and marked "Transfer." This memorandum can then be used in the office for the making of the necessary credit and debit.

Where transfers are numerous it is sometimes the practice to have special columns in the stock record sheets or bin cards for recording the details of the transfers.

Material transfer note

The transfer of material from one job to another in the works should be strictly prohibited unless the procedure is adequately recorded on the material transfer note (Fig. 10) showing all necessary data for crediting and debiting the cost accounts affected, as otherwise the records and cost accounts concerned would be incorrect. Such transfers occur where an urgent order has to be made, and work started on a less urgent order may be appropriated. In such a case there must be provision for the re-issue of material to the job from which material already issued has been transferred. Any excess material should be returned to the stores, when a shop credit note can be made out.

Considerable care must be taken to ensure that excess material is not left lying around departments, because this will lead to deterioration in the value of the materials as well as to congestion in the departments.

Scrutiny of the cost accounts may reveal excess material in any department, where the material charge is higher than expected. Action should then be taken to return the material to the stores and the department concerned credited with the value of material.

MATERIAL TRANSFER NOTE

Issuing Dept.: Engines   **No.** 57
Receiving Dept.: Tools   **Date:** 31 July, 19...

Quantity	Description	Code No.	Weight	Rate	£	Notes
5 ft	½″ Brass X.E.D.	B102	6 lb	£0·5 lb	3·0	

Authorised by: F.S.	**Received by:** E.R.	**Cost Office ref.:** MA 364
From Job No.: E513	**To Job No.:** T27	**Priced by:** G.B.

FIG. 10.—*Material transfer note*

A form like this is necessary to cover the transfer of material from one job to another and from one department to another; otherwise the costs will be wrongly charged.

NOTE: The pricing out is done in the cost office.

MATERIAL ISSUED IN EXCESS OF REQUIREMENTS

Bulk material has to be issued at times in excess of the needs for a particular job. This is the case with sheet iron or steel bars, which in some instances cannot be cut off in the stores to the exact size required, and which can be more advantageously operated upon in the works when full size. The procedure is to charge out the full quantity issued and, when the excess is returned to store, a stores debit note is filled in, signed by the foreman, and handed to the storekeeper.

Material return note

This note (Fig. 11) is an authorisation to return to the storekeeper raw material, finished parts or other stores no longer required by the factory. It is sometimes referred to as a stores debit note or shop credit slip. The various stock records and cost accounts are adjusted in due course from the details given on this form. These debit notes may be drawn up in the same form as a stores requisition, but printed in red to distinguish them.

MATERIAL RETURN NOTE						
Issuing Dept.: Engines					**Date**: 23 July, 19... **No.** 7	
Quantity	Description	Code No.	Weight	Rate	Amount £	Notes
5 ft	½″ Brass X.E.D.	B102	6 lb	£0·5 lb	3·0	
Authorised by: E.B. **From Job No.:** E513		**Received by:** A.S. **To Bin No.:** 975 **Stores Ledger Fo.:** 218			**Cost Office ref.:** MA 364 **Priced by:** G.B.	

FIG. 11.—*Material return note*

When excess material is returned to stores, a form like this is used to ensure that the job concerned receives credit for the material, and that the stores can keep its records correctly.

NOTE: The pricing out is done in the cost office.

MATERIAL RECORDS

Bin cards

Materials are kept in appropriate bins, drawers or other receptacles; some are stacked, others racked. For each kind of material or article, a separate record is kept on a bin card (Fig. 12), showing in detail all receipts and issues. The bin cards are used not only for detailing receipts and issues of materials but also to assist the storekeeper to control the stock. For each material, the maximum and minimum to be carried are stated on the card—these limits having been determined by the production department in the first instance as illustrated on page 39. From time to time these maxima and minima may be altered to suit current requirements.

To facilitate ordering of further supplies, the normal quantity to order is sometimes stated at the head of the card. When materials are of a kind requiring advance ordering, an ordering level may be specified on the bin card. The various receptacles in which materials are kept are numbered, the bin card for each being similarly numbered. Where identifying code numbers are used for materials, it is advantageous to attach these to the bin, and to quote them on the bin card.

Free balance

The increasing realisation of the importance of material control has resulted in the development of a more advanced design of bin card.

This bin card incorporates the information found in Fig. 12 but in addition shows such useful information as materials ordered, materials allocated and free balance of materials (*see* Fig. 13). As a result, this bin card shows the full cycle of material control: the order of new supplies; allocation of materials to jobs; receipt and issue of material; stock on hand; and free balance available.

BIN CARD

Description: ....   Bin No.: ....
....   Code No.: ....

Normal Quantity   Maximum: ....
to Order: ....   Minimum: ....
Stores Ledger Fo.: ....   Re-order Level: ......

Receipts			Issues			Balance	Remarks
Date	G.R. No.	Quan-tity	Date	Req. No.	Quan-tity	Quantity	Goods on Order and Audit Notes

FIG. 12.—*Bin card (1)*

This is the storekeeper's record of the movement "In" and "Out" of the materials under his control. It should show in the balance column the actual quantity of the particular material in stock at that time.

NOTE: The columns headed "quantity" may be ruled for tons, cwt, qrs, lb; cwt, qrs, lb, oz; gross, doz., units; or simply for units; yards, ft, in.; gallons, qts, pts, oz as may be necessary.

EXAMPLE

The following transactions occurred in respect of Material JD42 during the four months ended June 30:

	April	May	June	July
Allocated—units	1,000	1,500	1,300	3,200
Received—units	600	900	1,800	1,500
Issued—units	500	800	1,400	1,200

The following information is available:

Balance on order	1,000 units
Balance allocated	700 units
Stock on hand	500 units
Free balance	800 units

Orders are placed in 1,000 lots when the free balance falls to 600 or less.

Description: ....
Code No.: ....
Re-order Quantity: ....
Stores Ledger Folio: ....

Bin No.: ....
Maximum Stock Level: ....
Minimum Stock Level: ....
Re-order Level: ....

Date	Ordered				Allocated				Free Balance			Stock					Remarks
	P.O. No.	Qty.	Rec.	Bal.	Job No.	Qty.	Iss.	Bal.	Inc. Ord.	Dec. All.	Bal.	G.R.N. No.	Rec.	S.R.N. No.	Iss.	Bal.	
B/d. April				1000				700			800					500	
C/d. May		1000	600	1400		1000	500	1200	1000	1000	800		600		500	600	
C/d. June		2000	900	2500		1500	800	1900	2000	1500	1300		900		800	700	
C/d. July		1000	1800	1700		1300	1400	1800	1000	1300	1000		1800		1400	1100	
		3000	1500	3200		3200	1200	3800	3000	3200	800		1500		1200	1400	

FIG. 13.—*Bin card* (2) (*see* text and Example on page 48)

see text and Example on page 48

Key: P.O. No. = Purchase order number; G.R.N. No. = Goods received note number; S.R.N. No. = Stores requisition note number.

Reference should now be made to Fig. 13 and the following points observed:

Receipts. On receipt of materials, stock is increased while goods on order are reduced.

Allocations. When materials are allocated to specific jobs the balance allocated is increased and free balance available is reduced.

It should be appreciated that in this context, when materials are allocated to a job, they are not transferred physically from the stores to the process, but are reserved in the stores for a special job.

Issues. Issues of materials reduce the quantity of materials in stock and also reduce the balance allocated.

It is assumed in this context that materials issued to a job have been allocated previously to that job. However, if this were not the case, then the quantity issued would reduce the quantity of materials in stock, and would also reduce the free balance.

Orders. Materials are ordered when free balance falls to 600 or less. When orders are placed, balance on order increases and also balance on free balance is increased.

NOTE 1. Each month when the balances of each item are determined, a check should be made to ensure that the balances do, in fact, balance. Thus:

Balance on order + Stock balance = Balance allocated + Free balance, *e.g.* June 1,700 + 1,100 = 1,800 + 1,000.

NOTE 2. The quantity to be ordered is determined when the free balance falls below 600. Thus, for example, in May it is necessary to order two lots of 1,000 units in order to restore the free balance.

Readers should appreciate that this system follows the usual principles of double-entry book-keeping; in other words, there must be two entries in respect of each transaction.

Stores material control record

An alternative to bin cards is a stores material control record (Fig. 14) written up in the stores and/or by production control in a loose-leaf book or card file. On this record, as on the bin cards, quantities only are recorded, all money values being shown only in the stores ledger in the office. An advantage of this record is that the storekeeper has all details close at hand and can note in it such information as quantities ordered, probable requirements for particular contracts and other details. Where transfers between inter-departmental stores are numerous, an additional section may be included on the stock record sheets for details of the transfers as distinct from issues to the shops.

Stores Ledger

The Stores Ledger is kept in the cost department and is identical with the bin cards, except that money values are shown. Correct stores

STORES MATERIAL CONTROL RECORD

Description: ....
Code No.: ....
Re-order Quantity: ....

LIMITS
Maximum: ....
Minimum: ....
Re-order Level: ....
Bin No: ....
Unit: ....

Receipts			Issues			Balance	On Order				Delivered		Remarks and Stock Counts
Date	G.R. No.	Quantity	Date	Req. No.	Quantity	Quantity	Date	Pur. Req. No.	Supplier	Quantity	Quantity	Date	

Fig. 14.—*Stores material control record*

This record card is helpful for production control purposes, because, if desired, it can show transfers between departments as recorded in an additional section.

accounting is as important as accounting for cash, hence the separation of this clerical work from the actual handling of the materials. The ledger is usually of the loose-leaf or card type, each account representing an item of material in store. The ruling of the accounts may be as shown in Figs. 15(a) and (b).

It can be seen from Fig. 15(a) that, in addition to the stores available, the materials ordered from suppliers and the materials reserved for special jobs can be ascertained. The debit side is prepared either from the goods received notes or from the invoices and from stores debit notes; the credit side either directly from the stores requisition notes or from an abstract summary compiled from them.

STORES CONTROL

THE PERPETUAL INVENTORY SYSTEM

This may be defined as a method of recording stores balances after every receipt and issue, to facilitate regular checking and to obviate closing down for stock-taking. It is sometimes termed "continuous inventory."

The balance of any account in the Stores Ledger should agree with the balance shown on the bin card, or stock control record, for the same item of material, and a frequent checking of these dual records should be made, as well as of the actual quantity in stock.

Closely allied to the perpetual inventory system is the continuous checking of the stock. Under this continuous stock-taking system a number of items are counted daily or at frequent intervals, and compared with the bin cards and Stores Ledger by a stores audit clerk. Discrepancies are investigated; many may be clerical errors, which will be corrected. When, however, the stock is incorrect, an enquiry is made, after which any shortage or surplus is adjusted in the records to make them correspond with the physical count. This may be done conveniently by making out a credit note or debit note, as the case may be, for the difference, and then, after obtaining authority to pass for adjustment through the Cost Journal, debiting (or crediting) a Stock Adjustment Account. The balance on that account is written off direct to Profit and Loss Account at appropriate times.

The usual causes of differences are: incorrect entries, breakage, pilferage, evaporation, breaking bulk, short or over issues, absorption of moisture, price approximation or pricing method, and placing of stores in the wrong bin.

The advantages of the perpetual inventory and continuous stock-taking systems are as follows:

(a) The long and costly work of a stock-taking count is avoided, and the stock of materials, as shown by the Stores Ledger (but not

STORES LEDGER ACCOUNT

Material: .... Code: .... Maximum Quantity: .... Minimum Quantity: .... Folio: .... Location: ....

	Receipts				Issues				Stock		
Date	G.R. No.*	Quantity	Price	Amount £	S.R. No.†	Quantity	Price	Amount £	Quantity	Price	Amount £

FIG. 15(a).—*Stores Ledger Account, showing Receipts and Issues columns*

The Receipts and Issues columns are entered from the goods received notes and stores requisition notes, the totals of which are posted in the main books of account to Stores Ledger Control Account.

NOTE: The Receipts and Issues columns are part of the double-entry accounting system; the Stock column is memorandum only.
   * Goods received note number.   † Stores requisition number.

STORES LEDGER ACCOUNT

MATERIAL: .... Code: .... Maximum Quantity: .... Minimum Quantity: .... Re-order Level: .... Folio: .... Location: ....

Ordered			Reserved			Received					Issued				Stock			Stock Checked		
Date	Ref.	Quantity	Date	Ref.	Quantity	Date	G.R. No.	Quantity	Price	Amount	S.R. No.	Quantity	Price	Amount	Quantity	Price	Amount	Date	Initials	Remarks

FIG. 15(b).—*Stores Ledger Account, showing Reserved and Stock Checked columns*

In this form of account, the "reserved" stores show the amounts earmarked for production soon to commence. It helps to disclose the approach of the re-order level, and thus to prevent shortages of vital materials.

NOTE: The Receipts and Issues columns are part of the double-entry accounting system; the Ordered, Reserved and Stock columns are memoranda only. Stock Checked column is used when the stock checkers have physically counted the items in stock.

the work in progress), can be obtained quickly for the preparation of a Profit and Loss Account and Balance Sheet at interim periods if required.

(*b*) A detailed, reliable check on the stores is obtained.

(*c*) Experienced men can be employed to check the stock at regular intervals.

(*d*) It is not necessary to stop production so as to carry out a complete physical stock-taking, except possibly at the end of each year.

(*e*) Discrepancies are readily discovered and localised, giving an opportunity for preventing a recurrence in many cases.

(*f*) The moral effect on the staff tends to produce greater care, and serves as a deterrent to dishonesty.

(*g*) The audit extends to comparing the actual stock with the authorised maxima and minima, thus ensuring that adequate stock are maintained within the prescribed limits.

(*h*) The storekeeper's duty of attending to replenishments is facilitated, as he is kept informed of the stock of every kind of material, thus ensuring uninterrupted and safe manufacturing stocks.

(*i*) The stock being kept within the limits decided upon by the management, the working capital sunk in stores materials cannot exceed the amount arranged for.

(*j*) The disadvantages of excessive stocks are avoided, as, for example:

(*i*) loss of interest on capital locked up in stock;
(*ii*) loss through deterioration;
(*iii*) danger of depreciation in market values;
(*iv*) risks of obsolescence.

TURNOVER OF STORES MATERIAL

It is an advantage to compare the turnover of different grades and kinds of material as a means of detecting stock which does not move regularly, thus enabling management to avoid keeping capital locked up in undesirable stocks. It is not an infrequent occurrence for a particular item of stock to be overlooked for considerable periods, unless means are taken to prevent such accumulations.

Stock turnover is measured often in terms of the ratio of cost of materials consumed to the average stock held during the period. The formula is:

$$\frac{\text{Cost of materials consumed during period}}{\text{Average stock of materials during period}}$$

EXAMPLE 1

The following details have been extracted from the accounts of Marart Ltd. at the end of a year:

Opening stock £3,000
Purchases £26,000
Closing stock £5,000

$$\text{Stock turnover} = \frac{£24,000}{£4,000} = 6 \text{ times p.a.}$$

NOTES 1. Cost of goods sold = £3,000 + £26,000 − £5,000.

2. Average stock held = $\dfrac{£3,000 + £5,000}{2}$.

A stock turnover of six times p.a. shows that, on average, stock is being held for two months. This figure is, however, an *average* figure, so it must be borne in mind that some stock must be turning over less frequently than this, while, of course, other stock will be turning over more frequently than this. It may be mentioned in passing that such a high stock turnover rate as shown in this example is achieved only by the most efficient manufacturing companies, particularly those employing computer techniques for stock and production control.

An alternative method of measuring stock turnover is one involving the use of maximum and minimum stock levels. The formula is:

$$\frac{\text{Cost of materials consumed during period}}{\frac{1}{2}(\text{Maximum stock level} + \text{Minimum stock level})}.$$

EXAMPLE 2

In respect of Material 1296, data extracted from the bin card is as follows:

Maximum stock level £3,000
Minimum stock level £1,000
Issues during the period £10,000

$$\text{Stock turnover} = \frac{£10,000}{\frac{1}{2}(£3,000 + £1,000)} = 5 \text{ times per annum.}$$

A more refined method of measuring stores turnover is one involving the re-order quantity. The formula is:

$$\frac{\text{Materials consumed}}{\text{Minimum stock level} + \frac{1}{2} \text{Re-order quantity}}.$$

EXAMPLE 3

The bin card for Material 24769 shows the following position:

Maximum stock level 1,500 units
Minimum stock level 600 units
Re-order quantity 800 units
Issues during year 4,000 units

$$\text{Stock turnover} = \frac{4,000}{600 + \frac{1}{2}(800)} = 4 \text{ times per annum.}$$

It is not prudent to stipulate which of these methods is the best one. Much depends on the information available; for example, if a company is not operating a stock control system involving stock levels, then only the first method could be used. In an examination question, the method to be used depends on the amount of information available. However, if the authors were to generalise, given all the information required, they would opt for the third method.

Stores turnover figures may reveal the presence of slow-moving stocks, and, if so, it is important that a careful watch be maintained to reduce these items to as low a level as possible. Materials which are lying in store for long periods not only are subject to deterioration but are incurring storage cost in the form of locked-up capital, storage space, etc. Three types of stock must be investigated:

Slow-moving stocks

Materials which have a low turnover ratio are classified as slow-moving stock. Stocks should be maintained at the lowest level which is consistent with forecast demand and supply.

Dormant stocks

Materials which at present have no demand are regarded as dormant stock. There is a possibility that in future they may be required. Consultation between the buyer, chief storekeeper, production controller and cost accountant should result in a decision either to retain materials because of the good chance of future demand, or to cut losses by scrapping the materials while they may have some market value, thus reducing storage costs.

Obsolete stocks

These represent materials for which there is no longer a demand, possibly because the finished product in which the material was used is no longer in production, or because a better substitute has been found. If possible, these materials should be scrapped, or, if there is no scrap value, they should be discarded.

Stocks which are scrapped or discarded would be written off to Abnormal Loss Account, any scrap value received being credited to this account.

SCRAP MATERIALS

Scrap materials generally fall into three categories:

(a) Some manufacturing operations create trimmings, off-cuts, and other waste which is too small or otherwise unsuitable to treat as (a) and (b) below. Such waste will have to be collected for sale as scrap, destroyed or dumped.

(b) In some cases off-cuts may be suitable for making other things, and this material is returned to store. It is usually taken on charge in the Stores Ledger at a lower value than the original price; a corresponding credit is given to the operation in which it arose.

(c) Other scrap consists of rejected products arising from inspection, or which have been spoiled or damaged and are not capable of being made good. There is often some salvage or sales value.

All saleable or usable scrap should be passed to the care of the storekeeper, so that usual stores records and control can be ensured. The treatment of scrap materials is discussed in more detail in Chapter 20.

RECORDING
MATERIAL NOTES

GOODS RECEIVED NOTES ARE PRICED FROM ORDERS OR INVOICES

STORES REQUISITIONS ARE PRICED FROM THE STORES LEDGER

MATERIAL TRANSFER NOTES ARE PRICED FROM THE COST LEDGER OR COST CARD

BIN CARD	
IN	OUT
GOODS RECEIVED NOTES	STORES REQUISITIONS
STORES DEBIT NOTES	

STORES LEDGER	
DR	CR
GOODS RECEIVED NOTES	STORES REQUISITIONS
STORES DEBIT NOTES	

COST LEDGER	
DR	CR
STORES REQUISITIONS	STORES DEBIT NOTES
MATERIAL TRANSFER NOTES	

FIG. 16.—*Accounting for material*

MATERIALS ISSUED AT INFLATED PRICE

Wastage of materials frequently occurs in a store due to evaporation, deterioration in quality, or some similar cause. When this occurs, it is necessary to charge materials to production at an inflated price to ensure that the true cost is recovered. For example, if 1,000 lb of material are bought at £0·10 per lb, and it is known from past experience that the normal wastage of this material is 5%, the charge to production should be:

$$\frac{£100}{950} = £0 \cdot 10\frac{1}{2} \text{ per lb.}$$

SMALL TOOLS

In a general engineering factory such tools form a large and valuable stock, consisting as they do of such items as turning tools and bits, milling cutters, reamers, drills, tap, dies and many other items of small equipment. Storage, inspection and maintenance of such tools involves considerable expense and careful control. This control is effected by the use of check discs, foremen's requisitions or both.

Tool-store procedure is described in Chapter 18.

CATEGORIES OF STOCK

It is usual to keep separate stores for part-finished stocks, finished stocks, raw materials and indirect materials. The definitions of the kinds of stock are given below:

Raw materials

Primary materials purchased or produced in either a natural or manufactured condition. Manufactured materials of one industry are often the raw materials of another.

Bulk material

This is a term often used to describe material not in unit form directly suited to the work in hand, as, for example, material not measurable except by weight or volume, e.g. sheets, bars, tubes and bales.

Part-finished stock

This is work in progress that has not reached the stage of completion as a part or component. In the case of some chemical or food-manufacturing process the work in progress often consists of quantities of part-processed material or intermediate products.

Finished parts

These are items, or sub-assemblies, put into store awaiting final assembly, or sale as spares.

Finished stock

This is the completed product awaiting sale or despatch. Stock is so named after transfer from work in progress, physically and by entry in the accounts.

Stores expenses

If of a general nature stores expenses are included in stores overhead, but expenses particular to a specific order may be charged thereto in addition to the price of the material, as may the cost of carriage inwards and handling.

EXAMINATION QUESTIONS

1. List the advantages claimed for an effective stores record system.

(*C.I.A.*)

2. Draw up a specimen bin card for use in a general store and give your reasoned advice as to whether it should be kept in the store office or alongside the goods to which it relates.

(*R.S.A. Advanced*)

3. Departmental stores situated in a works frequently interchange various materials. Describe an accounting system showing how these transactions should be recorded.

(*I.C.W.A. Inter.*)

4. Design a stores issue note suitable for requisitioning direct or indirect materials in a large organisation. Describe how it should be used.

(*I.C.A.*)

5. Briefly describe a system of recording the receipt and issue of goods from store to departments in any manufacturing business with which you are familiar.

(*C.I.S. Inter.*)

6. Discuss the respective merits and demerits of keeping store records of quantities:

(*a*) alongside the stocks to which they relate;
(*b*) in cabinets in an office conveniently placed in the storehouse;
(*c*) in the cost office.

(*I.C.W.A. Inter.*)

7. Describe the arrangements you would make for stock-taking throughout a large works in order that completion may be reached as quickly as possible.

(*I.C.W.A. Inter.*)

8. The following comparisons have been taken from the material control records of a company:

	Material A		Material B		Material C	
	Quan-tity	Value	Quan-tity	Value	Quan-tity	Value
		£		£		£
Bin card	20	—	4	—	20	—
Stores Ledger	40	20·00	—	10·62½	25	—
Perpetual inventory (physical count)	15	—	5	—	20	—

Surmise as to the causes of these discrepancies and state how you would investigate them.

(*I.C.W.A. Inter.*)

9. The physical stock of Material D.7 is different from the quantity shown as stock on the bin card and also that shown as stock in the Stock Ledger Account.

You are required to:

(*a*) give possible reasons as to how the differences may have been caused; and

(*b*) describe how you would deal with such differences in the Stock Ledger Accounts and how you would correct the bin card.

(*I.C.W.A. Inter.*)

10. A manufacturing company has a comprehensive system of material recording and control.

You are required:

(*i*) to state the information required to be included in a goods received voucher;

(*ii*) to draw out a simple flow chart showing the movement of a goods received voucher from the time of its preparation at the works gate; and

(*iii*) to detail the actions which should arise throughout the course of its flow.

(*C.A. Final*)

11. You are asked to consider the advisability of issuing stores of minor value in bulk to user departments in order to save expense in handling and accounting for individual stores requisitions of small value. List the factors you would take into account before giving your views.

(*I.C.W.A. Inter.*)

12. During the year, your company has purchased and received 1,500 tons of bulky raw material which is stored in the factory yard. Issues have been recorded amounting to 1,200 tons. Physical stock-taking at the accounting year-end reveals only 200 tons in stock. How would you deal in your cost re-

cords with the deficit of 100 tons in physical stock? What procedure would you install to ensure that deficits will not occur in the future?

(I.C.W.A. Inter.)

13. As cost accountant to a manufacturing company, what information relating to materials and material costs would you supply to different levels of management?

(I.C.W.A. Inter.)

14. (a) Distinguish between slow-moving, dormant and obsolete stocks.

(b) What principles would you follow in pricing these stocks for stock-taking purposes?

(c) What practical steps should be taken to minimise the losses and costs arising from the existence of these stocks?

(I.C.W.A. Inter.)

15. At the time of the great American slump of the late 1920s, it was said that "stocks are the graveyard of a business." Give your views on this statement. Is it pertinent now? What steps would you take to avoid a similar situation today?

(I.C.W.A. Inter.)

16. You are employed by a manufacturing organisation where direct material costs average 75% of total cost. In spite of this, most attention in recent years has been given to the study of direct and indirect labour in the search for cost improvements. Attention is now to be turned to raw materials and component parts. State the possible fields of investigation into material costs and indicate briefly the approach you would propose to secure cost improvements.

(I.C.W.A. Final)

17. (a) Discuss the advantages of using code numbers in a system of stores classification.

(b) How would you construct a simple stores classification code? Give a brief illustration of such a code.

(c) T Limited produces timber which it sells in 10 feet lengths. The size of the timber produced varies from $\frac{1}{4}''$ to 12$''$ in width and from $\frac{1}{4}''$ to 2$''$ in thickness. A coding system is used, parts of which are as follows:

Softwood	$5'' \times 1\frac{3}{4}''$	Code 11014
Hardwood	$7\frac{1}{2}'' \times 1\frac{1}{4}''$	Code 21510

What codes should be used for the following materials?

Hardwood $1\frac{1}{2}'' \times \frac{5}{8}''$
Softwood $4\frac{1}{2}'' \times \frac{3}{4}''$

What do the following codes represent?

11915
21512

(d) T Limited decides to stock, as a new line, 6 feet dowelling in diameters from $\frac{1}{4}''$ to $\frac{3}{4}''$. Suggest a suitable coding within the system and give as an example the code for $\frac{3}{4}''$ diameter dowelling.

(I.C.W.A. Inter.)

18. You are helping a client to improve his accounting and control systems with a view to the introduction of standard costing. The following decisions have been reached:

1. Work in progress will be costed on the basis only of raw materials and direct labour valued at standard prices. All other expenditures, including the cost of consumable materials, will be treated as period costs.

2. Separate expense budgets will be prepared for the managers of each manufacturing cost centre and for the sales manager, the chief accountant and the general works manager, and expenditures must be analysed accordingly.

3. Each manufacturing process will be a cost centre with its own Work-in-progress Account.

You find, however, that the client is still experiencing considerable difficulty in identifying the manager responsible for the various elements of cost and expense and in reliably recording the following documentation:

(*i*) Invoices for raw materials in the appropriate stock accounts.

(*ii*) Invoices for consumable materials in the appropriate stock accounts.

(*iii*) Vouchers for: raw material issues from stock; labour cost incurred; and work-in-progress transferred.

(*iv*) Expense invoices; and vouchers for consumable material issues.

You are told that the solution lies in preparing and introducing a suitable code of accounts.

You are required, in the circumstances explained, to:

(*a*) illustrate the structure or groupings of the code which you would adopt;

(*b*) give two reasons each for (*i*) the number of digits chosen and (*ii*) the arrangement of the structure adopted;

(*c*) explain in a few lines how you would ensure reliable application of the code to solve each of the problems described under (*i*) to (*iv*) above.

(*I.C.A. Final.* May 1969)

19. State the comparative advantages to a manufacturing company of maintaining its stocks in: (*a*) central stores; (*b*) sub-stores.

(*I.C.W.A. Inter.*)

20. What are the advantages and disadvantages of operating sub-stores in a large engineering factory in which there are fifteen production departments and five service departments? In a factory of this nature, how would you ensure that a reasonable level of stock is maintained in each sub-store?

(*I.C.W.A. Inter.*)

21. Explain the imprest system of stores control and discuss its advantages and disadvantages.

(*I.C.W.A. Inter.*)

22. (*a*) Define the term imprest system of stores control and state:

(*i*) the steps taken in its use;

(*ii*) the conditions under which it should be used;

(*iii*) the benefits to be expected.

(b) Enumerate the advantages and disadvantages of a centralised stores system.

(*I.C.W.A. Inter.*)

23. How would you deal with the following in stores records and what procedure would you adopt?

(a) Breakages in stores.
(b) Scrap returned to stores.
(c) Gain or loss in weight through climatic conditions.
(d) Excess materials requisitioned and returned to stores without advice.

(*C.A.A. Part 2*)

24. In the cost accounts of a chemical manufacturing company, how would you deal with:

(a) losses of raw materials in manufacture;
(b) storage losses of raw materials?

(*C.A.A. Part 2*)

25. Define stores turnover and discuss briefly its importance in material control. Using your own figures, calculate the stores turnover of a business.

(*I.C.W.A. Inter.*)

26. What are the advantages of keeping stores by the perpetual inventory system?

(*C.A.A. Part 2*)

27. What is meant by perpetual inventory? List the advantages to be gained from operating such a system and draft a form which could be used by the staff of the inventory audit section to report on the results of their operations.

(*C.A.*)

28. (a) Outline the considerations you would have in mind in preparing for the annual stock-taking in a medium-sized engineering concern.

(b) Briefly set out the advantages which might accrue to the company if a system of perpetual inventory and continuous stock-taking were to be installed.

(*A.C.C.A. Inter.*)

29. Describe briefly how you would conduct the audit of a system of continuous stock-taking and what procedure you would adopt to deal with differences.

(*I.C.W.A. Inter.*)

30. In a factory where "continuous stock-taking" is carried out periodically discrepancies are discovered. Suggest possible causes of these discrepancies.

(*A.C.C.A. Final*)

31. (a) What are the most important features of perpetual inventory and continuous stock-taking?

(b) Design a stock check sheet.

(*I.C.W.A. Inter.*)

32. A system of continuous stock-taking is operated in a large engineering company. Stock-takers frequently discover discrepancies when checking stocks of raw materials.

As cost accountant of the company, you are required to submit a report to the board of directors, in which you should suggest possible causes for these discrepancies. Outline the cost-accounting treatment required for normal and abnormal losses in stores.

(*I.C.W.A. Inter.*)

33. Describe in detail a method of controlling the replenishment of stocks of manufactured component parts.

(*I.C.W.A. Inter.*)

34. What do you understand by maximum and minimum stocks and ordering level?

(*R.S.A. Advanced*)

35. In connection with a stock record the term "ordering level" is sometimes used. In what way does this differ from the terms "minimum" and "maximum" stocks?

(*I.C.W.A. Inter.*)

36. Discuss the considerations that influence the setting of maximum and minimum stock levels and re-ordering levels.

(*I.C.W.A. Inter.*)

37. As accountant you are concerned as to the amount of working capital invested in raw material stocks, and would like to see it reduced if possible.

The works manager, for his part, wishes to be sure that these stocks never fall too low.

You therefore agree to meet each other to discuss the possibility of fixing:

(*a*) maximum;
(*b*) minimum stock levels.

List the factors which in your opinion should be taken into consideration in fixing (*a*) and (*b*), and outline the procedure you would recommend for implementing the scheme of stock control.

(*A.C.C.A. Inter.*)

38. What steps would you take to ascertain and to eliminate over-investment of capital in stocks?

(*I.C.W.A. Inter.*)

39. Your managing director wishes to reduce the investment in stocks and stores as disclosed by a recent balance sheet and asks you to investigate and report. List the type of information you would submit and the factors to which you would draw attention.

(*I.C.W.A. Inter.*)

40. As cost accountant of a manufacturing concern of medium size, you have proposed to the directors that the stores control system should be improved. Your proposals are to be discussed by the directors at their next board meeting. To enable them to appreciate the basic requirements of an up-to-date system the directors have asked you to present a report concentrating on certain definite aspects.

Prepare a report to the directors dealing particularly with the following:

(*a*) The steps to be taken to introduce maximum, minimum and re-order stock levels, enumerating the factors to be considered in setting each level and stating the advantages to be gained by their use.

(*b*) The importance of stores turnover as a measure in considering requirements for working capital.

(*I.C.W.A. Inter.*)

41. (*a*) The following information is available in respect of component D20:

Maximum stock level: 8,400 units
Budgeted consumption: maximum 1,500 units per month
minimum 800 units per month
Estimated delivery period: maximum 4 months
minimum 2 months.

You are required to calculate:

(*i*) re-order level;
(*ii*) re-order quantity.

(*b*) Define the re-order level. What factors must be considered in setting this level?

(*c*) Does the re-order quantity have an effect on the average stock level of a component? Support your answer with a suitable explanation.

(*I.C.W.A. Inter.*)

42. Two components, A and B, are used as follows:

Normal usage 50 per week each
Minimum usage 25 ,, ,,
Maximum usage 75 ,, ,,
Re-order quantity A: 300; B: 500
Re-order period A: 4 to 6 weeks; B: 2 to 4 weeks

Calculate for each component:

(*a*) re-order level;
(*b*) minimum level;
(*c*) maximum level;
(*d*) average stock level.

Comment briefly on the difference in levels for the two components.

(*I.C.W.A. Inter.*)

43. In manufacturing its products, a company uses three raw materials, A, B and C, in respect of which the following apply:

Raw material	Usage per unit of product	Re-order quantity	Price £ per lb	Delivery period			Re-order level	Minimum level
	(lb)	(lb)		Weeks			(lb)	(lb)
				Min.	Av.	Max.		
A	10	10,000	0·10	1	2	3	8,000	
B	4	5,000	0·30	3	4	5	4,750	
C	6	10,000	0·15	2	3	4		2,000

Weekly production varies from 175 to 225 units, averaging 200.

(a) What do you understand by:

(i) minimum stock;
(ii) maximum stock;
(iii) re-order level?

(b) What would you expect the quantities of the following to be:

(i) minimum stock of A;
(ii) maximum stock of B;
(iii) re-order level of C;
(iv) average stock level of A?

(c) If Material B could be purchased in 10,000 lb lots at £0·29 per lb:

(i) what would be the increase in the value of the average stock of B?
(ii) what would be the reduction in raw material costs per unit of product?
(iii) what would be the annual saving (assuming a 48-week production-year) on material costs as a percentage of the average increase in investment in stocks?

(I.C.W.A. Inter.)

44. Graph the following information relating to a period of 30 working days:

Opening stock: 100 lb
Usage: 1st 10 days: 15 lb per day
 2nd 10 days: 12 lb per day
 3rd 10 days: 20 lb per day.

Re-order level is 70 lb, and re-order quantity is 120 lb. Any goods ordered are delivered at the end of the third day after reaching or passing the re-order level.

(a) From your graph read off:

(i) the maximum stock in the period;
(ii) the minimum stock in the period;
(iii) closing stock for the period.

(b) If 20 lb per day is the maximum usage and 15 lb is the average usage, comment on the re-order level and the minimum level.

(I.C.W.A. Inter.)

45. The moving of material from stores to, and in, departments involves both labour and overhead expenses. Do you consider these should all be recovered by a direct charge against material or as a departmental overhead? Briefly explain your reasons for the method you suggest.

(I.C.W.A. Final)

46. You are required to design a stock card for recording raw material stocks in a manufacturing business. The card should cover the recording of orders not yet received and of issues to production earmarked but not yet made. Describe the techniques that could be employed to determine appropriate stock levels.

(C.A. Final)

47. (a) Supply the missing entries in columns 1, 2, 3 and 4 in the following record card (which relates to units only):

	Allocated	Free Balance	Ordered	In	Balance on order	Out	Balance in stock
B/F	250	650	—	—	500	—	400
Week 1	550			700		640	
2	850			500		640	
3	200			720		640	

Orders are placed in 500 lots when the free balance is reduced to 400 or less.

(b) What other information may be included on a stores record card?

(c) If the value of the opening balances in stock is £1 per unit and the values of receipts in weeks 1, 2 and 3 is £1·20, £1·10 and £1·25 per unit respectively, tabulate the total values of weekly issues and of the balances in stock at the end of each week if:

(1) issues are priced on FIFO basis;
(2) issues are priced on LIFO basis.

(I.C.W.A. Inter.)

48. The following information in summary form has been extracted from the stores card of a manufacturing company for material code 1324:

Description of material: 6″ angles.
Code: 1324.   Unit: each.
Re-order quantity: 2,000.
Re-order level: 500 free balance.

Date	Free balance	Ordered		Allocated		Stock		
			Balance	For month	Balance	Received	Issued	Balance
1 Sept.		—	1,100	—	900	—	—	1,500
Month ended								
30 Sept.				1,800		2,400	1,500	
31 Oct.				3,700		1,200	1,900	
30 Nov.				900		2,800	3,100	

Any assumption that you consider it is necessary to make in compiling the answer should be stated.

You are required to show at the end of each month the following balances:

(a) Stock.
(b) On order.
(c) On allocation.
(d) Free balance.

(I.C.W.A. Inter.)

49. Design a stores record card which you consider would provide for the optimum information in respect of any material in store. Insert the following figures in respect of Material R2 in the stores record card and balance off the stores record card at the end of each month:

Balances brought down at October 1, included:

	Units
Allocated	2,000
Ordered	3,000
Stock	1,500

Transactions during the period included:

	October units	November units	December units
Issued	2,800	3,300	4,100
Allocated	3,200	4,700	2,200
Received	2,500	4,000	3,800
Returned to suppliers	400	—	200
Returned to stores	—	300	—

Orders for supplies of R2 are placed in lots of 3,000 units when the free balance falls to 1,000 units or less.

(*I.C.W.A. Inter.*)

50. (*a*) Tabulate the main factors which should be taken into consideration in determining the following:

(*i*) Maximum stock level.
(*ii*) Minimum stock level.
(*iii*) Re-order quantity.

(*b*) A Ltd. makes and sells product J2 among many others. Three raw materials are used exclusively in the manufacture of this product. You are given the following information:

Raw material	X lb	Y lb	Z lb
Standard quantity required per unit of product J2	60	40	20
Maximum stock levels	72,000	48,000	24,000
Stocks at April 1	62,000	38,000	24,000
Purchase orders placed but not delivered	18,000	12,000	6,000

	Product J2 Units
Maximum stock level	1,200

At April 1 there were:

Stock in work in progress (material complete)	100
Stock in finished goods store	1,000
Sales orders received but not delivered	400

An order from an important customer was received on April 1 for 1,800 units of Product J2. No further orders are expected to be received for this product during the quarter.

In addition to completing the export customer's order, the company has decided to increase the stock of this product to the maximum stock level, in anticipation of orders during the next quarter.

It is also decided to increase the stock of materials X, Y and Z to maximum stock level.

You are required to prepare a statement showing:

(i) the production order requirements in respect of J2;
(ii) the standard quantity of each material, X, Y and Z, needed for the production programme;
(iii) the purchase order requirements for materials X, Y and Z.

(I.C.W.A. Inter.)

Chapter 6

METHODS OF VALUING MATERIAL ISSUES

There are many methods of valuing material issues, the most important being the following:

1. FIFO (first in, first out).
2. LIFO (last in, first out).
3. Base stock.
4. Simple average.
5. Weighted average.
6. Periodic simple average.
7. Periodic weighted average.
8. Standard price.

The use, advantages and disadvantages of these methods may be illustrated by the following Stores Ledger Accounts compiled from these transactions:

Jan.   1   Received   1,000 units at £1·00 per unit.

Jan.	1	Received	1,000 units at £1·00 per unit.		
,,	10	Received	260	,,	£1·05	,,
,,	20	Issued	700	,,		
Feb.	4	Received	400	,,	£1·15	,,
,,	21	Received	300	,,	£1·25	,,
March	16	Issued	620	,,		
April	12	Issued	240	,,		
May	10	Received	500	,,	£1·10	,,
,,	25	Issued	380	,,		

NOTE: For simplicity, the amounts columns in the following accounts have been calculated to the nearest £1; in practice, calculations would show £1 and decimals of £1.

1. FIFO (Fig. 17)

This method ensures that materials are issued at actual cost, so no profits or losses will be incurred merely by adopting this price; it will be seen later in this chapter that when estimates or approximations are used a profit or loss on issue may be obtained.

It is assumed that the materials purchased are issued in strict chronological order. FIFO is easy to operate, but if the price of the materials purchased fluctuates considerably it involves a number of tedious calculations, which may increase the possibility of errors.

Comparison of the costs of one job with another may be difficult because issues to one job may be at, for example, £1·00, while the next job may be priced at £0·90 or £1·10, if the stock at 1·00 has been exhausted. In stock valuation a great advantage of FIFO is that not only is stock at cost but is as closely representative of current prices as possible. When prices are falling the material charge to production is high, while the cost of stock replacement will be low. Conversely, when prices are rising, the charge to production will be low, while the replacement cost will be high.

2. LIFO (Fig. 18)

This method also ensures that materials are issued at actual cost. It is assumed that the materials purchased are issued in the reverse order to FIFO; *i.e.* the last receipt is the first issue.

LIFO suffers from the disadvantages mentioned in FIFO, concerning tedious calculations and unfair comparisons of job costs. In addition, although stock is at cost, the price is that of the oldest material in store, so does not represent current price levels. Consequently it may be necessary to write off stock losses during periods of falling prices, as the book values of the materials will exceed market values.

A great advantage of this method is that the charge to production is as closely related to current price levels as possible. Assuming the purchase of materials was in recent times, it will not be necessary to ascertain market values.

3. BASE STOCK (Fig. 19)

This method also ensures that materials are issued at actual cost. It is assumed that a fixed minimum stock of the material is always carried at original cost. On page 38 it was mentioned that a minimum stock is calculated for each item of material in stock below which the stock is not allowed to fall. In effect, this minimum stock is always in store, and cannot be released unless an emergency arises, for instance when supplies of the material are delayed and production must continue, or the business ceases to continue, when the stock will be sold. This minimum stock is therefore regarded as being in the nature of a fixed asset.

Base stock is rather similar to FIFO in operation, and suffers from the same disadvantages, namely, tedious calculations and unfair comparisons of job costs.

In stock valuation the stock will normally contain the minimum stock plus any of the latest purchases which have not been issued to production. Figure 19 assumes that a minimum stock of 100 units was to be carried.

STORES LEDGER ACCOUNT

Material: Code: Folio: ....
Maximum Quantity: ....   Location: ....
Minimum Quantity: ....

Date	Receipts G.R. No.	Quantity	Price £	Amount £	Issues S.R. No.	Quantity	Price £	Amount £	Stock Quantity	Price £	Amount £
Jan. 1		1,000	1·00	1,000					1,000	1·00	1,000
10		260	1·05	273					1,260		1,273
20						700	1·00	700	560		573
Feb. 4		400	1·15	460					960		1,033
21		300	1·25	375					1,260		1,408
Mar. 16						620					
						300	1·00	300	640		766
						260	1·05	273	400		490
						60	1·15	69			
						240	1·15	276			
Apr. 12		500	1·10	550					900		1,040
May 10						100	1·15	115	520		575
25						380					
						280	1·25	350			
		520						£575			

FIG. 17.—*Stores Ledger Account: FIFO method*

This account has been entered on the "first in, first out" principle, which has the same effect as if materials were issued in strict chronological order.

NOTE: The closing stock represents:

20 units at £1·25 per unit = 25
500   "   £1·10   = 550
520   £575

STORES LEDGER ACCOUNT

Material: .... Code: .... Folio: ....

Maximum Quantity: .... Location: ....

Minimum Quantity: ....

Date	Receipts				Issues				Stock		
	G.R. No.	Quantity	Price £	Amount £	S.R. No.	Quantity	Price £	Amount £	Quantity	Price £	Amount £
Jan. 1		1,000	1·00	1,000					1,000	1·00	1,000
10		260	1·05	273					1,260		1,273
20						700 {260 440}	1·05 1·00	273 440	560		560
Feb. 4		400	1·15	460					960		1,020
21		300	1·25	375					1,260		1,395
Mar. 16						620 {300 320}	1·25 1·15	375 368	640		652
Apr. 12						240 {80 160}	1·15 1·00	92 160	400		400
May 10		500	1·10	550					900		950
25						380	1·10	418	520		532

FIG. 18.—*Stores Ledger Account: LIFO method*

This records the same facts as in Fig. 17, but on the "last in, first out" principle. This tends to charge current production with current prices.

NOTE: The closing stock represents:

400 units at £1·00 per unit = 400
120 ,, £1·10 ,, = 132
520 £532

STORES LEDGER ACCOUNT

Material: ....   Code: ....   Maximum Quantity: ....   Folio: ....

       Minimum Quantity: ....   Location: ....

Date	G.R. No.	Receipts Quantity	Price £	Amount £	S.R. No.	Issues Quantity	Price £	Amount £	Stock Quantity	Price £	Amount £
Jan. 1		1,000	1·00	1,000					1,000	1·00	1,000
10		260	1·05	273					1,260		1,273
20						700	1·00	700	560		573
Feb. 4		400	1·15	460					960		1,033
21		300	1·25	375					1,260		1,408
Mar. 16						200	1·00	200			
						260	1·05	273			
						160	1·15	184	640		751
						620					
Apr. 12						240	1·15	276	400		475
May 10		500	1·10	550					900		1,025
25						300	1·25	375			
						80	1·10	88	520		562
						380					

FIG. 19.—*Stores Ledger Account: base stock method*

The entries shown here conform to the base stock method of keeping stores. This supposes that each stores account carries a fixed minimum stock below which it must not be allowed to fall, and which is therefore never issued.

NOTE: The closing stock represents:

$$
\begin{array}{llll}
100 \text{ units at} & £1·00 \text{ per unit} & = & 100 \text{ (Base)} \\
420 \quad ,, & £1·10 \quad ,, & = & 462 \\
\cline{1-1}\cline{4-4}
520 & & & £562 \\
\end{array}
$$

4. SIMPLE AVERAGE (Fig. 20)

Under this method an approximated figure is obtained, owing to the fact that the total of the prices paid for the material is divided by the number of prices used in the calculation. Materials are not therefore charged out at actual cost, so a profit or loss may be incurred merely by adopting this price when evaluating materials charged to production.

The simple average is very easy to operate, and when prices of purchases do not fluctuate very much can give reasonably accurate results.

It will be noticed that in this illustration the design of the account has been changed slightly. Cumulative quantity columns have been introduced so that comparisons one with another can be made to ascertain which materials have been fully issued from stock. It is recommended that the cumulative issues column is not entered until after the price has been calculated. Thus:

In the first issue:

Cumulative receipts 1,260; Cumulative issues NIL, so price is:

$$(£1·00 + £1·05) \div 2 = £1·02\tfrac{1}{2};$$

In the second issue:

Cumulative receipts 1,960; Cumulative issues 700, so price is:

$$(1·00 + 1·05 + 1·15 + 1·25) \div 4 = £1·11;$$

In the third issue:

Cumulative receipts 1,960; Cumulative issues 1,320;

1,320 exceeds cumulative receipts to January 10 (1,260), so price is:

$$(1·15 + 1·25) \div 2 = £1·20;$$

In the fourth issue:

Cumulative receipts 2,460; Cumulative issues 1,560;

1,560 exceeds cumulative receipts to January 10 (1,260) but is still less than cumulative receipts to February 4 (1,660), so price is:

$$(1·15 + 1·25 + 1·10) \div 3 = £1·16\tfrac{1}{2}.$$

It was mentioned above that a profit or loss may be incurred by using this method. If we compare the value of closing stock (£527) with, for example, the value of closing stock under FIFO, which was £575, we find that we have charged more to production than was necessary, so have made a profit on issue of £48.

STORES LEDGER ACCOUNT

Material: ....   Code: ....   Maximum Quantity: ....   Folio: ....

Minimum Quantity: ....   Location: ....

Date	G.R. No.	Receipts Quantity Actual	Cum.	Price £	Amount £	S.R. No.	Issues Quantity Actual	Cum.	Price £	Amount £	Stock Quantity	Price £	Amount £
Jan. 1		1,000	1,000	1·00	1,000						1,000	1·00	1,000
10		260	1,260	1·05	273						1,260		1,273
20							700	700	1·02½	718	560		555
Feb. 4		400	1,660	1·15	460						960		1,015
21		300	1,960	1·25	375						1,260		1,390
Mar. 16							620	1,320	1·11	682	640		708
Apr. 12							240	1,560	1·20	288	400		420
May 10		500	2,460	1·10	550						900		970
25							380	1,940	1·16½	443	520		527

FIG. 20.—*Stores Ledger Account: simple average method.*

In this simple average method, the issue price is obtained by averaging the prices which have been paid on purchases. When prices are stable the average price will be fair and reasonable.

NOTE: Under the average methods the identity of materials in store disappears, so that the closing stock figure cannot be verified as under the previous system.

5. WEIGHTED AVERAGE (Fig. 21)

This method is similar to the simple average price in that a profit or loss on issue may be incurred owing to the approximation of figures; but it is more complicated to operate than the simple average price, owing to the fact that total quantities and total costs are considered. It is essential to calculate issue prices to a considerable degree of accuracy if the benefit of the system is to be obtained; usually calculations are to four decimal places. However, this greater accuracy is an advantage of this method, particularly where the prices paid for materials fluctuate considerably.

It should be noted that this method differs from all the other methods described in this chapter, in that issue prices are calculated on *receipt* of materials, not on issue of materials.

In the Stock section above, as each delivery of material is received the total cost in the Stock column is divided by the total quantity in the Stock column; thus:

$$\frac{£1,273}{1,260} = £1 \cdot 0103.$$

On issue the quantity issued is multiplied by the last stock calculation of price, thus:

$$700 \text{ at } £1 \cdot 0103 = £707.$$

6. PERIODIC SIMPLE AVERAGE PRICE (Fig. 22)

This method is similar to the two previous methods in that a profit or loss on issue may be incurred owing to the approximation of figures, here caused by dividing the *total* prices of the materials obtained during that period by the number of prices used in the calculation.

The periodic simple average price is extremely simple to operate; the only calculation of issue price occurs at the end of the period concerned. It is very similar to the simple average price, with the exception that it is calculated periodically, not on the occasion of each issue of material. The purchases during the period and closing stock are included in the calculation, but it must be noted that the opening stock does not enter into the calculation because it was not purchased during the current period, and would have been included in last year's calculation.

A disadvantage of this method is that, although the calculation of the issue price is relatively easy, the fact that the issue prices of all materials in store will have to be calculated at the end of each period leads to a considerable amount of work at one time.

This system can be utilised in process industries where each individual order is absorbed into the general cost of producing a large

STORES LEDGER ACCOUNT

Material: .... Code: ....
Maximum Quantity: .... Folio: ....
Minimum Quantity: .... Location: ....

Date	Receipts				Issues				Stock		
	G.R. No.	Quantity	Price £	Amount £	S.R. No.	Quantity	Price £	Amount £	Quantity	Price £	Amount £
Jan. 1		1,000	1·00	1,000					1,000	1·0000	1,000
10		260	1·05	273					1,260	1·0103	1,273
20						700	1·0103	707	560		566
Feb. 4		400	1·15	460					960	1·0688	1,026
21		300	1·25	375					1,260	1·1119	1,401
Mar. 16						620	1·1119	689	640		712
Apr. 12						240	1·1119	267	400		445
May 10		500	1·10	550					900	1·1056	995
25						380	1·1050	420	520		575

FIG. 21.—*Stores Ledger Account: weighted average method*

The weighted average is calculated afresh each time a purchase is made. The quantity bought is added to the stock in hand, and the revised balance is then divided into the new cash value of the stock. The effect of early prices is thus eliminated.

STORES LEDGER ACCOUNT

Material: .... Code: .... Maximum Quantity: .... Folio: ....

Minimum Quantity: .... Location: ....

Date	Receipts				Issues				Stock		
	G.R. No.	Quantity	Price £	Amount £	S.R. No.	Quantity	Price £	Amount £	Quantity	Price £	Amount £
Jan. 1		1,000	1·00	1,000					1,000	1·00	1,000
10		260	1·05	273					1,260		1,273
20						700			560		
Feb. 4		400	1·15	460					960		
21		300	1·25	375					1,260		
Mar. 16						620			640		
Apr. 12						240			400		
May 10		500	1·10	550					900		
25						380			520		
		2,460	£5·55	£2,658		1,940	£1·11	£2,153			505

FIG. 22.—*Stores Ledger Account: periodic simple average method*

This method follows the principle of the simple average price (Fig. 20) but a period is set over which the average will be calculated. The calculation made at the end of the period is then used as the issue price for the period in question.

NOTE

The periodic simple average price is:

$$\frac{\text{Total prices of the materials}}{\text{Number of prices}} = \frac{£5\cdot55}{5} = £1\cdot11 \text{ per unit.}$$

Receipts − Issues = Closing stock.
£2,658 − £2,153 = £505.

quantity of articles, but where each individual order must be priced at each stage up to completion the method would be unsatisfactory.

However, if closing stock is valued at £1·11 per unit, this would give 520 × £1·11 = £577. This shows the discrepancy of the system.

7. PERIODIC WEIGHTED AVERAGE PRICE (Fig. 23)

As in all the average-price methods mentioned above, a profit or loss on issue of materials is incurred due to approximations; in this case it is caused by dividing the *total* cost of the materials obtained during that period by the quantity purchased. However, any differences will be very small owing to greater accuracy. Unlike the weighted average price, this method is easy to operate, the only calculation of issue price occurring at the end of the period concerned. Owing to the fact that quantities and costs are considered, this method is much more accurate than the periodic simple average price; otherwise comments mentioned in (6) above apply equally well to this system.

8. STANDARD PRICE (Fig. 24)

The standard-price method also incurs a profit or loss on issue, but this is not due to approximation of calculations as noted in the average-price methods; it is due to variances from a pre-determined price for each material in store.

A pre-determined price is ascertained which takes into consideration a number of factors which may influence the prices of materials in a future period; such factors include the following:

(a) The quantity of materials to be purchased, which will affect quantity discounts.

(b) The possibility of a rise in prices due to expected wage increases.

(c) The likelihood of a rise or fall in prices due to market conditions.

(d) The charging of freight and warehousing expenses to the material.

(e) The charging of containers to the material.

The standard price will be set for each material, which can then be compared with the actual price paid. If the actual price paid exceeds standard, then a loss will be realised; if the actual price is less than standard, a profit will be obtained.

This method is relatively easy to operate, because all issues of the material are calculated at the same price. A great advantage is the opportunity to check the efficiency of the purchase of materials, by seeing whether or not the actual price exceeds standard.

It should be noted that this method can be utilised in most industries, even though a system of standard costing is not in operation, although

STORES LEDGER ACCOUNT

Material: .... Code: .... Maximum Quantity: .... Folio: ....

Minimum Quantity: .... Location: ....

Date	Receipts				Issues				Stock		
	G.R. No.	Quantity	Price £	Amount £	S.R. No.	Quantity	Price £	Amount £	Quantity	Price £	Amount £
Jan. 1		1,000	1·00	1,000					1,000		1,000
10		260	1·05	273					1,260		1,273
20						700			560		
Feb. 4		400	1·15	460					960		
21		300	1·25	375					1,260		
Mar. 16						620			640		
Apr. 12						240			400		
May 10		500	1·10	550					900		
25						380			520		563
		2,460		£2,658		1,940	£1·08	£2,095			

FIG. 23.—*Stores Ledger Account: periodic weighted average method*

The periodic weighted average price is also calculated at the end of a given period, and is obtained by dividing the total cost of purchases by the total quantity received.

The periodic weighted average price is:

NOTES

$$\frac{\text{Total cost of materials}}{\text{Quantity purchased}} = \frac{£2,658}{2,460} = £1\cdot08 \text{ per unit.}$$

Receipts — Issues = Closing stock.

£2,658 — £2,095 = £563.

If closing stock is valued at £1·08 per unit, this would give:

520 × 1·08 = £562 (approx.). This shows that the figures are approximately correct.

STORES LEDGER ACCOUNT

Material:............ Code:............ Maximum Quantity:............ Folio:............

Minimum Quantity:............ Location:............

Date	Receipts				Issues				Stock		
	G.R. No.	Quantity	Price £	Amount £	S.R. No.	Quantity	Price £	Amount £	Quantity	Price £	Amount £
Jan. 1		1,000	1·00	1,000					1,000		1,000
10		260	1·05	273					1,260		1,273
20						700	1·15	805	560		468
Feb. 4		400	1·15	460					960		928
21		300	1·25	375					1,260		1,303
Mar. 16						620	1·15	713	640		590
Apr. 12						240	1·15	276	400		314
May 10		500	1·10	550					900		864
25						380	1·15	437	520		427
		2,460		£2,658		1,940		£2,231			

FIG. 24.—*Stores Ledger Account: standard-price method*

The standard-price method ensures that production is charged always at the standard price for the commodity, variances from the actual price paid being transferred to Price Variance Account.

of course the greatest benefit will be obtained under a standard costing system.

Assume that the standard price for this material is £1·15 per unit.

It will be noticed that the closing value of stock is under-valued, owing to the fact that production has been charged at a higher price (the standard price) than the actual price. If the actual price of the material had exceeded the standard price, the stock would have been over-valued.

To ascertain whether or not the buying of materials has been efficiently performed:

(Actual receipts × Standard price) — Actual amount
$$= (2,460 \times £1·15) - £2,658$$
$$= £2,829 - £2,658$$
$$= £171.$$

It was expected that the cost of materials purchased would be £2,829, so £171 represents the efficiency in purchasing.

If the closing stock is valued at standard price, the value would be:

$$520 \times £1·15 = £598.$$

Compare this figure with the amount shown in the above account (£427), and the resulting difference is £171, which has been shown to be the efficiency in purchasing.

HIFO

The "highest in, first out" method has not been adopted widely, so it is not illustrated here, but nevertheless it warrants some brief comments. The prime aim of this method is to ensure that stock values are maintained at as low a level as possible, and that issues to work in progress are charged with the most expensive materials in stock. Under this method, issues are priced at actual prices, but it results in complicated calculations as regards the valuation of both issues and stock. As with the FIFO and LIFO systems, it leads to unfair comparisons of job costs.

NIFO

The "next in, first out" method, like the HIFO method, has not been widely adopted. It is a complicated system, which attempts to value issue prices at an actual price which is as near as possible to the market price. It will be appreciated that, if issues are to be made using the market price method, then theoretically, every time an issue is made, one should ascertain the current market price ruling at that time. Clearly, this is not very practicable. However, with the NIFO method, issues are made at the next price—*i.e.* the price of material which has been ordered but not yet received. In other words, issues are at the latest price at which the company has been committed, even though the materials have not yet been physically received. Under normal conditions, this price should be reasonably close to market prices.

In a rising market, this method will have rather similar results to HIFO, in that prices of issues will be high and stock valuations will be low. In a falling market, this method will be rather similar to LIFO, in that stock valuations will be high while issue prices will be low. In general, it is similar to the market-price method, except that it is based on actual prices rather than on prices which have been ascertained at the time of issue. Calculations of issue prices are complicated and, as with FIFO, LIFO and HIFO, lead to unfair comparisons of job costs.

INFLATED-PRICE METHOD

On page 58, it was mentioned that materials which deteriorate or evaporate may be charged out at an inflated price. This method may be used also to recover such items as storage and transport costs.[1] By using this method, costs are charged direct to each material consumed, rather than absorbed as an overhead recovery rate. It must be noted, however, that it is usually very difficult to ascertain accurately how much should be charged directly to any item of material, hence the adoption of the production overhead recovery rate by many companies.

The method adopted for pricing materials issued largely depends upon the nature of the materials, the undertaking concerned and the circumstances which require to be taken into consideration.

The purpose of cost accounts is to arrive at the actual cost of each job, or of each process or operation of manufacture, and to this end it is desirable to charge out stores material at cost.

Some businessmen prefer that material issued should be charged to cost accounts at market prices ruling at the time the materials are used, because these are the prices which would have to be paid if the material were purchased at that time. This procedure introduces considerable confusion into the accounts, and at once involves departure from the principle of showing actual costs in the cost accounts.

There are a few kinds of business, however, where the particular nature of the transactions leads the management to desire that the cost accounts should represent the current position, and correspond with estimates, as well as that the efficiency of buying should be revealed. This information is secured by charging stores at current market prices, regardless whether these are higher or lower than the actual figures paid. When this method is used a careful adjustment in a "Stores Adjustment Account" is necessary. The result of this procedure is that, in a period of falling prices, the costs of such manufacturers will show as lower than those of manufacturers who charge materials at actual prices paid at an earlier date. This does not mean that the first-named manufacturers are in a more competitive position, for the reason that when submitting estimates, or fixing prices, allowance must be made for the trend of market prices. Herein lies one of the chief points of difference between costs and estimates.

Mention must be made here also of materials which it is necessary to retain for purposes of maturing, of which perhaps the best example is timber. Logs are often sawn longitudinally and left in this rough state for seasoning, as also is timber cut into suitable sizes. In such cases the stock appreciates in value, and it is customary to increase the cost by at least the interest on the capital value the stock represents, and other special storage expenses may also be added. It is not considered that such an addition for interest to cost is valid; it is probably better to cover the value in the price.

There are many kinds of stock held for long periods for reasons other than maturing factors. Consider whisky and wines, which are held for many years. The storage, insurance, labour, etc., certainly add to the cost; but, better than charging interest in costs is to recognise that it must be included in the selling price. Profit for each year's tied-up capital must be included in the price, which therefore involves a calculation at compound interest.

It is important to realise that in this chapter we have been discussing methods of pricing issues from stores, not methods of issuing materials. Many candidates in examinations confuse these two functions. In stores control systems, it is assumed that the storekeeper will issue materials on a "first in, first out" basis, particularly if the materials are perishable, or, perhaps, he may issue the materials which are nearest to hand. However, the system chosen for pricing issues is operated quite independently of that used by the storekeeper in physically issuing the materials. It is a common error for students to say that under a LIFO system perishable materials will become valueless or that some items will rust; this is confusing the issue. One would assume that in such a situation the stores clerk would price out materials using the LIFO method, but the storekeeper would issue the materials which came into the stores first. Some readers may think that this is stating the obvious, but it is nevertheless pertinent in view of the many students who have this misunderstanding.

STOCK VALUATION

The method of valuing stores for the Annual Balance Sheet, it is important to observe, is quite independent of the system of pricing for costing purposes. The recognised methods of pricing stores for the balance sheet compiled from the financial accounts is at cost, net realisable value or replacement price, whichever is the lowest. The cost price referred to in this connection is the average cost price of the stores on hand which, it may be assumed, will consist of the most recent purchases.

The problem which arises from valuing stock in the cost accounts at one price and the stock in the financial accounts at another price is discussed fully in Chapter 15.

SMALL PARTS USED IN LARGE QUANTITIES

Such parts, when of little individual value, are not generally requisitioned and charged separately for each production order. The average quantity used may be pre-determined and charged on that basis to each job. A quantity of each of such materials may be issued by the stores to a shop and a Shop Stores Account debited at an average cost price. This account will be credited, say weekly, with the estimated quantity for the number of orders dealt with, thereby eliminating much unnecessary detail.

An alternative procedure is for the cost of small items, for example glue used for sealing labels on cans, to be treated as indirect materials and charged to production through production overhead recovery rates. These indirect materials, sometimes called *consumable stores*, include such items as lubricants and cleaning materials, and should be requisitioned in the same way as materials issued for manufacturing operations. The requisitions are summarised and charged to suitable expense accounts.

NORMAL LOSS IN STORES

In most stores there will occur an expected loss of materials due to, for example, evaporation, deterioration and petty pilferage. Where such losses are unavoidable, they should be provided for either by using the inflated price method or by recovery in work in progress through production overheads. In the former case, no specific accounting entries are required because the issue price will absorb the normal loss, but in the latter case accounting entries are required to record the transaction:

> Dr. Production Overhead Account
> Cr. Stores Control Account

ABNORMAL LOSS IN STORES

In addition to a normal loss in stores, there will almost invariably occur an abnormal loss due to such occurrences as fire, flood, theft and posting errors. Obviously such items cannot be foreseen so must be accounted for and where possible steps should be taken to reduce the trisk of future occurrences. The accounting entries would be as follows:

Dr. Abnormal loss in Stores Account
Cr. Stores Control Account
Dr. Profit and Loss Account
Cr. Abnormal loss in Stores Account } at end of period.

EXAMINATION QUESTIONS

1. State the various methods of pricing stores requisitions with which you are familiar, and discuss their respective merits.

(*R.S.A. Adv.*)

2. Outline the effects of rising prices in relation to pricing of issues and stock valuation.

(*I.C.W.A.*)

3. During periods of rapid increase or decrease in prices of materials used in production, which of the following methods of pricing stores issues results in the most accurate costing of goods manufactured and sold?

(*a*) "First-in, first-out" method.
(*b*) Actual cost method.
(*c*) Average cost method.
(*d*) "Last-in, first-out" method.
(*e*) Standard cost method.

Give reasons in support of your answer.

(*I.C.W.A. Inter.*)

4. The following transactions occur in the purchase and issue of a material:

January	29	Purchased	100 at £5·00 each
February	4	„	25 at £5·25 „
„	12	„	50 at £5·50 „
„	14	Issued	80
March	6	Purchased	50 at £5·50 „
„	20	Issued	80
„	27	Purchased	50 at £5·75 „

Complete the Stock Account showing the balance at March 31, the end of the accounting year. State clearly your method of pricing the issues, why this method has been adopted and the price and value of the closing stock.

(*I.C.W.A. Inter.*)

5. Discuss four of the accepted methods of pricing stores issues. Indicate which method will result in the most accurate costing of goods manufactured and sold during periods of rapid increases in prices of raw materials used in production.

(*A.I.A. Final*)

6. Midwest Engineers Ltd. charges stores out to jobs on the FIFO basis. Among the stores stocked is Component AZ, on which a provision for spoilage by rust is made of 1% on the balance on the Stores Account at the beginning of each month. Stock is taken physically at three-monthly intervals and the balances on the Stores Ledger Accounts are appropriately adjusted.

On July 31 the stock of Component AZ was 2,500, on which the cost was £0·47½ per 100. During the next three months the transactions were as follows:

	Purchases quantities	Price per 100 £	Issues
August	10,000	0·50	9,150
September	20,000	0·55	20,316
October	25,000	0·60	18,070

At October 31 stock-taking recorded a shortage of 150 components. You are required:

(a) to write up the Stores Ledger Account for component AZ for the three months to October 31; and

(b) to state how you would deal with the components spoiled by rust and the shortage in stock.

(C.A.A. Part 2)

7. What principles should be used in determining the price at which items from stock should be charged to cost accounts at a time when prices are rising? Is it correct practice to use the same rule as for balance sheet valuations— "cost or market price, whichever is the lower"? Give reasons for your answer.

(C.A.A. Part 2)

8. One of the most widely used bases for the valuation of inventories is "cost or market price, whichever is lower."

(a) What is the underlying principle of this procedure?

(b) Would you use this basis for all classes of stocks; viz. raw materials, work in progress, finished goods?

(c) Explain your choice of the "individual" method or the "global" method for calculating the valuation in this way.

Give reasons for your answers.

(C.I.A. Final)

9. Due to shortage of supplies in this country, raw materials (e.g. steel) are being imported into the country at a price considerably higher than that of the home product. How would you treat this extra cost? For example, would you charge it only to the products and orders using imported materials, would you absorb the cost as a spread charge to all production or would you charge it direct to profit and loss?

(Comm. A. Final)

10. A retail trading company sells goods at prices which are normally 25% above cost. Goods which cannot be sold at the normal selling price are "marked down" to a lower selling price.

The following figures were extracted from the company's books at December 31:

	£
Stock-in-trade, January 1, at cost	2,400
Purchases for the year	42,100
Sales for the year	49,965

The stock at January 1 had been marked down to £2,930, and the goods were afterwards sold for that amount, which is included in the sales shown above (£49,965).

Certain goods purchased at a cost of £8,600 (included in purchases £42,100) had been marked down to £10,120. Some of these goods (cost £100, marked down to £85) remained in stock at December 31, but the rest had been sold at the reduced prices to which they had been marked down. These sales are included in the figure of £49,965 above.

You are required to show your calculation of the stock at December 31, at cost price.

(Comm. A. Final)

11. The following is an extract from the stores bin card relating to Commodity A:

	Units		Units
April 1 Balance	5,000	April 16 Return to	
15 Received into store	12,500	suppliers	500
		22 Withdrawn from	
		stores for sale	360
		27 Destroyed by fire	200
		30 Issues to production	
		during month	12,000
		Wastage	300
		Balance	4,140
	17,500		17,500

Stores in hand and received into store are taken into the Stores Accounts at £0·25 per unit. The stores withdrawn for sale were sold to an associated business at £0·31 per unit. Issues to production are charged at £0·25½ to cover normal wastage. The cost of wastage not covered by this inflated charge is to be written off to Works Expenses Account. The stores wasted realised a scrap value of £25.

Write up the Stores Ledger Account for Commodity A for the month of April.

(A.C.C.A. Inter.)

12. (*a*) State and discuss briefly the principles you would recommend for balance-sheet valuations of the following:

(*i*) raw materials;
(*ii*) work in progress;
(*iii*) finished goods.

(b) (i) Would you recommend the principle(s) of pricing given in your answer to (a) (i) above to be adopted in the cost accounts for the charging to work in progress of raw materials from stores?

(ii) Discuss briefly any qualifications you would place on your recommendation given in your answer to (b) (i) above in a time of fluctuating raw-material prices.

(I.C.W.A. Inter.)

13. Show the Stores Ledger entries as they would appear when using:

(a) the weighted-average method,
(b) the simple-average method, and
(c) the LIFO method

of pricing issues, in connection with the following transactions:

			Units	Price
				£
April	1	Balance in hand b/f	300	2
	2	Purchased	200	2·2
	4	Issued	150	
	6	Purchased	200	2·3
	11	Issued	150	
	19	Issued	200	
	22	Purchased	200	2·4
	27	Issued	150	

In a period of rising prices such as the above, what are the effects of each method?

(A.C.C.A. Inter.)

14. (a) The following transactions in respect of Material T20 occurred during the six months ended December 31:

Date	Purchases	Price per lb	Issues
	lb	£	lb
July	220	2·50	250
August	250	2·40	220
September	240	2·60	200
October	220	2·30	240
November	260	2·50	210
December	200	2·27½	210

The opening stock on July 1 was 240 lb at £2·40 per lb.

The closing stock on December 31 was 300 lb at £2·35 per lb.

Do you consider the value of the closing stock shown above to be a justifiable one? Give reasons.

(b) In a non-integrated accounting system, can the closing-stock valuation as shown in the cost accounts differ from that shown in the financial accounts? Give brief reasons for your answer.

(I.C.W.A. Inter.)

15. The Kwikgro Fertiliser Co. uses as one of the ingredients in its products, a compound known as XYZ which it buys from several suppliers both in the

U.K. and abroad. Issues to production are in units of one hundredweight and are charged out on the weighted-average basis.

On November 1 the stock of XYZ was 60 cwt valued at £2·45 per cwt. Receipts for November were as follows:

> 4th 500 cwt at £3 per cwt less 10% trade discount, carriage paid. The consignment was delivered in 10 containers included on the invoice at £10 each, £6 per container being credited on return.
>
> 20th 1,000 cwt from Sweden for £2,000 bulk price, plus freight £150 and insurance £40.

Issues for November were as follows:

2nd	40 cwt
10th	100 cwt
18th	300 cwt
22nd	500 cwt
29th	300 cwt

Prepare an account for November for compound XYZ indicating clearly the value of each intake, the unit issue prices and the value of the closing stock. Your calculations should be taken to three decimal places.

(A.C.C.A. Inter.)

16. The directors of a small manufacturing concern are considering the possibility of expanding the business of their company. As a preliminary approach towards this end, you are asked to consider, as cost accountant, certain steps to be taken to introduce a stores control system.

Prepare a report to the directors in this connection concentrating on the following features:

(a) The method of pricing to be adopted, discussing three of the following methods:

> FIFO;
> LIFO;
> HIFO;
> NIFO;

and their relative effects on:

(*i*) the cost of production;
(*ii*) the stock valuation.

You may assume that the market is experiencing a period of falling prices.

(b) The factors to be considered in determining an efficient location and layout of stores.

(I.C.W.A. Inter.)

17. The following information for the three months ended November 30 in respect of a certain material has been extracted from the Stores Ledger Account of a manufacturing company:

Date	Receipts			Issues		
	Quantity units	Price £	Amount £	Quantity units	Price £	Amount £
Sept. 1						
Balance b/d	1,500	1·50				
Sept. 12	2,000	1·52½				
18				1,100		1,650
Oct. 10				800		1,210
16				1,000		1,525
18	2,400	1·60				
20				900		1,395
Nov. 2	5,000	1·62½				
6				900		1,440
15				2,400		3,870

At the physical stock-taking at November 30 3,600 units were in stock.
You are required to:

(a) state:

(i) the method of pricing you consider was employed;

(ii) whether the method was a suitable one;

(b) calculate the values of the transactions given and make any entries you consider necessary to complete the account for the three months; an explanation should be given of adjustments included;

(c) if the LIFO method of pricing had been in use show the value of the stock at November 30.

(I.C.W.A. Inter.)

18. Consideration is being given to the method to be used for the pricing of issues from a Raw Material Stores Ledger. The account for a certain material, for the month of April has been used for this. A comparison of the results achieved by two different pricing methods has been commenced and partially completed. These results are as below:

Date	Receipts		Issues		
				First method	Second method
April	Quantity units	Value	Quantity units	value	value
		£		£	£
1	600	750			
3	200	240			
8			400	500	500
9	500	575			
10			400	490	490
11	600	660			
14			400	460	460
16	500	600			
18			400	445	480
21			300	330	
22	500	575			
24			600	715	
25	400	480			
28			300	345	

There was no opening stock.

Stock in hand at April 30 was 480 units.

You are required to:

(a) identify and state both the first and second methods of pricing used;

(b) complete the account for the second pricing method;

(c) list briefly the merits and demerits of the second pricing method.

(I.C.W.A. Inter.)

19. From the data given, answer the following:

(a) What is the simple average price of the four weeks' receipts of material A?

(b) What is the weighted average price of the four weeks' receipts of material B?

(c) What is the value of the balance of material A in stores at the close of the fourth week if issues are priced on a LIFO ("last-in, first-out") basis?

(d) What is the value of the fourth week's issues of material B if they are priced on a FIFO ("first-in, first-out") basis?

(e) Show the entries in the Material Price Variance Account for weeks 1 and 2.

(f) What are the individual material usage variances for the four-weekly period for materials A and B? (Assume that there are no partly manufactured products at the commencement and end of the period.)

(g) If the total standard costs of products I and II are £15 and £5 respectively, and the proceeds of the sale of scrapped material are £3 and £1 respectively what are the scrap variances of each product for the four-weekly period?

Stores movements:

| | Raw material received | | | | Issues to works | |
| | A | | B | | A | B |
Week	lb	£	lb	£	lb	lb
1	500	1,000	1,250	1,690	350	1,500
2	600	1,260	1,400	1,960	500	1,200
3	400	880	750	1,050	600	1,300
4	500	960	1,600	2,400	600	1,100

Works production

| | Output | | Scrapped | |
| Week | Product I | Product II | Product I | Product II |
	units	units	units	units
1	200	500	10	—
2	150	600	5	—
3	175	400	—	50
4	150	500	12	—

Stores opening stocks: A   400 lb value £720
                         B   2,000 lb value £2,900

Works stocks:

	Opening	Closing
A	400 lb	300 lb
B	600 lb	1,100 lb

Standard prices: A £1·9 per lb
         B £1·375 per lb

Standard usage:

		A	B
Product	I	1 lb	3·8 lb
,,	II	¾ lb	1 lb

Standard scrap allowance: 3% of output

(I.C.W.A. Inter.)

20. The annual accounts of a trading company are to be made up to December 31 but it was not possible to carry out a stock-taking until January 5 at which date the stock was valued at cost at £68,567.

The following transactions took place between 1st and 5th January:

	£
Goods received	4,600
Goods returned	200
Sales	10,500
Returns by customer	625

The rate of gross profit is 25% of cost.

Prepare a statement to show the valuation of stock as at December 31.

(I.C.W.A. Inter.)

CHAPTER 7

LABOUR: ENGAGEMENT, TIME-KEEPING AND TIME-BOOKING

NEW PERSONNEL

ESTABLISHMENT

It is nowadays customary to fix an establishment of workers for each department of a business, and this will show the numbers of each grading permitted, the salary scale or wages rate, with space for any changes made and a reference to the minute authorising the change.

By this means it is possible for management to guard against any unauthorised growth in the numbers on the payroll, and ensures that a convincing case is made out for each addition.

ENGAGEMENT OF LABOUR

The engagement of labour is delegated by management to the personnel officer, or whoever in the particular business exercises that function. The personnel officer carries out this work in response to properly authorised requests for employees received from departmental managers, and always subject to the proviso that the vacancy exists within the allowed establishment.

A worker is not taken on, however, by the personnel manager alone, but likely candidates are sent by him to the departmental manager or foreman concerned, who may perhaps give them a practical test, and then report back as to the one he recommends for the vacancy.

A personnel record (Fig. 25) is kept for every employee, and this is designed to act as a history of all that takes place during the course of the employment. It will be seen from the illustration that on the front of the sheet are spaces for a number of personal particulars relating to the employee and his employment. On the reverse side of the form space is given for sickness records, lateness records, absenteeism, holiday periods and any comments as to the employee's special interests, training and abilities which may be a guide to promotion possibilities.

Upon engagement the following procedure is followed:

(a) *Notice is given to the department concerned.* A first notification is made at once that the employee is expected on a certain date. When the employee reports for duty he sees the personnel officer again, is given a copy of the works rules, and a duplicate of the notification to take to his new foreman.

NAME   CLOCK NUMBER   P/4

ADDRESS

DATE OF BIRTH	MARRIED OR SINGLE	CHILDREN

N.H.I NUMBER	R.D.P PARTS

DATE OF EMPLOYMENT	INTRODUCED BY

PARTICULARS OF EMPLOYMENT

Date	Department	Wk	Date	Wages	Date	Wages	DATE LEFT
							REASON
							RE-ENGAGED
							A
						B C D E

18 years of Age	Pensions Fund	Retirement Date

NAME	MARRIED / SINGLE	CHILDREN	CLOCK No.

REASONS	SICKNESS PAY								
	WEEK ENDING	No. OF DAYS	N.H.I.	WEEK ENDING	No. OF DAYS	N.H.I.	WEEK ENDING	No. OF DAYS	N.H.I.

FIG. 25.—*Personnel record*

Each employee's record is kept by the personnel department, and contains details of the history of his employment. If it is prepared in the form of a stiff envelope printed back and front, the relative papers may be conveniently filed inside. Adequate space should be provided for changes of address, and records of promotions and transfers from one department to another. It is also useful to include the employee's private telephone number, or that of someone living close by who will take a message in case of emergency. The names of those from whom references were obtained should also be stated, as well as those to whom they may be subsequently given. On the reverse side of the record, details of holidays taken are often listed. Sickness is also noted down, the date of the first sickness becoming the "anniversary date" from which all subsequent sickness entitlement at full pay and half pay is calculated.

(b) *Notice is given to the wages office.* This notifies them of the new employee's name, the name of the former employee whom he replaces, the date of commencement, department, rate of pay and clock number. Subsequently, the employee's National Insurance card and P.A.Y.E. record will also be passed on to this department.

TERMINATION OF EMPLOYMENT

When an employee leaves his employment for any reason, the personnel officer should seek to find out that reason. The truth is not always told on these occasions, but repeated labour changes in one particular department may point to a "difficult" foreman or to unsatisfactory working conditions.

A foreman should not have power to dismiss employees under him. That "hire and fire" mentality is quite out of keeping with modern ideas of employer–employee relationship. The foreman should therefore limit himself to making a recommendation to the personnel officer, who will then investigate all the facts before taking a decision. If the fault is not all on one side it may be possible to transfer the employee to another department. In such a case, however, the full co-operation of all concerned is necessary to secure a happy and permanent solution, and it is one of the fundamental tasks of personnel work to cultivate better "human relations" throughout the organisation.

LABOUR TURNOVER RATE

Any changing of employees occasions loss to a manufacturer. The cost of the personnel department itself, the loss of production while the new employees learn the routine of the works and the details of their duties, unabsorbed overhead, are all examples of these costs. For this reason, a check is kept on the rate at which employees who leave have to be replaced, and this is expressed as a labour turnover percentage:

$$\frac{\text{Number of leavers replaced}}{\text{Average total number of employees}} \times 100.$$

This figure may be compared with previous periods and, even more valuably, with the rate for the industry as a whole. In some trades, especially those which employ a high proportion of married women as part-time workers, the normal rate may be as high as 70–80%, whereas in others the rate may be as low as 10% or less. It does not always follow, however, that it is a good thing to have a very low labour turnover rate in the more senior grades of workshop employment, because it may mean that there are few possibilities of promotion within the concern, and all the best of the younger workers are forced to look elsewhere for future advancement.

TIME-KEEPING METHODS

The methods of recording the gate, or factory, time of workers vary considerably, and although in most modern works time-recording clocks are used, older methods are still occasionally to be found.

THE CHECK OR DISC METHOD

Metal discs bearing the workers' numbers are placed on hooks on a board kept at the entrance of the works. The worker, on entering, removes his disc and places it in a box provided. This box is removed at starting time, and another "late" box is substituted. A variation of this procedure requires the worker to take his disc to the department in which he works, where there are a series of drawers under the supervision of the departmental foreman. The worker puts his disc in the next available drawer, which may be locked successively by the foreman as time elapses. This acts as a deterrent to latecomers, and provides a tighter check on any attempt to book on for a friend who has not yet arrived.

The timekeeper uses the discs to record attendances, and if required the individual times of latecomers may be recorded by making latecomers present their discs at the timekeeper's window.

TIME-RECORDING CLOCKS

The substitution of mechanical for manual methods of time-keeping allows for greater accuracy and avoids much loss of time. However, the presence of a timekeeper is still necessary to prevent fraud and irregularities. The clocks in use fall into two main categories:

1. Dial time recorders

This type of time recorder consists of a large clock face, around the edge of which are about 150 holes, each of which bears a number which corresponds to the clock number of the worker concerned (*see* Fig. 26). All the worker has to do is to swing a radial arm mounted on the clock face and press it into the hole allotted to him. This automatically records the time on a roll of paper within the machine, and against his clock number. The numbering of these recorders can be arranged by departments, provided that more than sufficient are allocated in the first place, so that numbers do not have to be re-used immediately by a new employee when another leaves. Arrangements can also be made for the record of times to be an integral part of the payroll, thus avoiding the necessity of recopying the times.

It should be mentioned that, although quite a few of this type of time recorder are to be seen in operation, they are regarded by the manufacturers as "museum pieces."

2. Card time recorders

These give a weekly and, indeed, daily printed and tabulated record of the times of arrival and departure of employees, but use a separate card for each person. Some models give the incomings and outgoings in one-colour printing only, but others automatically print all lateness, overtime, or similar data in red, thus bringing it prominently to notice. This is of great help to the wages clerks, and also helps to reduce the number of latecomers.

FIG. 26.—*Dial time recorder*

Where large numbers of men have to clock on, this method helps to prevent the formation of queues. The metal arm is swung round the face of the dial and punched into the appropriate hole. This gives an automatic time record in number order on a paper roll.

FIG. 27.—*Card time recorder*

In this latest type of card recorder it is only necessary for the worker to insert his clock card into the machine. The time is then automatically stamped in the correct position, and in red ink if he is late.

Figure 27 shows one of the latest models, which merely requires the worker to insert his card in the machine. Racks are installed near each recorder, and cards bearing the workers' numbers are each week placed in numbered pockets in these racks. On entering, the card is taken by the worker from the "Out" rack, inserted in the recorder to have the time stamped and placed in the "In" rack. The machines print the day of the week, and the hour and minute a.m. and p.m. Some concerns have adopted 6 minutes as being equivalent to 0·1 of an hour, and therefore the clock changes from say 8·5 to 8·6 only after an elapsed time of 6 minutes. This decimal system is of much assistance to the wages clerks in calculating the weekly time of workers.

CALCULATION OF ATTENDANCE TIME

This can be done: (*a*) daily, by extending the hours, and totalling at the end of the week; (*b*) weekly, by fixing a standard week. The total standard hours, plus overtime, less lost time, may be speedily determined, especially when used with the two-colour printing system. No calculation is needed at all for cards showing time wholly in blue, *i.e.* normal standard hours.

The totalled hours are shown at the foot of the clock card as shown in Fig. 28, and space is provided for overtime, which may be counted as time and a quarter, time and a half or double time, as the case may be. It is suggested, however, that although it is important to know the hours of overtime worked, and the reasons therefor, a separation should be made between the actual hours and the premium hours (*see* Fig. 29). This would be of value for the reason that the standard weekly hours plus the actual overtime hours will, in the case of production departments, be chargeable as direct labour while the overtime premium hours will, generally speaking, be chargeable as overhead. Thus, assuming that overtime is paid at time and a half:

			£
Direct labour			
Standard weekly hours	44		
Overtime hours	3		
	47	£0·50	23·50
Overhead			
Overtime premium hours	3	£0·25½	0·75
Gross wages payable			£24·25

No. 525				
No...				
NAME..				
WEEK ENDING..........................19........				
Harlow				

	IN	OUT	IN	OUT	Total

	Hours	Rate	£	s.	d.
ORDINARY TIME...					
OVERTIME					
LESS NAT. INS. ... OTHER DEDUC'NS					
NET WAGES ...					

No._____					
NAME_____					
WEEK ENDING					

HOURS WORKED	HRS.		HRS.
OVERTIME ALLOWANCE	HRS.		HRS.
TOTAL	HRS.		HRS.

DAY	IN	OUT	IN	OUT	TOTAL
M AM PM					
TU AM PM					
W AM PM					
TH AM PM					
F AM PM					
S AM PM					
SUN AM PM					

NET AMOUNT PAYABLE_____
RECEIVED THE NETT AMOUNT PAYABLE AS STATED
Signed _____

FIG. 28.—*Clock card— usual type*

This shows the normal type of clock card for use with a card time recorder. It provides sufficient space for the calculation of the wages due, prior to entry on the wages sheets.

FIG. 29.—*Clock card— alternative type*

This type of card provides a means of differentiating between "straight time" and overtime premium. This is most valuable in the proper apportionment of wages.

TIME-BOOKING

In addition to registering workers' times of arrival and departure, it is necessary, in most instances, to record also particulars of work done, and the time spent on each order or operation.

In most cases, too, it is important that the information thus obtained should be capable of being reconciled with the gate times, which means,

JOINER'S TIME-SHEET

WORKMAN: ....

Clock No.: ....   Week ending:..................

Name of Job	No. of Job, or Rod *	Description of Work	S.	M.	T.	W.	Th.	F.	Total	
									Ordy.	O'time.

Workman's Signature: Foreman's Signature:

Sheet to be made up *each* day and handed to Foreman on Friday.

FIG. 30.—*Joiner's time sheet*

This type of hand-written weekly record is extensively used in the building trade. It is not very accurate and errors in charging time to jobs are likely to occur, as they are usually made up from memory at the end of the week.

* "Rod" is a term for job, used in joinery works.

DAILY TIME-SHEET

Man's Name: ....   Date:....................

Check No.: ....   Week No.: ....

Machine No.: ....

Works Order No.	Work done	Time		Hours	Rate	£
		Start	Finish			

Signed (worker):   Certified (foreman):   Office Ref.:

FIG. 31.—*Daily time sheet*

These records are used in small works which have not gone to the expense of a card time recorder. There is a check on their correctness, since the foreman gives a daily signature as well as the worker. One of the chief disadvantages is that as records they tend to arrive in the cost office in a dishevelled state, and are unpleasant to handle.

in effect, that it must be possible to account for the whole of each worker's day, including idle time. This degree of precision is essential in factories, but not necessarily in every industry, and this is reflected in the methods of time-booking employed.

WEEKLY TIME SHEETS

A typical weekly time sheet is shown in Fig. 30, and it will be seen that the workers are required to fill in particulars of the time spent on each separate job each day; a different-coloured sheet would be used for each trade, *e.g.* machinists, joiners, etc. This method is rather rough and ready, but it is extensively used by builders and decorators and by civil-engineering contractors, and is apparently found satisfactory in such cases.

DAILY TIME SHEETS

These have nearly the same disadvantages as the weekly time sheets. From the example given in Fig. 31 it will be observed that provision is made for recording the time spent on each job during the day, and there may be some advantage over the weekly sheet in that the worker must complete the sheet every day and hand it to the foreman for signature. Even so, there is a tendency for times to be approximate only, and periods of idle or wasted time are conveniently forgotten. If a conscientious foreman is in charge, greater accuracy may perhaps be obtained by having the job times entered on the forms in the foreman's office.

JOB TICKETS

The use of these for registering the time worked on each order is extensive. There is correspondingly a very large variety of forms, as nearly every manufacturer draws up his job tickets to suit the particular needs of his business. A typical form is shown in Fig. 32, but the student will be well advised not to endeavour to commit it to memory. He should rather note the salient points contained in it.

Only one ticket is issued to a worker at a time, usually by the foreman's office, and it serves the dual purpose of providing instructions as to the operation to be performed, and of recording the time spent in performing it. As the operator finishes the operation he is doing he submits his work with his job ticket, has the finishing time recorded (usually by clock), and is then issued with another job ticket with the starting time recorded, *i.e.* the same time.

If the operator cannot immediately carry on with a new job, as, for example, when he has to wait for work from a previous operation, an

---

JOB TICKET

Department: ....   Job No.: ....

Works Order No.: ....   Date ....

Drawing No.: ....   Time started: ....
Operation No.: ....   „   finished: ....
Machine No.: ....   Hours on Job: ....
Time allowance: ....

Description of Job	Hours	Rate	£

Worker's No.:	Certified	Office
Signature:	(foreman or	ref.:
	inspection):	

FIG. 32.—*Job ticket*

The purpose of these tickets is to keep a close check on the time spent by an operator on each job which he does during the day. They may be used with a card time recorder if so designed.

UNALLOCATED TIME

Man No.: ....

Machine No.: ....

Type of Machine: ....

REASONS FOR WAITING

1. Machine break down ....
2. Material ....
3. Inspection ....
4. Orders ....
5. Tools ....
6. Foreman's attention ....
7. Previous operation ....
8. Other reasons:
   ....
   ....
   ....
   ....

FIG. 33.—*Section of card showing reasons for idle time:*
time registrations are on other side of card

It is important to know how much time in a factory is unproductive, and for what reason. If an operator's time is not covered by a job ticket, he must make use of an idle time card in order to account for a full day's employment.

idle time card should be started, so that the record of his day's activities may be complete, and yet not be unfairly charged against production and reflect adversely upon his competence as a worker. Similarly if, during the course of an operation, there is a machinery breakdown, the idle time thus caused must be recorded on an idle time card, and not on the worker's job time ticket. A specimen idle-time card is shown in Fig. 33.

JOB COST CARD

ORDER No. 422 DRAWING No. 90 PATTERN No. 437

Special Instructions:...

DATE STARTED: 29/8 DATE FINISHED: 30/8

Work-man	Operation		Cost £	Rate £	Time Taken		Time Stamps
					Hours	Minutes	
17	Dressing	Off	0·19½	0·35	—	34	Aug 29 8.34
		On					Aug 29 8.00
15	Marking off	Off	0·67½	0·45	1	30	Aug 29 10.06
		On					Aug 29 8.36
9	Rough planing	Off	0·40½	0·40	1	01	Aug 29 11.09
		On					Aug 29 10.08
4	Rough turning	Off	1·21½	0·40	3	02	Aug 29 17.02
		On					Aug 29 14.00
3	Turning	Off	1·98½	0·50	3	58	Aug 30 11.58
		On					Aug 30 8.00
21	Planing	Off	0·23½	0·50	—	28	Aug 30 12.28
		On					Aug 30 12.00
8	Grinding	Off	0·74	0·50	1	29	Aug 30 15.01
		On					Aug 30 13.32
7	Drilling	Off	0·33½	0·40	—	50	Aug 30 15.54
		On					Aug 30 15.04
19	Cleaning off	Off	0·21½	0·35	—	37	Aug 30 16.34
		On					Aug 30 15.57
38	Finishing	Off	0·43½	0·40	1	05	Aug 30 17.40
		On					Aug 30 16.35
	Total Labour Cost		£6·43½				
	ENTER MATERIAL USED ON REVERSE SIDE						

Fig. 34.—*Labour cost card*

Instead of, or in addition to, a separate job ticket, a cost card sometimes travels with each job as it goes from operation to operation. In this way the times can be worked out and the total labour cost found. It will be noted that the illustration is headed "Job Cost Card" because it provides for materials to be entered on the reverse side. As this is somewhat unusual, the caption has been altered.

LABOUR COST CARDS

This is a variation of the job ticket method, for the tickets are combined on one card, which travels with the order. An illustration of this is given in Fig. 34. The total cost of the labour involved in completing the order may be calculated and totalled at the end of the card's circulation round the factory floor, and then if the coupons are made detachable, they may be sorted under the operators' clock numbers, and thus built up into a total to agree with their clock times.

Yet another variation of this idea is to be seen in Fig. 35, where a daily cost card is issued to each operator. He records the various jobs on which he has worked, with the starting and the stopping times of each, and these, when extended and totalled, give an agreement with his gate times for the day as recorded at the top of the card. In this case if

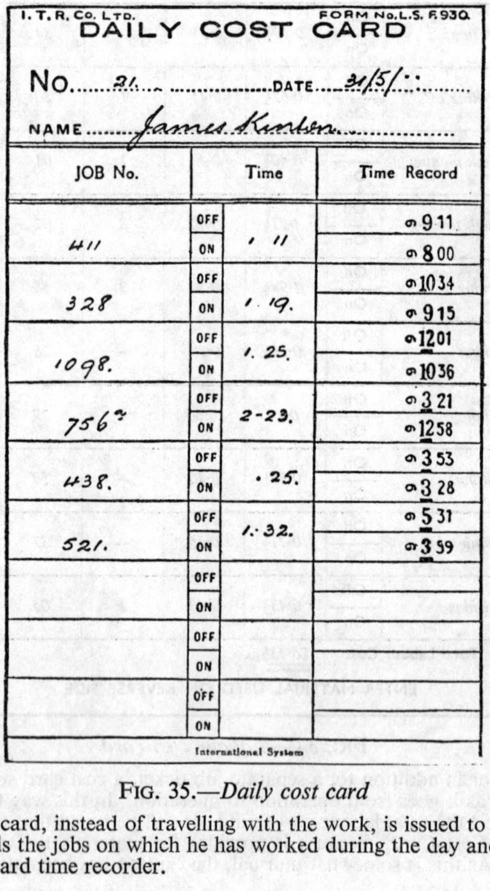

I. T. R. Co. LTD.		FORM No. L.S. F. 930
	DAILY COST CARD	
No. 21		DATE 31/5/..
NAME James Kinlen		

JOB No.		Time	Time Record
411	OFF	' 11	911
	ON		8 00
328	OFF	1. 19.	10 34
	ON		9 15
1098.	OFF	1. 25.	12 01
	ON		10 36
756²	OFF	2-23.	3 21
	ON		12 58
438.	OFF	. 25.	3 53
	ON		3 28
521.	OFF	1. 32.	5 31
	ON		3 59
	OFF		
	ON		
	OFF		
	ON		
	OFF		
	ON		

International System

FIG. 35.—*Daily cost card*

This type of card, instead of travelling with the work, is issued to each operator. On it he records the jobs on which he has worked during the day and the times are stamped by a card time recorder.

the coupons are detachable they are sorted under the various job numbers to build up the labour costs of each job, and one system allows for them to be inserted in slots, much as pictures may be mounted in a photographic album. The completed results may then be microfilmed to produce a permanent record.

No. Made	Passed	Rejected	Rate	£

PIECE-WORK ORDER

No.: ....
Worker's Name: ....
Date: ....
Clock No.: ....
Time Taken: ....
Part: ....
Price: ....
Operation: ....
Quantity: ....

Signed Worker: Signed Inspection:
                                  Foreman:

FIG. 36.—*Piece-work order*

These orders are the worker's entitlement to be paid for the quantity of pieces he has completed which satisfactorily pass inspection. The agreed piece-work price is stated as well as details of the work to be done.

PIECE-WORK TICKETS

Where a factory undertakes repetitive work, payment to the workers is often made on the basis of a rate per piece or number of pieces produced. In such cases the entitlement to wages is the possession of completed piece-work tickets, and a typical form is shown in Fig. 36.

It might be thought that under this system time records are unnecessary, and in some factories time is not, in fact, recorded for piece-workers. This is a mistake, however, because the apportionment of overhead is more often than not determined in relation to the time factor and, of course, when a premium or bonus is paid for time saved, then both quantities and time must be recorded. Furthermore, the fixing of accurate piece-work rates depends, in the last analysis, on an assessment of how many pieces of work it is reasonable to expect per hour. Time records, therefore, are highly necessary and important, and may be obtained by any of the methods already discussed.

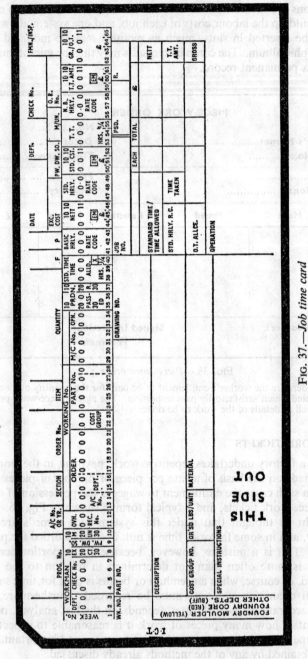

FIG. 37.—*Job time card*

The illustration is of a job time card suitable for punched-card accounting allied to standard costs.

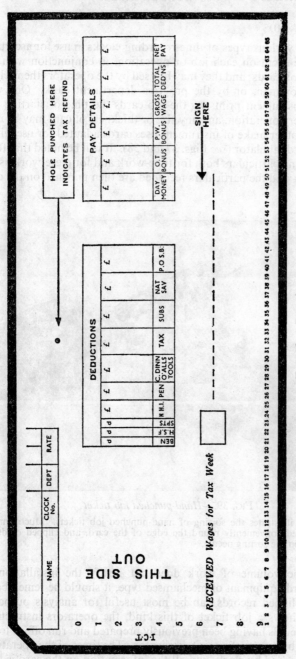

FIG. 38.—*Pay slip*

This is a hand-written record, but the information is then punched into the card itself, which is sorted and tabulated. After signature by the employee it is retained by the wages office.

EQUIPMENT AIDS

There are various types of time-recording clocks in use for ascertaining the time spent on each job or operation, in conjunction with job tickets and job cards; and they may be used by the operators themselves, or by the foreman, or by the progress department clerk. One very adaptable instrument prints on the job cards the time of starting and stopping every operation, and any size or thickness of card may be used with it. Another make of instrument uses cards adapted for use with a punched-card tabulator (*see* Figs. 37 and 38). It will be noted that these cards combine particulars both for time-work and for piece-work as the case may be, and the particulars recorded are then punched on the card itself.

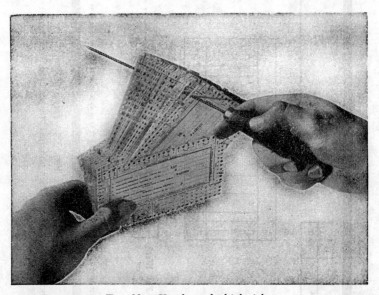

Fig. 39.—*Hand-punched job ticket*

This figure illustrates the sorting of hand-punched job tickets. Much analysis may be clipped conveniently round the edge of the card, and clipped cards are not retained on the sorting needle.

Where the volume of work does not justify the installation of punched-card equipment of mechanised type, it should be remembered that hand-clipped records can be most useful for analysis purposes. Figure 39 shows a job ticket of this kind, the operators instructions and order details having been previously prepared and run off on to the blank cards by means of a spirit duplicator. The times of the operations are then recorded by clock, and all the information on the card is then clipped on the edge of the card. The cards can then be sorted by means of sorting needles, one or two columns at a time, the clipped holes not being retained by the needle as it is pushed from front to back of the pack of cards.

TICKETOGRAPH COUPON SYSTEM FOR PIECE-WORK

The ticketograph system is constructed for controlling costs and progress in a factory and is particularly, though not solely, suitable for piece-work. The equipment is shown in Fig. 40. It imprints a ticket,

FIG. 40.—*Ticketograph equipment*

composed of coupons, one for each operation, and arranged in the same order as the work progresses through the factory. The coupon bears sufficient details to identify the work, and also gives the piece-work price to be paid. The card itself (Fig. 41) is usually about 10 in. × $5\frac{1}{2}$ in. in size, although this may vary according to the number of operations.

The tickets are perforated between each coupon, and as the work passes from one operator to another, each worker detaches the coupon referring to his or her particular operation. He inserts his clock number, and then files it in a small pocket of a coupon-holder book, which thus becomes the worker's entitlement to pay. In the card illustrated, ticket No. 12 shows that the order no. is 432, the type of cloth is 56 and that the price is £0·12½ per dozen. Twelve tickets must therefore be collected to obtain that amount.

At the end of each day the worker enters up a statement card, illustrated in Fig. 42, which is then checked by the office, and returned to him in time for the next day's entries. At the end of each week the entries are cross cast, and easily worked out at the appropriate rate.

Progress coupons, sometimes known as "trumps," are used to keep track of the progress of the work, and as the work reaches certain inspection points, or other agreed progress control points, the operator

1 I **432** **56** **12** **£0·15** V Cutting	3 H **432** **56** **12** VOID Back-making	5 G **432** **56** **12** **£0·15** Piecing Up	7 F **432** **56** **12** **£0·02½** Shaping	9 E **432** **56** **12** **£0·15** ***£0·03** Sew Round	11 D **432** **56** **12** **£0·10** Closing	13 C **432** **56** **12** **£0·04** Neck-making	15 B **432** **56** **12** **£0·20** Felling	17 A **432** **56** **12** **£0·15** Brushing and Pressing	Despatch V **432** **56** **12**	Warehouse or Cutting Room V **432** **56** **12**
1	3	5	7	9	11	13	15	17	PROGRESS (The four coupons attached to this portion form progress reports and must be put in the collecting box immediately operation is finished.)	
		1	2	3	4					
		Workers, before detaching Coupons, must place their Clock No. in the square corresponding to their operation. REMEMBER—the Coupon is your voucher for pay.								
2	4	6	8	10	12	14	16	18		
2 **432** **56** **12** **£0·09** V Fixing	4 **432** **56** **12** **DB** Sleeve Making	6 **432** **56** **12** **£0·04½** Under Pressing	8 **432** **56** **12** **£0·15** Linen to Edge	10 **432** **56** **12** **£0·05** Baist Under	12 **432** **56** **12** **£0·15** Baist Out	14 **432** **56** **12** **£0·09** Stitching	16 **432** **56** **12** **£0·15** Sleeving	18 **432** **56** **12** **£0·25** Buttons and Button-holes	Cost Office V **432** **56** **12** **DB**	Making Department V **432** **56** **12**

FIG. 41.—*Ticketograph piece-work coupons*

NOTE: The figures in bold type are printed a line at a time by one pressure of a lever.

* **£0·03** on coupon No. 9 is an "extra" added by a "plussing" device.

					Total	Doz. or Gross	Price	Amount £
STATEMENT CARD								
Name: .... No.: .... Operation:								
Dept.: .... Week Ending:								

TIME HAND		Hours	Rate	£	Checked by	Total Wages + Time-work as at back
Profit	Loss					
Received amount stated					Examined by	% Added
Signed................................						GROSS

Fig. 42.—*Statement card*

The worker uses this card to summarise the ticketograph coupons in the coupon holder book. It is checked by the wages office and is the voucher for payment.

who completes the operation at that point places the appropriate "trump" coupon in a box provided, which is cleared by the progress department at least once each day. These coupons are then placed on a control board, which thus shows at a glance the position of every order as it passes through the factory.

Examination questions on Chapters 7–9 are given at the end of Chapter 9.

CHAPTER 8

LABOUR: METHODS OF REMUNERATION

GENERAL CONSIDERATIONS

THE cost of labour is a factor which requires the most careful thought. It provides problems of major importance, and, on the solution of these, the success of any enterprise must largely depend.

Reduction in labour costs is one of the chief objectives of the production manager, and much guidance to this end may be secured from a suitably organised costing system. Low wages do not necessarily mean low costs—in fact, it is now widely recognised that efficiently organised factories may pay the highest wages, and yet have the lowest wages costs. A moment's reflection will be sufficient to grasp how this may come about. A firm using rather old-fashioned methods, and with only a moderately effective organisation, may pay its 100 employees at the rate of £0·50 per hour, and in a week of 44 hours there may be 4,000 pieces produced. The labour cost per piece in this case will be:

$$(100 \times 44 \times £0·50) \div 4,000, \quad \text{or} \quad £0·55.$$

With better organisation and more up-to-date machinery the firm might be able to obtain this result:

$$(90 \times 44 \times £0·60) \div 6,000, \quad \text{or, say,} \quad £0·39\tfrac{1}{2}.$$

Many schemes for remunerating labour have been devised with a view to increasing productivity, but they have not been uniformly successful.

FACTORS TO BE CONSIDERED

EFFICIENCY IN PRODUCTION

When the volume of production is the important factor, labour control and remuneration may be devised to this end; but, when the volume of output is less important than the care and accuracy which the work must be given, wage payments based on production quantities are undesirable unless competent inspection is arranged at all stages.

EFFECT ON WORKERS

The attitude of workers is of great importance, and every wage system should be thoroughly explained to them, and be capable of being under-

114

stood by those of average intelligence. Unless and until their co-operation is secured, the fullest advantage of the system will not be obtained;
indeed, it could not be implemented at all.

INCIDENCE OF OVERHEAD

Some of the indirect expenses, or overhead, of an undertaking are,
within limits, "fixed," that is to say, they do not fluctuate with changes
in the volume of output. In consequence, any reduction of output
results in an increased cost of production per unit of output (*see* Fig.
43, and example on page 116).

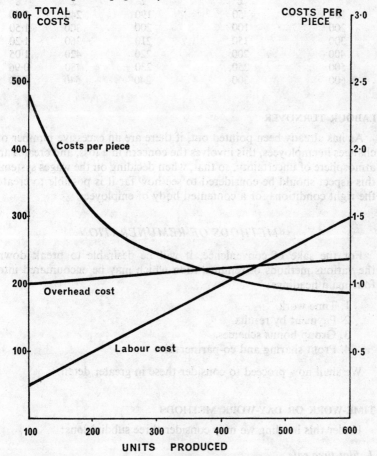

FIG. 43.—*Overhead cost curve*

This chart illustrates the fact that the presence of a fixed element in the overhead
has a marked effect on the cost per piece as the volume of output rises. Hence the
importance of achieving greater productivity by well-chosen schemes of remuneration.

This is a factor of outstanding significance, and lies at the basis of all schemes of remuneration. The following will be seen to be involved:

(*a*) Volume of output to be achieved.
(*b*) Time which can be saved in producing it.

EXAMPLE

Units produced	Labour cost at £0·50 per unit £	Overhead cost (including £180 fixed overhead) £	Total cost £	Cost per piece £
100	50	190	240	2·40
200	100	200	300	1·50
300	150	210	360	1·20
400	200	220	420	1·05
500	250	230	480	0·96
600	300	240	540	0·90

LABOUR TURNOVER

As has already been pointed out, if there are an excessive number of changes in employees, this involves the concern in a loss, and creates an atmosphere of uncertainty, so that, when deciding on the wages system, this aspect should be considered to see how far it is possible to create the right conditions for a contented body of employees.

METHODS OF REMUNERATION

For the sake of convenience, it will be desirable to break down the various methods of remuneration which may be encountered into four main headings:

1. Time work.
2. Payment by results.
3. Group bonus schemes.
4. Profit sharing and co-partnership.

We shall now proceed to consider these in greater detail.

TIME-WORK OR DAY-WORK METHODS

Under this heading we may consider three subdivisions:

1. Flat time rate

The payment to the workers is based on this formula:

$$\text{Earnings} = \text{Clock hours worked} \times \text{Rate per hour}$$

which may be conveniently shortened into:

$$E = CHW . RH.$$

NOTE: An extra premium is paid for overtime work.

Let it be said at once that many large works operate successfully under this method of payment, but keen management and supervision are essential because of the inherent tendency of employees:

(a) to work no harder than necessary to "get by";
(b) to refrain from seeking the next job to be done;
(c) to wait, rather than ask, for instructions from the foreman;
(d) to make the job last out until the next work break.

There are circumstances in which time wages are particularly advantageous, as, for example, in the tool-room and pattern shop. Here the work demands a high degree of skill—the error in a jig being only one-tenth of that allowed in the finished work—and it is far more important for accuracy to be maintained than it is for speed. Indirect labourers such as sweepers and cleaners, nightwatchmen, boiler-house stokers and inspection staff are all most suitably paid on a time basis.

The chief merit of the time-work basis of payment is its simplicity: it is easy to understand; it provides a steady rate of earnings each week; and it is easy to make the wage calculations required.

2. High day rate

The flat time-rate basis does not offer monetary reward for special effort, and thereby fails to secure anything like the maximum output. This means, as we have seen, that production costs tend to rise.

In consequence, many manufacturers, while wishing to keep the advantages of simplicity, have realised its weaknesses. To overcome these, they have instituted a high day-rate method. The most notable adherent of the high wages plan was Henry Ford, and he and others have proved that high wages do not necessarily imply high costs, but that many costs are higher than they should be because of low wages, which commend themselves only to the less efficient workers. The high wages plan may be summarised as follows:

(a) A high rate of wages per hour is paid.
(b) Special interest and effort in the work is demanded.
(c) The high wages offered attract those who are confident of their own abilities, and are willing to pit their skill against a rather exacting standard.
(d) Standards of efficiency and output are set, which foremen are required to maintain. Work is set for each man to do, and he must do it. Often the work progresses on a conveyor belt, and each man

must complete his operation within certain distance limits, and within the time set by the speed at which the conveyor belt is moving along. Supervision is strict throughout the day, and there may be frequent inspections.

(e) Nevertheless, the work set is not more than can be accomplished by a competent and conscientious worker, without undue fatigue, day after day. Overtime work, generally speaking, is not encouraged.

3. Measured day work

As a kind of variation of this high wages plan, many firms have introduced what has been called "measured day work." The employer pays an agreed level of wages for a specified level of performance. Although the worker has no direct incentive to improve upon the level of performance initially fixed, it is claimed that the better relations established between management and employees more than offset any possible drop in the level of output.

It will be seen that the general characteristic of all forms of time wages is that the employee receives nothing beyond his $CHW . RH$ (where CHW = Clock hours worked and RH = Rate per hour), and, conversely, nothing less. The employer takes all the loss arising from his employees' inefficiency, and all the gain arising from their extra efficiency.

PAYMENT BY RESULTS SCHEMES

When we speak of payment by results, it is at once apparent that we are thinking of methods of payment which are at the opposite end of the scale to time wages. Here it is the employee, not the employer, who stands to gain or lose as a result of the standard of efficiency which he attains, and, subject to certain provisos, the general principle may be stated as: produce more—earn more; produce less—earn less.

From the point of view of management, there are two matters which have to be borne in mind:

(a) Production may be encouraged at the expense of quality, so that a strict inspection of the work must be provided. This additional cost offsets the fact that less supervision of the work may be required.

(b) Employees may have fixed in their minds how much they want to earn each week, the incidence of taxation, for example, making further effort unattractive. They may then go home early, or absent themselves, forgetting, or not caring, that factory overhead is still being incurred.

For this reason, employees who are being paid by results should be required to record their gate times in the same way as those on time wages, and also job times can be stated. This information will be useful in computing overhead recovery rates, and in compiling the cost of idleness.

Attention may be drawn, at this point, to two sources of information which any student wishing to delve deeply into the subject should consult. These are Report No. 65, and its supplement on *Payment by Results Systems*, produced by the National Board for Prices and Incomes, and obtainable from H.M.S.O., and *Financial Incentives* by R. M. Currie, and published by the British Institute of Management.

Following Report No. 65, we shall attempt a classification of payment by results systems as follows:

1. Straight piece-work

Quoting from the Report, para. 11, we have the following statement:

"The oldest and simplest form of PBR is straight piece-work, where the employer pays a money price for each unit of output (*e.g.* x pence per piece, or ton, or yard produced) and where the whole wage then varies according to production."

We may state this concept in terms of the following formula:

$$\text{Earnings} = \text{Number of units} \times \text{Rate per unit.}$$

Or, put more briefly:

$$E = NU \,.\, RU.$$

The basis for the piece rate is usually the comparable time rate for the same class of worker, but this basic rate is increased to constitute an inducement to greater output.

EXAMPLE

In a particular job of work the following factors apply:

Basic hourly rate = £0·25.
Increase on rate to be 20%.
Adjusted hourly rate is therefore to be (1·2)(0·25) = £0·30.
Output expected = 12 units per hour.

Therefore the piece-work rate is £0·30 ÷ 12 = £0·02½, the formula for calculation being expressed in general terms as:

$$E = NU \,.\, RU = 120\% \; CHW \,.\, RH.$$

If, therefore, a worker produces 120 units in an 8-hour day he will be paid 120 × 0·02½ or £3, which is a gain of £1 over the comparable time wages for the day's work. On the other hand, if he produces only 80 units, he will be paid 80 × 0·025 or £2 which is the same as time wages for the day.

It will be seen that although the labour cost per unit remains the same, and the employer makes no payment for units not produced, yet the total cost will vary considerably, owing to the incidence of overhead, as has already been shown.

It should be borne in mind that there is almost always one qualification to the above remarks, in that provision is made for a time basis of payment to operate for piece-workers in cases where non-production is beyond their control, e.g. failure of machinery, waiting for work, etc.

Although, in the above example, we may suppose that care was exercised in determining the number of units which an employee might be expected to produce per hour, it was probably not done scientifically.

The introduction of work-study techniques, and the formulation of standard times, allows for the development of more sophisticated schemes of payment by results.

2. The 75–100 straight proportional scheme

The basis of this scheme is as follows:

(a) A "standard" performance is taken as being 100.
(b) The bonus begins when operator performance exceeds 75.
(c) The bonus is $33\frac{1}{3}\%$ of the job rate for a performance of 100, and below and above 100 it is in direct proportion.
(d) There is no theoretical limit to the bonus which may be earned.

EXAMPLE

Clock hours worked	8 hours
Less authorised "down time" for waiting, walking, etc.	1·5 hours
Net operating hours	6·5 hours

$$6\cdot5 \text{ hours} \times 60 = \underline{390 \text{ minutes.}}$$

Standard time allowed in minutes per unit we will say is 5·75 minutes.
Assume that 60 units were produced.
Then total standard time was $5\cdot75 \times 60 = \underline{345 \text{ minutes.}}$
Operator performance is 345/390 or $\underline{88\cdot5\%}$.
Suppose the job hourly rate of pay is £0·35.
Then:

because 88·5 exceeds 75 by 13·5, and because 100 exceeds 75 by 25, and the bonus is $33\frac{1}{3}\%$, it follows, by proportion:

$$(13\cdot5)/25 \text{ of } 33\tfrac{1}{3}\% = 54/100 \text{ of } 33\tfrac{1}{3}\% = 18\%.$$

Hence the bonus is 18% of job rate of £0·35 = £0·063.
The total rate per operating hour becomes

$$0\cdot35 + 18\% = 0\cdot35 + 0\cdot063 = 0\cdot413.$$

Therefore the earnings will be:

$$6\cdot5 \text{ hours} \times 0\cdot413 = 2\cdot68\tfrac{1}{2}$$
$$1\cdot5 \text{ hours} \times 0\cdot35 = 0\cdot52\tfrac{1}{2}$$

$$£3\cdot21$$

This can be seen from Fig. 44.

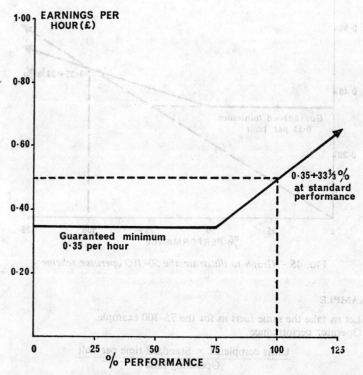

FIG. 44.—*Graph to illustrate the 75–100 straight proportional scheme*

As earnings may fluctuate rather widely in some cases when the 75–100 scheme is applied—because of variable factors which tend to make havoc of the measurement of operator performance—another scheme has been devised, as follows.

3. The 50–100 operator scheme

In Fig. 44 if the straight line showing the proportional bonus is rotated so that it cuts the guaranteed minimum line at performance 50, the incentive is less, as seen by the less steep slope of the line, but the earnings tend to be more stable. Figure 45 shows the result.

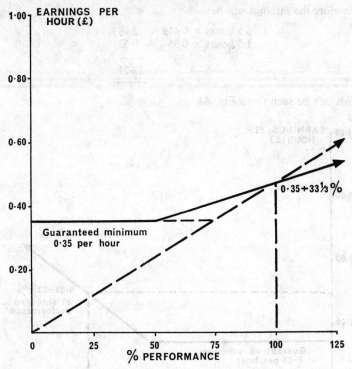

FIG. 45.—*Graph to illustrate the 50–100 operator scheme*

EXAMPLE

Let us take the same facts as for the 75–100 example.
Operator performance

$$\frac{\text{Units completed} \times \text{Standard time per unit}}{\text{Operating time}}.$$

$$\frac{60 \times 5 \cdot 75}{6 \cdot 5 \times 60} = \frac{345}{390} = 88 \cdot 5\%.$$

88·5% exceeds 50% by 38·5%,
100% exceeds 50% by 50%.

By proportion:

$$\frac{38 \cdot 5}{50}(33\tfrac{1}{3}\%) = 26\%.$$

The total rate per operating hour becomes:

$$0 \cdot 35 + 26\% = 0 \cdot 35 + 0 \cdot 09 = 0 \cdot 44$$

and this result can be read from the graph.

The total payment will therefore be:

$$6.5 \text{ hours} \times 0.44 = 2.86$$
$$1.5 \text{ hours} \times 0.35 = 0.525$$

$$£3.38\tfrac{1}{2}$$

From this it is seen that the earnings under the 75–100 scheme would be £3·21, and under the 50–100 scheme, slightly more, *viz.* £3·38½.

Both these schemes are designated as being directly proportional to output, but we now come to payment by results schemes in which payment is proportionately less than output.

4. *Premium bonus schemes*

These schemes introduce a different principle, because gains and losses in labour efficiency are shared by employer and employee. The premium bonus to be paid is calculated on the hours saved, that is, on the difference between the time allowed and the time taken. However, as the bonus is brought into operation at a low rate of efficiency, the incentive to greater production tends to be extremely ineffective.

Usually these schemes are invoked when it is difficult to be precise about the time to be allowed. We may illustrate this by thinking of a job like "washing down walls." Some walls are fairly clean; others are very dirty. Some rooms are large; some are quite small. Some walls have been painted with gloss paint; some have been painted with a matt surface. In any given situation, then, what time allowance is to be given?

The foreman, making use of his practical "know-how," may have a shrewd idea of what time it would take him to do the job well, but this is likely to be less than he can expect from others.

To this "element time" is therefore added a percentage of 66⅔% to cover contingencies of all kinds. This means, in effect, that if the "element time" be regarded as equivalent to 100%, *i.e.* normal efficiency, the bonus on the time saved will be payable from a much lower level— 60% upwards.

EXAMPLE

Element time for job	3 hours
Add 66⅔%	2 hours
Time allowed (60% efficiency)	5 hours

If the job is done in 4 hours, the man will be paid for 4 hours at the normal rate per hour and will qualify for bonus on the 1 hour saved.

He will then be ready, of course, to go on with the next job.

There are two main types of premium bonus scheme:

(a) The Halsey (and the Halsey–Weir) scheme

The essential feature of both these schemes is that the worker is given a fixed percentage of the time saved as a bonus. In the Halsey scheme it is 50%, but in the Halsey–Weir scheme it is 30%. Other percentages may be met with in practice, but the method is precisely the same in all cases.

Looking at the above example again, if the Halsey scheme is being applied, and the worker did the job in the 3 hours element time, he would qualify for a bonus of 50% of 2 hours, *i.e.* 1 hour, and he would be paid for 4 hours work in all. That is to say, the scheme is designed to allow him to earn time and one-third, if he completes his task in the basic element time.

We can therefore make up a table as follows:

Time allowed	Time taken	Time saved	Bonus
5	5	Nil	Nil
5	4	1	$\frac{1}{2}$ hour
5	3	2	1 hour

Reducing these schemes to a formula we have:

$$\text{Earnings} = \begin{pmatrix} \text{Clock} \\ \text{hours} \\ \text{worked} \end{pmatrix} \times \begin{pmatrix} \text{Rate per} \\ \text{hour} \end{pmatrix} + \frac{1}{2}(\text{Time saved}) \times \begin{pmatrix} \text{Rate per} \\ \text{hour} \end{pmatrix}$$

Or more briefly:

$$E = CHW \cdot RH + 0.5(TS)RH.$$

In theory, there is no limit to the amount of bonus which can be earned: more time saved will increase the bonus. There are, however, very practical limits to the ability of an employee to work faster, even if he wished to do so.

(b) The Rowan scheme

This scheme was introduced by David Rowan of Glasgow in 1901. As before, the premium to be paid, a bonus, is based on time saved, but instead of a *fixed* percentage being taken, as in the Halsey scheme, a *proportion* is taken. This proportion is:

$$\frac{\text{Time saved}}{\text{Time allowed}}.$$

The bonus may be calculated by either adjusting the rate per hour, or by adding it to the normal time wages. The final result is, of course, the same.

EXAMPLE

Time allowed for job	5 hours
Time taken	4 hours
Time saved	1 hour
Bonus ratio	$\frac{1}{5}$
Rate per hour	£0·40

Wage calculations:

Method (a):

$$4 \text{ hours} \times 0.48 = £1.92$$

Method (b):

4 hours × 0·40	£1·60
Add bonus $\frac{1}{5}$	0·32
	£1·92

As shown for the Halsey scheme, it is possible to reduce this Rowan scheme to a formula, but there seems little point in so doing.

The premium bonus under the Rowan scheme is also payable from about the 60% level of efficiency, and at first it compares favourably with the Halsey scheme from the employees' point of view. At 120% it yields the same earnings, but above 120% it yields a diminishing return. This may be illustrated thus:

Time allowed	Time taken	Time saved	Rate per hour	Basic pay	Bonus Halsey	Bonus Rowan
5	5	Nil	0·40	2·00	Nil	Nil
5	4	1	0·40	1·60	0·20	0·32
5	3	2	0·40	1·20	0·40	0·48
5	2	3	0·40	0·80	0·60	0·48

It will be seen from the above that the earnings *per hour* rise as follows:

	Total earnings		Earnings per hour	
Time taken	Halsey	Rowan	Halsey	Rowan
5	2·00	2·00	0·40	0·40
4	1·80	1·92	0·45	0·48
3	1·60	1·68	0·53	0·56
2	1·40	1·28	0·70	0·64

5. Barth scheme

This is another payments by results scheme, in which payment is proportionately less than output. It is quite unlike any others, and has been especially designed for apprentices and beginners, until, having been tested, they are deemed to be proficient enough to go on to some other scheme. It is as follows:

Earnings = Rate per hour × $\sqrt{(\text{Standard hours} \times \text{Clock hours})}$.

EXAMPLE

Rate per hour	£0·40
Standard hours allowed	3 hours
Time taken	5 hours

$$\text{Earnings} = 0.40 \times \sqrt{3 \times 5}$$
$$= 0.40 \times 3.873$$
$$= \underline{\text{£1·55.}}$$

Average earnings per hour = £1·55 ÷ 5 = £0·31.

6. Bedaux scheme, or schemes after this pattern

Very accurate time study is applied to every operation, and a standard minute's worth of work is evolved, which represents a fraction of work plus a fraction of rest for fatigue, etc. Thus, each standard minute of work is to be done in one minute, and each operation to be performed can be expressed as being so many standard minutes of work to be produced, or "B's." Payment is then made on the basis of the number of "B's" which have been credited to the worker.

Time wages are paid until 100% efficiency rate is reached, so that this scheme is a real incentive to reach higher output above that level. Moreover, since it is possible to put on a notice-board the "B's" earned yesterday, and the target for today, a competitive element is introduced which acts as an additional spur to production.

When the scheme was originally introduced the worker received only 75% of the bonus, the other 25% being diverted to supervision. For this reason the scheme is classified as being among the payment by results schemes in which payment is proportionately less than output.

However, one may encounter "points schemes" in which this unpopular feature has been amended, allowing up to 100% of the bonus to be paid to the worker.

For its successful operation, a good system of production control is required, and the "B's" allowed for each operation must be clearly indicated on the job tickets.

7. Accelerating premium bonus

This is a payment by results scheme, but payment is neither directly proportional to output, as in the 75–100 and 50–100 schemes, nor less than proportional to output, as in the premium bonus schemes, such as the Halsey and Rowan. On the contrary it offers a bonus which increases at a faster and faster rate.

It is not generally considered suitable for the machine operator, but it is valuable for supervisors and foremen as an encouragement to obtain the best possible level of productivity.

Unfortunately, there is no simple formula for such a scheme, and it would be necessary for each firm to devise its own. Merely by way of illustration, the graph of the function

$$y = 0 \cdot 8x^2$$

may be drawn. We take x as being equal to percentage efficiency $\div$ 100. Then we have:

Percentage efficiency	100	120	140	160	180
x	1	1·2	1·4	1·6	1·8
x^2	1	1·44	1·96	2·56	3·24
$y = 0 \cdot 8x^2$	0·8	1·15	1·57	2·05	2·59

Multiplying these results by 100 enables us to plot per-cent earnings against per-cent efficiency. On this basis, efficiency of 150% gives earnings of 175% of basic wages: this may or may not be considered too generous.

8. Payment in varying proportions

This classification contains three schemes which should be noted:

(a) The Taylor system

Many years ago, Dr. F. W. Taylor, the so-called "father" of scientific management, introduced a scheme in the United States as an attempt to increase the output of workers whom he considered were working far below capacity.

The scheme combined time taken, with the quantity of work produced, so that differential rates of pay operated. The rate rose abruptly as the output obtained in the allotted time increased beyond a stated quantity per hour. Rate-fixing for this scheme had to be scientific in order to be successfully applied, and workers had to be convinced that it had been done fairly, and reasonably. A reference to rate-fixing is on page 313.

The chief features of the scheme, as outlined by Dr. Taylor, were as follows:

(i) Day wages were not guaranteed.

(ii) A standard time for a job was computed by a rate-fixer so that the amount of work demanded was entirely just, and such as could reasonably be accomplished.

(iii) Two piece rates were fixed, so that if the worker did the work in less than the standard time, he received the higher rate, whereas if he took longer he received the lower rate.

(iv) Thus it was the declared intention to remunerate the workman well if he accomplished his task, but to make sure that when a worker failed to do so, he would be the loser thereby.

EXAMPLE

The following particulars apply to a certain work process:

Standard time allowed   100 units per hour
Normal time rate per hour   £0·50

Differential to be applied:

80% of piece rate when below standard.
120% of piece rate when above standard.

In an 8-hour day:

Worker A completes 700 units.
Worker B completes 900 units.

Combining time and quantity, we have:

$$RU \cdot NU = CHW \cdot RH$$
$$RU(800) = (8)(0 \cdot 50)$$
$$RU = £4 \div 800 = £0 \cdot 005.$$

This means that worker A, having produced less than the expected 800 units would be paid at the rate of 80% of 0·005, *i.e.* at 0·004.

$$700 \times 0 \cdot 004 = £2 \cdot 80.$$

On the other hand worker B would be paid at the higher rate of 120% of 0·005, *i.e.* at 0·006.

$$900 \times 0 \cdot 006 = £5 \cdot 40.$$

The sharp jump between 0·004 and 0·006 in the rate of pay will explain, perhaps, why the Taylor system has never been popular. Indeed, the lower rate has been regarded as "punitive" and "unfair."

(b) Gantt task and bonus scheme

This is a scheme which appeals only to the really competent and keen worker who is aiming at high wages, and it is regarded as an extremely adequate scheme for that purpose.

It may be considered in three stages:

(*i*) Day wages are guaranteed—but it is not contemplated that only day wages will be earned.

(*ii*) A definite task is set on which a bonus may be earned if it is completed within the standard time allowed. The standard time is arrived at by careful work study. The bonus is a fixed percentage on the time taken, if the standard is reached.

(*iii*) If the work is done in less than the standard time then a high piece rate takes the place of the bonus.

The time and bonus rates are fixed for each job, and when a job is completed the man goes on with the next. The pay thus earned consists of day wages plus the sum of all bonuses for which the worker has qualified—or the quantity × the high piece rate.

The foreman may also receive a bonus if the workers reach the standard of efficiency qualifying for a bonus.

EXAMPLE

Assume that the high piece rate is obtained thus:

$$F \times Hours \times RH = NP \times RP$$
$$1 \cdot 33\tfrac{1}{2} \times \quad 6 \quad \times 0 \cdot 50 = 10 \times £0 \cdot 40.$$

If a man performs the task in 7 hours, his earnings will be at the day wage rate:

$$7 \text{ hours} \times 0 \cdot 50 = \underline{£3 \cdot 50}.$$

If he performs it at standard, *i.e.* in 6 hours his earnings will be:

$$6 \text{ hours} \times 0 \cdot 50 = £3 \cdot 00$$
$$\text{Bonus } 33\tfrac{1}{3}\% \quad = \quad 1 \cdot 00$$
$$\underline{\underline{£4 \cdot 00}}$$

If he performs the task in 5 hours, *i.e.* his performance is above standard, his earnings will be:

$$10 \text{ pieces} \times 0 \cdot 40 = \underline{£4 \cdot 00}.$$

The comparative rate of earnings per hour is therefore:

(*i*) 0·50;   (*ii*) 0·66;   (*iii*) 0·80.

(c) Emerson's efficiency system

This scheme is not for the skilled and competent worker, but is designed to give encouragement to the slow worker to do a little better than before.

As the bonus begins at a low rate of efficiency, the scheme can be used as a means of transition from time wages to another payment by results scheme, but it is not effective when efficiency is much above standard, *i.e.* above 100%.

The main features of the scheme are as follows:

(*i*) Day wages are guaranteed.

(*ii*) A volume of output, decided upon from previous output records and test observations, is taken as standard (100% efficiency).

(*iii*) A bonus is paid to a worker whose output exceeds two-thirds (66⅔% efficiency) of the standard in any one week.

(*iv*) As efficiency rises in small steps, so the appropriate bonus percentage is read off from specially compiled tables. Emerson used about thirty-two differential steps.

Group bonus schemes

In the schemes so far considered, the bonuses to be paid have been calculated on an individual basis. In many factories, however, it is possible to arrange that a group of employees working together as a team, *e.g.* on assembly work, should share out a bonus based on the results of the team effort.

The intention is to create a collective interest in the work, and each group enforces its own standards of efficiency. Anyone who is an individualist and wants to work faster than the others, or anyone who cannot match the pace of the team, are alike unwelcome as members of the group. Often, when a member of the group leaves, the others suggest their own replacement, acceptable to them all.

When a group of ten to twenty work together harmoniously they may achieve high output and economical production.

EXAMPLE

Standard production is fixed at 20 units per day, and it is agreed that for every 20% increase in production, a bonus of £50 will be shared among the 20 members of the group, and *pro rata*.

In one day, 25 units were produced, which represents an increase of 25%.

By proportion, $25/20 \times £50 = £62 \cdot 50$.

Each member of the group therefore receives:

$$£62 \cdot 50 \div 20 = £3 \cdot 12\tfrac{1}{2} \text{ as bonus.}$$

Sometimes the idea of a group bonus has been extended in scope to include the whole factory, and there are three schemes which should be noted:

(a) Priestman's production bonus

A standard is set for the output to be achieved weekly by a factory; this standard being measured in terms of units or points. It is therefore similar to the Bedaux scheme already considered, but lacks its scientific approach. The actual output, valued on the same basis, is compared with the standard, and if actual exceeds standard the employees are all paid a bonus in proportion to the increase.

EXAMPLE

In a factory producing plastic toys, 200 workers are employed. The standard output for the week is set at 100,000 points. During one week in December the actual output is valued at 120,000 points. The employees will receive their basic wages, but in addition will receive a bonus calculated as follows:

Standard output	100,000 points
Actual output	120,000 points
Increase 20%	20,000 points

All employees will therefore receive a bonus of 20% of their wages.

(b) Rucker, or "share of production" plan

This scheme is based on the concept that labour is to receive a constant proportion of the "added value." This term is defined in the *Terminology of Cost Accountancy* as follows:

"The change in market value resulting from an alteration in the form, location or availability of a product or service, excluding the cost of bought-out materials or services.
NOTE: Unlike conversion cost it includes profit."

In introducing such a scheme consideration is given to the history of the concern over a number of years, and a ratio is agreed which represents the normal relationship between earnings and "added value." Any reduction in the ratio of earnings to added value produces appropriate bonus payments.

(c) Scanlon plan

This is similar to the Rucker plan, but the ratio adopted is that which wages bears to the sales value of production.

Both the Rucker and the Scanlon plans presuppose that there will be a great deal of joint consultation between management and employees, "so that the total intelligence of the organisation can be applied to the task of making effort more effective."

PROFIT SHARING AND CO-PARTNERSHIP SCHEMES

The idea of giving employees additional remuneration in line with the prosperity of the concern is becoming more widespread, and is growing in importance.

In one such scheme the amount shared among employees amounted to more than six times the sum paid in net dividends to the shareholders.

On the other hand, if the concern has to face bad times, the prospect of not having a bonus at all, is from the employees' point of view, rather a bleak one.

The principle of participation in schemes of this kind is usually a certain length of unbroken service, so that labour turnover tends to be reduced. The longer an employee stays with a firm, the more does he experience the sense of "belonging" to it. He becomes personally involved in the growth and prestige of the firm, as its products become more widely known and accepted at home and abroad. As morale improves, so does productivity increase, and greater care is exercised in handling valuable machines.

After the shareholders have received a dividend of not less than a stated amount, the bonus is payable to the employees, and this may then increase *pari passu* with any further dividend to the shareholders.

A co-partnership scheme is often arranged in conjunction with a profit-sharing scheme, allowing the bonus to be left as an investment in the company. This investment may be in the form of special shares, not carrying voting rights, and only saleable to trustees, but entitled to a fixed dividend, or it may be left in the form of a loan carrying generous interest.

The student should be aware that details of profit-sharing and co-partnership schemes are given from time to time in companies' annual reports, and they will repay study.

SUMMARY

We have now surveyed the field. A great many schemes for the remuneration of labour exist, and we have examined the most important of them. Now, however, it is recognised that more and more power resides with the men on the shop floor, and we can expect a much greater increase in joint consultation, and wages to be very closely geared to productivity.

New agreements will be reached in most of the major industries of the country, and the student must note the details of the terms agreed to see whether they can be fitted into the existing pattern, or whether they constitute a new departure.

Examination questions on Chapters 7–9 are given at the end of Chapter 9.

CHAPTER 9

WAGES

PREPARATION AND PAYMENT OF WAGES

WAGES SHEETS

Whichever method of time-keeping is adopted, the wages due to the workers are entered up on the payroll or wages sheets, a specimen of which is shown in Fig. 46.

Before making any entries, however, the calculation of the wages payable to each worker must have been checked, especially noting that all overtime has been properly authorised; and the gate times upon which payment is made must have been reconciled with the job time records and idle time cards for each worker.

All this work takes time, and often it is necessary to arrange for several days "lying time." This is the time which elapses before workers are paid for the week's work which they have completed. This temporary hardship at the end of their first week's employment is overcome by making them a temporary "sub" or loan. At the termination of their employment, however, they receive payment right up to the date of leaving, so that they lose nothing in the long run.

If the numbers employed are fairly large it may be considered desirable to preprint the wages sheets and employees' pay slips with certain standard information. Addressograph Ltd. make a metal plate on which can be recorded the following details:

(a) The worker's name.
(b) His rate of pay.
(c) His income tax code number.
(d) His clock number.
(e) Standard deductions.

The metal of the plate is soft enough to allow for any alterations to be made should they become necessary.

It is convenient if a separate wages sheet is commenced for each department or cost centre, because in this way the actual wages incurred may be compared with the budgeted amount for that department, and a departmental labour rate may be easily calculated by dividing the total wages for the department by the direct labour hours incurred. It also materially assists in spreading the amount of work to be done.

As each clock card is entered, it is easy to check that it refers to the person whose particulars have been pre-printed on the wages sheet.

PAYROLL

No.	Name	Total hours worked	Rate	Basic pay	Over-time premium	Gross pay	Free pay	Taxable pay to date	Tax due to date	Tax refunds	Deductions			Net pay	Employer
											Tax	Nat. Ins	Total		Nat. Ins.
				£	£	£	£	£	£	£	£	£	£	£	£

FIG. 46.—*Payroll*

This specimen of a payroll allows for additional lines for wages to be used for particular purposes such as Overtime premium. Most firms have them specially printed to suit their own requirements.

The entries may be made either by hand or by accounting machine. In very large factories the wages are automatically tabulated from punched cards.

It is strongly recommended that in drawing up the wages sheet a distinction be made between:

(a) normal time worked;
(b) overtime hours worked;
(c) overtime premium hours.

This is because (a) and (b) are both wanted for record purposes, and will be charged as direct labour in the case of production departments. The sum of (a) and (b) divided into the gross wages payable under these headings will also give the direct labour cost per hour for the department concerned, and this is important for comparative purposes; (c), on the other hand, will almost always be charged as overhead.

The wages sheets are now passed to another clerk for the income tax record cards and the tax columns on the wages sheets to be completed. This division of labour acts as a valuable internal check, for this second clerk would be specifically instructed to report any extraordinary increase in the earnings of any worker, and to list the names of those without tax records and to whom the emergency coding had been applied. Some firms, indeed, go so far as to withhold the pay of any worker who has not produced his tax record card, and his National Insurance card.

The remaining deduction columns, the net payable column and the employer's contribution column, are now completed, and, if possible, by a third clerk. This clerk will also total the wages sheets, section by section, check the cross casts and prepare the grand summary sheet.

CASH

As each section of the wages sheet is completed it is passed to the cashier, who forthwith enters it on a cash summary sheet. This shows the breakdown of the net payable column into £, 50p, 10p, 5p and bronze required in order to make up the wage packets (*see* Fig. 47).

When the money is drawn from the bank it is checked in the Cashier's department in total, and ranged in bundles of twenty £ notes and columns of new pence. The amounts required to make up the wages of the first section, as shown on the cash summary sheet, are now counted out on to a "making-up" table. The pay envelopes for the section having been filled, there should be no cash remaining on that table. The amounts for the second and subsequent sections are similarly dealt with until all the wages have been put into the pay envelopes.

By following this routine carefully, any discrepancy is localised at once, and any checking over is confined to relatively few wage packets.

Department	£		50 p		10 p		5 p		Bronze	

FIG. 47.—*Cash summary sheet*

This is useful for summarising the cash required to make up the wages of each department. It could be provided with a total column if thought necessary, but it is not difficult to manage without it.

PAYING OUT WAGES

Payment of wages in a factory will be made, if possible, at one and the same time in all or several departments, to prevent any opportunity of a worker being in two places. The clerk in the cashier's department should be a responsible person, and he should have the help of the departmental foreman, who will be present at the paying out, in order to identify the workers under him. In some cases workers are provided with brass discs bearing their clock number, and may be asked to call their names and show their discs. Alternatively, workers are often given their completed clock cards for prior examination. They initial these, and hand them in as a receipt for their wage packet.

The wage packets of absentees are entered in an "unclaimed wages book" before being returned to the safe; and they should be signed for when subsequently claimed. No wages should be handed to anyone purporting to act on behalf of an absentee unless and until a written authority has been received from the employee. This authority should then be filed for reference.

A close check should always be kept on National Insurance card and tax records, as they are an excellent guide to the correctness of the names and attendance of those on the wages sheets, but addresses should be checked with the personnel record sheet. In the case of men working on civil-engineering contracts, where a foreman can give a man his cards at a moment's notice, it used to be possible for the wages sheets to carry fictitious names of men supposed to have been engaged and sacked within a week. There is now no longer such a possibility, as it is usual for National Insurance cards and holidays with pay cards to be sent to head office, and wages are not paid until the cards are received. Any employee who has left in such circumstances as envisaged above must also make application in writing, and any pay due to him is sent by post direct.

ACCOUNTING ENTRIES FOR WAGES

In considering the entries to be made in the books to record wages, two matters have first to be decided:

(a) How is overtime to be treated?

(b) What is to be done with the employer's part of National Insurance?

Overtime

It has already been suggested that the ordinary hours of overtime be treated as direct labour hours, in the case of workers in production departments. Most overtime is called for because of general factory conditions, and, therefore, in considering the quantity of work produced we are not particularly concerned whether it was done at 11 a.m. or at 4 p.m. or 8 p.m. On the other hand, the overtime *premium* incurred is an additional indirect cost, and is not chargeable to the cost of the job or process, but should be treated as overhead. The only exception to this method of treatment would be when the overtime is specifically worked for a particular order or contract, and it can then be charged as part of the direct cost of the job (*see* page 181).

National Insurance (*Employers*)

In financial book-keeping the custom is to charge the employers' part of National Insurance as an addition to the wages and salaries, and this is quite reasonable so long as detailed and analysed accounts are not required. When, however, as in job costing, each operative's time has to be divided between a number of jobs or operations, practical difficulties are raised, and these may be overcome in one of two ways:

(a) either an additional rate per hour may be charged to cover the employers' National Insurance;

(b) or the National Insurance may be treated as an overhead.

As method (a) is usually time-wasting to apply, especially when the hours worked are different from the normal expected, it is recommended that method (b) be adopted.

WAGES ANALYSIS BOOK

With these assumptions, the accounting entries may now be prepared, and it will be found convenient in practice to make use of a wages analysis book for the purpose.

The ruling for such a book is shown in Fig. 48, and it will be seen that

Date	Total	Work in Progress	Production Overhead Control	Administration Overhead Control	Selling and Distribution Overhead Control
Department					

Total	Net Cheque	Deduction Accounts			
		Tax	Graduated Pension	National Insurance	National Savings

Fig. 48.—*Wages analysis book*

An analysis of the wages to the main control accounts is essential for accounting purposes. The lower half of the figure is the credit side, for use in an integral system of accounts. If the cost accounts are separate from the financial accounts only one credit posting would be required—to the General Ledger Adjustment Account.

provision is made for entering the wages by department, and extending them to the various control accounts, *viz.* Work-in-progress, Production Overhead Control Account, Administration Overhead Control Account, and Selling and Distribution Overhead Control Account.

The sources of information for compiling this series of extensions are as follows:

1. Wages sheets.
2. Job time cards for work in progress.
3. Idle time cards.

If the wages sheets have been properly departmentalised there should be no difficulty in allocating the wages to the proper controls. It will be remembered especially that the overtime premium and National Insurance (Employers) are to be regarded as overhead.

The opening of these control accounts in the Ledger accords with a system of integral accounts, and the student will perhaps recall the definition of this term given in the *Terminology of Cost Accountancy*: "a single book-keeping system which contains both financial and cost accounts."

Below the summary of debit entries in the wages analysis book is a single line of credit entries, representing the postings to be made to the various "deduction" accounts, such as Income Tax Collections Account, National Insurance Collections Account—which contains both employee's and employer's contributions, sick club collections and so on. The cross cast to agree the total is completed by the amount of the cheque for the net wages payable, and is posted from the cash book.

Putting the matter in diagrammatic form, the Ledger Accounts in the main books of account will be as shown in Fig. 49.

Furthermore, the job time cards or Wages Abstract (Fig. 62) which provided the total for work in progress will also provide the detailed entries on the job cost cards. Similarly, the Production Overhead Control Account will be supported by the details contained in the standing order numbers, which is the name often given to the subsidiary records relating to factory overhead. The details of the Administration Overhead Control Account and the Selling and Distribution Overhead Control Account will be contained in sets of cost account numbers. A suggested ruling for a job cost card is given in Fig. 50, but rulings for standing order numbers and cost account numbers are given in the chapters dealing with overhead.

There are, of course, still many concerns which have separate financial and costing systems, and entries for wages on this basis are not difficult to arrange.

The financial accountant will no doubt keep a wage analysis book himself, and allocate the wages to such headings as he may wish. He will also pick up the postings for the deduction accounts. Most important of all for the cost accountant, the financial accountant will post the total of the wages to a Cost Ledger Control Account. This is merely a memorandum account in his books, and forms no part of his double entry.

The cost accountant, for his part, will pick up the same figures as before in his wages analysis book, and post the total to the *credit* of a General Ledger Adjustment Account. His cost books are now on a double-entry basis, and agreement between the cost and financial books is easily obtained through the Cost Ledger Control Account and

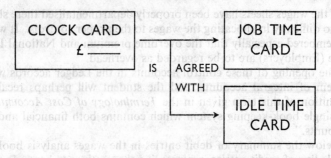

AND IS ENTERED ON THE WAGES SHEETS

WHICH ARE ANALYSED

DATE & DEPARTMENT	TOTAL	WORK IN PROGRESS	FACTORY O.CONTROL	ADMINISTN O.CONTROL	SELLING & DISTN O.CONTROL

WAGES ANALYSIS BOOK

FROM THIS WAGES ANALYSIS BOOK POSTINGS
ARE MADE TO WORK IN PROGRESS ACCOUNT
AND THE OTHER CONTROL ACCOUNTS

SUBSIDIARY RECORDS ARE IN LEDGERS OR

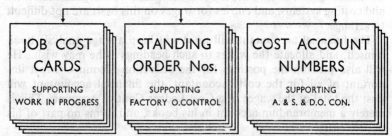

FIG. 49.—*Flow of information for labour costs*

This chart summarises what has been stated in the text and in other figures. It shows how the information regarding direct labour cost originates. Clock cards (but not job tickets) are used for indirect labour as well, and the information flows down in the same way. (Factory overhead is the same as production overhead.)

the General Ledger Adjustment Account. The cost books will not, of course, now include the deduction accounts, nor the posting from the cash book.

Date...............	Order No................	Job No................
Customer..		Estimate Ref.........
Job Description		
....		

MATERIALS		
....		
....		
....		
LABOUR		
....		
....		
....		
PRIME COST		
PRODUCTION OVERHEAD		
....		
....		
PRODUCTION COST		
Estimate £		
Gross Profit %		

FIG. 50.—*Job cost card or Ledger Account*

The entries for materials will be picked up from stores requisitions, while those for labour will come from summaries of job tickets or from a Wages Abstract (Fig. 62). Production Overhead will be added at pre-determined rates as described in Chapter 11. For another specimen of this type of record *see* Fig. 64.

EXAMPLE

A company has gross wages (including Employers' National Insurance £400) of £5,000. Deductions have been made from the wages of the following sums:

Employees' National Insurance £420
P.A.Y.E. taxation £1,050
Sickness club £165

The wages are apportionable as follows:

Department A

Direct wages	£2,050
Indirect wages	£1,000
National Insurance	£300

Department B

Direct wages	£700
Indirect wages	£850
National Insurance	£100

(a) Write up, in the form of journal entries, the postings required to record these facts, when there are separate cost and financial records.

(b) Indicate what changes would be necessary if the accounts were later to be integrated.

(a) (i) *Entries in the financial books*

		£	£
Wages Account Dr.		5,000	
To Wages Payable Account			5,000

To record gross wages £4,600 and Employers' National Insurance £400 as per payroll.

		£	£
Wages Payable Account Dr.		5,000	
To National Insurance collections			820
P.A.Y.E. collections			1,050
Sickness club			165
Cash book—posting of net cheque for wages			2,965

Transfers and posting required to clear Wages Payable Account

In addition, a memorandum entry would be made in the Cost Ledger Control Account, debit wages £5,000. This account is not part of the double-entry system.

(ii) *Entries in the cost books*

		£	£
Wages Control Account Dr.		5,000	
To General Ledger Adjustment Account			5,000

To record gross wages paid per Cost Ledger Control Account, and payroll

		£	£
Work-in-progress Account Dr.			
Direct wages Dept. A		2,050	
„ B		700	
Production Overhead Control Account			
Indirect wages Dept. A		1,000	
National Insurance „ A		300	
Indirect wages „ B		850	
National Insurance „ B		100	
To Wages Control Account			5,000

Apportionment of gross wages and National Insurance per details in the wages analysis book folio.

(b) In order to integrate the records, that is, to have one system of accounts only, the following steps would be taken:

(i) Omit the Cost Ledger Control Account.

(ii) Omit the General Ledger Adjustment Account.

(iii) Omit the Wages Account now kept in the financial books.

As a result, the remaining accounts will constitute a double-entry system of accounts, the first entry from the payroll now being:

Wages Control Account   Dr.
     To Wages Payable Account

EXAMINATION QUESTIONS
Also includes questions on Chapters 7 and 8.

1. What do you understand by labour turnover? Discuss its significance in industry today, and its effect on the production costs of a company manufacturing a specialised product.

(I.C.W.A. Final)

2. You are required to submit a report on labour turnover in a factory. Indicate in the form of a skeleton report (without figures) the general contents of such a report.

(C.A.A. Inter.)

3. As cost accountant of a factory in a very busy industrial area, you find that there is a high rate of labour turnover in certain departments. Write a report to management drawing attention to this fact, and suggesting practical methods of retaining your labour.

(I.C.W.A. Final)

4. Where workers are paid by results, describe the method you would adopt to ensure that piece-rates and/or bonus payments are entered correctly on job cards.

State the system you would install in the factory to ensure maintenance of accurate labour cost records.

(I.C.W.A. Inter.)

5. Is it necessary to keep time records for piece-workers? Give full reasons for your answer.

(C.A.A. Inter.)

6. Outline a practical method of keeping records of labour cost in an industry where the average number of jobs on which each man is engaged is three per day.

(C.A.A. Inter.)

7. As cost accountant of a large company, you are charged by the financial controller with the task of ensuring that the system of computing earnings, the payroll routine and the payment of wages is adequate. List the internal checks you would perform. What types of deliberate fraud would you need to guard against?

(I.C.W.A. Inter.)

8. A small company manufacturing a single complex product has three separate production departments, but the nature of the organisation and work does not lend itself readily to piece-work wage rates.

It is proposed to introduce a group bonus scheme to include all the workers, by fixing a monthly added value standard, and distributing a proportion of any monthly excess achieved as a percentage increase to wages. What criticisms would you make of such a scheme, and what difficulties would you expect to arise? (Added value is the sales price of a product, less the cost of direct materials in it.)

(I.C.W.A. Final)

9. What do you understand by accelerating premium plans? State their purpose, effects, advantages and disadvantages.

By means of a diagram show the shape of the earnings and labour-cost curves related to output for such plans.

(I.C.W.A. Inter.)

10. In a factory where workers under 20 years of age are paid weekly rates varying according to age, similar work is done by workers earning different rates. What method of charging out wages costs can be used to ensure uniformity for different jobs?

(C.A.A. Inter.)

11. Describe, briefly, three methods of payment by results, indicating in each case the formula by which the payment to the employee is computed. State what, in your opinion, are the respective advantages and disadvantages of each method.

(C.A.A. Inter.)

12. It is proposed to institute a system of payment of wages by results in a general engineering factory, and you are required to consider the safeguards that should be provided for both employer and employee in order to ensure that the proposed system will operate on an equitable basis.

Submit your report to the board of directors, assuming any data that may be relevant.

(C.A.A. Final)

13. (a) Comment on the following methods of remunerating direct labour:

Premium bonus.
Piece-work.
Time-work.

State the advantages of each method to the employer and to the employee.

(b) Draft a form of weekly time sheet for an employee, using specimen figures which will provide a record of hours worked and wages paid on a variety of jobs in any one week.

(C.A. Final)

14. (a) Explain the following terms used in connection with wage payments:

(i) Time-work or day-work.
(ii) Piece-work system.
(iii) Bonus or premium system.
(iv) Shift premium.

(*b*) State the main advantages claimed for piece-work and bonus systems of wage payment. What difficulties may arise with these systems?

(*C.A. Final*)

15. The term "tradesman's labourer" is generally understood to describe those workers whose job it is to work with, and provide unskilled assistance to, a skilled tradesman.

Discuss the problems involved in paying a bonus as an incentive to increase productivity to a tradesman's labourer whose work is related to a skilled tradesman. Also, consider the effectiveness of such a bonus.

(*A.C.C.A. Inter.*)

16. The directors of the X.Y. Engineering Co. Ltd. are concerned about the ever-increasing labour costs at their Alpha factory. It is also felt that labour efficiency is very low although this is difficult to establish because production at the Alpha factory is quite dissimilar from any of the other production units in the company and, accordingly, comparisons are not made. You are required to prepare a memorandum for the directors outlining a system of accounting for labour costs which will both control the level of expenditure and give some indication of labour efficiency. Your memorandum should indicate the records, and their source documents, which would have to be kept and *pro-formas* of the reports (figures are not required) which would be presented to management should also be given.

(*A.C.C.A. Final*)

17. (*a*) Define piece rates.
(*b*) Briefly distinguish between:

   (*i*) straight piece rates;
   (*ii*) piece rates with guaranteed day rates;
   (*iii*) differential piece rates.

(*c*) Tabulate the advantages and disadvantages of piece rates.
(*d*) Define time rates.
(*e*) Briefly distinguish between:

   (*i*) ordinary time rates;
   (*ii*) high-wage level time rates;
   (*iii*) graduated time rates.

(*f*) Tabulate the advantages and disadvantages of time rates.

(*I.C.W.A. Inter.*)

18. Explain the fundamental differences between:

   (*a*) straight piece-work;
   (*b*) differential piece-work;
   (*c*) the Rowan system of premium bonus.

In what circumstances would you recommend the use of each of the three systems?

(*I.C.W.A.Inter.*)

19. What factors must be borne in mind where, by reason of increased demand for a product, a decision has to be made between:

(*a*) introducing a second shift;

(*b*) sub-contracting the work.

Embody in your answer a report to your managing director covering the cost of these alternatives.

(*I.C.W.A.Final*)

20. Distinguish between direct and indirect labour. What difficulties are experienced in practice in making this distinction? Illustrate each type of labour with *two* clear examples taken from a particular industry.

(*I.C.W.A. Inter.*)

21. In what circumstances would you propose that the bonus paid for overtime or for night-shift work should be charged to:

(*a*) the particular jobs worked upon during the overtime or night-shift periods;

(*b*) the shop overheads; or

(*c*) general overheads?

(*A.I.A. Final*)

22. How would you deal in the cost accounts with wages paid for the following?

(*a*) The excavation of foundations for the installation of a large press, abandoned after several weeks' work, the site being discovered geologically unsuitable.

(*b*) Transfer of direct labour from a slack department, the employees retaining their existing wage rates, which exceed the rate normally paid in their new department.

(*c*) Work on a project to manufacture an existing product more cheaply.

(*d*) Wages, including overtime premiums, paid to inspectors employed on direct productive operations during overtime only.

Give reasons.

(*I.C.W.A. Inter.*)

23. For some selected industry, describe the cost accounting treatment you would give to wages cost relating to defective work of all kinds, and to its correction where correction is possible.

(*I.C.W.A. Inter.*)

24. Job evaluation is to be used as the basis of the wage structure for a firm employing over 1,000 production and ancillary workers. List six evaluation factors which might be used in such a scheme giving a brief definition of each.

(*I.C.W.A. Inter.*)

25. Explain the meaning of the following terms in relation to time and motion study:

(*a*) Element time.

(*b*) Contingencies allowance.

(*c*) Standard time.

Illustrate your answer by an example showing how the standard time is computed where an operation is done on a machine tool.

(*C.A.A. Final*)

26. In a factory where a system of piece-work is in operation outline the necessary forms and records. How would you deal in the cost account records with "make-up" wages—that is, those cases where the operators' piece-work earnings are less than the minimum weekly rate?

(*I.C.W.A. Inter.*)

27. Distinguish between profit-sharing and co-partnership. Estimate the value of such schemes as incentives to employees and list their defects. Describe briefly two methods used in such schemes.

(*I.C.W.A. Inter.*)

28. A business operates a large fleet of delivery vans to distribute a perishable product from depots to retailers on a nation-wide scale. What factors do you consider should be taken into account in devising a monetary incentive scheme for the van drivers? Describe briefly how you would set about measuring the work of a driver.

(*I.C.W.A. Inter.*)

29. Analysis of labour turnover indicates a large proportion of leavers who have joined other firms in the locality for higher wages. As a consequence, the wages structure is to be reviewed. List and annotate the factors which would need examination for this purpose.

(*I.C.W.A. Inter.*)

30. How would you deal in your cost accounts with:

(*a*) wages paid for idle time during a shortage of work owing to seasonal fluctuation in demand;
(*b*) compensatory payment on account of redundancy, the payment depending on the length of service of the employee;
(*c*) payments made in lieu of bonus to operators unable to work owing to a major machine breakdown?

Give your reasoning in each case.

(*I.C.W.A. Inter.*)

31. From the following details calculate the labour cost chargeable to job no. 873 in respect of an employee who is paid according to:

(*a*) the Rowan scheme;
(*b*) the Halsey 50% scheme.

Job No. 873

Time allowed	5 hours 30 minutes
Time taken	4 hours 25 minutes
Rate of pay	£0·60 per hour

(*A.C.C.A. Inter.*)

32. Ten men work as a group. When the weekly production of the group exceeds standard (200 pieces per hour) each man of the group is paid a bonus for the excess production in addition to his wages at hourly rates. The bonus is computed thus:

The percentage of production in excess of the standard amount is found and one half of this percentage is considered as the men's share. Each man in the group is paid as a bonus this percentage of a wage rate of £0·66½ per hour. There is no relationship between the individual workman's hourly rate and the bonus rate. The following is one week's record:

	Hours worked	Production
Monday	90	22,100
Tuesday	88	20,600
Wednesday	90	24,200
Thursday	84	20,100
Friday	88	20,400
Saturday	40	10,200
	480	117,600

(a) Compute the rate and amount of bonus for the week.

(b) Compute the total pay of Jones who worked 41½ hours and was paid £0·47½ per hour basic, and of Smith who worked 44¼ hours and was paid £0·52½ per hour basic.

(I.C.W.A. Inter.)

33. Prepare a labour cost sheet for a machined component, using your own figures, assuming three operations and the following additional information:

Commenced with 300 units.
10 units scrapped in Operation 1.
12 units scrapped in Operation 2 and 14 units rejected for adjustment.
8 units scrapped in Operation 3.

(A.I.A. Final)

34. A manufacturer introduces new machinery into his factory, with the result that production per worker is increased. The workers are paid by results, and it is agreed that for every 2% increase in average individual output an increase of 1% on the rate of wages will be paid. At the time the machinery is installed the selling price of the product falls by 8⅓%.

Show the net saving in production costs which would be required to offset the losses expected from reduced turnover and bonus paid to workers.

	1st Period	2nd Period
Number of workers	175	125
Number of articles produced	168,000	140,000
Wages paid	£33,600	—
Total sales	£75,600	—

(I.C.W.A. Final)

35. An article passes through five hand operations as follows:

Operation No.	Time per article	Grade of worker	Wage rate per hour
1	15 minutes	A	£0·65
2	25 minutes	B	£0·55
3	10 minutes	C	£0·45
4	30 minutes	D	£0·40
5	20 minutes	E	£0·35

The factory works a 40-hour week, and the production target is 600 dozen per week. Prepare a statement showing for each operation and in total the number of operators required, the labour cost per dozen and the total labour cost per week to produce the target output.

(C.A. Final)

36. (a) Define standard hour.
(b) Using the following information, calculate and show separately each of:

(i) the basic wage earned;
(ii) the hours and money value of bonus earned;
(iii) the total gross wage payable.

The basic working week is 40 hours, and the basic rate is £0·66½ per hour. Overtime work is paid for as follows:

Week-days: the first 3 hours at time and a third
Week-days: after the first 3 hours at time and a half
Saturdays: all hours at time and a half
Sundays: all hours at double time

The employee worked a 52½ hour week of which 4 hours were on a Saturday and 3½ hours were on a Sunday.
A bonus scheme is in operation based on work study. Bonus is paid at the basic rate per hour for time saved on accepted output from measured work only. 530 dozen units were issued, but 60 units were rejected. Time spent on measured work was 38 hours and 72 standard minutes are allowed for each gross of accepted units.

(I.C.W.A. Inter.)

37. A factory department operates a group bonus scheme in which three skilled, two semi-skilled, four unskilled male operatives and six female operatives participate. Time saved on good units produced on group bonus jobs is shared in proportion to the time spent on them.
In a certain week when 42 hours were worked by each employee and no overtime was worked, the following information is recorded:

	Male skilled	Male semi-skilled	Male un-skilled	Female
Hours spent by each on bonus job	24	24	30	40
Base rate per hour	£0·45	£0·40	£0·37½	£0·30
Percentage of base rate at which hours saved are paid	66⅔	50	33⅓	25

Hours spent on jobs other than those on bonus are paid for at base rate only. Production details for the week are:

	Base units	Side units	Top units
Bonus time allowed, minutes each	20	15	12
Gross units produced	600	1,750	1,550
Units rejected and bonus time allowance withdrawn	60	150	50

Calculate and summarise for presentation:

    (a) percentage of hours saved to hours taken;
    (b) bonus hour entitlement of each labour grade;
    (c) bonus payable to:
        (i) the group;
       (ii) each labour grade;
      (iii) each operative;
    (d) gross wage payable to each operative for the 42-hour week.

                                                  (*I.C.W.A. Inter.*)

38. Jobs are issued to operative X, to make 189 units, and to operative Y, to make 204 units, for which a time allowance of 20 standard minutes and 15 standard minutes per unit respectively, is credited. For every hour saved, bonus is paid at 50% of the base rate, which is £0·66½ per hour for both employees. The basic working week is 42 hours. Hours in excess are paid at time plus one third.

X completes his units in 45 hours and Y completes his in 39 hours (but works a full week). Due to defective material, six of X's units and four of Y's units are subsequently scrapped, although all units produced are paid for.

You are required to calculate for each of X and Y:

    (a) the amount of bonus payable;
    (b) the total gross wage payable;
    (c) the wages cost per good unit made.

                                                  (*I.C.W.A. Inter.*)

39. In a factory bonus system, bonus hours are credited to the employee in the proportion of time taken which time saved bears to time allowed. Jobs are carried forward from one week to another. No overtime is worked and payment is made in full for all units worked on, including those subsequently rejected.

From the following information you are required to calculate for each employee:

    (a) the bonus hours and amount of bonus earned;
    (b) the total wage costs;
    (c) the wage cost of each good unit produced.

Employee	A	B	C
Basic wage rate, per hour	£0·50	£0·80	£0·75
Units issued for production	2,500	2,200	3,600
Time allowed per 100 units	2 hrs 36 min	3 hrs	1 hr 30 min
Time taken	52 hrs	75 hrs	48 hrs
Rejects	100 units	40 units	400 units

                                                  (*I.C.W.A. Inter.*)

40. (a) Distinguish between:

(i) straight piece-work;
(ii) differential piece-work.

(b) Calculate the earnings arising under each method for each of the following jobs issued to make a common product. Under one system a rate of £0·05 per unit is paid. Under the other, the first 480 units for each job are paid at £0·01 per unit increasing by the same amount for each subsequent 240 units produced.

Job	Units
D	720
E	1,200
F	480
G	1,680

(c) For each method give:

(i) the total cost of the total output;
(ii) the average cost per unit.

(I.C.W.A. Inter.)

41. Using the information given below you are required to:

(a) Calculate the amounts earned by each employee under each of the following remuneration methods:

(i) piece-work (with guaranteed hourly rates);
(ii) hourly rates;
(iii) bonus system (under which the employee receives $66\frac{2}{3}\%$ of time savings).

(b) Calculate the gross wages paid to each employee under each of the above methods:

	Employee A	Employee B	Employee C
Time allowed: hours per 100 units	23	32	38
Price per unit	£0·12½	£0·05	£0·07½
Guaranteed hourly rate	£0·60	£0·75	£0·50
Actual time taken: hours	40	42	39
Actual units produced	200	125	150

(I.C.W.A. Inter.)

42. A company's basic wages rate is £0·45 per hour and its overtime rates are:

Evenings—time and one-third;
Week-ends—double time.

During the previous year the following hours were worked:

Normal time	440,000 clock hours
Time plus one-third	40,000 ,, ,,
Double time	20,000 ,, ,,

The following times have been worked on the stated jobs:

	Job X	Job Y	Job Z
	Clock hours	Clock hours	Clock hours
Normal time	6,000	10,000	8,000
Evening overtime	600	1,200	2,100
Week-end overtime	200	100	600

You are required to calculate the labour cost chargeable to each job in each of the following circumstances:

(a) Where overtime is worked regularly throughout the year as company policy due to labour shortage.

(b) Where overtime is worked irregularly to meet spasmodic production requirements.

(c) Where overtime is worked specifically at the customer's request to expedite delivery.

State briefly the reason for each method chosen.

(*I.C.W.A. Inter.*)

43. The following information relates to a certain week for three employees:

Employee	A	B	C
Work issued (dozens)	150	264	60
Bonus time allowed (hours)	0·5	3·0	0·75
	per dozen	per gross	per dozen
Output rejected (dozens)	37	63	20
Basic hourly wage rate	£0·66½	£1·00	£0·50
Hours worked	48	54	42
Hours on indirect work	—	—	12

Bonus is paid at 66⅔% of the base rate for all time saved.

Owing to faulty materials creating an abnormally high rate of rejection, it was agreed to credit all output for bonus purposes.

The basic working week is 42 hours, the first six hours overtime are paid at time plus one third, and the next six hours at time plus one half.

Using the information given above, present in tabulated summary form for each employee:

(a) number of bonus hours earned;

(b) basic wages including overtime premium;

(c) amount of bonus earned;

(d) gross wages;

(e) direct wages cost per dozen when overtime is worked:

    (i) regularly throughout the year as company policy due to labour shortage; and

    (ii) specifically at the customer's request to expedite delivery.

For (e) (i) and (e) (ii) the cost per dozen should be calculated on:

1. accepted output; and
2. work issued.

(*I.C.W.A. Inter.*)

CHAPTER 10

OVERHEAD: CLASSIFICATION AND DISTRIBUTION

OVERHEAD is defined in the *Terminology of Cost Accountancy* as "the aggregate of indirect material cost, indirect wages and indirect expense," and by the word "indirect" in this connection is meant, "that which cannot be allocated, but which can be apportioned to, or absorbed by cost centres or cost units."

These sections of overhead may also be analysed into groups, *viz.*:

> production overhead;
> administration overhead;
> selling and distribution overhead.

Or again, for the purposes of budgetary control, they may be incorporated in departmental budgets.

And yet again, when marginal costing principles are to be applied, they may be sub-divided into:

> fixed overhead;
> semi-fixed overhead;
> variable overhead.

It is important, however, to grasp the fact that *it is the same overhead*, from whatever angle we are looking at it.

INDIRECT MATERIALS

In the course of manufacture of a product, various materials have to be purchased which do not themselves enter into the finished product. To take a simple example, a dustbin is made of galvanised metal, which is a *direct* cost. The side of the dustbin is either spot welded or seam welded, and the welding equipment requires the use of electrodes. These electrodes are an *indirect* material cost, and would be included within the "production overhead" group.

Again, some materials are used in such small quantities that it is often considered best to regard them as an indirect expense. In the manufacture of brooms and brushes, for example, pitch is sometimes used to assist in holding the tufts of fibres in place. This pitch is used in small, unmeasured quantities, and may satisfactorily be treated as production overhead.

On the other hand, there are cases when materials which, at first sight, are "indirect" are regarded as "direct." In brick-making, for example, large amounts of coal or coke may be used in firing the kilns. This fuel does not enter into the finished product directly, but it may be said to do so in the form of applied heat to make a hard-baked brick, and therefore the fuel cost is treated as a "direct" cost.

As a general rule, it may be accepted that indirect materials are those which are used ancillary to manufacture and cannot be traced into the finished product.

INDIRECT WAGES

This comprises wages paid for all labour which does not help directly in changing the shape or composition of the raw materials from which a product is made. Obvious examples are the wages of factory foremen, the salaries of office executives and the commission payable to representatives "on the road."

INDIRECT EXPENSES

Most expense items of expenditure are classified as "indirect," since they are incurred for the business as a whole rather than in regard to any particular order received or product made. Some items fall clearly under the head of production, administration, or selling and distribution, *e.g.* repairs of factory machinery; office stationery; advertising and catalogues. Other items, such as fire insurance, have to be suitably apportioned.

STANDING ORDER NUMBERS AND COST ACCOUNT NUMBERS

In order to systematise the analysis of overhead, and to ensure the grouping of like items with like in a convenient and expeditious manner, it is necessary to devise a syllabus of account headings, suitably coded. The guiding principle must be that the headings selected shall be clear and not be confused one with another, and at the same time be sufficient in number to cover every contingency.

Standing order numbers are, by custom, applied to factory expense headings; and cost account numbers to administration, and selling and distribution expense headings. The method of compilation is, however, the same in each case, and to term them all "nominal headings" would seem to be sensible.

Some cost accountants like to use letter symbols as mnemonic aids, *e.g.* "R" for repairs, "A" for administration expenses, "S" for selling expenses and so on. Others prefer a decimal arrangement:

22 *Repairs to buildings*

    2211 Repairs to foundry building
    2212 Repairs to power-house
    2213 Repairs to machine shop

Or again:

27 *Maintenance of plant*

    2711 Steam plant
    2712 Transmission
    2713 Electric-power plant

It should be noted that every business has its own particular scheme of nomenclature compiled to suit its own particular accounting organisation—the exception being that some industries have adopted a uniform system of accounting to which many of the firms engaged therein will conform.

The classification of standing order numbers given below is a partial example only, and has been arranged on the decimal system because this is preferred for mechanical sorting and tabulating in conjunction with punched cards.

SECTION A—DEPARTMENTAL CODING

01 *Raw material store*
02 *Press shop*
03 *Lathes*

    031 Capstans
    032 Turrets
    033 Centre

04 *Drilling machines*

    041 Horizontal
    042 Vertical
    043 Multiple

05 *Welding shop*

    051 Multiple spot
    052 Single spot
    053 Seam
    054 Arc

06 *Grinding shop*

    061 Surface
    062 Internal

SECTION B—CLASSIFICATION OF PRODUCTION OVERHEAD

11 *Supervision*

111 Foremen

111.01 Grade 1
111.02 Grade 2

112 Inspection

112.01 Senior
112.02 Assistants

12 *Internal transport*

121 Drivers

121.01 Fork lift truck
121.02 Crane

13 *Sweepers and cleaners*

131 Mechanical floor-scrubber
132 Others

132.01 Male
132.02 Female

14 *Supplies*

141 Machine tools

141.01 Oils and grease
141.02 Cotton waste

142 Operators

142.01 Overalls
142.02 Goggles
142.03 PVC gloves

143 Factory—general

143.01 Brooms
143.02 Brushes
143.03 Dustpans
143.04 Dustbins
143.05 Detergent powder
143.06 Soap—green
143.07   —liquid
143.08   —toilet
        and so on

15 *Insurance—factory*

151 Fire
152 Third party

It follows from the above classification that if a requisition were received from the press shop for a broom it would be referenced 143.01.02, and again, if an overall were requisitioned for a capstan-lathe operator it would be coded 142.01.031, the last number in each case giving the department concerned.

The classification would be continued to include the various headings required for service departments such as the boiler-house, plant maintenance department, canteen, etc.

Entirely separate classifications would be prepared for the cost account numbers required for administration and selling and distribution analysis, but care must be taken to ensure that the reference numbers chosen do not in any way conflict with those used for production overhead.

Thus, suppose that the last main number used in the production overhead classification were 37, it would be advisable to leave a gap in the numbers and begin the administration classification with 51, and the selling and distribution classification with, say, 81.

CLASSIFICATION OF ADMINISTRATION OVERHEAD

51 *Salaries*

511 Executive and management

511.01 Managing director
511.02 Secretary
511.03 Cost accountant

512 Clerks

512.01 Grade A
512.02 Grade B

52 *Rent*
53 *Rates*

531 General
532 Water

54 *Printing and stationery*

and so on

CLASSIFICATION OF SELLING AND DISTRIBUTION OVERHEAD

81 *Salaries*

811 Sales manager
812 Travellers
813 Clerks

82 *Commissions*

    821 Sales manager
    822 Travellers

83 *Catalogues*

    831 Catalogues
    832 Circulars and price lists

84 *Advertising*

    841 Newspapers
    842 Trade magazines
    843 Posters

and so on

APPORTIONMENT OF OVERHEAD

The object of classifying overhead is to facilitate the correct apportionment to various departments, and thence to the cost units of production. The procedure follows the general pattern given below:

1. All overhead is collected under the separate headings provided, *i.e.* the standing order numbers and the cost account numbers.

2. All the separate totals of expense in standing order numbers are then apportioned to production departments and service departments.

3. The total overhead for each service department is then apportioned to the departments which use those services, and this is repeated if necessary until all the overhead has been apportioned to production departments.

4. The final totals of overhead for the production departments are absorbed in such a way that each works order number, or unit of production, is charged with its share of the overhead of the departments through which it passes.

How the plan operates is described in the remainder of the chapter.

1. COLLECTION OF OVERHEAD

There are four main sources of overhead:

    (*a*) Invoices.
    (*b*) Stores requisitions.
    (*c*) Wages analysis book.
    (*d*) Journal entries.

These are examined below, together with types of subsidiary records.

Invoices

In a hand-written accounting system the usual practice is for invoices to be entered in a Purchase Journal and extended into columns so that postings may be made to the nominal headings to be charged. In an integral costing system, however, these nominal headings may be conveniently grouped together under control accounts, and to make this clear a specimen ruling of a Purchase Journal is given in Fig. 51. By

Date	Suppliers	Total Creditors	Materials Control	Production Overhead Control	Administration Overhead Control	Selling and Distribution Overhead Control	Payments in Advance	Accrued Charges

FIG. 51.—*Purchase Journal*

This is a specimen ruling of a Purchase Journal for costing purposes. The invoices are entered and allocated or apportioned to their respective control accounts. Note particularly the explanation of the two columns on the right as given in the text.

this arrangement, all materials, of whatever kind, and for whatever purpose, find their way into the "Materials Control Account" and from thence the total of the goods received notes will already have been posted to the Stores Ledger Control Account. Invoices for expense items are extended to one or more of the Overhead Control Accounts, as the case may be. The basis of this apportionment has to be the one most suitable to the type of expense. In some cases it might be relative areas of factory as compared with offices; in others there would be meter readings to act as a guide; and in yet others there would be technical estimates.

The accounting entries would therefore be:

Sundries   Dr.
    To Total Creditors Account
Materials Control Account
Production Overhead Control Account
Administration Overhead Control Account
Selling and Distribution Overhead Account

It will be noted that in addition to the columns for the control accounts two others are provided, headed respectively:

   (*a*) payments in advance;
   (*b*) accrued charges.

The reason for these two headings is entirely one of practical convenience. In cases where invoices are received which cover a period, say January 1 to June 30, it is better to make use of these columns than to post the full amount at once to one of the control accounts, and thus throw out the agreement of the month's entries posted to the standing order numbers.

Stores requisitions

Stores requisitions for "direct" materials are not now within our consideration, having already been dealt with in Chapter 5.

Those, however, which are for "indirect" materials will have been coded, and will therefore be posted to the debit of the respective control accounts, and credited to Stores Ledger Control Account.

Wages analysis book

The accounting entries from the wages analysis book have already been dealt with in Chapter 9, and it will be recalled that in addition to the Work-in-progress Account the various Overhead Control Accounts were also affected by items of indirect wages.

Journal entries

The Journal entries referred to are the monthly apportionments from payments in advance and accrued charges.

The picture which the student should have in mind is therefore as shown in Fig. 52.

Subsidiary records

   (*a*) *Standing order numbers*—giving details of the Production Overhead Control Account.

   (*b*) *Cost account numbers*—giving details of the Administration Overhead Control Account and Selling and Distribution Overhead Control Account.

In the manner shown above the control accounts are built up from period to period, and indicate the cumulative amount of overhead incurred, while the subsidiary records give the information which would otherwise be given in Nominal Ledger Accounts.

Invoices received for materials

and expenses, etc.,

are entered in the

Purchase Journal

Total	Materials Control	Prod. Overhead Control	Admin. Overhead Control	S. and D. Overhead Control	Payments in advance	Accrued charges

The totals are posted as follows:

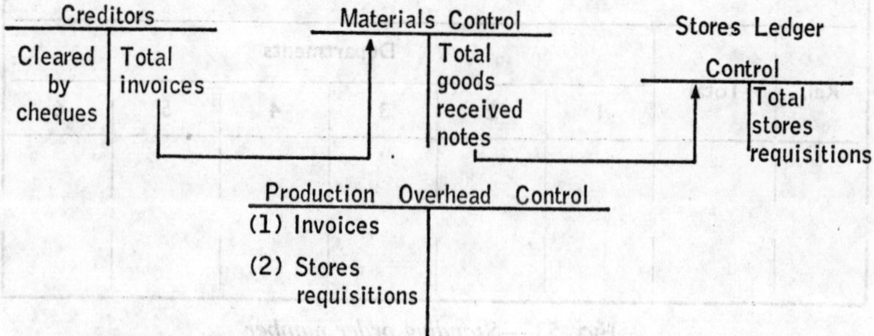

Creditors		Materials Control		Stores Ledger
Cleared by cheques	Total invoices		Total goods received notes	Control — Total stores requisitions

Production Overhead Control

(1) Invoices

(2) Stores requisitions

NOTES

Administration Overhead Control and Selling and Distribution Overhead Control are both similar in form to Production Overhead Control.

Materials Control Account can be dispensed with if goods received notes are priced from invoices and not from copies of orders.

FIG. 52.—*Flow chart for invoices*

The Materials Control Account proves the agreement of invoices and goods received notes. Only part of the stores requisitions credited to Stores Ledger Control Account are debited to Production Overhead Control Account: the bulk going to Work-in-progress Account (*see* Fig. 50).

2. ALLOCATION AND APPORTIONMENT

Standing order numbers

The second stage of the general plan is to apportion the periodic total shown in the Production Overhead Control Account to the production and service departments.

This may be conveniently done as part of the ruling of the standing order numbers. Whether these order numbers are composed of cards or loose-leaf sheets depends on the number of departments concerned. A specimen ruling is suggested in Fig. 53.

The entry in the Production Overhead Control Account which has been posted from the Purchase Journal is the first to be dealt with. For this purpose it is necessary to go back to the Journal and exhaust the items in the Control Account column, one by one, on to the appropriate standing order numbers.

		Departments					
Ref.	Total	1	2	3	4	5	6

HEADING: ....   CODING: ....

Basis of Apportionment:

FIG. 53.—*Standing order number*

This is a suggested ruling for an account used for the collection of factory overhead. The departments 1–6 might be extended as necessary: for example, as in Fig. 54.

Let it be supposed that one particular item in the Purchase Journal is a bill for the repair of a piece of equipment in the power-house. It will appear in the total column and be extended to the Production Overhead Control Account column. The coding on the invoice will be read, and the standing order number for "Maintenance of plant and equipment" will be turned up. The necessary entry will then be made under the period concerned, both in the total column and also in this case in the power-house column.

In the same way the stores requisitions are used as the basis for exhausting the entry in the Control Account for indirect materials; and the wages sheets for apportioning the indirect wages.

When all the required entries have been made on the standing order numbers they are ruled off for the month, and summarised as shown in Fig. 54. The total of this summary must then be agreed with the total of the month's entries to the Control Account.

Cost account numbers

An attempt used to be made to deal with administration and selling and distribution overhead on exactly the same lines as production

DEPARTMENTAL DISTRIBUTION SUMMARY

Four Weeks to February 28, 19…

Items	Total as per Summary	General Production Overhead	Buildings	Services — Electricity Supply	Services — Steam Supply	Services — Motive Power	Services — Stores Expenses	Services — Heating Service	Services — Lighting Service	Production — Dept. A	Production — Dept. B	Production — Dept. C
	£	£	£	£	£	£	£	£	£	£	£	£
Indirect Labour:												
Foremen	199		20	25	20	25	16	10	10	33	20	20
Storemen	40						40					
Shop clerks	32	32										
Labourers	256		20	10	40	10				50	76	50
Works salaries	797	797										
National Insurance	269		2	1	1	1	1	1	1	92	84	84
Workmen's Compensation Insurance	32									9	8	8
Fire Insurance	30		1	1	1	1	10	1	1			
Rent	257		257									
Rates	298		272		26							
Stationery, etc.	20	20										
Indirect Material	179			5	5	15	4	3	2	45	52	48
Water	14	3			11							
Electricity and Gas	120					100			20			
Coal	582			240	220			122				
Service Wages	250	6	70	50	80	32		10	3			
Repairs	536		130	40	26	47		14	8	61	134	75
Maintenance	20			7	9	8						
Stores adjustment	70						20					
Dining-room	70	70										
Welfare	40	40										
Lighting Material	30								30			
Fire Protection	8	8										
Depreciation	365		85	45	80	30	2	25	3	35	30	32
Transport (internal)	100									36	24	40
Sundry Expenses	257	257										
Experimental	32	32										
	£4903	£1268	£902	£424	£519	£269	£93	£186	£78	£370	£435	£362

FIG. 54.—*Departmental distribution summary*

After the standing order numbers have been completed each month, they are ruled off and summarised on a statement as shown.

overhead. It has been realised, however, that this attempt must largely be based on guesswork, since the connection between these kinds of overhead and the production departments is hard to discover. For this reason among others it has largely been abandoned, and a simple ruling for cost account numbers can therefore be recommended, as shown in Fig. 55.

HEADING:		CODING:						
			Months					
Ref.	Details	Total	J.	F.	M.	A.	M.	J.

FIG. 55.—*Cost account number*

This is a possible ruling for accounts used for the collection of administration overhead. The columns for the months could be extended to cover the full year.

The procedure with regard to exhausting the items in the control accounts should be followed as before, and the periodic totals must be summarised and agreed with the control accounts.

For management purposes, it is useful to prepare summaries of the cost account numbers, period by period, and on a cumulative basis, so that expenditure incurred under each heading can be carefully watched. Apart from this, however, these sections of overhead dealing with administration and selling and distribution overhead drop out of our consideration for the time being.

Basis of apportionment of overhead to departments

This varies according to the type of overhead being considered, but similar factors will apply, as when apportioning between the Overhead Control Accounts. The main bases in use, and specimen examples of each, are as below:

(*a*) *Direct allocation*

Overtime premium of men engaged in a particular department.
Power, when separate meters are available.
Jobbing repairs.

(b) *Capital values*

Depreciation of plant and machinery.
Fire insurance.

(c) *Relative areas of departments*

Lighting and heating.
Fire-precaution service.
Building service.

(d) *Direct labour hours and/or machine hours*

Majority of general overhead items.

(e) *Number employed*

Canteen expenses.
Recreation room expense.
Time-keeping.

(f) *Technical estimate*

Electric light—number of lights or watts used.
Electric power—operating time in conjunction with horse-power of machines.
Steam—based on a consumption return, or on potential consumption.
Water—when for process use it is usually metered.

Departments for costing purposes

These are not necessarily only production departments or shops. Sometimes a production "centre" is treated as a "department," instead of, or in addition to, the larger factory divisions. A centre may be an isolated work-bench, a machine, or a group of machines of one type, or an activity. By this arrangement closer distribution of expense and more detailed control are aimed at. This method of minute departmentalisation of cost involves a considerable amount of analysis and, in the majority of cases, the expense of the work would not be warranted. The value of the method lies in the more precise costs which are obtained, regardless of the variation in the product or the equipment. Unless great care is used in analysis, this elaboration may lead to erroneous results.

3. APPORTIONMENT OF SERVICE DEPARTMENTS TO PRODUCTION AND OTHER SERVICE DEPARTMENTS

The departmental distribution summary having been prepared by summarising the standing order numbers, it now becomes necessary to apportion the cost of the service departments to the production departments, and possibly to other service departments. Figure 54 shows aecds imen departmental distribution summary, and from this it can be seen that there is a considerable problem in regard to the redistribution of the service department costs.

It is necessary to consider the use made of each of the service departments by every other department, in terms of time and money values. The service departments will normally keep time sheets showing the hours spent on work done, and for whom it was done, and these records may well form the basis of calculation. In other cases estimates must suffice.

It is a good plan to tackle the work in two stages:

(a) Make the inter-service departments transfers.
(b) Apportion the totals so obtained to the production departments.

There are three methods available for dealing with inter-service departments transfers:

(a) Simultaneous equations.
(b) Matrices.
(c) Repeated distribution.

In the first place let us take a simple case.

A company has three production departments and two service departments, and for a period the departmental distribution summary has the following totals:

	£
Production department A	800
B	700
C	500
Service department 1	234
2	300
	£2,534

The expense of the service departments is charged out on a percentage basis as follows:

	A	B	C	1	2
SD 1	20%	40%	30%	—	10%
SD 2	40%	20%	20%	20%	—

You are required to show the apportionment of overhead.

(a) Simultaneous-equation method

Let x = total overhead of department 1.
And y = total overhead of department 2.

Then:

$$x = 234 + 0 \cdot 2y$$
$$y = 300 + 0 \cdot 1x$$

Rearranging, and multiplying to eliminate decimals:

$$10x - 2y = 2,340 \quad \cdot \quad \cdot \quad \cdot \quad \cdot \quad \cdot \quad (1)$$
$$- x + 10y = 3,000 \quad \cdot \quad \cdot \quad \cdot \quad \cdot \quad \cdot \quad (2)$$

Multiply equation (1) by 5, and add result to (2):

$$49x = 14,700$$
$$x = \underline{300.}$$

Substituting this value in equation (1):

$$y = \underline{330.}$$

All that now remains to be done is to take these values $x = 300$ and $y = 330$ and apportion them on the basis of the agreed percentages to the three production departments, thus:

	Total	A	B	C
	£	£	£	£
Per distribution summary	2,000	800	700	500
Service Department 1	270	60	120	90
„ „ 2	264	132	66	66
	2,534	992	886	656

Thus the amount of £60 apportioned for service departmental to production department A is 20% of £300, and the £66 apportioned for service department 2 to production department C is 20% of £330.

This method is not to be recommended when there are more than two service departments, as each creates an additional "unknown."

(b) Matrices

For those who may have learned modern mathematics this method is included, since the use of inverse matrices enables the solution to be obtained even if there are several unknowns.

We have:

$$x - 0 \cdot 2y = 234$$
$$-0 \cdot 1x + y = 300$$

In matrix form this is:

$$\begin{bmatrix} 1 & -0 \cdot 2 \\ -0 \cdot 1 & 1 \end{bmatrix} \begin{bmatrix} x \\ y \end{bmatrix} = \begin{bmatrix} 234 \\ 300 \end{bmatrix}$$

The inverse matrix of:

$$\begin{bmatrix} 1 & -0 \cdot 2 \\ -0 \cdot 1 & 1 \end{bmatrix} \text{ is } \begin{bmatrix} 1 & 0 \cdot 2 \\ 0 \cdot 1 & 1 \end{bmatrix}.$$

Therefore:

$$\begin{bmatrix} 1 & 0{\cdot}2 \\ 0{\cdot}1 & 1 \end{bmatrix}\begin{bmatrix} 1 & -0{\cdot}2 \\ -0{\cdot}1 & 1 \end{bmatrix}\begin{bmatrix} x \\ y \end{bmatrix} = \begin{bmatrix} 1 & 0{\cdot}2 \\ 0{\cdot}1 & 1 \end{bmatrix}\begin{bmatrix} 234 \\ 300 \end{bmatrix}$$

$$\longrightarrow \quad \begin{bmatrix} 0{\cdot}98 & 0 \\ 0 & 0{\cdot}98 \end{bmatrix}\begin{bmatrix} x \\ y \end{bmatrix} = \begin{bmatrix} 294 \\ 323{\cdot}4 \end{bmatrix}$$

$$0{\cdot}98x = 294$$
$$0{\cdot}98y = 323{\cdot}4$$

Hence:

$$x = 300$$
$$y = 330.$$

(c) Repeated distribution method

In this case the totals as shown in the departmental distribution summary are put out in a line, and then the service department totals are exhausted in turn repeatedly according to the agreed percentages, until the figures become too small to matter:

	A	B	C	1	2
	£	£	£	£	£
Per distribution summary	800	700	500	234	300
Service Department 1	47	94	70	(234)	23
,, ,, 2	129	65	65	64	(323)
,, ,, 1	14	25	19	(64)	6
,, ,, 2	2	2	2		(6)
	992	886	656		

NOTE: The italicised figures are credits, necessary to exhaust the service department columns.

A quicker method is sometimes to settle the position, first of all, as between the service departments themselves: it depends on how many there are.

In this case, there are only two, and we have this position:

10% of service department 1 is charged to service department 2.
20% of service department 2 is charged to service department 1.

Therefore:

	Department 1	Department 2
Original apportionment	234	300
	(234)	23 (10% of 234)
	65 (20% of 323)	(323)
	(65)	7 (10% of 65)
	1 (20% of 7)	(7)
Cast of positive figures	300	330

The procedure from this point is the same as when the values of x and y were found by methods (a) and (b).

In many ways the repeated distribution method appears to be the easier method.

Now let us tackle the example given in Fig. 54.

Let us assume that as a result of investigation it is agreed that the general factory overhead and other services are charged out on the following percentage basis.

NOTE: Any agreed proportion may be expressed for convenience in percentage terms.

	Service departments								Production departments		
	a 1	b 2	c 3	d 4	e 5	f 6	g 7	h 8	A	B	C
1 a Fy. Gen. O	—	5	5	5	5	5	5	5	30	20	15
2 b Buildings	—	—	10	20	10	—	—	—	20	20	20
3 c Electricity	—	—	—	—	75	—	—	25	—	—	—
4 d Steam	—	—	—	—	—	—	40	—	30	15	15
5 e Motive Power	—	—	—	—	—	—	—	—	40	30	30
6 f Stores	—	—	—	—	—	—	—	—	30	35	35
7 g Heating	—	—	—	—	—	10	—	—	30	30	30
8 h Lighting	—	—	—	5	—	5	—	—	30	30	30

Simultaneous-equation method

The cumbersome nature of this method can now be seen.

Let a, b, c, d, e, f, g, h represent the total overhead of service departments 1–8 inclusive.

As there are several unknowns, a means of building up the equations by substituting one value for another is worth trying, thus:

$$a = 1,265 \qquad\qquad\qquad = 1,265$$

$$
\begin{aligned}
b &= 902 + 0.05a \\
&= 902 + 63.25 &&= 965.25
\end{aligned}
$$

$$
\begin{aligned}
c &= 424 + 0.05a + 0.1b \\
&= 424 + 63.25 + 96.53 &&= 583.78
\end{aligned}
$$

$$
\begin{aligned}
h &= 78 + 0.05a + 0.25c \\
&= 78 + 63.25 + 145.94 &&= 287.19
\end{aligned}
$$

$$
\begin{aligned}
d &= 519 + 0.05a + 0.20b + 0.05h \\
&= 519 + 63.25 + 193.05 + 14.36 &&= 789.66
\end{aligned}
$$

$$
\begin{aligned}
e &= 269 + 0.05a + 0.10b + 0.75c \\
&= 269 + 63.25 + 96.53 + 437.84 &&= 866.62
\end{aligned}
$$

$$
\begin{aligned}
g &= 186 + 0.05a + 0.40d \\
&= 186 + 63.25 + 315.86 &&= 565.11
\end{aligned}
$$

$$
\begin{aligned}
f &= 93 + 0.05a + 0.10g + 0.05h \\
&= 93 + 63.25 + 56.51 + 14.36 &&= 227.12
\end{aligned}
$$

Having thus apportioned the service departments as between themselves, we now apply the production department percentages to the figures we have obtained. Thus factory general overhead shows:

30% for dept. A, *i.e.* 30% of £1,265 = £380
20% for dept. B, *i.e.* 20% of £1,265 = £253
15% for dept. C, *i.e.* 15% of £1,265 = £190

Again, steam service shows:

30% for dept. A, *i.e.* 30% of £790 = £237
15% for dept. B, *i.e.* 15% of £790 = £118
15% for dept. C, *i.e.* 15% of £790 = £119

The result, therefore, is as follows:

	A	B	C
	£	£	£
Per distribution summary	370	435	362
Factory general overhead	380	253	190
Buildings	193	193	193
Electricity	—	—	—
Steam	237	118	119
Motive power	347	260	260
Stores expense	68	79	79
Heating service	169	170	169
Lighting service	86	86	86
	£1,850	£1,594	£1,458

Repeated distribution method

	1	2	3	4	5	6	7	8	A	B	C
	£	£	£	£	£	£	£	£	£	£	£
Totals	1,265	902	424	519	269	93	186	78	370	435	362
1	(1,265)	63	63	63	63	63	63	64	380	253	190
2		(965)	97	193	96				193	193	193
3			(584)	193	438			146			
4				(775)			310		233	116	116
5					(866)				346	260	260
6						(156)	56		47	55	54
7						56	(559)		168	167	168
8				14	14			(288)	86	87	87
4				(14)			6		4	2	2
6						(70)			21	25	24
7							(6)		2	2	2
									£1,850	£1,595	£1,458

Whether the period being dealt with is a calendar month or a four-weekly period, the Production Overhead Control Account has now been distributed to the various production departments or cost centres. It may be considered desirable to close off the Production Overhead Control Account to separate accounts such as Production Department "A" Incurred Overhead Account, etc., but this is not really necessary, provided running totals are kept in some subsidiary record book: this might well be the file in which the distribution summaries are kept.

The fourth stage of the overhead plan is now ready for development, but as the subject of overhead application is such a large one, it is best to defer it until the following chapter.

Examination questions on Chapters 10–13 *are given at the end of Chapter* 13.

OVERHEAD: CLASSIFICATION AND DISTRIBUTION 171

subsidiary record book; this might well be the file in which the distribution summaries are kept.

The fourth stage of the overhead plan is now ready for development, but as the subject of overheads is in such a large one, it is best to defer it until the following chapter.

Examination questions — Chapters 10–13 are given at the end of

CHAPTER 11

OVERHEAD: ABSORPTION BY PRODUCTION

BY the phrase "application of overhead to production" is meant the charge to be made to each works order, process or unit of production, over and above the prime cost, and which is intended to cover a proportion of the factory overhead incurred.

In the early days of cost accounting, just after the First World War, it was the era of the "cost-plus" contract. In order to avoid delays in estimating for urgent contracts, the Government had placed contracts for war work on the basis that they would reimburse the cost, plus a percentage to cover the administration and other overhead expense incurred.

Firms who took on several contracts were forced to account separately for each, and had to watch carefully lest their overhead should swallow up their percentage allowance. This might occur because they had taken a contract which provided relatively little by way of percentage addition. For example:

	Contract A	Contract B
	£	£
Wages	500,000	200,000
Materials	100,000	100,000
Prime cost	600,000	300,000
Add 10%	60,000	30,000
	£660,000	£330,000

Contract A provided £60,000 to cover overhead: on the other hand, contract B required the use of as much material, and perhaps a higher degree of managerial skill, and yet provided only £30,000.

Inevitably, questions discussed after the war revolved upon what was the "cost" of a contract, and particularly, what was the best method of recovering indirect expenses as part of the cost of a product.

At first the ease with which a percentage addition to wages, or to materials, or to prime cost, could be made, seemed to provide a solution. But it was soon observed that where two products were being made side by side, and were taking the same time to make, the application of overhead by any of these "rule-of-thumb" methods might be quite unsound.

172

It requires but a simple example to show this:

Cost of Metal Caps

	In brass	In steel
	£	£
Materials	4·00	2·00
Labour	0·90	0·90
Prime cost	4·90	2·90
Production overhead 75% on material cost	3·00	1·50
Production cost	£7·90	£4·40

It must be concluded therefore that, except in the simplest cases, these methods are obsolete. The only circumstances in which they could be used would be when:

(a) one product is being made;
(b) material prices are stable;
(c) labour rates are steady;
(d) equipment used remains unchanged.

As soon as it was realised that the cost of materials and labour had no direct relation to the amount of overhead incurred, cost accountants began to recognise the importance of the time factor. Overhead is incurred from year to year, from month to month, from day to day, and from hour to hour; and the overhead which is thus incurred "in time" may be satisfactorily related to the production hours worked in the factory.

Thus the following information may be available:

Dept.	Estimated production overhead	Men	Weeks p.a.	Hours p.wk.	Total direct labour	Rate per D.L.H.
	£				Hours	£
A	12,000	30	50	50	75,000	0·16
B	17,000	40	50	50	100,000	0·17
C	14,000	70	50	50	175,000	0·08

The prime cost of the work done each week will be increased by the appropriate departmental rate or rates per direct labour hour worked, and thus the overhead will be absorbed. It will be recalled that in the previous chapter it was seen how production overhead was departmentalised, and it is necessary to estimate in advance for each department separately, since perhaps some items produced do not pass through all departments. The method depends for its accuracy on two prior estimates, *viz.* what the production overhead is likely to amount to, and how many direct labour hours are expected to be worked.

With these provisos, however, it is a satisfactory scheme of overhead application. It must, however, be stressed that the estimated direct labour hours have to take into account annual holidays, public holidays and all anticipated normal idle time: only then can there be any hope that the application rate her hour will recover most of the overheads actually incurred.

A variation of the *direct-labour-hour method* is the *production-unit method*. Thus, if in the case just considered there were 2 units produced per direct labour hour, it would be expected that, on the assumption that the work of Departments A and B met at an assembly point, and then passed through Department C, there would be a total production of $175,000 \times 2$ complete units. The total estimated overhead is £43,000, so that production overhead would be applied on the basis of £0·123 per unit of production.

This method is satisfactory when the works are producing uniform units, as is often the case in process and single-output manufacturing. As soon as the units vary, however, conversions have to be made on a "points" basis into a common unit equivalent, and this introduces an element of arbitrary judgment which is not desirable. An illustration of this is seen in the somewhat doubtful practice by which hospitals equate a number of out-patients attendances with one in-patient day.

The departmental direct-labour-hour method of overhead absorption has certain drawbacks, which can sometimes be seen when a comparison is made between the classes of work carried on in a department, or between the work of one department and another.

In Department B shown above the production overhead was estimated to be £17,000, which is high by comparison with the other departments. Let it be supposed that the figure is made up as follows:

	£
Supervisory wages	2,500
Rent	1,200
Insurance	
Fire—machinery	350
building	150
Power	3,000
Depreciation of machinery	2,000
Lighting	800
Supplies	2,500
Service department E	3,000
Service department F	1,500
	£17,000

Clearly a large part of the overhead is incurred by the use of machinery, and for this reason, in such cases the use of *machine hour rates* is advocated.

The principle is that production overheads of a machine cost centre are distributable in proportion to the operating hours of the machines. In factories where production is largely by machinery this method gives greater accuracy than any of those previously mentioned.

A machine rate can be set up for each machine, but as this would probably create too many different rates for convenience, and be too costly in administration, it is often the practice to fix a rate for each group of machines of similar type.

COMPUTATION OF A MACHINE HOUR RATE

METHOD 1

(*a*) All production overhead is departmentalised as already shown, and the overhead of the service departments is apportioned to the production departments.

(*b*) More detailed analysis is carried out, however, because each cost centre is regarded as a separate production centre.

NOTE: The *Terminology of Cost Accountancy* defines a cost centre as a location, person or item of equipment (or group of these) in relation to which costs may be ascertained and used for the purpose of cost control.

(*c*) By this means every cost centre will be charged with its proportion of general production overhead.

(*d*) The machine cost centres will, in addition, have been charged with their appropriate machine running expenses.

(*e*) Separate rates can now be calculated for machine cost centres:

$$\frac{\text{Estimated overhead}}{\text{Machine hours anticipated}}$$

and for bench work cost centres:

$$\frac{\text{Estimated overhead}}{\text{Direct labour hours anticipated}}$$

These calculations will follow the same pattern as the actual overhead incurred, and will probably be based to a large extent on the previous year's results.

METHOD 2

(*a*) All production overhead is departmentalised, but only to main accounts.

(*b*) The overhead of the service departments is apportioned to the main production departments, and the totals thus obtained are then sub-divided for each department into:

(*i*) machine running costs;
(*ii*) other overhead.

(*c*) Two rates or more will therefore be applied in respect of each production department to cover these classes of overhead.

MACHINE EXPENSE SCHEDULE
Machine No. B.23; Shop "A"

Description: Grinder   **Date bought:** 5th June 19...
Maker: Samson   **Cost:** £600
Power: 4 h.p.   **Estimated life:** 10 years
Additions:......................   **Depreciation:** 9% p.a.

Item	Basis of Estimate	Cost per Annum £
Depreciation	9% to reduce to £60 in 10 years	54
Insurance	Actual	2
Repairs and maintenance	Estimated from records or otherwise	64
Indirect materials: oil, cotton-waste, etc.	Estimated on average issues	10
Rent of floor space allotted	300 sq. ft at £0·067	20
Superintendence and shop expenses	$\frac{300}{3000} \times$ £1,800 (say)	180
Power	302 days of 8 hours less 20% idle time, estimated	190
Cost per annum		**£520**
Cost per operating hour (1,933 hours) **Use, say, £0·27 per hour**		**£0·269**

FIG. 56.—*Computation of a machine hour rate*

Each piece of machinery is the subject of such a computation, and the overhead is recovered on production by means of an hourly rate for the time during which the machine operates.

Figure 56 gives a schedule showing the computation of a machine hour rate under method 1, and it will be noted that the machine operator's time is not included. A machine hour rate does not cover this, because this item is already dealt with as direct labour.

While the machine hour rate gives a fairly reliable basis for absorption of overhead, the following reasons may be cited as possible causes of discrepancies:

(*a*) The inevitable irregularities of operating times.

(*b*) The necessity of using an estimated number of machine hours in advance.

(*c*) The amount of abnormal idle time, waiting time and overtime. The qualifying word "abnormal" is used, because any normal, and therefore anticipated, idle time will have been taken into account when estimating. If there is a decided trend of increase in non-operating time a revision of rates might be called for, but generally speaking, this is not desirable, because comparisons are made difficult. (Students may, with advantage, refer at this point to page 182, where the question of idle facilities and the cost of idleness is more fully discussed.)

Stand-by, or spare, machines, such as boilers, electric motors, etc., will be provided for in computing the rate, and their "idleness" is not included under (*c*) above.

ACCOUNTING ENTRIES

So far, in the main books there is a Production Overhead Control Account, the details of which are to be found in the subsidiary records under standing order numbers. When the departmental distribution summary was completed there was the option of transferring the period's entries in the Production Overhead Control Account to:

(*a*) production overhead incurred—Department A

(*b*) production overhead incurred—Department B

and so on, or, on the other hand, of keeping the details in some kind of running record.

What, then, happens when production overhead is to be applied? In Fig. 50 was shown a specimen job cost card and it will be seen that in addition to space being given for materials and direct labour, room is provided for the inclusion of production overhead. As each job or works order is carried out, the production overhead is applied at the end of each period on the cost card or cost sheet concerned, by one or more of the methods already outlined, and having regard to the departments through which the work has passed.

The production overhead thus applied to each cost sheet is summarised, and forms the basis of the following journal entry:

> Work-in-progress Account   Dr.
>
>   To Production Overhead Applied Accounts
>
>   Department A
>
>   Department B
>
>   and so on.

Alternatively, if the details are to be kept outside the ledger, then the only entry would be:

Work-in-progress Account   Dr.

    To Production Overhead Applied Account

The entry to Work-in-progress Account adds to those already made for direct materials and expenses, and direct labour, so that the Work-in-progress Account now shows "in total" what the cost sheets reveal in detail.

It will be noted that the opening of Production Overhead Applied Account(s) are suggested. In practice, it is useful to have these accounts separate so that the position may be seen at a glance at any time, but they are not strictly essential, and have not always been shown.

On completion of each works order the cost sheet is totalled and set aside. Then, at the end of the current period these completed cost sheets are summarised and the following Journal entry is put through:

Finished Goods Stock Account   Dr.

    To Work-in-progress Account

In this way the Work-in-progress Account is reduced to show the balance of work now going through the factory, and is supported by the details on the file of uncompleted cost sheets.

ADJUSTMENT OF PRODUCTION OVERHEAD

It will be apparent that whatever basis is used for applying production overhead there is little probability that the amount absorbed will exactly agree with the amount incurred. There will be a balance under- or over-recovered. Under-recovery will take place, for example, when:

    (a) the total expense incurred for a department exceeds the estimate;

    (b) the output or hours worked are less than anticipated.

Alternatively, there would be over-recovery when:

    (a) the total overhead incurred is less than estimated;

    (b) the output or hours worked exceed the estimate.

There are three methods of disposing of the balance:

    (a) Carry down the balance, on the assumption that it may be counterbalanced next time. This should be done only in intermediate periods during the year, and when the balance is comparatively small.

    (b) Transfer the balance to Production Overhead Under- and Over-absorbed Account, for eventual transfer to Costing Profit and Loss Account.

(c) Transfer the balance, in proportion, to:

- (i) work in progress;
- (ii) finished stock;
- (iii) cost of sales.

EXAMPLE

An amount of £1,238 is disclosed in the books as under-recovered overhead. It is decided to transfer this to cost of work done, rather than show it as a separate item in the Costing Profit and Loss Account.

	Balance	Addition required
	£	£
Work in progress	6,000	33
Finished stock	18,000	100
Factory cost of goods sold	200,000	1,105
	£224,000	£1,238

NOTE: 6/224 of 1,238 = 33, and so on.

The entries should always be made in the Production Overhead Applied Accounts, where these are kept, on the ground that no adjustment should be made in the Production Overhead Incurred Accounts, as these represent actual expenditure incurred.

At the end of the year, and after these entries have been made, the debit on Production Overhead Control Account will correspond to the credit figure on Production Overhead Applied Account, and the two accounts may be closed off by transfer from one account to the other.

CLASSES OF PRODUCTION OVERHEAD

It is opportune to consider at this point certain kinds of Production overhead, and their method of treatment.

Estimating and drawing office expenses

These are often apportionable as between production and selling overhead.

Royalties

Royalties payable are in the nature of a rent which is paid for the right to make use of a patent process or component in the course of manufacture, or possibly for the right to sell the finished product. In each case the payment is made to the owner of the rights in question.

Whether or not the royalties are to be regarded as a production cost or a selling cost depends on the fact of the case, and they may be apportionable between the two. If they are regarded as a production cost it may be possible to charge them as a direct expense, and consideration should be given to this, before putting them to production overhead.

Depreciation and interest

Students are asked to refer to Chapter 13, where this subject is more fully discussed.

Fixing new plant

The cost should be capitalised and written off with the asset as depreciation.

Moving and refixing existing plant

This cost adds nothing to the value of the asset: it must therefore be charged as production overhead.

Rent charges for premises owned

No rent is actually payable in cash, but nevertheless it is considered reasonable to raise a charge in the overhead. Credit could be given to Accrued Charges Account, and from thence, at the end of the year, it would be transferred to the credit of Costing Profit and Loss Account.

Inspection

This is generally a production overhead, and is apportioned to the production departments on the basis of the amount of work for each.

Tool setting

If the setting is for a specific order it may be conveniently made a direct charge to that order. When, however, a number of orders are dealt with on a machine with one setting only the expense is included in the overhead rate for the machine or department concerned.

Wages of engineers and millwrights

This is a service department cost, and will be apportioned to production departments and/or cost centres, and thus will be included in the machine hour rate. Work done of a capital nature will be charged to a capital order number on suitable authority. To distinguish it from other work it is often found convenient to use different coloured stationery; the entry, on completion, will be:

> Capital Expenditure Account   Dr.
> To Work-in-progress Account.

Overtime and special night-work wages

When overtime or night work is necessary, owing to the desire of a customer to have an order completed or rushed through within a specified time, the extra payment for overtime is legitimately charged to the job as direct labour.

When, however, the overtime is regular, or intermittent but recurring, and is for the purpose of generally increasing the output of the factory, *e.g.* to keep up with stock requirements, the cost of the overtime premium is charged to production overhead, a standing order number being provided for the purpose (*see* page 154).

EXAMPLE

6 hours overtime	
Rate per hour £0·50	
Paid at time and a half	£4·50
Charge	
Direct labour	£3·00
Standing order number	£1·50

Distinction should be made between special intermittent overtime and night work, and that which is regular and budgeted. The latter can be recovered in overhead rates; the former, if not chargeable to a particular job, or if not suitable for inclusion in production overhead, will be written off to Costing Profit and Loss Account.

Carriage inwards of stores materials

As is well known, this is usually treated in manufacturing accounts as an addition to the cost of raw materials purchased. In costing, however, it sets a problem in stores accounting, for the carriage is not normally known at the time of purchase, and has to be estimated. This throws out the easy agreement of the stores accounts. For this reason it may be better to regard it as overhead.

Idle time

Broadly speaking, idle time falls into two main categories:

(*a*) Idle facilities.
(*b*) Idleness.

Idle facilities means that the machine is available for work but is not being used. It is not usual, in fact, to work a machine all the available time, because it has to be serviced, and is possibly of a kind which is only used intermittently during the process. The percentage of expected use has to be worked out for each machine, and, even if standard costing is not in force, it is convenient to refer to it as the standard capacity usage ratio. This is defined in the *Terminology of Cost Accountancy* as:

"the relationship between the budgeted number of working hours and the maximum number of working hours in a budget period."

Idleness, as distinct from idle facilities, is due to such causes as:

(*i*) waiting for work;
(*ii*) waiting for foreman's instructions;
(*iii*) breakdown of machinery, etc.

In such cases it is generally regarded as correct to charge the unproductive labour element to a special standing order number, or to a series of them, in order to analyse the cost by causes. However, there is far more to it than that: the unrecovered standing charges of a machine, and also a proportion of the fixed overhead of the concern as a whole, are legitimately to be regarded as the cost of idle time, and if management is to be fully aware of the true position the cost accounts must be designed to bring out the necessary information.

SPECIMEN QUESTION

The standing charges, maintenance cost and depreciation for a machine are estimated to total £2,400 per annum. The machine is capable of working 50 weeks × 46 hours, or 2,300 hours, but it is anticipated that it will only work 80% of that time, or 1,840 hours. The actual hours recorded for the machine were 1,750 hours, and the operator's idle time is analysed by causes in standing order numbers. These disclose that:

30 hours were spent in waiting for work,
10 „ „ „ waiting for foreman,
30 „ „ „ breakdowns of machine.

The operator's rate of pay was £0·6 per hour. The fixed administration overhead was £10,000, and the anticipated machine hours of the factory as a whole is 14,000 hours.

Prepare a machine utilisation statement to bring to the notice of management the true cost of idle time.

ANSWER

Machine Utilisation Statement—Machine No. 84

Year ended..................

(*a*) Maximum possible hours	2,300
Standard capacity expected	1,840

Standard capacity usage ratio

$$\frac{1,840}{2,300} \text{ or } 0{\cdot}8 \text{ or } 80\%.$$

(b) Standard capacity expected   1,840
    Actual hours recorded   1,750

Capacity utilisation ratio

$\dfrac{1,750}{1,840}$ or 0·95 or 95%.

(c) Causes of idle time   Hours
  (i) Unavoidable
    Idle facilities 2,300 − 1,840   460
  (ii) Avoidable
    Idle facilities (above anticipated figure)   20
    Idleness of operator due to:

Waiting for work	30
Waiting for foreman	10
Breakdown of machine	30
	—
	70
	550

(d) Cost involved   £

Labour of operator charged to Production Overhead
in standing order numbers—70 hours at £0·60   42

    (NOTE: Operator assumed to have been working
    with another machine during the 20 hours the
    machine was available for work.)

Fixed overhead   £
Machine standing charges   2,400
Administration
  Total £10,000
  Proportion for machine No 84:

$\dfrac{\text{Standard capacity of this machine}}{\text{Standard capacity of whole factory}}$

i.e. $\dfrac{1,840}{14,000} \times 10,000$ 1,314

£3,714

This must be apportioned as follows:

$\dfrac{\text{Hours lost}}{\text{Maximum hours}} \times 3,714$

$\dfrac{550}{2,300} \times 3,714$ 888

£930

The maximum hours are used for the denominator of this fraction, because it is our intention to show the total cost of idleness, for unavoidable as well as for avoidable.

However, if the statement is to show avoidable cost only, the fraction would be $\dfrac{90}{1,840} \times 3,714$.

(e) Breakdown of cost

		£
Unavoidable causes:		
Idle facilities	$\dfrac{460}{550} \times 888$	743
Avoidable causes:		
Labour cost of idle time		42
Idle facilities	$\dfrac{20}{550} \times 888$	32
Waiting for work	$\dfrac{30}{550} \times 888$	49
Waiting for foreman	$\dfrac{10}{550} \times 888$	16
Breakdown of machine	$\dfrac{30}{555} \times 888$	48
		£930

NOTE: A transfer will be made from the Overhead Control Accounts to the Costing Profit and Loss Account of the total cost of idle time for all machines in the factory.

AUTOMATION

The growth of automatic processes will tend to merge direct wages with production overhead. As a result the "conversion cost" concept will doubtless be developed. By this is meant that production overhead is collected by cost centres, and the cost-centre costs, including labour, are recovered at predetermined rates for the time which the work spends within each centre. Thus the total factory cost becomes, e.g.

	£	£
Raw materials		25
Cost centre 3—5 hours at £2·40	12	
Cost centre 4—3 hours at £2·00	6	
Cost centre 7—4 hours at £2·50	10	
	—	28
		£53

"Conversion cost" therefore covers the cost of conversion of the raw materials into finished product, i.e.:

(*a*) direct labour, plus

(*b*) production overhead.

"Added value," as shown on page 131, covers conversion cost, plus gross profit, or, in other words, is equivalent to sales value less material cost.

Where an automatic machine can perform either of several processes at the touch of the appropriate button, one of the problems is to apportion the operator's time. The single cost centre has become, for all intents and purposes, several cost centres: and in one case, at least, it has been thought necessary to assess "cam-cycle" hours as a basis of apportionment.

This may be explained thus. A cam is designed to guide the movements of the tools of a machine, and may assume various shapes to produce an "eccentric" action.

As the cam rotates round its axis a "follower," *i.e.* a spring-loaded roller, follows the shape of the cam, and this controls the tools. The more complex the shape of the cam, the longer the operation cycle is likely to be.

If button "A" is operated, one series of cams come into use, and later on, if button "B" is operated, an entirely different series of cams take the place of those previously used. It is possible to calculate for each the cam-cycle hours required for a batch of work, and thus without asking the operator to book his time on to various jobs, his hours can be apportioned on the basis of the cam-cycle hours.

Examination questions on Chapters 10–13 *are given at the end of Chapter* 13.

CHAPTER 12

OVERHEAD: ADMINISTRATION, AND SELLING AND DISTRIBUTION

IN Chapter 10 it was seen that these types of overhead are collected in cost account numbers, and that these in turn are agreed with the respective Overhead Control Accounts. It now remains to consider the nature of this overhead, and its proper treatment in the books of account.

ADMINISTRATION OVERHEAD

Generally speaking, the overhead incurred in administrative offices is incurred for the business as a whole. Production in a certain department may rise or fall, but the administration overhead goes on unchanged. Indeed, it is more likely to be geared to sales than to manufacture. As, therefore, it has little or no connection with production in any direct kind of way, it is considered unrealistic to add little amounts of administration overhead as part of the cost of production of a unit.

Again, to charge any part of administration overhead to work in progress inflates the stock values at the end of the year, and carries forward to next year part of the overhead which should be borne in the current year.

In all normal financial accounting administration overhead is shown in the Profit and Loss Account, and has to be provided from year to year out of the gross profit for that year. There is no need, it is suggested, to depart from this time-honoured practice.

For these reasons it is recommended that students should "apply" administration overhead in the following manner:

Finished Goods Stock Account   Dr.

     To Administration Overhead Applied Account

If the year is divided up, for example, into 13 four-weekly periods, then each period will bear $\frac{1}{13}$ of the estimated annual expense.

At the same time a close watch will be kept on the details given in the cost account numbers, as has already been suggested, to see that the incurred overhead is not far astray from the estimates.

With the entry above having been made, the Finished Goods Stock Account will look as follows:

Finished Goods Stock Account

Balance	b/d	Transfer to Cost of Sales	
Transfer from Work-in-progress Account, production cost of goods completed		Account	
		Balance	c/d
Administration Overhead Applied Account			

In order to comply with normal accounting conventions the balances on the above account should be valued at factory cost, so that the whole allocation of administration overhead finds its way into the Cost of Sales Account.

It may well be argued that the administration overhead should have been put there in the first place, and there is little to be said against this point of view. However, as cost accountants were originally, and to some extent still are, imbued with the idea that it should be charged to work in progress, the method advocated represents a compromise between the two positions: the student may make up his own mind.

The difference between Administration Overhead Control Account and Administration Overhead Applied Account will be written off from the latter account, at the end of the year, to Costing Profit and Loss Account.

Examples of administration expenses are as follows:

General office expenses.
Managing director's remuneration.
Stationery.
Postage and telephones.
Rent of offices.
Professional fees.

None of them calls for special comment.

SELLING AND DISTRIBUTION OVERHEAD

For costing purposes these are generally considered together, although it is quite possible, and it may in some circumstances be desirable, to deal with them separately.

It is convenient to identify such expenses as those which are incurred subsequently to the manufactured goods being placed in the warehouse or finished goods store. The definitions given in the *Terminology of Cost Accountancy* are as follows:

Selling cost

The cost of seeking to create and stimulate demand (sometimes termed "marketing") and of securing orders.

Distribution cost

The cost of the sequence of operations which begins with making the packed product available for despatch and ends with making the re-conditioned returned empty package, if any, available for re-use.

NOTE: As well as including expenditure incurred in transporting articles to central or local storage, distribution cost includes expenditure incurred in moving articles to and from prospective customers as in the case of goods on sale or return basis. In the gas, electricity and water "distribution" means pipes, mains and services which may be regarded as the equivalent of packing and transportation.

As with administration overhead, the details of the expenditure incurred are given in a set of cost account numbers, and if these are suitably ruled for the purpose it is possible to carry out a useful analysis from them. A suggested ruling is given in Fig. 57.

The monthly or periodical totals of these cost account numbers will be analysed (as was done when dealing with production overhead) to a distribution summary, so that finally all the selling and distribution overhead is apportioned to the sales areas. A satisfactory basis for making this distribution of departmental costs will be in proportion to sales, *i.e.*:

Total sales £15,000
Leeds sales £5,000
Advertising department overhead £1,200

$$\text{Apportionment to Leeds £1,200} \times \frac{5,000}{15,000} = \underline{£400}$$

Having thus arrived at the selling and distribution overhead for each sales area, it is possible to break it down still further, *viz.* by salesmen. This might be done in one of three ways:

(*a*) By equal division.
(*b*) In proportion to sales achieved by each salesman.
(*c*) By sales quotas.

The advantage of the sales quota method is that it takes account of the differing conditions of the areas, and of the abilities of the salesmen:

Overhead for Brighton area   £700
Sales quotas

Salesman A   £3,000
Salesman B   £4,000

Sales achieved £4,000 in each case.
On a quota basis, Salesman A is "charged" with $\frac{3}{7}$ of £700, or £300.
On a sales basis, the figure would have been £350.

A further analysis can be made by classes of products sold, and the basis for distribution of the overhead would be "sales," or "gross profit on sales."

Whether these subsidiary analyses are carried out by the sales department or the costing department is a matter of policy, but the costing department would certainly take the work as far as the accounting entry out of the Selling and Distribution Overhead Control Account.

HEADING		CODING				
Basis of Apportionment:						
Details	Total	Sales Areas				
		N.W.	N.E.	S.W.	S.E.	London

FIG. 57.—*Cost account number*

This ruling is suggested for a series of accounts in which the Selling and Distribution Overhead may be collected. The precise ruling is dictated by the needs of the business.

This is as follows:

Area 1. Selling and Distribution Overhead Incurred Account   Dr.
Area 2. Selling and Distribution Overhead Incurred Account   Dr.
     etc.

    To Selling and Distribution Overhead Control Account

Of course, as in the case of production overhead, it may be considered sufficient to keep this information in the form of running totals outside the Ledger.

The application of selling and distribution overhead is carried out very simply by the entry:

Cost of Sales Account   Dr.

    To Selling and Distribution Overhead Applied Account

It is not necessary to detail the overhead for each area, but the amount is made up by taking, for example, $\frac{1}{13}$ of the total estimate.

The accounting position is now as follows:

Costs of Sales Account

Transfer from Finished Goods Stock Account	Transfer to Costing Profit and Loss Account
Selling and Distribution Overhead Applied Account	

Costing Profit and Loss Account

Transfer from Cost of Sales Account	Sales
Overhead under-absorbed [details]	Overhead over-absorbed [details]
Abnormal losses to be written off [details]	Abnormal gains or income to be brought in [details]
Net Profit per Cost Accounts	

Examples of selling overhead are as follows:

(*a*) Advertising, catalogues, samples, folders, etc. Advertising by permanent signs would be regarded as capital outlay to be apportioned over the estimated effective life of the sign. The cost of shop displays, catalogues and an extensive advertising campaign may similarly be spread over a period.

(*b*) Rent and other expenses of sales department.

(*c*) Royalties. Sometimes these are more closely connected with production than with sales, and may be treated as a direct expense.

(*d*) Travellers' salaries and commissions.

(*e*) Market research. The amount to be spent in any year is usually a policy decision, to be modified by events.

(*f*) Bad debts. When a fairly regular percentage of bad debts is incurred this item may be reasonably included in selling overhead. When a large bad debt is exceptional and abnormal it is better to exclude it from the cost accounts.

Examples of distribution overhead are as follows:

(*a*) Warehouse rent.

(*b*) Warehouse labour and other expenses.

(*c*) Depot expenses.

(*d*) Finished stock waste and loss. Distinguish between:

(*i*) unavoidable waste due to inherent qualities, *e.g.* shrinkage, evaporation, breaking bulk, etc.;

(*ii*) deterioration due to lapse of time, obsolescence, and abnormal damage or abnormal loss;

(*iii*) avoidable waste caused by faulty handling and storage.

Losses such as (ii) should be written off direct to Costing Profit and Loss Account, but (i) and (iii) should be included as part of the distribution overhead.

(*e*) Carriage. Carriage on goods despatched may be:

(*i*) charged to customers direct;
(*ii*) charged as a distribution overhead;
(*iii*) charged as a selling overhead, being regarded as an inducement to potential customers.

(*f*) Packages and containers for despatch purposes.
(*g*) Finished stock insurances.

Examination questions on Chapters 10–13 *are given at the end of Chapter* 13.

OVERHEAD: DEPRECIATION AND INTEREST ON CAPITAL

HITHERTO it has been the practice to regard depreciation as representing the loss in value of the capital sunk in buildings, mines, quarries, leases, plant, machinery and other equipment, owing to the normal and inevitable process of making use of the asset over a number of years.

Nowadays, however, there is a school of thought which considers that "replacement cost" and not "original cost" is the important factor. In this view the term "depreciation" should no longer be used, and "replacement provision" should take its place. It is pointed out that in a period of rising prices merely to write down an asset over a period of years from its original cost to its scrap value provides no internal strength to meet replacement costs; and these may be considerably more than the original capital invested.

The factory cost of production, it is argued, should reflect not only rising wages costs and rising material prices, which it does automatically, but also rising costs of overhead, including capital replacement.

In periods of stable or falling prices the call for this additional provision would obviously not exist. It is entirely a matter of policy, but the student should note that no accounting difficulty would be caused by a decision to provide for replacement costs. The entry would merely be:

Manufacturing Account   Dr.
        To Depreciation Provision Account
            Asset Replacement Provision Account

and in the cost accounts the debit entry would be to Production Overhead Control Account.

METHODS OF CALCULATING DEPRECIATION

The *Terminology of Cost Accountancy* sets out the following methods of calculating depreciation and, of course, any of them can be adapted for use to conform to the orthodox view of depreciation or to the replacement cost theory.

1. STRAIGHT-LINE METHOD

"The method of providing for depreciation by means of equal periodic charges over the assumed life of the asset."

EXAMPLE

Cost of machine = £5,000.
Estimated residual value after 10 years = £500.
Write off £4,500 over 10 years, *i.e.* £450 per year.

This is a much used and recommended method, which is simple and effective and has the great advantage that the uniform annual charge affords better comparative costs. It requires little work for computing the amounts.

It has the recommendation of the Institute of Chartered Accountants (*Depreciation of Fixed Assets*, 1945).

2. REDUCING BALANCE METHOD

"The method of providing for depreciation by means of periodic charges calculated as a constant proportion of the balance of the value of the asset after deducting the amounts previously provided."

EXAMPLE

Cost of machine = £5,000.
To be written down at the rate of 20% per annum.

Year	Cost and balance b/f	Depreciation	Balance c/f
	£	£	£
Year 1	5,000	1,000	4,000
2	4,000	800	3,200
3	3,200	640	2,560
		and so on	

It is argued, in favour of this method, that a heavier depreciation charge is borne in the earlier years when repairs are lighter, and that the assumed increasing repair cost is counterbalanced, in later years, by the reduced annual charge for depreciation. Such a relationship between depreciation and repairs is obviously most haphazard.

It is found, in practice, that assets appear to hold their book values for an inordinate length of time, and it not infrequently happens that, when this method is used in the financial accounts, heavier rates or other methods are employed in the cost accounts. A graphical comparison of written-down values, using both straight-line and reducing-balance methods, is given in Fig. 58.

One of the most frequent problems in practice is to find the rate per cent to be used in order to write a machine down to a given figure.

The formula to be used is:

$$A = PR^n$$

when $R = \left(1 - \dfrac{r}{100}\right).$

Now for an asset costing £5,000 to be written down to £2,560 in 3 years we have:

$$2{,}560 = 5{,}000\left(1 - \frac{r}{100}\right)^3$$

$$\left(\frac{100 - r}{100}\right)^3 = \frac{2{,}560}{5{,}000}$$

$$\frac{100 - r}{100} = \sqrt[3]{\frac{2{,}560}{5{,}000}}$$

$$100 - r = \sqrt[3]{0{\cdot}512} \times 100$$

$$- r = (\sqrt[3]{0{\cdot}512} \times 100) - 100$$

$$r = 100 - (\sqrt[3]{0{\cdot}512} \times 100)$$

$$= 100 - (0{\cdot}8 \times 100)$$

$$= 100 - 80$$

$$= \underline{20}$$

That is, the rate required is 20%.

3. PRODUCTION UNIT METHOD

"The method of providing for depreciation by means of a fixed rate per unit of production calculated by dividing the value of the asset by the estimated number of units to be produced during its life."

EXAMPLE

Machine to work 10 years × 50 weeks × 46 hours = 23,000 hours.
Estimated rate of production = 10 per hour.
Total estimated units = 230,000.
Cost, less residual value of machine = £5,000.
Write off depreciation at the rate of:

$$\frac{\text{£}5{,}000}{230{,}000} \text{ or £0·02174 per unit.}$$

This is a somewhat uncertain method, because it depends on the accuracy of the estimate of the number of units which a machine will produce in a given number of years.

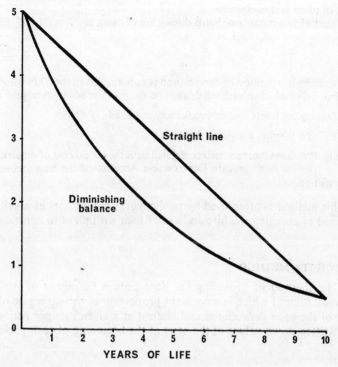

COST OF MACHINE
(£'000)

FIG. 58.—*Comparison of writing-down methods*

Chart to show the comparison between written-down values, using (*a*) the straight line, (*b*) the reducing balance methods, applied to examples in the text.

4. PRODUCTION HOUR METHOD

"The method of providing for depreciation by means of a fixed rate per hour of production calculated by dividing the value of the asset by the estimated number of working hours of its life."

This method is so similar to (3) above that it calls for no special comment.

5. REPAIR PROVISION METHOD

"The method of providing for the aggregate depreciation and maintenance cost by means of periodic charges, each of which is a constant proportion of the aggregate of the cost of the asset depreciated and the expected maintenance cost during its life."

EXAMPLE

Cost of plant and equipment	£5,000
Add cost of two major overhauls during life of asset, say 2 × £1,000	£2,000
	£7,000

The straight-line method of depreciation is now applied to the £7,000 less any residual value which is estimated, and the entry in the books each year is:

Sundry contracts and/or production overhead   Dr.

To Repairs Provision Account

Repairs Provision Account will be debited with the actual cost of repairs, and with a transfer to Aggregate Depreciation Account of the true amount of depreciation.

This method is often used by public works contractors as a suitable method of charging the hire and use of their own plant to contracts.

6. ANNUITY METHOD

"The method of providing for depreciation by means of periodic charges, each of which is a constant proportion of the aggregate of the cost of the asset depreciated and interest at a given rate per period on the written-down values of the asset at the beginning of each period."

EXAMPLE

For the purposes of illustration, a short period is taken.
Cost of asset = £3,000.
Interest to be taken at the rate of 4% per year (compound).
Period 4 years.
Annuity tables give the fact that £1 paid now will purchase an annuity of £0·27549 for 4 years at 4%.

$$\text{The formula is } PR^n = \frac{A(R^n - 1)}{R - 1}$$

where P = value of the asset, $R = 1 + \dfrac{r}{100}$,

n = term of years, and A = annual sum.

The annual sum to be provided is, therefore:

£3,000 × 0·27549, *i.e.* £826·47.

PROOF

Year	Cost and balance b/f	Interest at 4%	Annual provision	Balance c/f
	£	£	£	£
1	3,000	120·00	826·47	2,293·53
2	2,293·53	91·74	826·47	1,558·80
3	1,558·80	62·35	826·47	794·68
4	794·68	31·79	826·47	—

This method is generally used for the redemption of leases over a fairly long period, since money invested for a lengthy period in a capital asset should be deemed to be earning interest.

7. SINKING FUND METHOD

"The method of providing for depreciation by means of fixed periodic charges which aggregated with compound interest over the life of the asset would equal the cost of that asset. Simultaneously with each periodic charge, an investment of the same amount would be made in fixed interest securities which would accumulate at compound interest to provide, at the end of the life of the asset, a sum equal to its cost."

EXAMPLE

Cost of asset £3,000.
Interest at the rate of 4% (compound).
Period = 3 years.
Sinking fund tables state that £0·320348 invested annually at 4% will amount to £1 at the end of 3 years.
The formula is:

$$P = A\frac{(R^n - 1)}{R - 1}$$

the meanings to be attached to these letters being the same as above.
The annual sum to be provided is, therefore:

£3,000 × 0·320348, *i.e.* £961·044.

PROOF

Year	Balance b/f	Interest at 4%	Annual provision	Annual investment	Balance c/f
	£	£	£	£	£
1	—	—	961·044	961·044	961·044
2	961·044	38·443	961·044	999·487	1,960·531
3	1,960·531	78·425	961·044	*Not invested*	3,000·000

This is the only method so far considered which provides cash for the replacement of the asset at the end of the useful life forecast for it. It may not provide sufficient cash, unless replacement costs are fully covered.

At the end of the period, if the investments are sold and the proceeds added to the cash retained, there will be £3,000 available for the purchase of a new asset. The depreciation fund will also be £3,000, which will be written off to the Asset Account: the annual provision having been credited to the fund and debited to Production Overhead Control Account.

8. ENDOWMENT POLICY METHOD

"The method of providing for depreciation by means of fixed periodic charges equivalent to the premiums on an endowment policy for the amount required to provide, at the end of the asset, a sum equal to its cost."

This is similar in effect to the sinking fund method. Cash is taken out of the business to pay the insurance premiums, and is made available again at the end of the period for the purchase of another asset.

9. REVALUATION METHOD

"The method of providing for depreciation by means of periodic charges, each of which is equivalent to the difference between the values assigned to the asset at the beginning and the end of the period."

This is the method commonly used for loose tools, laboratory glassware, horses and, sometimes, patterns. The procedure often adopted is to open a Loose Tools Account, etc., to which the cost is debited of all new tools (other than those purchased or made for a particular job, which are debited direct to the job) and of repairs to tools. At the end of each accounting period the amount of the revalued stock is credited and carried down, and the difference on the account is the depreciation (or appreciation) to be taken into the accounts.

10. REDUCING PROPORTION METHOD

In addition to the above methods of depreciation, all of which are used as thought appropriate, there is a method of quick depreciation for motor vehicles, which may be of interest.

The method is based on the idea of taking each year a reduced proportion of the sum of an arithmetical progression in respect of the years of life forecast, multiplied by the cost, less residual value, of the asset.

EXAMPLE

Cost of vehicle = £950.
Residual value = £200.
Period = 5 years.
Years   1 2 3 4 5.
Sum of years $n/2$ (a plus l) = $\frac{5}{2}$ (1 plus 5) = 15.

Where n = no. of years; a = 1st term; and l = last term.

Write off:

Year 1	$\frac{5}{15}$ of £750 =	£250
2	$\frac{4}{15}$	£200
3	$\frac{3}{15}$	£150
4	$\frac{2}{15}$	£100
5	$\frac{1}{15}$	£50

The advantage claimed for this method is that it realistically takes account of the immediate drop in value of a new vehicle, however recently purchased. It also makes the decision to sell and repurchase before the estimated time an easier one, as after the first two years a loss on sale will not be apparent.

PLANT AND MACHINERY REGISTER

In order that the annual charge for depreciation may be easily ascertained, it is a good plan to record particulars of each piece of plant and major equipment in a plant and machinery register. This register may be designed to show the following:

(*a*) One machine on each page, with details of cost, purchase price, date of purchase, name and address of suppliers, particulars of any guarantees given as to performance, estimated life, estimated residual value, rate of depreciation, method of depreciation to be used and details and cost of repairs undertaken, with dates on which the work was carried out. Figure 59 shows a suggested layout for this type of register, but it will be appreciated that a depreciation schedule will also be necessary in order to summarise the annual figures. Such a schedule is shown in Fig. 60.

(*b*) All machines of one type together, which probably means that one rate and method of depreciation is in force for them all. The depreciation schedule can be made integral with the plant record.

(*c*) All machines in one department together. This enables the charge for depreciation against each production department to be easily ascertained.

J	F	M	A	M	J	Jy	A	S	O	N	D

Description: .... Reference: ....

....

Makers: .... Suppliers: ....

Date Purchased: .... Estimated Life: ....

Purchase Price: .... Scrap Value: .... Net to W/OFF: ....

Method of Depreciation to Be Used: ....

....

Folio of Deptn. Schedule: .... Frequency of Maintenance: ....

Date	Men employed	Time taken	Maintenance carried out	Approx. cost

FIG. 59.—*Plant and machinery register*

A record of each piece of plant or machinery is kept with details of major expenditure on maintenance. Guides may be clipped in position along the top of the card to indicate when items are due for preventive maintenance.

Ref. No.	Date of purchase	Brief Description	Cost Price	Depreciation			Date of Sale	Sale Price	Profit or Loss on Sale
				19...	19...	19...			

FIG. 60.—*Depreciation schedule*

Such a schedule is indispensable for arriving at the total annual depreciation. The headings shown are a minimum and might be extended to include Depreciation Rate and Total Depreciation.

OBSOLESCENCE

As distinct from depreciation, though akin to it, obsolescence is generally used to indicate a sudden loss in value of an asset not due to wear and tear. It arises because a machine has to be discarded in favour of one better adapted to its purpose and giving better results. It is difficult to provide for this in advance, since a machine of new and revolutionary design may be put on the market at any time. It therefore becomes a difficult and important management problem to decide whether the point has been reached when it would be more profitable to exchange one machine for another.

MACHINE REPLACEMENT CALCULATION

From the data shown below it can be seen that the new machine shows a saving of £0·00145 per unit of cost, and the purchase would be recommended, provided the increased production could be disposed of satisfactorily.

Particulars	Existing machine	Proposed machine
Rate of production per hour, units	500	800
	£	£
Present realisable value	1,000	—
Replacement cost	—	2,000
Annual annuity charge	350	700
Maintenance, power, supplies, etc.	2,100	2,300
Operators' wages	1,500	1,000
	£3,950	£4,000
Estimated production for 2,000 hours in millions of units	1·0	1·6
Cost per unit	0·00395	0·0025

Although the *book value* of the existing machine will probably be higher than the realisable value, the difference between the two figures does not have to be brought into calculation. In the event of the sale and purchase taking place, then the difference would be regarded as a loss to be written off, which had arisen through insufficient depreciation having been written off in the past. It has no bearing on the profitability of the new plant in the future.

Other points to be noticed in the illustration are that an annuity calculation has been assumed over a period of five years, and that interest on the capital invested has thereby been taken account of, as well as the reduction of the asset value.

The student will have encountered the formula for an annuity, which combines the notions of interest on investment and depreciation of the investment, earlier in this chapter. Repeating it for convenience, it is:

$$PR^n = \frac{A(R^n - 1)}{R - 1}$$

in which $R = 1 + r/100$, $n =$ the term of years, $P =$ cost of asset, and $A =$ annual sum to be written off.

Usually, this type of calculation involves finding A, the amount to be written off each year, and an example of this has already been given (*see* page 196).

For present purposes, however, let us suppose that we know the following facts:

$P =$ Cost of asset = £1,000.

$n =$ 5 years.

$A =$ Annual sum to be set aside, which the company does not wish to exceed, £350.

We require to find R.

We proceed thus:

Multiply both sides of the equation by $R - 1$.

Then	$PR^n(R - 1) = A(R^n - 1)$.
Therefore	$PR^{n+1} - PR^n = AR^n - A$.
Transposing	$PR^{n+1} - PR^n - AR^n + A = 0$,
or	$PR^{n+1} - (P + A)R^n + A = 0$.
That is:	$1,000R^6 - 1,350R^5 + 350 = 0$.

We now have to find R by trial and error methods, and we find that the equation is approximately true when $R = 1 \cdot 22$, that is when $r = 22\%$. The calculations are as follows:

$$R^6 = 6\log R, \text{ or } 6\log 1 \cdot 22 = 0 \cdot 5184$$

$$1,000 \text{ by logarithms} \qquad 3 \cdot 0000$$

$$3 \cdot 5184 \text{ Antil. } 3,299$$

$$R^5 = 5\log R \text{ or } 5\log 1 \cdot 22 = 0 \cdot 4320$$

$$1,350 \text{ by logarithms} \qquad 3 \cdot 1303$$

$$3 \cdot 5623 \text{ Antil. } 3,651$$

$$3,299 - 3,651 + 350 = -2$$

which is as near zero as we can expect to get.

The annuity charge for the proposed machine, shown in the second column of the table on page 201, is £700, since the cost of the asset is

£2,000 and not £1,000. We shall use $r = 22\%$ again, and the following statement shows the writing down of the asset:

b/f	Interest at 22%	Total	Annual sum	c/f
2,000	440	2,440	700	1,740
1,740	386	2,126	700	1,426
1,426	314	1,740	700	1,040
1,040	228	1,268	700	568
568	126	694	694	—

INTEREST ON CAPITAL

Although interest on capital invested has often to be considered in making calculations, as, for example, in the illustration given above regarding plant replacements, the consensus of opinion is against including it in the cost accounts.

The arguments for and against doing so may be summarised thus:

For	Against
(a) Wages are the reward of labour. Interest is the reward of capital. It is as much a production cost as labour.	(a) This argument is economics, not costing.
(b) Real profit is not made until interest on capital is paid or provided.	(b) Interest is merely an anticipation of profit.
(c) Stocks held for maturing, such as timber, whisky, beer, etc., cost more for rent and interest. The same is really true of the fixed assets.	(c) If interest is included in manufactured stock it has to be written back for balance sheet purposes.
(d) Comparative costs of differing methods and processes are untrue unless interest on plant used is taken into account.	(d) Charging interest is unnecessarily complicated, and comparisons involving interest are best done on separate statements.
(e) Interest has to be paid on capital borrowed. If the borrowing is to assist production, the interest paid is part of the production cost. A manufacturer who uses his own capital should similarly be credited with a sum representing interest.	(e) Interest on capital borrowed is a matter of finance, not of costing.

The important point to remember, in relation to accounting entries is this: if interest on capital is charged, thus increasing the costs, a corresponding account—say, "Provision for Interest on Capital"—has to be credited, since the cost books are kept on a double-entry basis. Thus, in the final analysis, the profit per the cost books remains unaltered.

The same is true in regard to all notional charges, and this fact must be borne in mind later on, when we come to deal with the reconciliation of cost and financial accounts.

EXAMINATION QUESTIONS

Also includes questions on Chapters 10–12

1. Outline the chief methods used for the recovery of factory overhead expense as a charge to the products made, and state the circumstances in which each might be most suitably applied.

(A.C.C.A. Inter.)

2. The allotment of overheads and their absorption by individual products often presents difficulties to the cost accountant. Discuss this point in relation to a manufacturing concern which produces a variety of products with different classes of labour, and where each class of overhead (factory, administration and selling) includes elements of fixed, variable and semi-variable expenses.

(I.C.W.A. Final)

3. Criticise the statement "the more machinery employed, the more the manufacturer is at the mercy of the market."

(I.C.W.A. Final)

4. Your company operates an engineering works which acts as a service department to its several factories. The management decide to use the idle capacity of the works by accepting work for outside customers in order to reduce overheads and thus cheapen the cost of the work done for the company. As cost accountant you are asked to advise regarding:

   (a) the make-up of the minimum price at which work for third parties can be executed; and
   (b) the method of crediting any profit earned on outside work.

Give your reasons for the advice tendered.

(I.C.W.A. Final)

5. What are the two basic causes of under-absorption of works overhead? Mention two examples, which may be met in practice, of each cause.

Where such under-absorption at the end of a month applies to production delivered, work in progress and finished products awaiting despatch, show a composite journal entry indicating the general ledger accounts affected.

(I.C.W.A. Final)

6. State what you understand by:

    (*a*) depreciation;
    (*b*) obsolescence;

and outline four methods commonly used for calculating depreciation, and three ways in which depreciation may be provided for.

You should say, in your answer, in what circumstances any particular method of depreciation or ways of making provision for it might be considered suitable.

(*A.C.C.A. Inter.*)

7. A jobbing manufacturer assesses the overhead to be absorbed by each job by adding to the prime cost a fixed percentage of direct material cost and direct wages. This percentage is calculated on his previous year's accounts.

Although each individual job appears to show a reasonable profit, his Profit and Loss Account for the year shows a loss. His total overhead, however, has not varied to any appreciable extent from that of the previous year.

    (*a*) How can you explain this position?
    (*b*) In view of the adverse position revealed by the annual accounts, what alteration to the system would you recommend?

(*I.C.W.A. Inter.*)

8. Owing to the exclusive nature of his product, a manufacturer is forced to undertake the manufacture of his own machinery. Discuss the problem of the application of overheads to this part of his activities and the valuation of such machinery for capital and depreciation purposes.

(*I.C.W.A. Final*)

9. The overheads incurred in a certain department are estimated to amount to 250% of direct wages, but at the end of a year's working you find that they have risen to 350% of direct wages. Explain what factors must be considered, and how they would be evaluated in assessing the significance of the variation.

(*I.C.W.A. Final*)

10. In computing rates of overhead absorption, what consideration would you give to cost classification, allocation and apportionment? Explain how the three procedures mentioned must be used in order to make the computation, and give illustrations of bases used for cost apportionment and overhead absorption.

(*I.C.W.A. Final*)

11. Discuss the statement: "You make progress only when you raise your overhead rates."

(*I.C.W.A. Final*)

12. As cost accountant in a large factory, draw up a memorandum on stock valuation of raw materials, work in progress and finished goods.
    Assume:

    (*a*) that market prices of some materials have changed since purchases were made;
    (*b*) that departmental rates of overhead absorption include:

(i) percentage on labour;
(ii) labour hour rate;
(iii) machine hour rate;

(c) that administration, selling and distribution expenses are usually absorbed as a percentage of production cost.

(*I.C.W.A. Final*)

13. In every manufacturing business there is usually a considerable amount of idle time for which payment is made but for which no return is received in productive effort. Thus, there may be considerable loss of time by stopping of machinery for cleaning purposes, lack of materials, etc. Enumerate other similar examples of idle time and explain how you would deal with this loss in the costing records.

(*C.A.A. Final*)

14. Show how overhead costs are affected by each of the following:

(a) Idle capacity.
(b) Variety of products.
(c) Contraction and expansion of size of the production facilities.

(*I.C.W.A. Inter.*)

15. Explain concisely what is meant by:

(a) idle capacity;
(b) excess capacity.

Mention *three* possible ways in which production capacity may be expressed, and outline the circumstances in which each of the three may be used in practice, naming an industry to which each may apply.

(*I.C.W.A. Final*)

16. As cost accountant in a business you observe that, although the volume of business in a certain department is increasing, productivity is decreasing.

Using suitable figures, present a report to the works manager drawing attention to the facts which have given rise to this situation.

(*I.C.W.A. Final*)

17. Your directors have decided to manufacture an entirely new product to utilise spare capacity within the works. Describe in detail how you would compute the approximate selling price of this new product.

(*I.C.W.A. Final*)

18. A tool-room in a general engineering factory:

(a) makes tools for sale;
(b) makes new tools for use in the factory;
(c) repairs tools for use in the factory.

What problems of cost ascertainment, allocation and apportionment arise, and how are these problems dealt with?

(*I.C.W.A. Final*)

19. In a certain business it has been the custom to absorb administration costs as a percentage of production costs. A customer buys otherwise identical

products in different materials, one cheap, one expensive, and complains about the difference in the prices quoted, which he contends should amount to the difference in material price only. Give fully your views on the problem.

(I.C.W.A. Final)

20. What method would you recommend for the absorption of administration costs in product costs? Point out the virtues and defects (if any) of the method suggested.

(I.C.W.A. Inter.)

21. Your company manufactures five varieties of product, distributed nation-wide at fixed retail prices. Selling and distribution costs form a substantial part of total cost. Design a summarised statement to inform your board of the monthly results of their operations.

(I.C.W.A. Final)

22. Do you consider that amounts charged to cost for depreciation should vary with changes in productive activity? Give your reasons, and state also the opposite arguments.

(I.C.W.A. Final)

23. When considering the rate of depreciation of plant and machinery, what influence would expenditure on repairs have upon your recommendation? Give your reasons for your answer.

(I.C.W.A. Final)

24. What are the advantages to be gained by maintaining separate accounts for "fixed assets at cost" and "accumulated depreciation relating to the fixed assets."

What are your views on depreciation provided on a replacement-cost basis? What method of provision for depreciation do you prefer and want?

(A.I.A. Final)

25. A very expensive machine has recently been purchased, for which the normal rate of depreciation is regarded as $12\frac{1}{2}\%$ per annum on diminishing value. Your management feels that due to the introduction of improved machinery there will be a serious risk of obsolescence in about five years' time. Using suitable figures, write a report to your management, making appropriate recommendations.

(I.C.W.A. Final)

26. A company is about to produce two articles whose prime cost is composed as follows:

	Cost per dozen A £	Cost per dozen B £
Direct material	1·50	2·25
Direct wages		
8 hours at £0·45 including 5 machine hours	3·60	
4 hours at £0·67½ including 2 machine hours		2·70
Prime Cost	£5·10	£4·95

For the three months ending September 30, 19.., the budget shows the following information:

Budgeted output of A   1,000 dozen
    „   „   B   2,000 dozen

Overhead £18,000.
You are requested:

(a) to name three cost rates by which overhead to be absorbed by each product could be calculated;

(b) to calculate the overhead to be absorbed by each product under each of the cost rates that you name.

Show your workings.

(I.C.W.A. Inter.)

27. "The Modern Company" is divided into four departments; A, B and C are producing departments, and D is a service department. The actual costs for a period are as follows:

	£		£
Rent	1,000	Supervision	1,500
Repairs to plant	600	Fire insurance	500
Depreciation of plant	450	Power	900
Light	100	Employers' liability insurance	150

The following information is available in respect of the four departments:

	Dept. A	Dept. B	Dept. C	Dept. D
Area, sq. ft	1,500	1,100	900	500
Number of employees	20	15	10	5
Total wages	£6,000	£4,000	£3,000	£2,000
Value of plant	£24,000	£18,000	£12,000	£6,000
Value of stock	£15,000	£9,000	£6,000	—

Apportion the costs to the various departments by the most equitable method.

(I.C.W.A. Inter.)

28. A company manufactures a product in three qualities of material. The value of the material used in these products is £2·00, £2·50 and £3·00 per unit. The direct labour cost remains constant at £0·50 per unit. The company absorbs overhead expenditure by:

(a) a percentage addition to the material content calculated to recover the fixed overheads on the budgeted output;

(b) a percentage addition to direct wages calculated to recover the variable overheads on the budgeted output.

Describe the effect of this method of absorption on the cost of the products, and state with reasons whether you consider it to be an equitable method in the circumstances.

(I.C.W.A. Final)

29. (a) The following costs were incurred by a company for the six months ending 31st March:

	£
Materials	14,229
Wages	10,490
Factory overhead	11,921
Factory cost	36,640
Other overhead	6,412
	£43,052

(b) All units of the finished product pass in sequence through each of three factory departments—A, B and C.

An analysis of departmental expenditure for the period shows:

	A £	B £	C £
Materials	5,220	6,306	2,703
Wages	2,420	4,130	3,940
Factory overhead	2,904	3,304	5,713

(c) Unit prime cost charges may be taken as:

	A £	B £	C £
Materials	1·30	1·50	0·50
Wages	0·62½	0·83½	0·75

Prepare a statement of *cost per unit* for each department, recovering factory overhead by the per cent of wages method; and other overhead by the per cent of factory cost shown in (a) above.

(*A.C.C.A. Inter.*)

30. In Department X a group of six machines produce an article, the factory cost of the output of which has been calculated for a 13-week period as follows:

Group output	13,500 units
	£
Raw materials used	1,800
Wages—machine operators	1,440
	3,240
Factory overheads, say 60% on wages	864
	£4,104

Each machine is of equal size and capacity, and fully occupies the attention of one operator.

In the above period Department X was closed for the equivalent of one week in respect of holidays and roof repairs.

A 40-hour week is worked, which includes 1½ hours and 1 hour per machine for setting and cleaning time, respectively.

The standard wage rate is £0·50 per hour.

The management want to know what is the factory cost per unit of output in the light of the above, recovering factory overheads by a machine hour rate instead of as a percentage on cost.

The following further particulars are available:

Department X	Per annum
	£
Foreman, salary	2,000
Rent and rates	320
Light and heat	240
Machine stores	176
Machine repairs	288
Machine repairs and setting	48

Each machine costs £1,200 and depreciation is provided at the rate of 10% per annum on cost.

Submit a brief report as required by management.

(*I.C.A. Final*)

31. The following figures have been extracted from the books of a manufacturing company. All jobs pass through the company's two departments:

	Working dept.	Finishing dept.
Material used	£6,000	£500
Direct labour	£3,000	£1,500
Factory overheads	£1,800	£1,200
Direct labour hours	12,000	5,000
Machine hours	10,000	2,000

The following information relates to Job A. 100:

	Working dept.	Finishing dept.
Material used	£120	£10
Direct labour	£65	£25
Direct labour hours	265	70
Machine hours	255	25

You are required:

(*a*) to enumerate four methods of absorbing factory overheads by jobs, showing the rates for each department under the methods quoted;

(*b*) to prepare a statement showing the different cost results for Job A. 100 under any two of the methods referred to.

(*I.C.W.A. Final*)

32. As cost accountant you are asked to advise a company on the best method of absorbing overheads and to compute the rate or rates to be applied. No cost accounts have been kept, but estimates have been prepared for jobs undertaken on the following basis:

Estimated materials and direct wages, plus 150% on direct wages for factory overheads, plus 15% on factory cost for all other overheads. To this figure a further 15% is added for profit.

The accounts for the year show the following figures:

	£
Direct material	21,000
Factory overheads	27,500
Selling overheads	3,000
Sales	75,000
Direct wages	18,500
Administration overheads	5,000
Distribution overheads	1,500
Net loss	1,500

There are two production departments, and the overhead rates for the departments vary considerably.

(a) Summarise your computation and observations.

(b) State what advice you would give to the management.

(c) Suggest lines on which further investigation should proceed.

(*I.C.W.A. Final*)

33. (a) The following expenditure was incurred in installing new boilers:

	£
Removal of old boilers	90
Demolition of old foundations	60
Erection of new foundations	350
Demolition of wall	20
Extension of boiler-house to take additional boiler	1,780
Installation of new boilers	5,500
Architect's fees	120

State in respect of each of the above items of expenditure and each item of old plant replaced, what amounts would be charged to revenue and/or to capital.

(b) Where fixed assets are revalued and show a surplus over book values, how would you treat the excess in the accounts of the business? What effect will such increase have on future profits?

(c) What are the merits of the straight-line method of calculating depreciation?

(*I.C.W.A. Final*)

34. (a) "The most important factor in determining overhead rates is the level of output." What is meant by this statement?

(b) A machine has a potential capacity per annum of 48 weeks at 40 hours per week; however, it is forecast that the machine will have an actual capacity usage of only 90% because of normal idle time. When the machine is in operation two operatives are required who are paid on a time basis of £0·80 per hour each. Fixed expenses directly associated with the use of the machine such as depreciation and maintenance, etc., are £3,840 and general factory overheads total £30,000. General overheads are allocated to machines on the basis of capacity usage which for the factory as a whole is 25,920 machine hours. During the year the machine was actually in operation for 1,650 hours. The abnormal idle time records indicate that time lost was as follows: shortage of materials 10 hours, excess repairs 50 hours, labour dispute 5 hours and re-runs 20 hours. From the above information, prepare a statement analysing the cost of idle time, both normal and abnormal.

(A.C.C.A. Final)

35. The budgeted costs of a manufacturing business for a normal year are as follows:

	£	£
Direct materials		68,273
Direct wages:		
Machine shop (100,000 hours)	27,382	
Assembly (80,000 hours)	22,780	
		50,162
Works overheads:		
Machine shop	33,490	
Assembly	16,237	
		49,727
Administration overheads		12,268
Selling expenses		15,481
Distribution expenses		13,290

The absorption method of costing is in operation.

Prepare a schedule of overhead rates suitable for practical use in this business.

Complete a cost estimate for a job, the technical data for which are as follows:

Material: 20 lb A at £0·64 per lb
             15 lb B at £0·08½ per lb
Direct labour:
  Machine shop: 15 hours at £0·60 per hour
  Assembly: 25 hours at £0·70 per hour

(I.C.W.A. Final)

36. The recovery of overheads as part of the cost of production must include not only the expense directly allocated to the production departments, but also a share of the service department costs, which are apportioned to them.

Discuss the method by which allocation may be achieved and establish the amount of overhead (to the nearest £100) to be allocated to both production departments, A and B, given the following details:

Amounts directly allocated:
                          A   £12,000
                          B   £13,000

Amounts to be apportioned: service department
                          X   £2,000
                          Y   £4,000

It is forecast that:

Department X will do 40% of its work for A; 30% for B; 30% for Y and Department Y will do 50% for A; 30% for B; 20% for X.

(A.C.C.A. Inter.)

37. Briefly describe two ways of dealing with the problem of apportioning service department costs among service departments which, in addition to doing work for the main operational departments, also serve one another.

(I.C.W.A. Inter.)

38. The Blank Manufacturing Company Ltd. consists of four production departments and two service departments. For the month of September the direct departmental expenses were as follows:

Production departments—A, £4,800; B, £5,600; C, £6,800; D, £2,400.
Service departments—X, £1,800; Y, £2,400.

The cost of service departments X and Y are allocated to the other departments on a percentage basis, viz.:

	A	B	C	D	X	Y
X	30	20	25	15	—	10
Y	20	30	10	25	15	—

Prepare a statement showing the distribution of the service department expenses.

(C.A.A. Final)

39. One of the budget centres of the X.Y. Manufacturing Company is the boiler-house, which raises and supplies steam for all manufacturing budget centres in the company.

The foreman of one of the manufacturing budget centres has complained to the works manager that in his accounts he is charged at different rates each month per lb of steam used. The highest rates have been as much as 20% above the lowest.

You are required to explain in a report to the works manager:

(*a*) how such different rates per lb of steam can be incurred in the boiler-house;

(*b*) why being charged at different rates should present a difficulty to the foreman of the manufacturing budget centre;

(*c*) what procedure, as management accountant of the X.Y. Manufacturing Company, you would propose to install to remedy this position.

(I.C.W.A. Inter.)

40. A company makes a product in a standard model whose ratio of direct materials cost to direct wages was 7 to 3. In 1965, total prime costs were £100,000 and no direct expense was incurred. The company uses a direct wages percentage rate of overhead absorption; for 1965 this was 230%, but there was an under-absorption of overhead of £6,000, even though total direct wages were as budgeted. The profit margin on total costs incurred was 20%.

For 1966, the company proposes to take up a contract for a different model which will require more processing per unit than the standard model, and will have a direct material cost to direct wages ratio of 3 to 7.

For 1966, the company expects the total prime cost to remain the same as in 1965, though 20% of that total will relate to the new contract model. It also expects to incur an additional £8,600 of overhead above the 1965 actual total overhead incurred. It cannot, however, alter the selling price of the standard model.

The contract customer is prepared to accept a price which covers prime cost, overhead at the prime cost percentage rate that would have applied for 1965, and a 20% profit margin on total costs.

You are required to:

(a) calculate the total price that would be payable for the contract models for 1966 if the company were to accept the contract:

(i) on the customer's terms;

(ii) on its present method of overhead absorption calculated on the basis of the 1966 budgeted figures, plus a 20% margin on total costs;

(b) show budgeted trading and profit and loss statements for the company for 1966 for each of the situations in (a) (i) and (a) (ii) above.

(I.C.W.A. Inter.)

41. A productive department of a manufacturing company has five different groups of machines, for each of which it is desired to establish machine hour rates.

A budget for this department for the year ending June 30, shows the following overhead:

	£	£
Consumable supplies—		
Machine group 1	150	
2	300	
3	500	
4	600	
5	950	
		2,500
Maintenance—		
Machine group 1	350	
2	400	
3	600	
4	850	
5	500	
		2,700
Power		700
Rent and rates		2,400
Heat and light		400
Insurance of buildings		200
Insurance of machinery		500
Depreciation of machinery		8,000
Supervision		4,800
General expenses		600
		£22,800

Additional operating information is available as follows:

Group	Effective h.p.	Area occupied (sq. ft)	Book value of machinery £	Working hours
1	5	250	2,500	12,000
2	20	750	12,500	20,000
3	10	100	5,000	8,000
4	25	500	20,000	10,000
5	40	400	10,000	30,000

You are required to:

(a) calculate a machine hour rate for each of the five groups of machines, showing clearly the basis of apportionment that you use;

(b) calculate the overhead that will be absorbed by one unit of Product X and one unit of Product Y on the manufacture of which the following times (in hours) are spent in the machine groups of this department:

	Machine groups				
	1	2	3	4	5
Product X (each unit)	2	—	7	1	2
Product Y	4	1	—	6	1

(I.C.W.A. Inter.)

42. It is the practice of a manufacturing business to charge overhead to jobs as a percentage of direct labour cost. The rate in use is 120%.
The overhead budget for the year is as follows:

	£
Supervision	7,525
Indirect workers	6,000
Holiday pay, S.E.T., company's National Insurance	6,200
Tooling cost	9,400
Machine maintenance labour cost	4,500
Power	1,944
Small tools and supplies	1,171
Insurance of machinery	185
Insurance of buildings	150
Rent and rates	2,500
Depreciation of machinery	9,250
	£48,825

While overhead at present is absorbed into the cost of products by means of a single rate it is proposed to consider absorbing overhead by use of a separate machine hour rate for each of the four different groups of machines.

The following data are accordingly made available:

	Machine groups				
	Q	R	S	T	Total
Floor space, square feet	1,800	1,500	800	900	5,000
Kilowatt hours '000s	270	66	85	65	486
Capital cost of machines £'000s	30	20	8	16	74
Indirect workers, persons	3	3	1	1	8
Total workers, persons	19	24	12	7	62
Machine maintenance hours '000s	3	2	3	1	9
Tooling costs £	3,500	4,300	1,000	600	9,400
Supervision costs £	2,050	2,200	1,775	1,500	7,525
Small tools and supplies £	491	441	66	173	1,171
Machine running hours '000s	30	36	19	8	93

As adviser to the business recommending the change to the machine hour basis you are required to:

(a) state the arguments in favour of the change;

(b) calculate a machine hour rate for each of the four groups of machines;

(c) calculate the overhead to be absorbed by Job "A" involving 4 hours in group Q, 5 hours in group R, 1 hour in group S and 6 hours in group T, using the machine hour rates calculated by you in answer to (b);

(d) calculate the overhead to be absorbed by Job "A" when the labour cost is £7 and the present method is used.

(I.C.W.A. Inter.)

43. Factory A has a lower rate of overhead absorption than Factory B. Both factories produce the same type of goods.

Discuss whether this can be taken as a sign that Factory A is more efficient than Factory B.

(I.C.W.A. Inter.)

44. A manufacturing company has three production departments and two service departments.

Overhead allocated for a period to these departments is as follows:

Production department:

		£
	A	15,000
	B	27,000
	C	19,000

Service department:

		£
	X	3,000
	Y	5,000

A technical assessment for the apportionment of the costs of the service departments shows:

Department:	A	B	C	X	Y
X	45%	15%	30%	—	10%
Y	60%	35%	Nil	5%	—

You are required to show the total overhead chargeable to the three production departments by two methods:

(a) Ignoring the fact that the two service departments serve one another.

(b) Using the method known as "continued allotment" or "repeated distribution" of apportioning service department costs between the two service departments.

(I.C.W.A. Inter.)

45. X.Y. Ltd. operates a factory whose annual budget shows the following budgeted trading account for the year ending November 30:

	£	£	£	£
Selling value of goods produced				300,000
Production cost:				
Direct wages		70,000		
Direct material cost		90,000		
			160,000	
Indirect wages and supervision:				
Machine department X	3,800			
„ „ Y	4,350			
Assembly department	4,125			
Packing department	2,300			
Maintenance department	2,250			
Stores	1,150			
General department	2,425			
		20,400		
Maintenance wages:				
Machine department X	1,000			
„ „ Y	2,000			
Assembly department	500			
Packing department	500			
Maintenance department	500			
Stores	250			
General department	450			
		5,200		
Indirect materials:				
Machine department X	2,700			
„ „ Y	3,600			
Assembly department	1,800			
Packing department	2,700			
Maintenance department	900			
Stores	675			
General department	400			
		12,775		
Power		6,000		
Rent and rates		8,000		
Lighting and heating		2,000		
Insurance		1,000		
Depreciation (20%)		20,000		
			75,375	
				235,375
Budgeted factory profit				£64,625

The following operating information is also available:

Department	Effective h.p.	Area occupied (sq. ft)	Book value of machinery and equipment £	Productive capacity		Machine hours
				Direct labour		
				Hours	Cost £	
Productive:						
Machine X	40	10,000	30,000	100,000	28,000	50,000
„ Y	40	7,500	40,000	75,000	21,000	60,000
Assembly	—	15,000	5,000	75,000	14,000	
Packing	10	7,500	5,000	50,000	7,000	
Service:						
Maintenance	10	3,000	15,000			
Stores	—	5,000	2,500			
General	—	2,000	2,500			
		50,000	£100,000			

The general department consists of the factory manager, and general clerical and wages personnel.

You are required to:

(a) prepare an overhead analysis sheet for the departments of the factory for the year ending November 30 (showing clearly the bases of apportionment);

(b) calculate hourly cost rates of overhead absorption for each productive department (ignore the apportionment of service department costs among service departments).

(I.C.W.A. Inter.)

46. A manufacturing company has three cost centres: two production departments X and Y and a cost centre Z to which all common costs are charged.

The information taken from the standard costs of the three products made and from the budgets for the year, is as follows:

Products:	Per unit		
	A	B	C
Direct labour hours:			
Department X	10	12	8
Department Y	15	22	8
Prime cost (£)	21·5	29·0	21·0
Sales price of spoilt work (£)	25	46	20
	For year		
Sales and production (units)	200	500	400
Department:	X	Y	Z
	For year		
Overhead (£)	9,240	11,352	6,248
Direct labour hours	12,320	18,920	—

Overhead of the common centre Z is apportioned to the production departments according to direct labour hours. Overhead is absorbed into production costs by a direct labour hour rate.

The company budgeted for spoilt work to the extent of 10% of its budgeted production. The spoilt work is sold at the sales prices given above while the overhead shown does not include any loss arising from the work spoilt.

To aid the company to choose the method they are to adopt for the treatment of spoilt work, you are required to take the information given above and to calculate:

(a) the rate of overhead absorption for department X and department Y;

(b) the cost of each unit of products A, B and C if there were no spoilt goods;

(c) the overhead cost of each unit of products A, B and C with spoilt goods as budgeted, if the loss on spoilt goods is charged entirely to cost centre Z overhead.

(I.C.W.A. Inter.)

47. A company manufacturing one product in three departments finds that, to meet its orders during the current year, it must increase its hours worked by 5%. To do this it will have to introduce overtime which will incur a premium of 50% of wages for the extra hours worked.

During last year the hours worked, output, direct wages and overhead were as follows:

Department	Hours worked 1st half-year	Hours worked 2nd half-year	Overhead Fixed per half-year £	Overhead Variable per hour £	Direct wages per hour £
A	27,000	18,000	40,000	0·75	0·60
B	54,000	36,000	36,000	0·50	0·50
C	143,000	100,000	30,000	0·75	0·40
Output (in units)	40,000	29,000			

During the current year budgeted direct wage rates and fixed overhead are the same as last year, but an extra 10% on last year's variable overhead is budgeted for increased lighting, heating, etc. However, output per hour is expected to rise by 5%.

The company at present calculates its product costs each half-year based on the actual data for the half-year.

Because of the seasonal nature of its work it is proposed to change to a single rate of overhead absorption for calculation of product costs for the whole year instead of for each half-year.

You are required to:

(a) calculate the overhead cost content per unit of production per half-year under the present basis of overhead absorption:

(i) for last year;

(ii) budgeted for the current year;

(b) calculate the overhead cost content per unit of production budgeted for this year using the proposed new method of overhead absorption;

(c) (i) calculate the over/under-absorption per half-year that will arise with the new method; and (ii) briefly explain how this over/under-absorption should best be treated in the company's half-yearly accounts.

Calculations should be made correct to one decimal place.

(I.C.W.A. Inter.)

48. A machine was purchased by a manufacturing company for £2,000. The estimated operating costs for each year of its maximum possible working life and its estimated scrap value (if sold) at the end of each year, are set out in the following table:

	Annual operating costs	*Scrap value at end of year*
	£	£
1st year	1,000	1,200
2nd ,,	1,300	800
3rd ,,	1,500	600
4th ,,	1,800	400
5th ,,	2,200	200

When and why will it pay to replace the machine by a new one of the same type, assuming that a new machine can be purchased at any time for £2,000?

(C.I.S. Final, Part question)

49. A factory makes two products whose unit prime costs and selling prices are:

	Product X	*Product Y*
	£	£
Direct materials cost	1·00	1·50
Direct wages	2·50	4·00
	(Grade A—1 hour	(Grade A—6 hours
	,, B—2 hours)	,, B—1 hour)
Selling price	£10·50	£18·25

Fixed overhead is budgeted at £120,000 per annum, budgeted total direct labour cost is £40,000 and budgeted total direct labour hours are 60,000, which is well below capacity.

Grade A labour is easily available, but grade B labour is very difficult to obtain and no more than 20,000 hours of grade B labour are expected to be worked. Wage rates for grade A labour are £0·50 per hour and for grade B labour £1·00 per hour.

The company absorbs its fixed overhead by a direct labour hour method, though there have been suggestions that it should use a direct labour percentage rate.

You are required to:

(a) calculate the profit or loss per unit of X and Y that would be earned if overhead is absorbed on the present basis;

(b) state on which product the company should concentrate to give the largest profit, and support your statement by suitable calculations;

(c) calculate the profit or loss per unit of X and Y that would be earned if overhead were absorbed on a direct labour percentage rate;

(d) state on which product the company should concentrate to give the largest profit if it changed its method of absorption of overhead to a direct labour percentage rate. Support your statement with a suitable calculation.

(I.C.W.A. Inter.)

CHAPTER 14

COST CONTROL ACCOUNTS

THE system of double-entry book-keeping has been widely adopted. At first, bound ledgers were used for the recording of transactions, but in many industries these have been replaced by loose-leaf ledgers, card ledgers and tabulations produced by machines from punched cards or tape. However, even in the modern systems, the theory of "every debit must have a corresponding credit" still applies.

There are three types of accounts, as follows:

    (*a*) Personal accounts: accounts of persons, *e.g.* debtors.
    (*b*) Real accounts: accounts of tangible items, *e.g.* cash.
    (*c*) Nominal accounts: accounts of gains or losses, *e.g.* discount.

In most firms, except perhaps the very small ones, a cost department is operated in which detailed cost statements, reports, etc., are produced. This department is particularly interested in the nominal accounts, and, to some extent, real accounts, which may be considered as impersonal accounts. The accounting department is interested in personal accounts, real accounts and nominal accounts. Thus, in the main, the cost department is concerned with the income and expenditure of the business.

In Chapter 16 integrated accounts will be discussed, and there it will be shown how the accounting and costing departments operate together, using only one set of books. However, in a business using Cost Control Accounts, each of the two departments operates separate ledgers. In this chapter the main consideration is cost book-keeping, but to understand thoroughly the system it is essential to discuss some of the financial transactions which complete the book-keeping entries.

LEDGERS REQUIRED

The most important ledgers required are as follows:

FINANCIAL LEDGERS

    (*a*) *General Ledger.*
    (*b*) *Debtors Ledger.*
    (*c*) *Creditors Ledger.*

COST LEDGERS

(a) *Cost Ledger*. This is the principal ledger of the cost department, in which is recorded the impersonal accounts.

(b) *Stores Ledger*. In this ledger all the stores accounts are maintained, a description of which was given in Chapter 6. An account will be opened for each item in store.

(c) *Work-in-progress Ledger*. This ledger records production during a period and the cost incurred. Each job, unit, batch or process will be assigned a number—a job number—and an account will be maintained for each job. All expenditure incurred will be posted to the respective job accounts as is described in Chapter 18.

(d) *Finished Goods Ledger*. The completely finished products are recorded in this ledger. An account will be opened for each type of product.

These are the four important ledgers in the cost department, and it is suggested that each ledger should have a Control Account, one for each ledger; the Cost Ledger will consequently contain these four control accounts, plus perhaps others, such as the Materials Control Account.

1. General Ledger Adjustment Account

This account is often referred to as Cost Ledger Control Account. Into this account are posted all items of income or expenditure which have been extracted from the financial accounts. In effect, this account represents the personal accounts shown in the financial books. Any transfer from the cost books to the financial books, *e.g.* cost of capital work performed by the factory, will be entered in this account. The main object of this account is to complete the double entry in the Cost Ledger. It is important to note that no entry should be made direct from the financial books to the cost books; entries must pass through the General Ledger Adjustment Account. The balance on this account represents the total of all the balances of the impersonal accounts.

2. Materials Control Account

This account is sometimes dispensed with but shows the total transactions of materials, *e.g.* total receipts, per invoices; and total transfers to Stores Ledger Control per goods received notes. These are brought into agreement.

3. Stores Ledger Control Account

This shows the receipts of materials per goods received notes, and issues per stores requisitions. The balance represents in total the detailed balance of the stores accounts.

4. Work-in-progress Ledger Control Account

This account represents the total work in progress at any time. At the end of any period the total balances of the Job Accounts should equal the balance on this account.

5. Finished Goods Ledger Control Account

The total value of finished goods in stock is represented in this account.

LINK BETWEEN FINANCIAL AND COST BOOKS

In the financial books a Cost Ledger Control Account is opened in which is recorded all the items of income and expenditure which affect the cost accounts (it will be shown on page 255 that there are a number of items which are regarded as purely financial items and are not shown in the cost accounts). This account contains the same items as in the corresponding account in the cost books, but of course they are on the opposite side of the account.

A simple illustration will show how the Cost Ledger Control Account is operated:

Materials priced at £1,000 are bought during January.

In the financial books

The financial accountant will be requested to open a Cost Ledger Control Account in which will be recorded all items of expenditure and income which affect the cost accounts. This account is memorandum only, so, in addition to the ordinary posting, there will be a memorandum entry as follows:

	£	£
Dr. Materials Account	1,000	
Cost Ledger Control Account (memorandum)		
Cr. Creditors Account		1,000

In the cost books

	£	£
Dr. Materials Control Account	1,000	
Cr. General Ledger Adjustment Account		1,000

Purchase of materials on credit for £1,000.

COST ACCOUNTS

When the elements of cost were discussed in Chapter 2 it was suggested that the different types of expenditure can be grouped as follows:

Direct material ⎫
Direct labour   ⎬ PRIME COST
Direct expenses ⎭
Production overhead
Administration overhead
Selling and distribution overhead

It is now suggested that, when answering examination questions, it is useful to open accounts in the Cost Ledger in rather the same order as shown above. The accounts will then be as follows:

(a) General Ledger Adjustment Account.
(b) Materials Control Account.
(c) Stores Ledger Control Account.
(d) Wages Control Account.
(e) Production Overhead Account.
(f) Administration Overhead Account.
(g) Selling and Distribution Overhead Account.

It will be observed that no account is opened for direct expenses: this is because direct expenses are charged direct to production.

The main items of expenditure will be recorded in the above-mentioned accounts, so it is now possible to find the cost of production by opening:

(h) Work-in-progress Ledger Control Account (or Work-in-progress Account).

(i) Finished Goods Ledger Control Account (or Finished Goods Stock Account).

These two accounts were referred to on pages 177 and 178.

The finished goods which are sold are transferred to:

(j) Cost of Sales Account.

In this account is shown the total selling and distribution overheads recovered, which, together with the cost of finished goods, represent the cost of sales.

It is now possible to produce:

(k) Costing Profit ant Loss Account.

Briefly the above accounts are the main accounts to be opened in the Cost Ledger, but it may often be necessary to open additional accounts, e.g. Overhead Adjustment Account or accounts for special repairs or capital work, but these accounts will be explained later in this chapter.

SPECIMEN BOOK-KEEPING ENTRIES

Materials

Financial books

1. During a financial period materials amounting to £10,000 are purchased on credit.

	£	£
Dr. Purchases Account	10,000	
Cost Ledger Control Account (memorandum)		
Cr. Creditors Account		10,000

2. Returns to suppliers amounted to £200.

Dr. Creditors	200	
Cr. Purchases Returns		200
Cost Ledger Control Account (memorandum)		

3. Cash purchases of £1,000 are effected.

Dr. Purchases Account	1,000	
Cost Ledger Control Account (memorandum)		
Cr. Cash		1,000

Cost books

1. Credit purchases £10,000 of which £500 was purchase for special job.

Dr. Materials Control Account	10,000	
Cr. General Ledger Adjustment Account		10,000
Dr. Stores Ledger Control Account	9,500	
Work-in-progress Ledger Control Account	500	
Cr. Materials Control Account		10,000

2. Returns £200.

Dr. General Ledger Adjustment Account	200	
Cr. Stores Ledger Control Account		200

3. Cash Purchases £1,000.

Dr. Materials Control Account	1,000	
Cr. General Ledger Adjustment Account		1,000
Dr. Stores Ledger Control Account	1,000	
Cr. Materials Control Account		1,000

The following entries do not affect the financial accounts; they are merely transactions or transfers in the Cost Ledger and therefore will not appear in the General Ledger Adjustment Account.

	£	£

4. Materials amounting to £9,000 are issued to production.

Dr. Work-in-progress Ledger Control Account   9,000
Cr. Stores Ledger Control Account   9,000

The individual Job Accounts in the Work-in-progress Ledger will be debited and individual Stores Accounts in Stores Ledger credited.

5. Issue of indirect materials amount to £500.

Dr. Production Overhead Account   500
Cr. Stores Ledger Control Account   500

Individual Stores Accounts will be credited in the Stores Ledger, and the total of overhead analysis debited to Production Overhead Account.

6. Materials returned from production to stores at cost of £50.

Dr. Stores Ledger Control Account   50
Cr. Work-in-progress Ledger Control Account   50

Individual Stores Accounts in the Stores Ledger will be debited and Job Accounts in the Work-in-progress Ledger credited.

7. Materials amounting to £100 were transferred from Job No. 29 to Job No. 57.

Dr. Job No. 57 Account   100
Cr. Job No. 29 Account   100

In the Work-in-progress Ledger, only these two accounts are affected. No entry is required in Work-in-progress Ledger Control Account or Stores Ledger Control Account.

Labour

Financial books

1. During the same period wages amounting to £5,000 are earned; deductions, etc., amounting to £500 are effected, *viz.*:

National Insurance (employers and employees)	£60	
P.A.Y.E. income tax	£400	
Superannuation contributions	£40	
Dr. Wages Account (including N.I. employers)	5,000	
Cost Ledger Control Account (memorandum)		
Cr. National Insurance Suspense Account		60
P.A.Y.E. Income Tax Account		400
Superannuation Fund Account		40
Cash		4,500

	£	£

Cost books

1. Dr. Wages Control Account   5,000

     Cr. General Ledger Adjustment Account   5,000

2. This amount is analysed in the wages analysis book.

Direct labour	£4,000
Indirect labour	£1,000

The indirect labour is further analysed:

Production staff	£600
Administration staff	£300
Selling and distribution staff	£100

Dr. Work-in-progress Account   4,000

     Cr. Wages Control Account   4,000

The individual Job Accounts will be charged as per the analysis of job time records.

Dr. Production Overhead Account   600

     Administration Overhead Account   300

     Selling and Distribution Overhead Account   100

Cr. Wages Control Account   1,000

Overhead

Financial books

1. During the period services were supplied by creditors amounting to £2,000.

Dr. Expense Accounts   2,000

     Cost Ledger Control Account (memorandum)

     Cr. Creditors   2,000

2. This amount owing to creditors was paid.

Dr. Creditors   2,000

     Cr. Cash   2,000

This transaction does not affect the cost accounts.

3. Petty cash expenditure £100.

Dr. Expense Accounts   100

     Cost Ledger Control Account (memorandum)

     Cr. Cash   100

Cost books

1. Services £2,000; analysed, *e.g.*:

Production overhead	£1,200
Administration overhead	£600
Selling and distribution overhead	£200

Dr. Production Overhead Account   1,200

     Administration Overhead Account   600

     Selling and Distribution Overhead Account   200

Cr. General Ledger Adjustment Account   2,000

	£	£

2. Petty cash expenditure £100 analysed, *e.g.*:

Administration overhead	£60	
Selling and distribution overhead	£40	
Dr. Administration Overhead Account	60	
Selling and Distribution Overhead Account	40	
Cr. General Ledger Adjustment Account		100

The Cost Ledger now shows the total overhead incurred on behalf of production, administration, selling and distribution. It is now necessary to record in the Cost Ledger the amount of overheads which have been absorbed by production. This information is obtained from the Work-in-progress Ledger; as each period is completed the respective accounts will be debited with the appropriate charge for production overheads; thus by totalling these charges the total overheads recovered can be ascertained.

3. *Production overhead*, £2,250, has been absorbed by production (stores, wages and services).

Dr. Work-in-progress Ledger Control Account	2,250	
Cr. Production Overhead Account		2,250

4. Invariably there will be a difference between overheads incurred and overheads absorbed. In this illustration £2,300 was incurred and £2,250 absorbed. The difference is due to such factors as increased or decreased production, actual expenditure being above or below estimated; this was discussed more fully in Chapter 11. The balance on the account, representing over- or under-recovered overhead, is transferred to Overhead Adjustment Account or exceptionally direct to Costing Profit and Loss Account.

Dr. Overhead Adjustment Account	50	
Cr. Production Overhead Account		50

5. *Administration overhead*, £1,000, has been absorbed by production of finished goods.

Dr. Finished Goods Ledger Control Account	1,000	
Cr. Administration Overhead Account		1,000

6. The balance of the account is transferred:

Dr. Administration Overhead Account	40	
Cr. Overhead Adjustment Account		40

	£	£

7. *Selling and distribution overhead*, £325, has been recovered on goods sold.

	£	£
Dr. Cost of Sales Account	325	
Cr. Selling and Distribution Overhead Account		325

Selling and distribution overheads are not apportioned to production, but form part of the cost of sales. It is therefore necessary to record the amount of selling and distribution overheads which have been recovered from sales.

8. The balance of the account is transferred:

	£	£
Dr. Overhead Adjustment Account	15	
Cr. Selling and Distribution Overhead Account		15

SPECIMEN QUESTION

The following balances appeared in the books of the Marart Engineering Co. Ltd. as at the beginning of the financial year:

	£	£
General Ledger Adjustment Account		15,237
Stores Ledger Control Account	8,751	
Work-in-progress Ledger Control Account	4,287	
Finished Goods Ledger Control Account	2,199	
	£15,237	£15,237

At the end of the year the following information is supplied:

	£	£
Purchases for stores		57,640
Purchases for special jobs		1,750
Direct wages	38,627	
Indirect factory wages	9,543	
Administrative salaries	6,731	
Selling and distribution salaries	4,252	
		59,153
Production expenses		12,432
Administration expenses		8,546
Selling and distribution expenses		5,437
Stores issued to production		54,701
Stores issued to maintenance account		2,476
Returns to supplier		207
Production overheads absorbed by production		24,500
Administration overheads absorbed by finished goods		15,250
Selling overhead recovered on sales		9,600
Products finished during year		117,717
Finished goods sold—at cost		132,292
Sales		150,000

You are required to record the entries in the Cost Ledger for the year and prepare a trial balance.

ANSWER

COST LEDGER

General Ledger Adjustment Account

			£				£
Dec. 31	Stores Ledg. Control A/c—returns		207	Jan. 1	Balance b/d		15,237
,, 31	P. & L. A/c—sales		150,000	Dec. 31	Stores Ledg. Control A/c—purchases		57,640
,, 31	Balance c/d		18,029	,, 31	W.I.P. A/c—special purchases		1,750
				,, 31	Wages A/c		59,153
				,, 31	Production Overhead A/c		12,432
				,, 31	Administration Overhead A/c		8,546
				,, 31	Selling Overhead A/c		5,437
				,, 31	Costing P. & L. A/c—profit		8,041
			£168,236				£168,236
				Jan. 1	Balance b/d		18,029

Stores Ledger Control Account

			£				£
Jan. 1	Balance b/d		8,751	Dec. 31	W.I.P. Ledg. Control A/c		54,701
Dec. 31	Gen. Ledg. Adj. A/c—purchases		57,640	,, 31	Production Overhead A/c		2,476
				,, 31	Gen. Ledg. Adj. A/c		207
				,, 31	Balance c/d		9,007
			£66,391				£66,391
Jan. 1	Balance b/d		9,007				

Wages Control Account

			£				£
Dec. 31	Gen. Ledg. Adj. A/c		59,153	Dec. 31	W.I.P. Ledg. Control A/c		38,627
				,, 31	Production Overhead A/c		9,543
				,, 31	Administration Overhead A/c		6,731
				,, 31	Selling Overhead A/c		4,252
			£59,153				£59,153

Production Overhead Account

			£				£
Dec. 31	Gen. Ledg. Adj. A/c		12,432	Dec. 31	W.I.P. Ledg. Control A/c		24,500
,, 31	Stores Ledg. Control A/c		2,476				
,, 31	Wages A/c		9,543				
,, 31	Overhead Adjustment A/c		49				
			£24,500				£24,500

Administration Overhead Account

			£				£
Dec. 31	Gen. Ledg. Adj. A/c		8,546	Dec. 31	F. Goods Ledg. Control A/c		15,250
,, 31	Wages A/c		6,731	,, 31	Overhead Adjustment A/c		27
			£15,277				£15,277

Selling and Distribution Overhead Account

		£			£
Dec. 31	Gen. Ledg. Adj. A/c	5,437	Dec. 31	Cost of Sales A/c	9,600
,, 31	Wages A/c	4,252	,, 31	Overhead Adjustment A/c	89
		£9,689			£9,689

Work-in-progress Ledger Control Account

		£			£
Jan. 1	Balance b/d	4,287	Dec. 31	Fin. Goods Ledg. Control A/c	117,717
Dec. 31	Gen. Ledg. Adj. A/c	1,750	,, 31	Balance c/d	6,148
,, 31	Stores Ledg. Control A/c	54,701			
,, 31	Wages A/c	38,627			
,, 31	Production Overhead A/c	24,500			
		£123,865			£123,865
Jan. 1	Balance b/d	6,148			

Finished Goods Ledger Control Account

		£			£
Jan. 1	Balance b/d	2,199	Dec. 31	Cost of Sales A/c	132,292
Dec. 31	Administration Overhead A/c	15,250	,, 31	Balance c/d	2,874
,, 31	W.I.P. Ledg. Control A/c	117,717			
		£135,166			£135,166
Jan. 1	Balance b/d	2,874			

Cost of Sales Account

		£			£
Dec. 31	Selling Overhead A/c	9,600	Dec. 31	P. & L. A/c	141,892
,, 31	Finished Goods Ledg. Control A/c	132,292			
		£141,892			£131,892

Overhead Adjustment Account

		£			£
Dec. 31	Administration Overhead A/c	27	Dec. 31	Production Overhead A/c	49
,, 31	Selling Overhead A/c	89	,, 31	Costing P. & L. A/c	67
		£116			£116

Costing Profit and Loss Account for year ending December 31

	£		£
Cost of Sales	141,892	Sales	150,000
Overhead Adjustment A/c	67		
General Ledger Adjustment A/c: profit for year	8,041		
	£150,000		£150,000

Trial balance as at December 31

	£	£
Stores Ledger Control Account	9,007	
Work-in-progress Ledger Control Account	6,148	
Finished Goods Ledger Control Account	2,874	
General Ledger Adjustment Account		18,029
	£18,029	£18,029

OVERHEAD ADJUSTMENT ACCOUNT

Into this account is transferred all over- or under-recovered overhead; the balance being taken to Costing Profit and Loss Account. Exceptionally this account may not be opened, any balances on overhead accounts being transferred direct to Costing Profit and Loss Account.

CAPITAL ORDERS

Improvements to plant, machinery, tools, buildings, etc., are frequently carried out by a manufacturing company's own workmen, and on many occasions tools and equipment are actually produced in the firm. It is absolutely essential that a record is kept of all expenditure incurred on these operations, so that successful work may be "capitalised." By this is meant the transfer of all expenditure incurred to an asset account; *e.g.* if materials amounting to £2,000 and wages £1,000 were incurred in producing a machine for use in the factory the accounting entries would be:

	£	£
Dr. Capital Order Account	3,000	
Cr. Work-in-progress Ledger Control Account		3,000

A capital order would be opened for each item of capital work to be performed, and on this order would be recorded all expenditure involved in each job. When the work was finished the above transfer would be effected. At the end of the period the asset would be transferred from the cost accounts to the financial accounts, as follows:

	£	£
Dr. General Ledger Adjustment Account	3,000	
Cr. Capital Order Account		3,000

It will be observed that no addition of production overhead has been made to the amount to be capitalised in the above illustration. Opinions differ on whether this ought to be done, but it is thought that, provided such overhead is incurred in consequence of the capital work undertaken, it is legitimate to do so. It is obviously unsound practice, however, to load normal overhead on to capital projects to such an extent as to vitiate comparisons of product manufacture.

REPAIR ORDERS

Special repair and maintenance work is recorded in a rather similar way to capital equipment work. A repair order is issued, on which is recorded all expenditure incurred on that special job. When the repair is completed the repair order would be closed and the necessary adjustment effected in the Cost Ledger:

	£	£
Dr. Special Repair and Maintenance Account	3,500	
Cr. Work in-progress Ledger Control Account		3,500

Assuming that this expenditure had been incurred on behalf of departments as follows: production department £2,000; administration department £1,000; selling and distribution department £500—the entries would be:

	£	£
Dr. Production Overhead Account	2,000	
Administration Overhead Account	1,000	
Selling and Distribution Overhead Account	500	
Cr. Special Repairs and Maintenance Account		3,500

SPECIAL ORDERS

Sometimes orders are received for a special delivery of goods to a customer. A production order will be issued on which will be recorded all expenditure incurred on this special job. When the job is completed the goods can be despatched to the customer without being taken into finished stock. The entry will then be:

Dr. Special Order Account
Cr. Work-in-progress Ledger Control Account

CARRIAGE INWARDS

Where possible the cost of carriage inwards is often added to the purchase price of the materials. However, this is frequently found to be impracticable, so this expense is recovered on production through production overhead.

Dr. Production Overhead Account
Cr. General Ledger Adjustment Account

SPECIMEN QUESTION

The balances appearing in the Cost Ledger of the Jervid Engineering Co. Ltd. at January 1 were as follows:

	£	£
General Ledger Adjustment Account		58,750
Stores Ledger Control Account	25,247	
Work-in-progress Ledger Control Account	12,560	
Finished Goods Ledger Control Account	20,943	
	£58,750	£58,750

At the end of the year the following information is supplied:

	£	£
Purchases for stores		180,742
Purchases for Special Job No. 57		10,638
Materials issued to production:		
Materials used on Special Repairs and Maintenance Order No. 29	3,527	
Material used on Capital Order No. 10	8,974	
Material used on Special Job No. 57	20,748	
Material used in products	140,916	
		174,165
Materials issued to repairs and maintenance		2,468
Materials returned to suppliers from stores		1,253
Materials lost by theft		126
Carriage inwards on stores		3,264
Total wages paid to employees:		
Labour incurred on Special Repairs and Maintenance Order No. 29	2,431	
Labour incurred on Capital Order No. 10	6,328	
Labour incurred on Special Job No. 57	18,643	
Labour incurred on products	106,065	
		133,467
Indirect wages	15,346	
Idle time due to power failure	575	
Normal idle time	993	
		16,914
Direct expenses		597
Production expenses		21,263
Administration expenses		18,462
Selling expenses		10,572
Distribution expenses		5,433
Sales	330,000	
Selling price of Special Job No. 57	70,000	
		400,000

At the end of the year the following balances were ascertained:

	£
Stores Ledger Control Account	27,844
Work-in-progress Ledger Control Account	14,106
Finished Goods Ledger Control Account	22,167

Production overheads were recovered as follows: 15% on prime cost.

Administration overheads were recovered on finished production, amounting to £20,000.

Selling and distribution overheads were recovered on products sold, amounting to £17,500.

Capital Order No. 10 was completed during the year and is to be "capitalised."

Special Repair and Maintenance Order No. 29 was completed and is to be charged to production, administration and selling and distribution departments in the ratio of 5 : 3 : 2.

Special Job No. 57 was also completed and was despatched to customer. Production overhead is not to be charged to Capital Order No. 10. Administration overhead and selling and distribution overhead are not to be charged to Special Order No. 57.

You are required to enter the amounts in the Cost Ledger, prepare the Costing Profit and Loss Account and show a trial balance at the end of the period.

ANSWER

General Ledger Adjustment Account

	£		£
Stores Ledger Control A/c—returns	1,253	Balance b/d	58,750
Capital Order No. 10	15,302	Stores Ledger Control A/c: materials purchased	180,742
Profit & Loss A/c—sales	330,000		
Special Job No. 57	70,000	W.I.P. Ledger Control A/c: materials for special orders	10,638
Balance c/d	64,117	Production Overhead A/c: carriage inwards	3,264
		Wages Control A/c	150,381
		W.I.P. Ledger Control A/c: direct expenses	597
		Production Overhead A/c	21,263
		Administration Overhead A/c	18,462
		Selling Overhead A/c	10,572
		" "	5,433
		Costing P. & L. A/c: profit for year	20,570
	£480,672		£480,672
		Balance b/d	64,117

Stores Ledger Control Account

	£		£
Balance b/d	25,247	W.I.P. Ledger Control A/c: materials issued to production	174,165
Gen. Ledger Adj. A/c: purchases	180,742	Production Overhead A/c: materials used for repairs	2,468
		Gen. Ledger Adj. A/c: materials returned	1,253
		Abnormal Loss A/c: materials lost by theft	126
		Production Overhead A/c: normal loss of materials	133
		Balance c/d	27,844
	£205,989		£205,989
Balance b/d	27,844		

Wages Control Account

	£		£
Gen. Ledger Adj. A/c: Wages	150,381	W.I.P. Ledger Control A/c: direct wages	133,467
		Production Overhead A/c: indirect wages	15,346
		Abnormal Loss A/c: idle time	575
		Production Overhead A/c: normal idle time	993
	£150,381		£150,381

Production Overhead Account

	£		£
Stores Ledger Control A/c: materials for repairs	2,468	W.I.P. Ledger Control A/c: overhead recovered	45,303
Gen. Ledger Adj. A/c: carriage inwards	3,264	Overhead Adj. A/c (under-recovered)	1,590
Wages Control A/c:			
Indirect wages	15,346		
Normal idle time	993		
Gen. Ledger Adj. A/c	21,263		
Stores Ledger Control A/c: normal loss	133		
Special Repairs & Maintenance O. 29	3,426		
	£46,893		£46,893

Administration Overhead Account

	£		£
Gen. Ledger Adj. A/c	18,462	Finished Goods Ledger Con. A/c: overhead recovered	20,000
Special Repairs & Maintenance O. 29: repairs	2,056	Overhead Adj. A/c (under-recovered)	518
	£20,518		£20,518

Selling and Distribution Overhead Account

	£		£
Gen. Ledger Adj. A/c	10,572	Cost of Sales A/c: overhead recovered	17,500
" "	5,433		
Special Repairs & Maintenance O. 29: repairs	1,370		
Overhead Adj. A/c (over-recovered)	125		
	£17,500		£17,500

Work-in-progress Ledger Control Account

	£			£	£
Balance b/d	12,560		Special Repair & Maintenance		
Gen. Ledger Adj. A/c: purchases	10,638		O. 29:		
Stores Ledger Control A/c: materials			Materials	3,527	
issued	174,165		Labour	2,431	
Wages Control A/c: direct wages	133,467		Production overhead	894	
Gen. Ledger Adj. A/c: direct expenses	597				6,852
Production Overhead A/c	45,303		Capital Order No. 10:		
			Materials	8,974	
			Labour	6,328	
					15,302
			Special Job No. 57:		
			Materials	20,748	
			Labour	18,643	
			Production overhead	7,505	
			Special purchases	10,638	
					57,534
			Finished Goods Ledger Control A/c		282,936
			Balance c/d		14,106
	£376,730				£376,730
Balance b/d	14,106				

Finished Goods Ledger Control Account

	£		£
Balance b/d	20,943	Cost of Sales A/c: finished goods sold	301,712
W.I.P. Ledger Control A/c	282,936	Balance c/d	22,167
Administration Overhead	20,000		
	£323,879		£323,879
Balance b/d	22,167		

Special Repair & Maintenance Order No. 29

	£	£		£
W.I.P. Ledger Control A/c:			Production Overhead A/c	3,426
Materials	3,527		Administration Overhead A/c	2,056
Labour	2,431		Selling Overhead A/c	1,370
Production overhead	894			
		6,852		
		£6,852		£6,852

Capital Order No. 10

	£	£		£
W.I.P. Ledger Control A/c:			Gen. Ledger Adj. A/c: cost of capital	15,302
Materials	8,974		work	
Labour	6,328			
		15,302		
		£15,302		£15,302

Special Job No. 57

	£	£		£
W.I.P. Ledger Control A/c:			Gen. Ledger Adj. A/c: sales	70,000
Materials	20,748			
Labour	18,643			
Overhead	7,505			
Special purchases	10,638			
		57,534		
P. & L. A/c: profit		12,466		
		£70,000		£70,000

Abnormal Loss on Materials Account

Stores Ledger Control A/c	£126	Costing P. & L. A/c	£126

Abnormal Idle Time Account

Wages Control A/c	£575	Costing P. & L. A/c	£575

Overhead Adjustment Account

	£		£
Production Overhead A/c	1,590	Selling Overhead A/c	125
Administration Overhead A/c	518	Costing P. & L. A/c	1,983
	£2,108		£2,108

Cost of Sales Account

	£		£
Finished Goods Ledger	301,712	Costing P. & L. A/c	319,212
Selling & Distribution Overhead A/c	17,500		
	£319,212		£319,212

Costing Profit and Loss Account for period ending December 31

	£	£		£
Cost of Sales		319,212	Sales	330,000
Abnormal loss:			Profit on Special Job No. 57	12,466
Materials	126			
Labour	575			
		701		
Overhead Adj. A/c: overhead under-recovered		1,983		
Gen. Ledger Adj. A/c: profit for year		20,570		
		£342,466		£342,466

Trial balance as at December 31

	£	£
General Ledger Adjustment Account		64,117
Stores Ledger Control Account	27,844	
Work-in-progress Ledger Control Account	14,106	
Finished Goods Ledger Control Account	22,167	
	£64,117	£64,117

NOTES

Production overhead recovered

Production overheads are to be recovered at 15% on prime cost. This is cal-culated:

	£	£
Balance of work in progress	12,560	
Special purchases	10,638	
Materials	174,165	
Wages	133,467	
Direct expenses	597	
	331,427	
Less Balance c/d	14,106	
		£317,321

$$£317,321 \times \frac{15}{100} = £47,598.$$

This is analysed:

	£	£	£
Special Repair and Maintenance Order No. 29			
Prime cost	5,958		
15%		894	
Capital Order No. 10			
Prime cost	15,302		
15%		2,295	
Special Job No. 57			
Prime cost	50,029		
15%		7,505	
Finished production			
Prime cost	246,032		
15%		36,904	
			£47,598

However, in this illustration, it is suggested that production overhead should not be charged to capital orders, so that the actual overheads recovered will be:

	£
	47,598
Less Capital Order No. 10	2,295
	£45,303

The profit for the year is debited to Costing Profit and Loss Account and credited to General Ledger Adjustment Account. If a loss has been realised the entries would have been reversed.

It has been shown in the above exercise how the cost accountant has ascertained the profit for the year. The financial accountant would also have prepared final accounts and ascertained the profit for the year. If management is to have any confidence in the information provided it is obvious that the profit for the year as ascertained by the financial accountant and cost accountant must be capable of reconciliation. This will be discussed in the next chapter.

OVER- OR UNDER-ABSORBED OVERHEAD

In the above illustration over- or under-absorbed overhead was transferred to an Overhead Adjustment Account and the balance taken to Profit and Loss Account. This was because many accountants consider that overhead incurred in a financial period should be recovered during the same period. However, some accountants prefer to carry forward the balances on the various overhead accounts to the next year, so they show the balances in the trial balance. Where the latter method is used there will be a difference in profit shown in the cost accounts compared with that in the financial accounts.

WORK-IN-PROGRESS LEDGER

It will be observed that all work performed, whether routine, special, maintenance or capital, has been recorded in the Work-in-progress Ledger. Job Accounts will be maintained for each job, and possibly different colours will be used to denote the various types of job, such as capital, maintenance orders. When, for example, a capital order is completed, the total material and labour cost can be transferred from the Work-in-progress Ledger to the Capital Order Account in the Cost Ledger, which will thus reveal the cost of the project to be capitalised.

EXAMINATION QUESTIONS

1. Define "Cost Control Accounts" and give examples.

Show their relation to the financial accounts and the details of cost summaries, presenting your answer in the form of a chart.

(*I.C.W.A. Final*)

2. You wish to institute Control Accounts in respect of materials purchased and used in your factory. What purposes do Control Accounts serve? What accounts would you institute and from what sources would the entries be derived?

(*I.C.W.A. Inter.*)

3. The following balances are shown in a Cost Ledger as at October 1:

	Dr.	Cr.
	£	£
Work-in-progress Account	7,840	
Finished Stock Account	5,860	
Works Overhead Suspense Account	400	
Office and Administration Overheads Suspense Account	200	
Stores Ledger Control Account	10,500	
Cost Ledger Control Account		24,800

Transactions for the year ended September 30 were:

	£
Wages—direct labour	61,200
Wages—indirect labour	2,800
Works overheads allocated to production	18,700
Office and administration overheads allocated to production	6,200
Stores issued to production	39,300
Goods finished during year	120,000
Finished goods sold	132,000
Stores purchased	36,000
Stores issued to factory repair orders	1,500
Carriage inwards on stores issued for production	600
Works expenses	14,000
Office and administration expenses	6,000

Write up accounts in the Cost Ledger to record the above transactions, make the necessary transfers to Control Accounts, and prepare a trial balance as at September 30. Compute the profit or loss for the year.

(*C.A.A. Final*)

4. The balances in the Cost Ledger of a manufacturing company on January 1 were:

	£
Stores Ledger Control Account	7,000
Work-in-progress Account	12,800
Finished Stock Account	2,000
Cost Ledger Control Account	21,800

You are given the following information for the year:

	£
Purchases of materials	40,000
Direct factory wages	60,000
Manufacturing expenses	34,600
Selling and distribution expenses	5,400
Materials issued to production	37,200
Manufacturing expenses recovered	34,440
Selling and distribution expenses recovered	5,320
Sales	150,000
Stock of material at December 31	9,800
Stock of finished goods at December 31	4,700
Work in progress at December 31	14,700

You are required to show the accounts in the Cost Ledger for the year, to prepare the Costing Profit and Loss Account for the year, and extract a trial balance.

(C.I.S. Final)

5. The following balances are shown in a Cost Ledger as at January 1:

	Dr.	Cr.
	£	£
Work-in-progress Account	3,920	
Finished Stock Account	2,930	
Works Overheads Suspense Account	200	
Office and Administration Overheads Suspense Account	100	
Stores Ledger Control	5,250	
Cost Ledger Control Account	——	12,400

Transactions for the year ended December 31 were:

Wages—direct labour	30,600
Wages—indirect labour	1,400
Works overheads allocated to production	9,350
Office and administration overheads allocated to production	3,100
Stores issued to production	19,650
Goods finished during year	60,000
Finished goods sold	66,000
Stores purchased	18,000
Stores issued to factory repair orders	750
Carriage inwards on stores issued for production	300
Works expenses	7,000
Office and administration expenses	3,000

Write up accounts in the Cost Ledger to record the above transactions, make the necessary transfers to Control Accounts, and prepare a trial balance as at December 31. Compute the profit or loss for the year.

(C.A.A. Final)

6. From the following balances extracted from the Cost Ledger construct a Cost Control Account and show the trial balance of the Cost Ledger:

	£		£
Stores	1,366	Finished stock	17,508
Direct material	25,346	Direct wages	48,682
Works overheads	46,548	Sales from stock	2,006
Job No. 794	1,142	Profit on completed jobs	22,138
Job No. 852	1,964	Office Overhead Suspense	
Profit on sale from stock	460	A/c	416
Office overheads	10,648	Completed jobs	131,578
Direct expenses	456	Works Overhead Suspense	
		A/c	1,030

(A.I.A. Final)

7. The following is an extract from the accounts of a contractor for the year to March 31:

Trading and Profit and Loss Account

	£		£
Stock of materials	3,400	Contracts completed	38,000
Work in progress	6,300	Stocks of materials	4,000
Purchases, materials	14,200	Work in progress	7,800
Wages	16,300		
Gross profit	9,600		
	£49,800		£49,800
Establishment charges	3,900	Gross profit	9,600
Net profit	5,700		
	£9,600		£9,600

The costing system is separate from the financial books, and includes Stores and Contract Ledgers.

Work in progress is valued in the financial accounts at prime cost, and the figures are identical with those shown by the Contract Ledger at the relevant dates, the breakdown of the valuations being as follows:

	April 1 £	March 31 £
Direct materials	2,090	4,500
Direct labour	4,210	3,300
	£6,300	£7,800

Materials used, as shown in the Trading Account after adjusting stocks, include wastage in stores £420 and indirect material £760; wages in the Trading Account include indirect labour £450; apart from these exceptions, all materials used and wages incurred as shown above are charged in detail to the Contract Accounts. Establishment charges (including indirect expenditure) are debited in the Contract Ledger by adding $27\frac{1}{2}\%$ of the direct labour cost to each contract on completion of the work when the invoice is sent to the customer.

Prepare on a double-entry basis suitable accounts for the costing books, which will reveal the financial results, act as Control Accounts where necessary and also serve to reconcile the cost records with the financial books after taking into account establishment charges under- or over-recovered.

(C.C.S. Final)

8. From the following figures (standard, except where otherwise stated) relating to a month's activities draw up the various Control Accounts required, showing the total variances from standard:

	£	£
Stock brought forward:		
Steel bars	7,000	
Pressings	5,000	
Tools	1,000	
Consumable stores	2,000	
		15,000
Work in progress brought forward		11,000
Direct wages:		
Machine shop	3,000	
Assembly shop	7,000	
Tool-room	2,000	
		12,000
Overheads:		
Machine shop	6,000	
Assembly shop	3,500	
Tool-room	3,000	
		12,500
Sales (actual)		42,000

Purchases:	Actual	Standard	
	£	£	
Steel bars	6,140	6,000	
Pressings	6,090	6,000	
Tools	1,050	1,000	
Consumable stores	1,020	1,000	
			14,000
	14,300		

Issues from stores:		£	£
Steel bars to machine shop		6,500	
Pressings to assembly shop		5,500	
Tools		500	
Consumable stores:			
Machine shop	750		
Tool-room	250		
		1,000	
			13,500
Production:			
Machine shop			20,500
Assembly shop			16,750
Scrapped work in progress:			
Machine shop		750	
Assembly shop		250	
			1,000
Work in progress carried forward			12,000
Cost of sales			35,250
Allocation of tool-room cost:			
Machine shop		5,000	
Assembly shop		750	
			5,750

NOTE: Total variance only is required, and no attempt should be made to analyse by causes.

(*I.C.W.A. Final*)

9. Given the following information, you are required to write up the appropriate accounts, bring down the closing balances at June 1 and take out a trial balance, under account code numbers, at May 31. The following balances existed in the company's Cost Ledger as at April 30:

Code		£	£
1	Control Account		397,576
2	Cost of sales	315,631	
3	Material price variance		1,025
4	Material wastage	14,187	
5	Wages over/under-absorbed	346	
6	Overhead over/under-absorbed		763
7	Finished stock	29,864	
	Work in progress:		
8	Process A—Materials	8,613	
	Wages	856	
	Overhead	1,712	
9	Process B—Materials	6,424	
	Wages	689	
	Overhead	689	
10	Process C—Materials	3,987	
	Wages	420	
	Overhead	630	
11	Raw materials	15,316	
		£399,364	£399,364

During May the following transactions took place:

	£	£
Actual cost of materials purchased		12,008
Actual wages incurred		1,266
Wages were allocated to: Process A	784	
„ B	232	
„ C	168	
		1,184
Actual overhead incurred		2,346
Raw materials issued from store to Process A		7,200
Work in progress, valued and transferred:		
From Process A to B:		
Material	9,206	
Wages	986	
		10,192
From Process B to C:		
Material	8,614	
Wages	790	
		9,404
From Process C to finished stock:		
Material	6,308	
Wages	510	
		6,818
Finished stock sold (at cost)		15,719

Overhead is absorbed by processes on the basis of wages.

Inter-process and finished stock transfers also carry overhead on the same basis.

Materials purchased are taken into stock at standard cost, which allows for a 0·5% price loss.

Standard material wastage allowances (based on cost of material input) are: Process A, 3%; Process B, 1%; Process C, 2%.

(*I.C.W.A. Inter.*)

10. The Manufacturing and Trading Accounts of B. Limited for the year are as follows:

Manufacturing Account

	£	£	£
Raw material:			
Opening stock		15,634	
Purchases	98,746		
Returns	6,324		
		92,422	
		108,056	
Closing stock		14,831	
			93,225
Direct wages		84,723	
Overhead		87,531	
			172,254
Work in progress:			
Opening stock		8,375	
Closing stock		8,058	
			317
			£265,796

Trading Account

	£
Cost of goods manufactured	265,796
	£265,796

Trading Account

	£	£		£
Finished goods:			Sales	417,548
Opening stock	24,326			
Cost of goods manufactured	265,796			
	290,122			
Closing stock	24,941			
		265,181		
Gross profit		152,367		
		£417,548		£417,548

The statement prepared to reconcile the gross profits in the financial and the cost accounts at the end of the year is as follows:

	£	£	£
Gross profit in financial accounts			152,367
Difference in stock valuations:			
Add Raw material, closing stock		176	
Work in progress, opening stock		265	
Finished goods, opening stock		321	
		—	762
Less Raw material, opening stock		198	
Work in progress, closing stock		243	
Finished goods, closing stock		365	
		—	806
			—
			44
Gross profit in cost accounts after adjustment of overheads			£152,323

The cost accounts revealed that overheads had been under-absorbed by £2,808. This amount was written off to the Costing Profit and Loss Account for the year.

Show the following Control Accounts in the Cost Ledger:

(*a*) Raw material.
(*b*) Work in progress.
(*c*) Finished goods.

(I.C.W.A. Inter.)

11. The L. Manufacturing Company Limited maintains separate cost and financial accounts. In the Cost Ledger for the six months ended June 30 the Stock Control Accounts were as follows:

Stores Ledger

		£			£
Jan. 1	Balance b/d	44,900	June 30	Returns	9,000
June 30	Purchases	216,900		Work in pro-gress	205,600
				Balance c/d	47,100
		£261,800			£261,700
July 1	Balance b/d	47,100			

Work-in-progress Ledger

		£			£
Jan. 1	Balance b/d	10,200	June 30	Finished goods	430,800
June 30	Stores	205,600		Balance c/d	10,600
	Wages	71,400			
	Production over-head	154,200			
		£441,400			£441,400
July 1	Balance b/d	10,600			

Finished Goods Ledger

		£			£
Jan. 1	Balance b/d	22,100	June 30	Cost of sales	430,900
June 30	Work in progress	430,800		Balance c/d	22,000
		£452,900			£452,900
July 1	Balance b/d	22,000			

Production overhead has been absorbed in the above Work-in-progress Control Account on the basis of 75% of direct material costs. A charge of £5,000 for the six months ended June 30, in respect of capital invested in stocks has been added in the Cost Ledger to the actual production overhead incurred.

A simplified Revenue Account prepared from the financial accounts for the six months ended June 30, was:

	£	£		£
Direct materials:			Production cost carried	
Opening stock		43,600	down	427,800
Purchases	216,900			
Less Returns	9,000			
		207,900		
		251,500		
Less closing				
stock		46,200		
		205,300		
Direct wages		71,400		
Production over-head		151,400		
Gross production cost		428,100		
Work in progress:				
Closing	11,300			
Opening	11,000			
		300		
Net production cost		£427,800		£427,800

	£	Sales	£
Finished goods:		Sales	747,800
Opening stock	22,400		
Production cost			
brought down	427,800		
	450,200		
Less Closing stock	21,900		
	428,300		
Gross profit	319,500		
	£747,800		£747,800

You are required to:

(*a*) state the accounting treatment of interest on capital invested in stocks used in the Cost Ledger and discuss results arising from its inclusion;

(*b*) enumerate briefly the possible reasons for, and the recognised methods of dealing with, the under-absorption of production overhead in the cost accounts;

(*c*) calculate the profit shown in the cost accounts, before final adjustments are made, using the information given above, and prepare a statement to reconcile the profits shown in the financial accounts and the cost accounts.

(I.C.W.A. Inter.)

12. A manufacturing company makes two products, X and Y. The standard selling prices and details on which standard costs are calculated of these products are:

		Per unit	
		X	Y
Selling price		£10	£20
	Standard price per lb		
	£	lb	lb
Materials: A	0·50	4	6
B	0·25	4	8
C	0·20	5	5

Product X is made in Department X and Product Y is made in Department Y.

During the month of April, the following raw materials were purchased and consumed:

		X	Y
	Actual price per lb		
	£	lb	lb
Materials: A	0·550	14,200	18,800
B	0·22½	15,000	25,800
C	0·200	17,600	18,100

All products made during the month were sold.

Raw material purchases are charged to the Raw Material Stores Accounts at actual prices and price variances are declared when materials are issued. Separate Work-in-progress Accounts are kept for departments X and Y and they are charged with actual quantities of materials used and actual costs of direct wages and overhead.

The Profit and Loss Account for the month of April, which is in course of preparation, shows the following information:

NOTE: Adverse variances are indicated by (A) and favourable variances by (F).

	X £	Y £	Total £
Budgeted sales	40,000	60,000	100,000
Sales variances:			
Price	800 (F)	600 (A)	200 (F)
Quantity	4,000 (A)	6,000 (F)	2,000 (F)
Total	3,200 (A)	5,400 (F)	2,200 (F)
Actual sales			
Less Standard cost of sales:			
Direct materials			
Direct wages	5,400	8,250	13,650
Production overhead	12,600	21,450	34,050
Total			
Standard profit			
Production variances:			
Direct materials:			
Price			
Mix			
Total			
Direct wages:			
Rate	220 (F)	130 (A)	90 (F)
Efficiency	100 (A)	120 (F)	20 (F)
Total	120 (F)	10 (A)	110 (F)

	X £	Y £	Total £
Production overhead:			
Expenditure	150 (F)	100 (A)	50 (F)
Volume	300 (A)	100 (F)	200 (A)
Total	150 (A)	—	150 (A)
Total			
Actual profit			

You are required to prepare, with details of variance for the month of April:

(a) Raw Material Stores Accounts for materials A, B and C;

(b) Work-in-progress Accounts for departments X and Y, showing each element of cost;

(c) Summary Control Accounts for raw material stores and for work in progress.

(*I.C.W.A. Inter.*)

CHAPTER 15

THE RECONCILIATION OF COST AND FINANCIAL ACCOUNTS

WHERE accounts are maintained on the integral accounts system there are no separate cost accounts and financial accounts; consequently the problem of reconciliation does not occur. However, where there is a financial accounting system and a separate cost accounting system, it is imperative that the accounts be reconciled. A Memorandum Reconciliation Account is prepared, as will be illustrated later in the chapter.

At this stage it might be expedient to consider in more detail the General Ledger Adjustment Account which was prepared in the previous chapter. The account appeared thus:

General Ledger Adjustment Account

	£		£
Stores Ledger Control A/c— returns	1,253	Balance b/d	58,750
Capital Order No. 10	15,302	Stores Ledger Control A/c: materials	
Profit & Loss A/c—sales	330,000	purchased	180,742
Special Job No. 57	70,000	W.I.P. Ledger Control A/c: materials	
Balance c/d	64,117	for special orders	10,638
		Production Overhead A/c: carriage	
		inwards	3,264
		Wages Control A/c	150,381
		W.I.P. Ledger Control A/c: direct	
		expenses	597
		Production Overhead A/c	21,263
		Administration Overhead A/c	18,462
		Selling Overhead A/c	10,572
			5,433
		Costing P. & L. A/c: profit for year	20,570
	£480,672		£480,672
		Balance b/d	64,117

The items appearing in the above account may be analysed as follows:

DEBIT ITEMS

1. Returns

This figure should be the same as that appearing in the financial books, where the entry would have been:

	£	£
Dr. Creditors	1,253	
Cr. Purchase Returns Account		1,253
Cr. Cost Ledger Control Account		
(memorandum)		

253

2. Capital work

It is a policy decision of management as to whether or not the value of capital improvements completed will be shown in the Asset Account in the financial books at the cost price as recorded in the Cost Ledger. If the value is the same, then this item will not affect the reconciliation of the cost and financial accounts. However, if the value is lower, then the profit shown by the cost accounts will be greater than that shown by the financial accounts, so must be reconciled in the Reconciliation Account.

In the financial books:

	£	£
Dr. Asset Account	15,302	
Cr. Purchases Account		8,974
Wages Account		6,328
Cost Ledger Control Account		
(memorandum)		

3 and 4. Sales

This figure is obtained from the financial accounts.

	£	£
Dr. Sundry Debtors Account	400,000	
Cr. Sales Account		400,000
Cr. Cost Ledger Control Account		
(memorandum)		

5. Balance

This represents the various Asset Accounts, *e.g.* Stock, Work-in-progress, Finished Goods, at end of period.

CREDIT ITEMS

1. Balance

This represents the various Asset Accounts, *e.g.* Stock, Work-in-progress, Finished Goods, at beginning of period.

2. Materials
3. Special materials
4. Carriage inwards
5. Wages
6. Direct expense
7. Production overhead
8. Administration overhead
9. Selling overhead
10. Distribution overhead

As illustrated in the previous chapter, these charges were obtained from the financial accounts through the Memorandom Cost Ledger Control Account.

11. Profit

The financial accountant will have ascertained the year's profit in the Profit and Loss Account, so will not wish to record the costing profit also in his ledger. Consequently this item will be shown only in the Memorandum Cost Control Account as a debit, thus corresponding with the credit in the General Ledger Adjustment Account.

It can be seen from the General Ledger Adjustment Account that most of the figures have been posted from the financial accounts, so in respect of these items no reconciliation is necessary. The only exceptions were the following:

(a) Opening and closing balances.
(b) Capital order.
(c) Profit for year.

Thus, when preparing a Memorandum Reconciliation Account, these three items are the only ones to be considered in relation to the cost accounts. If, however, over- or under-absorbed overheads are carried forward to the next period (as was mentioned in the previous chapter as an alternative to the method illustrated there), then this item will also affect reconciliation.

ITEMS SHOWN ONLY IN THE FINANCIAL ACCOUNTS

There will invariably be a number of items which appear in the financial accounts and not in the cost accounts. All such items of expenditure will have reduced the financial profit for the year, while any items of income will have increased the financial profit. When reconciling the cost and financial accounts, any items under this category must be considered. The main items are as follows:

1. Purely financial charges

(a) Losses of capital assets, arising from sale, exchange or un-insured destruction. Fees of assessors and advisers on such destruction losses (fire, etc.) come under this heading, being unrelated to operating cost.

(b) Stamp duty and expenses on issues and transfers of capital stock, shares and bonds, etc.

(c) Losses on investments.

(d) Discounts on bonds, debentures, etc.

(e) Fines and penalties.

(f) Interest on bank loans, mortgages, etc.

2. *Purely financial income*

(*a*) Rent receivable; if, however, the rent is received from sub-letting part of the business premises, then allowance will probably have been made in the cost accounts.

(*b*) Profits arising from sale of fixed assets.

(*c*) Fees received on issues and transfers of shares, etc.

(*d*) Interest received on bank deposits, loans, etc.

(*e*) Dividends received.

3. *Appropriation of profit*

(*a*) Donations to charities.

(*b*) Items which appear in the Profit and Loss Appropriation Account, *e.g.*:

(*i*) taxation;

(*ii*) dividends paid;

(*iii*) amounts transferred to sinking funds for repayment of liabilities;

(*iv*) transfers to reserves;

(*v*) amounts written off goodwill.

The items included in (*b*) above will not, of course, affect the net profit shown in the Financial Profit and Loss Account.

ITEMS SHOWN ONLY IN THE COST ACCOUNTS

There are very few items which appear in the cost accounts and not in the financial accounts. All expenditure incurred, whether for cash or credit, passes through the financial accounting system, so the type of entry which can appear in the cost accounts only is a nominal charge. The following two items are examples of this type of entry.

1. *Interest on capital*

Sometimes management policy is to charge interest on capital employed in production in order to show the nominal cost of employing the capital rather than investing it outside the business.

2. *Charge in lieu of rent*

Again it is sometimes policy to charge a nominal amount for rent of premises owned, so as to be able to compare costs of production in a factory owned by a company with similar costs in a leasehold or rented factory.

However, these two items will not affect the Financial Profit or Loss because they are merely a transfer in the cost accounts, *e.g.*:

Dr. Production Overhead Account.
Cr. Interest on Capital Account.
Dr. Work-in-progress Ledger Control Account.
Cr. Production Overhead Account.
Dr. Interest on Capital Account.
Cr. Profit and Loss Account.

It should be appreciated that the above entries will result in an elimination of the amount of the charge. If one follows through this charge, one can see that the debit was transferred from production overheads to work in progress. From there it would be transferred eventually to Finished Goods Account, then to Cost of Sales Account and finally to Costing Profit and Loss Account. The credit was transferred to Costing Profit and Loss Account from Interest on Capital Account at the end of the accounting period. Thus the cost accounting cycle is complete. If anyone thinks that this complicated cycle has been unnecessary, it should be realised that it has not been in vain; the fact that the charge has been absorbed as a production overhead will result in an increase in the cost of the product, which is the object of the exercise. The arguments for and against the inclusion of interest on capital in costs were discussed on page 203.

A brief example of a Memorandum Reconciliation Account will illustrate the points mentioned above.

SPECIMEN QUESTION

Profit and Loss Account for year ending December 31

	£		£
Office salaries	5,641	Gross profit b/d	27,324
„ expenses	3,257	Dividend received	200
Salesmen's salaries	2,461	Interest on bank deposit	75
Sales expenses	4,652		
Distribution expenses	1,495		
Loss on sale of machinery	975		
Fines	100		
Discount on debentures	50		
Net profit for year c/d	8,968		
	£27,599		£27,599
Taxation	4,000	Net profit b/d	8,968
Reserve	500		
Dividend	2,000		
Balance c/d	2,468		
	£8,968		£8,968

The above accounts have been prepared by the accountant of W.R. Ltd. The cost accountant has prepared his accounts for the year, from which he ascertains a profit of £9,818. Reconcile the two sets of accounts.

ANSWER

Memorandum Reconciliation Account

	£	£		£	£
Items not charged in cost accounts:			Profit as per cost accounts		9,818
Loss on machinery	975		Items not credited in cost account:		
Fines	100		Dividend received	200	
Discount on debentures	50		Interest on bank deposit	75	
	—	1,125		—	275
Profit as per financial accounts		8,968			
		£10,093			£10,093

OVERHEAD

The recovery of overhead is always based on an estimate, *e.g.* percentage on prime cost, percentage on sales, etc., so that the amount recovered and the amount actually incurred will invariably disagree. As was illustrated in the previous chapter, differences may be written off to an Overhead Adjustment Account or direct to Costing Profit and Loss Account, with the result that the actual amount shown in the financial accounts will now agree with that finally charged in the cost accounts. Consequently, when reconciling cost and financial accounts no further adjustment in respect of overheads is necessary.

In some costing systems selling and distribution overheads are ignored, as a result of which the Costing Profit and Loss Account will show a greater profit or smaller loss than that shown by the financial accounts, in which obviously selling and distribution expenses would be included. When preparing a Memorandum Reconciliation Account an adjustment must be made in respect of any such expenses.

SPECIMEN QUESTION

The Profit and Loss Account of B.B. Ltd. is as follows:

Profit and Loss Account for the year ending December 31

	£		£
Office salaries	4,834	Gross profit b/d	25,000
Office expenses	3,214		
Sales manager's salary	1,000		
Salesmen's salaries	4,256		
Sales expenses	3,419		
Packing costs	875		
Distribution expenses	1,246		
Net profit c/d	6,156		
	£25,000		£25,000

The cost accounts revealed a profit for the year of £16,952; selling and distribution overheads had been ignored. Reconcile the cost and financial accounts.

ANSWER

Memorandum Reconciliation Account

	£	£		£
Items not charged in cost A/c:			Profit as per cost accounts	16,952
Sales manager's salary	1,000			
Salesmen's salaries	4,256			
Sales expenses	3,419			
Packing costs	875			
Distribution expenses	1,246			
		10,796		
Profit as per financial A/cs		6,156		
		£16,952		£16,952

DIFFERENT BASES OF STOCK VALUATION

Frequently stocks will appear in the cost accounts at one figure, and in the financial accounts at a different figure, owing to the use of different bases of stock valuation. The financial accountant invariably bases the valuation of his stock on the principle of cost, replacement price or net realisable value, whichever is the lowest, as a matter of financial prudence. However, the cost accountant will value his stock according to the system adopted in the stock accounts, *e.g.* FIFO or LIFO, whichever system he thinks best portrays the cost of the material. As will be appreciated, differences in stock valuations will affect the profits or losses shown by the two sets of books. In preparing a Reconciliation Account, consideration must be given to this important point.

Valuation of work in progress often proves to be very difficult. There are three main bases:

(*a*) Prime cost.
(*b*) Prime cost + Production overhead.
(*c*) Prime cost + Production overhead + Administration overhead.

It is suggested that the second base is perhaps the most suitable because production overhead is usually incurred all the time production is proceeding, but administration overhead is incurred whether production is nil or 100%. It may be remembered that, in the previous chapter, production overhead was charged to work in progress while administration overhead was charged either to finished goods or to Cost of Sales Account.

SPECIMEN QUESTION

The Manufacturing Account of G.B. Ltd. is as follows:

Manufacturing Account for year ended December 31

	£	£		£
Raw materials:			Trading Account:	
Opening stock	25,246		Cost of goods manufactured trans-	
Purchases	112,648		ferred	263,092
	137,894			
Less Closing stock	29,461			
Materials consumed		108,433		
Wages—direct		87,461		
PRIME COST		195,894		
Production overheads:				
Power	21,468			
Wages—indirect	27,428			
Rent and rates	10,641			
Heating and lighting	2,467			
Depreciation	5,835			
Expenses	975			
		68,814		
GROSS WORKS COST		264,708		
Deduct Work in progress:				
Closing stock	17,468			
Less Opening stock	15,852			
		1,616		
		£263,092		£263,092

The Profit and Loss Account reveals a profit of £57,634 for the year. In the cost accounts the valuations placed on stocks were:

Raw materials— Opening stock £25,348
Closing stock £29,371

Work in progress—Opening stock £15,763
Closing stock £17,409

Profit shown in the Costing Profit and Loss Account was £57,472. Prepare a Reconciliation Account.

ANSWER

Memorandum Reconciliation Account

	£			£
Difference in stock:		Profit as per cost accounts		57,472
Work in progress—		Difference in stocks:		
Opening stock	89	Raw materials—	£	
Profit as per financial accounts	57,634	Opening	102	
		Closing	90	
		Work in progress—		
		Closing	59	
				251
	£57,723			£57,723

NOTES

Raw material—Opening stock

The figure used in the cost accounts is £25,348, compared with £25,246 in the financial accounts; thus £102 more was charged in the cost accounts, so financial profit must be reduced.

Raw material—Closing stock

Cost accounts £29,371; financial accounts £29,461.
£90 more credit was taken in the financial accounts, so financial profit must be reduced.

Work in progress—Opening stock

Cost accounts £15,763; financial accounts £15,852.
£89 more was charged in the financial accounts, so financial profit must be increased.

Work in progress—Closing stock

Cost accounts £17,409; financial accounts £17,468.
£59 more credit was taken in the financial accounts, so financial profit must be reduced.

Many students find considerable difficulty in reconciling the different valuations of stocks. To show the effects of a change in stock values, let us consider simplified Trading Accounts for three non-consecutive months:

January	£		£	July	£		£	October	£		£
Opening		Sales	800	Opening		Sales	800	Opening		Sales	800
stock	100	Closing		stock	300	Closing		stock	100	Closing	
Purchases	500	stock	200	Purchases	500	stock	200	Purchases	500	stock	400
Gross				Gross				Gross			
profit	400			profit	200			profit	600		
	£1,000		£1,000		£1,000		£1,000		£1,200		£1,200

During the month of January, it will be noted that the gross profit was £400. In July, the opening stock was greater than that for January by £200 and the profit was correspondingly reduced by that amount. In October, the closing stock was greater than that for January by £200 and the profit was correspondingly increased by that amount. Thus a rule can be propounded:

The larger the opening stock, the lower is the profit.
The larger the closing stock, the larger is the profit.

To consider this in the context of reconciliation of the cost and financial accounts, if the opening stock in the cost accounts is greater than that in the financial accounts, the profit in the cost accounts will be ower than that in the financial accounts. Similarly, if the closing stock in the cost accounts is lower than that in the financial accounts, the profit in the former will be lower than that in the latter.

SPECIMEN QUESTION

The Manufacturing, Trading, Profit and Loss and Profit and Loss Appropriation Accounts of S.B. Ltd. for the year ending December 31 are as follows:

	£	£		£
Raw materials:			Trading Account:	
Opening stock	27,458		Cost of goods manufactured trans-	
Purchases	134,762		ferred	318,466
	162,220			
Less Closing stock	29,326			
		132,894		
Wages—direct		112,378		
PRIME COST		245,272		
Production overhead:				
Power	23,246			
Wages—indirect	31,351			
Rent and rates	10,724			
Heating and lighting	2,841			
Depreciation	6,015			
Expenses	1,020			
		75,197		
GROSS WORKS COST		320,469		
Deduct Work in progress:				
Closing stock	21,382			
Less Opening stock	19,379			
		2,003		
		£318,466		£318,466
Finished goods:			Sales	500,000
Opening stock	20,642			
Goods manufactured	318,466			
	339,108			
Less Closing stock	22,435			
		316,673		
Gross profit c/d		183,327		
		£500,000		£500,000
Office salaries	35,642		Gross profit b/d	183,327
,, expenses	20,326		Dividend received	300
Salesmen's salaries	18,421		Interest on bank deposit	50
Selling expenses	15,263			
Distribution expenses	13,248			
Loss on sale of plant	1,250			
Fines	200			
Interest on mortgage	150			
Net profit for year	79,177			
		£183,677		£183,677
Taxation	25,000		Balance b/d	35,246
General reserve	10,000		Net profit for year	79,177
Ordinary share dividend	20,000			
Preference share dividend	10,000			
Goodwill written off	4,000			
Balance c/d	45,423			
		£114,423		£114,423

The cost accounts revealed a profit of £127,411. In preparing this figure, stocks had been valued as follows:

Raw materials— Opening stock £27,342
Closing stock £29,457

Work in progress—Opening stock £19,488
Closing stock £21,296

Selling and distribution expenses had been ignored in the cost accounts. Prepare a Reconciliation Account.

ANSWER

Memorandum Reconciliation Account

	£	£			£
Items not charged in cost accounts:			Profit as per cost accounts		127,411
	£	£	Items not credited in cost accounts:	£	
Loss on sale of plant	1,250				
Fines	200		Dividend received	300	
Interest	150		Interest	50	
		1,600			350
Salesmen's salaries	18,421		Difference in stocks:		
Selling expenses	15,263		Work in progress—		
Distribution expenses	13,248		Opening	109	
		46,932	Closing	86	
					195
		48,532			
Difference in stocks:					
Raw materials—					
Opening	116				
Closing	131				
		247			
Profit as per financial accounts		79,177			
		£127,956			£127,956

Sometimes in examination questions the profit as per the cost accounts is not revealed, and one is required to ascertain the profit and also prepare a Reconciliation Account. The account should be prepared in the usual way shown above, a blank being left for the profit figure; the account is then balanced and the balancing amount inserted in the blank space provided.

It is possible to prepare a Memorandum Reconciliation in the form of a statement as an alternative method of presentation. The statement would appear as follows:

Memorandum Reconciliation Statement

	£	£
Profit as per cost accounts		127,411
Less Items not charged in cost accounts:		
Loss on sale of plant	1,250	
Fines	200	
Interest	150	
		1,600
		125,811
Add Items not credited in cost accounts:		
Dividend received	300	
Interest	50	
		350
Carried forward		126,161

		Brought forward	126,161

Less Selling and distribution expenses:

Salesmen's salaries		18,421	
Selling expenses		15,263	
Distribution expenses		13,248	
		——	46,932
			79,229

Add Difference in stocks:

Work in progress—Opening		109	
Closing		86	
		——	195
			79,424

Less Difference in stocks:

Raw materials—Opening		116	
Closing		131	
		——	247
Profit as per financial accounts			£79,177

EXAMINATION QUESTIONS

1. Indicate the reasons why it is usually necessary for the cost and financial records of a factory to be reconciled and explain the main sources of difference which might enter into such a reconciliation.

(*C.A.A. Final*)

2. The profit disclosed by the Manufacturing Account prepared from the cost books is in excess of that shown by the Trading Account prepared from the financial books. To what could such difference be attributable, and what steps would you take to obviate or minimise similar differences in future?

(*A.I.A.Final*)

3. A business expanding rapidly uses historical costing methods. Towards the end of a year the reconciliation of cost and financial accounts reveals considerable difference between overheads incurred and overheads absorbed in production. It is suggested that the differences would not have occurred if a standard costing system had been used.

Give your views on this suggestion, indicate the type of difference likely to have arisen, and show how the difference would have been avoided and/or indicated in standard costing.

(*I.C.W.A. Final*)

4. (a) Why is it important that cost and financial accounts should be capable of reconciliation one with the other?

(b) Give three examples of items which would not normally appear in the cost accounts, though they would quite properly be taken into account in the Financial Revenue Accounts.

(I.C.A. Final)

5. You are requested to investigate the costing system in operation in a manufacturing business where the profit shown by the cost accounts is greatly in excess of the profit shown by the financial accounts. Assuming any data you deem advisable, indicate any defects you found in the present system with particular reference to the discrepancy between the results shown by the two sets of accounts, and suggest any amendments you consider advisable to ensure closer agreement between the results shown by the cost and financial accounts.

(C.A.A. Inter.)

6. During the year a company's profits have been estimated from the costing system to be £23,063, whereas the final accounts prepared by the auditors disclose a profit of £16,624. Given the following information, you are required to:

(a) prepare a Reconciliation Statement showing clearly the reasons for the difference;

(b) describe an alternative accounting system which would obviate the need for reconciling the financial and cost accounts.

Profit and Loss Account
year ended March 31

	£	£		£
Opening stocks	247,179		Sales	346,500
Purchases	82,154			
	329,333			
Closing stocks	75,121			
		254,212		
Direct wages		23,133		
Factory overhead		20,826		
Gross profit c/d		48,329		
		£346,500		£346,500
Administration		9,845	Gross profit b/d	48,329
Selling expenses		22,176	Sundry income	316
Net profit		16,624		
		£48,645		£48,645

The costing records show:

(a) a Stock Ledger closing balance of £78,197;

(b) a Direct Wages Absorption Account with a closing credit balance of £24,867;

(c) a Factory Overhead Absorption Account with a closing credit balance of £19,714;

(d) administration expenses calculated as 3% of the selling price;

(e) selling prices include 5% for selling expenses;

(f) no mention of sundry income.

(I.C.W.A. Inter.)

7. The following is a summary of the Trading and Profit and Loss Account of A.B. Ltd. for year ending December 31:

	£			£
Materials consumed	68,500	Sales (60,000 units)		150,000
Wages	37,750	Finished stock (2,000		
Factory expenses	20,750	units)		4,000
Administration expenses	9,560	Work in progress—	£	
Selling and distribution		Materials	1,600	
expenses	11,250	Wages	900	
Preliminary expenses w/o	1,000	Factory expenses	500	
Goodwill w/o	500			3,000
Net profit	8,140	Dividends		450
	£157,450			£157,450

The company manufactures a standard unit.

In the cost accounts factory expenses have been allocated to production at 20% of prime cost, administration expenses at £0·15 per unit, and selling and distribution expenses at £0·20 per unit. The net profit shown by the cost accounts was £8,200.

Prepare:

(a) control accounts for factory expenses, administration expenses, and selling and distribution expenses;

(b) a statement reconciling the profit disclosed by the cost records with that shown in the financial accounts.

(I.C.W.A. Inter.)

8. You are required, as the cost accountant of a manufacturing organisation, to prepare a statement reconciling the financial records with the cost records. You are also required to write briefly on the possible causes of such differences between the two sets of records as disclosed by the comparison. The following information relating to the operations for a given month has been supplied to you:

(a) Extract from Profit and Loss Statement prepared from financial books:

	£	£	£
Sales			36,128
Less Cost of goods sold			
Stock at beginning of period—			
Raw material	3,984		
Work in progress	2,216		
Finished goods	7,842		
		14,042	
Raw materials		10,224	
Direct wages		7,163	
Manufacturing expenses		5,289	
		36,718	
Less Stock at end of period—			
Raw material	4,285		
Work in progress	3,072		
Finished goods	8,177		
		15,534	
			21,184
Gross profit			£14,944

(b) Data obtained from costing records:

	£	£
Work in process at beginning of period—		
Material	956	
Wages	700	
Expenses, 80% of wages	560	
		2,216
Work in process at end of period—		
Material	1,398	
Wages	930	
Expenses, 80% of wages	744	
		3,072
Material and wages charged to work in process during period—		
Material		9,528
Wages		6,634

(I.C.W.A. Final)

9. (a) Discuss how the results shown by the costing books and those shown by the financial books may be reconciled, and the reasons why such reconciliation is important.

(b) According to the cost books the profit for the year was £48,390.

The financial books of the company disclosed the following position:

Manufacturing Account

	£	£		£
Raw materials opening stock	1,900		Transfer to Finished Stock Account	111,400
Purchases, *less* Returns	54,900			
	56,800			
Less Closing stock	1,800			
		55,000		
Direct labour		35,500		
Factory overhead		21,400		
		111,900		
Work in progress:				
Opening	8,400			
Closing	8,900			
		500		
Factory cost of production		£111,400		£111,400

Finished Stock Account

	£		£
Opening stock	11,600	Cost of sales transferred to Trading Account	110,700
Transfer from Manufacturing Account	111,400	Closing stock	12,300
	£123,000		£123,000

Trading Account

	£		£
Factory cost of sales transferred from Stock Account	110,700	Sales	184,500
Gross profit c/d	73,800		
	£184,500		£184,500

Profit and Loss Account

	£		£
Administration expenses	15,600	Gross profit b/d	73,800
Distribution expenses	10,182	Discounts received	1,806
Discounts allowed	1,511	Bank interest received	37
Debenture interest	850	Dividends received	300
Fines	500		
Losses of a non-trading nature	350		
Net profit	46,950		
	£75,943		£75,943

The valuations in the cost books were as follows:

	Opening balance	Closing balance
	£	£
Raw materials	1,969	1,850
Work in progress	8,280	8,730
Finished stock	11,396	12,810

Depreciation amounting to £6,146 was charged in the cost books, whereas factory overhead in the financial books included £5,873 for this expense heading.

The profit shown in the cost books has been arrived at after charging notional rent £1,500 and interest on capital £3,000.

You are requested to show the reconciliation of the cost and financial books in an orderly manner.

(A.C.C.A. Inter.)

10. L. Engineering Co. Ltd. keep their financial accounts separate from their cost accounts. In the Cost Ledger on January 1, the balances were as follows:

	£
Stores Ledger control	10,000
Work-in-progress control	15,500
Finished stock control	3,500
Cost Ledger control	29,000

Transactions for the year ended December 31 were:

		£
Purchase of raw materials		55,000
	£	
Wages—direct	79,000	
indirect	21,000	
		100,000
Factory overhead expenses: incurred		36,000
absorbed		55,000
Administration overhead expenses: incurred		12,500
absorbed		12,400

	£
Selling overhead expenses: incurred	7,500
absorbed	7,600
Materials issued to production	57,500
Sales	265,000
Work in progress: value at December 31	13,500
Finished stock: value at December 31	4,000

It is established that the following items have been recorded in the financial accounts only:

	£
Debenture interest paid	8,000
Loss on sale of investment	2,500
Dividends received	3,000

The value of stocks and work in progress in the company's balance sheets were as follows:

	£
As at January 1	31,000
As at December 31	24,500

You are required to:

(a) show the accounts in the Cost Ledger for the year ended December 31;

(b) prepare a statement reconciling the profit disclosed by the cost accounts with the profit prior to taxation shown in the financial accounts.

(I.C.W.A. Final)

CHAPTER 16

INTEGRAL ACCOUNTS

In many large firms the system of integral or integrated accounts has been adopted. Under this system one set of accounts only is operated, as distinct from the costing section keeping their records and the financial section maintaining their accounts. This eliminates the necessity of operating Cost Ledger Control Accounts and of reconciling the cost and financial accounts. In some of the earlier chapters in this book a brief introduction to integral accounting was given, especially in connection with wages accounting. It is proposed in this chapter to give two comprehensive illustrations taken from the examinations of the Institute of Cost and Works Accountants.

Basically, the integral accounts system is similar to the separate accounting and costing systems, except that of course it eliminates the duplication of entries, and the maintenance of unnecessary accounts.

EXAMPLE 1

Purchases of £10,000 of raw materials on credit.

This would be recorded in an accounting system:

	£	£
Dr. Purchases Account	10,000	
Cr. Creditors Account		10,000
(Dr. Cost Ledger Control Account—memorandum only)		

In the cost accounting system, omitting Materials Control Account.

	£	£
Dr. Stores Ledger Control Account	10,000	
Cr. General Ledger Adjustment Account		10,000

However, in an integral accounting system the entries would be:

	£	£
Dr. Stores Account	10,000	
Cr. Creditors Account		10,000

It will be observed that the essential points are recorded in both systems, *viz.* stores and creditors.

EXAMPLE 2

Paid wages in cash £5,000.

In financial books:

	£	£
Dr. Wages Account	5,000	
Cr. Cash Account		5,000
(Dr. Cost Ledger Control Account—memorandum only)		

In cost books:

	£	£
Dr. Wages Control Account	5,000	
Cr. General Ledger Adjustment Account		5,000

However, in an integral accounting system:

	£	£
Dr. Wages Control Account	5,000	
Cr. Cash Account		5,000

It will again be observed that the essential points are recorded in both systems, *viz.* wages and cash.

Readers may care to refer to the accounting entries in Chapter 14 on cost control accounts and try to visualise how the entries would appear in an integrated accounting system.

THE THIRD-ENTRY METHOD

There is a method of integral accounting known as the third-entry method. This system is very similar to the one described above, except that a third entry is made in respect of elements of cost. All items of cost, *e.g.* purchases, are debited in total in a Cost Ledger Control Account, and credited to a Creditor's Account. The cost is then analysed into Third-entry Accounts (which are not part of a double-entry system) in respect of materials, factory overheads, administration overheads, etc. The totals of these accounts are then transferred to Finished Goods Account, Profit and Loss Account, etc., the double entry being in the Cost Control Account. However, it is felt that ordinary double-entry principles are sufficient, because the analysis work described in the third-entry method would be obtainable from the job cards, standing order cards, etc. This method is discussed and illustrated in *Principles and Practice of Management Accountancy*, by J. L. Brown and L. R. Howard (Macdonald and Evans Ltd., 1969).

Two further illustrations of integral accounting are now included which should show clearly how the principles of double-entry accounting are observed. Both examples are taken from examinations of the Institute of Cost and Works Accountants.

SPECIMEN QUESTION

As at November 30, the following balances existed in a company's integrated Standard Costs and Financial Accounts:

Balance Sheet Accounts

	£'000	
Capital and reserves	300	
Creditors and accruals	88	
Fixed assets	140	
Raw materials in store and process	80	
Direct wages in process	20	(at standard)
Factory overheads in process	10	
Finished stock	90	
Debtors	100	
Cash at bank	10	

Trading Accounts

Budgeted sales	585	
Sales variances	12	(Debit)
Standard factory cost of sales	493	
Material variance	5	(Credit)
Direct wages variance	7	(Debit)
Factory overhead variance	2	(Debit)
Administration and selling expenses	14	

During December the following transactions took place:

Budgeted sales	105	
Actual sales	98	
Cash received—from debtors	95	
Cash paid—to creditors	63	
Cash paid—direct wages	23	
Raw materials purchased	40	(actual cost)
Excess materials issued	1	(at standard)
Factory expenses incurred	17	
Administration and selling expenses incurred	3	
Output finished (at standard cost):		
Materials	50	
Direct wages	26	
Factory overhead	13	
Standard factory cost of actual sales	82	

The standard cost of materials purchased is £42,000.
The closing valuations of Work-in-progress Accounts (which are debited at actual and credited at standard) are:

	£
Direct wages (at standard)	15,000
Factory overhead (at standard)	13,000

You are required to:

    (*a*) write up and close off the ledger accounts; and
    (*b*) prepare a trial balance of the closing balances.

ANSWER

    NOTE: For illustration purposes a Profit and Loss Account and Balance Sheet have been prepared, but the trial balance called for by the question has not been shown.

Capital and Reserves Account

	Balance b/d	£300,000

Creditors and Accruals Account

	£		£
Bank	63,000	Balance b/d	88,000
Balance c/d	85,000	Purchases	40,000
		Expenses:	
		Factory	17,000
		Administration	3,000
	£148,000		£148,000
		Balance b/d	85,000

Fixed Assets Accounts

Balance b/d	£140,000

Raw materials in Store and in Process Account

	£		£
Balance b/d	80,000	Finished goods	51,000
Creditors	42,000	Balance c/d	71,000
	£122,000		£122,000
Balance b/d	71,000		

Direct wages in Process Account

	£		£
Balance b/d	20,000	Finished goods	26,000
Bank	23,000	Wages Variance Account	2,000
		Balance c/d	15,000
	£43,000		£43,000
Balance b/d	15,000		

Factory overhead in Process Account

	£		£
Balance b/d	10,000	Finished goods	13,000
Creditors	17,000	Overhead variance	1,000
		Balance c/d	13,000
	£27,000		£27,000
Balance b/d	£13,000		

Finished Stock Account

	£		£
Balance b/d	90,000	Sales	82,000
Raw materials	50,000	Balance c/d	97,000
Labour	26,000		
Factory overheads	13,000		
	£179,000		£179,000
Balance b/d	97,000		

Debtor's Account

	£		£
Balance b/d	100,000	Bank	95,000
Sales	98,000	Balance c/d	103,000
	£198,000		£198,000
Balance b/d	103,000		

Cash at Bank Account

	£		£
Balance b/d	10,000	Creditors	63,000
Debtors	95,000	Wages	23,000
		Balance c/d	19,000
	£105,000		£105,000
Balance b/d	19,000		

Budgeted Sales Account

	£		£
Profit and loss	690,000	Balance b/d	585,000
		Debtors	105,000
	£690,000		£690,000

Sales Variance Account

	£		£
Balance b/d	12,000	Profit and loss	19,000
Debtors	7,000		
	£19,000		£19,000

Cost of Sales Account

	£		£
Balance b/d	493,000	Profit and loss	575,000
Finished goods	82,000		
	£575,000		£575,000

Materials Variance Account

	£		£
Raw materials	1,000	Balance b/d	5,000
Profit and loss	6,000	Purchases	2,000
	£7,000		£7,000

Direct Wages Variance Account

	£		£
Balance b/d	7,000	Profit and loss	9,000
Wages	2,000		
	£9,000		£9,000

Factory Overhead Variance Account

	£		£
Balance b/d	2,000	Profit and loss	3,000
Overhead	1,000		
	£3,000		£3,000

Administration and Selling Expenses Account

	£		£
Balance b/d	14,000	Profit and loss	17,000
Creditors	3,000		
	£17,000		£17,000

Profit and Loss Account for period ending December 31

	£		£
Cost of sales	575,000	Budgeted sales	690,000
Sales variance	19,000	Material variance	6,000
Wages variance	9,000		
Factory overhead variance	3,000		
Administration and selling	17,000		
Net profit	73,000		
	£696,000		£696,000

Balance Sheet as at December 31

	£	£		£	£
Capital	300,000		Fixed assets		140,000
Net profit	73,000		Stock	97,000	
		373,000	Materials	71,000	
Creditor		85,000	Wages in process	15,000	
			Overhead in process	13,000	
					196,000
			Debtors	103,000	
			Bank	19,000	
					122,000
		£458,000			£458,000

SPECIMEN QUESTION

Record in ledger accounts in integral account form the under-noted transactions, give effect to the additional information provided and close off the accounts as at the end of the period.

Trial balance at beginning of period

	£	£
Cash	3,000	
Debtors	26,000	
Stock—Raw materials	22,000	
Work in progress	14,000	
Finished goods	6,000	
Plant and machinery	60,000	
Buildings	10,000	
Share capital		100,000
General reserve		10,000
Profit and loss		2,000
Creditors		29,000
	£141,000	£141,000

Transactions during period

	£
Purchases—credit—materials	15,000
"expenses"	500
cash— "expenses"	500
Materials used—product direct	12,000
service dept. A direct	1,000
service dept. B direct	500
production dept.	2,500
"Expense" allotted to products	200
to service dept. A	200
to service dept. B	400
to production dept.	200
to administration and selling	100

Wages and salaries—service dept. A		200
service dept. B		400
production dept.		3,500
administration and selling		900
Deductions from salaries—P.A.Y.E.		700
funds		100
Sales—production cost plus 16⅔%		28,000

Additional information

Rate of apportionment of cost of service dept. A	30% of cost of all materials
Rate of apportionment of cost of service dept. B	40% of production dept. wages and salaries
Rate of apportionment of cost of production dept.	£2 per unit of product
Number of units of product produced and completed at cost of at £5 each	4,000
Depreciation	1% of value of plant and machinery and ½% of value of buildings to be charged to production dept.

ANSWER

Cash Account

	£		£
Balance b/d	3,000	Expenses	500
Balance c/d	1,700	Wages	4,200
	£4,700		£4,700
		Balance b/d	1,700

Debtors Account

	£		£
Balance b/d	26,000	Balance c/d	54,000
Sales	28,000		
	£54,000		£54,000
Balance b/d	54,000		

Stock—Raw Materials Account

	£		£
Balance b/d	22,000	Work in progress	12,000
Purchases	15,000	Service dept. A	1,000
		Service dept. B	500
		Production dept.	2,500
		Balance c/d	21,000
	£37,000		£37,000
Balance b/d	21,000		

Work-in-progress Account

	£		£
Balance b/d	14,000	Finished goods	20,000
Raw materials	12,000	Balance c/d	15,450
Production dept.	9,250		
Expenses	200		
	£35,450		£35,450
Balance b/d	15,450		

Stock—Finished Goods Account

	£		£
Balance b/d	6,000	Profit and loss	24,000
Work in progress	20,000	Balance c/d	2,000
	£26,000		£26,000
Balance b/d	2,000		

Plant and Machinery Account

Balance b/d	£60,000		

Buildings Account

Balance b/d	£10,000		

Share Capital Account

		Balance b/d	£100,000

General Reserve Account

		Balance b/d	£10,000

Profit and Loss Appropriation Account

	£		£
Balance c/d	4,800	Balance b/d	2,000
		Net profit	2,800
	£4,800		£4,800
		Balance b/d	4,800

Creditor's Account

	£		£
Balance c/d	44,500	Balance b/d	29,000
		Purchases	15,000
		Expenses	500
	£44,500		£44,500
		Balance b/d	44,500

Expenses Account

	£		£
Creditors	500	Work in progress	200
Cash	500	Service dept. A	200
Profit and loss	100	Service dept. B	400
		Production dept.	200
		Administration and selling	100
	£1,100		£1,100

Wages and Salaries Control Account

	£		£
To wages payable	5,000	Service dept. A	200
		Service dept. B	400
		Production dept.	3,500
		Administration and selling	900
	£5,000		£5,000

Wages Payable Account

	£		£
P.A.Y.E.	700	Wages control	5,000
Funds	100		
Cash	4,200		
	£5,000		£5,000

P.A.Y.E.

			£
		Wages payable	£700

Funds Account

			£
		Wages payable	£100

Service Dept. A Account

	£		£
Stores	1,000	Service dept. B	200
Expenses	200	Production dept.	1,000
Wages	200	Profit and loss	200
	£1,400		£1,400

Service Dept. B Account

	£		£
Stores	500	Production dept.	1,400
Expenses	400	Profit and loss	100
Wages	400		
Service dept. A	200		
	£1,500		£1,500

Production Dept. Account

	£		£
Stores	2,500	Work in progress—	
Expenses	200	Units completed	8,000
Wages	3,500	Units not completed	1,250
Service dept. A	1,000		
Service dept. B	1,400		
Depreciation on plant	600		
Depreciation on buildings	50		
	£9,250		£9,250

Administration and Selling Expenses Account

	£		£
Expenses	100	Profit and loss	1,000
Wages	900		
	£1,000		£1,000

Depreciation Provision on Plant and Machinery Account

			£
		Production dept.	£600

Depreciation Provision on Building Account

			£
		Production dept.	£50

Profit and Loss Account for period

	£		£
Finished goods	24,000	Expenses—over-recovered	100
Administration and selling expenses	1,000	Sales	28,000
Service dept. A } under-recovered	200		
Service dept. B }	100		
Net profit	2,800		
	£28,100		£28,100

Trial Balance at end of period

	£	£
Cash		1,700
Debtors	54,000	
Stock:		
Raw material	21,000	
Work in progress	15,450	
Finished goods	2,000	
Plant and machinery	60,000	
Buildings	10,000	
Share capital		100,000
General reserve		10,000
Profit and loss appropriation		4,800
Creditors		44,500
P.A.Y.E.		700
Funds		100
Depreciation provision on plant and machinery		600
Depreciation provision on buildings		50
	£162,450	£162,450

NOTES

1. Cost of goods sold is calculated:

Sales = Production cost + $16\frac{2}{3}\%$ = £28,000.
Therefore cost   = £24,000.

2. Service dept. A apportionment:

Materials used by depts.	A	1,000
	B	500
	Production	2,500
		£4,000

$$4,000 \times \frac{30}{100} = 1,200.$$

This cost is allocated between:

Dept. B $\frac{500}{3,000} \times 1,200 = £200.$

Production dept. $\frac{2,500}{3,000} \times 1,200 = £1,000.$

3. Service dept. B is apportioned:

$$\frac{40}{100} \times 3,500 = £1,400.$$

4. Production dept. is absorbed:

4,000 units at £2 = £8,000.

The total cost of the dept. was £9,250, and, since only £8,000 has been absorbed, the balance of £1,250 has been regarded as being the production dept.'s contribution to work in progress.

This can be checked:

	£	£
Work-in-progress balance at beginning		14,000
„ „ „ end		15,450
Increase of		£1,450

Represented by:		
Direct expenses	200	
Production dept.	1,250	
		£1,450

5. It will be observed that there is a credit balance on the Cash Account. In practice, this should not happen, but in this question full information has not been given; *e.g.* there has been no cash received from debtors.

EXAMINATION QUESTIONS

1. What do you understand by "integrated" accounts, and what are the principles involved?

(Com. A. Final)

2. Set out your views on the separation and integration of costing and financial accounting records.

(*A.I.A. Final*)

3. It is proposed to integrate the cost and financial accounts in a company in which they have previously been separate. State the advantages to be derived from this process and the main adjustments to procedure which will be needed.

Also show how the process might affect the organisation of the cost department and its relation to other departments.

(*I.C.W.A. Final*)

4. (*a*) What do you understand by integral accounts?

(*b*) Design a code of accounts illustrating the principles of integral accounts in a limited-liability company selling a single standardised product which passes through one production department.

(*I.C.W.A. Inter.*)

5. From the following information relating to a year's operations, you are required to compile and close off the cost and financial accounts of a company whose accounts are integrated and prepare a trial balance:

Balances at beginning of period	Actual £	Standard £
Customers	185,000	
Suppliers	84,000	
Cash	39,000	
Materials		40,000
Fixed assets	200,000	
Depreciation provision	94,000	
Work in progress		60,000
Investments	12,000	
Ordinary share capital	300,000	
Profit and Loss Account (credit)	58,000	

Transactions during year		
Sales	404,000	385,000
Cost of sales		249,000
Wages (gross) (70% direct)	112,000	
Materials issued (85% direct)		106,000
Materials purchased	137,000	131,000
Materials returned	4,000	5,000
Cash paid—		
Wages	102,000	
Expenses	7,000	
Suppliers	125,000	
Interim dividend	23,000	

Transactions during year		*Actual*	*Standard*
		£	£
Cash received—			
From customers		416,000	
Income from investments		4,000	
Overhead allowance			65,000
Variances—adverse:			
Direct wages—rate	3% of actual		
efficiency	4% ,, ,,		
methods	3% ,, ,,		
Indirect materials—price	4% of standard		

Depreciation at 10% is to be charged to costs.

(I.C.W.A. Final)

6. Give journal entries (narratives are not required) to give effect to the double-entry principles of integral accounting in respect of the following:

	£
(a) Payment of—	
Net wages cheque	800
National Insurance cheque	100
And the deduction from wages of P.A.Y.E. tax	100
(b) Allocation of gross wages and National Insurance—	
Direct wages (in progress)	600
Departmental indirect wages	150
(Wages are paid a week in arrear.)	
(c) Credit purchases of raw materials	2,000
and returnable packages	120
(d) Charging into departmental costs of a proportion of annually paid insurances	70
(e) Credit charging by outside engineers of departmental plant repairs	240
(f) Payment of supplier's accounts (after £60 taken for cash discounts)	1,130
(g) Factory cost of production of finished stocks	10,000
(Ratios: direct materials, 12; direct wages, 2; factory overheads, 6.)	
(h) Factory cost of finished stocks sold	8,000
(i) Sale of finished stocks on credit (after allowing £370 sales rebates)	10,370
(j) Payment by customers of credit sales (after taking £120 in cash discounts)	13,380

(I.C.W.A. Inter.)

7. For a certain week the wages and costing records of a company with two production departments show the following:

	Department A	Department B
Gross wages paid:	£	£
Direct	862	700
Indirect and supervision	224	137

	Total
	£
Employer's contributions:	
National Insurance	82
Selective employment tax	126
State graduated pension	110
Employees' deductions:	
P.A.Y.E. tax	186
National Insurance	82
State graduated pension	110
Hospital fund	42

	Department A	Department B
Production in units:		
Product X	2,763	2,644
Product Y	4,632	1,302
Standard minutes allowed per unit:		
Product X	20	30
Product Y	15	40
Actual hours worked	2,469	1,710
Standard rate per hour	£0·33½	£0·40

NOTES

1. With the exception of National Insurance, all other employees' deductions and employer's contributions remain unpaid.

2. Employer's cost of National Insurance and state graduated pension are charged to a "Works Overhead Account."

3. Employer's cost of selective employment tax is to be charged to a "Selective Employment Tax Recoverable Account."

4. Work in progress is to be charged with actual cost and credited with standard cost and variances.

Using the above information you are required to:

(a) calculate the appropriate wage variances for each department;

(b) prepare a summary of (a) for presentation to works management;

(c) open the appropriate accounts and post the entries as they would appear in an integrated accounting system;

(d) give the make-up of the net wages cheque.

(*I.C.W.A. Inter.*)

8. R. Ltd. operates an integrated accounting system. Materials received into store are recorded at actual prices and issued from store at standard prices. Direct materials price variance is calculated at the time of issue. The following transactions relate to Material 1568 which has a standard price of £0·25 per unit:

April 1   Ordered 1,200 units at £0·27½ each.
       17   Received 800 units, which were invoiced.
       18   Issued to production maintenance 60 units.
       19   Returned to supplier 100 units which were faulty; full credit was allowed.
       22   Issued to production 200 units.
       23   Fire destroyed 100 units; claim submitted to insurance company.
       24   Transferred 40 units from production department to production maintenance.
       25   Returned to store from production department 20 units.
       26   Received 500 units, which were invoiced.
       29   Issued to production 300 units.
       30   Insurance company agreed fire claim in respect of stock destroyed on April 23.
       30   Paid supplier £180 on account.
       30   Physical inventory of 550 units recorded.

Record the above transactions by means of journal entries. All accounting entries including cash should be shown but narrations are not required.

(I.C.W.A. Inter.)

9. Record in ledger accounts in integral form the following transactions giving effect to the additional information provided, and closing off at the end of the month.

Trial balance at beginning of month

	£	£
Share capital		100,000
General reserve		15,000
Profit and Loss Appropriation Account		8,000
Plant and machinery	87,000	
Plant and machinery depreciation		20,000
Stock (materials)	14,200	
Work in progress	12,000	
Stock (finished products)	20,600	
Sales Ledger control	38,400	
Bought Ledger control		40,000
Bank	10,800	
	£183,000	£183,000

Transactions for month	£	£
Purchases:		
Materials for stock	18,720	
Materials (direct to products)	1,480	
Works overheads (materials and services)	1,700	
Administration, selling and distribution overhead (materials and services)	2,320	
Plant and machinery	1,180	
		25,400
Wages:		
Cash drawn for wages	7,300	
Cash drawn for N.I. stamps	485	
P.A.Y.E. deductions not yet paid to the Inland Revenue	365	
		8,150
Wages direct to products	7,085	
Factory indirect labour	1,065	
	£8,150	
Salaries (administration, selling and distribution)		825
Other cash disbursements (administration, selling and distribution)		255
Depreciation to be provided at 10% of original cost for one month (ignore additions)		
Rent £1,200 per annum. One month to be provided for and apportioned 75% factory and 25% offices		
Issues:		
Production	14,870	
Expense materials	1,250	
		16,120
Works overheads—recovery rate 65% of direct wages		26,840
Factory cost of work in progress at end of month		13,200
Stock of finished products at end of month		22,450
Sales for month		29,700
		(I.C.W.A. Final)

10. At the beginning of the current financial year the following list of balances was extracted from the integrated accounts of a manufacturing company:

	£
Debtors	180,000
Creditors	115,000
Cash	54,000
Fixed assets at cost	350,000
Raw materials at standard	85,000
Finished goods at standard	50,000
Work in progress at standard	90,000
Depreciation, fixed assets	95,000

	£
Investments	20,000
Ordinary share capital	500,000
Profit and loss, credit balance	119,000

The following information is provided of transactions in the first quarter of the current financial year:

	Actual £	Standard £
Direct wages	22,000	21,000
Materials issued to production at standard prices	36,500	35,000
Purchase of raw materials, on credit	41,500	40,000
Factory overhead, including indirect wages and £4,000 depreciation	20,100	
Factory overhead absorbed, at 95% normal capacity		19,000
Administration, selling and distribution expenses	13,000	
		Budget
Sales, on credit	97,600	£100,000

The cash transactions are as follows:

		£
Payments:	Net wages	26,500 (after subtracting deductions £3,500)
	Creditors	70,000
Receipts:	Debtors	100,000

Overhead expenses (except wages) should be regarded as credit transactions.

At the end of the quarter the following balances have been calculated on a basis of standard costs:

	£
Work in progress	95,000
Finished goods	48,000

Wages earned during the quarter have all been paid.

The following adverse variances have been calculated and with the other variances to be ascertained are to be charged against profit:

	£
Overhead expenditure	100
Sales price	1,400
Labour rate	1,200

You are required to:

(a) record the above information in integral form in the books of the company;
(b) prepare for presentation to management the interim:

(i) Profit and Loss Account for the quarter;
(ii) balance sheet at end of the quarter.

(*I.C.W.A. Final*)

11. You are required to record the under-noted transactions in the accounts in the Financial and Cost Ledgers which are affected by them. The cost and

financial books are integrated. You are required to prove the accuracy of
your work by taking out a trial balance.

	£
Materials purchased during period—	
At cost	32,856
At standard	29,324
Salaries—	
Research and development	3,900
Production	5,400
Selling	3,800
Distribution	1,600
Administration	2,100
Wages—	
Research and development	950
Production	14,680
Selling	1,300
Distribution	4,920
Administration	1,150
Supplies—	
Research and development	940
Production	1,350
Selling	540
Distribution	2,920
Administration	750
Expenses—	
Research and development	1,800
Production	3,640
Selling	980
Distribution	430
Administration	1,340
Cheques drawn in favour of trade creditors	46,500
Cheques drawn for salaries, wages, supplies and expenses	41,000
Deductions made from wages and salaries	4,900
Stock of materials on hand at beginning of period at standard	10,640
Trade creditors at beginning of period	29,440
Cash at bank at beginning of period	56,820
Sales during period—	
At actual	97,500
At standard	72,100
Trade debtors at beginning of period	51,430
Cash received from trade debtors	48,600

Discount allowed—
  To customers   1,250
  By suppliers   1,890

Depreciation—
  Financial provision   4,200
  Charge against costs   4,950

Research expenditure capitalised   2,000
Cost of work carried out on new factory extension by building
    maintenance department   2,600
Notional rent of freehold factory   1,000

                                        (*I.C.W.A. Final*)

CHAPTER 17

CONTRACT COSTS

IN contract costing the principles of job costing are applied, and a separate cost account is kept for each individual contract or job undertaken. Builders, civil-engineering contractors, constructional and mechanical-engineering firms and similar concerns make use of this type of cost accountancy. Factory job costing is more detailed, and is dealt with in the next chapter.

THE PROCEDURE

It is usual to give each contract a distinguishing number, to facilitate reference in the books and on the various forms which are used. This number identifies the cost account to which are charged the labour, materials and expenses.

THE COST OF MATERIALS

Stores material

Materials from the store are issued against a material requisition (Fig. 9) which is the authority of the storekeeper to issue. Each requisition bears the number of the job for which it is required, and a weekly or monthly summary may be made, called a material issue analysis, in which an analysis of materials chargeable to job numbers may be made (*see* Fig. 61). The total value of the material under each job number is then debited to the appropriate cost account bearing the same number.

In most cases no analysis sheet is now prepared, postings being made direct from the priced requisitions, or, rather, from machine-added summaries for each job number.

Direct material

Sometimes material is purchased outside, or manufactured in the works, for a particular job or contract. The cost of this material will usually be debited direct to the cost account for the job concerned.

In the case of large constructional contracts, sub-contracts for specialised work or material—*e.g.* polished granite or heavy steel girders—are placed with specialist suppliers, and the cost is a direct debit to the contract.

291

Materials returned to store

It is sometimes necessary to issue certain kinds of material in excess of requirements, as, for instance, cement, bricks, pipes, man-hole covers, etc. The surplus is later returned to the store, accompanied by a material return note, which gives details of the material returned, and states the job to be credited.

													No. 12		
												Week ending: February 7, 19...			
Job No. 90		Job No. 91		Job No. 98		Job No. 100		R. 13		N. 31		Summary			
I.R. No.	£	I.R. No.	£	I.R. No.	£	I.R. No.	£	I.R. No.	£	I.R. No.	£	Job No.	£	Cost Led. fol.	
91	4	93	1	92	8	94	2	96	8	88	6	90	7	
95	3	97	3			98	1	99	3	89	6	91	4	
								90	1			98	8	
												100	3	
												R. 13	12	
												N. 31	12	
	£7		£4		£8		£3		£12		£12		£46	

FIG. 61.—*Material issue analysis sheet*

A form like this is admirable for summarising stores requisitions when the office has no equipment to provide machine-added summaries.

Materials on site

At the end of each accounting period the value of materials on site is carried forward as a charge against the next period. It should be noted that, although this is the usual practice, in a few special cases the terms and conditions of the contract may allow for payment on account to be made in respect of materials on site.

THE COST OF LABOUR

Method of remuneration

Generally speaking, the method employed on contracts is by means of an hourly rate, with a bonus addition if work is completed to time.

Calculation of wages

On large engineering contracts it is customary to have a resident timekeeper—one for about every 300 men—who is responsible for noting down the attendance of the men, working out their pay on the time sheets and sending the pay sheets complete to head office by a specified time each week.

Payment of wages

The pay packets are made up by the head office's cashier, after the pay sheets have been checked, and the packets and a copy of the sheets are taken out to the contract by a responsible member of the staff— possibly an engineer who is visiting the site. On more distant sites arrangements have to be made with a bank to cash the weekly wages cheque for the contract cashier, subject to an agreed maximum. The foreman, or ganger, will be present when wages are paid out, and only those present to receive their wages will be paid. Any packets left over will be taken or sent back to head office, and not left on the contract. On written request, head office will post off a money order to the address given, if it agrees with that on the National Insurance card, or is vouched for by the contract foreman. Payment of wages by cheque, if it becomes common, will save a great deal of trouble for all concerned; however, it is doubtful whether such a method of payment could ever be applied to the changing population on civil-engineering contracts.

Wages analysis sheet

A wages analysis sheet is not required on contracts for which separate pay sheets are prepared, but smaller firms, such as builders and decorators, need them so that the men's time can be apportioned to the various jobs on which they have been working during the week. The information is compiled from the time sheets, and the sheet is usually in sections, according to trades, so that separate totals for each job for each class of work are obtained—*e.g.* bricklayers, plumbers, joiners, etc. The total against each job is posted to the appropriate cost account (*see* Fig. 62), and the grand total is agreed with the total of the pay sheets to ensure that the wages charged in the detailed cost accounts agrees with the summary figure posted to Work-in-progress Account.

THE COST OF OVERHEAD

In some cases indirect expense may easily be allocated to the contract concerned, but where this cannot be done it is posted to appropriate standing order numbers. A distribution summary is then prepared, and an apportionment of overhead is made on the basis, for example, of a rate per direct labour hour.

FORM OF CONTRACT COST LEDGER ACCOUNTS

The exact form of each Contract Cost Account will depend on individual requirements, but in Fig. 63 is shown a specimen ruling for a firm of builders.

WAGES ANALYSIS SHEET

No. 32

Week ending: February 7, 19...

Clock No.	Job No. 90 Hrs.	Job No. 90 Amount £	Job No. 91 No.	Job No. 91 Hrs.	Job No. 91 Amount £	Job No. 98 No.	Job No. 98 Hrs.	Job No. 98 Amount £	Job No. 100 No.	Job No. 100 Hrs.	Job No. 100 Amount £	R. 13 No.	R. 13 Hrs.	R. 13 Amount £	N. 31 No.	N. 31 Hrs.	N. 31 Amount £	Summary Job No.	Summary Hrs.	Summary Amount £	Cost Led. folio
12	4	1·40	22	5	1·38	23	4	1·40	12	4	1·40	22	3	0·80	14	8	2·80	90	15	5·99	
13	8	2·83	23	4	1·40	17	40	14·00	18	2	1·25	18	14	8·75	17	3	2·80	91	9	2·78	
18	2	1·25							21	2	1·03	21	2	1·03	21		1·50	98	44	15·40	
21	1	0·51										12	20	7·00	22	40	11·05	100	8	3·68	
												19	6	2·40				R. 13	45	19·98	
																		N. 31	59	18·15	
	15	£5·99		9	£2·78		44	£15·40		8	£3·68		45	£19·98		59	£18·15		180	£65·98	

FIG. 62.—*Wages analysis sheet*

This is useful for the analysis of job tickets and idle time cards of workers whose wages are charged as direct labour. The total will be posted partly to Work-in-progress Account and partly to Production Overhead Control Account, probably via the wages analysis book (Fig. 47).

The total shown in the summary column must agree with the direct wages on the payroll.

CONTRACT COST LEDGER ACCOUNT

Name:...

The Southern Bank Ltd.
New Premises, 296 High Street,
London.

Contract No.:......

| Week Ending | Ref. | Debits | | | | | | Credits | | | Prime Cost | Over-head Charges | Total Cost to date |
		Stores Materials	Direct Materials	Use of Plant etc.	Wages	Direct Expenses	Total	Stores Returned	Other Income	Total			
		£	£	£	£	£	£	£	£	£	£	£	£

FIG. 63.—*Contract Cost Ledger Account*

A ruling of this kind would be suitable for a firm of builders and contractors. The plant sent to the contract might be recorded on the reverse side, and the charge raised for the use of it would be calculated there each month before entry on the front side of the account form.

Use of plant on contracts

In some cases the book value of plant and tools sent to the site of a contract is debited to the contract and the Plant Account is credited. In due course, when the plant is returned to the yard, the depreciated value is credited to the contract.

However, it is not considered that this is the best way to deal with plant sent to contracts. An "Upkeep Account" should be opened for each major piece of plant, to which is debited the cost of maintenance, depreciation, obsolescence provision, fuel oil, etc. A hire rate is then fixed and charged weekly to the contract. This rate, although it may be lower than the charge from an outside plant-hiring firm, is sufficient to cover the upkeep of the plant. By receiving this charge against his contract, the contract agent or foreman will take steps to see that the plant is returned or made the responsibility of head office when no longer wanted. From a book-keeping point of view, this method has the advantage that the Contract Accounts are not swamped with the capital cost of plant which is eventually to be returned for credit.

Sub-contracts

When a sub-contractor is engaged for a special piece of work the accounts received are dealt with as direct materials, even though the cost may largely consist of labour.

Jobbing work

During the course of completion of major contracts the contractor is often approached to do jobbing work of a minor nature, *e.g.* the use of an excavator to clear a site for some garages; the use of a roller on a footpath; the use of a concrete mixer and the supply of sand and cement for putting roughcast on the walls of a house. The charges made are treated as income to the contract.

CERTIFICATION OF WORK DONE

As the work proceeds, the architect or surveyor appointed by the contractees issues certificates to the effect that so much money is now due to the contractors in accordance with the terms of the contract. These payments on account are credited either to the Contract Account or to the account of the contractees, depending on the precise book-keeping method being used. The contract will usually stipulate that a retention of, say, 10% is held back for twelve months after the contract is completed. At that time the surveyor will go round with the contractor and indicate any faults in the work which have been disclosed within the year, and which have to be remedied before release of the retention money.

PROFIT ON UNCOMPLETED CONTRACTS

In view of the hazards involved in contract work, such as the discovery of a spring of water in the middle of a contract site or of a bed of running sand in the course of digging the foundations, and in view of the liability to make good any defects in the work which develop within the retention period, it is an accepted principle that no profit should be taken on uncompleted contracts, except in the case of very long contracts when a conservative sum may be credited. This is usually based on the formula:

$$\tfrac{2}{3} \times \text{Notional profit} \times \frac{\text{Cash received}}{\text{Work certified}}.$$

When a large contract is nearing successful completion, use is sometimes made of the formula:

$$\text{Notional profit} \times \frac{\text{Work certified}}{\text{Contract price}}$$

and, of course, individual firms may have their own particular basis of calculation.

SPECIMEN CONTRACT ACCOUNTS

In order to illustrate the way in which Contract Cost Accounts may be kept, the following examples are given of:

(a) a builder's business;
(b) a civil-engineering contract.

SPECIMEN QUESTION

Short & Co. are in business as builders and decorators, and they undertake small contracts and also jobs for local residents most of which are below £100 in value. They employ bricklayers, joiners, painters and paperhangers. In the three months ending March 31 the results of their business are as follows:

	£
Materials	
In store January 1	860
Purchases:	
January	710
February	760
March	970
Issues to contracts:	
January	410
February	270
March	350
Issues to Jobbing Account:	
January	300
February	520
March	460
Issues to joiners' shop:	
March	300
Wages	
Gross wages paid:	
January	1,590
February	1,630
March	1,720
Allocated direct to contracts	2,460
Apportioned to:	
Joiners' shop	1,070
Jobbing Account (joiners)	790
Overhead Control Account	620

£

Overhead

Rent and rates	900
Haulage	300
Office expenses	600
Lighting and heating	125
Repairs	170
Depreciation	235

Overhead *applied* as follows:

To contracts	2,049
To joiners' shop	375
To Jobbing Account	520

Work done on contracts completed

To March 31	8,160

NOTE: A loss of £130 was sustained on one contract.

Work in progress

On contracts:

January 1	1,200
March 31	1,400

On Jobbing Accounts:

January 1	200
March 31	300

In joiners' shop:

January 1	—
March 31	145

Jobbing sales for quarter   4,140

The work done in the joiners' shop

Charged to:

Contracts	600
Jobbing Account	1,000

It is required to show the main Control Accounts in the ledger, the assumption being made that individual Contract Accounts are kept only on a card index, subsidiary to the book-keeping system.

ANSWER

Stores Ledger Control Account

	£		£
Balance b/f	860	Issues	410
Purchases	710		300
	760		270
	970		520
			350
			460
			300
		Balance c/d	690
	£3,300		£3,300
Balance b/d	690		

Wages Control Account

	£		£
Gross wages	1,590	Contracts	2,460
	1,630	Joiners	1,070
	1,720	Jobbing	790
		Overhead control	620
	£4,940		£4,940

Work in Progress—Contracts

	£		£
Balance b/f	1,200	Completed work	8,160
Stores	410	Loss on contract	130
	270	Balance c/d	1,400
	350		
Wages	2,460		
Overhead	2,049		
Joiners	600		
Profit to date	2,351		
	£9,690		£9,690
Balance b/d	1,400		

Joiners' Shop Account

	£		£
Wages	1,070	Contracts	600
Stores	300	Jobbing	1,000
Overhead	375	Balance c/d	145
	£1,745		£1,745
Balance b/d	145		

Jobbing Account

	£		£
Balance b/f	200	Sales	4,140
Stores	300	Balance c/d	300
	520		
	460		
Wages—joiners	790		
Work done in joiners' shop	1,000		
Overhead	520		
Profit	650		
	£4,440		£4,440
Balance b/d	300		

Overhead Control Account

	£		£
Wages	620	Applied Overhead A/c	2,950
Rent and rates	900		
Haulage	300		
Expenses	600		
Heating	125		
Repairs	170		
Depreciation	235		
	£2,950		£2,950

Applied Overhead Account

	£		£
Transfer to Overhead Control A/c	2,950	Contracts	2,049
		Joiners' shop	375
		Jobbing A/c	520
		Balance, overhead under-absorbed to	
		P. & L. A/c	6
	£2,950		£2,950

Contracts Summary Account

	£		£
Loss on contract (detail)	130	Profits on contracts (set out in detail)	2,351
Balance to Profit & Loss A/c	2,221		
	£2,351		£2,351

Profit and Loss Account

	£		£
Under-absorbed overhead	6	Contracts	2,221
Net profit	2,865	Jobbing	650
	£2,871		£2,871

SPECIMEN QUESTION

The South Park Construction Co. Ltd. have undertaken the construction of a bridge over the River Till for the Champton Council. The value of the Contract is £125,000, subject to a retention of 20% until one year after the certified completion of the contract, and final approval of the council's surveyor. The contractors have given the contract number 86 for reference, and the following are the details as shown in the books:

	£
Labour on site	40,500
Materials direct to site, *less* returns	42,000
Materials from store and workshops	8,120
Plant Upkeep Account—hire and use of plant	1,210
Direct expenses	2,300

	£
General overhead apportioned to this contract	3,710
Materials on hand June 30	630
Wages accrued at June 30	780
Direct expenses accrued	160
Work not yet certified, at cost	1,650
Amount certified by the council's surveyor	110,000
Cash received on account	88,000

Prepare the Contract Accounts to show the position at June 30, retaining an adequate provision against possible losses before final acceptance of the contract.

ANSWER

Contract No. 86—Expenditure Account

	£		£
Materials direct	42,000	Materials on hand c/d	630
Other materials	8,120	Cost of contract to date c/d	96,500
Wages	40,500	Work done, not yet certified, at cost	1,650
Direct expenses	2,300		
Plant Upkeep A/c	1,210		
General overhead	3,710		
Wages accrued c/d	780		
Direct expenses accrued c/d	160		
	£98,780		£98,780
Cost to date b/d	96,500	Wages b/d	780
Materials on site b/d	630	Direct expenses b/d	160
Work done, not yet certified, at cost	1,650		

Contract No. 86—Certificates Account

	£		£
Balance c/d	110,000	Certificates 1–17	110,000
		Balance b/d	110,000

Contract No. 86—Retentions Account

	£
Certificates Account	£22,000

Champton Council's Account—Contract No. 86

	£		£
Certificates Account	£88,000	Cash on A/c	£88,000

Contract No. 86—Profit Suspense Account

	£		£
Transfer to P. & L. A/c	7,200	Profit to be taken c/d	7,200
Balance b/d	7,200		

NOTE: The calculation of the profit to be taken is arrived at by taking two-thirds of the notional profit £110,000 − £96,500 = £13,500, and still further reducing the result in the proportion which the cash received bears to work certified, thus:

$$£13,500 \times \frac{2}{3} \times \frac{88,000}{110,000}$$

$$= £7,200.$$

It will be noted that by this method the Expenditure Account is maintained at cost, as work in progress.

If this contract represented the whole of the work in hand the figures could be shown on the balance sheet as follows:

Assets side of the balance sheet

	£	£
Work in progress, including profit taken to date	105,350	
Less Cash on account	88,000	
		17,350
Materials on site		630

Liabilities side of the balance sheet

	£	£
Accrued charges:		
Wages	780	
Direct expenses	160	
		940

The chief merit of this method is that it is simple, does not give a false impression of the amount of the assets and especially does not disclose the amount of Retentions Account, which is not immediately realisable.

ALTERNATIVE METHOD

This method is alternative to that described previously. It is possibly not as useful in practice as the previous one, but for examination purposes is widely used and is probably more easily understood. The main difference between the two methods is in the presentation in the accounts; principles involved and records to be maintained are unchanged.

SPECIMEN QUESTION

Towering

The Beeches Construction Co. is engaged on two contracts during the year. The following information relates to these contracts, which were commenced on January 1 and July 1 respectively:

	Contract A J	Contract D B
	£	£
Contract price	300,000	400,000
Direct materials issued	55,000	40,000
Materials returned to store	500	1,000
Direct labour payments	48,000	32,000
Accrued wages December 31	2,000	2,500
Plant installed at cost	30,000	45,000
Establishment charges	25,000	15,000
Direct expenses	15,000	10,000
Direct expenses accrued December 31	1,000	500
Work certified by architect	160,000	80,000
Cost of work not yet certified	10,000	15,000
Value of plant December 31	20,000	40,000
Materials on site December 31	5,500	4,000
Cash received from contractor	150,000	60,000

Show the accounts for these contracts and for the contractees, also extract from the company's balance sheet as at December 31.

ANSWER

Contract J

	£	£		£	£
Direct materials	55,000		Materials on site c/d		5,500
Less Returns	500		Cost c/d		150,000
		54,500			
Direct wages	48,000				
Accrued c/d	2,000				
		50,000			
Establishment charges		25,000			
Direct expenses	15,000				
Accrued c/d	1,000				
		16,000			
Plant depreciation		10,000			
		£155,500			£155,500
Cost b/d		150,000	Value of work certified		160,000
Profit:			Cost of work not yet certified c/d		10,000
Profit and Loss Account	12,500				
Balance c/d	7,500				
		20,000			
		£170,000			£170,000
Balance b/d:			Balance b/d:		
Stores	5,500		Wages	2,000	
Work not yet certified	10,000		Expenses	1,000	
		15,500	Profit	7,500	
					10,500

Contractee

	£		£
Value of work certified	160,000	Cash	150,000
		Balance c/d	10,000
	£160,000		£160,000
Balance b/d	10,000		

NOTE: *Calculation of profit.* The proportion which it is normally considered prudent to include in the Profit and Loss Account for the year is:

$$\tfrac{2}{3} \times \text{Notional profit} \times \frac{\text{Cash received}}{\text{Value of work certified}}$$

$$\tfrac{2}{3} \times 20,000 \times \frac{150,000}{160,000}.$$

Contract D

	£	£		£	£
Direct materials	40,000		Materials on site c/d		4,000
Less Returns	1,000		Cost c/d		100,000
		39,000			
Direct wages	32,000				
Accrued c/d	2,500				
		34,500			
Establishment charges		15,000			
Direct expenses	10,000				
Accrued c/d	500				
		10,500			
Plant depreciation		5,000			
		£104,000			£104,000
Cost b/d		100,000	Value of work certified		80,000
			Cost of work not yet certified c/d		15,000
			Loss on contract		5,000
		£100,000			£100,000
Balance b/d:			Balance b/d:		
Stores	4,000		Wages	2,500	
Work not yet certified	15,000		Expenses	500	
		19,000			3,000

Contractee

	£		£
Value of work certified	80,000	Cash	60,000
		Balance c/d	20,000
	£80,000		£80,000
Balance b/d	20,000		

NOTE: The loss is written off to Profit and Loss Account, not apportioned as in the case of profits. It is not considered prudent to carry forward losses to a future year.

Balance sheet (extract)

	£	£		£	£
Profit and Loss Account			Plant at cost	75,000	
This will include:			Depreciation	15,000	
Profit J	12,500				60,000
Loss D	5,000		Stores		9,500
		7,500	Work in progress*		47,500
Sundry creditors					
This will include:					
Wages accrued	4,500				
Expenses accrued	1,500				
		6,000			

Work in progress

This can be calculated as follows:

	£	£
J Cost of work not yet certified	10,000	
Contractee's balance	10,000	
	20,000	
Less Profits provision	7,500	
		12,500
D Cost of work not yet certified	15,000	
Contractee's balance	20,000	
	35,000	
Less Profit provision	—	
		35,000
		£47,500

Alternatively:

	£	£
J Cost incurred	150,000	
Profit taken	12,500	
	162,500	
Less Cash received	150,000	
		12,500
D Cost incurred	100,000	
Profit taken	(5,000)	
	95,000	
Less Cash received	60,000	
		35,000
		£47,500

It may be observed that in the first method of calculating work in progress the balance on Contractee's Account was included. It is considered preferable to show this balance here rather than in the debtor's balance, because frequently in contract work the contractee is entitled to withhold payment of part of the value of work certified (this was referred to earlier under retention money), and this money will not be received by the contractor until after satisfactory completion of the contract. This amount owing by the contractee is not regarded as a current debt, so should not be shown as such.

SECTIONALISATION OF CONTRACTS

On large civil-engineering contracts it is often possible for the accountant, in conjunction with the engineering staff, to divide the bill of quantities into sections, especially when the work is to begin simultaneously at several places. By suitably coding these sections the contract costs can be made to correspond more closely to the monthly certificates, and then, if the estimates are seen to have been low in certain directions, the engineer is able to give special attention to those sections of the work.

EXAMINATION QUESTIONS

1. J. Smelt & Co. Ltd. are public works contractors, and maintain a separate account for each contract. Contract No. 142 was commenced in January 19.., and the expenditure to December 31 of that year was as follows:

	£
Materials purchased direct	11,960
Materials issued from stores	590
Plant (purchased April 1)	6,500
Wages	7,890
Direct expenses	740

The stock of materials at December 31 was £1,410.

The life of the plant is 5 years, and an addition for overheads has to be made equal to 50% of wages. On December 1 the architect certified the value of work done at £25,000. The total contract price is £100,000. The contract will take three years to complete, and at December 31 it is estimated that 30% of the total cost (£90,000) had been incurred.

From the above information prepare the Contract Account, and state the amount which, in your opinion, should be brought into work in progress at December 31.

(A.I.A. Final)

2. A firm of speculative builders have in the past delegated the work of roofing and wall-tiling to sub-contractors. In future they propose to undertake the work themselves by direct labour. You are required to state what alterations will require to be made in the costing system.

(C.A.A. Final)

3. A Contract Account in the books of J. McHugh Ltd. appears as follows:

19..		£
June 30	Materials issued to site	5,000
	Plant issued to site	12,500
	Direct labour	4,600
	Indirect labour	640
	Overhead expenses	1,950

You are informed that it is the practice of the firm to take credit for two-thirds of the profit earned on the contracts in progress after taking into account the value of the work certified for payment by professional surveyors. You are required to complete this account to June 30 and show the transfer to Profit and Loss Account, for which purpose you are supplied with the following further information as at that date:

	£
Value of work certified for payment	10,000
Cost of work carried out, but not certified	3,800
Stock of materials not used	950
Value of plant on site, after depreciation	11,875
	(*C.C.S. Final*)

4. Dominion Erectors Ltd. undertook three contracts in one year; one on January 1, one on July 1 and one on October 1. On December 31, when the company's accounts were prepared, the position was as follows:

Contract No.	1	2	3
	£	£	£
Contract price	150,000	101,250	37,500
Expenditure—			
Materials	27,000	21,750	2,500
Wages	41,250	42,150	1,750
General expenses	1,500	1,050	125
Plant installed	7,500	6,000	1,500
Materials on site	1,500	1,500	250
Wages accrued	1,275	1,350	200
General expenses accrued	225	150	25
Work certified	75,000	60,000	4,500
Cash received on work certified	56,250	45,000	3,375
Work completed, but uncertified	2,250	3,000	275

The plant was installed on the commencing dates of the contracts, and depreciation is calculated at 10% per annum.

Prepare the respective accounts in the Contracts Ledger and give suitable entries in the company's balance sheet at December 31. A columnar layout may be adopted and calculations approximated to the nearest £.

(*A.I.A. Final*)

5. The following trial balance was extracted on April 30 from the books of General Contractors Ltd.:

	Dr.	Cr.
	£	£
Share Capital Account, shares of £1		35,180
Profit and Loss Account, May 1		2,500
Provision for depreciation on plant and tools		6,300
Cash received on account, Contract 123		128,000
Creditors		8,120
Land and buildings, cost	7,400	
Plant and tools, cost	5,200	
Bank	4,500	
Contract 123—		
Materials issued	60,000	
Direct labour	83,000	
Expenses	4,000	
Plant and tools on site, cost	16,000	
	£180,100	£180,100

Contract 123 was begun on May 1. The contract price is £240,000, and the customer has so far paid £128,000, being 80% of the work certified. The cost of work done since certification is estimated at £1,600.

On April 30, after the above trial balance was extracted, plant costing £3,200 was returned to store, and materials then on site were valued at £2,700.

Provision is to be made for direct labour accrued due £600, and depreciation of all plant and tools at $12\frac{1}{2}\%$.

You are required to:

    (a) write up the contract;

    (b) compute the profit (if any) for which credit may be taken.

                                            (I.C.A. Final)

6. Arnold Maidstone Ltd. are public works contractors, and are successful in securing a contract for building a large swimming pool and sports arena at a price of £275,000. Work commenced on July 1 and the contract is due to be completed in 18 months from that date.

By December of the first year most of the preliminary excavations and piling had been completed, and the expenditure relating to the contract was as follows:

	£
Value of plant sent to the site	125,000
Stores sent from depot	320
Materials purchased—	
Cement	4,600
Reinforcing rods	9,200
Sand and ballast	2,720
Fuel oil for bulldozers	2,970
Wages paid	13,660
Wages accrued	520
National Insurance	1,800
Insurance	400
Miscellaneous expenses and overhead	30,200

The last certificate for work done was dated December 15, and the total amount certified under the contract to that date was £80,000. The cost of work from that date to the end of the year was estimated at £7,000. Payment of the certificates is subject to 15% retention, and all money due has been received.

At December 31, the valuation put upon the plant was £106,000, and materials on site amounted to £1,750.

You are required to show:

(a) the Contract Account;

(b) the Contractee's Account;

and to show as part of your answer the amount of profit which you consider might be fairly taken on the contract, and how you have calculated it.

(A.C.C.A. Inter.)

7. Stannard and Sykes Ltd. are contractors for the construction of a pier for the Seafront Development Corporation. The value of the contract is £300,000, and payment is by engineer's certificate subject to a retention of 10% of the amount certified, this to be held by the Seafront Development Corporation for six months after completion of the contract.

The following information is extracted from the records of Stannard and Sykes Ltd.:

	£
Wages on site	41,260
Materials delivered to site by supplier	58,966
„ „ „ from store	10,180
Hire of plant	21,030
Expenses charged to contract	3,065
Overheads charged to contract	8,330
Materials on site at November 30	11,660
Work certified	150,000
Payment received	135,000
Work in progress at cost (not the subject of a certificate to date)	12,613
Wages accrued November 30	2,826

You are to prepare the Pier Contract Account to November 30, and to suggest a method by which profit could be prudently estimated.

(A.C.C.A. Inter.)

8. Brickworkers Ltd., building contractors, commenced work on a certain contract on January 1, 19... The agreed price for the contract was £200,000, and the work was to be finished by December 31 in the *following* year.

Expenditure charged to the Contract Account during the first year was:

	£
Materials purchased	38,000
Plant purchased	16,000
Wages	42,000
Administrative expenses	6,500

The stock of unused materials on the site at December 31 amounted at cost to £2,500. It was estimated that the residual value of the plant at the termination of the contract will be £4,000. Depreciation is to be apportioned over the period of the contract by the straight-line method.

All work completed up to the end of November was certified by the architect in December, and in that month the company received a payment of £96,000, representing the contract price of the work certified less 20% retention money.

When the company's accounts for the year to December 31 were prepared it was decided to take credit in the Profit and Loss Account for a proportion of the total estimated profit on the contract, the proportion being that which the contract price of the work certified in the first year bears to the total contract price. For the purposes of this calculation it was estimated that the expenditure from January 1 (second year) to completion, including a provision of £10,000 for contingencies, would amount to £56,000 in addition to the cost of materials on site brought forward, and to depreciation of plant.

You are required to set out the entries in the Contract Account for the year ended December 31 (first year), showing the transfer to Profit and Loss Account; and show how any balances resulting from the above matters would appear in the balance sheet.

(C.I.S. Final)

9. The following particulars are extracted from the books of Constructors Ltd. for the year to June 30, 19..:

Contract No.	Work in progress brought forward from previous year £	Wages £	Materials £	Sales £
11	8,640	7,030	6,090	30,500
12	4,050	4,810	4,600	18,500
13		10,400	6,240	23,250
14		6,080	4,570	4,450
15		2,930	1,800	2,100

In respect of work in progress (valued consistently at wages and material costs) it is the company's practice to provide, for balance sheet purposes, 10% for contingencies.

On June 30:

(*a*) Contract 14 was 75% complete. In April the customer was invoiced with 25% of the contract price and has paid £2,500 on account. This latter amount has been credited to Work-in-progress Account.

(*b*) Contract 15 was 50% complete. In May the customer paid an instalment of 20% of the contract price. This amount has been credited to Sales Account. Wages include a payment of £645 to sub-contractors, yielding a profit to them of $7\frac{1}{2}\%$.

Submit:

(1) corrective journal entries as you think necessary;
(2) a summarised Trading Account;
(3) a reasoned comment on the profits for which you think credit might be taken.

(C.C.A. Final)

10. The following are details of a contract (No. 21A) undertaken by M.N. Ltd.:

Date commenced July 1, year 1.
Date completed October 31, year 2.
Contract price £100,000.

	In year 1 £	In year 2 £
Direct expenditure		
Materials	13,824	24,699
Wages	14,287	30,298
Expenses	944	1,324
	£29,055	£56,321

Plant purchased for cash at beginning of contract	12,000	—
Payments for plant on hire purchase		2,000
Penalty for failure to complete by September 30, year 2		1,000
Cash received	36,000	63,000

The plant purchased for cash was sold for £3,250 on October 31, year 2.

An initial deposit of £2,000 was paid on March 1, year 2, for the plant acquired on hire purchase. The hire purchase agreement called for three further payments at six-monthly intervals each of £2,000, which included interest at the rate of 10% per annum. This plant, the cost price of which was £7,445, was used on the contract until August 31 when it was transferred to another contract, its value for depreciation purposes then being fixed at £5,800.

The cash received in each year represented the contract price of all work certified in that year less, in the case of uncompleted contracts, 10% for retention and in the case of the cash received in year 2 the penalty.

When the annual accounts for the year ended December 31, year 1, were completed, it was expected that the contract would be completed by September 30, year 2, when it was estimated that the realisable value of the plant would be £3,855 at September 30, year 2, and that expenditure still to be incurred would total £53,000 but the necessity to hire plant in year 2 was not foreseen.

For the purpose of the annual accounts:

(a) all depreciation was charged to contracts by the straight-line method and was calculated by reference to the expected market value of the plant at the completion of the contract;

(b) credit was taken for that proportion of the estimated profit on uncompleted contracts which the contract price of the work certified bore to the total contract price.

You are required to prepare the Contract Account for the years 1 and 2 showing the transfer to the Profit and Loss Account.

Ignore taxation.

(I.C.W.A. Final)

11. Mike Ltd. is an engineering company and prepares accounts half yearly to June 30 and December 31. During the eighteen months ended December 31, 1965, the company entered into three major contracts. Customers were provided periodically with certificates prepared by an engineer and showing the value of work done up to particular dates. The following information relates to the contracts:

	Contract A		Contract B		Contract C	
	Date	£	Date	£	Date	£
Contract price		5,000		8,000		4,000
Budgeted profits		2,000		3,000		1,600
Work certified	30.9.64	2,000	30.11.64	4,000	28.2.65	1,000
Work certified	—		31. 5.65	2,000	31.8.65	2,000
Work certified (final certificate)	30.4.65	3,000	31. 7.65	2,000		—

The half yearly costs for each contract are tabled below:

	Labour			Material			Overheads		
	A	B	C	A	B	C	A	B	C
	£	£	£	£	£	£	£	£	£
Six months to:									
December 31, 1964	600	800	—	500	800	—	300	400	—
June 30, 1965	700	1,200	600	600	700	1,100	350	600	300
December 31, 1965	—	200	175	—	—	—	—	100	75

Each half year a proportion of budgeted profit on every uncompleted contract is credited to Profit and Loss Account. The proportion is based on the value of work certified in relation to the contract price. When a contract is completed the balance of the profit is transferred to Profit and Loss Account.

A provision for losses and claims is recorded at the rate of 20% of the profit credited to Profit and Loss Account in respect of the half year's profit on each contract. The whole of the provision on each contract is released and transferred to the credit of Profit and Loss Account at the end of the accounting period immediately following that in which the final certificate is issued to the customer.

You are required:

(a) to prepare in columnar form for the three half years ended December 31, 1965, (i) the Contract Account and (ii) the Account for Provision for Losses on Contracts;

(b) to show the figures relating to contracts appearing in the Profit and Loss Account for the half year ended June 30, 1965; and

(c) to set out an acceptable method of describing the work in progress in the balance sheet as on June 30, 1965.

(I.C.A. Final June, 1966)

CHAPTER 18

FACTORY JOB COSTING

THE PRODUCTION ORDER NUMBER

Factory job costing is concerned with those undertakings, mostly of a general engineering kind, which may undertake jobs of the "one-off" type, or orders for a batch of similar components. Costs are therefore generally recorded against each individual job or order, and this requires careful routing and scheduling, since there is no predetermined flow line for the work to follow. In consequence, this type of costing is characterised by a great deal of paper work.

The costs are collected and recorded under the production order number, a separate cost account such as shown in Fig. 64 being set up for each number. By using a well-arranged numbering scheme, work of different categories, and work done in different departments, can be readily identified.

The method of numbering and some of the procedure varies according to whether the order is for:

   (a) repetition work;
   (b) work involving sectional operations, or the making of components for assembly;
   (c) a simple straight job.

When an order is received, production control allots a number to it. If necessary, the work will be divided into sections, and in this case a master order number would be given to the order as a whole, and sub-section order numbers to the parts composing it, e.g. sub-numbers for components.

In some works this is an elaborate process, often involving the setting up of many operations, for each of which the planning department and the rate-fixing department decide the extent of each operation, and the time allowed for performing each.

EXAMPLE

The rate-fixer has observed an operation being done by a worker twenty or thirty times. The average time taken (or, maybe, the mode) is 0·8 minutes. He rates performance as 65/60. 15% relaxation factor is to be allowed for the class of work being done.

$$\text{Normal time} = \frac{65}{60} \times 0\cdot 8 = 0\cdot 87$$

$$\text{Add relaxation factor } 15\% = 0\cdot 13$$

$$\text{Standard time allowed} \quad \underline{1\cdot 00}$$

NOTE: If the Halsey, Halsey–Weir or Rowan schemes of remuneration are used it will be remembered that the time allowed would be $166\frac{2}{3}\%$ of the standard element time, *viz.* $0\cdot 87 \times 166\frac{2}{3}\% = 1\cdot 45$ minutes.

			COST CARD		
Description:.................			**Quantity:**.................		**Job No.:**.........
....					

Date	Ref.	Particulars		Cost	
				Detail	Total
		MATERIAL:			
		LABOUR			
		FACTORY OVERHEAD:			
		ADMINISTRATION AND SELLING OVERHEAD:			

Make-up of Estimate					
Ref.	Material	Labour	Production Overhead	A.D. & S.O.	Total

FIG. 64.—*Factory job cost card*

This, as in Fig. 50, shows a ruling for a job cost card or Job Cost Account. These cards constitute the details of the Work-in-progress Account, and when the job is finished the card which applies is removed; the total of such removed cards is used as the basis of a transfer from work in progress to finished work.

Clipper Card Sheath.

Illustration	Index Letter	Description
	R.C.A.	Milling Card Sheath Castings.
	R.C.B	Drilling to Jig.
	R.C.C.	Mouthpieces, Drill & Oxidise
	R.C.D¹	Cutter Holder, Boring & Turning.
	R.C.D²	Cutter Holder, Machining
	R.C.D³	" " Drilling to Jig & Tapping.
	R.C.E¹	Cutter Plates, Punching
	R.C.E²	" " Flatten Drill & Tap.
	R.C.F¹	Cutters, Machining.
	R.C.F²	" File to Jig.
	R.C.F³	" Grinding after Hardening.
	R.C.G¹	Cutter Shanks, Cut off Straighten & Drill
	R.C.G²	" " Machining.
Casting.	R.C.H¹	Brass Top Plate Making.
Casting.	R.C.H²	" Bottom Plate "
	R.C.I	Aligning Stud, Make in Captan.
	R.C.J	Springs for Card Cutters.
	R.C.K	Assembling Clipper Card Sheath Complete

Fig. 65.—Schedule of operations

For repetition work, the planning department decides how the work is to be split up, draws up a schedule of jobs and identifies each job or operation by a distinguishing number or index letter. An index letter or symbol, combined with an operation number, is often used with great advantage. The example in Fig. 65 shows how a schedule of operation can be indexed; in this case the operations for making a clipper card sheath for a Gledhill-Brook time recorder are shown.

THE PRODUCTION ORDER

After the production planning department has made out the production orders for the various parts to be made, the requisite information given on them is run off by spirit duplicator or other means on to a number of other forms arranged in sets. Figure 66 illustrates such a production order and Fig. 67 the flow of information for Part 2, under

PRODUCTION ORDER

Progress Copy to
Circulate with Work

Date to commence	Number required	Machine Yes/No	Production Order Number			
Part Name	Part No.	Material Required				
		Per Part		This Order		
Operation Nos.						
Machine Nos.						

Clock Times	Op. No.	Dept. No.	Operation		Quantity		
			No.	Details	Made	Rej.	c.f.

FIG. 66.—*Production order*

These are made out by the planning department in respect of each type of part required either for a particular job or for finished parts stock.

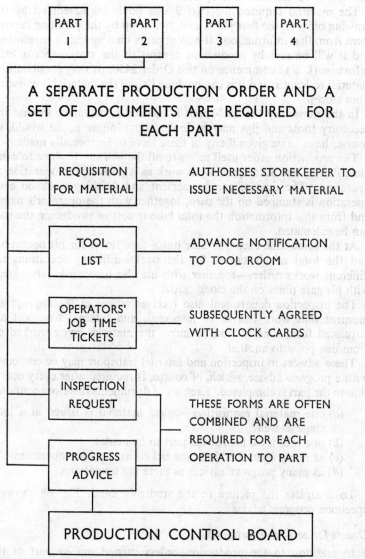

PRODUCTION OR WORKS ORDER

PART 1   PART 2   PART 3   PART 4

A SEPARATE PRODUCTION ORDER AND A SET OF DOCUMENTS ARE REQUIRED FOR EACH PART

REQUISITION FOR MATERIAL — AUTHORISES STOREKEEPER TO ISSUE NECESSARY MATERIAL

TOOL LIST — ADVANCE NOTIFICATION TO TOOL ROOM

OPERATORS' JOB TIME TICKETS — SUBSEQUENTLY AGREED WITH CLOCK CARDS

INSPECTION REQUEST

PROGRESS ADVICE — THESE FORMS ARE OFTEN COMBINED AND ARE REQUIRED FOR EACH OPERATION TO PART

PRODUCTION CONTROL BOARD

FIG. 67.—*Production department documents*

The flow of information required in jobbing and batch production: much paperwork is involved in ensuring that the production is completed by the date required.

Production Order No. 2456. It will be seen that the actual issue of the forms to the factory is made by the control section of production control, for the planning department's responsibility ended with the decision as to the route and operations necessary.

The material required for Part 2 was doubtless scheduled by the drawing office in the first place, and picked up by the planning department from that information. It now appears on a materials requisition, and it will be sent by production control to the storekeeper a little before work is to commence on this Order 2456. It may entail cutting material to length, and this can be done before the material is collected from stores.

In the same way the tool-room is advised in advance, so that the necessary tools and jigs may be looked out; longer notice would, of course, have to be given if any of these have to be specially made.

The production order itself refers to all the work to be done to complete Part 2, and accompanies the work as it passes from operation to operation. The time of commencement and finishing work on each operation is stamped on the card, together with the operator's name, and from this information the total labour cost of producing the part can be calculated.

At the same time each operator has a time ticket for his operation, and the total of his tickets for the week—different operations for different works orders—together with his idle time cards, are agreed with his gate times on the clock cards.

The inspection department also receives advice at the appropriate moment that work has to be inspected, and internal transport are requested from time to time to move the material being worked on from one point to another.

These advices to inspection and internal transport may be combined with a progress advice, which, of course, is required after every operation to the part is completed. Each set of documents therefore contains:

> (a) one material requisition—unless material is issued at a later stage as well;
> (b) one tool issue list for the part to be made;
> (c) as many operators' job time tickets as there are operations;
> (d) as many progress advices as there are operations.

To complete the picture in the student's mind, Fig. 68 shows a specimen progress advice.

Orders for service departments

In addition to the production orders carried out as part of the planned production, there are many jobs which are done in a factory for service departments, and which are therefore in the nature of overhead. Often it is the practice to open a special standing order number for such jobs, but it is suggested that there is no need to vary the procedure outlined above. The same routine can be followed, using perhaps stationery of a distinctive colour, or a reference number which will clearly identify it as being an internal works order.

PROGRESS ADVICE			
For the Attention of Production Control			
Date commenced	Number required	Machine Yes/No	Production Order Number
Date finished	Part Name	Part No.	Operators No.
From Dept. No.		To Dept. No.	

Quantity produced	Quantity inspected	Quantity passed	Quantity rejected	Inspector

FIG. 68.—*Progress advice*

One of the documents referred to in Fig. 67 was of this type. After the operator has completed his operation the work goes by internal transport to the inspector. This form notifies production control of the stage reached by the work.

Orders carried out by service departments

In some cases certain parts can be made for stock by a service department—such as the tool-room or the plant maintenance department—whenever they have time and opportunity to spare. Such orders remain in force until countermanded, and are therefore sometimes referred to as "standing orders." This is bound to cause confusion, since the term "standing order numbers" is by custom applied to overhead. It would be best therefore to refer to them as "stock orders."

On the other hand, such service departments will, for the most part, use their time in maintaining the workshop tools, carrying out maintenance, etc., so that the labour cost of each has to be carefully recorded and accounted for. No new problems arise, however, and the student is referred to one of the methods outlined in Chapter 7.

TIME AND MATERIALS SPENT IN REPLACING REJECTED WORK

There is no need to vary the normal procedures, except to use stationery of a distinctive colour. This will make the compilation of a scrap report easier.

It is suggested that the additional charges incurred under these headings become a direct charge to the job concerned. Of course, if standard costing is in force, they would constitute material usage and labour efficiency variances.

OVERTIME

A distinction must be drawn between overtime, that is the time worked over and above the normal working hours, and overtime premium, which is the additional payment made over the normal rate for those additional hours.

When the overtime is worked on a special job, say outside the works, or when it is due to the insistence of a customer that a job be completed within the time specified, the extra payment for overtime premium is legitimately charged to the job as direct labour. On the other hand, if the overtime is for the purpose of generally increasing the output of the factory, *e.g.* to keep up with stock requirements or to take on additional jobs, the cost of the overtime premium is treated as overhead and charged to a standing order number.

PAYROLL AND WAGES ANALYSIS

The payroll is made up from the clock cards, and/or piece-work tickets. When a premium bonus, or other output or efficiency bonus, is paid, an extra column will be provided for the inclusion of these amounts.

In the cost office the wages, having been agreed with the time tickets, are dissected so that the correct allocation of direct wages to the job cost cards and of indirect wages to the appropriate standing order numbers can be made. Statistical data regarding labour cost rates per department may also be prepared.

The student is referred to page 271 for the relative accounting entries on the basis of integral accounts, and to page 227 for those where separate cost and financial systems are in operation.

STORES MATERIALS

There is a good deal to be said for arranging that all materials received in the factory, even for special jobs, pass through exactly the same routine as for stores materials proper. In the first place they are covered by goods received notes, and then, when issued to the factory, they, like the usual stores items, are all covered by requisitions. These requisitions, when priced, are charged out to the various job cost cards, and the total will then support the entry from Stores Ledger Control Account to work in progress.

TOOL-ROOM AND TOOL-STORE PROCEDURE

The careful selection, and the making and maintenance, of tools for manufacturing purposes are of great importance. In connection with the organisation dealing with tools, there are three divisions:

1. Manufacturing.
2. Maintenance and inspection.
3. Storage and issue.

1. Tool manufacture

The making of tools for production will be costed by the job-costing methods already described in this chapter.

2. Tool maintenance and inspection

As tools are returned from the factory floor to the tool store they are inspected before being placed on the racks ready for reissue. No doubt the tool inspector is highly skilled and experienced, and is able, by training and adherence to agreed tolerances, to decide on what maintenance treatment is required. Such work becomes part of the cost of running the tool-room, and will be apportioned with other items of expense as service department overhead.

3. Tool storage and issue

The tool stock can be conveniently recorded by the use of the bin-card procedure outlined in Chapter 5. If, as has been suggested, written requisitions are used for the issue of tools they should be made out in triplicate. One copy is kept by the workman, one in a file at the bin in numerical order of the recipients, and one in a file on the tool-stores clerk's desk arranged numerically according to tool nomenclature. When a tool is returned the requisitions are withdrawn from the files, and completed as to time and date of return.

An alternative method is to issue brass checks to the workmen, numbered according to their clock numbers. A check is given in, in exchange for a tool, and is hung on a peg on the bin. Each tool bin has checks also, bearing the symbol and number of the tools. When the workman's check is placed by the bin a tool check is removed to correspond, and is hung on a control board under the workman's number. Track of the tools is therefore easily kept. This method provides none of the useful data obtainable from the requisition-note procedure, and therefore a combination of both methods is sometimes used.

Tools returned

These are examined and reconditioned before being replaced, and the cost is charged to a standing order number for upkeep of tools.

Apportionment of tool expense

All the expense of running the tool room and tool store are collated and apportioned as overhead to the machine departments, except for the value of tools capitalised. Regard must also be paid to the fact that tools are made for:

(a) tool-room use;
(b) other centres;
(c) sale.

The basis on which apportionment may be made is the machine hours worked in the tool-room.

PRODUCTION OVERHEAD

The procedure to be adopted in the collection, apportionment and absorption of production overhead has already been described in Chapters 10 and 11, and factory job costing does not call for any variation.

BATCH COSTING

This is used when the production consists of limited repetition work and a definite number of articles are manufactured in one batch. Where a number of different parts enter into the article, sufficient for each batch are passed through the works for the quantity required. The cost of the operations is ascertained as described for job costing, the batches being given a production order number.

In determining the optimum quantity to constitute an economical batch there are five main considerations:

1. The cost and time taken in setting up the tools on the machines.
2. The cost and time taken in manufacturing the parts.
3. The rate of interest on the capital invested in the parts.
4. The cost of storage.
5. The rate at which the parts are demanded.

In addition, it is necessary to postulate an agreed period, say one month. We have, then, the following position:

1. Setting up cost per piece $= \dfrac{\text{Total setting up cost}}{\text{Quantity in batch}} = \dfrac{S}{X}.$

2. Manufacturing cost per piece =

Cost of material, labour and production overhead per piece = C.

3. Interest charge on capital invested. This raises some preliminary considerations:

(*a*) The average stock of units. This ranges from the minimum quantity which is in stock when a new batch is put in hand, to this figure plus the quantity in the batch. If M be used to denote the minimum, then the *average* is:

$$\frac{M + (M + X)}{2} \text{ or } M + \frac{X}{2}.$$

(*b*) The average investment in stock is therefore:

$$\left(\frac{S}{X} + C\right)\left(M + \frac{X}{2}\right).$$

(*c*) Assuming I represents the annual rate of interest, then the interest charge per month is:

$$\frac{I}{12}\left(\frac{S}{X} + C\right)\left(M + \frac{X}{2}\right).$$

4. The monthly storage charge. This is arrived at as follows:

(*a*) The total annual storage charges, including wages of storekeepers, rent, provision for obsolescence, etc., are calculated.

(*b*) A proportion of this figure is taken to represent that part of the storage space allotted for the type of components under consideration.

(*c*) This result is divided by 12 to obtain the monthly storage charge to be borne by the average quantity.

As in the present context this is a constant, we may denote the final answer by the mnemonic for "bin":

$$\frac{B}{12}.$$

5. The rate of demand per month, which may be denoted by D.

Now, let the total cost of a month's supply = Y.

Then:

$$Y = \frac{\text{Cost of units}}{\text{demanded}} + \frac{\text{Monthly interest on}}{\text{cost of average}} + \frac{\text{Monthly storage cost}}{\text{of average quantity.}}$$
$$\text{quantity}$$

Using the symbols suggested:

$$Y = D\left(\frac{S}{X} + C\right) + \frac{I}{12}\left(\frac{S}{X} + C\right)\left(M + \frac{X}{2}\right) + \frac{B}{12}.$$

Multiplying out:

$$Y = \frac{DS}{X} + \frac{DC}{1} + \frac{ISM}{12X} + \frac{ISX}{24X} + \frac{ICM}{12} + \frac{ICX}{24} + \frac{B}{12}.$$

This may be put in the index form:

$$Y = DSX^{-1} + DC + \frac{ISMX^{-1}}{12} + \frac{IS}{24} + \frac{ICM}{12} + \frac{ICX}{24} + \frac{B}{12}.$$

Using the calculus, if Y is a minimum, then $\frac{dx}{dy} = 0$,

and

$$\frac{dy}{dx} = \frac{-DS}{X^2} - \frac{ISM}{12X^2} + \frac{IC}{24} = 0.$$

Rearranging:

$$\frac{12DS + ISM}{12X^2} = \frac{IC}{24}.$$

Multiply both sides by $24X^2$:

$$24DS + 2ISM = X^2(IC).$$

Hence:

$$X^2 = \frac{24DS + 2ISM}{IC},$$

and

$$X = \sqrt{\frac{24DS + 2ISM}{IC}}.$$

In order to shorten this formula, it is often arranged that M, the minimum quantity, is to be regarded as too small to affect the calculation, so that:

$$X = \sqrt{\frac{24DS}{IC}}.$$

EXAMPLE

Let the monthly demand for a certain part be   200
Let the set up cost be (per batch)   £120
Let the annual rate of interest be   6%
Let the cost of manufacture per unit be   £6

Then X, the economic batch quantity, is:

$$\sqrt{\frac{24 \times 200 \times 120}{0.06 \times 6}} = 1,265.$$

NOTE: In the above illustration, had the rate of interest been taken as 25%, it would have offset the diminishing total cost per piece for larger batches to such an extent that the economic batch would be only 620.

GRAPHICAL METHODS

It is possible to find the economic batch quantity by graphical methods, and in order to illustrate this, the following question set by the I.C.W.A. may be considered:

SPECIMEN QUESTION

A manufacturing company, in addition to its work for outside customers, has an internal requirement for 200 units a day for a speciality product it manufactures and markets itself. At present several operations are performed manually in meeting this requirement.

Mechanised batch production is contemplated. This will involve a set-up cost of £700 for each batch put into production. The largest single batch size is 12,000 units. After each batch has been made the set-up cost, which includes maintenance and cleaning, must be incurred before a new batch can be started.

The variable cost of each unit is £10. The annual storage cost is £1 per unit and the cost of financing the inventory is 8% per annum.

The speciality products are required for 240 working days a year, and the average inventory is one half of the number of units made in each batch.

(a) Selecting 4, 6, 8, 12, 24 and 48 as the number of batches each year upon which to base the calculations, determine the annual cost for the required quantity of the speciality product for the selected number of batches.

(b) Draw a graph, plotting three curves to illustrate:

    (i) the annual total costs;
    (ii) the set-up costs;
    (iii) the inventory carrying costs

as determined in (a) and ascertain from the graph the optimum number of batches to produce each year to minimise the total cost of setting-up and carrying the inventory.

ANSWER

The annual requirements of speciality product are:

$$200 \text{ units} \times 240 \text{ working days} = 48,000.$$

We have therefore:

Number of batches	4	6	8	12	24	48
Size of each batch ('000)	12	8	6	4	2	1
Average no. of units in stock ('000)	6	4	3	2	1	0·5

	£	£	£	£	£	£
Set-up costs at £700 per batch	2,800	4,200	5,600	8,400	16,800	33,600
Variable costs per annum at £1 per unit	480,000	480,000	480,000	480,000	480,000	480,000
Storage costs at £1 per unit in stock	6,000	4,000	3,000	2,000	1,000	500
(a)	488,800	488,200	488,600	490,400	497,800	514,100

Inventory finance

We take the proportion of total cost which the number of units in stock bears to the total units made, to obtain the cost of inventory. The cost of financing the inventory is then 8%.

$$6/48(488,800) - 61,100$$
$$4/48(488,200) = 40,684$$

Thus:	61,100	40,684	30,538	20,433	10,375	5,355
at 8% per annum (b)	4,888	3,254	2,443	1,635	830	428
(a) + (b)	493,688	491,454	491,043	492,035	498,630	514,528

For the purpose of drawing the graph (Fig. 69), we may subtract from these total costs the amount of the variable costs per annum. This leaves the total of set-up costs, storage costs and inventory finance:

13,688	11,454	11,043	12,035	18,630	34,525

Line (a) + (b) gives the answer to part (a) of the question, and the graph (Fig. 69) gives the answer to part (b) of the question, and it shows that the optimum number of batches to produce each year is between 7 and 8 batches, or, say, 8 to the nearest round number.

SIMPLIFICATION OF COSTING WORK IN JOB COSTING

Owing to the vast amount of paperwork involved in obtaining the separate cost of each job undertaken, it is often found that the expense incurred is out of all proportion to the value of the result. Measures may therefore be taken to simplify the work, as follows:

(a) Estimates for each job are carefully prepared when submitting the quotation to the customer. These estimates are based on data sheets giving information on similar time-studied operations.

(b) The factory or works is split up into cost centres.

(c) Costs are collected as to:

(i) direct materials used;
(ii) labour costs per cost centre;
(iii) cost-centre production overhead incurred.

(d) No attempt is made to allocate these costs to particular jobs, the original estimates being assumed to be approximately correct.

(e) The material content of the estimates is compared in total with the direct materials issued and used.

(f) The labour content of the estimates is analysed to cost centres and compared with the total direct labour hours recorded for the cost centre. At the same time the average direct labour hour rate for the cost centre is found and compared with those recorded for previous periods.

(g) The production overhead content of the estimates is summarised and compared with the production overhead applied to the cost centre.

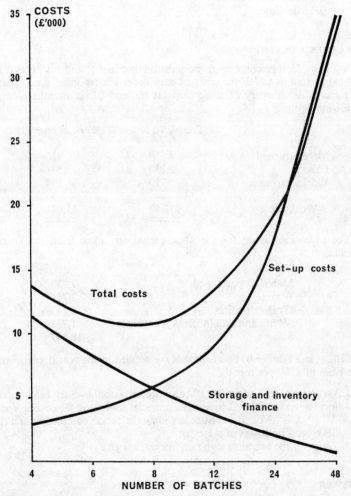

FIG. 69.—*Graph to illustrate annual total costs, set-up costs and inventory carrying costs in relation to a speciality product*

Adjustments have to be made on the analysis of the estimates to take care of beginning and ending work in progress, but this is not too difficult, since the progress advice gives the necessary information as to the stage of completion reached. By arranging the work in this way:

(a) material requisitions are dealt with in total and not one by one;
(b) operators' individual job time tickets are not required;
(c) payment to the operators is made on the basis of the clock card alone, split as to:

(i) productive time;
(ii) idle time.

SPECIMEN QUESTION*

A joinery factory commences business on January 1, and institutes a job-costing system in which the costs of each order are recorded on a separate cost card. A summary of these cards at the end of six months gives the following figures:

	Completed orders £	Work in progress £
Materials used	4,610	916
Labour	2,130	581
Works expenses	710	194
Works cost	£7,450	£1,691

The following figures for the same period are taken from the financial books:

	£
Materials purchased	7,430
Wages	2,711
Works expenses	1,142
Selling and administration expenses	1,793
Sales	10,547

Selling and administration expenses are applied in the cost department on the basis of £300 per month.

1. Write up Cost Ledger Total Accounts on a double-entry basis so as to form a reconciliation between the financial books and the costing system. All work is invoiced to customers immediately on completion and there have been no losses of materials.
2. Write up the accounts using an integral system.

ANSWER

In the answer given, figures only are used, the entries being numbered where necessary to show the double entry. A Materials Control Account is used so that the agreement of invoices and goods received notes can be demonstrated.

* This question is based on one given in the Intermediate Examination of the Corporation of Secretaries.

1. USING COST ACCOUNTS SEPARATE FROM FINANCIAL ACCOUNTS

Financial books

Materials Account	Wages Account	Works Expenses Account
7,430		2,711		1,142	

Selling and Administration Expenses Account	Sales Account
1,793			10,547

Cost Ledger Control Account—Memorandum

	7,430		10,547
	2,711	c/d	2,529
	1,142		
	1,793		
	13,076		13,076

Costing books

General Ledger Adjustment Account

	10,547 (10)		7,430 (1)
c/d	2,529		2,711 (4)
			1,142 (5)
			1,793 (7)
	13,076		13,076

Materials Control		Work in Progress	
7,430 (1)	7,430 (2)	5,526 (3)	7,450 (8)
		2,711 (4)	c/d 1,691
		904 (6)	

Stores Ledger Control			
7,430 (2)	5,526 (3)	9,141	9,141

Works Expenses Incurred

1,142 (5)	

Works Expenses Applied		Cost of Sales	
	904 (6)	7,450 (8)	
		1,800 (9)	

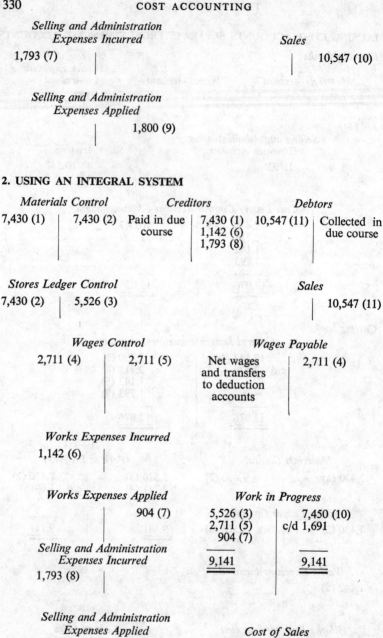

*Selling and Administration
Expenses Incurred*

1,793 (7)

Sales

10,547 (10)

*Selling and Administration
Expenses Applied*

1,800 (9)

2. USING AN INTEGRAL SYSTEM

Materials Control

7,430 (1) | 7,430 (2)

Creditors

Paid in due
course | 7,430 (1)
1,142 (6)
1,793 (8)

Debtors

10,547 (11) | Collected in
due course

Stores Ledger Control

7,430 (2) | 5,526 (3)

Sales

10,547 (11)

Wages Control

2,711 (4) | 2,711 (5)

Wages Payable

Net wages
and transfers
to deduction
accounts | 2,711 (4)

Works Expenses Incurred

1,142 (6)

Works Expenses Applied

904 (7)

Work in Progress

5,526 (3)
2,711 (5)
904 (7)
9,141 | 7,450 (10)
c/d 1,691

9,141

*Selling and Administration
Expenses Incurred*

1,793 (8)

*Selling and Administration
Expenses Applied*

1,800 (9)

Cost of Sales

7,450 (10)
1,800 (9)

In both systems of accounting shown above there will be certain subsidiary costing records:

(*a*) Stores Ledger in agreement with the Stores Ledger Control.

(*b*) Job cost cards giving details of work in progress: cards for completed work will be transferred to another cabinet, so that the "live" cards agree with the balance of work in progress carried forward.

(*c*) Standing order numbers in agreement with, and giving details of works expenses incurred.

(*d*) Cost account numbers giving details of selling and administration expenses incurred.

It will be seen that when separate systems of accounting are used, some work is duplicated, but agreement between the records is made through the Cost Ledger Control Account in the financial books, and the General Ledger Adjustment Account in the costing books.

For a fuller treatment of the subject the student is referred to Chapter 15.

EXAMINATION QUESTIONS

1. From the following information, prepare a job cost sheet for Order B. 1329 for the A.B. Company Ltd. for 120 identical castings.

Metal used	40 cwt at £0·65 per cwt
Mould labour	20 hours at £0·60 per hour
Core-making labour	10 hours at £0·57½ per hour
Finishing labour	86 hours at £0·47½ per hour

Overhead absorption rates:

Moulding	233%	on direct process labour	
Core-making	265%	,,	,,
Finishing	180%	,,	,,

Three pounds of scrap metal are fettled off each finished casting. One hundred and twenty-six castings were made, but six were found defective after pouring and scrapped. Scrap value is £0·20 per cwt. Show the cost per casting and per cwt of finished casting.

(*I.C.W.A. Inter.*)

2. In an organisation making a wide variety of engineering products each order is the subject of a job cost. It is found that for a number of smaller jobs the cost of compiling these costs is up to 50% of the total production cost of the job.

Give your reactions to this situation, suggesting alternative procedures. Would the introduction of mechanical accounting equipment have any effect on the basic problem?

(*I.C.W.A. Inter.*)

3. A company manufacturing components for the motor-car industry consists of a light machine shop and an assembly department. In a normal year, when sales amounted to £120,683, its costs were made up as follows:

	£
Direct materials	24,832
Direct wages, machine shop	16,694
Direct wages, assembly	8,090
Factory overhead, machine shop	31,742
Factory overhead, assembly	7,264
Administration costs	8,767
Selling costs	4,445
Distribution costs	6,427

Direct labour hours amounted to 67,284 in the machine shop and 40,073 in the assembly department.

It is the custom of the company to absorb overheads as follows:

Factory overhead:

Machine shop at £0·95 per direct labour hour.
Assembly department at £0·36½ per direct labour hour.
Administration, selling and distribution costs at 22½% on production cost.

A certain component is made from 50 lb of steel strip costing £112·00 per ton and requires 3½ hours of machine shop labour charged at £0·50 per hour, and 1¾ hours of assembly labour charged at £0·40 per hour. The customer is being charged a price of £12·00 each, and asks for quotations for exactly the same component: (a) made in "free issue" material, and (b) made from brass strip requiring 50 lb per article at a cost of £0·22½ per lb.

Management asks for information to enable quotations to be made as required, and also to see whether the present selling price is reasonable.

Present figures as required.

(I.C.W.A. Final)

4. In a manufacturing organisation short runs are almost invariably more costly than long runs.

Using appropriate figures, produce a report to management illustrating this fact, first indicating the nature of the industry and the size of the business.

(I.C.W.A. Final)

5. A production order is issued for the manufacture of 3,000 Type "X" Machines, for which will be required, among other things, 9,000 Components "Y." Trace by means of a diagram the progress of such components through the cost and financial books from the time of purchase to their subsequent use in fulfilling the production order, assuming that under inspection 110 of the components are scrapped as being not up to standard.

(C.A.A. Final)

6. The Diarmid Co. Ltd. has a job order costing system. The factory expenses incurred in the month of January (as shown by the Factory Overhead Control Account), were as follows:

	£
Cutting shop	36,250
Finishing and sanding shop	7,900
Fitting and assembly shop	4,755
Spraying shop	670

Overheads have been debited to jobs as follows:

Cutting £1·30 per machine hour for 22,000 hours.
Finishing and sanding £0·75 per direct labour hour for 11,000 hours.
Fitting and assembly 140% of direct labour cost. Direct labour £3,300.
Spraying £0·60 per piece for 925 pieces.

All expenses are charged to a Factory Overhead Control Account and are transferred from this account at the end of each month to Departmental Overhead Accounts. During the month the overhead charge to each job is transferred from the Departmental Overhead Account concerned.

You are required:

(a) by means of a journal entry, to close the Factory Overhead Control Account by making the necessary transfer to the Departmental Overhead Accounts;

(b) to journalise the factory overhead absorbed;

(c) to state the amount of over- or under-absorption of overhead in each department, and, where this is considered significant, comment on this position;

(d) to explain the costing treatment of such over- and under-absorbed overhead, at the end of the financial year.

(C.C.A. Inter.)

7. The summarised Profit and Loss Account of the Light Engineering Company Limited for the year ended July 31, is as follows:

	£	£	£
Sales			1,192,900
Material		491,724	
Labour—Department 1	96,000		
Department 2	128,000		
		224,000	
Factory expenses—Department 1	72,000		
Department 2	102,400		
		174,400	
Administrative expenses		53,500	
Selling expenses		80,000	
			1,023,624
Profit			£169,276

In October the sales manager was negotiating for a particular job—1A2—and he was supplied with the following information:

Job 1A2

	£
Lowest price acceptable	1,372
Target price to give 12½% profit on selling price	1,568

The above figures were taken from the cost estimate of Job 1A2:

Job 1A2 cost estimate sheet

	£	£
Material		600
Labour—Department 1 544 hours at £0·50 per hour	272	
Department 2 176 hours at £0·50 per hour	88	
	——	360
		960
Add 43% to cover other expenses		412
Total cost		£1,372

(*a*) Discuss the method adopted by the company for estimating cost and using the information available recalculate the cost of Job 1A2 using a method which you consider to be superior to that adopted by the company.

(*b*) Comment on the additional information which you would consider necessary to enable the cost estimate to be prepared in a form more suitable for both negotiating tender prices and controlling costs.

(*A.C.C.A. Final*)

8. You have recently been appointed as cost accountant to a manufacturing organisation which produces a wide range of products. It consists of a machine shop, electro-plating department and assembly department, together with the usual service departments. A preliminary analysis of the accounts for the year just ended reveals the following figures:

	£
Direct materials	90,000
Direct wages	50,000
Factory overheads	80,000
Administration overheads	13,000
Selling overheads	27,000
Distribution overheads	30,000
Sales	300,000

Sales estimates are made on the following basis:

(*a*) Direct materials: at cost, with what is stated to be an adequate allowance for loss in process.

(*b*) Direct wages: as paid to the workers.

(*c*) Factory overheads: at 175% of direct wages.

(*d*) An addition of 35% on factory cost to cover all other overheads.

(*e*) An addition of 10% to this total cost for profit.

List the main points which would be made in a preliminary report to management.

(*I.C.W.A. Final*)

9. A foundry finds it very difficult to obtain and retain moulders, particularly skilled moulders.

It is ascertained that a skilled moulder on floor work expects to earn at least £0·75 per hour, while a moulder on machine work expects to earn £0·50 per hour.

A certain job can be done by the floor moulder at a piece-work price of £0·12½ per box, or it can be put on the moulding machine at a piece-work price of £0·05 per box.

The variable overhead rates attributable to the two sectors are respectively:

Floor moulding, £0·12½ per box.
Machine moulding, £0·20 per box.

Prepare figures for management to indicate the more economic method of manufacture.

(I.C.W.A. Final)

10. X Limited manufactures a number of products including Product D which is sold under contract to J Limited. Using the information given below:

(a) calculate the selling price of 100 units of D;
(b) evaluate 1,000 units of D held in stock by X Limited.

This valuation is for inclusion in the balance sheet. Give brief reasons in support of the method you recommend.

Standard production data for 100 units:

	£
Direct materials 200 lb of material Z at	0·25 per lb
Direct wages 50 hours at	0·50 per hour
Variable production overhead	5·00
Machine hours 10	

Budgeted data for year:

		£000's
Production variable cost		1,000
Overhead:	fixed production	400
	administration	350
	selling and distribution	700
Profit 20% of selling price		
Machine hours 100,000		

(I.C.W.A. Inter.)

CHAPTER 19

OPERATING COSTS

OPERATING cost is defined in the *Terminology of Cost Accountancy* as "the cost of providing a service." Such a service might consist of transport, steam and hot water, catering and so on, as departments of a firm, or it might be applied to large public-utility undertakings, such as Gas and Electricity Boards.

This method of costing is different from that used in connection with production manufacturing, and the difference lies chiefly in the manner of assembling the cost data, and in its allocation to cost units.

TRANSPORT COSTING

PURPOSE

The records are designed to show the total cost of operating each vehicle, and then to apply this cost to particular units, *e.g.* per ton, per mile run, per ton-mile or per hour worked. These units have to be chosen with care, because, when materials are being carried which vary in bulk, weight and type, to cost per ton, per mile run, or per ton-mile is somewhat unsuitable. The costs ascertained are useful for the following:

(*a*) Comparing the cost of using motor vehicles owned and that of using alternative forms of transport.

(*b*) Determining what should be charged against departments, or others, using the service.

(*c*) Deciding at what price the use of a vehicle can be charged, profitably, to anyone hiring a vehicle.

(*d*) Comparing the cost of maintaining one vehicle with another, or one group of vehicles with another group.

COLLECTION OF DATA

Most of the details required by the transport manager for controlling the vehicles under his authority is obtained from the daily log sheet, a specimen of which is to be seen in Fig. 70. In addition, he will doubtless inaugurate a system of requisitions for transport, so that he may allocate them to the most suitable vehicles available. His aim will be to avoid idleness of vehicles, to prevent waste of capacity by too much light running and to guard against unnecessary duplication of journeys.

336

LOG SHEET

Vehicle No.: .... **Date:** ....19...
Driver: .... **Time left Garage:** ....
Route No.: .... **Time returned:** ....

Trip Record.

| Trip No. | From | To | Tons or Packages | | Miles | Time | |
			Out	Collected en route		Out	In
1							
2							
3							
4							
5							
6							
etc.							
		Totals					

Supplies	Workers' Time	Exceptional Delays
Petrol:	Driver:	Loading delays: ....
Oil:	Assistant:	Traffic delays: ....
Grease:	Cleaners:	Accidents: ....
etc.	Mechanics:	

FIG. 70.—*Log sheet*

Each driver hands in daily a log sheet of this kind, from which the transport manager can extract details by which he maintains control.

EXPENDITURE ON REPAIRS

If the driver has to arrange for any repairs or adjustments when away from his own garage he may be required to note the fact on the back of the log sheet, so that the account, when received, may be linked up and checked from his record. Work done by the firm's own garage staff is usually recorded on repair tickets, and is then costed. The cost of repairs may be collected for each individual vehicle, or for groups of similar vehicles, and should be stated as so much "per mile run."

Special statistics on tyre performances are often kept, and this is not so difficult as it might seem, since reference numbers are marked on the wall of the tyre.

If the repair tickets are filed for reference a handy repair history for each vehicle can be accumulated, and will be most useful when a decision has to be taken on whether to incur further repair expenditure or not. It is considered advisable to prepare an estimate for each proposed major repair: if these estimates are done conscientiously experience will lead to greater and greater accuracy, and finally it may then be found unnecessary to find the actual cost of each job done.

EXPENDITURE ON FUEL

Each night or morning the tanks of all vehicles are filled, and the gallons supplied are noted at once on the log sheet. Any fuel obtained *en route* has to be accounted for by garage tickets, and also noted on the log sheet.

The basis of control in this case will be "miles per gallon."

COST SUMMARY AND PERFORMANCE STATEMENT

This is shown in Fig. 71. It will be seen that there are three main subdivisions of cost:

(a) *Operating and running costs.* These vary from day to day, and are incurred by the actual operation of the vehicle; expenses which would not be incurred if the vehicle were "laid up" come under this heading, *e.g.* petrol, oil, grease and part of the driver's wages.

(b) *Maintenance charges.* These include wear on tyres, repairs and overhauls, painting, hire of spare vehicles when the firm's own are under repair, garaging, etc.

(c) *Fixed charges.* These are incurred whether a vehicle is operating or not. They include insurance, tax, depreciation and part of the driver's wages. Interest on capital might also be included.

RECOVERY OF TRANSPORT COSTS

It is customary to charge a rate per hour or a rate per mile, based on the cost summary figures, to the various departments making use of the transport.

BOILER-HOUSE COSTING

The necessary statistics for arriving at the cost of steam produced and used are based on accounts prepared by the cost office and technical data provided by the engineering department as to steam pressures, evaporations, meter readings and distribution to processes, factory heating, turbines, losses, etc.

The costs may be considered under the following headings:

(a) *Supervision.* Wages of foreman, and a proportion of the works engineer's salary.

(b) *Labour.* Coal handlers, stokers and ash removers.

COST SUMMARY AND PERFORMANCE STATEMENT

No. of Car: 19   Month ended April 19...
Chassis No.: 14966A   Capacity in lb............

MONTHLY CHARGES

A. Operating Charges		B. Maintenance Charges	
	£		£
Petrol		Tyres	
Oil		Repairs	
Grease		Overhaul	
etc.		Spare Car	
Driver		Garage Charge	
Assistant		etc.	
Mechanics			
Total	102·00	Total	26·00

C. Fixed Charges	Proportion for Month
	£
Insurance at £ ...... per year	
Interest at ...... per cent per year	
Depreciation at .... per cent per year	
Tax, licence at £ ...... per year	
Other items at £ ...... per year	
Total	70·00

MONTHLY COST SHEET

1. Total Capital cost, complete	£1123·95
Performance Record	
2. Days operated	26
3. Days idle	4
4. Days maintained (Item 2 + Item 3)	30
5. Total hours operated	232
6. Total miles covered	803
7. Total trips made	28
Performance Averages	
8. Average miles per day maintained (Item 6 ÷ Item 4)	26·76
9. Average miles per day operated (Item 6 ÷ Item 2)	30·88
10. Average miles per trip (Item 6 ÷ Item 7)	28·67
Costs for the Month	
11. Total expenses for month (Sum of Items A, B and C above)	£198
12. Cost per day operated (Item 11 ÷ Item 2)	£7·61
13. Cost per day maintained (Item 11 ÷ Item 4)	£6·6
14. Cost per mile operated (Item 11 ÷ Item 6)	£0·24½
15. Cost per hour (Item 11 ÷ Item 5)	£0·85

FIG. 71.—*Cost summary and performance statement*

This provides summarised details in regard to the running of each vehicle or group of similar vehicles. Comparison of period with period and of one vehicle with another should yield useful information for control purposes.

(c) *Maintenance.* Furnace repairs, renewal of fire bars, replacement of fire irons, etc.

(d) *Indirect materials.* Service materials and small tools.

(e) *Fuel.* This may be coal, or fuel oil. The cost will include cartage, handling and storage.

(f) *Water.* The cost of purification and softening is included, as well as the cost of supply.

(g) *Fixed overhead.* Rent, rates, depreciation, insurance and possibly interest on capital. It should be noted that the capital value of the boiler-house plant is included in the rating assessment, whereas that in manufacturing machinery is not. This must be borne in mind when apportioning rates as between shops, departments and boiler-house.

A specimen boiler-house cost sheet is shown in Fig. 72. The costs are apportioned to departments in the basis of technical data of consumption supplied by the engineer. Separate consumption returns are required for processes, heating and domestic hot water.

A simple system is to ascertain by technical calculation the rate of consumption of steam in pounds per hour for each appliance connected with the mains and service pipes. Then, by estimating or recording the times during which each unit is consuming steam, a reasonably reliable record for steam allocation is obtained.

CANTEEN COSTING

The main headings of expense will be as follows:

(a) *Provisions.* Meat; fish and poultry; vegetables; fruit (fresh and dried); flour; cakes; milk and cream; tea; coffee; sugar; soft drinks; and often cigarettes are included too under this heading.

(b) *Labour.* Supervision; cooks; waitresses; kitchen assistants; porters.

(c) *Services.* Steam; gas; electricity; power and light; water.

(d) *Consumable stores.* Table linen; cutlery; crockery; glassware; mops and washing-up cloths; drying-up cloths; cleaning materials; dustpans and brushes, etc.

(e) *Miscellaneous overhead.* Rent and rates; depreciation; insurances, etc.

(f) *Credit.* Charges for meals, teas and other sales; sale of swill.

The canteen manageress will have the duty of estimating the quantities of food required each day. Adequate cold-store facilities will greatly help her in the avoidance of waste and in economical buying.

She will probably have a general responsibility to the personnel manager, or to the works manager, and from time to time, with her

BOILER-HOUSE COST SHEET
For the month of June 19...

S.O. Nos.	Expense Items	Total Cost		Cost per 1,000 lb of Steam		Incr. or decr. %
		This Year	Last Year	This Year	Last Year	
		£	£	£	£	
	Fuel					
	Fuel Handling					
	Ash Removal and Disposal					
	Electric Power					
	Stokers and Coal Wheelers					
	Water Purchased					
	„ Softening					
	Boiler Cleansing					
	Sundry Indirect Materials					
	Gas and Electric Light					
	Maintenance Services:					
	Fixed Plant					
	Meters					
	Boilers					
	Economisers					
	Softening Plant					
	Mechanical Stokers					
	Steam Service Pipes					
	Barrows					
	Weighing Machine, Tools, etc.					
	Coal Bunkers					
	Furnace					
	Miscellaneous Expenses:					
	Supervision					
	Sweepers, Cleaners, and General Labour					
	Rent, Rates, etc.					
	Depreciation Plant					
	„ Buildings					
	Renewals					
	Steam Mains					
	Allocation of General Charges					
	Total					

Steam Produced in 1,000 lb:......	Less Boiler House Use:.........	Less Mains Losses:.........	Total Consumption:.........

Remarks:

Fig. 72.—*Boiler-house cost sheet*

The main points to notice here will be the fuel costs, the labour costs and the maintenance costs as against the steam raised. Other information, of a more technical kind, as for example the CO_2 recording, will be watched by the engineer.

The expense headings would be modified should the fuel used be oil and not coal.

co-operation, he should initiate an examination of the swill bins, which more than anything will reveal whether food is being wasted unnecessarily.

Whether it is possible to introduce a choice of dishes each day depends largely on the numbers being catered for. An experienced canteen manageress will, however, aim at a weekly cycle, without repetition, of main joints and entrées, and about a ten-day cycle in

	Actual		Budget	
CANTEEN COST STATEMENT For the month of .... 19...	This Month	Cumulative Total	This Month	Cumulative Total
Wages and Salaries: Supervisor Cooks Vegetable Preparation Counter Helpers				
Provisions: Meat Fish and Poultry Vegetables and Fruit Eggs Butter Tea Bread and Cakes Biscuits Coffee Cheese Milk Soft Drinks Groceries Miscellaneous: Maintenance Crockery and Glassware Insurance Table Linen Consumable Stores Rent Steam Gas Electricity				
Deduct Income from: Sales Company Subsidy				

Fig. 73.—Canteen cost statement

respect of sweets. Generally speaking the average worker likes plain food, well cooked and attractively served.

Costing with a view to fixing a price for main meals and subsidiary meals is difficult to arrange, as it necessitates equating one type of meal with another. However, by recording the numbers of persons served, using different coloured dockets according to the type of meal provided, experience will be gained from which the cost involved may be approximated. Canteen-management training also helps by providing knowledge as to the quantities which can be expected from various joints of meat and kinds of fish; the numbers of cups of tea from one pound of tea and one pint of milk; the number of slices of bread and butter from a quartern loaf and a pound of butter; and so on.

Most factory canteens have to be subsidised to some extent, since to charge prices sufficient to cover not only the direct costs but full overhead as well would result in the canteen being neglected—and on production grounds this may be undesirable.

It is therefore suggested that the best kind of operating-cost statement to prepare will be on the lines of the expense headings already given, with comparative figures for the last period and the corresponding period last year (*see* Fig. 73).

By the use of moving-average charts for the main headings of expense, the income received and the numbers of each type of meal provided, a close watch can be obtained on the trends which are significant.

EXAMINATION QUESTIONS

1. A brewery maintains a motor service consisting of twelve lorries, delivering barrelled and bottled beer, and bringing back empties.

Outline a system of cost control, covering the cost of running, maintenance and depreciation, recommending the unit of measurement to be applied.

(I.C.W.A. Inter.)

2. In a group organisation consisting of twelve individual companies it has been the practice for each company to maintain its own transport department. Top management has decided to pool all vehicles and staff into a central transport department which will in future give service to all companies within the group. Approximately thirty vehicles are involved, ranging in type from saloon cars to 5-ton lorries, and the vehicles are used for purposes ranging from inter-company communication to direct sales delivery service.

Discuss the effect of this change on costs. Outline the bases upon which you would propose to absorb the operating costs of this new service department.

(I.C.W.A. Final)

3. With a mixed fleet of a hundred goods-transport vehicles how would you calculate an hourly rate per vehicle for charging to jobs and services?

(I.C.W.A. Final)

4. A factory which uses a large amount of coal is situated between two collieries, "A" and "B," the former being 5 miles and the latter 10 miles distant from the factory. A fleet of lorries of 5-ton carrying capacity is used for the collection of coal from the pit-heads. Records reveal that the lorries average a speed of 20 miles an hour when running and regularly take 10 minutes in the factory yard to unload. At Colliery "A" loading time averages 30 minutes per load; at Colliery "B" 20 minutes per load.

Drivers' wages, licences, depreciation, garage and similar charges are found to cost £1·20 per hour operated. Fuel, oil, tyres, repairs and similar charges are found to cost £0·10 per mile run.

Draw up a statement showing the cost per ton-mile of carrying coal from each colliery. If the coal is of equal quality and price at pit-head, from which colliery should the purchases be made?

(I.C.W.A. Final)

5. Describe a method to ensure recovery of all expenditure on repair work in a motor garage when immediate charges are made to customers.

(C.A.A. Inter.)

6. Draw up a *pro-forma* cost statement for a canteen subsidised by the company, serving a firm of 1,500 employees.

What measures of efficiency would you use in such a case, and on what basis would canteen prices be fixed?

(I.C.W.A. Final)

7. The works canteen of a large industrial organisation shows a considerable loss on the first year's trading, although it was intended that the amounts charged for meals, etc., should just cover the cost. You are instructed to investigate the matter and to suggest any improvements you consider necessary in the existing costing system. You may assume whatever facts you consider appropriate as having been discovered during your investigation. Submit the main headings of your report.

(C.A.A. Final)

8. What is a departmental operating statement?

Prepare such a statement to indicate the efficiency of the use of each element of cost.

(I.C.W.A. Final)

9. Your company employs three different types of transport vehicle in bringing into the factory heavy steel bars, and delivering to customers finished tubes and fabricated tube products. Detail the procedures necessary to install satisfactory costing arrangements for the transport, and suggest cost control measures which might be introduced.

(I.C.W.A. Final)

CHAPTER 20

PROCESS COSTING

Introduction and General Principles

PROCESS costing is a method of costing used to ascertain the cost of the product at each process, operation or stage of manufacture, where processes are carried on having one or more of the following features:

(a) Where the product is produced in one single process.

(b) Where the product of one process becomes the material of another process or operation.

(c) Where there is simultaneous production, at one or more processes, of different products, with or without by-products.

(d) Where, during one or more processes or operations of a series, the products, or materials, are not distinguishable from one another, as, for instance, when finished products differ finally only in shape or form.

The system provides for showing the cost of the main products and of any by-products, and thus is very different from job costing, where each job is separately costed. Orders may be combined for common process production to a certain state, and then be costed for subsequent operations by job cost methods.

In most cases process costing requires fewer forms, and less details, than are needed for job costs, but a closer analysis of operations is needed. For example, there is not the need for the allocation of labour to so many order numbers, and material is issued in bulk to departments, rather than to many specific jobs. In continuous processes, as in a coal distillation plant, the men are occupied continuously on each process.

In process costing the terms by-product, joint product, scrap and wastage frequently occur, so it might be expedient to define these terms before proceeding.

BY-PRODUCTS

The Cost Accountants' Handbook,* from which this and the other definitions given below are taken, defines these as:

"any saleable or usable value incidentally produced in addition to the main product."

* *The Cost Accountants' Handbook*, edited by Theodore Lang (The Ronald Press Company, 1944, New York).

345

In the process of producing the main product it frequently occurs that materials or other products emerge which are of smaller value. These are the by-products, and, even if subsequent processing enhances their value, the resulting profit will be less than that from the main product, otherwise of course the by-product would become the main product, and vice versa. A typical example of the creation of by-products is in the oil refinery industry, where the crude oil is processed and refined oil might be the main product, with sulphur, bitumen and chemical fertilisers among the many by-products.

It is possible for a main product of one industry to be the by-product of another. An example of this occurs in the production of coke and gas. In coke ovens production is concentrated on the main product—coke—and gas is incidentally produced, and thus becomes a by-product. However, in a gas-works gas is the main product, while coke is a by-product. This situation may raise a difficult problem when the by-product of one firm is being sold at a cheaper rate than the same commodity which is a main product of another firm.

JOINT PRODUCTS

The definition of these is that they:

"represent two or more products separated in the course of the same processing operations, usually requiring further processing, each product being in such proportion that no single product can be designated as a major product."

In a process where two or more products are inevitably produced, and each one earns approximately the same profit as another, the products would be considered joint products. The term is also used to describe various qualities of the same product, as, for example, the many grades of coal which may be used.

SCRAP

This is defined as:

"the incidental residue from certain types of manufacture, usually of small amount and low value, recoverable without further processing."

Products which are found to be defective or raw materials which prove to be not up to standard may be used in other departments of the firm or sold at a much lower price than the cost. In many firms off-cuts are unavoidably produced, as, for example, when can lids are pressed out of a sheet of tin-plate; the remaining tin-plate may be collected and returned to the supplier, who can re-process the tin and credit the firm returning the material with the scrap value.

It is essential to keep the quantity of scrap produced to a minimum and, if possible, make it more profitable by further processing; *e.g.* metal turnings could be made into pan scrapers.

WASTE

The *Handbook* defines this as:

"that portion of a basic raw material lost in processing, having no recovery value."

Anything which has no value is considered to be waste. An example of waste is a tank of soup into which broken glass has fallen, with the result that the soup is unfit for consumption and must be destroyed.

THE APPLICATION OF THE METHOD

The industries in which process costs may be used are very many; in fact, except where job, batch or unit operation costing is necessary, a process costing system can usually be devised. In particular, the following may be mentioned as a few examples:

Chemical works	Textiles, weaving, spinning, etc.
Soap-making	Food products
Box-making	Canning factories
Distillation processes	Coking works
Paper mills	Paint, ink, and varnishing, etc.
Biscuit works	Meat products factory
Oil refining	Milk dairy

Process costing is used by firms having a continuous flow of identical products, where it is not possible to distinguish one unit from another. The amount of production is determined to a large extent by supply and demand for the product, rather than by a specific order. The cost per unit is averaged over a period, *e.g.* a week or a month.

To illustrate the above statement, let us assume the following details:

Production for the month of January was 60,000 units.
Direct materials consumed amounted to £6,000.
Direct labour costs were £4,000.
Production overhead incurred was £2,000.

The cost per unit is determined by dividing the total cost by the total number of units produced.

$$\frac{£12,000}{60,000} = £0\cdot20 \text{ per unit.}$$

This might be shown in a cost statement, thus:

XYZ, Ltd.
Cost Statement January 19..
Production 60,000 units

	£	£
Prime cost		
Direct materials consumed	6,000	
Direct labour	4,000	
		10,000
Production overhead		
50% of direct labour cost		2,000
Production cost		£12,000

Production cost per unit

$$\frac{£12,000}{60,000} = £0·20 \text{ per unit.}$$

This cost of £0·20 per unit will relate to each one of the 60,000 units produced, irrespective of the fact that on one day the units produced cost £0·21 while on another day the cost was £0·19. The important fact is that £0·20 per unit is the average cost for the period.

THE GENERAL FEATURES OF THE PROCESS COST SYSTEM

The factory is divided into departments or processes, which are limited to a certain operation; *e.g.* in a canning factory one department may bake the beans and another department may prepare the sauce for the beans. The process may perform a certain operation or operations, each of which completes a special stage in the production routine. Each process is usually the responsibility of one person, who may be a foreman or a supervisor.

An account is kept for each process or operation. Materials, labour and overhead are debited, by-products and scrap are credited, while the material as modified at the first operation is passed on to the next process. If by-products require further treatment the same procedure is followed.

Put in another way, the "finished product" of the first process becomes the "raw material" of the next one, and so on, until the final products are completed. Each Process Cost Account, in fact, represents a sub-division of a Manufacturing Account, so that the works cost of each process is separately ascertained, and from which the unit cost at each operation may be calculated.

Single or output costing resembles process costing, in which there is but one process where every unit is identical. Sometimes unit costing is combined with process costing, the method being to cost by the unit of production, where manufacture is continuous and the units are identical, or can be made equivalent by means of ratios.

Departmental costing differs in that separate products are generally dealt with in each department, whereas in process costing the same material passes from one operation or process to another in altered form. When two or more distinct varieties of goods are manufactured separate departmental costs are desirable, so that the profit made by each department may be revealed. Any normal loss suffered in a process is borne by the good production, thus increasing the average cost per unit. Any abnormal loss is valued at the ordinary rate and the amount transferred to an Abnormal Loss Account, which reveals to management any losses due to inefficiency, accidents, etc.

STANDARD COSTS IN PROCESS COSTING

In industries where process costing is suitable, standard costs may be used with great advantage. Standard costs provide a measure against which actual costs may be compared. Standard costing, in connection with process costs, gives the management an excellent measure of the efficiency of production, and it may be mentioned that accounting systems on these lines are being more widely used every year. This method is dealt with fully in another chapter.

THE USE OF NUMERICAL NOMENCLATURE

In an earlier chapter the use of works order numbers and standing order numbers was described. The identification of cost to processes by means of process order numbers facilitates the collection of the necessary details, ensures a proper apportionment of expenditure to each process and simplifies overhead analysis.

The adoption of departmental or process numbers is necessary when mechanical sorting and tabulating machines are used, as is the case in many large firms today. Numbers are also essential where electronic computing machines are in operation. Mechanical or electronic machines are indispensable in large factories if prompt cost and production figures are required.

THE ELEMENTS OF PRODUCTION COST
Materials

Frequently in process costing all the material required for production is issued to the first process, where after processing it is passed to the next process, and so on: each process merely performs some operation on the material which has been passed from the first process. In other systems material may pass from the first process to the second process, where extra or new materials are added, then more material added in the next process; this may continue until completion.

Whichever method is used, sufficient supplies of raw materials must be available to meet production needs. Materials may be requisitioned in the way described in Chapter 5 or bulk requisitions may be issued. When bulk requisitions are used, materials are issued from the stores to the department in bulk quantities, where they are held in departmental stock until such time as they are needed.

Labour

Generally, the cost of direct labour is a very small part of the cost of production in industries adopting process costing; for example, in one large firm in the chemical industry, the cost of direct labour represents 4% of the total cost. With the introduction of more and more automatic machinery the direct-labour element becomes smaller and smaller, while the overhead element increases.

Compared with, for example, job costing, the recording and allocating of time spent on production is relatively easy. Where employees are engaged continuously on one process, as is frequently the case, the time spent by the employees is analysed and posted to the debit of the Process Account concerned. However, if employees are engaged on more than one process it will be necessary to record the time spent on each one, or an approximate apportionment of the total time will be allocated to each process concerned.

Direct expenses

Each item of expenditure which can be directly attributed to a process will be debited to the relative Process Account. An example of direct expense is the design cost of a can used in canning vegetables.

Production overhead

In process costing the overhead element of total cost is normally very high. Great care will be needed to ensure that each process is charged with a reasonable share of the production overhead. The actual overhead to be debited to each Process Account will be calculated as suggested in Chapter 11.

EXAMPLE

The manufacture of Product "Exe" requires four distinct processes, numbered 1–4. On completion, the product is passed from Process 4 to finished stock. During Period 10, the following information was obtained in relation to Product "Exe":

Element of cost	Total	Process			
		1	2	3	4
	£	£	£	£	£
Direct material	2,600	1,500	400	—	700
Direct labour	2,650	250	300	900	1,200
Direct expense	800	100	—	200	500
Production overhead	7,950				

Production overhead is absorbed by processes on the basis of 300% of direct wages.

Production during the period was 1,000 tons.

There was no stock of raw material or work in progress either at the beginning or at the end of the period.

Process 1

Description: Period No. 10
                                                                             Output 1,000 tons

	Amount	Cost per ton			Amount	Cost per ton
	£	£			£	£
Direct material	1,500	1·50	Output transferred to Process 2		2,600	2·60
Direct labour	250	0·25				
Direct expense	100	0·10				
Production overhead	750	0·75				
	£2,600	£2·60			£2,600	£2·60

Process 2

Description: Period No. 10
                                                                             Output 1,000 tons

	Amount	Cost per ton			Amount	Cost per ton
	£	£			£	£
Output transferred from Process 1	2,600	2·60	Output transferred to Process 3		4,200	4·20
Direct material	400	0·40				
Direct labour	300	0·30				
Production overhead	900	0·90				
	£4,200	£4·20			£4,200	£4·20

Process 3

Description: Period No. 10
                                                                             Output 1,000 tons

	Amount	Cost per ton			Amount	Cost per ton
	£	£			£	£
Output transferred from Process 2	4,200	4·20	Output transferred to Process 4		8,000	8·00
Direct labour	900	0·90				
Direct expense	200	0·20				
Production overhead	2,700	2·70				
	£8,000	£8·00			£8,000	£8·00

Process 4

Description:

Period No. 10
Output 1,000 tons

	Amount	Cost per ton		Amount	Cost per ton
	£	£	Output transferred to Finished Stock	£	£
Output transferred from Process 3	8,000	8·00		14,000	14·00
Direct material	700	0·70			
Direct labour	1,200	1·20			
Direct expense	500	0·50			
Production overhead	3,600	3·60			
	£14,000	£14·00		£14,000	£14·00

It will be observed that the "finished" product of Process 1 is the "raw material" of Process 2 and so on, each transferred at cost. Sometimes these transfers are made to show the transferring process a profit; the reason and stock valuation problems arising, are dealt with later in Chapter 21. The finished output of Process 4 is transferred to Finished Stock Account.

Finished Stock Account—Product "Exe"

	Tons	Cost per ton	Amount		Tons	Cost per ton	Amount
		£	£			£	£
Output of 1,000 tons transferred from Process 4 at cost	1,000	14·00	14,000				

PROCESS LOSS, SCRAP AND WASTAGE

Some loss, scrap and/or wastage is inevitable in process industries, so it is essential that accurate records are maintained to enable control of these items to be effected. The cost department must be kept well informed through the medium of scrap tickets, material credit notes and loss reports.

It should be pointed out to foremen and supervisors that scrap, etc., should be measured and recorded, otherwise production costs will be adversely affected. Materials which have been processed and are then found to be defective and scrapped have incurred their share of labour and variable overhead up to the point of rejection, so obviously the financial loss to the firm increases with each stage of production. Where possible, scrap should be baled as it is incurred, because baled scrap is usually valued higher than loose scrap, and needs less storage space.

In most process industries the loss of material which is inherent in the processing operation can be worked out in advance. Usually this is calculated by formula or by experience, and it reveals the loss which would be expected in normal conditions. Process loss is often caused by such factors as evaporation and that loss which is inherent in large-scale production, and may often include scrap and waste already defined. This is considered to be the normal process loss.

Abnormal process loss is that loss caused by unexpected or abnormal conditions, such as sub-standard materials, carelessness and accidents. All losses under this category must be thoroughly investigated, and, where necessary, steps should be taken to try to prevent any recurrence.

The accounting treatment of normal and abnormal losses differ. In the first case the cost of any normal loss is absorbed in the cost of production of good products, while a separate account is opened for abnormal losses, to which is debited the cost of material, labour and appropriate overhead incurred by the wastage. Abnormal losses should be written off to the Costing Profit and Loss Account.

WASTE

Waste has no value. If waste is part of the normal process loss the cost will be absorbed by the good production. On the other hand, if it is part of the abnormal process loss, the cost will be transferred from the Process Account to Abnormal Loss Account.

SCRAP

The problem of scrap is more complex than that of waste, and may be treated as follows:

(a) Scrap resulting from one process which is to be utilised in another process should be credited to the first process at the value at which it was originally debited, and debited to the relevant Stores Account. This value is thus related to the market price of the good material. On issue to the next process it is valued at the same price as that which it would have been charged if bought specifically for the purpose. This method is advantageous in that, if a comparison of the cost of production of a firm is to be made with the cost of having the product produced elsewhere, accurate costs will be obtainable.

(b) Scrap which cannot be utilised for subsequent production should be credited to the Process Account and debited to the appropriate Stores Account at a value which is not greater than the market price of such scrap material.

(c) Scrap which is of small value may be sold periodically, and the amount realised credited to Production Overhead Account. This method saves the expense of allocating credit to each process which has incurred the scrap.

To illustrate the different treatment of normal loss and abnormal loss in process costing, the following illustration is given:

In the manufacture of product "Wye," 1,000 lb of material at £0·20 per lb were supplied to the first process. Labour costs amounted to £50 and production overheads of £25 were incurred. The normal process loss has been estimated at 10% of which half can be sold as scrap at £0·10 per lb. The actual production realised was 850 lb.

Process 1

Description:

Period No. 1
Output 850 lb

	lb	Cost per lb	Amount		lb	Cost per lb	Amount
			£				£
Direct material	1,000	£0·20	200	Normal loss	100	£0·05	5
Direct labour			50	Abnormal loss	50	£0·30	15
Production overhead			25	Process 2 output	850	£0·30	255
	1,000		£275		1,000		£275

Normal loss is calculated as follows:

Estimated loss 10% of production (1,000 lb) = 100 lb.
Half can be sold as scrap = 50 lb.

$$50 \text{ lb at } £0·1 \text{ per lb} = \underline{£5.}$$

Abnormal loss is calculated as follows:

Estimated production	900 lb
Actual production	850 lb
Abnormal loss	50 lb

Cost of normal production = £275 − £5 = £270.

$$\text{Cost of normal production per lb} = \frac{£270}{900}.$$

$$\text{Cost of abnormal loss } \frac{£270}{900} \times 50 = \underline{£15.}$$

However, some of the abnormal loss will probably possess scrap value, so, if we assume for purposes of illustration that half can be sold, then 25 lb at £0·10 per lb will be realised.

In the Abnormal Loss Account will appear the debit of £15 transferred from Process 1, while on the credit side will be shown the £2·50 realised on sale of the scrap. The net cost of the abnormal loss is thus £12·50.

ABNORMAL GAIN

Mention was previously made of allowances being made for losses which would be expected in process industries in normal conditions. Then it was shown how abnormal losses occur when the allowances were exceeded. Sometimes, however, the actual loss in a process is smaller than was expected, in which case an abnormal gain results.

The value of the gain will be calculated in a similar manner to an abnormal loss previously described, then posted to an Abnormal Gain Account.

EXAMPLE

In the manufacture of Product "Wye," 1,200 lb of material at £0·20 per lb were supplied to the first process in Period 2. Labour costs amounted to £60 and production overheads of £30 were incurred. The normal process loss has been estimated at 10%, of which half can be sold as scrap at £0·10 per lb. The actual production realised was 1,120 lb.

Process 1

Description: Period No. 2
                                                                             Output 1,120 lb

	lb	Cost per lb	Amount		lb	Cost per lb	Amount
			£				£
Direct material	1,200	£0·20	240	Normal loss	120	£0·05	6
Direct labour			60	Process 2 output			
Production overhead			30	transferred	1,120	£0·30	336
Abnormal gain	40	£0·30	12				
	1,240		£342		1,240		£342

Normal loss is calculated as follows:

Estimated loss 10% of production (1,200 lb) = 120 lb.
Half can be sold as scrap = 60 lb.

$$60 \text{ lb at £0·10 per lb} = £6.$$

Abnormal gain is calculated as follows:

Estimated production	1,080 lb
Actual production	1,120 lb
Abnormal gain	40 lb

Cost of normal production £330 − £6 = £324.

Cost of normal production per lb: $\dfrac{£324}{1,080}$.

Cost of abnormal gain $\dfrac{324}{1,080} \times 40 = £12.$

In the Abnormal Gain Account will appear the credit of £12 transferred from Process 1, while on the debit side will be shown an item of £2 calculated as follows:

Normal loss estimated at 120 lb.
Half is sold as scrap at £0·10 per lb.

$$60 \text{ lb at £0·10} = £6.$$

However, the actual loss realised was only 80 lb. Assuming for the purpose of illustration that half is sold as scrap, then the value realised will be:

$$40 \text{ lb at } £0·10 = £4.$$

This means that there is a reduced income of £2 from scrap, so the loss of income will partly offset the gain of £12 arising from the abnormal gain in production.

Abnormal Gain Account

	£		£
Process 1	2	Process 1	12
Profit and loss	10		
	£12		£12

It will be observed that in the two illustrations above the cost per lb of output transferred to the next process has not changed: £0·30 per lb in each case. The introduction of Abnormal Loss and Abnormal Gain Accounts should ensure that minor variations in production do not cause the cost of production to fluctuate. In addition, the attention of management is drawn to these accounts, which may reveal efficiencies or inefficiencies, or a possible need for revision of allowances.

A complete illustration of process costing involving normal loss, abnormal loss and abnormal gain is now shown.

Product "Zed" passes through three processes to completion. In Period 3 the costs of production were as follows:

		Process		
Element of cost	*Total*	*1*	*2*	*3*
	£	£	£	£
Direct material	8,482	2,000	3,020	3,462
Direct labour	12,000	3,000	4,000	5,000
Direct expense	726	500	226	—
Production overhead	6,000			

1,000 units at £5 each were issued to Process 1.
Output of each process was:

Process 1	920 units
,, 2	870 ,,
,, 3	800 ,,

Normal loss per process was estimated as:

Process 1	10%
,, 2	5%
,, 3	10%

The loss in each process represented scrap which could be sold to a merchant at a value as follows:

Process 1	£3 per unit
„ 2	£5 „
„ 3	£6 „

There was no stock of materials or work in progress in any department at the beginning or end of the period. The output of each process passes direct to the next process and finally to finished stock. Production overhead is absorbed by each process on a basis of 50% of the cost of direct labour.

Process 1

Description: Period No. 3
                                                Output 920 units

	Units	Cost per unit	Amount		Units	Cost per unit	Amount
			£				£
Units introduced	1,000	£5	5,000	Normal loss	100	£3	300
Direct material			2,000	Process 2 output			
Direct labour			3,000	transferred	920	£13	11,960
Direct expense			500				
Production overhead			1,500				
Abnormal gain	20	£13	260				
	1,020		£12,260		1,020		£12,260

Process 2

Description: Period No. 3
                                                Output 870 units

	Units	Cost per unit	Amount		Units	Cost per unit	Amount
			£				£
Process 1	920	£13	11,960	Normal loss	46	£5	230
Direct material			3,020	Abnormal loss	4	£24	96
Direct labour			4,000	Process 3 output			
Direct expense			226	transferred	870	£24	20,880
Production overhead			2,000				
	920		£21,206		920		£21,206

Process 3

Description: Period No. 3
                                                Output 800 units

	Units	Cost per unit	Amount		Units	Cost per unit	Amount
			£				£
Process 2	870	£24	20,880	Normal loss	87	£6	522
Direct material			3,462	Finished stock out-			
Direct labour			5,000	put transferred	800	£40	32,000
Production overhead			2,500				
Abnormal gain	17	£40	680				
	887		£32,522		887		£32,522

Abnormal Loss Account

	Units	Cost per unit	Amount		Units	Cost per unit	Amount
Process 2	4	£24	£ 96	Debtor Profit and loss	4	£5	£ 20 76
	4		£96		4		£96

Abnormal Gain Account

	Units	Cost per unit	Amount		Units	Cost per unit	Amount
Process 1 Process 3 Profit and loss	20 17	£3 £6	£ 60 102 778	Process 1 Process 3	20 17	£13 £40	£ 260 680
	37		£940		37		£940

Finished Stock Account

To Process 3	800	40	£32,000

NOTES

PROCESS 1

Normal loss

$$10\% = \frac{10}{100} \times 1,000 = 100 \text{ units.}$$

Scrap value £3 per unit. $100 \times £3 = \underline{£300.}$

Abnormal gain

Normal cost £12,000 − £300 = £11,700.
Normal production 1,000 units − 100 = 900.

$$\frac{£11,700}{900} \times 20 = \underline{£260.}$$

PROCESS 2

Normal loss

$$5\% = \frac{5}{100} \times 920 = 46 \text{ units.}$$

Scrap value £5 per unit. $46 \times £5 = \underline{£230.}$

Abnormal loss

Normal cost £21,206 − £230 = £20,976.
Normal production 920 units − 46 = 874.

$$\frac{£20,976}{874} \times 4 = \underline{£96.}$$

PROCESS 2

Normal loss

$$10\% = \frac{10}{100} \times 870 = 87 \text{ units.}$$

Scrap value £6 per unit. $87 \times £6 = £522.$

Abnormal gain

Normal cost £31,842 − £522 = £31,320.
Normal production 870 units − 87 = 783.

$$\frac{£31,320}{783} \times 17 = £680.$$

ABNORMAL GAIN ACCOUNT

This account is debited with £60 and Process 1 Account credited with £60. This figure is calculated as follows:

Normal loss 10% of 1,000 units =	100 units
Actual loss	80 "
Abnormal gain	20 "

Process normal loss of 100 units would realise £300, but as only 80 units were scrapped, only £240 would be received as scrap value. Consequently the difference (300 − 240) = £60 must reduce the gain on Abnormal Gain Account. Thus the item normal loss in Process 1 is built up as follows:

Scrap value	80 units at £3	240
Transfer to Abnormal Gain Account	20 " "	60
	100 " "	£300

A similar calculation would be effected in respect of Process 3.

Examination questions on Chapter 20 are given at the end of Chapter 21.

CHAPTER 21

PROCESS COSTING

Work in Progress, Joint Products and By-products

THE problem of work in progress in process industries has not yet been discussed; it is, however, a very important problem and frequently a difficult one. In most firms manufacture is on a continuous basis, as a result of which a process may frequently be uncompleted at the end of an accounting period. How is the cost to be related to the uncompleted work? One way of solving this problem is by calculating what is known as the equivalent or effective production, to which is apportioned the cost incurred.

EQUIVALENT PRODUCTION

This represents the production of a process in terms of completed units. Thus, it is considered that an opening stock of 10 units which is 50% completed is equivalent to a stock of 5 units which is 100% completed. In each process an estimate is made of the percentage completion of any work in progress. A production schedule and a cost schedule will then be prepared.

The work in progress is inspected and an estimate is made of the degree of completion, usually on a percentage basis. It is most important that this estimate is as accurate as possible, because a mistake at this stage would affect the stock valuations used in the final accounts and balance sheet.

There are two main methods of calculating equivalent production:

(a) The FIFO method.
(b) The average-price method.

These methods operate in a similar way to those discussed in Chapter 6. In the FIFO method, one assumes that the raw materials issued to work in progress pass through to finished goods in a progressive cycle; in other words what comes in first goes out first. This method is satisfactory when prices of raw materials and rates of direct labour and overheads are relatively stable. Work in progress at the end of the period becomes the opening work in progress for the next period; the closing work in progress will be valued at costs ruling during the old period, while the opening work in progress will be valued at costs ruling during

360

the new period. Thus, where costs are more or less the same in each period, the FIFO system is adequate.

The average-price method is useful when prices fluctuate from period to period. The closing valuation of work in progress, in the old period is added to the costs of the new period and an average rate obtained which tends to even out any price fluctuations. Both these methods will be discussed in this chapter. The FIFO system will be used to illustrate some of the simple stages in calculating equivalent units; then in the more advanced stages the FIFO method will be used followed by similar illustrations using the average-price method.

EXAMPLE

During January 2,000 units were introduced into Process 1. The normal loss was estimated at 5% on input. At the end of the month 1,400 units had been produced and transferred to the next process; 460 units were uncompleted and 140 units had been scrapped. It was estimated that the uncompleted units had reached a stage in production as follows:

Material	75% completed
Labour	50% „
Overhead	50% „

The cost of the 2,000 units was £5,800.
Direct materials introduced during the process amounted to £1,440.
Direct wages amounted to £3,340.
Production overheads incurred were £1,670.
Units scrapped realised £1 each.
The units scrapped had passed through the process, so were 100% completed as regards material, labour and overhead.

FIFO METHOD

Statement of Production

Process 1   January

Input	Units	Output	Units	Equivalent production (units)					
				Material		Labour		Overhead	
				Quantity	%	Quantity	%	Quantity	%
Units	2,000	Normal loss	100	—	—	—	—	—	—
		Abnormal loss	40	40	100	40	100	40	100
		Finished production	1,400	1,400	100	1,400	100	1,400	100
		Work in progress	460	345	75	230	50	230	50
	2,000	TOTAL	2,000						
		EQUIVALENT PRODUCTION		1,785		1,670		1,670	

Statement of Cost

Process 1   January

Element of cost	Cost		Equivalent production (units)	Cost per unit
	£	£		£
Materials:				
Units introduced	5,800			
Direct	1,440			
	7,240			
Less Scrap value of normal loss	100			
		7,140	1,785	4
Labour: direct		3,340	1,670	2
Overhead: production		1,670	1,670	1
TOTAL		£12,150		£7

Statement of Evaluation

Process 1   January

Production	Element of cost	Equivalent production (units)	Cost per unit	Cost	Total cost
			£	£	£
Abnormal loss	Material	40	4	160	
	Labour	40	2	80	
	Overhead	40	1	40	
					280
Finished production	Material	1,400	4	5,600	
	Labour	1,400	2	2,800	
	Overhead	1,400	1	1,400	
					9,800
Work in progress	Material	345	4	1,380	
	Labour	230	2	460	
	Overhead	230	1	230	
					2,070
					£12,150

Process 1 Account

	Units	£		Units	£
Units introduced	2,000	5,800	Normal loss	100	100
Material		1,440	Abnormal loss A/c	40	280
Labour		3,340	Process 2 A/c	1,400	9,800
Overhead		1,670	Balance c/d	460	2,070
	2,000	£12,250		2,000	£12,250
Balance b/d	460	2,070			

Process 2 Account

	Units	£		Units	£
Process 1	1,400	£9,800			

Abnormal Loss Account

	Units	£		Units	£
Process 1	40	280	Debtors	40	40
			Profit and loss		240
	40	£280		40	£280

Normal loss

Normal loss is absorbed by the good production, as was illustrated in the previous chapter.

This procedure has been followed throughout the examples given because it is normal and correct practice to do so when using the FIFO method. However, in strict theory, care should always be taken to establish:

(*a*) the degree of completion of the scrap;
(*b*) the cost of it;
(*c*) upon whom the cost should fall.

In this particular example the scrap is not discovered until fully processed. There is, therefore, none in the closing work in progress, and it is suggested that, had we been using the average-price method, the cost of the scrap (less scrap value) *ought* to be borne only by the completed units transferred to the next process. This, in some instances, could make a substantial difference to the valuation of the closing work in progress. However, in practice, this will probably be regarded as a "counsel of perfection."

Finished production

These units have been completed, so obviously will have incurred total cost per unit of material, labour and overhead.

Abnormal loss

These units have been completed, then found defective, but must still bear the total cost per unit of material, labour and overhead.

Work in progress

These units are not yet completed, but according to the estimate will be charged with 75% of material cost, and 50% of labour and overhead charges.

Credit of £1 per unit has been effected in the cost statement in relation to units scrapped owing to normal loss.

Material, labour and overhead costs have been divided by the equivalent production units, to obtain a cost per unit.

Finished production, abnormal loss and work in progress have been evaluated at the equivalent production unit rate.

(*a*) £9,800, the cost of finished production, will be transferred to the next process.

(*b*) £280, the cost of abnormal loss, will be credited to Process 1 Account and debited to Abnormal Loss Account. The scrap value of these units (40 at £1), £40, will be credited to Abnormal Loss Account and debited to the Scrap Merchant's Account on sale of the scrap.

(*c*) £2,070 is the estimated value of work in progress and will be carried forward to the next accounting period.

Where there is an opening stock in a process which is only partially completed, this requires careful consideration, particularly in a process which is not the first stage of a production routine. Thus Process 2 will receive the finished output of Process 1; if in Process 2 direct materials are added to the units transferred from the previous process, then any opening stock in Process 2 will be fully completed as far as the material transferred is concerned, but not necessarily completed as regards the material added in process. It is therefore necessary to calculate two material rates of equivalent production:

(a) Rate for material transferred from previous process.
(b) Rate for material added in process.

EXAMPLE

The following information is obtained in respect of Process 2 for the month of June:

Opening stock: 600 units £105
Degree of completion: Materials 80%
        Labour 60%
        Overhead 60%
Transfer from Process 1: 11,000 units at £550
Transfer to Process 3:   8,800 units
Direct material added in Process 2: £241
Direct labour amounted to £715·50
Production overhead incurred £954
Units scrapped: 1,200
  Degree of completion: Material 100%
         Labour 70%
         Overhead 70%
Closing stock: 1,600 units
  Degree of completion: Material 70%
         Labour 60%
         Overhead 60%

There was a normal loss in the process of 10% of production. Units scrapped realised £0·05 per unit.

FIFO METHOD

Statement of Production

Process 2   *June*

Input	Units	Output	Units	Material (1) Quantity	%	Material (2) Quantity	%	Labour Quantity	%	Overhead Quantity	%
Opening stock	600	Opening stock	600	—	—	120	20	240	40	240	40
Process 1	11,000	Normal loss	1,000	—	—	—	—	—	—	—	—
		Abnormal loss	200	200	100	230	100	140	70	140	70
		Completely processed during period	8,200	8,200	100	8,200	100	8,200	100	8,200	100
		Closing stock	1,600	1,600	100	1,120	70	960	60	960	60
	11,600	TOTAL	11,600								
		EQUIVALENT PRODUCTION		10,000		9,640		9,540		9,540	

NOTES
Material (1) refers to transfer from previous process.
Material (2) refers to materials added in this process.
Material (1) will always be 100% completed, because it is the *finished* product of the previous process.

Statement of Cost

Element of cost	Cost		Equivalent production (units)	Cost per unit
Material:	£	£		£
1. Transferred from previous process	550			
Less Scrap value of normal loss 1,000 units at £0·05 per unit	50			
	—	500·00	10,000	0·05
2. Added in process		241·00	9,640	0·02½
Labour: direct		715·50	9,540	0·07¾
Overhead: production		954·00	9,540	0·10
TOTAL		£2,410·50		£0·25

Statement of Evaluation

Production	Element of cost	Equivalent production (units)	Cost per unit	Cost	Total cost
			£	£	£
Opening stock	Material (1)	—	0·05	—	
	Material (2)	120	0·02½	3·00	
	Labour	240	0·07¾	18·00	
	Overhead	240	0·10	24·00	
					45·00
Abnormal loss	Material (1)	200	0·05	10·00	
	Material (2)	200	0·02½	5·00	
	Labour	140	0·07¾	10·50	
	Overhead	140	0·10	14·00	
					39·50
Completely processed during the period	Material (1)	8,200	0·05	410·00	
	Material (2)	8,200	0·02½	205·00	
	Labour	8,200	0·07¾	615·00	
	Overhead	8,200	0·10	820·00	
					2,050·00
Closing stock	Material (1)	1,600	0·05	80·00	
	Material (2)	1,120	0·02½	28·00	
	Labour	960	0·07¾	72·00	
	Overhead	960	0·10	96·00	
					276·00
	TOTAL				£2,410·50

NOTES

Statement of production

Opening stock. 20% Material (2) and 40% labour and overhead required for completion.

Normal loss. Absorbed in good production.

Closing stock. Not yet completed.

Completely processed during period. 8,800 units were transferred to Process 3, comprising opening stock of 600 and 8,200 completely processed during period.

Statement of cost

Material. 11,000 units valued at £550 were transferred. 600 units were opening stock and 1,600 units closing stock. Therefore 10,000 units were processed (11,000 + 600 − 1,600 units). 10% normal process loss = 1,000 units.

The equivalent production is as follows:

Goods completed during period	8,200
Abnormal loss	200
Work in progress at close	1,600
	10,000 units

Opening stock. No material from Process 1 required; the material would have been calculated last period. The only requirements are Material (2), labour and overhead in Process 2.

Closing stock. There are 1,600 units in stock, so there will be 1,600 units worth of the output of Process 1 included in this valuation. There is also 70% of Material (2) and 60% of labour and overhead added in Process 2.

The accounts in respect of the above transactions would appear as follows:

Process 2 Account

	Units	£		Units	£
Balance b/d	600	105·00	Normal loss	1,000	50·00
Process 1 A/c	11,000	550·00	Abnormal Loss A/c	200	39·50
Material		241·00	Process 3 A/c*	8,800	2,200·00
Labour		715·50	Balance c/d	1,600	276·00
Overhead		954·00			
	11,600	£2,565·50		11,600	£2,565·50
Balance b/d	1,600	276·00			

Process 3 Account

	Units	£		Units	£
Process 2 A/c	8,800	2,200·00			

Abnormal Loss Account

	Units	£		Units	£
Process 2 A/c	200	39·50	Debtors	200	10·00
			Profit and Loss A/c		29·50
	200	£39·50		200	£39·50

				£
* Units completely processed during period 8,200 at £0·25 per unit				2,050
Opening stock completed during period	600	,,	,,	150
				£2,200

In the previous illustration the question of evaluating equivalent production of a process in which there was an opening and closing stock of work in progress was considered; a process in which an abnormal loss was incurred. What would have been the effect of an abnormal gain? Briefly the position would be as follows:

(*a*) The transfer to the next process would be greater than expected.

(*b*) If faulty units are normally scrapped before they are completed, then any production in excess of normal will necessitate an increased cost of the factors of production. Thus in the previous illustration, units scrapped had reached this stage of completion:

Material 100%, labour 70% and overhead 70%.

Any above-normal production will therefore incur 30% labour costs and 30% overhead costs to bring these units up to completion.

EXAMPLE

The following information is obtained in respect of Process 2 for the month of July:

Opening stock: 1,600 units £276
Degree of completion: Material 70%
                              Labour 60%
                              Overhead 60%
Transfer from Process 1: 10,200 units at £510
Transfer to Process 3:   9,200 units
Direct material added in Process 2 = £224
Direct labour amounted to £657
Production overhead incurred: £876
Units scrapped: 800

Degree of completion: Material 100%
                              Labour 70%
                              Overhead 70%

Closing stock = 1,800 units

    Degree of completion: Material 60%
                              Labour 40%
                              Overhead 40%

There was a normal loss in the process of 10% of production. Units scrapped realised £0·05 per unit.

At this stage it is considered expedient to introduce a new presentation for the evaluation of equivalent units. In the previous two examples, three statements have been built up to show production, cost and evaluation. Having introduced each stage separately, we can now proceed to speed up the presentation of figures by combining these three statements into one grand presentation. It should be possible to follow through each stage as before, but, by combining the statements, one can eliminate some of the repetition which was experienced previously.

FIFO METHOD

Process 2   *Statement of Production, Cost and Evaluation*   July

Input		Output		Equivalent production								Total
				Direct materials (1)		Direct materials (2)		Direct labour		Production overheads		
Details	Units	Details	Units	Quantity	%	Quantity	%	Quantity	%	Quantity	%	
Opening stock	1,600	Opening stock	1,600	—	—	480	30	640	40	640	40	
Process 1	10,200	Normal loss	1,000	—	—	—		—		—		
		Completely processed during the month	7,600	7,600	100	7,600	100	7,600	100	7,600	100	
		Closing stock	1,800	1,800	100	1,080	60	720	40	720	40	
			12,000	9,400		9,160		8,960		8,960		
		Abnormal gain	200	200	100	200	100	200	100	200	100	
	11,800		11,800									
		Equivalent units		9,200		8,960		8,760		8,760		
				£		£		£		£		£
Cost												
This period			510									
Scrap value of normal loss			50									
			—	460		224		657		876		2,217
		per equivalent unit		£0·05		£0·02½		£0·07½		£0·10		£0·25
Evaluation												
Opening stock				—		12		48		64		124
Normal loss				—								
Completely processed during the month				380		190		570		760		1,900
Closing stock				90		27		54		72		243
				470		229		672		896		2,267
Abnormal gain				10		5		15		20		50
			£	460		224		657		876		2,217

The accounts would appear as follows:

Process 2 Account

	Units	£		Units	£
Balance b/d	1 600	276·00	Normal loss	1,000	50·00
Process 1	10,200	510·00	Process 3 A/c	9,200	2,300·00
Material		224·00	Balance c/d	1,800	243·00
Labour		657·00			
Overhead		876·00			
Abnormal gain A/c	200	50·00			
	12,000	£2,593·00		12,000	£2,593·00
Balance b/d	1,800	243·00			

Abnormal Gain Account

	Units	£		Units	£
Process 2 Profit and loss	200	10·00 40·00	Process 2	200	50·00
	200	£50·00		200	£50·00

NOTES

Statement of production

Opening stock. 100% Material (1), 70% Material (2), 60% labour and 60% overhead costs would have been charged to opening stock last period.

Normal loss. Absorbed by good production.

Abnormal gain. These units have been completely processed, so will be transferred to Process 3. However, as illustrated earlier in this chapter, abnormal gains or abnormal losses must be shown in separate accounts so as to show clearly any losses or gains which were not expected.

Statement of cost

Material. For convenience, the value of scrap realised has been deducted from Material (1). This is an arbitrary decision: the scrap value is fairly small, so it is felt that it is not necessary to apportion the value in any greater detail.

Process 2 Account

Process 3. The amount transferred from Process 2 to Process 3 is 9,200 units valued at £2,300.

$$
\begin{array}{lrr}
\text{This is composed of opening stock 1,600 units at £0·25} & 400 \\
\text{Completed process 7,600 ,, £0·25} & 1,900 \\
\hline
9,200 & £2,300 \\
\end{array}
$$

Abnormal Gain Account

It was expected that 1,000 units would be scrapped and would realise £50. However, only 800 were actually scrapped, so the credit would be only £40. It is therefore necessary to debit Abnormal Gain Account with £10 so as to offset the balance of £10. In Process 2 Account the corresponding entry of £10, together with the £40 received for scrap, makes up a total of £50.

Stocks

It is very important to realise that opening stock of work in progress is partially completed, and therefore requires only a given percentage of cost to complete the process. The statement of production shows the production for the current period only. Closing stock will be valued at cost price, and so will include the cost incurred to that date. In this illustration it was assumed for convenience that costs did not fluctuate from one period to another. Thus opening stock was valued as follows:

Element of cost	Units	Cost per unit	Amount	Percentage completed	Cost
		£	£		£
Material (1)	1,600	0·05	80·00	100	80·00
Material (2)	1,600	0·02½	40·00	70	28·00
Labour	1,600	0·07½	120·00	60	72·00
Overhead	1,600	0·10	160·00	60	96·00
TOTAL		£0·25	£400·00		£276·00

$$
\begin{array}{rll}
& & \text{£} \\
\textit{Check} \quad \text{Work done in June} & 276 \\
\text{,, \quad ,, \quad July} & 124 \\
\hline
& \text{£400} \\
\end{array}
$$

1,600 units at £0·25 = £400

Two further illustrations are shown now, in which the average-price method is used. The first illustration shows the calculations involved when an abnormal loss results from the operation. It should be noted how under this method it is unnecessary to show separately the opening work in progress which has now been completed and the units which have been completely processed during the period. These two items are replaced by only one item—the transfer to the next process.

EXAMPLE

The following information is obtained in respect of Process 3 for the month of August:

Opening stock: 1,000 units

Value: Direct material (1) £390.   Direct material (2)   £75
Direct labour   £112.   Production overhead £118

Process 2 transfer: 6,000 units at £2,360
Process 4 transfer: 4,700 units
Direct materials added in process: £520
Direct labour employed: £1,036
Production overhead absorbed: £1,541
Units scrapped: 300

Degree of completion: Direct material   100%
Direct labour   80%
Production overhead   60%

Closing stock: 2,000 units

Degree of completion: Direct material 60%
Direct labour 50%
Production overhead 40%

Normal loss: 5% of production.
Units scrapped realised £0·20 each.

AVERAGE PRICE METHOD

Statement of Production, Cost and Evaluation

Process 3   August

Input		Output		Equivalent production								Total
				Direct materials (1)		Direct materials (2)		Direct labour		Production overhead		
Details	Units	Details	Units	Quantity	%	Quantity	%	Quantity	%	Quantity	%	
Opening stock	1,000	Normal loss	250	—	—	—	—	—	—	—	—	
Process 2	6,000	Abnormal loss	50	50	100	50	100	40	80	30	60	
		Process 4	4,700	4,700	100	4,700	100	4,700	100	4,700	100	
		Closing stock	2,000	2,000	100	1,200	60	1,000	50	800	40	
	7,000		7,000									
		Equivalent units		6,750		5,950		5,740		5,530		
				£		£		£		£		£
Cost												
Opening stock				390		75		112		118		695
This period				2,360		520		1,036		1,541		5,457
				2,750		595		1,148		1,659		6,152
		Scrap value of normal loss		50								50
Total				£2,700		£595		£1,148		£1,659		£6,102
		per equivalent unit		£0·40		£0·10		£0·20		£0·30		£1·00
Evaluation												
Normal loss				—		—		—		—		—
Abnormal loss				20		5		8		9		42
Process 4				1,880		470		940		1,410		4,700
Closing stock				800		120		200		240		1,360
Total				£2,700		£595		£1,148		£1,659		£6,102

NOTES

Scrap value of normal loss

It may have been observed throughout the examples in this chapter that the scrap value received in respect of normal loss has been deducted from direct material (1). This is purely a matter of convenience. There are four possible choices:

(*a*) Deduct from Material (1).
(*b*) Deduct from Material (2).

　　　　(c) Apportion between Material (1) and Material (2).
　　　　(d) Apportion between materials, labour and overhead.

With regard to (d) above, this is clearly inadvisable because costs of direct labour and production overhead are of no value to the raw material if it is to be scrapped because it is below standard. Choice (c) is too involved a calculation to warrant its being used in most circumstances. It is not very important which element of cost is reduced by the scrap value, so to apportion costs is a waste of time. Choice (b) could be used, but, because the material added in process is usually of less value than the material transferred from the preceding process, then choice (a) is usually the most satisfactory solution.

Normal loss (5% of production)

　　This is calculated as follows:

Opening stock	1,000 units
Process transfer	6,000 ,,
	7,000
Closing stock	2,000 ,,
	5,000
Normal loss 5%	250 units

　　The accounts for the month would appear as follows:

Process 3 Account

	Units	£		Units	£
Balance b/d	1,000	695	Normal loss	250	50
Process 2 A/c	6,000	2,360	Abnormal Loss A/c	50	42
Direct materials		520	Process 4 A/c	4,700	4,700
Direct labour		1,036	Balance c/d	2,000	1,360
Production overhead		1,541			
	7,000	£6,152		7,000	£6,152
Balance b/d	2,000	£1,360			

Process 4 Account

	Units	£		Units	£
Process 3 A/c	4,700	4,700			

Abnormal Loss Account

	Units	£		Units	£
Process 3 A/c	50	42	Debtors	50	10
			Profit and Loss A/c		32
	50	£42		50	£42

An abnormal gain in process is treated in the average-price method in a similar way to that shown in the FIFO method. It must be understood that an abnormal gain will be processed completely and passed on to the next process, unlike an abnormal loss, which is not necessarily processed completely. If the inspection point is at the beginning of the process, *e.g.* Process 2, then any units which fail inspection will have incurred only direct Material (1) costs. If inspection is carried out at the half-way stage in Process 2, then costs incurred would be 100% direct materials (1) and 50% direct materials (2), labour and overheads (assuming that each element of cost is introduced at an even rate). If a unit is scrapped at such a stage as, for example, in Process 2, 60% direct materials, 50% direct labour and 40% production overheads, then costs incurred would be 100% direct materials (1), 60% direct materials (2), 50% direct labour and 40% production overheads.

EXAMPLE

The following information is shown in respect of Process 2 for the month of September:

Opening stock: 1,000 units

Value: Direct materials (1) £400. Direct materials (2)   £200.
       Direct labour   £35. Production overheads £80.

Process 1 transfer: 16,000 units at £8,100
Process 3 transfer: 14,500 units
Direct materials added in process: £4,375
Direct labour employed: £1,430
Production overheads absorbed: £2,850
Units scrapped: 500

        Degree of completion: Direct materials   100%
                       Direct labour   60%
                       Production overhead 20%

Normal loss in process: 5% of production.
Units scrapped realised £0·50 each.

AVERAGE PRICE METHOD

Statement of Production, Cost and Evaluation

Process 2   September

Input		Output		Direct materials (1)		Direct materials (2)		Direct labour		Production overhead		Total
Details	Units	Details	Units	Quantity	%	Quantity	%	Quantity	%	Quantity	%	
Opening stock	1,000	Normal loss	750	—	—	—	—	—	—	—	—	
Process 1	16,000	Process 3	14,500	14,500	100	14,500	100	14,500	100	14,500	100	
		Closing stock	2,000	2,000	100	1,000	50	400	20	400	20	
			17,250	16,500		15,500		14,900		14,900		
		Abnormal gain	250	250	100	250	100	250	100	250	100	
	17,000		17,000									
		Equivalent units		16,250		15,250		14,650		14,650		
				£		£		£		£		£
COST												
Opening stock				400		200		35		80		715
This period				8,100		4,375		1,430		2,850		16,755
				8,500		4,575		1,465		2,930		17,470
Scrap value of normal loss				375		—		—		—		375
TOTAL			£	8,125		4,575		1,465		2,930		17,095
per equivalent unit				£0·50		£0·30		£0·10		£0·20		£1·10
EVALUATION												
Normal loss				—		—		—		—		
Process 3				7,250		4,350		1,450		2,900		15,950
Closing stock				1,000		300		40		80		1,420
				8,250		4,650		1,490		2,980		17,370
Abnormal gain				125		75		25		50		275
TOTAL			£	8,125		4,575		1,465		2,930		17,095

NOTE: It should be ensured that the totals of each element of cost shown in the cost section of the above statement are the same as those shown in the evaluation section of the statement. Thus, for example, total cost of direct labour is £1,465 and total evaluation of direct labour is £1,465.

The accounts for the month would be as follows:

Process 2 Account

	Units	£		Units	£
Balance b/d	1,000	715	Normal loss	750	375
Process 1 A/c	16,000	8,100	Process 3 A/c	14,500	15,950
Direct materials		4,375	Balance c/d	2,000	1,420
Direct labour		1,430			
Production overheads		2,850			
Abnormal Gain A/c	250	275			
	17,250	£17,745		17,250	£17,745
Balance b/d	2,000	1,420			

Process 3 Account

	Units	£		Units	£
Process 2 A/c	14,500	15,950			

Abnormal Gain Account

	Units	£		Units	£
Debtors		125	Process 2 A/c		275
Profit and Loss A/c		150			
		£275			£275

JOINT PRODUCTS

Joint products were discussed on page 346, but it is now necessary to mention some of the methods which may be employed in costing joint products. The difficulties inherent in valuing the various products passing through the same process will be appreciated in this simple example.

In a meat-products factory, pork may be the raw material. The carcase is carved, boned, etc., cut into pieces, then divided and allocated to various production lines. Some meat may be used for making sausages, some for pies, some for luncheon meat, etc. The problem is how to evaluate the meat which is to be used in each of the various lines. Once the meat is separated into the various requirements, the normal process-costing procedure will apply, but it is the apportioning of costs up to the point of separation which creates the problem. Much will, of course, depend upon the special conditions and circumstances prevailing in the factory or type of industry, but some of the methods which may be used in apportioning these costs up to the point of separation are as follows.

1. MARKET VALUE AT POINT OF SEPARATION

The market value of the joint products at the separation point is ascertained, and the total cost is apportioned in the ratio of these values.

Products "Exe" and "Wye" are jointly produced in a factory. The values at separation point are known to be £5 and £6 respectively. The cost will then be apportioned $\frac{5}{11}$ to "Exe" and $\frac{6}{11}$ to "Wye." This is subject to giving weight to the quantities produced.

This method is useful where further processing of the products incurs disproportionate costs.

2. MARKET VALUE AFTER FURTHER PROCESSING

This method is easy to operate because the selling prices of the various joint products will be readily available. Sales values are used as the basis for apportioning costs up to the point of separation, in that the pre-separation costs are apportioned in proportion to the sales values of the finished products.

The sales of "Exe" and "Wye" are 10,000 and 8,000 units at prices of £10 and £8 respectively. The pre-separation costs are £82,000.

The pre-separation costs will be apportioned thus:

$$£82,000 \times \frac{100,000}{164,000} \text{ to "Exe" and } £82,000 \times \frac{64,000}{164,000} \text{ to "Wye"}$$

$$\underline{£50,000} \qquad\qquad\qquad\qquad \underline{£32,000}$$

This system is, however, unfair where further processing costs of products are disproportionate: these further costs should therefore be deducted from the sales values to arrive at adjusted figures which are fair and reasonable.

3. PHYSICAL MEASUREMENT

A physical base, *e.g.* raw material, is the proportion used to apportion pre-separation-point costs to joint products.

There is 40% beef in Product "Exe" and 60% beef in Product "Wye." $\frac{4}{10}$ of the costs up to separation point will be charged to "Exe" and $\frac{6}{10}$ to "Wye."

This system is not suitable where, for example, one product is a gas and another a liquid.

It should also be borne in mind that where this system is used it presupposes that each joint product is equally valuable, which is probably not the case.

Decision taking

The attempt to apportion the costs up to the point of separation may obscure the real position. The decision whether or not to process a joint product after separation depends on whether the sales value at the end of processing minus the sales value which could be obtained if no further processing was done is more than sufficient to cover the additional costs incurred. This may be lost sight of if too much of the common costs are apportioned to the product.

EXAMPLE

Pre-separation costs	£ 10,000		

	A £	B £	C £
Apportionment of the separation costs on a tonnage basis	6,000	3,000	1,000
Additional processing costs	1,000	800	1,200
	7,000	3,800	2,200
Sales value	12,000	3,100	1,200
Profit/(Loss)	5,000	(700)	(1,000)

From this it might be concluded that further processing of B and C was unprofitable.

If the pre-separation costs were not apportioned one might obtain the following result:

	A £	B £	C £
Sales value before further processing	600	600	500
Sales value after further processing	12,000	3,100	1,200
Change of value	+11,400	+2,500	+700
Additional processing costs	1,000	800	1,200
Surplus/Deficit	£10,400	£1,700	£−500

We should now decide to process C no further and our results would be:

	£	£	£
Sales	12,000	3,100	500
Additional costs	1,000	800	—
Contribution towards profit	£11,000	£2,300	£500

Total contribution	13,800
Less Pre-separation costs	10,000
Profit	£3,800

BY-PRODUCTS

By-products were discussed on page 345, but it is now necessary to detail some of the systems utilised in costing by-products. In some industries there are many by-products produced, and it is frequently very difficult to ascertain the cost of production of any one by-product. The special conditions pertaining to any factory or industry will affect the choice of system. However, some methods which may be used are as illustrated below.

1. MARKET VALUE

The market value of the by-product is obtained, and this figure is used as a base for calculating the amount to be credited to the Process Account. If any further processing costs are required to make the by-product saleable, or any selling and distribution overheads are incurred, these amounts must be subtracted from the market value, and the resulting figure is regarded as being the value of the by-product at separation point.

In the manufacture of 1,000 units of Product A, 100 units of Product B, a by-product, are produced. The market value of Product B is £0·25 per unit. After Product B is separated from the process in which Product A is produced, further processing costs amounting to £5 are necessary, and selling and distribution overheads amounting to £2·50 are incurred. The amount to be credited to the Process Account in respect of Product B will be:

	£	£	Total £	Per unit £
Sales price			25·00	0·25
Less Processing costs	5·00	0·05		
Selling and distribution overheads	2·50	0·02½		
			7·50	0·07½
			£17·50	0·17½

This method suffers from the disadvantage that, if the market value of Product B fluctuates, the credit to the Process Account of Product A will fluctuate accordingly. Owing to the fact that credits to the main Process Account fluctuate, inefficiencies in that process may be concealed.

2. STANDARD COST

A standard cost is set for each by-product produced. The standard may be determined by averaging costs recorded in the past, or by adopting arbitrary figures.

During the past five years records have been kept of the production costs of Product C and Product D, which is a by-product of Product C. These records show the following data in respect of Product D:

1st year produced	100	tons estimated cost		£500
2nd year	„	150	„	„	£800
3rd year	„	120	„	„	£620
4th year	„	160	„	„	£840
5th year	„	140	„	„	£735
TOTAL	„	670	„	„	£3,495

The average cost per ton is $\frac{£3,495}{670} = £5\cdot20$ (approx.).

The standard cost of Product D would be £5·20. If in future periods costs fluctuated, then the standard would probably be revised.

3. COMPARATIVE PRICE

Under this method, the value of the by-product which will be credited to the main product is ascertained by reference to the price of a similar or an alternative material. Thus, for example, in a large motor-car factory a blast furnace not only provides the steel required for the car bodies but also produces gas which is utilised in the factory. This gas is a by-product, which can be valued at the price which would have to be paid to the gas industry for the supply of gas which would be required if the factory was unable to produce its own supply. On the other hand, the price of an alternative material, *e.g.*, in this case, electricity, could be used as the base for ascertaining a price for the by-product.

In the production of Product E a by-product F is obtained. In one month 100 units of Product F are produced, which are transferred to another department where they are consumed. If Product F was purchased from outside suppliers, the price would be £0·25 each. The amount to be credited to Product E in respect of by-product F would be 100 × £0·25 = £25.

WHERE BY-PRODUCTS ARE OF LITTLE VALUE

It will be appreciated from the above examples of pricing of by-products that ascertaining a reasonable price is not an easy task; in fact, in many cases, it can be an extremely difficult one. Consequently, if the by-product is of little value, it may be considered uneconomic to incur the expense of calculating the price of each unit produced. Where this is so, the amount realised on the sale of by-products may be treated as a profit and shown in the Profit and Loss Account. Alternatively, the amount realised may be credited to the main product, thus reducing the cost of the product.

INTERNAL PROCESS PROFITS

Sometimes the output from one process is transferred to a subsequent process, not at cost as shown in the preceding examples, but at a price showing a profit to the transferor process. Transfer may be made, for instance, at a price corresponding to current wholesale market prices or at cost plus an agreed percentage. The object is:

(a) to show whether the cost of production competes with market prices;
(b) to make each process stand on its own efficiency and economies; i.e. the transferee processes are not given the benefit, when comparing the cost at that stage with external prices, of economies effected in the earlier process.

The system involves a rather unnecessary complication of the accounts, as the desired comparisons could be prepared on separate cost reports for each process or by adopting a standard costing system, when standards could be set for each process. The complexity brought into the accounts arises from the fact that the inter-process profits so introduced remain included in the price of process stocks, finished stocks and work in progress. For balance sheet purposes, inter-process profits cannot be included in stocks, because a firm cannot make a profit by trading with itself, so a provision must be created to reduce the stocks to actual cost price. This problem arises only in respect of stocks on hand at the end of the period, because goods sold will have realised the internal profits. The procedure is illustrated in the examples shown below.

EXAMPLE

Product A passes through three processes before it is completed and transferred to finished stock. There were no stocks in hand at June 1, and no work in progress at June 1. The following data were available in respect of Processes 1, 2 and 3 for the month of June:

Details	Process		
	1	2	3
	£	£	£
Direct material	20,000	5,000	4,000
Direct wages	15,000	10,000	20,000
Stock of material	5,000	6,500	9,500

Sales of finished goods amounted to £110,000; stock was valued at £5,000. The output of each process is transferred to the next process at an amount which will yield 20% profit on the transfer price; the transfer from Process 3 to finished stock is to be similarly treated.

For this illustration, overheads have been excluded. It will be noted that, in the accounts illustrated below, three columns have been used in preference to the usual one-column ledger. This method is adopted to facilitate the calculation of the provision for profit in closing stocks. It was mentioned previously that the calculation of this provision is difficult, which will be appreciated when one considers that, for example, the stock of finished goods includes a proportion of profit added by Processes 1, 2 and 3.

The Process Accounts would appear as follows:

Process 1 Account

	Total	Cost	Profit		Total	Cost	Profit
	£	£	£		£	£	£
Materials	20,000	20,000	—	Stock c/d	5,000	5,000	—
Labour	15,000	15,000	—	Transfer to Process 2	37,500	30,000	7,500
	35,000	35,000	—				
Profit (20% on transfer, 25% on cost)	7,500	—	7,500				
	£42,500	£35,000	£7,500		£42,500	£35,000	£7,500
Stock b/d	5,000	5,000	—				

Process 2 Account

	Total	Cost	Profit		Total	Cost	Profit
	£	£	£		£	£	£
Transfer from Process 1	37,500	30,000	7,500	Stock c/d	6,500	5,571	929
Material	5,000	5,000	—	Transfer to Process 3	57,500	39,429	18,071
Labour	10,000	10,000	—				
	52,500	45,000	7,500				
Profit (20% on transfer, 25% on cost)	11,500	—	11,500				
	£64,000	£45,000	£19,000		£64,000	£45,000	£19,000
Stock b/d	6,500	5,571	929				

Process 3 Account

	Total	Cost	Profit		Total	Cost	Profit
	£	£	£		£	£	£
Transfer from Process 2	57,500	39,429	18,071	Stock c/d	9,500	7,394	2,106
Materials	4,000	4,000	—	Transfer to finished stock	90,000	56,035	33,965
Labour	20,000	20,000	—				
	81,500	63,429	18,071				
Profit (20% on transfer, 25% on cost)	18,000	—	18,000				
	£99,500	£63,429	£36,071		£99,500	£63,429	£36,071
Stock b/d	9,500	7,394	2,106				

Finished Stock

	Total	Cost	Profit		Total	Cost	Profit
	£	£	£		£	£	£
				Stock c/d	5,000	3,113	1,887
Transfer from Process 3	90,000	56,035	33,965	Sales	110,000	52,922	57,078
Profit	25,000	—	25,000				
	£115,000	£56,035	£58,965		£115,000	£56,035	£58,965
Stock b/d	5,000	3,113	1,887				

NOTES

Stocks

Stocks are calculated as follows:

Process 2. This includes a proportion of the transfer from Process 1 and part of the prime cost of Process 2:

$$\frac{\text{Cost}}{\text{Total}} \times \text{Stock} = \frac{45,000}{52,500} \times 6,500 = £5,571.$$

Total £6,500 — Cost £5,571 = Profit £929.

Process 3. This includes a proportion of the transfer from Process 2 and part of the prime cost of Process 3:

$$\frac{\text{Total}}{\text{Cost}} \times \text{Stock} = \frac{63,429}{81,500} \times 9,500 = £7,394.$$

Total £9,500 — Cost £7,394 = Profit £2,106.

Finished stock. This includes a proportion of the transfer from Process 3:

$$\frac{56,035}{90,000} \times 5,000 = £3,113.$$

Total £5,000 — Cost £3,113 = Profit £1,887.

Profit

Provision for internal process profits not yet realised will be:

	£
Process 2	929
„ 3	2,106
Finished stock	1,887
	£4,922

Gross profit for the year will be:

	£	£
Process 1		7,500
Process 2	11,500	
Less Provision	929	
		10,571
Process 3	18,000	
Less Provision	2,106	
		15,894
Finished stock	25,000	
Less Provision	1,887	
		23,113
TOTAL		£57,078

Balance sheet

Stocks will appear in the balance sheet at cost as revealed in the cost column above:

	£
Stock in Process 1	5,000
„ „ 2	5,571
„ „ 3	7,394
Finished stock	3,113
TOTAL	£21,078

In the above illustration the question of production overhead, opening stocks in process and previous provisions for unrealised profit were ignored. These items can now be considered.

EXAMPLE

Product B passes through three processes before it is completed and transferred to finished stock. The following data were available for the month of June:

Details	Process			Finished stock
	1	2	3	
	£	£	£	
Opening stock	5,000	8,000	10,000	20,000
Direct material	40,000	12,000	15,000	—
Direct labour	35,000	40,000	35,000	—
Production overhead	20,000	24,000	20,000	—
Closing stock	10,000	4,000	15,000	30,000

Output of Process 1 is transferred to Process 2 at 25% on the transfer price.

    „   „   2   „   „   „   3 „ 20%   „   „

    „   „   3   „   „   Finished stock at 10% on the transfer price.

Stocks in process have been valued at prime cost.

Finished stock has been valued at the price at which it was received from Process 3.

Sales amounted to £400,000.

Provisions for internal process profits as at June 1 were:

		£
Included in Process 2		1,395
„	„ 3	2,690
„	Finished stock	6,534
		£10,619

These provisions would be created in the previous month in respect of closing stock. Consequently, they are brought into the accounts for June as provisions in respect of internal process profits in opening stock.

A three-column ledger is again used for the Process Accounts, but, in order to conform to the usual method of setting out accounts to obtain the prime cost, the closing stock has been deducted on the debit side. Students must remember, however, not to forget its existence, and be careful to bring it down after ruling off the account.

Process 1 Account

	Total	Cost	Profit		Total	Cost	Profit
	£	£	£		£	£	£
Stock b/d	5,000	5,000	—	Transfer to Process 2	120,000	90,000	30,000
Direct materials	40,000	40,000	—				
Direct labour	35,000	35,000	—				
	80,000	80,000	—				
Less Stock c/d	10,000	10,000	—				
PRIME COST	70,000	70,000	—				
Production over-head	20,000	20,000	—				
PROCESS COST	90,000	90,000	—				
Gross profit (25% on transfer, 33⅓% on cost)	30,000	—	30,000				
	£120,000	£90,000	£30,000		£120,000	£90,000	£30,000
Stock b/d	10,000	10,000	—				

Process 2 Account

	Total	Cost	Profit		Total	Cost	Profit
	£	£	£		£	£	£
Stock b/d	8,000	6,605	1,395	Transfer to Process 3	250,000	169,303	80,697
Transfer from Process 1	120,000	90,000	30,000				
Direct material	12,000	12,000	—				
Direct labour	40,000	40,000	—				
	180,000	148,605	31,395				
Less Stock c/d	4,000	3,302	698				
PRIME COST	176,000	145,303	30,697				
Production overhead	24,000	24,000	—				
PROCESS COST	200,000	169,303	30,697				
Gross profit (20% on transfer, 25% on cost)	50,000	—	50,000				
	£250,000	£169,303	£80,697		£250,000	£169,303	£80,697
Stock b/d	4,000	3,302	698				

Process 3 Account

	Total	Cost	Profit		Total	Cost	Profit
	£	£	£		£	£	£
Stock b/d	10,000	7,310	2,690	Transfer to finished goods stock	350,000	235,648	114,352
Transfer from Process 2	250,000	169,303	80,697				
Direct material	15,000	15,000	—				
Direct labour	35,000	35,000	—				
	310,000	226,613	83,387				
Less Stock c/d	15,000	10,965	4,035				
PRIME COST	295,000	215,648	79,352				
Production overhead	20,000	20,000	—				
PROCESS COST	315,000	235,648	79,352				
Gross profit (10% on transfer, ⅑ on cost)	35,000	—	35,000				
	£350,000	£235,648	£114,352		£350,000	£235,648	£114,352
Stock b/d	15,000	10,965	4,035				

Finished Stock

	Total	Cost	Profit		Total	Cost	Profit
	£	£	£		£	£	£
Stock b/d	20,000	13,466	6,534	Sales	400,000	228,916	171,084
Transfer from Process 3	350,000	235,648	114,352				
	370,000	249,114	120,886				
Less Stock c/d	30,000	20,198	9,802				
	340,000	228,916	111,084				
Gross profit	60,000	—	60,000				
	£400,000	£228,916	£171,084		£400,000	£228,916	£171,084
Stock b/d	30,000	20,198	9,802				

Stocks

Stocks are calculated as follows:

Process 2:

$$\frac{148,605}{180,000} \times 4,000 = £3,302.$$

Total £4,000 − Cost £3,302 = Profit £698.

Process 3:

$$\frac{226,613}{310,000} \times 15,000 = £10,965.$$

Total £15,000 − Cost £10,965 = Profit £4,035.

Finished stock:

$$\frac{249,114}{370,000} \times 30,000 = £20,198.$$

Total £30,000 − Cost £20,198 = Profit £9,802.

Profit

Provision for Unrealised Profit in Stock Account

	£	£		£	£
Profit and Loss A/c:			Balance b/d:		
Proportion of provision in respect of Process 2 not required		697	Process 2	1,395	
Balance c/d:			3	2,690	
Process 2	698		Finished stock	6,534	10,619
3	4,035		Profit and Loss A/c:		
Finished stock	9,802	14,535	Additional provision required:		
			Process 3	1,345	
			Finished stock	3,268	4,613
		£15,232			£15,232
			Balance b/d:		
			Process 2	698	
			3	4,035	
			Finished stock	9,802	14,535

Gross profit for the month will be:

	£	£
Process 1		30,000
Process 2	50,000	
Plus Provision w/o	697	
		50,697
Process 3	35,000	
Less Provision	1,345	
		33,655
Finished stock	60,000	
Less Provision	3,268	
		56,732
		£171,084

Balance sheet

Stocks will appear in the balance sheet as:

	£
Process 1	10,000
„ 2	3,302
„ 3	10,965
Finished stock	20,198
TOTAL	£44,465

NOTE: The gross profit for the month of £171,084 should be checked with the Profit column on the Sales side of the Finished Stock Account on page 385.

EXAMINATION QUESTIONS

Also includes questions on Chapter 20.

1. What do you regard as the special feature of process costs? To what classes of manufacture are they generally applied?

(*R.S.A. Advanced*)

2. Explain what is meant by (*a*) normal, (*b*) abnormal scrap and waste of materials during the process of manufacture.

What treatment would you give them in the cost accounts?

(*A.C.C.A. Inter.*)

3. Define each of the terms given below, when used in connection with materials, in a business operating on a process cost basis:

(*a*) (*i*) Normal losses and gains.
   (*ii*) Abnormal losses and gains.
(*b*) (*i*) By-products.
   (*ii*) Joint products.

How would you evaluate and deal in the process accounts with each of these items?

(*I.C.W.A. Inter.*)

4. How would you deal with scrap material in process costs? Give a concrete example.

(*I.C.W.A. Inter.*)

5. In crediting the proceeds from sale of by-products to the cost account for a primary product, would you include the profit realised on the by-product, or would you credit it at a value which excludes profit? Give reasons for your preference.

(*I.C.W.A. Final*)

6. How should a scheme of costing be designed to suit the conditions operating in a concern which has a number of by-products? Mention the factors which tend to govern the choice of any effective scheme.

(*I.C.W.A. Final*)

7. A factory having its own gas-making plant utilises in its manufacturing processes the whole of the residual coke. How would you determine the price at which to credit the gas factory for the coke so used?

(I.C.W.A. Inter.)

8. A chemical undertaking manufactures a number of products. The early processes in the manufacturing chain are joint for all products.

The cost department allocates the corresponding joint costs of these processes to the various products on the basis of the final sales value of each product. A director argues that this procedure is a waste of time and money because it provides no information on which any useful action can be taken. You are asked to give your reasoned opinion.

(A.C.C.A. Final)

9. Discuss the treatment of by-products in the cost accounts when:

    (a) the by-product has a considerable market value;
    (b) the by-product is subjected to further processes before utilisation as the raw material of a new product;
    (c) the by-product is unsaleable and expense is incurred in its disposal.

(C.A.A. Final)

10. How should by-products be dealt with in costing:

    (a) where they are of small total value;
    (b) where they are of considerable total value;
    (c) where they require further processing?

The yield of a certain process is 80% as to the main product, 15% as to by-product and process loss 5%. The material put in process (500 units) cost £3 per unit and all other charges £1,000 of which power is £230. It is ascertained that power is chargeable as to by-product and main product in the ratio of 2:1.

Draw up a statement showing the cost of the by-product.

(A.C.C.A. Inter.)

11. "In the treatment of joint costs, as in many other fields, the accountant is quite unconsciously a source of error. He all too often insists on setting off a particular cost against a particular revenue in some subordinate or departmental account, instead of boldly carrying forward joint . . . costs into a consolidated account, there to be met out of general revenue" (an economist).

"The allocation of joint costs among joint products is essential if we are to know just how profitable each of our products is" (a salesman).

Comment on the above quotations making particular reference to the reasons why most organisations allocate common costs to joint products.

(A.C.C.A. Final)

12. A company making a number of different products in separate factories has asked you to prepare, for issue to the staff and approval of the auditors, instructions for the taking and valuation of work-in-progress stock in two of its factories, A and B, at the year end. Factory A manufactures a toilet preparation and costs its production as a continuous process. Factory B

makes a variety of small metal products, each consisting of several components, and employs a system of costing by batches.

You are required to give in brief note form, in preparation for the writing of the work-in-progess stock-taking instructions, details of the procedures you would adopt to take and to value the work in progress at Factory A and at Factory B.

(I.C.W.A. Inter.)

13. Many of the problems associated with Process Cost Accounts relate to the treatment of wastage and the valuation of partially completed work in progress. What are these problems and how can they be dealt with in a cost accounting system?

(A.C.C.A. Final)

14. From the following particulars you are required to prepare a process cost statement, showing:

(a) the cost of input of material in total, and per lb;
(b) the manufactured cost of yield in total, and per unit.

Direct materials

	In stock July 1	Purchased during year	In stock June 30
A	1,300 lb at £0·25 per lb	14,000 lb at £0·26	1,450 lb
B	1,500 lb at £0·20 per lb	16,500 lb at £0·22½	1,600 lb
C	1,175 lb at £0·15 per lb	12,500 lb at £0·16½	1,300 lb

Direct labour

Department 1   10,000 hours at £0·5 per hour
           2   12,000 hours at £0·55 per hour
           3   9,000 hours at £0·47½ per hour

Works overhead

Absorption rates—Department 1   £0·80 per hour
                       2   £0·70 per hour
                       3   £0·60 per hour

The quantities used produced a yield of 4,250 units. The loss of yield was scrap which was sold for £0·10 per lb.

One unit requires 10 lb of mixed material.

(A.C.C.A. Inter.)

15. The metal charged to a cupola in an iron foundry during a period was as follows:

                76 tons pig-iron "A" at £23 per ton
                52   „   „   "B" at £21   „
                17   „   steel scrap   at £12   „
                55   „   iron scrap   at £20   „

During the period 100 tons of good castings were produced and 85 tons of scrap work, runners, heads, etc., were returned to stock.

Draw up a statement for management showing the costs of metal charged, metal poured and good castings produced in total and "per ton."

Show also the savings in cost which would have been effected if the loss in melt had amounted to 5% of metal charged, and the same weight of scrap work, runners, heads, etc., had been returned to stock. It is the practice of the business to credit scrap, etc., returned to stock at average cost of metal content.

(I.C.W.A. Final)

16. The Excelsior Company Ltd. manufactures a single product in two successive processes. The following information is available for the month of July:

Process 1

1. No opening work in process on July 1.
2. During the month 815 units costing £2,415 were put into process.
3. Labour and overhead incurred amounted to £1,600.
4. During the month 600 units were finished and passed to Process 2.
5. On July 31, 190 units remained in process, the operations on which were half completed, but the materials for the whole process have been charged to the process.

Process 2

1. No opening work in process on July 1.
2. The cost of labour and overhead in this process was £900, and material costing £350 was added at the end of operations.
3. On July 31, 400 units had been transferred to finished stock.
4. At that date 180 units remained in process, and it was estimated that one-third of the operations had been completed.

You are requested to show the Process Accounts, treating any process losses as a normal loss.

(A.C.C.A. Inter.)

17. A brass alloy of 70% copper and 30% zinc is made into extruded brass section by the two consecutive processes of casting and extrusion. Copper costs £170 per ton and zinc £65 per ton.

In casting there is a loss in melt of 3%, and 10% of total input is returned to stock as scrap brass. Casting process costs in addition amount to £24 per ton of total input. In extrusion, 30% of the input of the process is returned to stock as scrap brass, and other extrusion process costs amount to £27 per ton of the input of this process.

Administration, selling and distribution costs amount to £21 per ton sold. Scrap brass is credited to the process in which it arises and debited to Scrap Brass Stock Account at the cost of metal content.

Present figures showing the process and total costs per ton of output.

(I.C.W.A. Final)

18. (a) Discuss briefly how you would treat in the cost accounts of a manufacturing process the following:

(i) Normal loss.
(ii) Abnormal loss.

(b) The following particulars for Process 4 are given:

	Units	£
Transfer from Process 3 at cost	2,000	
Direct wages		1,000
Direct materials		1,500
Production overhead		2,000
Transfer to finished stock	1,620	
Direct wages		1,000
Direct materials used		1,500

Production overhead is absorbed at a rate of 400% of direct materials.
Allowance for normal loss is 20% of units worked.
Scrap value of £2·50 per unit.
Evaluate the cost of the transfer to finished stock.

(c) Using the information supplied in (b) above show the amount for losses or gains in process to be entered in the Costing Profit and Loss Account.

(I.C.W.A. Inter.)

19. A foundry produces castings in a number of different alloys, in each of which scrap metal from previous meltings is used. It is the practice to charge this scrap metal at the average price of metal content; but, as the market price of scrap metal of an identical mixture is lower, a suggestion is made that this market price should be used in the cost accounts in respect of the foundry's own scrap.

As cost accountant, present a report to management on the subject, illustrating your recommendations by the use of figures in respect of your most important product, the material content of which is:

50% Material A costing £200 per ton
20%   „   B   „   £580   „
10%   „   C   „   £120   „
20% scrap metal of identical mixture.

The market price of this scrap metal is £100 per ton, and, in making the alloy, 5% of metal charged is lost in melting, and, from the production of the product in question, 30% is returned to scrap metal stock to be used in future meltings.

In making the report, give consideration to the positions which arise when:

(a) all scrap cannot be used in future melting processes;
(b) the scrap returned to store after pouring is (i) lower than, (ii) equal to and (iii) higher than, the input of scrap.

(I.C.W.A. Final)

20. A foundry produces brass castings consisting of 70% copper, costing £450 per ton, and 30% zinc, costing £120 per ton. 10% of the metal charged is lost in melting, i.e. before pouring. Melting costs, other than materials, amount to £50 per ton of metal poured.

Good castings produced vary, according to product type, from 50% to 70% of metal poured. The balance, consisting of runners, heads and scrap, is returned to stock for subsequent use, being valued at cost of metal content only.

Prepare costs of metal and melting for products with (a) 50%, (b) 60% and (c) 70% yields.

What difference (if any) is made to these figures when the charge of metals in the ratio 70:30 is supplemented by 40% addition of scrap metal of this mixture?   (*I.C.W.A. Final*)

21. (a) X Ltd. manufactures a chemical product passing through two consecutive processes A and B. Waste material from A is used to form the basis of a by-product C and is charged to C at the ex-stores price (below).

Cost summaries for the 3 months to December 31 show:

	A		B		C	
	Tons	£	Tons	£	Tons	£
Materials ex-raw stores	72	2,076	18	1,272	5	192
Direct labour		3,220		830		428
Indirect shop labour and variable overheads		1,050		370		160

Fixed shop overheads for the three months amounted in total to £1,400, and are to be charged on the basis of conversion cost: A, 20%; B, 40%; and C, 25%; any balance being carried temporarily in suspense. Interest is to be charged in the costing at 4% per annum on the process capital employed, which is A, £10,100; B, £8,400; and C, £3,300. During the three months to December 31, 6 tons of waste material were transferred to By-product C and 66 tons to Process B.

Compute the cost per ton of output from A, B and C.

(b) Discuss concisely the method of overhead allocation adopted in (a) above in relation to the provision of information to management.

(*A.C.C.A. Final*)

22. X.Y. Ltd. manufactures Product A, which yields two by-products B and C. The actual joint expenses of manufacture for a period were £8,000.

It was estimated that the profit on each product as a percentage of sales would be 30%, 25% and 15%, respectively. Subsequent expenses were as follows:

	A	B	C
	£	£	£
Materials	100	75	25
Direct wages	200	125	50
Overheads	150	125	75
	£450	£325	£150
Sales were	£6,000	£4,000	£2,500

Prepare a statement showing the apportionment of the joint expenses of manufacture over the different products.

(*I.C.W.A. Final*)

23. The costs of a manufacturing company for a year are as follows:

	£
Direct material	120,000
Direct wages	80,000
Production overhead (variable)	60,000
„ „ (fixed)	40,000
Selling and distribution costs (variable)	20,000
„ „ (fixed)	40,000

During the period sales were as follows:

	£
Main product	340,000
By-product A (8,000) units	40,000
„ B (5,000) „	20,000

It is discovered that a further process combining by-product B with some of by-product A and adding further material will yield a saleable product C. Investigation shows that if the 5,000 units of B are combined with 4,000 units of A, together with additional material costing £60,000, and an additional direct wages cost of £30,000, the production of C will give a sales value of £180,000.

Plant, machinery and facilities are available in the business to accommodate this extra work, but it is estimated that additional fixed expenses amounting to £12,000 will be incurred during a year if the additional process is carried out.

Present a report to management, making recommendations on the course of action you suggest.

(*I.C.W.A. Final*)

24. A chemical plant produces two industrial products, A and B. In addition, there is a by-product, C, for which there is a steady demand. By-product C is obtained from Process No. 1, the remaining output from which passes on to Process No. 2, of which A and B are joint main products.

You are given the following information relating to the plant for the month of October:

1. Production costs:

	Process No. 1	Process No. 2
Materials	£9,000	£5,000
Operating expenses	£12,000	£15,000

2. Production:

Product A	15,000 tons
B	6,000 tons
C	10,000 gallons

3. Sales (at ex-works prices):

Product A	14,000 tons at £2 per ton
B	5,000 tons at £4·62½ per ton
C	11,000 gallons at £0·05 per gallon

4. Stocks at the commencement of the month:

Product A	1,500 tons at cost, £1·50 per ton
B	1,000 tons at cost, £3·75 per ton
C	1,200 gallons at £0·05 per gallon

Costs are divided between Products A and B according to a ratio provided by the chief chemist. By-product C is valued at its market price of £0·05 per gallon.

5. Work in process is negligible.

You are required to:

(a) calculate the value of stocks of processed materials at the end of October;

(b) prepare a statement of gross profit for the month of October.

(*I.C.A. Final, November 1966*)

25. A company produces three joint products A, B and C by the operation of a process. The standard costs for a period are as follows:

Input: Materials 600 tons at £20 per ton
Labour at £5 per ton of input
Overheads at 200% on labour
Output: 400 tons Product A at £30 per ton
100 „ „ B at £40 „ „
5,000 gallons „ C at £1 „ gallon

Product A is sold at a price of £35 per ton.

Product B is passed to a second process, in which labour costs are £10 per ton of input, and overhead is at 200% on labour. The output is 98 tons of Product M, which is sold at £80 per ton.

Product C is passed to another process in which labour costs are £0·20 per gallon, and overhead is again at 200% on labour. The output is 50 tons of Product N, which is sold at £200 per ton.

Present figures to management to show the profitability of operating the processes. All process losses should be regarded as normal.

(*I.C.W.A. Final*)

26. A textile company has a department which concentrates upon one style of garment which is re-designed annually. Since high-grade production is aimed at, a proportion of the output, usually 20%, is sold without the brand name, being sub-standard. A further 2% has no value except for certain pieces of salvaged material, usable for trimming.

The figures for a batch of 100 were as follows:

	£
Direct materials	3·00 per garment
Direct wages	1·50 „ „
Variable overhead	2·00 „ „
Fixed overhead	150·00 (total)

Output:

			£
First grade	78 garments:	sales value	15·00 each
Sub-standard	20 ,,	sales value	8·00 ,,
Scrap	2 ,,	value	0·50 ,,

No difficulty is experienced in using salvaged material from scrap up to 5%, but beyond this level scrap is virtually of no value.

Sickness and holiday absence make the engagement of temporary staff necessary. The employment of temporary staff increases sub-standard output to 30% and scrap to 7%. Fixed overhead is unaffected.

Using the figures given, show how the joint costs would be allocated.

Determine profits on first grade and sub-standard output in (a) normal conditions, and (b) where the use of temporary staff has produced 7% scrap and 30% sub-standard garments.

What advice would you give to management?

(I.C.W.A. Final)

27. A company receives steel in strip form from a nearby steel-mill. On a specialised machine, from one kind of steel strip, there are produced three products A, B and C. Product A is taken from the machine and further processed to make it available for sale at £1·25 each. The additional processing cost for product A is £176 per month. Products B and C are run through a dipping vat to make them heat-resistant. The dipping material costs are calculated at £0·07½ per cubic foot of product. Product B will then sell at £1·80 each and Product C at £3·00 each.

In the month of May, the costs of running the machine for the month were:

	£
Materials	2,835
Direct labour	600
Maintenance and depreciation	435
	£3,870

Production and sales for the month were: Product A 600 units, Product B 800 units and Product C 1,000 units, and this can be regarded as a typical product mix.

Product B has a volume of ½ cubic foot and Product C of ⅘ cubic foot.

The dipping vat is being depreciated at the rate of £24 per month. It requires six men for its operation at a total cost of £540 per month and necessitates other operating costs of £60 per month; these costs are regarded as fixed costs.

(a) Produce a cost statement for May assigning the joint costs to each product.

(b) Make your recommendations on the advisability of the company selling, on a long-run basis, Product B undipped, at £1·70 each.

(I.C.W.A. Final)

28. For the month ended May 31, the following particulars are submitted in respect of Process X:

	£
Raw materials used	27,690
Direct labour	14,625

Factory overhead, allocated at 100% on labour £14,625.

During the month 3,800 units were begun and 3,600 units passed to finished stores.

Certain losses were incurred in process, but are not to be regarded as part of the cost of production of the finished units.

Opening and closing work in progress were as follows:

	Units		£
May 1	200	25% complete	1,955
May 31	250	80% complete	?

All works records are maintained on the FIFO basis.

It can be assumed that the material, labour and overhead cost all accrue evenly over time, so that if a unit is half finished it can be assumed to have absorbed half its material cost, half its labour cost and half its overhead cost. The FIFO principle is to be applied to partly finished units; i.e. all unfinished units in work in process at the beginning of the year are to be costed so far as the balance of the work on them is concerned on the basis of current unit costs.

Draft the Process Total Account, reconciling the quantities and money values, and bringing down the balances.

(A.C.C.A. Final)

29. The P.Q. Company Limited is considering an order for an additional 2,000 lb per month of Beta Powder at a price of £1·37½ per lb.

On the basis of the following cost information—the only information available—prepare a Process Account and a report advising management as to whether or not it should accept this order.

Beta Powder—Final Process Account for November

	lb	£
Opening work in process	1,800	1,772
Transferred from previous process	19,000	18,050
Direct process costs—labour	—	6,000
Direct process costs—expenses	—	2,200
Transferred to finished goods store	16,500	—
Closing work in process	2,400	—

NOTE:

1. Normal process loss is estimated at 5% of input from the previous process—no value for this is credited to the Process Account but excessive losses are charged to the account. Losses are only identified when the goods are complete and then have no scrap value.

2. Opening and closing work in process can be assumed to be 50% complete as to labour and expenses while material is complete.

(A.C.C.A. Final)

30. Product M is manufactured in three processes. For the month of November the following information is given for Process 2:

Transfers from Process 1 to Process 2:

| 4,500 units at cost | £3,325 |
| Materials issued to Process 2 | £480 |

Processing costs are charged to Process 2 on the basis of 300% of the value of material issued.

Work in progress:

	Units	Stage of completion and material issued in Process 2
At start:	500	50%
At end:	1,000	30%

A total of 250 units were scrapped, of which 200 were fully processed and considered a normal loss, while 50 with 80% of Process 2 material issued were considered an abnormal loss.

Units scrapped are sold at £0·50 each. The value received for those considered a normal loss are credited to the value of products transferred from Process 1.

Using a FIFO basis you are required for Process 2 for November to:

(a) calculate the unit cost and total cost of the products:

(i) transferred to Process 3;

(ii) treated as an abnormal loss;

(b) compile the Work-in-progress Account. You are to assume that the costs per unit brought forward at start of month are the same as for those incurred in November;

(c) compile the Abnormal Loss Account.

(*I.C.W.A. Inter.*)

31. The following details relate to a process costing system:

	Percentage degree of completion	No. of units	Cost £
Opening stock—		300	1,230
(a) Material	50		
(b) Labour	80		
(c) Overhead	80		
Material			790
Wages			3,710
Overhead			1,484
Transferred from previous process	100	3,800	13,680
Transferred to next process	100	3,500	
Scrap—		100	
(a) Material	100		
(b) Wages	50		
(c) Overhead	50		
Closing stock—		500	
(a) Material	100		
(b) Wages	80		
(c) Overhead	80		

(a) Prepare a statement of production, showing opening and closing stocks, output completed and scrap, in terms of (i) material and (ii) wages and overhead, converted from the percentages into equivalent completed "effective units."

(b) Prepare a statement of unit valuations, grouped as to quantity and value, into cost of scrap and cost of good production.

(c) Prepare a cost of production analysis, giving effective units from (a), actual issued quantity, total costs and unit costs.

(I.C.W.A. Final, Adapted)

32. The following information is obtained in respect of Process 2 for the month of August:

Opening stock: 800 units valued at £352.

Degree of completion—
Material	60%
Labour	40%
Overheads	40%

Transfer from Process 1: 16,000 units at £0·20 each.
Transfer to Process 3: 14,000 units.

	£
Direct material added in Process 2	1,521·00
Direct labour amounted to	2,240·25
Production overhead incurred	4,480·50

Units scrapped: 1,000.

Degree of completion—
Materials	100%
Labour	70%
Overheads	70%

Closing stock: 1,800 units.

Degree of completion—
Materials	80%
Labour	60%
Overhead	60%

There was a normal loss of 5% of production.
Units scrapped realised £0·20 each.

Prepare:

(a) statement of production;
(b) statement of cost;
(c) statement of evaluation;
(d) Process 2 Account.

33. The following figures relate to a single industrial process:

Quantity of work in process at commencement: 8,000 units
Costs of work in process at commencement:
Material	£29,600
Wages	£6,600
Overhead	£5,800

During the period under review, a further 32,000 units were introduced, and the additional costs were:

Material: £112,400;   Wages: £33,400;   Overhead: £30,200.

At the end of the period, 28,000 units were fully processed, and 12,000 units remained in process. This closing stock was complete as regards material cost, and one-third complete as regards wages and overhead.

Using the average method of valuation, tabulate these production and cost figures to give quantities, unit values and total values for completed output, and for each of the three elements comprising the closing work in process.

Attention should be paid to the form of presentation.

(I.C.W.A. Final)

34. A manufacturing company makes a product by two processes. For the month of April the information recorded for the second process was:

A work-in-process balance of 300 units brought forward from March was valued at cost as follows:

	£
Direct material, complete	820
Direct wages, 60% complete	400
Overhead, 60% complete	545

During April, 4,500 units were transferred from the first to the second process at a cost of £2·50 each, while costs incurred by the second process were:

	£
Direct materials issued	890
Direct wages	9,490
Overhead	13,301

The transfer of finished goods to the warehouse amounted to 3,900 units, a loss of 300 units in the processing having occurred.

Work in process at the end of the month consisted of 200 completed units awaiting transfer to warehouse and a balance of unfinished units, which were complete as regards direct material and half complete as regards direct wages and overhead.

Prepare for the month of April the account for the second process to show direct material, direct wages and overhead separately for:

(a) production cost per unit of the finished product;
(b) total cost of production transferred to the warehouse;
(c) total cost of finished goods in closing work in process;
(d) total cost of uncompleted goods in closing work in process.

(I.C.W.A. Final)

35. A company operates a department producing a component which passes through two processes. During November, materials for 40,000 components were put into process. There was no opening process stock. 30,000 were finished and passed to the next process. Those not passed forward

were calculated to be one-half finished as regards wages and overhead. The costs incurred were as follows:

	£
Direct material	10,000
Factory overhead	12,000
Direct wages	8,000

Of those passed to the second process, 28,000 were completed and passed to finished stores. 200 were scrapped, which was not abnormal. 1,800 remained unfinished in process, one-quarter finished as regards wages and overhead. No further process material costs occur, after introduction at the first process, until the end of the second process, when protective packing is applied to the completed components. The process and packaging costs incurred at the end of the second process were:

	£
Direct material	4,000
Factory overhead	4,500
Direct wages	3,500

Prepare a cost analysis statement for November, accounting for total costs incurred, analysed into elements of cost for each process, covering finished and part-finished items.

(I.C.W.A. Final)

36. A structural engineering contractor has a contract to supply and erect light steelwork transmission pylons estimated to number 12,000. The estimating engineers and cost department have produced the following figures for a single pylon:

Light Construction Department

	Amount	Standard cost	Total
			£
Sundry steelwork	18 cwt	£4·50 per cwt	81
Direct wages	30 hours	£0·50 per hour	15
Overhead (machine)	30 ,,	£0·60 ,, ,,	18
			£114

Site Fabrication and Erection Department

	Amount	Standard cost	Total
Bolts, rivets, etc.	80	£0·02½ each (average)	2
Direct wages	16 hours	£0·62½ per hour	10
Overhead	16 ,,	£0·25 ,, ,,	4
			£16

The contract extends over several months. The following are the figures for the month under review:

	Light construction department	Site fabrication and erection department
Opening stock	160 pylons	50 pylons
Percentage completed (wages and overhead)	30	40
Standard costs of stock:	£	£
Materials: steelwork, rivets, etc.	12,960	100
Steelwork transferred to site	—	5,700
Direct wages	720	200
Overhead	864	80
Costs for month (actual):		
Materials bought and issued	95,000	2,100
Direct wages	16,500	10,000
Overhead	19,000	4,400
Closing stock	250 pylons	150 pylons
Percentage completed	50	75

During the month, 950 pylons were finished, of which 900 were certified as accepted by the electricity generating company and passed for payment.

Using the "first-in, first-out" method for production and sales, prepare an account in tabulated columnar form for each of the two departments to show the classified costs for production, transfers, opening and closing stocks of work in progress and variances. Add a tabulated summary of units and amounts in respect of finished pylons transferred, sold and in stock at the end of the period.

(I.C.W.A. Final)

37. A company makes a product which passes through two separate processes, botching and fletching. The material changes composition in each of these processes, so that the unit of measurement also changes.

The costs of these two processes for November were as follows:

	Botching £	Fletching £
Materials out of stores	14,550	4,200
Process labour	5,460	16,800
Process overhead	8,100	31,500

Output of the processes for the month was as follows:

Botching: 2,000 units were completed and passed to the Fletching process. 800 units were still in process at month-end, complete as to material, and 50% complete as to conversion cost.

Fletching: 5,000 units were completed and passed into the finished stock warehouse, while 2,000 units were still in process at month-end, complete as to material, and 50% complete as to conversion cost.

On November 1 the work-in-progress figures were:

	Units	Cost £
Work in progress, botching	1,000	
Direct material (complete)		7,500
Process labour (75% complete)		3,000
Process overhead (75% complete)		4,500
		£15,000
Work in progress, fletching	3,000	
Direct material (complete)		25,500
Process labour (50% complete)		5,700
Process overhead (50% complete)		9,000
		£40,200

Prepare Process Accounts for November, treating material passing from botching to fletching as direct material in the Fletching Process Account, and valuing closing work in progress at average cost. Show appropriate unit cost information.

(I.C.W.A. Final)

38. Explain fully the principles you would adopt for the valuation of work in progress at the end of an accounting period.

(I.C.W.A. Inter.)

39. (*a*) What bases may be adopted in fixing the prices at which transfers from process to process are made?

(*b*) What bearing would these prices have on the value of the stock at the end of the accounting period?

(C.A.A. Final)

40. Your company produces a chemical product X from materials which are passed through two distinct processes A and B.

A summary of production details and costs incurred for a certain month which is under review is given below:

	Process A gallons	Process B gallons
Materials put into process	500,000	
Transferred from Process A to Process B	450,000	450,000
Work in process:		
at beginning of month	—	30,000
at end of month	50,000	20,000
	£	£
Costs:		
Work in process, at beginning of month	—	4,700
Materials, added at beginning of process	60,000	—
Labour and overhead	13,800	9,100

In Process A the work in process at the end of the month was one-fifth complete as to labour and overhead.

In Process B the work in process at the beginning of the month was one-third complete and at the end of the month one-quarter complete.

Chemical product X is sold to a subsidiary company for £19 per 100 gallons.

As an alternative, the output from Process B could be subject to further processing at an estimated additional cost of £11,500 and sold as Product Y on the open market at £23 per 100 gallons. The setting up of the extra process would incur an estimated capital cost of £400,000. If it were decided to adopt this alternative and produce Product Y, the subsidiary company could obtain supplies of Product X from another and adequate source at a cost of £92,000 for the output of the month under review, which represents the normal and consistent monthly requirement of the subsidiary company.

Prepare for management in a suitable form the following:

(a) Accounts for the month for Process A and Process B, with the cost per gallon of Product X produced.

(b) A report on whether the suggested alternative as stated above should be adopted to produce Product Y and to sell it on the open market and to allow the subsidiary company to obtain supplies of X from another source. Your company expects a return on capital employed of 15% prior to tax.

(I.C.W.A.)

CHAPTER 22

UNIFORM COSTING

UNIFORM OR STANDARDISED COSTING SYSTEMS

THE DEVELOPMENT OF UNIFORM COSTING

Amalgamations and close working arrangements between groups of manufacturers in particular industries, and organisation for rationalisation, have necessitated, to a certain extent, the establishment of some degree of uniform costing by industries. In the case of particular manufacturers who control a number of factories situated in different districts, co-ordinated uniform costing has been introduced in order that the costs at each factory may be properly comparable. Uniformity of application of principles; of apportionment and absorption of overhead; and of determining cost and selling prices are found to be advantageous for comparing efficiencies and as a means of controlling unit costs.

In a different class may be considered those uniform systems which have been devised and introduced into particular industries by various federations or associations of manufacturers, as, for example, in such industries as paper-bag making, printing, tin-box making, etc. One of the purposes of these particular schemes is to render competition less destructive, by ensuring that all the members know what is included in cost, and how to arrive at it, but this does not include any provision for disclosure of members' costs. Other purposes of this type of uniform costing are connected with a standardised method of collecting figures in order to fix selling prices on a basis acceptable to those engaged in the industry.

Various associations and federations have issued a uniform costing system for their respective industries. The adoption by individual firms is voluntary, and many of them do not put the approved uniform system into operation, although in some cases some of its features may be introduced into their existing system.

A disadvantage of a system of uniform costing is that it may introduce a certain amount of rigidity into the costing system, in as much as it is difficult to bring about a change in the system if it may affect other firms involved in the scheme. A further disadvantage may be that the system may tend to become out of date unless all the firms involved agree to update the scheme.

Of the systems organised by trade associations, that of the British Master Printers' Federation was the first serious attempt at devising a uniform system of costing, and is probably the most complete. An official outline of the system is given in this chapter.

REQUIREMENTS FOR UNIFORM COSTING

Apart from any decision whether single, process or job costing is desirable, the following details require to be determined:

(a) The bases for the apportionment and absorption of overhead.

(b) The departments, sections or production centres to be used for analysis and comparison of costs.

(c) What items shall be regarded as factory as distinct from administration expense.

(d) How expenses of administration, distribution and selling shall be applied to prime cost, i.e. the basis of recovery rates.

(e) How expenses in connection with the buying, storing, handling and issuing of stores materials shall be treated.

(f) What rates of depreciation shall be applied to plant and machines.

(g) Whether interest on capital is to be included, and, if so, how, and on what basis.

(h) What rent charge is to be made for building if freehold or leasehold.

(i) How service departmental costs shall be arrived at.

(j) The demarcation between direct and indirect wages.

(k) In the case of time- and piece-work, whether the time or wage basis, or both, shall be used for determining overhead rates.

(l) What organisation can be set up to prepare comparative statistics for the use of those adopting the uniform system. Privacy of individual data and confidence in the co-ordinating office are essential factors.

THE PURPOSES AND VALUE OF UNIFORM COSTING

In a group of amalgamated manufacturers, or in the case of a firm controlling a number of factories, actual detailed costs can be compared, standard costs may be set up and controls by comparisons secured. The most economical and suitable distribution of orders received can be made. Actual and relative efficiencies of production can be compared. By suitable organisation costs may be reduced.

Where manufacturers are only associated, or where the system is organised by a manufacturers' federation, less precise cost comparisons may be provided, as, for instance, the following:

(a) The cost value of production on some common basis, *e.g.* per £ of direct wages or other factor.

(b) The cost of rent, light, heat, etc., on the basis of, say, per 1,000 square feet.

(c) The ratio of indirect labour to direct labour, say by units, by operations or by processes.

(d) The number of plant-hours worked, and the output per hour for similar operations.

(e) The ratio of each kind of overhead to prime cost, or to direct wages.

(f) An index number as a guide to the degree of utilisation of capacity.

(g) The quantity of output to which the above information relates.

By these means comparison of efficiencies, of costs by selected units and of periodical averages of costs of different firms, etc., can be made.

It will be obvious that greater advantage is obtained by those actually controlling a group of factories than by individual manufacturers operating a common system organised for their particular industry owing to the dangers of disclosure of facts to competitors.

The British Institute of Management has for some time operated a department for carrying out inter-firm comparisons, and information of great value to the participants has come to light. Much more of this kind of interchange of information is done in the United States than in Great Britain, and has not been found to harm the business interests of those taking part. On the contrary, "spreading the light" has benefited the industry. This topic is dealt with fully in *Principles and Practice of Management Accountancy* (Macdonald and Evans Ltd., 1969).

THE BRITISH MASTER PRINTERS' COSTING SYSTEM

OUTLINE OF THE SYSTEM

In 1911 the Federation of Master Printers set up a special committee charged with the responsibility of compiling a system of costing that could be uniformly applied to printing businesses of all sizes. To-day the cost of probably more than 80% of the work produced by printers in Britain is found by means of this system as modified, by official agreement, to make it more up to date.

Budget of expenses. Operational costs are established by means of a budget, based on the expenses incurred over a year or, where deemed necessary, a shorter period. Direct allocation of expenses to departments and, later, to operations (both hand and machine) is one of the main principles of the system.

Use of hourly cost rates. Inclusive hourly cost rates are set up for all operations. These rates comprise wages, direct expenses as departmentalised and overhead expenses that are not possible of departmentalisation.

Expenses of stores, etc. The cost of buying, receiving, storing, issuing and delivering direct material is ascertained and recovered as "handling charges" by adding to the cost of material a fixed percentage of the invoice price.

Interest on capital. Interest on capital employed in the business is taken in as an item of cost, owing, partly, to the fact that hand and machine operations are essential to the production of every order, and, sometimes, a choice of these operations may be deemed desirable; machines vary enormously in price, and one type of machine may serve equally as well for certain classes of work as another type of a higher value. Depreciation is taken in on the basis of diminishing value.

Testing the rates used

In order to prove the correctness, or otherwise, of the set-up hourly rates, and also to ascertain whether the full costs are being recovered on the volume of the work produced, two *weekly* statements are prepared:

(*a*) On a form, Federation Form No. 4, called the "Value of Production," is tabulated the whole of the hours of "chargeable" (*i.e.* productive) time for all operations, gathered from daily time-dockets. This time is shown against the name of each hand-worker and each machine. In addition, the non-chargeable time is collated. Thus, not only is the total of each worker shown, but the ratio of chargeable to non-chargeable time of each individual is apparent. Columns are provided for progressive totals of both sets of figures, and it is thus possible to make comparisons over chosen periods.

(*b*) On another form (Federation Form No. 3) are tabulated weekly the departmental wages and expenses, the latter being fixed on a basis of a fiftieth part of the annual budget figures. To the sum of these two items is added the ascertained percentage to recover the overhead expenses, and the total represents the cost of production for the department concerned.

Effect of the overhead rates used. The application of overhead expenses by a percentage of the departmental cost has the effect of increasing the cost of production when pressure of work increases the departmental wages, and correspondingly decreases the cost of production when lack of work reduces the departmental wages bill. This applies to the normal fluctuations, and not to abnormal conditions, which would necessitate a recasting of the budget.

The departmental totals of value of production from Form 4 can be compared with the cost of production, and the difference shown as a surplus, or a deficit, as the case may be.

These two forms provide the management with information of great value as to whether the capacity of the factory to produce is being maintained.

The Federation publishes a booklet containing full details of the system, and illustrations of a great variety of forms for use in connection with the system, but these are too numerous to reproduce in this book.

THE BASIS OF ALLOCATION USED

The *departments* into which costs are divided are dependent upon the size and nature of the business. For a large firm they might be as follows: composing, foundry, machining, ruling, binding, lithography, materials. The composing may be further divided into hand composing, monotype and linotype.

Rent, rates, heat, light and water are in most cases apportioned to departments on the basis of square feet of area.

Fire insurance. That on buildings by area; on plant and contents according to value in each department; on standing formes and work on litho stones and plates, separate accounts with a view to recovery by a definite charge. Insurance for consequential loss (profits and standing charges) is treated as general overhead.

Interest on capital. A charge of at least 5% is debited to each department on the value of the plant and stock therein. Interest on the balance of the capital in the business is included in general overhead.

Depreciation. Usually, type 10%, plant 7½% on the diminishing value. Replacement values of pre-war plant should be used. Loss in melt of metal used by monotype and linotype plant depends on the frequency of melting; 2% per melt (of which there are two) is usually taken, and, by multiplying 4% by the total value of metal melted, the depreciation per annum is arrived at.

Holiday payments. The cost of fixed holidays, and annual holidays given to employees, is included in the annual expense budget for each department; thus the cost is evenly distributed over the year.

General expenses on materials. Handling charges, *e.g.* buying, receiving, storing, issuing, delivering, are added to the cost of materials; also a proportion for management and office expenses.

The remaining general expenses, *i.e.* travellers' salaries, commission, expenses, spoilage and the sundry expenses, are also applied as a percentage on materials. In the case of customers' own paper, an addition is made for handling and storage cost.

Cost sheets. A convenient form of cost sheet is shown in Fig. 74.

PRINTERS COST SHEET

Customer's Name: F. Smith & Co.

Work Ticket No. 391

Address: High Street, London

Details: 20,000 Annual Reports as per Work Ticket, La. Post 4to fly, printed black and red.

Composing Room *				Materials			
19 ..	State Hand or Mono.	Hrs.	£	19 Aug. 2			£
July 30	W. Jones, Hand Comp.				10,080 Sheets Cr. Ld. L. Post		
,, 31	W. Jones, Hand Comp.				Ink No. 8		
Aug. 3	W. Jones, Author's corrections				,, No. 4 20 M. Envelopes *Add* handling charges		

Machine Room					Outwork		
19 Aug. 2	Man 15	Machine E 3	Time	Rate £	19 .. Aug. 7		£
,, 3	,,	,,				Addressing Enve- lopes *Add* charges	
,, 4	,,	,,					
,, 5	,,						

Binding Room				Summary		
19 .. Aug. 5	Folding Cutting Piecework	Hrs.	At. £	Composing Machining Binding Materials Sundries		£

FIG. 74.—*Printers cost sheet*

It will be seen that this follows the general pattern of cost cards as shown in Figs. 50 and 64, but makes no provision for showing the amount of the estimate given to the customer: this might be added with advantage.

* Where mono- or linotype composing is used a separate section may be introduced, as this will be charged at a different hourly rate from hand composing.

The form is kept in the office and entered up daily from the daily dockets, and on completion is filed with the work ticket.

EXAMINATION QUESTIONS

1. "Some progressive businesses would like to have the advantages of uniform cost accounting and are prepared to exchange costs with other businesses with the object of ascertaining the best production and commercial methods" (*Uniform Cost Accounting*, I.C.W.A., Paragraph 8).

What are "the advantages of uniform cost accounting"? What type of cost information would be exchanged and how would this best be done without the disclosure of confidential information?

(*I.C.W.A. Final*)

2. A group of factories producing similar products has different costing systems. Tabulate the costing principles, with an example of each, necessary to establish a similar costing system for each factory.

(*I.C.W.A. Inter.*)

3. Printing machines are made to print appropriate sizes of paper and usually cost more as the sizes increase. To meet the requirements of customers it frequently happens that a small sheet must be printed on a large machine. What procedures should be adopted when assembling the costs of the job?

(*I.C.W.A. Final*)

4. What information from a uniform cost system would you suggest as *particularly* useful to manufacturers in the same line of business?

(*I.C.W.A. Final*)

5. What steps would you take to establish a system of uniform costing for fixing price standards in an industry controlled by a combine?

(*I.C.W.A. Final*)

6. What items of general expense would you expect to show most change per centum as a result of a combine? Indicate the direction of, and reasons for, these changes.

(*I.C.W.A. Inter.*)

7. Your firm propose making an amalgamation with another, and wish you, as cost accountant, to investigate and report. What especial features would you take into consideration for that report?

(*I.C.W.A. Final*)

8. The studio and design department of a printing business prepares ideas which are sometimes accepted by clients, but a large proportion of the work so produced is abandoned as unsuitable. How do you consider the cost of such a service should be recovered? Give your reasons.

(*I.C.W.A. Inter.*)

9. A proposal is being considered to amalgamate two factories at an estimated cost of £50,000. The savings expected to result therefrom are estimated at £20,000 per annum. State broadly the details of the savings, aggregating £20,000, that you would assume to follow on the amalgamation, and how you, as cost accountant, could contribute to the discussion of the proposal.

(*I.C.W.A. Final*)

10. How would you propose to deal with the following items in your costs:
(*a*) Warehousing expenses incurred in a printing business?

(*R.S.A. Part of question*)

11. From the following data prepare six prices per thousand for printing an art wrapper, *viz.*:

    (*a*) first orders of 50,000; 100,000, and 250,000;
    (*b*) repeat orders for 50,000; 100,000, and 250,000.

Cost of sketch and lithographic work, £40. Making machines ready for printing, £20. All other work (per thousand), £2. Add for general overhead and profit, 25%.

(I.C.W.A. Final)

12. State as fully as possible what you consider are the advantages and disadvantages of uniform costing to:

    (*a*) an individual firm;
    (*b*) an industry;
    (*c*) the public.

(I.C.W.A. Final)

13. As cost consultant to a trade organisation, you are requested to investigate the cost systems of various concerns with a view to the introduction of a uniform cost system. Describe the general lines upon which you would proceed, and indicate the principal preliminary difficulties to be overcome.

(I.C.W.A. Final)

14. A company has acquired a new undertaking. Because the accounting systems of the parent and subsidiary companies differ, results are not comparable. Uniformity of methods would render void for either company comparisons with previous periods. Suggest a compromise.

(I.C.W.A. Final)

15. Explain the objectives of uniform costing and outline the main causes of differences in costs between undertakings within the same industry.

(I.C.W.A. Final)

16. Design a form of cost statement suitable for a number of concerns engaged in the manufacture of the same standard product, adding a note as to the factors which you would consider in order to ensure that the results of the various concerns are strictly comparable.

(C.A.A. Final)

17. What is meant by "uniform costing"? What advantages would you expect to accrue from its adoption in an industry?

(A.I.A. Final)

18. The chief accountant of a group of companies in the same industry wishes to introduce uniformity of costing methods—and you are charged with investigating this objective. Tabulate the fundamental costing principles which need agreement and in respect of each give an example.

(I.C.W.A. Inter.)

19. The following figures were taken from the annual accounts of two electricity supply boards working on uniform costing methods:

Meter reading, billing and collection costs:

	Board A £000's	Board B £000's
Salaries and wages of:		
Meter readers	150	240
Billing and collection staff	300	480
Transport and travelling	30	40
Collection agency charges	—	20
Bad debts	10	10
General charges	100	200
Miscellaneous	10	10
	600	1,000
Units sold (millions)	2,880	9,600
Number of consumers (thousands)	800	1,600
Sales of electricity (millions)	£18	£50
Size of area (square miles)	4,000	4,000

Prepare a comparative cost statement using suitable units of cost. Brief notes should be added, commenting on likely causes for major differences in unit costs so disclosed.

(I.C.W.A. Final)

CHAPTER 23

MARGINAL COSTING

MARGINAL costing is not a system of costing, such as job costs, process costs, operating costs, etc., but is a special technique concerned particularly with the effect which fixed overheads has on the running of a business.

As was pointed out at the beginning of Chapter 10, overhead can be analysed in various ways. Instead of dividing it up into production overhead, administration overhead and selling and distribution overhead, the division is now into:

(a) variable overhead;
(b) semi-variable overhead;
(c) fixed overhead.

Nevertheless, it is the *same* overhead.

A costing system may be so arranged as to give information under the former headings, and there is no reason to make any change. All the introduction of marginal cost principles does is to give the management a fresh, and perhaps a refreshing, insight into the progress of their business; if this leads eventually to a weakening of those ties which bind overhead so closely to unit product cost, then the revolution can be peacefully achieved. It has already been suggested that administration overhead should be excluded from manufacturing cost. That is the first step: marginal costing goes further in the same direction.

First of all, it is necessary to begin with the realisation that certain items of overhead vary "up" or "down" with changes in the volume of production, while others do not. Those which do not vary constitute the fixed overhead.

EXAMPLE

Fixed overhead	= £5,000
Variable overhead cost per unit	= £0·25
Production—Period 1	= 5,000 units
Period 2	= 10,000 units

From the above figures it can be seen that in Period 1 the fixed overhead works out at £1 per unit, and in Period 2 it is only £0·50 per unit. The variable overhead, on the other hand, remains at the rate of £0·25 per unit throughout both periods.

413

The above example is, of course, over-simplified, but it is possible to deduce a general principle of the first importance, *viz.*:

> Other things being equal, the fixed overhead will, in total, remain "fixed" during changes in production achieved, and the rate per unit will consequently vary; whereas the variable overhead will remain constant per unit of production, and vary in total.

Consider now the figures given below. A chart, as shown in Fig. 75, can be made from these figures to show the cost per unit for any number of units within the range of readings available.

Number of units	Average variable cost per unit £	Total variable cost £	Fixed cost £	Total cost £	Total cost per unit £
5	5	25	300	325	65
10	5	50	300	350	35
15	5	75	300	375	25
20	5	100	300	400	20
25	5	125	300	425	17
30	5	150	300	450	15

Thus, as the fixed overhead is spread over more units, its influence on the cost per unit becomes less and less marked, and, if 300 units were produced, the total cost per unit would only be £0·30.

Again, consider the following results, as presented by two methods of accounting:

OLD METHOD

	£	£
Direct materials		3,000
Direct wages:		
Department A	1,200	
Department B	800	
		2,000
Prime cost		5,000
Production overhead:		
Department A	1,000	
Department B	600	
		1,600
Production cost		6,600

Administration, selling and distribution overhead:

20% on factory cost	1,320
Total cost	7,920
Profit	2,080
Sales	£10,000

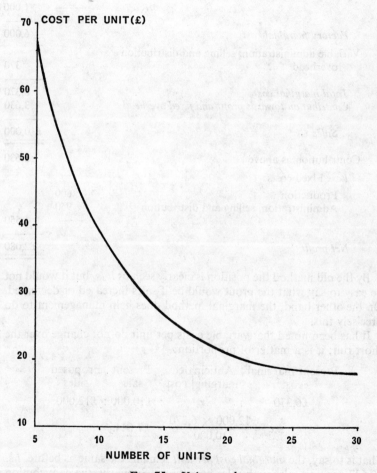

FIG. 75.—*Unit cost chart*

This chart depicts the fall in the cost per unit achieved as production rises. This is due to the lessening incidence of fixed overhead.

MARGINAL METHOD

		£	£
Direct materials			3,000
Direct wages:			
Department A		1,200	
Department B		800	
			2,000
Variable production overhead:			
Department A		600	
Department B		400	
			1,000
Factory marginal cost			6,000
Variable administration, selling and distribution overhead			370
Total marginal cost			6,370
Contribution towards profit and fixed overhead			3,630
Sales			£10,000
Contribution as above			3,630
Less Fixed costs:			
Production		600	
Administration, selling and distribution		950	
			1,550
Net profit			£2,080

By the old method the position is clearly seen *as it is*, but it would not be easy to say what the profit would be if sales increased or decreased. On the other hand, the marginal method does help management to do precisely this.

It has been noted that variable costs per unit do not change over the short run: it is a matter of proportion:

Present marginal cost	.	Anticipated marginal cost	..	Present sales	.	Proposed sales
£6,370	:	x	::	£10,000	:	£12,000

$$x = \frac{12,000 \times 6,370}{10,000} = £7,644.$$

That is to say, the *marginal cost per unit* remains the same as before, *i.e.* £0·637 per unit, although sales have risen. Similarly, the contribution available towards profit is 36·3% of sales, and this tends to be a stable percentage which management may and should watch.

If, then, it is desired to know what profit will be made when sales go up from £10,000 to £12,000:

$$36 \cdot 3\% \text{ of } £12,000 \text{ is } \underline{£4,356.}$$

The fixed costs, by definition, will remain the same (though this is true only within limits) and so the profit will be:

$$£4,356 - £1,550 \text{ or } \underline{£2,806.}$$

MARGINAL COST EQUATION

For the sake of convenience, it is possible to make an equation in general terms as follows:

Sales — Direct and variable costs = Fixed costs + Profit
(*i.e.* the contribution)

and this is shortened to:

$$S - V = F + P.$$

In any given problem, therefore, if we know three of the above factors, it is always possible to find the fourth. The equation is of the greatest importance to all students.

PROFIT/VOLUME RATIO

This is one of the most important ratios to watch in business, and is given by the formula:

$$\frac{S - V}{S}.$$

If the result arrived at by the use of the formula is multiplied by 100 the product will be a percentage, and this may be desired. The profit/volume (P/V) ratio expresses the relation between "contribution" and sales, and marks the change in the percentage of contribution in relation to changes in the volume of sales. In making investigations into the records of businesses, it is instructive to take the past five or six years' results and analyse all expenditure so that the variable costs are segregated. If the business is going along steadily it will be found, in all probability, that its P/V ratio has also remained steady.

If the term P/V had not become so firmly established C/S, or Contribution/Sales, would be a better one.

SPECIMEN QUESTION

If a business finds its profits fall to nil it is at break-even point. The contribution is only just sufficient to cover the fixed overhead. What would be the sales at break-even point?

ANSWER

$$Let\ S - V = F + P.$$

And $(S - V)/S$ = Contribution ratio, or P/V ratio.

Going back to the illustration:

$$S = £10,000;\quad V = £6,370;\quad F = £1,550.$$

Therefore the P/V ratio $= (£10,000 - £6,370)/10,000$
$$= 0·363.$$

The break-even point of sales is:

$$\frac{F}{P/V} = 1,550/0·363 = £4,270.$$

Check

	£
When S =	4,270
V for 4,270 units × £0·637 =	2,720
Leaving F =	£1,550

BREAK-EVEN CHARTS

As an aid to management, and in order to obtain a clearer view of the position of a business, it is often desirable to construct what is known as a "break-even chart." There are two ways of doing this, shown in Figs. 76 and 77. In either case make the y axis (vertical) correspond to sales and costs, and the x axis (horizontal) to output or capacity.

EXAMPLE

Output in thousands	5	10	15	20	25
Fixed costs	£2,000	£2,000	£2,000	£2,000	£2,000
Variable cost per unit £0·20	£1,000	£2,000	£3,000	£4,000	£5,000
Sales at £0·40 per unit	£2,000	£4,000	£6,000	£8,000	£10,000

It will be seen that Method 2 (Fig 77) helps in showing clearly that below (that is, to the left of) the break-even point, the sales fail to cover all the fixed overhead.

By formula:

$$Sales\ at\ BEP = F ÷ P/V\ ratio.$$

$$\frac{£2,000}{0·50} = £4,000.$$

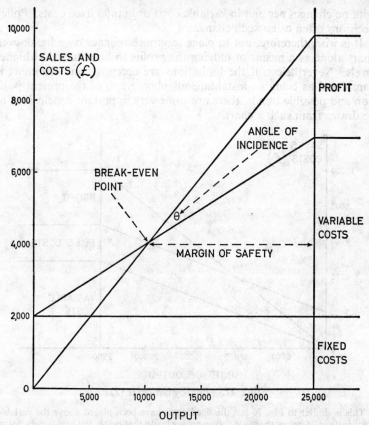

FIG. 76.—*Break-even chart (1)*

The usual form of break-even chart, showing in this case a break-even point at £4,000 sales, and what appears to be a healthy position for the firm.

On the charts the break-even point (BEP) can be seen at the point of intersection between the sales line and the total cost line.

LIMITATIONS OF BREAK-EVEN CHARTS

In actual practice, these break-even charts are quite unlikely to look like straight-line graphs, and it would not be surprising to find that it took on the appearance of Fig. 78. In this case there is one break-even point, but there might have been more.

One of the most frequent mistakes made with regard to break-even charts is to suppose that, as output rises, a proportional increase in sales revenue can be achieved; and, moreover, that this can be done with no changes per unit in variable costs or in total fixed costs. Policy decisions often cause such changes.

It is wise, therefore, not to place too much reliance on a break-even chart alone as a means of judging the profits to be obtained at higher levels. Nevertheless, if the limitations are accepted, and the chart is considered as being an instantaneous photograph of the present position and possible trends, there are some very important conclusions to be drawn from such a chart.

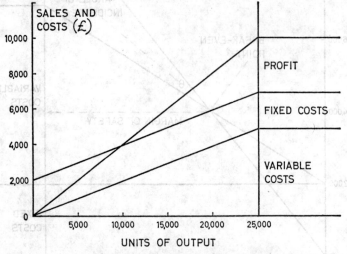

FIG. 77.—*Break-even chart* (2)

This is similar to Fig. 76 but the fixed costs have been placed above the variable costs instead of below them. It shows more clearly that below the break-even point, it is the fixed costs which are not being covered.

MARGIN OF SAFETY

This is represented on the chart as the distance between the BEP and the output being produced. If the distance is relatively short it indicates that a small drop in productive capacity or sales will reduce profits considerably. If the distance is long it means that the business could still be making profits after a serious drop in production. It should be noted that, as will be shown on page 423:

$$P \div P/V \text{ ratio} = M/S.$$

ANGLE OF INCIDENCE

This is the angle at which the sales line cuts the total costs line. If the angle is large (*see* Fig. 76) it is an indication that profits are being made

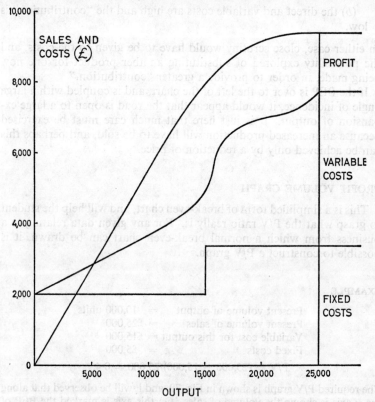

FIG. 78.—*Break-even chart (3)*

From this chart it can be seen that, when fact rather than theory is considered, a break-even chart is unlikely to be a series of straight lines. There might be several break-even points at different levels of output and sales.

at a high rate. Taken in conjunction with the margin of safety, it can be seen that a large angle of incidence with a high margin of safety indicates an extremely favourable position, and even the existence of monopoly conditions.

On the other hand, if the angle of incidence is small, it indicates that, while profits are being made, they are being achieved under less favourable conditions.

POSITION OF BREAK-EVEN POINT

If the break-even point appears well over to the right of the chart, the margin of safety is low and the cause may be that either:

(*a*) the amount of fixed overhead is too great for the amount of sales being achieved; or (*b*) the direct and variable costs are high and the "contribution" is low.

In either case, close scrutiny would have to be given to the costs, and the possibility explored of substituting another product for one now being made, in order to provide a greater "contribution."

If the BEP is over to the left of the chart, and is coupled with a large angle of incidence, it would appear that the road is open to a large expansion of output. It is just here that much care must be exercised because an increased production will have to be sold, and perhaps this can be achieved only by a reduction of price.

PROFIT VOLUME GRAPH

This is a simplified form of break-even chart, and will help the student to grasp what the P/V ratio really is. For any given data relating to a business from which a normal break-even chart can be drawn, it is possible to construct a P/V graph.

EXAMPLE

Present volume of output $\quad$ = $\quad$ 10,000 units
Present volume of sales $\quad$ = £25,000
Variable cost for this output = £15,000
Fixed costs $\quad$ = $\quad$ £5,000

$$P/V = (25,000 - 15,000)/25,000 = 0\cdot4.$$

The required P/V graph is shown in Fig. 79, and it will be observed that along the x axis is shown the volume of sales. On this axis is marked the BEP of sales, which can be obtained either by first drawing a normal break-even chart or by calculation, using the formula as before:

$$\text{Sales at BEP} = F \div P/V$$

$$\frac{5,000}{0\cdot4} = £12,500.$$

The y axis is drawn vertically through the point of origin; above the x axis it represents profits, while below it represents fixed costs. The amount of fixed costs is therefore marked on the y axis as though it were a loss, and this point is joined by a straight line to the BEP of sales, being extended to a position a little beyond the present volume of sales. Looking at this graph, it will be seen that the tangent of angle A is the side opposite divided by the side adjacent, so that when, in triangle XYZ, sales are £25,000, the length of YZ is 5,000, representing profit, and the length of XZ is 25,000 − 12,500, or 12,500, representing the margin of safety.

Then:

$$\tan A \text{ is } \frac{P}{M/S} \text{ and is } \frac{5,000}{12,500} \text{ or } \underline{0\cdot4}.$$

Now, since:

$$S - V = F + P.$$
$$V = S - F - P.$$

That is:

$$V = 25,000 - 5,000 - 5,000 = £15,000.$$

And:

$$P/V = \frac{S - V}{S} = \frac{10,000}{25,000} = 0.4.$$

So then:

$$\tan A = \frac{P}{M/S} = \text{the P/V ratio. Therefore, } M/S = P \div P/V$$

and changes in sales are accompanied by changes in profits, assuming always that:

variable costs remain steady,
fixed cost remain unaltered,

and the rate of this change is measured by the P/V ratio.

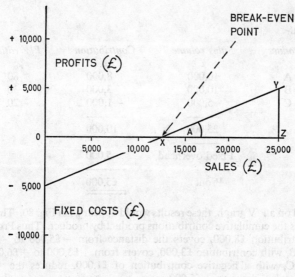

FIG. 79.—*Profit graph (I)*

This is a simplified form of break-even chart. It can be drawn if any two points on the contribution line are known, *i.e.* fixed costs, break-even point or profits at a given level. From the graph can be read the probable profits at any other level within the range.

IMPROVEMENT OF THE P/V RATIO

Clearly it is always advantageous to increase the P/V ratio, for by doing so the contribution towards meeting fixed overhead and profit is increased. It can be done:

(a) if sales prices are increased;

(b) if direct and variable costs can be reduced by improved methods of manufacture;

(c) if production can be switched to those products showing a higher P/V ratio.

It should be noted that a reduction in the fixed overhead does not affect the P/V ratio, although it increases the amount of profit available.

P/V RATIOS FOR INDIVIDUAL PRODUCTS

The slope of the profit line in the P/V graph indicates the degree of contribution made, so that a 60% contribution would be steeper than the 40% shown. Instead of drawing one profit graph for the concern as a whole, it is possible, and indeed desirable, to show the cumulative effect of various products.

EXAMPLE

Product	Sales volume	Contribution	P/V ratio
	£	£	%
A	10,000	8,000	80
B	10,000	3,000	30
C	5,000	−1,000	−20
	25,000	10,000	
Fixed overhead		5,000	
Profit		£5,000	

Plotted on a P/V graph, these results would appear as in Fig. 80. The dotted line shows the cumulative contributions product by product. Thus Product A, with contribution £8,000, covers the distance from −£5,000 to +£3,000; Product B, with contribution £3,000, covers from +£3,000 to +£6,000; and Product C, with a negative contribution of £1,000, reduces the +£6,000 already reached down to +£5,000.

The solid line in the diagram shows the overall contribution of £10,000, covering the distance from −£5,000 to +£5,000. It cuts the sales line at the break-even point:

$$\text{Fixed} \div \text{P/V ratio}$$

$$£5,000 \div \frac{10}{25}$$

$$= £12,500.$$

It would be concluded that Product C should no longer be made and that the manufacture of Product A should be developed, provided the plant available was flexible enough to cope with more of the same product.

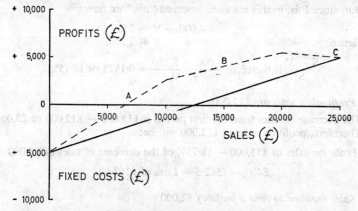

FIG. 80.—*Profit graph (2)*

This shows a profit graph similar to that in Fig. 79, but in addition to the single contribution line for the business as a whole, those for the individual products are shown as well, revealing which gives the greatest contribution.

USES OF THE P/V RATIO

When the P/V ratio has been found, it is often possible to make good use of it in answering management enquiries.

SPECIMEN QUESTION

Given:

Period 1	Sales £15,000	Profit £400
2	Sales £19,000	Profit £1,150

Calculate:

(a) the P/V ratio;
(b) the profit when sales are £12,000;
(c) the sales required to earn a profit of £2,000.

ANSWER

(a) The P/V ratio

The change in sales is £4,000.
The change in profits is £750.
The change in fixed costs assumed nil.

We may set these changes up in marginal equation form:

$$S - V = F + P$$
$$4,000 - V = F + 750$$

But, since F is, in this instance, assumed "nil," we have:

$$4,000 - V = 750$$

Hence $$V = 3,250.$$

$\dfrac{S - V}{S}$ is therefore $\dfrac{4,000 - 3,250}{4,000} = 0.1875$ or $\underline{18.75\%}$.

(b) Profit when sales are £12,000

The decrease of sales from the first period is £15,000 — £12,000 or £3,000. Therefore, profit on sales at £12,000 will be:

Profit on sales of £15,000 — 18·75% of the decrease of sales of £3,000

$$£400 - £562.5 = \underline{\text{Loss of £162·50.}}$$

(c) Sales required to earn a profit of £2,000

The increase of profit over the profit earned in the first period is:

$$£2,000 - £400 = £1,600.$$

Therefore the additional sales to produce £1,600 additional profit will be:

$$\frac{£1,600}{18.75} \times 100 = £8,533.$$

The total sales required to earn a profit of £2,000 under these conditions will therefore be:

$$£15,000 + £8,533 = \underline{£23,533.}$$

EFFECT OF REDUCTION OF PRICES

There is sometimes a temptation to reduce prices in order to encourage sales, but the effects of doing so have always to be considered most carefully.

EXAMPLE

The sales of a product are at the rate of 100 per month at £5 per unit. The total sales revenue per month is therefore £500. The fixed overhead is £100 per month, and the variable costs amount to £3 per unit.

The proposal is to reduce prices by 10%.

Note first of all that a 10% reduction in prices will result in an immediate loss of profit of £50, and this will have to be counterbalanced:

(a) by additional sales; and/or
(b) by reduced costs.

For the purposes of the illustration it is assumed that (b) is considered unlikely.

As we have seen:

$$S - V = F + P.$$

Dividing both sides by S:

$$\frac{(S - V)}{S} = \frac{F + P}{S}.$$

Hence:

$$S = \frac{F + P}{P/V}.$$

The profit in the above illustration is:

$$P = S - V - F$$
$$500 - 300 - 100 = £100,$$

and it is assumed that this has to be maintained.

Now, the P/V ratio falls thus (using unit figures) from:

$$\frac{5 - 3}{5} \text{ to } \frac{4 \cdot 5 - 3}{4 \cdot 5}$$
$$40\% \text{ to } 33\tfrac{1}{3}\%.$$

The new figure of sales will therefore have to be:

$$\frac{F + P}{33\tfrac{1}{3}\%} = \frac{100 + 100}{33\tfrac{1}{3}\%} = £600.$$

That is to say, $133\tfrac{1}{3}$ units will have to be sold at £4·50 per unit to maintain a profit of £100.

$$S - V = F + P$$
$$600 - 3(133\tfrac{1}{3}) = 100 + 100.$$

The number to be sold can be obtained directly by dividing the contribution required by the new unit contribution, *i.e.*:

$$£200/(£4 \cdot 50 - £3) = 200 \div 1 \cdot 50 = 133\tfrac{1}{3}.$$

From this it can be seen that if management carry out their proposals to reduce prices by 10% sales must go up by a third to achieve exactly the same result as before. The effect of a price reduction is always to reduce the P/V ratio, to raise the BEP and to shorten the margin of safety.

It is therefore a serious decision to make.

SELLING AT OR BELOW MARGINAL COST

There are occasions when to reduce prices to marginal cost, or even below it, may be justified for a short while. Some of the reasons for doing so would be as follows:

(*a*) To maintain production and to keep employees occupied.

(*b*) To keep plant in use in readiness to go "full steam ahead." Plant may also depreciate more quickly when standing than when being used. This is said to be true of the hosiery industry.

(*c*) To prevent loss of future orders. If a firm's product is in short supply other firms, or other products, take its place: and later on it may be difficult to recover the trade.

(*d*) If a loss has already occurred because prices have fallen throughout the market it may be advisable to follow suit.

(e) To dispose of perishable goods.

(f) To eliminate the competition of weaker rivals.

(g) To popularise a new product.

(h) To help in the sales of a conjoined product which is making a considerable profit.

There are dangers in price cutting, however, as it may start a landslide in prices which becomes permanent and does damage to the whole industry.

DIFFERENTIAL SELLING

Sometimes there is a limited market for a certain brand of goods. This is made to bear all the fixed overhead. The remainder of the production is then sold unbranded or under another brand name, at a lower price, and in a different market.

APPLICATION OF MARGINAL COSTING

OPTIMUM LEVEL OF PRODUCTION

The assumption often made that direct and variable unit costs will not vary is based on the following two underlying assumptions:

(a) That the present methods of production are to remain unchanged.

(b) That the skill and output of additional workers will not diminish.

However, it ought to be borne in mind that large-scale production would probably induce a change in methods of manufacture, and this would in turn cause a variation in the variable cost rate.

Similarly, the fixed costs vary in total because additional supervision, office staff and plant depreciation are incurred.

It will be seen, therefore, that there is an optimum level of production for the capacity of any plant, and this is the point at which the plant is fully occupied in producing goods which can be sold to give the maximum profit without disproportionate increase in the fixed overheads.

This can be put in another way by saying that a business with a given capital can only support a certain turnover of sales, for if it goes beyond its capabilities it will run into the serious dangers arising from over-trading.

This means that break-even charts can be extended to the right only within the limits of capital availability.

We may illustrate this by putting the turnover v. capital employed chart directly below the break-even chart, as in Fig. 81.

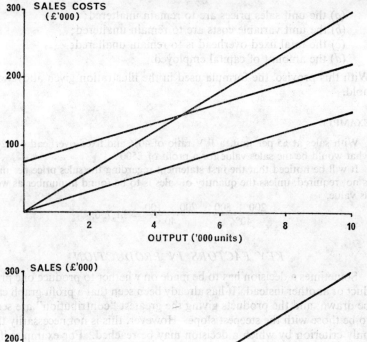

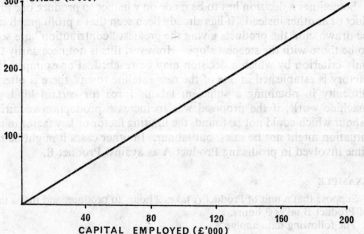

FIG. 81.—*Area of significance in a break-even chart*

A break-even chart showing the turnover in relation to capital employed. These graphs illustrate that the area of significance in a break-even chart is between the break-even point and the turnover which a given amount of capital can support. In this case the turnover is 1·5 times the amount of capital.

SALES VALUE AT WHICH A PROFIT IS EARNED

Sufficient has already been said to warn the student against applying the marginal cost formula indiscriminately: that is to say, given certain trading results, it is not possible to think of *any* figure of profit, and then apply the formula with certainty to find what the sales would be. Within limits this can be done, and these limits are:

(*a*) the unit sales prices are to remain unaltered;
(*b*) the unit variable costs are to remain unaltered;
(*c*) the total fixed overhead is to remain unaltered;
(*d*) the amount of capital employed.

With this proviso, the formula used in the illustration given above will hold.

EXAMPLE

With sales at £5 per unit, a P/V ratio of 40% and fixed overhead of £200 what would be the sales value for a profit of £500?

It will be noticed that the first statement regarding the sales price per unit is not required, unless the quantity of sales is to be found in number as well as value.

$$\frac{200 + 500}{40\%} = \frac{700 \times 100}{40} = \underline{\underline{£1,750.}}$$

KEY FACTORS IN PRODUCTION

Sometimes a decision has to be made on whether to produce one product or another instead. It has already been seen that a profit graph can be drawn, and the products giving the greatest "contribution" are seen to be those with the steepest slope. However, this is not necessarily the only criterion by which a decision may be reached. For example, if a factory is established in one of the new satellite towns, there is often a difficulty in obtaining a sufficient labour force for certain kinds of machine work; if the proposal was to increase production requiring labour which could not be found, the limiting factor or key factor in the situation might not be sales, but labour. In other cases it might be the time involved in producing Product A as against Product B.

EXAMPLE

Suppose that a unit of Product A takes 2 hours to produce, and that a unit of Product B takes 3 hours.

The following data apply:

	A	B
	new pence	
Direct material	25	15
Direct labour at £0·25 per hour	10	15
Variable overhead at £0·15 per hour	6	9
Marginal cost	41	39
Contribution	59	81
Selling price	100	120
P/V ratio	0·59	0·67

It would seem from this that as Product B has the better P/V ratio, the manufacture of this product should be encouraged. The key factor, however, is the time involved. The contribution *per hour* is:

$$A \quad \frac{59}{2} \text{ or } £0 \cdot 30 \text{ approx.}$$

$$B \quad \frac{81}{3} \text{ or } £0 \cdot 27$$

so that Product A becomes more important, especially if the labour force is limited as well.

COMPARISONS OF METHODS OF MANUFACTURE

Marginal costing principles are often used to disclose whether there is an advantage in using one machine instead of another; one machine with one operator or two machines with one operator; hand work or machine work; and so on.

	Machines	
	1	2
Production per hour	3 doz.	6 doz.
Unit costs disclosed by normal costing (new pence):		
Material	36	36
Labour	60	70
Overhead	84	79
	180	185
Selling price	200	200
Apparent net profit	20	15
Unit costs disclosed by marginal costing (new pence):		
Material	36	36
Labour	60	70
Marginal overhead	46	41
	142	147
Selling price	200	200
Contribution	58	53
Contribution per minute	34·8	63·6

This illustration is given to bring home to the student that, in examination work, weight *must always* be given to the time factor whenever it is stated. It is, of course, quite unsound to say that with Machine 2 there is an apparent net profit of 15 new pence per unit, without thinking of how many are to be made; and, when marginal principles are applied, the key factor is again time—the contribution per unit is 53 new pence for Machine 2, but the contribution per minute is 64 new pence approx. against 35 new pence approx. for the other machine.

At this stage the attention of students is drawn to Chapter 29, and the discussion on the subject of profitability.

However, the following link-up of ratios should be noted at once:

$$P/V \times \frac{M/S}{S} = \frac{P}{S}, \; i.e. \left(\frac{S-V}{S} \times \frac{P}{S/V} \times \frac{I}{S} = \frac{P}{S} \right)$$

and:

$$\frac{P}{S} \times \frac{S}{CE} = \frac{P}{CE}.$$

P = Profit, and CE = Capital employed, and the other letters carry the meanings already explained.

FIXING SELLING PRICES

If a firm has an overall turnover of £800,000 and wishes to maintain a 40% P/V ratio marginal costing will help in fixing approximate selling prices for products. This is done by dividing the variable costs by (100% − P/V%).

Thus in the above instance we have:

	£
Sales	800,000
Variable costs	480,000
Contribution	320,000
P/V ratio	40%

If we divide the variable costs £480,000 by (100% − 40%) we have:

$$\frac{480,000 \times 100}{60} = £800,000.$$

This is also true of any individual product line. It is possible to assess the direct and variable cost, say £6. Then the selling price, if a P/V ratio of 40% is wanted, is:

$$\frac{6 \times 100}{60} = £10.$$

A concern with many sales lines is thus able to experiment with prices, making a better P/V ratio on some products than others, but ensuring an overall P/V ratio of the percentage required.

However, the turnover rate has to be taken into account when fixing selling prices, and this is something which the large multiple stores take into careful consideration.

Since $S - V =$ Contribution, there is a relationship not only between contribution and sales, but also between contribution and variable cost.

The following table sets this out:

Contribution as a % of sales (a)	Variable cost as a % of sales (b)	Ratio between contribution and variable costs $(a \div b)$
20	80	0·25
30	70	0·43
40	60	0·67
50	50	1·00
60	40	1·50
70	30	2·33
80	20	4·00

Now, taking the previous example by way of illustration, suppose we want a 40% contribution, and the variable costs are £6. Our first shot at fixing the selling price was $6/(1 - P/V)$ or $6/(1 - 0·4) = £10$. But, if we now say that our expected rate of turnover is four times each year, the selling price should be:

$$\text{Variable cost} \left(1 + \frac{r}{100}\right)^{\frac{1}{4}}$$

where $r =$ the target rate per cent on variable cost. In this case, from the above table, it is 67%.

Therefore: $6(1·67)^{\frac{1}{4}}$.

By logarithms, $\log 1·67^{\frac{1}{4}} = \frac{1}{4} \log 1·67 = \frac{1}{4}(0·2227) = 0·0557$

Antil. $0·0557 = 1·137$

Hence $6 \times 1·137 = 6·822$.

On the first turn the contribution of $6·822 - 6·0 = 0·822$ would be made. This is assumed to be reinvested in the business for the nine months remaining in the year, and by compound interest amounts to:

$$0·822(1·67)^{\frac{3}{4}}$$

By logarithms: $\frac{3}{4}(0·2227) = \frac{1}{4}(0·6681) = 0·1670$

$\log. 0·822 = \bar{1}·9149$

$$0·0819$$

Antil. $0·0819 = 1·208$.

Similarly, on the second turn, the contribution of 0·822 is deemed to be reinvested for the remaining six months, and will amount to 1·063.

On the third turn, three months' interest added to the contribution yields a total of 0·9346.

On the fourth turn, the contribution of 0·822 is obtained.

Putting these together, we have:

1st turn	1·208
2nd turn	1·063
3rd turn	0·935
4th turn	0·822
	4·028

This is equivalent to getting the contribution of £4 with a selling price of £10, in one turn only, so that, according to all the circumstances. one could fix the selling price somewhere between £10 and £6·822.

SEPARATION OF SEMI-VARIABLE OVERHEAD INTO FIXED AND VARIABLE ELEMENTS

In the theoretical discussion of marginal costing, no attempt has yet been made to indicate the practical difficulties there may be in deciding which items of overhead are to be classed as "fixed" and which as "variable."

In fact, those which are entirely fixed can usually be agreed without much difficulty. For example, the managing director's salary, rent, rates, fire insurance, etc., may be regarded as fixed within the limits of a particular situation.

The majority of items of overhead, however, fall at first into the classification of "semi-variable," since they are partially variable and yet have a hard core within them of fixed expense. In most cases it is best to regard *all* overhead, other than that which can be definitely labelled as fixed, as being semi-variable.

The problem now becomes one of apportioning these items between fixed and variable, so that eventually all overhead is in one camp or the other. A great deal of work is involved in doing this for each overhead expense heading separately, but as each may vary in different ways it is not really sufficient to deal with the total of all semi-variable overhead in one set of calculations.

There are two usual ways of making the apportionment:

Method 1. Comparison of periods.
Method 2. Regression line.

METHOD 1

In this case the levels of expense reached in two periods are compared with one another, and related to output achieved in those periods. This output may be measured in any convenient unit, such as number of units, direct labour hours, machine hours or even sales.

EXAMPLE

Period 1	1,300 direct labour hours	£2,000
Period 2	1,500 direct labour hours	£2,200

Since it is to be assumed that fixed overhead is "fixed" for the two periods, and for the levels of overhead observed, it becomes clear that the "change" in the levels must be due to variable overhead. From this it is easy to deduce the variable cost per direct labour hour:

$$\frac{\text{Change in level of expense}}{\text{Change in level of hours}} = \frac{£200}{200} = \underline{£1{\cdot}00}.$$

Therefore:

Period 1	1,300 hours at £1·00	£1,300 variable and £700 fixed
Period 2	1,500 hours at £1·00	£1,500 variable and £700 fixed

This must be regarded as "rough and ready."

METHOD 2

This is based on finding a "line of best fit" for a number of observations. This is perhaps rather advanced for most first-year students.

It is necessary to go back to first principles. The reader will recall from school algebra the graph of a straight line in the form of:

$$y = mx + c.$$

We are going to find the best straight line in this form, which will fit a set of points, but we cannot do this convincingly without making use of statistical methods.

It will be best if we take a series of observations, and follow the procedure through step by step. If any student has forgotten correlation and regression, he will do well to revise the subject.

SPECIMEN QUESTION

The following data have been collected over a period of five years, relating to a particular expense heading of a factory:

Year No.	x = Units of output	y = Level of expense (£)
1	10,000	300,000
2	25,000	500,000
3	20,000	350,000
4	30,000	450,000
5	15,000	400,000

It is required to draw the best straight line to fit these pairs of observations, and to state the estimate of the fixed expense contained in the figures.

ANSWER

In the first place we must satisfy ourselves that there is a correlation between output and expense, as we have supposed, for this expense may not, in fact, vary with output at all, but with something else which we have not considered.

The formula for the coefficient of correlation is:

$$\frac{\text{Covariance of } x, y}{\substack{\text{Standard deviation of } x, \text{ multiplied} \\ \text{by the standard deviation of } y}}$$

or

$$\frac{\frac{1}{N}\Sigma(x - \bar{x})(y - \bar{y})}{\sqrt{\frac{1}{N}\Sigma(x - \bar{x})^2}\sqrt{\frac{1}{N}\Sigma(y - \bar{y})^2}}$$

where

N = the number of observations;
Σ means "the sum of things like . . .";
$\bar{x}$ = the arithmetic mean of the x's;
$\bar{y}$ = the arithmetic mean of the y's.

If the top line of this fraction is expanded it becomes:

$$\frac{\Sigma xy}{N} - \frac{\Sigma x}{N} \cdot \frac{\Sigma y}{N}$$

and if the bottom line is expanded it becomes:

$$\sqrt{\frac{\Sigma x^2}{N} - \left(\frac{\Sigma x}{N}\right)^2}\sqrt{\frac{\Sigma y^2}{N} - \left(\frac{\Sigma y}{N}\right)^2}.$$

These expansions make it easier to do the computations. It will be remembered that in working out the coefficient of correlation we may add to or deduct from the x's and y's, or multiply or divide by any number, and in this case we shall elect to divide the x's by 1,000 and to divide the y's by 10,000.

Arranging the figures in a table, we have:

x	y	xy	x^2	y^2
10	30	300	100	900
25	50	1,250	625	2,500
20	35	700	400	1,225
30	45	1,350	900	2,025
15	40	600	225	1,600
100	200	4,200	2,250	8,250
Averages 20	40	840	450	1,650

Substituting these values we have:

$$\frac{\dfrac{\Sigma xy}{N} - \dfrac{\Sigma x}{N} \cdot \dfrac{\Sigma y}{N}}{\sqrt{\dfrac{\Sigma x^2}{N} - \left(\dfrac{\Sigma x}{N}\right)^2}\sqrt{\dfrac{\Sigma y^2}{N} - \left(\dfrac{\Sigma y}{N}\right)^2}}$$

$$= \frac{840 - (20 \times 40)}{\sqrt{(450 - 400)}\sqrt{(1,650 - 1,600)}} = \frac{40}{\sqrt{50}\sqrt{50}} = \frac{40}{50} = 0 \cdot 8.$$

This result shows that there is indeed a strong positive correlation between the two sets of variables, for perfect positive correlation would be $+1$.

We now justifiably proceed to find the regression of y on x, in the form of $y = mx + c$.

There are two ways of doing this:

METHOD 1: Simultaneous equations

Imagine that for each period we have an equation in this form:

$$y = mx + c$$
$$y' = mx' + c$$
$$y'' = mx'' + c$$

and so on.

If these are added together they will give:

$$\Sigma y = m\Sigma x + N \cdot c.$$

We require to solve for m and c, but, as these are two unknowns, we need another equation to make a pair of simultaneous equations. It has been found that this second equation may be obtained by taking each of the previous equations in turn, and multiplying both sides by x.

They then become:

$$xy = mx^2 + c \cdot x$$
$$x'y' = mx'^2 + c \cdot x'$$
$$x''y'' = mx''^2 + c \cdot x''$$

and so on, which, when added together, become:

$$\Sigma xy = m \cdot \Sigma x^2 + c \cdot \Sigma x.$$

Putting the two equations together, we now have a pair of simultaneous equations:

$$\Sigma y = m \cdot \Sigma x + N \cdot c \quad . \quad . \quad . \quad . \quad . \quad (1)$$
$$\Sigma xy = m \cdot \Sigma x^2 + c \cdot \Sigma x \quad . \quad . \quad . \quad . \quad . \quad (2)$$

However, it will be seen that using these equations will involve squaring the values of x and calculating the values of xy. It could be most unwieldy to do this, and if a means of cutting down the work was available it would be most welcome. Fortunately there is such a device.

To explain this, go back to the figures of the specimen question.

We form variates from the x's and y's for working purposes, but we shall have to remember afterwards to reconvert our answer back into our original terms. Suppose, therefore, that we say:

$$X = x/1,000$$
and:
$$Y = y/10,000.$$

Then:

x	y	X	Y	XY	X^2
10,000	300,000	10	30	300	100
25,000	500,000	25	50	1,250	625
20,000	350,000	20	35	700	400
30,000	450,000	30	45	1,350	900
15,000	400,000	15	40	600	225
		100	200	4,200	2,250
		ΣX	ΣY	ΣXY	ΣX^2

If we substitute these values in our equations (1) and (2), using variates, of course, we have:

$$200 = 100m + 5c \quad . \quad . \quad . \quad . \quad . \quad . \quad (3)$$
$$4,200 = 2,250m + 100c \quad . \quad . \quad . \quad . \quad . \quad (4)$$

Multiply (3) by 20:

$$4,000 = 2,000m + 100c \quad . \quad . \quad . \quad . \quad . \quad (5)$$

Subtract (5) from (4):

$$200 = 250m$$

Hence:

$$m = 0\cdot8.$$

Now, substituting this value in equation (3) leads to:

$$200 = 80 + 5c$$

and thus:

$$c = 24.$$

We now have:

$$Y = 0\cdot8X + 24.$$

Finally, we translate our variates back into original terms, and the equation becomes:

$$y/10,000 = 0\cdot8(x/1,000) + 24.$$

Multiply both sides by 10,000:

$$\underline{y = 8x + 240,000.}$$

This shows that £240,000 is the amount of fixed expenses inherent in the total expense.

METHOD 2

The second method is to use the equation:

$$y - \bar{y} = \frac{\text{Cov}_{xy}}{\text{Var}_x}(x - \bar{x}).$$

The covariance of xy is:

$$\frac{1}{N}\Sigma(x - \bar{x})(y - \bar{y})$$

or as we have seen is:

$$\frac{\Sigma xy}{N} - \frac{\Sigma x}{N} \cdot \frac{\Sigma y}{N}.$$

and the variance of x is:

$$\frac{1}{N}\Sigma(x - \bar{x})^2$$

or

$$\frac{\Sigma x^2}{N} - \left(\frac{\Sigma x}{N}\right)^2$$

but it will be remembered that, when calculating the regression equation, we cannot use variates as we did for the coefficient of correlation, because the location as well as the direction of the line is important.

We have, then:

x	y	x^2 (millions)	xy (millions)
10,000	300,000	100	3,000
25,000	500,000	625	12,500
20,000	350,000	400	7,000
30,000	450,000	900	13,500
15,000	400,000	225	6,000
100,000	2,000,000	2,250	42,000
Averaging: 20,000	400,000	450	8,400

Then:

$$\frac{\text{Cov}_{xy}}{\text{Var}_x} = \frac{8,400,000,000 - (20,000 \times 400,000)}{450,000,000 - (20,000)^2}$$

$$= \frac{400}{50} = 8$$

Then:

$$y - 400,000 = 8(x - 20,000).$$

Hence, as before:

$$\underline{y = 8x + 240,000.}$$

The graph of the linear equation is shown in Fig. 82, in which the levels of expenditure given in the illustration have been plotted against the output.

Having faced some of the problems to be overcome in installing marginal costing, we are now in a position to pursue the matter a little further.

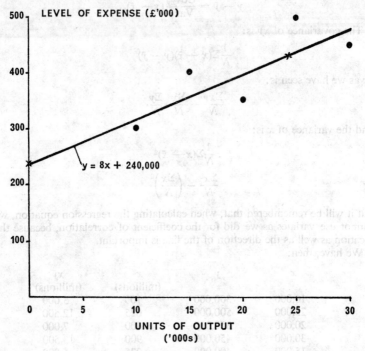

FIG. 82.—*Graph of a linear equation*

This graph shows the best straight line to fit the sets of points given in the specimen question. Where the line cuts the *y* axis is the amount of fixed cost in the expense.

MULTIPLE BREAK-EVEN CHARTS

These may be drawn either in the traditional form of a break-even chart or, most commonly, in the form of a profit or contribution graph.

EXAMPLE 1

A company is at present operating at 70% capacity and is producing and selling 1,400 units. The sales price obtained is £3 per unit, and the variable costs are £1·80 per unit. The fixed costs are £800.

The company wishes to expand its activities to 90% capacity, *i.e.* to 1,800 units, but it considers that to achieve this target it will have to reduce its selling price. This may be compensated for to some extent by using a substitute cheaper material. On the other hand, direct wages may increase per unit, because of the introduction of a bonus system. At the 1,600 units level the fixed costs will jump to £1,200.

The cost accountant sets out the present and proposed positions as follows:

	Present 1,400 units £	Proposed 1,800 units £
Unit selling price	3·00	2·75
Direct material	0·90	0·55
Direct labour	0·60	0·65
Factory overhead (variable)	0·30	0·30
	1·80	1·50
Unit contribution	1·20	1·25
P/V ratio	0·40	0·455
Fixed costs	£800	£1,200
Break-even point (Fixed ÷ P/V)	£2,000	£2,640

He supports these figures by a profit graph, shown in Fig. 83, from which it will be seen that the profit, now at about £900, may be expected to increase to about £1,050.

The cost accountant, having thus disclosed the facts, concludes his presentation by making a recommendation, namely that before embarking on this expansion, yielding such a small increase of profit, and depending on so many assumptions—as for example customer approval of a product made of lower-grade material—it would be advisable to consider diversification into some other product.

EXAMPLE 2

A company is thinking of introducing another product on to the market, and, having undertaken market research, arrives at the following estimates:

Volume of sales expected

From 10,000 at £5 per unit to 15,000 at £4 per unit.

Variable costs

These are likely to be between £1 and £2 per unit.

Additional fixed costs

At low volume: £15,000. At higher volume: £20,000.

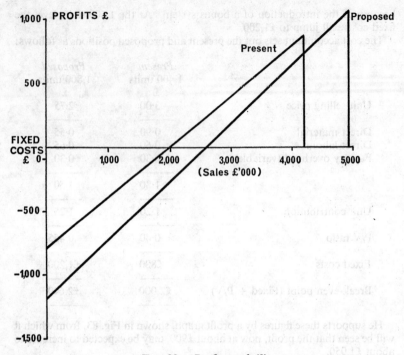

FIG. 83.—*Profit graph* (3)

The cost accountant now proceeds to calculate the range between high and low P/V ratios, thus:

$$\frac{\text{High sales price} - \text{Low variable cost}}{\text{High sales price}} = \frac{5 - 1}{5} = 0 \cdot 8.$$

$$\frac{\text{Low sales price} - \text{High variable cost}}{\text{Low sales price}} = \frac{4 - 2}{4} = 0 \cdot 5.$$

With this information, four break-even points can now be found:

    1. High fixed cost ÷ Low P/V 20,000 ÷ 0·5 = £400,000
    2. Low fixed cost ÷ Low P/V 15,000 ÷ 0·5 = £300,000
    3. High fixed cost ÷ High P/V 20,000 ÷ 0·8 = £250,000
    4. Low fixed cost ÷ High P/V 15,000 ÷ 0·8 = £187,500

The contribution chart is now drawn with upward-sloping lines from the high and low fixed-cost points, through the corresponding break-even points. This is seen in Fig. 84. The vertical lines mark the upper and lower range of sales.

The area of the chart to which particular attention must be directed is the inner parallelogram, and the point at which the diagonals intersect is the most probable position. At this point, the sales are likely to be £55,000 and the additional contribution about £17,500.

The chart also shows that, in the most unfavourable set of circumstances:

lowest sales volume,
highest fixed costs,
lowest P/V ratio,

an additional contribution of £5,000 would be obtained.

A fuller discussion of this subject is to be found in an article by Douglas Gould entitled "Opportunity Accounting by Product Line Decisions" (*Management Accounting*, April 1969, The National Association of Accountants, New York).

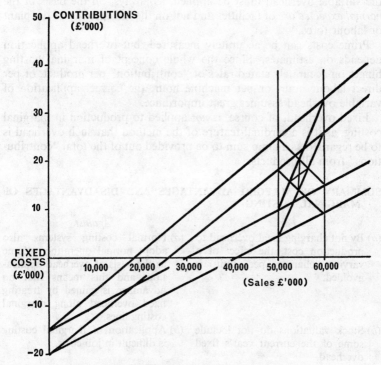

FIG. 84.—*Multiple break-even chart*

ACCOUNTING ENTRIES IN MARGINAL COSTING

When all overhead has been duly apportioned between "variable" and "fixed," whether or not any accounting entries are put through the books will depend to the extent to which marginal costing has been adopted as a thorough-going philosophy. In many cases it is only used for *ad hoc* investigations such as have been discussed, but, if entries are to be made, it is quite a simple matter to make the following journal transfers:

Variable Overhead Incurred Account Dr.
Fixed Overhead Incurred Account Dr.
  To Production Overhead Incurred Account
     Administration Overhead Incurred Account
     Selling and Distribution Overhead Incurred Account

APPLICATION OF OVERHEAD

It is essential, in making use of marginal principles, to remember that the variable overhead must be applied, as always, on the basis of the *normal expected use* of facilities and not on the full capacity of the plant or labour force.

Prime costs can be accurately measured, but overhead application depends on estimates. Since the whole concept of marginal costing hinges on accurately stated rates of "contribution" per product, or per direct labour hour, or per machine hour, the correct application of variable overhead assumes great importance.

Fixed overhead, of course, is *not* applied to production in marginal costing, as it is a cardinal feature of the method that such overhead is to be regarded as a lump sum to be provided out of the total "contributions" from all products.

SUMMARY OF ALLEGED ADVANTAGES AND DISADVANTAGES OF MARGINAL COSTING

For	*Against*
(a) By not charging fixed overhead to production cost, the effect of a varying charges per unit is avoided.	(a) Normal costing systems also adopt normal operating volume as the basis of overhead application, and this means that no advantage is gained by treating fixed overhead along marginal costing lines.
(b) Stock valuations do not include some of the current year's fixed overhead.	(b) Application of marginal costing is difficult in job costs.
(c) Simple to understand, and can be combined with standard costing.	(c) Difficult to analyse overhead into "fixed" and "variable."
(d) Eliminates large balances being left in Overhead Control Accounts.	(d) The application of variable overhead still depends on estimates, so that there is bound to be some over- or under-recovery.
(e) Attention is concentrated on controllable features of the business.	(e) A selling price cannot reasonably be determined simply by looking at "contribution." Some reference must be made as to how much fixed overhead is justified in the price.

For	Against
(f) Effects of alternative sales and production policies are more easily grasped and appreciated.	(f) Standard costing provides the answers just as well. Volume variance figures disclose the effect of fluctuating output on fixed overhead.

EXAMINATION QUESTIONS

1. "The technique of marginal costs can be a valuable aid to management." Discuss this statement and give your views.

(*C.A.A.*)

2. What do you understand by the expressions "break even" and "margin of safety"? Outline a simple chart to illustrate the meanings you would attach to these terms, taking as your data assumed figures for fixed expenses, marginal profit and normal sales.

(*C.A.A. Final*)

3. A well-known writer commenting on the break-even chart said, "It [the break-even chart] must be applied with an intelligent discrimination, with an adequate grasp of the assumptions underlying the technique and of the limitations surrounding its practical application." Expand on this statement giving illustrations of the points which the writer had in mind.

(*A.C.C.A. Final*)

4. What are the arguments for and against the inclusion of fixed overhead in the valuation of stock at the end of an accounting period?

What difference in profit for a period will result from the adoption of each method?

(*I.C.W.A. Inter.*)

5. What do you understand by the optimum production level of a business? Outline the matters you would consider to determine the optimum of a small concern with which you are familiar.

(*I.C.W.A. Final*)

6. The results displayed by a break-even chart must be qualified by the assumptions underlying its construction. What are these assumptions and to what extent do you regard them as reasonable.

(*A.C.C.A. Final*)

7. (a) Define marginal costing.

(b) Present the following information to show clearly to management:

    (i) the marginal product cost and the contribution per unit;

    (ii) the total contributions and profits resulting from each of the following sales mixtures.

	Product	£ per unit
Direct materials	A	10
„	B	9
Direct wages	A	3
„	B	2
Fixed expenses		£800

(Variable expenses are allotted to products as 100% of direct wages)

Sales price	A	20
„	B	15

Sales mixtures:

   (a) 100 units of Product A and 200 of B
   (b) 150   „   „   150 „
   (c) 200   „   „   100 „

(I.C.W.A. Inter.)

8. The cost of two products are as follows:

	A £	B £
Direct labour	0·28	0·77
Direct materials	1·36	0·90
Variable factory overheads	0·22	0·57½
Fixed factory overheads	0·14	0·38
	2·00	2·62½
Administration, selling and distribution overheads	0·50	0·62½
Total cost	£2·50	£3·25

The factory is short of work, and a good customer offers a large contract for Product A at £2·25 each and/or for Product B at £3·00 each.

Present these figures to management in the most suitable way, indicating whether it is desirable to take on the production for either, or both products.

(C.A.A. Final)

9. The following information is available for X.Y. Ltd., which manufactures a standard product:

Quarterly budget for each of Quarters 3 and 4:

	£	Total £	£	Per unit £
Sales (30,000 units)		30,000		1·00
Production cost of sales:				
Variable	19,500		0·65	
Fixed overhead	6,000	25,500	0·20	0·85
		4,500		0·15
Selling and administration cost (fixed)		2,100		0·07
Profit		£2,400		£0·08

Actual production, sales and stocks in units for Quarters 3 and 4:

	Quarter 3	Quarter 4
Opening stock	—	6,000
Production	34,000	28,000
Sales	28,000	32,000
Closing stock	6,000	2,000

You are required to show in tabular form Trading and Profit and Loss Accounts for each of the quarters:

(a) when fixed production overhead is absorbed into the cost of the product at the normal level shown in the quarterly budget; and

(b) when fixed production overhead is not absorbed into the cost of the product, but is treated as a cost of the period and charged against sales.

(N.B. The bases of calculations should be shown.)

(I.C.W.A. Inter.)

10. The following figures apply to a manufacturing company:

	£
Annual sales at 100% effective capacity	1,200,000
Fixed overhead	400,000
Total variable costs	600,000

It is proposed to increase the capacity by the acquisition of 30% additional space and plant. One result will be to increase fixed overhead by £100,000 per annum.

Plot the foregoing on a single break-even chart, and determine from the chart at what capacity-utilisation the same profit as before will be produced after the extensions have been made.

(I.C.W.A. Final)

11. The budget of Nalgonut Ltd. includes the following data for the forthcoming financial year:

(a) Fixed expenses—£30,000.
(b) Contributions per unit—

    Product A—£5.
    Product B—£2·50.
    Product C—£3.

(c) Sales forecast—

    Product A—2,000 units at £10 each.
    Product B—10,000 units at £6·50 each.
    Product C—5,000 units at £7 each.

You are required to:

    (i) calculate the P/V ratio for each product;
    (ii) plot the above data on a graph;
    (iii) also show on the same chart, the break-even point for the company as a percentage of the budgeted activity.

(C.A.A. Final)

12. The Makem Manufacturing Co. produces 10,000 units per annum by employing 50% of the factory capacity. The selling price of the unit is £5, and the total costs were:

	£
Materials	10,000
Wages	20,000
Fixed overhead	10,000
Variable overhead	4,000
	£44,000

Variable overhead maintains a constant ratio to the number of units produced.

The company accepts an order for an additional 10,000 units at a selling price of £3·87½ each.

The increased volume of purchases reduces the material prices by 2½%. Wage-rates remain constant, but due to the employment of new workers there is a drop in labour efficiency of 5% on all production.

Prepare a statement showing the variation of net profits resulting from the acceptance of the order.

(*I.C.W.A. Final*)

13. Two businesses A.B. Ltd. and C.D. Ltd. sell the same type of product in the same type of market. Their budgeted Profit and Loss Accounts for the year ending 19.., are as follows:

	A.B. Ltd.		C.D. Ltd.	
	£	£	£	£
Sales		150,000		150,000
Less: Variable costs	120,000		100,000	
Fixed costs	15,000		35,000	
		135,000		135,000
Net profit budgeted		£15,000		£15,000

You are required to:

(*a*) calculate the break-even points of each business;
(*b*) calculate the sales volume at which each of the businesses will earn £5,000 profit; and
(*c*) state which business is likely to earn greater profits in conditions of:

(*i*) heavy demand for the product;
(*ii*) low demand for the product.

Give your reasons.

(*I.C.W.A. Inter.*)

14. A manufacturing company concentrates its resources upon one single product which it sells to wholesale merchants at £4·80 per unit. The following details apply:

Output (units)	75,000	85,000	100,000
	£	£	£
Variable overhead (production)	40,000	48,000	55,000
Variable selling and administration overhead	15,000	17,500	22,000

Material costs £2 per unit, but quantity rebates of 10% and 15% apply to purchase contracts for 85,000 and 100,000 units respectively. Average wages cost is £0·50 per unit. Fixed overhead is £70,000 (production); and £25,000 (selling and administration).

In order to sell the whole output selling price reductions of 5% and 10% are contemplated, for the output levels of 85,000 and 100,000 units respectively.

An offer to purchase 10,000 units at £4 per unit has been received from abroad.

(a) Tabulate the necessary figures to show marginal costs and the increases in selling value for the three output levels, and indicate which of the three is the most profitable.

(b) Prepare a simple statement to show profit or loss at each output level and indicate which of the three is the most profitable.

(c) Prepare a statement showing the effect upon net income if the offer from abroad is accepted, assuming that other prices will not be affected, and the output level indicated in your answer to (a) is adopted.

(*I.C.W.A. Final*)

15. A small jobbing foundry quotes for pattern equipment and castings on the basis of the following:

Pattern cost	£75
Labour cost	£0·75 per casting
Metal cost	£3·26½ per cwt
Variable overhead	£0·80 per casting.

Each casting weighs 84 lb and the price quoted is £7 per casting, to include the cost of pattern equipment.

From the foregoing information, prepare a break-even chart and determine from it at what sales level contribution to fixed overhead will begin.

(*I.C.W.A. Final*)

16. The trading results of Lear Ltd. for two years were as follows:

	£	£
Wages	60,000	67,500
Materials	100,000	133,000
Variable overhead	11,000	15,000
Fixed overhead	18,000	23,600
Profits	8,000	16,500
	£197,000	£255,600

Materials prices and wage-rates increased in the second year by 10% and 12%, respectively, and the sale prices were increased by 10%.

What general factors have contributed to the increase in profit percentage?

Prepare a statement showing how much each factor has contributed to the variation in profit.

(*C.A.A. Inter.*)

17. A wine and spirit importer, with four retail trade outlets, is reviewing the previous year's results. The summarised figures are as follows:

Retail branches	A	B	C	D
	£	£	£	£
Branch sales	90,000	80,000	140,000	90,000
Branch costs:				
Salaries	6,000	5,700	8,500	5,500
Commissions	1,000	950	1,500	900
Travelling expenses	1,200	1,250	1,500	1,000
Advertising (local)	1,750	1,800	2,200	2,000
Depreciation	1,750	1,600	1,800	1,600
Insurance	250	250	300	250
Rates	250	250	300	250

Fixed costs for the central distributing and administrative agency, which are apportioned to branches on the basis of branch sales, are as follows:

	£
Central office	30,000
Regional advertising	15,000
Receiving and distributing	15,000

30% of the sales value represents gross profit, the sales mix being fairly constant. For several years, Branch B has incurred a net operating loss, and its closure, which would not affect the central agency costs, is contemplated.

Prepare:

(a) comparative Branch Profit and Loss Statement to show profit or loss for each branch;
(b) comparative Branch Profit and Loss Statement using the marginal technique.

What are your recommendations?

(*I.C.W.A. Final*)

18. A manufacturing company operating in a single region contemplates expanding its activities by stages to cover the whole country. Market research and extensive cost investigation indicate that the following figures will be applicable to the first stage of expansion:

	£
Additional buildings required	500,000
Additional equipment	845,000
Additional sales annually	600,000

Depreciation of buildings (5% per annum) and of equipment (10% per annum) is by the straight-line method. Fixed overhead, other than depreciation, is estimated to increase by £10,500.

Present figures, before the expansion, are summarised as follows:

	£
Fixed overhead annually	200,000
Materials annually	200,000
Wages and variable overhead annually	400,000
Annual sales	900,000

The proposed scale of operations is expected to yield some minor economies in material purchase price for all of the output so that the proposed sales total will be reached if a further £120,000 annually is spent on materials. Similarly, other economies will result in a less than proportional increase in the wages and variable overhead, upon which annual outlay will be increased by £90,000.

Present the information represented by the above figures graphically on a single break-even chart. Extract from the chart summarised details of interest to the management.

(I.C.W.A. Final)

19. The following sales figures for a year apply to a manufacturing company with three main product lines:

	Sales quantity	*Selling price*
		£
Product A	650	1,500 each
Product B	580	1,800 each
Product C	700	1,200 each

The unit standard costs of the products are:

	Material	*Factory wages and variable overhead*	*Variable selling and distribution costs*
	£	£	£
Product A	600	300	60
Product B	800	400	100
Product C	500	220	50

The variances for the year are summarised below:

	Product A	*Product B*	*Product C*
	£	£	£
Factory wages and variable overhead	10,000 (loss)	12,000 (gain)	3,000 (gain)
Material usage	10,000 (gain)	16,000 (loss)	2,000 (gain)
Material price	4,000 (loss)	3,000 (loss)	2,000 (loss)

There are no variances in variable selling and distribution costs.

The fixed costs were budgeted at £200,000 for Product A, £170,000 for Product B, and £174,000 for Product C. Favourable variances occurred of £27,000 (Product A) and £10,000 (Product C).

(*a*) From the foregoing details prepare a columnar income and expenditure statement to show individual product results and total results. Insert in the statement in total, and for each product, the following:

(*i*) Contributions at standard.

(*ii*) Contributions at actual.

(*iii*) Actual fixed costs.

(*iv*) Net operating profits or losses.

(*v*) Express (*i*), (*ii*) and (*iv*) as percentages of the relevant sales value.

(*b*) What is the overall margin of safety for the year?

(*I.C.W.A. Final*)

20. A manufacturing company produces and sells three products X, Y and Z. From the accounts of the past year, the following information is available:

Product	Selling price per unit £	Profit volume ratio %	Percentage of total sales by units
X	50·0	10	50
Y	37·5	20	40
Z	25·0	40	10

Total fixed costs £32,500.

Management is concerned that the overall profit picture might be improved by selling a greater proportion of more profitable lines. After a full investigation it is found that the following sales mix should be possible in future.

	Percentage by units
Product X	30
Product Y	50
Product Z	20

Present the following information to management:

(*a*) A break-even chart for the existing sales mix showing the combined units of sale in 1,000 unit intervals up to a maximum of 7,000 units.

(*b*) A profit-volume graph for both the existing and proposed sales mix over the same range as in (*a*) above.

(*I.C.W.A. Final*)

21. A company manufactures a machine which is sold at £100. In one year 19.., monthly accounts showed the following figures:

	Units made and sold	Total costs £	Profit £
January	1,500	120,000	30,000
February	1,375	105,000	32,500
March	1,200	100,000	20,000
April	1,700	127,500	42,500
May	1,300	107,500	22,500
June	1,825	130,000	52,500
July	1,100	100,000	10,000
August	825	85,000	2,500 (*loss*)
September	2,175	145,000	72,500
October	1,900	140,000	50,000
November	1,575	115,000	42,500
December	975	85,000	12,500

Present these figures graphically to show:

(a) the effect of volume on profit;
(b) the fixed expenses of the company per month;
(c) the profit–volume ratio;
(d) the profits which it would be expected to earn in future months, assuming that the structure of the business is unaltered, if sales were:

(i) 1,000 units;
(ii) 1,400 units;
(iii) 2,000 units.

(I.C.W.A. Final)

22. An engineering company receives an enquiry for the manufacture of certain products where the costs are estimated as follows, per product:

	£
Direct materials	3·50
Direct labour (5 hours)	1·25
Direct expenses	0·25
Variable overheads	1·50

The manufacture of these products will necessitate the provision of special tooling costing approximately £375. The sales manager, from his knowledge of the market, envisages a selling price of £10·62½ per product. For an order to be considered profitable, it is necessary for it to yield a target contribution rate of £0·40 per labour hour.

Prepare a chart showing:

(a) the sales level at which a contribution to fixed costs commences;
(b) the sales level at which the contribution rate meets the target.

(I.C.W.A. Final)

23. W. Limited manufactured and sold during the past year 300,000 units of Product A and 150,000 units of Product B. The accounts for the year were as follows:

	£
Sales	1,650,000
Direct materials	300,000
Direct wages	400,000
Factory overhead: variable	200,000
fixed	150,000
Other overhead: variable	100,000
fixed	100,000

The following details for the year are given concerning the two products:

Product:	A	B
Per unit:	£	£
Selling price	3·00	5·00
Direct materials	0·50	1·00
Direct wages	0·60	1·30
Other overhead, half variable and half fixed	0·50	0·30

Factory overhead variable is absorbed as a percentage of direct wages.
During the coming year it is expected that, owing to a fall in demand, the

production and sales of Product A will be reduced by 20% and of Product B by 40%. It is therefore decided to manufacture a further Product C, based on the following information:

Production and sales	100,000 units
Per unit:	£
Selling price	3·50
Direct materials	0·70
Direct wages	1·20

Other overhead variable will be the same as Product A.

Total fixed overhead, factory and other, will remain the same and variable overhead, factory and other, will continue to be incurred at the rates as in the past year.

Present to management the following information:

(a) A budget showing the anticipated results for the coming year.

(b) A profit-volume graph to compare the results of the past year with those anticipated for the coming year.

(c) Conclusions that can be drawn from information prepared in answer to (a) and (b) above and any recommendations you may wish to make.

(I.C.W.A. Final)

CHAPTER 24

BUDGETARY CONTROL

DEFINITIONS OF BUDGETARY CONTROL AND A BUDGET

The Institute of Cost and Works Accountants gives the following definitions:

A budget

"A financial and/or quantitative statement, prepared and approved prior to a defined period of time, of the policy to be pursued during that period for the purpose of attaining a given objective. It may include income, expenditure and the employment of capital."

Budgetary control

"The establishment of departmental budgets relating the responsibilities of executives to the requirements of a policy, and the continuous comparison of actual with budgeted results, either to secure by individual action the objectives of that policy or to provide a firm basis for its revision."

A budget is thus a standard with which to measure the actual achievements of people, departments, firms, etc. Budgetary control is the planning in advance of the various functions of a business so that the business as a whole can be controlled.

In many large firms in this country, and particularly in the U.S.A., a system of budgetary control is used. Usually budgetary control is operated with a system of standard costing because both systems are interrelated, but it must be emphasised that they are not interdependent. Budgetary control can be operated without standard costing, and this occurs in industries in which it may be difficult to operate a system of standard costing, but budgetary control is certainly facilitated where standard costing is in operation. On the other hand, it would be difficult to operate a system of standard costing if budgets were not in use.

Budgetary control relates expenditure to the person who incurs the expenditure, so that actual expenses can be compared with budgeted expenses, thus affording a convenient method of control. This is in contrast to standard costing, which relates expenditure to a product, or a service.

THE OBJECTIVES OF BUDGETARY CONTROL

The general objectives of a system of budgetary control are as follows:

(*a*) To plan the policy of a business.

(*b*) To co-ordinate the activities of a business so that each is part of an integral total.

(*c*) To control each function so that the best possible results may be obtained.

PREPARATION OF THE BUDGET

In large companies the preparation of the budget is usually the responsibility of a budget committee. Normally the chief executive is chairman of the committee, but the responsibility for operating the system is undertaken by a budget officer. The budget officer is generally a senior member of the accounting staff. Other members of the committee may be representatives of various departments, *e.g.* sales, purchases, production and works engineering. In small companies the preparation of the budget is usually the responsibility of the cost accountant or the accountant.

The budget committee will formulate a general programme for the preparation of the budget, and then the budget officer will be responsible for functions such as those given below:

(*a*) Issuing instructions to various departments.

(*b*) Receiving and checking budget estimates.

(*c*) Providing historical information to departmental managers to help them in their forecasting.

(*d*) Suggesting possible revisions.

(*e*) Discussing difficulties with managers.

(*f*) Ensuring that managers prepare their budgets in time.

(*g*) Preparing budget summaries.

(*h*) Submitting budgets to the committee and furnishing explanations on particular points.

(*i*) Co-ordinating all budget work.

THE BUDGET PERIOD

No specific period of time can be formulated as being the best budget period, although it can be said that many firms regard the period of a year as being a natural period for budgeting. The determining of the budget period is usually related to two factors:

1. The type of business

In industries in which capital expenditure is high and long-term planning is necessary, budget periods of up to twenty years may be required. Examples of this occur in the shipping trade and the electrical supply industry, where future requirements must be planned in advance.

On the other hand, many firms experience seasonal fluctuations in demand for their products, so must adopt a shorter budget period, of perhaps six months. Examples of this occur in the clothing and food industries, where fashions and weather exert a great influence on demand.

2. The control aspect

Budgetary control implies control, and it is obvious that long budget periods cannot be effective means of controlling a business. Particularly is this so in respect of expenditure, which must be rigidly scrutinised at short intervals, usually monthly. It is therefore usually arranged that the budget period should be divided into months so that actual results can be compared with those budgeted; this ensures that if any adverse variances have resulted immediate action can be undertaken.

The effect of the above two factors is that a long-term budget is prepared showing future expectations, while monthly budget periods assure speedy control of the business. In this respect the Institute of Cost and Works Accountants' *Terminology* gives the following definitions:

Basic budget

"A budget which is established for use unaltered over a long period of time."

Current budget

"A budget which is established for use over a short period of time and is related to current conditions."

THE KEY FACTOR

In the preparation of budgets it is essential to consider the key factor, or as it is sometimes termed in budgeting the principal budget factor. This is the factor, the extent of whose influence must first be assessed in order to ensure that the functional budgets are reasonably capable of fulfilment. For example the time taken to obtain delivery of motor vehicles will influence the budget of a road-transport firm. Key factors are discussed further in Chapters 23 and 28.

FUNCTIONAL BUDGET

A functional budget is one which relates to any of the functions of an undertaking. Functional budgets are subsidiary to the *master budget*, which is the summary budget, incorporating its component functional budgets, which is finally approved, adopted and employed.

There are many types of functional budgets, of which the following are frequently used:

1. Sales budget.
2. Production budget.
3. Production cost budget.
4. Plant utilisation budget.
5. Capital expenditure budget.
6. Selling and distribution cost budget.
7. Purchasing budget.
8. Cash budget.

1. SALES BUDGET

This is probably the most difficult functional budget to prepare. It is not easy to estimate consumers' future demands, especially when a new product is being introduced. It is possibly the most important subsidiary budget, because if the sales figure is wrong, then practically all the other budgets will be affected, especially the master budget.

The sales budget is usually prepared in terms of quantities, then evaluated at budgeted unit prices. It is classified under a number of headings, of which the following are in common use:

(a) *Products*. Not many businesses sell only one product, so estimates must be prepared of sales for each product.

(b) *Territories*. Sales of each product, expressed in quantities and values to be sold in each territory.

(c) *Type of customer*. This may be important if different customers receive special discounts, special rates, etc.

(d) *Salesmen*. The sales to each salesman or agent in a territory. This may be useful also for comparative purposes.

(e) *Month*. Comparison of actual results with those budgeted for each period is important. In addition, it is necessary when calculating budgeted stock positions to know monthly sales.

The sales manager will be responsible for the preparation of the sales budget, particularly as regards to the quantities part of the budget.

He may have many aids in estimating sales, of which the following may be important:

(a) *Historical analysis of sales.* Statistical measurements, *e.g.* cyclical movement, trends and seasonal fluctuations may provide valuable information.

(b) *Business conditions.* International and political influences on markets.

(c) *Reports by salesmen.* Salesmen are in frequent contact with customers and can report on customers' habits, demands, etc., as well as possible competitors' activities.

(d) *Market analysis.* In large firms market analysts may be employed, while smaller firms may engage specialist agents to investigate potential market demands.

(e) *Special conditions.* There may be events planned outside the business which will have an effect on the sales of the business, *e.g.* the introduction of electricity to a village will lead to a demand for heaters, radios, etc.

If the principal budget factor or key factor is production capacity, then the sales budget will be determined by output, and preparation of the budget will be relatively easy. However, if sales is the key factor, then the production budget will be determined by estimated sales.

SPECIMEN QUESTION

In the Stansales Co. Ltd. there are four sales divisions, each consisting of four areas, N., S., E. and W. The company sells two products, "Exe" and "Wye." Budgeted sales for the six months ended June 30, 1970, in each area of division 1 were as follows:

N.	"Exe"	10,000 units at £10 each
	"Wye"	6,000 units at £5 each
S.	"Wye"	12,000 units at £5 each
E.	"Exe"	15,000 units at £10 each
W.	"Exe"	8,000 units at £10 each
	"Wye"	5,000 units at £5 each

Actual sales for the same period in division 1 were as follows:

N.	"Exe"	11,500 units at £10 each
	"Wye"	7,000 units at £5 each
S.	"Wye"	12,500 units at £5 each
E.	"Exe"	16,500 units at £10 each
W.	"Exe"	9,500 units at £10 each
	"Wye"	5,250 units at £5 each

SALES BUDGET

Division No. I

Area	Product	Budget June 30, 1971			Budget June 30, 1970			Actual June 30, 1970 — Six months to: June 30, 1971		
		Q.	P.	V.	Q.	P.	V.	Q.	P.	V.
NORTH	Exe	12,000	10	120,000	10,000	10	100,000	11,500	10	115,000
	Wye	6,500	5	32,500	6,000	5	30,000	7,000	5	35,000
	Total	18,500		£152,500	16,000		£130,000	18,500		£150,000
SOUTH	Exe	3,000	10	30,000	—	—	—	—	—	—
	Wye	13,000	5	65,000	12,000	5	60,000	12,500	5	62,500
	Total	16,000		£95,000	12,000		£60,000	12,500		£62,500
EAST	Exe	17,000	10	170,000	15,000	10	150,000	16,500	10	165,000
	Wye	5,000	5	25,000	—	—	—	—	—	—
	Total	22,000		£195,000	15,000		£150,000	16,500		£165,000
WEST	Exe	9,000	10	90,000	8,000	10	80,000	9,500	10	95,000
	Wye	5,500	5	27,500	5,000	5	25,000	5,250	5	26,250
	Total	14,500		£117,500	13,000		£105,000	14,750		£121,250
TOTAL	Exe	41,000	10	410,000	33,000	10	330,000	37,500	10	375,000
	Wye	30,000	5	150,000	23,000	5	115,000	24,750	5	123,750
	Total	71,000		£560,000	56,000		£445,000	62,250		£498,750

Fig. 85.—*Sales budget*

This shows the sales budget as compiled from details given in a specimen question in the text. The budget is compiled in the light of the budget for the corresponding period last year and the actual achievement attained.

From the salesmen's reports and observations of the area sales managers, it is thought that sales could be budgeted for the six months ended June 30, 1971, as follows:

N.	"Exe"	Budgeted increase of 2,000 units on June 1970 budget
	"Wye"	„ „ 500 „ „ „
S.	"Wye"	„ „ 1,000 „ „ „
E.	"Exe"	„ „ 2,000 „ „ „
W.	"Exe"	„ „ 1,000 „ „ „
	"Wye"	„ „ 500 „ „ „

At a meeting of area sales managers with the divisional sales manager it is decided that sales campaigns will be undertaken in areas S. and E. It is anticipated that these campaigns will result in additional sales of 3,000 units of "Exe" in the S. area and 5,000 units of "Wye" in the E. area.

Prepare for presentation to top management the sales budget for the six months ended June 30, 1971, showing also the budgeted and actual sales for June 30, 1970, which are to be provided as a guide in fixing the sales budget.

ANSWER

The required sales budget, when completed, will appear as shown in Fig. 85. Similar budgets will be prepared for each division, then a sales budget prepared for the company as a whole showing sales by divisions rather than areas. Sales in each division will be further analysed to show sales by salesmen and by customer.

2. PRODUCTION BUDGET

This shows the quantity of products to be manufactured. It is prepared by the production manager and is based upon the following:

(a) The sales budget.
(b) The factory capacity.
(c) The budgeted stock requirements.

The production budget is classified under various headings:

(a) Products.
(b) Manufacturing departments.
(c) Months.

PRODUCTION BUDGET

Six months to 30 June 19..

Product X	£
Requirements to fulfil sales programme	41,000
Forecast closing stock June 30	4,000
	45,000
Less Forecast opening stock January 1	3,000
	42,000
Add for defectives 2½%	1,050
Quantity to be put into production	£43,050

When required:

January	7,050
February	7,000
March	8,000
April	8,000
May	8,000
June	5,000
	£43,050

These may be allocated to departments (assuming each department is able to make the parts):

Part No.	No. per unit	Dept. A	Dept. B	Dept. C
X 1	1	43,050	—	—
X 2	1	21,000	22,050	—
X 3	2	—	—	86,100

and so on.

When the production budget is completed it forms the basis of the production cost budget.

3. PRODUCTION COST BUDGET

This is the quantity of products to be manufactured, expressed in terms of cost. It is classified under various headings, *e.g.*:

(*a*) Products.
(*b*) Manufacturing departments.
(*c*) Months.
(*d*) Element of cost.

Many companies prepare a raw material budget, labour budget and overheads budget, which give analysed figures of the element-of-cost section of the production cost budget.

4. PLANT UTILISATION BUDGET

This represents the plant requirements to meet the production budget. This budget may be very important because:

(*a*) it details the machine load in every manufacturing department;

(*b*) it draws attention to any overloading in time for any corrective action to be taken, *e.g.* shift working, purchasing of new machinery, overtime working, sub-contracting; and

(*c*) it draws attention to any underloading so that the sales manager can be requested to investigate possible increased sales.

5. CAPITAL EXPENDITURE BUDGET

This represents the estimated expenditure on fixed assets during the budget period. It is based on information such as the following:

(*a*) Overloading shown in the plant utilisation budget.

(*b*) Reports of the production manager requesting new production machinery.

(*c*) Reports of the works engineer requesting new service machinery.

(*d*) Reports of the distribution manager requesting new transport.

(*e*) Reports of the sales manager requesting new cars.

(*f*) Reports of the accountant requesting new office machinery.

(*g*) Decisions of the board to extend buildings, etc.

CAPITAL EXPENDITURE BUDGET

Covering the five years from 19.. to 19..

Project No.	Short description	Estimated cost £	Allow for extras £	Total £	Spent already £	Balance to spend £

(*a*) *Projects commenced before budget date*

(*b*) *Projects approved in principle, but not yet begun*

(*c*) *Projects for which consideration is now requested*

NOTE: There would be analysis columns for the years covered by the budget to the right of the columns shown above.

Authority for Capital Expenditure No.

Project No.
Short description
Original budget estimate approved   £
Proportion of work now completed   %   Value £

————————   £

Proportion of budgeted cost approved last time
   Add Extras to cost already approved

                                                          ————————

Additional proportion of budgeted cost this month
   Add Extras to budgeted cost incurred this month

                                                          ————————

                                                          ————————

Estimated balance required to finish this project
                                                          ════════

Remarks

                                        Signed.......................

6. SELLING AND DISTRIBUTION COST BUDGET

This represents the cost of selling and distributing the quantities shown in the sales budget. The sales manager, advertising manager and sales office manager will co-operate with the budget officer in the preparation of this budget.

SPECIMEN QUESTION

Selling expenses in Division No. 1 were budgeted for the six months ended June 30, 1970, as shown in the table on the next page.

The sales budget illustrated previously is used as a basis for the preparation of this budget.

For the budget for the six months ending June 30, 1971:

   (*a*) Sales commission is based on 2% of the sales.
   (*b*) Salesmen's salaries to be increased by 5%.
   (*c*) Salesmen's expenses to be increased by 10%.
   (*d*) Car expenses to be increased by 10%.
   (*e*) Warehouse wages to be increased by 5%.
   (*f*) Lorry expenses to be increased by 10%.
   (*g*) Sales office salaries to be increased by 10%.
   (*h*) One extra clerk to be engaged by E. area at £10 per week.

(*i*) Postage, stationery and telephone to be increased by 5%.
(*j*) Press and T.V. advertising to be increased in all areas by 10%.
(*k*) Coupon offers in areas S. and E. to be £2,000 and £3,000 each, respectively.
(*l*) Shop-window schemes in areas S. and E. to be £1,000 and £1,500 each, respectively.

An additional commission of 5% will be paid to salesmen in areas S. and E. for sales of the introductory offer of "Exe" and "Wye."
Prepare the selling cost budget for the six months ended June 30, 1971.

Element of cost	Area				Total
	North	South	East	West	
Direct selling expenses					
Salesmen's salaries	4,500	2,250	4,680	3,120	14,550
Salesmen's commission	2,600	1,200	3,000	2,100	8,900
Salesmen's expenses	440	220	538	352	1,550
Car expenses	3,000	1,500	3,600	2,400	10,500
	10,540	5,170	11,818	7,972	35,500
Distribution expenses					
Warehouse wages	2,000	1,500	2,500	1,500	7,500
Warehouse rent, rates, electricity	300	300	400	250	1,250
Lorry expenses	2,500	1,800	2,800	1,900	9,000
General expenses	400	400	500	450	1,750
	5,200	4,000	6,200	4,100	19,500
Sales office					
Salaries	2,600	1,900	3,000	2,500	10,000
Rent, rates, electricity	600	300	700	400	2,000
Depreciation	300	100	400	200	1,000
Postage, stationery, telephone	1,300	500	1,500	700	4,000
General expenses	600	400	500	500	2,000
	5,400	3,200	6,100	4,300	19,000
Advertising					
Press	1,000	1,000	1,000	1,000	4,000
Television	2,000	2,000	2,000	2,000	8,000
Coupon offers	1,500	—	—	1,200	2,700
Shop window displays	500	200	200	400	1,300
	5,000	3,200	3,200	4,600	16,000
TOTAL	£26,140	£15,570	£27,318	£20,972	£90,000

ANSWER

Figure 86 shows the type of budget that would be prepared. Similar budgets would be made out for each division, then a summarised budget prepared for the company as a whole, showing sales by divisions rather than areas.

7. PURCHASING BUDGET

This represents the total purchases to be made in the budget period. It is composed of direct materials, indirect materials and research and development requirements.

Purchases will normally be in line with budgeted requirements, with the exception of orders already placed with suppliers and any adjustments to budgeted stock positions.

8. CASH BUDGET

This represents the cash receipts and payments, and the estimated cash balances for each month of the budget period. Its main functions are:

(*a*) to ensure that sufficient cash is available when required;

(*b*) to reveal any expected shortage of cash, so that action may be taken, *e.g.* a bank overdraft or loan arranged;

(*c*) to reveal any expected surplus of cash, so that if the management desire, cash may be invested or loaned.

SPECIMEN QUESTION

Prepare a cash budget in respect of the six months to December 31 from the information given in the table below.

Cash balance on July 1 was expected to be £75,000.

Month	Sales	Materials	Wages	Overheads				
				Pro-duction	Adminis-tration	Selling	Distri-bution	Research and develop-ment
April	50,000	20,000	5,000	2,200	1,500	800	400	500
May	60,000	30,000	5,600	2,400	1,450	850	450	500
June	40,000	20,000	4,000	2,500	1,520	750	350	600
July	50,000	30,000	4,200	2,300	1,480	850	450	600
August	60,000	35,000	4,600	2,600	1,510	950	550	700
September	70,000	40,000	5,000	2,700	1,540	1,000	600	700
October	80,000	45,000	5,200	2,900	1,560	1,025	625	800
November	90,000	50,000	5,400	3,000	1,570	1,075	675	800
December	100,000	55,000	5,800	3,200	1,600	1,150	750	800

SELLING AND DISTRIBUTION COST BUDGET

Division No. I

Period Six months to: June 30, 1971

Element of Cost	Budget June 30, 1971					Budget for six months to June 30, 1970				
	Area					**Area**				
	North	South	East	West	Total	North	South	East	West	Total
DIRECT SELLING EXPENSES										
Salesmen's salaries	4,725	2,363	4,914	3,276	15,278	4,500	2,250	4,680	3,120	14,550
Salesmen's commission	3,050	3,400	5,150	2,350	13,950	2,600	1,200	3,000	2,100	8,900
Salesmen's expenses	484	242	592	387	1,705	440	220	538	352	1,550
Car expenses	3,300	1,650	3,960	2,640	11,550	3,000	1,500	3,600	2,400	10,500
	11,559	7,655	14,616	8,653	42,483	10,540	5,170	11,818	7,972	35,500
DISTRIBUTION EXPENSES										
Warehouse wages	2,100	1,575	2,625	1,575	7,875	2,000	1,500	2,500	1,500	7,750
Warehouse rent and rates, electricity	300	300	400	250	1,250	300	300	400	250	1,250
Lorry expenses	2,750	1,980	3,080	2,090	9,900	2,750	1,800	2,800	1,900	9,000
General expenses	400	400	500	450	1,750	400	400	500	450	1,750
	5,550	4,255	6,605	4,365	20,775	5,200	4,000	6,200	4,100	19,500
SALES OFFICE										
Salaries	2,860	2,090	3,560	2,750	11,260	2,600	1,900	3,000	2,500	10,000
Rent, rates, and electricity	600	300	700	400	2,000	600	300	700	400	2,000
Depreciation	300	100	400	200	1,000	300	100	400	200	1,000
Postage, stationery and telephone	1,365	525	1,575	735	4,200	1,300	500	1,500	700	4,000
General expenses	600	400	500	500	2,000	600	400	500	500	2,000
	5,725	3,415	6,735	4,585	20,460	5,400	3,200	6,100	4,300	19,000
ADVERTISING										
Press	1,100	1,100	1,100	1,100	4,400	1,000	1,000	1,000	1,000	4,000
Television	2,200	2,200	2,200	2,200	8,800	2,000	2,000	2,000	2,000	8,000
Coupon offers	1,500	2,000	3,000	1,200	7,700	1,500	—	—	1,200	2,700
Shop window displays	500	1,000	1,500	400	3,400	500	200	200	400	1,300
	5,300	6,300	7,800	4,900	24,300	5,000	3,200	3,200	4,600	16,000
	£28,134	£21,625	£35,756	£22,503	£108,018	£26,140	£15,570	£27,318	£20,972	£90,000

FIG. 86.—Selling and distribution cost budget

This budget has been compiled after taking into account all the relative facts and trends known to the budget officer: these are referred to in the text.

Expected capital expenditure:

Plant and machinery to be installed in August at a cost of £20,000 will be payable on September 1.

Extension to research and development department amounting to £5,000 will be completed on August 1. Payable £1,000 per month as from completion date.

Under a hire-purchase agreement £2,000 is to be paid each month.

A sales commission of 5% on sales is to be paid within the month following actual sales.

Period of credit allowed by suppliers	3 months
„ „ „ to customers	2 months
Delay in payment of overheads	1 month
„ „ wages	$\frac{1}{8}$ month

Taxation of £50,000 is due to be paid on October 1.

Preference shares dividend of 10% on capital of £1,000,000 is to be paid on November 1.

10% calls on ordinary share capital of £200,000 is due on July 1 and September 1.

Dividend from investments amounting to £15,000 expected on November 1.

Cash sales of £1,000 per month are expected; no commission payable.

ANSWER

The cash budget prepared from the above information is shown in Fig. 87.

NOTES

In preparing the figures for debtors and creditors, the student may find it convenient to arrange the work first on a spare sheet of paper:

	b/f	July	Aug.	Sept.	Oct.	Nov.	Dec.	c/f
Sales ('000)		50	60	70	80	90	100	
Debtors May	60							90 Nov.
June	40	60	40	50	60	70	80	100 Dec.
Materials ('000)		30	35	40	45	50	55	
Creditors Apr.	20							45 Oct.
May	30							50 Nov.
June	20	20	30	20	30	35	40	55 Dec.

This gives a check on opening and closing debtors and creditors, which is useful if a balance sheet has to be prepared, and it also gives the figures to be copied into the cash budget.

Wages are calculated thus:

	£	£
July—$\frac{1}{8}$ June (£4,000)	500	
$\frac{7}{8}$ July (£4,200)	3,675	
		£4,175
August—$\frac{1}{8}$ July (£4,200)	525	
$\frac{7}{8}$ August (£4,600)	4,025	
		£4,550

CASH BUDGET

Period Ending: December 31, 19...

Details	Month					
	July	August	September	October	November	December
RECEIPTS						
Balance b/d	75,000	122,105	117,375	131,115	93,900	25,615
Debtors	60,000	40,000	50,000	60,000	70,000	80,000
Cash sales	1,000	1,000	1,000	1,000	1,000	1,000
Capital	20,000	—	20,000	—	15,000	—
Dividend	—	—	—	—	—	—
Total	£156,000	£163,105	£188,375	£192,115	£179,900	£106,615
PAYMENTS						
Materials	20,000	30,000	20,000	30,000	35,000	40,000
Wages	4,175	4,550	4,950	5,175	5,375	5,750
Production overhead	2,500	2,300	2,600	2,700	2,900	3,000
Administration overhead	1,520	1,480	1,510	1,540	1,560	1,570
Selling overhead	750	850	950	1,000	1,025	1,075
Distribution overhead	350	450	550	600	625	675
Research overhead	600	600	700	600	800	800
Commission	2,000	2,500	3,000	3,500	4,000	4,500
Capital	—	3,000	23,000	3,000	3,000	3,000
Taxation	—	—	—	50,000	100,000	—
Dividend	—	—	—	—	—	—
Total	£33,895	£45,730	£57,260	£98,215	£154,285	£60,370
Balance c/d	£122,105	£117,375	£131,115	£93,900	£25,615	£46,245

Fig. 87.—*Cash budget*

A cash budget is an essential requirement of budgetary control: it enables a business to plan in advance to meet heavy commitments and to avoid being caught unawares.

It will be noted that cash resources have been built up to meet the large amount of payments budgeted for October and November. At the end of November the cash balance is down to £25,615, which, if the budget is reasonably accurate, should be sufficient. In any case where it is not it may be necessary to arrange for a bank overdraft.

It can be observed how invaluable is a cash budget, as one can see at a glance if there will be sufficient cash, or too much cash at any time in the budget period.

ADDITIONAL BUDGETS

In addition to the budgets detailed above, there may be many more budgets prepared, but it is not necessary to detail them here. For example, budgets will be prepared for the administration and research and development departments, but these are rather similar to the selling and distribution cost budget already detailed.

THE MASTER BUDGET

When the functional budgets have been completed the budget officer will prepare a master budget in the form of a Budgeted Profit and Loss Account (shown on p. 472), in which he will incorporate the production sales and costs estimated for the budget period. The board of directors will then consider the budget, and if they are not satisfied will call for amendments. However, when the budget is finally approved it represents a standard which should be achieved by each department in the business.

Notes would be given to management explaining why the budgeted net profit for the current budget period was lower than for the corresponding budget period in the previous year. Information would be readily available in the subsidiary budgets which make up this master budget.

THE OPERATION OF BUDGETARY CONTROL

The head of each department or section will receive a copy of the budget appropriate to his activity. Each month he will receive a copy of the departmental budget report, a simple illustration of which is given in Fig. 88.

The head of the department receiving the report (in this illustration the cost accountant) can see immediately where he has over- or under-spent his budgeted allowance. From the performance percentage he can see that he has been efficient this month (102%), and cumulatively he has also been efficient (101%).

On investigating the variances it is apparent that the most important item was code 11, clerical salaries. It would appear that the department has been operating below strength, which has resulted in increased overtime costs and reduced National Insurance charges. Code 28, personnel service costs, are over-spent, presumably caused by advertising and interviewing candidates to fill the vacancy.

Budgeted Profit and Loss Account

Details	Current year		Previous year	
	Amount	%	Amount	%
Net sales	1,800,000	100·0	1,700,000	100·0
Production cost	960,000	53·3	910,000	53·5
GROSS PROFIT	840,000	46·7	790,000	46·5
Less Operating expenses:				
Administration	77,000	4·3	71,000	4·2
Selling	106,000	5·9	98,000	5·8
Advertising	330,000	18·3	300,000	17·6
Distribution	112,000	6·2	106,000	6·2
Research and development	14,000	0·8	12,000	0·7
Financial	21,000	1·2	20,000	1·2
TOTAL	660,000	36·7	607,000	35·7
OPERATING PROFIT	180,000	10·0	183,000	10·8
Add Other income	2,000	0·1	2,000	0·1
NET PROFIT before taxation	182,000	10·1	185,000	10·9
Less Provision for taxation	85,000	4·7	86,000	5·1
NET PROFIT	£97,000	5·4	£99,000	5·8

It must be emphasised that speed of presentation, and corrective action if necessary, is essential in budgetary control. Unless monthly budget reports are issued soon after the monthly period in question, adverse costs may go undetected for a considerable time, and will be much more difficult to locate.

Budget reports will be issued for each department or budget centre, then summarised reports issued for divisions of the business. A report to management concerning all significant variances will be presented, explaining how the variances occurred, and any corrective action which may have been taken.

BUDGET REPORT ON CONTROLLABLE EXPENSES

Budget Centre: 57

Department: Cost Accounting

Date Issued: 6th July

Prepared by: C.G.B.

Checked by: P.J.B.

Performance %

		Month			
		Month	Cumulative		
		102	101		

Element of Cost		Month			Cumulative		
		Expense			Expense		
Code	Description	Budget	Actual	Variance	Budget	Actual	Variance
	INDIRECT MATERIAL						
01	Printing and stationery	75	70	5	450	460	(10)
02	Photographic supplies	30	32	(2)	180	185	(5)
03	Cleaning materials	10	8	2	60	50	10
04	General	5	5	—	30	28	2
	INDIRECT LABOUR						
11	Clerical salaries	1,020	987	33	5,800	5,680	120
12	Executive salaries	400	400	—	2,200	2,200	—
13	Overtime	30	36	(6)	90	120	(30)
14	Absence	28	24	4	160	154	6
15	National insurance	40	39	1	220	210	10
	MISCELLANEOUS						
21	Repairs: Buildings	10	12	(2)	40	45	(5)
22	Transport	—	—	—	—	—	—
23	Equipment	4	3	1	60	75	(15)
24	Depreciation: Buildings	20	20	—	120	120	—
25	Transport	—	—	—	—	—	—
26	Equipment	10	10	—	60	60	—
27	Heat, Light, and Power	15	12	3	120	110	10
28	Personnel Service	8	12	(4)	60	80	(20)
29	Postage	5	6	(1)	30	34	(4)
30	Telephone	30	28	2	180	166	14
31	Staff expenses	8	10	(2)	50	55	(5)
32	General expenses	2	1	1	10	8	2
		£1,750	£1,715	£35	£9,920	£9,840	£80

FIG. 88.—*Budget report*

Every month the head of each budget centre receives a report like this. It enables him to pay particular attention to those items of expense which call for it because of their "exception" to the rule.

FLEXIBLE BUDGETARY CONTROL

In order to avoid the wide discrepancies which may emerge when comparisons of actual results are made with a fixed budget, the use of flexible budgets is to be recommended.

Such a budget is defined in the *Terminology of Cost Accountancy* as:

"A budget which, by recognising the difference between fixed, semi-fixed and variable costs, is designed to change in relation to the level of activity attained."

In order to explain how such a budget operates, consider a simple hypothetical case. This must be done in two circumstances:

1. Flexible budget without standard costing.
2. Flexible budget with standard costing.

CASE 1: WITHOUT STANDARD COSTING

Department A, for which a flexible budget is to be set up, consists of five similar machines. At normal practical rates of working these machines are estimated to work in a 13-week period.

Machines		Weeks		Hours per week		Estimated utilisation		
5	×	13	×	44	×	75%	=	2,145 machine hours.

NOTE: In other departments, it should be noted, the capacity might well be measured in direct labour hours.

This normal practical capacity is taken as 100% capacity, and it will be necessary to take capacities on either side of this, in case the actual capacity achieved is less or more than the norm.

The next matter to be considered is the expenditure budgeted to be incurred at these various levels of activity. It is desirable to separate all expenditure into "fixed" and "variable," as the behaviour of them differs in circumstances which are themselves subject to fluctuation. Thus as production increases, economies of large-scale buying may reduce the direct material costs, but an increase in the fixed costs may take place. The semi-fixed costs must first be sub-divided as shown in the chapter on marginal costing.

As a result, the flexible budget, simplified into main headings, might be as follows:

Budgeted machine hours	1,287	1,716	2,145	2,574	3,003
Capacity %	60	80	100	120	140

	Unit cost	£	Unit cost	£	Unit cost	£	Unit cost	£	Unit cost	£
Direct and vari-able costs	3	3,861	3	5,148	3	6,435	2·7	6,950	2·7	8,108
Fixed costs		4,000		4,000		4,000		4,500		4,500
		£7,861		£9,148		£10,435		£11,450		£12,608

Now if in the actual period 2,000 machine hours were recorded, comparison of actual costs would be made with the flexible budget at this level, thus:

Direct and variable costs	2,000 × 3	= £6,000
Fixed costs		= £4,000
		£10,000

The difference between the actual expense incurred and the allowance would reflect in the budget comparison statement as a variance requiring explanation.

Thus one will suppose that the actual cost of overhead was:

Variable £6,200;
Fixed £4,146.

As far as the variable cost is concerned, there would be an expenditure variance ($-£200$); but the difference between the actual fixed overhead incurred and the budgeted figure would be explained thus:

Volume change due to working only 2,000/2,145 hours = 97·5% of normal capacity

	£
Absorbed 97·5% of £4,000	3,900
Volume capacity 2½%	100
Expenditure variance	
Actual overhead incurred, *less* budgeted fixed overhead at the flexible budget level, £4,146 − £4,000	146
Expenditure incurred	£4,146

CASE 2: WITH STANDARD COSTING

The same details as for the case above apply, but standards have been set up.

It has been found that in department A the five operators who look after the machines are a little more skilled than the average, and have been given a rating of 62/60. The relaxation factor has been fixed at 5% and 10% is also allowed to cover set-up time, gauge time, etc.

Time study establishes that the average time required by these operators to finish a unit of production is 70 minutes. The standard time per unit is therefore:

$$70 \times \frac{62}{60} \times 1 \cdot 15 = \underline{83 \cdot 2 \text{ minutes.}}$$

It follows that the budgeted standards hours will be

$$2{,}145 \text{ machine operating hours} \times 60 = 128{,}700 \text{ machine}$$
$$\text{minutes}$$
$$128{,}700 \text{ minutes} \div 70 = 1{,}838 \cdot 6 \text{ expected}$$
$$\text{units}$$
$$1{,}838 \cdot 6 \text{ units} \times 83 \cdot 2 \text{ standard time in minutes} = 153{,}072 \cdot 52 \text{ minutes}$$
$$153{,}072 \cdot 52 \div 60 = 2{,}550 \text{ standard}$$
$$\text{hours (approx.)}$$

If the level of activity of the operators, as measured in standard hours of work produced, rises or falls, it will mean either:

(a) they have worked faster or slower than they were rated; or
(b) the relaxation and other factors have been fixed incorrectly; or
(c) the machine hours available have been varied.

There are, therefore, two measures of achievement now open for consideration:

(a) *The actual usage of budgeted capacity ratio*

Either (i) $\dfrac{\text{Machine hours recorded}}{\text{Budgeted machine hours}} \times 100.$

Or (ii) $\dfrac{\text{Direct labour hours recorded}}{\text{Budgeted direct labour hours}} \times 100.$

The budgeted machine operating hours may not be the same as the budgeted direct labour hours because a machine is not in operation for the full length of an operator's day.

The relationship between machine hours and direct labour hours may be explained by the following diagram:

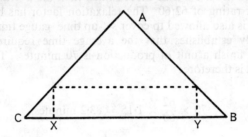

In a working day of, say, 8 hours represented by *CB* the periods *CX* and *BY* are cut off to cover the time spent by the operator in making ready and set-ups and in cleaning down and gauge time. The machine hours are represented by *XY*, but *XY* is in proportion to *CB*. Let us now suppose that the normal machine operating time is 6 hours.

Capacity is often measured in terms of machine hours, so that if the operating hours are virtually 5, the capacity ratio is $\frac{5}{6} \times 100 = 83\frac{1}{3}\%$.

On the other hand, if we measure capacity in terms of direct labour hours we should probably include set-up time and gauge time as part of those hours and the ratio might be $\frac{7}{8} \times 100 = 87\frac{1}{2}\%$.

(b) The activity ratio

$$\frac{\text{Standard hours actually produced}}{\text{Budgeted standard hours}} \times 100.$$

With regard to the denominator in this fraction "budgeted standard hours," if the definition in *Terminology* is adhered to we recognise that a standard hour is a measure of the work to be performed in one hour.

According to the interpretation we place on the actual usage of budgeted capacity ratio, so we may say:

one budgeted standard hour = the work to be performed in one budgeted machine hour, or the work to be performed in one budgeted direct labour hour.

The flexible budget in Case 2 is likely to be drawn up on the basis of budgeted standard hours, so that it might be:

Budgeted standard hours	1,530		2,040		2,550		3,060		3,570	
Activity level, %	60		80		100		120		140	
	Unit cost	£	Unit cost	£	Unit cost	£	Unit cost	£	Unit cost	£
Direct and variable costs	2·52	3,861	2·52	5,148	2·52	6,435	2·27	6,950	2·27	8,108
Fixed costs		4,000		4,000		4,000		4,500		4,500
		£7,861		£9,148		£10,435		£11,450		£12,608

If 2,400 standard hours of work are produced the level of activity achieved, in terms of standard hours is:

$$\frac{2,400}{2,550} \times 100 = \underline{94 \cdot 1\% \text{ approx.}}$$

Comparison of actual costs would therefore be made with the flexible budget at this level.

As far as the direct and variable expense is concerned, the matter is straightforward:

$$2,400 \times 2 \cdot 52 = \underline{£6,048.}$$

But what is to be done regarding the fixed expense? What is the "allowance" to be?

In considering the level of activity achieved, it is seen that it is interrelated with standard capacity attained; and the Institute of Cost and Works Accountants, in its publication on *Budgetary Control and Standard Costing*, considers that both ratios should be used.

Suppose, therefore, at the same time as 94·1% activity level was reached, the actual usage of budgeted capacity ratio was 98%.

The "allowance" in this case is:

$$£4,000 - £4,000 \ (98\% - 94 \cdot 1\%)$$
$$= 4,000 - (4,000 \times 3 \cdot 9\%)$$
$$= 4,000 - 157$$
$$= \underline{£3,843.}$$

Had the actual usage of budgeted capacity ratio been used alone, the result would have been:

$$£4,000 \times 98\% = \underline{£3,920.}$$

On the other hand, the activity level percentage alone would give:

$$£4,000 \times 94 \cdot 1\% = \underline{£3,764.}$$

The allowance of £3,843 allows for the fact that both capacity and activity have had a share in producing the result.

The total allowed expense will therefore be £6,058 variable, plus £3,843 fixed, *i.e.* £9,901.

For the benefit of the advanced student it is as well to follow this through to its conclusion. It should not, however, be attempted on the first reading of the book.

This may be illustrated by an example based on the figures used already, supplemented by others.

> Actual overhead: fixed £4,100; variable £6,500
> Budgeted machine hours 2,145, which converted to standard machine hours = 2,550
> Actual machine hours operated 2,500
> Standard hours of work produced 2,400
> Budgeted overhead: fixed £4,000; variable £6,435

The hourly budgeted rates of recovery are therefore:

$$\text{Fixed } £4,000 \div 2,550 = £1 \cdot 57$$
$$\text{Variable } £6,435 \div 2,550 = £2 \cdot 52.$$

By the use of the flexible budget the allowance for variable overhead is

$$2,400 \times 2 \cdot 52 = £6,048.$$

As the actual expenditure was £6,500, there is a variable overhead expenditure variance of £6,500 − £6,048 = £452 (A).

When we come to the fixed overhead we find the allowance by the use of the following formula:

$$FB = BFO - BFO(BCR - AR)$$

BFO budgeted fixed overhead; BCR actual usage of budgeted capacity ratio; AR activity ratio.

We have therefore:

$$
\begin{aligned}
FB &= £4,000 - 4,000\left(\frac{2,500}{2,550} \times 100 - \frac{2,400}{2,550} \times 100\right) \\
   &= £4,000 - 4,000(98\% - 94 \cdot 1\%) \\
   &= £4,000 - 4,000 \times 3 \cdot 9\% \\
   &= £4,000 - 157 \text{ (approx.)} \\
   &= \underline{£3,843.}
\end{aligned}
$$

Again we compare this allowance with the actual expenditure.

$$£4,100 - £3,843 = £257 \text{ (A)}$$

and this is a controllable variance, which is made up of the expenditure variance (budget £4,000 − actual £4,100) = £100 (A), plus the volume efficiency variance shown above = £157 (A).

By this method we might set up the Overhead Control Account thus:

Overhead Control Account

	F £	V £		F £	V £
Actual expenditure	4,100	6,500	Allowed overhead transferred to Work-in-progress Account	3,843	6,048
			Controllable variance c/d	257	452
	£4,100	£6,500		£4,100	£6,500

It will be seen that this does not disclose the capacity usage variance for fixed overhead, although it can be measured by comparing the allowance with the standard:

		£
Standard achieved	= 2,400 standard hours of work at 1·57 =	3,768
Allowance expected	=	3,843
Capacity usage variance =		£75 (A)

The student may like to see these variances disclosed in the normal manner (although this is more fully dealt with in the next chapter):

	£	£
A—Actual expenditure	4,100	6,500
B—Budgeted expenditure	4,000	
C—Capacity utilised 2,500 × 1·57	3,925	
S—Standard achieved 2,400 × 1·57	3,768	
× 2·52		6,048
A − B = Expenditure variance F	100 (A)	
A − S = Expenditure variance V		452 (A)
B − C = Capacity usage variance	75 (A)	
C − S = Volume efficiency variance	157 (A)	

Again setting up the Overhead Control Account we have:

Overhead Control Account

	F £	V £		F £	V £
Actual expenditure	4,100	6,500	Transfer to:		
			Work in progress	3,768	6,048
			Expenditure variance	100	452
			Capacity usage variance	75	
			Volume efficiency variance	157	
	£4,100	£6,500		£4,100	£6,500

EXAMINATION QUESTIONS

1. What do you consider to be the main objectives of budgetary control? List, with brief descriptions, three of the main subsidiary budgets which go to make up the main budget.

(*C.A.A. Inter.*)

2. "Standard costing is always accompanied by a system of budgeting, but budgetary control may be operated in businesses where standard costing would be impracticable." Discuss this statement, and indicate the method and use of budgetary control systems in the type of business mentioned in the latter part of the question.

(*I.C.W.A. Final*)

3. Where would the following types of material be included in a production cost budget and how would the amounts to be included be assessed?

(*a*) Direct material.
(*b*) Supplies consumed directly in production processes.
(*c*) Supplies consumed in supplying a service, *e.g.* coal for steam generation.
(*d*) Consumable stores, *e.g.* oils, greases, waste.
(*e*) Materials for repairs to buildings, plant and machinery.

(*I.C.W.A. Inter.*)

4. What do you understand by a master budget? Into what sections is it usually divided, and what are the purposes of the divisions? Explain, with any necessary figures, how you would present to management a report on variances occurring on one of the sections.

(*I.C.W.A. Final*)

5. In outlining a plan for a "production" budget, what main bases would you use?

(*Comm. A. Final*)

6. Having completed budgets for all the functions of a company how would you ensure that they were put to use?

(*Comm. A. Final*)

7. You are chief accountant of a manufacturing company which operates a fully integrated system of budgetary control and standard costing. The company manufactures a wide range of products involving a large number of manufacturing processes. You have been asked by the managing director to prepare a memorandum setting out your views on how the profit might be improved.

(*C.A. Final*)

8. You are required to give a *pro-forma* layout to illustrate how a long-term cash forecast or budget on broad lines might be prepared, covering four future accounting periods. The illustration should include assumed figures for the first two periods.

(*I.C.A. Final, November 1964*)

9. "It has been said that the sign of a good manager is his ability to delegate responsibility and this is especially true of expenditure control. If control of expenditure is delegated, as it should be, the means to enable those responsible to exercise control must be provided. The means is the *budget*."

Discuss the implications of the above statement in relation to the procedure you would adopt when called on to install a budgeting system in an organisation.

(*A.C.C.A. Final*)

10. An essential part of profit planning is the budgeting of sales and selling costs. In the circumstance where sales can be regarded as the principal budget factor, what checks would you apply upon receiving the first draft of the sales and selling cost budgets before using them as the basis for production and other budgets?

(*I.C.W.A. Final*)

11. Itemise a procedure for scheduling the material requirements of a production budget.

(*I.C.W.A. Inter.*)

12. X.Y.Z. Ltd. manufactures three products P1, P2 and P3. These are made in three production departments from four materials M1, M2, M3 and M4. The following information is supplied:

Standard product cost detail:

Product			P1	P2	P3
Material	*Used in dept.*	*Cost per unit in* £	*units per article*		
M1	D1	0·5	—	1	2
M2	D2	0·2	1	—	2
M3	D2	0·25	2	1	—
M4	D3	0·15	2	2	1
Rejection on final inspection at end of process considered normal			5%	10%	10%

Budget details:	£	£	£
Sales for the year in '000s	260	580	450
Sales price each	5	10	6

Stocks:	*in thousands of articles*		
January 1	5	10	15
December 31	10	15	30

Raw materials:

Stocks:	M1	M2	M3	M4
	in thousands of units			
January 1	30	40	10	60
December 31	40	30	20	50

You are required to prepare:

(a) standard material costs per article for P1, P2 and P3;
(b) for the year:

(i) the production budget;
(ii) production cost budgets for direct materials for departments D1, D2 and D3;
(iii) the purchasing budget.

(I.C.W.A. Inter.)

13. Product P is manufactured from 10 lb of raw material M at a cost of £0·2 per lb. The selling price of P is £5 per unit and the sales budget for 1968 was:

Month 1968	Sales value £'000	Month 1968	Sales value £'000
January	10	July	40
February	10	August	40
March	15	September	30
April	20	October	20
May	30	November	15
June	40	December	10

In preparation for the budget for the coming year the sales manager has forecast the following increases in sales for 1969 over the budgeted figures given above:

1969	%
January to April inclusive	10
May to August, inclusive	20
September to December, inclusive	10

It is estimated that the stock at December 31, 1968, will be:

Product P	500 units
Material M	4,000 lb

The monthly average stock levels for 1969 have been forecast to be as given below:

Month 1969	Product P (units)	Material M (lb)	Month 1969	Product P (units)	Material M (lb)
January	400	3,000	July	1,600	15,000
February	400	4,000	August	1,600	16,000
March	600	6,000	September	1,100	12,000
April	800	7,000	October	700	10,000
May	1,200	13,000	November	500	8,000
June	1,600	16,000	December	400	5,000

It may be assumed that stocks increase or decrease evenly throughout each month.

You are required, in preparation for the 1969 budget, to prepare the "purchase budget" for material M for 1969 in total and for each month.

(I.C.W.A. Inter.)

14. A company manufactures two models of a machine and distributes them in three sales areas. The budgeted Profit and Loss Account for the year ended December 31, is:

Sales:

Area	Large £	Small £	Total £
A	12,500	25,000	37,500
B	25,000	37,500	62,500
C	37,500	62,500	100,000
	£75,000	£125,000	200,000

Production cost of sales:	£	
Large (60% of sales)	45,000	
Small (70% „)	87,500	
		132,500

Gross profit		67,500

	Area			
	A £	B £	C £	Total £
Direct selling and distribution costs:				
Salesmen's salaries	3,625	4,000	1,875	9,500
„ expenses	1,125	750	625	2,500
Sales office costs	1,750	1,550	1,200	4,500
Advertising	350	850	400	1,600
Carriage	675	600	725	2,000

Indirect selling and distribution costs:		
	£	
Advertising	6,000	
Carriage	1,100	
Warehousing	3,850	
Credit control	2,200	
General administration	4,000	
		17,150
		37,250

Budgeted net profit		£30,250

The budgeted analysis of sales is:

	Large			Small	
Sales area	Sales volume (machines)	No. of orders		Sales volume (machines)	No. of orders
A	2,000	300		2,000	400
B	4,000	500		3,000	500
C	6,000	200		5,000	300

The cost manual of the company states that:

1. Indirect selling and distribution costs are to be apportioned to sales areas as follows:

	On basis of:
Advertising and general administration:	sales values
Carriage and warehousing:	sales volume
Credit control:	number of orders

2. Selling and distribution costs of sales areas are to be apportioned to models on the basis of sales values.

You are required to:

(a) prepare a comparative statement showing an analysis of budgeted selling and distribution costs by sales areas;
(b) prepare a comparative budgeted Profit and Loss Statement for each model by sales areas;
(c) show the budgeted average net profit per unit for each model in each sales area.

(I.C.W.A. Inter.)

15. The following details apply to an annual budget for a manufacturing company:

Quarter	1st	2nd	3rd	4th
Working days	65	60	55	60
Production (units per working day)	100	110	120	105
Raw material purchases (% by weight of annual total)	30	50	20	—
Budgeted purchase price (per lb)	£1·00	£1·05	£1·12½	

Quantity of raw material per unit of production: 2 lb.
Budgeted opening stock of raw material: 4,000 lb (cost £4,000).
Budgeted closing stock of raw material: 2,000 lb.

Issues are priced on FIFO basis.
Calculate the following budgeted figures:

(a) Quarterly, and annual purchases of raw material, by weight and value.
(b) Closing quarterly stocks by weight and value.

If the purchases in the second and third quarters were equal (at 35% of the annual total) what would be the effect on the value of the closing stocks of the second and third quarters, and in the budgeted annual cost of materials consumed?

(I.C.W.A. Inter.)

16. The month by month forecast of profitability of a company for the five months May to September is given below:

	May	June	July	Aug.	Sept.
			£000's		
Materials consumed	60	70	80	102	90
Wages	32	32	32	40	32
Depreciation	7	7	7	7	7
Factory expenses	5	5	5	5	5
Rent	3	3	3	3	3
Salaries and office expenses	32	32	32	32	32
Advertising and publicity	12	14	10	16	20
Sales commission	8	9	10	13	11
	159	172	179	218	200
Sales	160	180	200	260	220
Profit	1	8	21	42	20
Raw material stock (end-month)	70	80	90	70	60

The following additional information is given:

1. On average, payment is made to suppliers one month after delivery.
2. The lag in payment of wages is one-eighth of a month.
3. Factory expenses are paid during the month incurred.
4. Rent is paid quarterly on the last day of March, June, September and December.
5. Salaries and office expenses are paid in the month in which they arise.
6. Advertising and publicity expenditure is paid monthly but two months' credit is taken.
7. Sales commission is paid one month in arrear.
8. On average, debtors take two months' credit.
9. Cash balance at July 1 is £52,000.
10. In September £30,000 will be paid for machinery. A dividend and tax thereon amounting to £6,000 will be paid in August. Investment grants of £20,000 will be received in September.

You are required to prepare a cash budget for each of the three months to September 30. (Give figures to the nearest £1,000.)

(I.C.A. Final May 1969)

17. Predetermined product costs for the year are as follows:

Product	Material	Labour	Variable overhead	Fixed overhead	Total
A	£0·50	£0·25	£0·50	£0·25	£1·50
B	£1·12½	£0·37½	£0·75	£0·45	£2·70
C	£1·50	£1·00	£2·00	£0·90	£5·40
D	£1·25	£0·50	£1·00	£0·55	£3·30

The preliminary sales budget upon which the predetermined costs are based is:

Product			
A	3,000 units at £1·75 each
B	6,000 ,, ,, £2·75 ,,
C	4,000 ,, ,, £5·25 ,,
D	10,000 ,, ,, £3·50 ,,

It is suggested that additional sales promotion expenditure would bring additional sales as below:

Product	Suggested expenditure £	Additional sales (units)
A	2,000	3,000
B	3,000	7,000
C	2,000	4,000
D	3,000	6,000

Prepare a statement for management summarising the sales, costs and profit positions of the preliminary budget and of the other possibilities.

(*I.C.W.A. Final*)

18. The output of a factory is sold through three salesmen who are each paid a salary of £3,000 per annum plus a commission of 2% on sales.

In the budget the cost and gross profit make-up of the products as a percentage of selling price were:

		Pumps %	Motors %	Compressors %
Production cost:	Variable	40	50	45
	Fixed	30	25	35
Gross profit		30	25	20
Selling price		£100	£100	£100

The sales for the year were:

	Salesmen		
	A £'000	B £'000	C £'000
Pumps	90	80	70
Motors	40	60	50
Compressors	30	50	50

The expenses were:

	A £	B £	C £
Travelling costs	1,260	1,100	1,400
Bad debts	500	150	380
Local advertising		4% on sales	
Carriage and other selling expenses		2% on budgeted production cost	

Prepare a budgeted annual profit statement for each salesman, so that they share the year's fixed production cost on the basis of £50,000 each for A and C and £55,000 for B.

(*I.C.W.A. Final*)

19. Your company manufactures two products A and B. A forecast of the number of units to be sold in the first seven months of the year is given below:

	Product A	Product B
January	1,000	2,800
February	1,200	2,800
March	1,600	2,400
April	2,000	2,000
May	2,400	1,600
June	2,400	1,600
July	2,000	1,800

It is anticipated that:

(*i*) there will be no work in progress at the end of any month;

(*ii*) finished units equal to half the sales for the next month will be in stock at the end of each month (including December of the previous year).

Budgeted production and production costs for the year ending December 31 are as follows:

	Product A	Product B
Production (units)	22,000	24,000
	£	£
Direct materials per unit	12·5	19·0
Direct wages per unit	4·5	7·0
Total factory overhead apportioned to each type of product	66,000	96,000

Prepare for the 6 months' period ending June 30 a production budget for each month and a summarised production cost budget.

(*I.C.W.A. Final*)

20. The general manager of a manufacturing company asks you to examine a proposition to purchase some labour-saving equipment at a price of £7,000. This will have the following effect:

(*a*) Output will be increased by 15% p.a. (This can all be sold at present selling prices.)

(*b*) Direct wages at the increased output level will be £3,000 p.a. lower than at present.

(*c*) The ratio of overhead to prime cost, which is 30% at present, will rise to 45%.

The general manager is worried about the increase in the ratio of overhead to prime cost that would result from the introduction of this equipment. Sales at present are £60,000 p.a., for which the prime costs are: direct material cost, £16,000; direct wages, £24,000.

You are required to:

(*a*) prepare a simple budgeted Profit and Loss Statement for the year if the proposition is accepted;

(*b*) state whether the general manager's worry about the increase in the ratio of overhead to prime cost is justified. Give brief reasons.

(*I.C.W.A. Inter.*)

21. A manufacturing company of which you are the chief accountant produces three different products, X, Y and Z. The processes by which they are produced are independent of one another, and in no case are the sales of any one product affected by prices or sales of the others. The following budgeted Profit and Loss Statement for the year ending November 30, is presented to you by your assistant:

	Total £	X £	Y £	Z £
Sales	100,000	15,000	10,000	75,000
Variable production cost	60,000	8,000	4,000	48,000
Fixed production cost (apportioned to products)	20,000	1,000	3,000	16,000
	80,000	9,000	7,000	64,000
Gross profit	20,000	6,000	3,000	11,000
Variable selling cost	8,000	2,700	2,600	2,700
Fixed selling cost (apportioned to products)	2,000	700	700	600
	10,000	3,400	3,300	3,300
Net profit	£10,000	£2,600	—	£7,700
Net loss	—	—	£300	—

NOTE: The basis of apportionment of fixed costs are known and acceptable to you.

Your assistant recommends that, to improve the profit position, product Y should be eliminated from the range of articles produced by the company, thus leaving only two articles to be produced.

You are required:

(a) to re-draft the budgeted Profit and Loss Statement to show the profit that would result if product Y were eliminated;
(b) to state whether or not you agree with your assistant's recommendation. Give brief reasons.

(I.C.W.A. Inter.)

22. A manufacturing business has drawn up a budget for the current year, the proportion of the expected costs, etc., being as follows:

	%
Direct material	34·0
Direct labour	22·0
Variable factory overheads	16·5
Fixed factory overheads	12·0
Other variable costs	5·5
Other fixed costs	4·0
Profit	6·0
Total	100·0

After six months working it becomes apparent that the volume of business anticipated will not be obtained, and management considers that a figure of approximately 75% of budgeted sales will be obtained, *i.e.* £330,000 for the full year. As cost accountant of the business, present information to management at this stage, which will enable decisions to be made on matters of policy.

(I.C.W.A. Final)

23. Define activity percentage and efficiency percentage, explaining the significance of each.

The Baker Company Ltd. is a holding company controlling many subsidiary companies carrying on quite diverse activities differing from those of the holding company. Although the group is run on decentralised principles, the holding company keeps a close check on expenditure on overheads, because certain of the subsidiaries do not manage to cover their overheads and the deficiency has to be made good out of profits. This is especially true of the companies which have no selling organisation of their own but which sell to other members of the group on a cost-plus basis. This is negotiated at the beginning of the accounting year and remains constant for the period. All of the companies divide their accounting year into thirteen equal periods. The following relates to the activities of one of the subsidiary companies for period five. From this information you are required to prepare a report for the holding company commenting on the variances in fixed overhead expenses which have arisen and analysing such variances as you think necessary.

The budget of subsidiary company A shows that budgeted fixed overheads for the year are £26,000 and that during this period the estimated production is 1,040,000 units, production to be carried on evenly throughout the year. This production will require 130,000 hours to complete. During period five actual expenditure on fixed overheads was £2,500, bringing the total to date to £9,975 and actual output was 88,000 units, for which the time taken was 9,000 hours.

(A.C.C.A. Final)

24. You are employed in a seasonal trade, where the volume of sales has been declining in recent years. This decline has been met by increased advertising on television, in journals, and the national press and by increased expenditure on presentation and packaging of the domestic consumer products.

The advertising expenditure is planned to occur in those periods immediately before seasonal events such as Christmas, Easter and Whitsuntide, whereas the presentation and packaging expenditure is more or less directly variable with sales at all times.

State how you would propose to exercise control over these costs, and how you would absorb them in periodic accounts.

(I.C.W.A. Final)

25. What difficulties would you expect to find in the compilation of a flexible budget? Give sufficient detail to justify any assumptions you make. How would such a budget be used?

(I.C.W.A. Final)

26. What is meant in a system of flexible budgeting by:

    (a) budget overhead allowance;
    (b) overhead incurred;
    (c) absorbed overhead?

How are these costs related?

                                            (*I.C.W.A. Inter.*)

27. What is a flexible budget?
Prepare a table showing in detail the relative variances arising out of the following:

	Standard	Actual
Output (units)	12,000	13,500
Overhead	£1,600	£1,750

Standard overhead for output of 13,500 units: £1,700.

                                            (*A.C.C.A. Final*)

28. In order to meet increased orders, a manufacturing company proposes for the whole of the next year to undertake half-shift working from 6 p.m. to 10 p.m. for five days a week by additional labour. The company's labour force works a 40-hour week for fifty weeks per year and at present comprises 200 direct workers in shop X at an average wage rate of £0·6 per hour and 100 direct workers in shop Y at an average wage rate of £0·37½ per hour.

The additional workers will need to be paid one-third above the normal average wage rate for the shop. There will be 50 additional direct workers in shop X and 25 additional direct workers in shop Y. The budgeted overhead for the year, excluding any shift work, and the expected changes in that overhead resulting from shift work, are as follows:

	Before shift work		After shift work	
	Shop X £	Shop Y £	Shop X	Shop Y
Indirect wages	30,000	20,000	plus 20%	plus 15%
Works weekly salaries	9,000	14,000	„ £3,175	„ £3,250
Works monthly salaries	21,000	12,500	„ £1,000	„ £1,000
Repairs to plant	7,500	1,500	„ 20%	„ 10%
General expenses	3,000	1,500	„ 15%	„ 15%
Light and heat	2,400	1,800	proportionate to increased direct labour hours	
Consumable stores	1,800	600		
Indirect materials	6,000	1,800		
Power	4,800	1,800		
Other overhead items (not affected by shift work)	34,500	16,500		
	£120,000	£72,000		

You are required to:

(a) calculate the budgeted direct labour hour rates of overhead for shop X and shop Y if no shift work is undertaken;

(b) prepare a budgeted statement of the overhead costs for shop X and shop Y if shift working is undertaken as planned;

(c) calculate the budgeted direct labour hour rates of overhead for shop X and shop Y resulting from the statement prepared in answer to (b) above.

(*I.C.W.A. Inter.*)

29. The costing budget of a department for a year of normal activity of 50,000 hours is as follows:

	£
Fixed expenses	21,600
Variable expenses	12,000
	£33,600

During the first three months of the year for which the budget was prepared the expenses and activities of the business are as follows:

	Activities (hours)	Fixed expenses £	Variable expenses £
January	2,000	1,570	750
February	4,000	1,865	875
March	5,000	2,060	1,000

Show the variations in percentage form for each month as against the original budget, and prepare an amended budget for the remaining nine months to bring the year's figures to the original estimates.

(*C.A.A. Final*)

30. Explain the control of expense in relation to output by the method of flexible budgeting.

(*C.A.A. Final*)

31. Production costs of a factory for a year are as follows:

	£	£
Direct wages		80,000
Direct materials		60,000
Production overheads—fixed	20,000	
variable	30,000	
		50,000

During the forthcoming year it is anticipated that:

(a) the average rate for direct labour will fall from £0·66½ per hour to £0·62½ per hour;

(b) production efficiency will be unchanged;

(c) direct labour hours will increase by 33⅓%; and

(d) the purchase price per unit of direct materials, and of the other materials and services included among overheads will remain unchanged.

Draw up a budget and compute a factory overhead rate, the overheads being absorbed on a direct wages basis.

(*C.A.A. Final*)

32. The budget of a large manufacturing company shows that for the following twelve months fixed overheads are estimated at £10,000. The production budget indicates that during this period 200,000 units will be produced, for which variable overheads will be £30,000. Each unit of production requires two machine hours, and these figures have been used to calculate a predetermined overhead (absorption) rate per machine hour which is applied to each unit of output. To indicate the possible effects of any under- or over-absorption of cost you are requested to prepare a graph on which is plotted the total budget overhead cost line for output levels in machine hours from 0 to 600,000. On the same graph, and for the same range of output levels, plot the line of absorbed cost based on the predetermined rate calculated from the above. From the graph read the over- or under-absorption of overheads for the following levels of output:

180,000 machine hours
300,000 ,, ,,
370,000 ,, ,,
400,000 ,, ,,
450,000 ,, ,,
600,000 ,, ,,

(*A.C.C.A. Final*)

33. The flexible budget for a service department of an engineering company for a four-week period is as follows:

At normal capacity

Budgeted hours of service: 3,200

Budgeted costs:	Variable £	Fixed £	NOTES
Wages	1,600		
Holiday and sick pay	80	70	
Indirect wages		75	Above normal capacity add £5 after each additional 200 hours.
Supervision		250	Above 3,500 hours increase to £260.
Consumable supplies	20		
Repairs	50	50	
Depreciation and insurance of machinery and equipment		300	
Heat and light	5	20	
Rent and rates		40	
General factory expense and supervision		320	
Total	£1,755	£1,125	

The hours recorded and the expenditure incurred during the four weeks ended October 29 were:

Actual hours worked: 3,840

Actual costs:	£
Wages	1,902
Holiday and sick pay	154
Indirect wages	95
Supervision	258
Consumable supplies	20
Repairs	105
Depreciation and insurance of machinery and equipment	300
Heat and light	26
Rent and rates	40
General factory expense and supervision	320
Total	£3,220

You are required to:

(a) calculate:

(i) the overhead rate per hour of service that would need to be used for absorption of the budgeted costs of the department;

(ii) the over- or under-absorption in the four weeks ended October 29;

(b) tabulate the variances from budget for each item of expenditure which is controllable by the departmental supervision.

(*I.C.W.A. Inter.*)

34. Describe the two basic methods whereby the cash position of a firm at a given future date may be forecast.

(*C.A.A. Final*)

CHAPTER 25

STANDARD COSTING

Introduction; Simple Variances

STANDARD costs are pre-determined, or forecast estimates of cost to manufacture a single unit, or a number of units of a product, during a specific immediate future period. They are used as a measure with which the actual cost, as ascertained, may be compared. Standard costs are usually the planned costs of the product under current and anticipated conditions, but sometimes they are the costs under normal or ideal conditions of efficiency, based upon an assumed given output, and having regard to current conditions. They are revised to conform to super-normal or sub-normal conditions, but more practically to allow for persisting alterations in the prices of material and labour.

Standard costing is a method of ascertaining the costs whereby statistics are prepared to show:

(a) the standard cost;
(b) the actual cost; and
(c) the difference between these costs, which is termed the *variance*.

The utility of standard costs has been widely recognised in recent years, particularly in the U.S.A., and to a considerable extent in Great Britain. In the principal factories in Britain producing on a large scale, as, for example, in the textile industry, electrical and other engineering, biscuit-making and chemical industries, standard costs are in use, and there is every indication that standard costing will be used to a very large extent in future.

Much depends upon the arrangement of the records as to whether a standard costing system entails additional clerical work. In some instances it has resulted in less work. In a certain American factory making a standard product, cost variances only are recorded. It may be said that, even if the procedure does involve additional clerical work, the close control effected enables considerable saving to be made in production costs.

ADVANTAGES

The chief advantages secured may be summarised as follows:

(a) Actual performance is readily comparable with the pre-determined standards, showing separately favourable or adverse variances.

(b) The variances can be analysed in detail, enabling the management to investigate the cause. Any inefficiencies of labour, of the use of materials and of the operation of machines, for example, will be discovered.

(c) The principle of "management by exception" can be applied. Managements do not spend time and effort searching through unnecessary information, but can concentrate their attention on important matters.

(d) Gains or losses due to market fluctuations in prices of raw materials, as distinct from variations due to manufacturing conversion, are revealed.

(e) The effects on costs of variations in the price and use of materials, the ratio of labour wages, the volume of production and altered expenses are demonstrated at short intervals.

This information enables the management to see whether shops or processes are being worked economically, and are producing a satisfactory output. It further serves as a guide as to whether prices can be adjusted to meet competition. In periods of trade depression the records show at what price work may be undertaken to secure trade sufficient to cover overheads; this is discussed in more detail in the chapter on marginal costing.

LEVEL OF ATTAINMENT

When setting standard costs it is obviously necessary to determine at which level of attainment the firm should aim. There are three levels normally considered:

(a) *That which past performances suggest is capable of attainment.* This level may be considered satisfactory in that the standard achievement should be easily attained, but may lead management into complacency.

(b) *That which would necessitate maximum possible efficiency.* This level is rather unrealistic and will almost invariably reflect adverse variances due to the high standard demanded. These variances may stimulate management to greater effort, but frequently may have the effect of discouraging staff.

(c) *That which is possible by efficient working and management.* This level is usually the most satisfactory as it is realistic. Any adverse variances reflected will point the way to possible economies. Management will feel that with a reasonable amount of effort the standards should be achieved.

These levels of attainment may be better understood by means of an illustration:

EXAMPLE

In Process Department No. 1 of the G.B. Manufacturing Co. Ltd. the output for last year was 50,000 units. This year it is considered that if the department is operated at maximum possible efficiency the output could be 60,000 units; this estimate does not allow for such possible occurrences as plant breakdowns, power failures, shortage of material, etc. It is considered that under existing conditions an output of 52,000 units might be achieved, but if better planning were introduced an output of 55,000 units could be produced. Which level of attainment should be adopted as the standard?

Level (a) above was said to suffer from the disadvantage of leading management into complacency, while (b) above suffered from being unrealistic. However, (c) was said to be usually the most satisfactory. Thus in this illustration it would be considered that an output of 55,000 units should be the standard output.

The budgetary control of sales, production and finance is almost a necessity for the most advantageous and successful use of a standard costing system. For budgetary control all factors affecting production and cost are pre-determined as closely as possible. Sales quotas are determined in consultation with the sales manager and the selling staff. The cost of financing is carefully considered. The volume of production and its planning are fixed. From the budget so prepared, the standard cost of each product is calculated.

In the setting up of these standards, consideration is given to statistics of production costs in the preceding periods, but total reliance on these is inadvisable, it being more satisfactory to have regard to the tendency of prices of materials and labour and to the prospects of the immediate future. It will be apparent that marketing conditions, financing methods, selling methods, purchasing power, mechanical equipment, production possibilities and labour conditions all have an influence on standards and for determining standard costs they must be taken into consideration.

The determination of standards is a long and difficult task, and, consequently, it is not usual to vary the standards unduly. By the use of cost ratios, or efficiency percentages, such a course may be rendered unnecessary. It is convenient, however, to alter the standards if labour costs or prices of materials are definitely changed for the future.

REVISION VARIANCE

The *Terminology of Cost Accountancy* defines revision variances as

"the variance between the basic standard cost and the revised standard cost."

After standards are set, circumstances may change which could not have been envisaged. If the changes are of a temporary or a minor nature, then rather than revise standards, it is possible to create a revision variance. Any changes in cost will be posted to a Revision Variance Account, so that management can be informed of the extent of the change in cost.

In the next chapter mix variances will be illustrated; these may be a form of revision variance. It is sometimes necessary to change the mix of a product for a short period, in which case the standard may be "revised" by means of a revision variance—which is regarded as a mix variance.

THE STANDARD HOUR

Production is frequently expressed in terms of units, pounds, gallons, etc. This may be satisfactory in many cases, but as will be appreciated, it may be inconvenient when considering different types of products, especially when the products are measured in different units, for example, gases and liquids.

In standard costing systems production can be expressed in terms of a measure common to all products—this measure is termed the "standard hour."

The "standard hour" is the quantity of output or amount of work which should be performed in one hour. For example, if 100 units of product X can be produced in 10 hours, and 60 units of product Y can be produced in 12 hours, a standard hour represents 10 units of X and 5 units of Y. Thus an output of 600X and 300Y would represent 120 standard hours.

By using the standard hour it is not difficult to calculate the production for a period. Thus if there are 1,050 hours in a budget period, and it is desired to produce an equal number of product X and product Y, the production expected would be:

Product X—1 standard hour represents 10 units.
Product Y—1 standard hour represents 5 units.
Therefore Y takes twice as much time to manufacture as X.
Therefore $\frac{2}{3}$ of the period will be devoted to Y and
$\frac{1}{3}$ of the period will be devoted to X.
700 hours represents 3,500 units of Y.
350 hours represents 3,500 units of X.
The output is thus 3,500 units of both products.

EXAMPLE

A company manufacturing food products markets three brands: "Exe" jam, "Wye" marmalade and "Zed" lemon curd. It is estimated that 2,000 jars of jam, 6,000 jars of marmalade and 4,000 jars of curd could be filled in 1

hour. The output for the month of February was 300,000 units of "Exe,"
1,000,000 units "Wye" and 600,000 units "Zed."

Production could be measured in terms of standard hours as follows:

Actual production

February

Product	Production	Standard units per hour	Production in standard hours
"Exe" jam	300,000	2,000	150
"Wye" marmalade	1,000,000	6,000	166⅔
"Zed" curd	600,000	4,000	150
			466⅔

EFFICIENCY RATIO

The I.C.W.A. *Terminology of Cost Accountancy* defines efficiency
ratio as:

"the standard hours equivalent to the work produced, expressed
as a percentage of the actual hours spent in producing that work."

This can be expressed:

$$\frac{\text{Actual production in terms of standard hours}}{\text{Actual hours worked}} \times 100.$$

This ratio measures the efficiency with which the firm is operating.

EXAMPLE

A company manufactures office chairs and desks. It is estimated that 1
chair can be made in 2 hours and 1 desk in 10 hours. In March the actual
production is 100 chairs and 24 desks. Actual hours worked were 320.
Actual production in terms of standard hours is therefore:

Chairs: 100 units at 2 hours per unit   200
Desks: 24 units at 10 hours per unit   240

——
440

The efficiency ratio is: $\frac{440}{320} \times 100 = 137 \cdot 5\%$.

ACTIVITY RATIO

The *Terminology of Cost Accountancy* gives the activity ratio as:

"the number of standard hours equivalent to the work produced,
expressed as a percentage of the budgeted standard hours."

This can be expressed:

$$\frac{\text{Actual production in terms of standard hours}}{\text{Budgeted production in terms of standard hours}} \times 100.$$

This ratio measures the level of activity at which the firm is operating.

EXAMPLE

Continuing the illustration above and assuming the budgeted production for the month to be 125 chairs and 20 desks one can now calculate the activity ratio.

Budgeted production in terms of standard hours is:

Chairs: 125 units at 2 hours per unit	250
Desks: 20 units at 10 hours per unit	200
	450

The activity ratio is: $\frac{440}{450} \times 100 = 97 \cdot 8\%$.

ACTUAL USAGE OF BUDGETED CAPACITY RATIO

The *Terminology* expresses this ratio as:

"the relationship between the actual number of working hours and the budgeted number."

In the example above we have:

$$\frac{320}{450} \times 100 = 71\%.$$

We can check our results thus:

$$\frac{\text{Activity ratio}}{\text{Capacity ratio}} = \text{Efficiency ratio}$$

$$\frac{0 \cdot 978}{0 \cdot 710} \times 100 = 137 \cdot 5\%.$$

THE ESTABLISHMENT OF STANDARD COSTS

Standards of performance, usage of material, quantity of production and cost rates must be established. Usually the cost accountant will be responsible for setting the standard, but he must work in very close co-operation with time-and-motion-study engineers, production engineers, buyers and other personnel.

Standard costs must be ascertained for each of the following elements of cost:

1. Direct material.
2. Direct labour.
3. Variable overhead.
4. Fixed overhead.

1. DIRECT MATERIAL

(a) Standard quantities of material should be set for each product. It is thus necessary to establish a standard drawing, formula or specification, which should be adhered to except in special circumstances, when a revision may be necessary.

(b) If there is a normal loss in process, a standard loss should be set based on past experience or by scientific analysis.

(c) Standard prices of all materials consumed should be set for each product. Prices should be fixed in co-operation with the buyer, and allowing for the following:

(i) Stocks in hand.
(ii) The possibility of price fluctuations.
(iii) The extent of contracts already placed for materials.

2. DIRECT LABOUR

(a) The different grades of labour required in the production of various products should be ascertained. It should be then possible to establish the labour cost by evaluating the grades of labour at the standard rates per hour set by the personnel department. These are more often than not nationally agreed rates.

(b) Standards of performance should be set in conjunction with the work-study engineers. Thus the number of units produced per hour at the number of hours required per unit can be established.

3. VARIABLE OVERHEAD

It is assumed that variable overheads move in sympathy with production; therefore it is necessary to consider only the cost per unit or cost per hour. Irrespective of production, the variable overheads per unit or per hour will remain the same. Thus if packing costs are £0·02½ per unit of production, then the variable overhead cost of 1,000 units will be £25 and of 10,000 units, £250. This is obviously only true within limits.

4. FIXED OVERHEAD

Fixed overhead relates to all items of expenditure which are more or less constant irrespective of fluctuations in the level of output, within reasonable limits. The following points must be considered:

(a) The total cost of fixed overheads for the period.
(b) The budgeted production for the period.
(c) The number of hours expected to be worked during the period.

It should now be possible to estimate the standard fixed overhead cost for each product manufactured. A standard cost per unit can now be prepared, an example of which is as follows:

Standard cost of Product A

		£	£
1 *unit*			
Direct material:	60 lb of "Exe" at £0·25 per lb	15	
	40 lb of "Wye" at £0·30 per lb	12	
100		27	
10	Normal loss 10%		
90 lb		27	
	Scrap value	1	
			26
Direct labour:	Process 1—2 hours at £0·5 per hour	1	
	Process 2—5 hours at £0·4 per hour	2	
	Process 3—2 hours at £0·5 per hour	1	
			4
Variable overhead:	Process 1—£2 per unit	2	
	Process 2—£2·5 per unit	2·5	
	Process 3—£1·5 per unit	1·5	
			6
Fixed overhead:	Production 50% of labour cost	2	
	Administration 25% of labour cost	1	
	Selling and distribution 25% of labour cost	1	
			4
	TOTAL		40
Profit			10
	Selling price		£50

If during a period 10,000 units of Product A are manufactured and sold, and the actual costs are ascertained as below, the standard costs and actual costs could be compared as follows:

Total variances

Product A   Period

Element of cost	Standard	Actual	Variances	
			Favourable	Adverse
	£	£	£	£
Direct material	260,000	280,000		20,000
Direct labour	40,000	36,000	4,000	
PRIME COST	300,000	316,000	4,000	20,000
Variable overhead	60,000	55,000	5,000	
Fixed overhead	40,000	41,000		1,000
TOTAL COST	400,000	412,000	9,000	21,000
Profit	100,000	108,000	(8,000)	
Sales variance			20,000	
SALES	£500,000	£520,000	£21,000	£21,000

The above illustration demonstrates the main advantage of a standard costing system: management are given clear information to enable them to decide on future policy. It can be clearly seen that the total cost of Product A during the period was £12,000 more than the standard set. The adverse variance of £20,000 on direct material should be closely investigated. Despite adverse costs, profit is £8,000 higher than anticipated, due to selling prices exceeding those budgeted.

VARIANCES

The variances illustrated above show only the main variances. However, there are many other variances which can be calculated and which show why costs differed from the standards set. Thus, for instance, a material price variance would denote that a variance was caused as a result of differences in prices rather than as a result of inefficient use of material; similarly a labour efficiency variance would reveal a difference due to the efficiency or inefficiency of labour, not due to rates of pay being above or below the standard set. It is therefore easy to ascertain who is responsible for any cost variances from standard, so that the necessary action can be taken.

There are many variances used in practice, some of them particular to a certain industry, e.g. flight-time variance in the air-transport trade, but there are a number of variances common to many industries, and these are explained and illustrated below:

1. DIRECT MATERIALS

(a) *Direct materials cost variance.* The difference between the standard cost of direct materials specified for the output achieved and the actual cost of direct materials used.

(b) *Direct materials price variance.* That portion of the direct materials cost variance which is due to the difference between the standard price specified and the actual price paid.

(c) *Direct materials usage variance.* That portion of the direct materials cost variance which is due to the difference between the standard quantity specified and the actual quantity used.

(d) *Direct materials mixture variance.* That portion of the direct materials usage variance which is due to the difference between the standard and actual composition of a mixture. (Applicable only when direct materials are physically mixed.)

(e) *Direct materials yield variance.* That portion of the direct materials usage variance which is due to the difference between the standard yield specified and the actual yield obtained.

2. DIRECT LABOUR

(a) *Direct wages variance.* The difference between the standard direct wages specified for the activity achieved and the actual direct wages paid.

(b) *Direct wages rate variance.* That portion of the direct wages variance which is due to the difference between the standard rate of pay specified and the actual rate paid.

(c) *Direct labour efficiency variance.* That portion of the direct wages variance which is due to the difference between the standard labour hours specified for the activity achieved and the actual labour hours expended.

NOTE: Where efficiency is measured by a line speed or cost centre output, as distinct from the output of an individual worker, it may be possible to sub-analyse this variance between efficiency and amount of direct labour usage.

3. OVERHEAD

(a) *Overhead variance.* The difference between the standard cost of overhead absorbed in the output achieved and the actual overhead cost.

(b) *Volume variance.* That portion of the overhead variance which is the difference between the standard cost of overhead absorbed in actual output and the standard allowance for that output. (This represents the over- or under-absorption of fixed costs in the period concerned.)

(c) *Seasonal variance.* That portion of the volume variance which is due to the difference between the seasonally budgeted output and the average output on which standards have been calculated. (The sum of the seasonal variations over a complete year would be zero.)

(d) *Calendar variance.* That portion of the volume variance which is due to the difference between the number of working days in the budget period and the number of working days in the period to which the budget is applied. (The sum of the calendar variances in a complete year would be zero.)

NOTE: This variance arises from the convention that fixed costs are the same for each period, whatever the number of working days, and it can be eliminated by apportioning standard allowances and actual fixed costs on a working day basis.

(e) *Capacity usage variance.* That portion of the volume variance which is due to working at higher or lower capacity usage than standard.

(f) *Volume efficiency variance.* That portion of the volume variance which reflects the increased or reduced output arising from efficiency above or below the standard which is expected.

(g) *Overhead expenditure variance.* That portion of the overhead variance which represents the difference between the standard allowance for the output achieved and the actual expenditure incurred.

(h) *Overhead price variance.* That portion of the overhead expenditure variance which is due to the difference between the standard price of the service specified and the actual price paid.

(i) *Overhead efficiency variance.* That portion of the overhead expenditure variance which is the difference between the standard allowance for the activity (standard hours achieved) and the standard allowance for the actual hours worked.

NOTE: This variance only arises on costs which vary with time taken rather than with volume of output.

(j) *Overhead utilisation variance.* That portion of the overhead expenditure variance which is due to the difference between the standard quantity of the service specified and the actual quantity of the service used.

4. SALES VARIANCE

The difference between budgeted value of sales and the actual value of sales achieved in a given period.

NOTE: Sales variance can be analysed in many ways to suit a particular business, *e.g.* to isolate the effects of price changes, discounts and allowances from the effect of differing quantities of sales. A distinction is sometimes drawn between quantity and mixture variances. A mixture variance which is based on sales values only may be misleading because the effect of selling a different product mix than was budgeted is not only the difference in sales values but also the difference in standard cost of the mixture. In other words it is a difference in sales margins. The following definitions of sales margin variances are offered in preference to simple sales variances.

(a) *Total sales margin variance*. The difference between the standard margin appropriate to the quantity of sales budgeted for a period and the margin between standard cost and the actual selling price of the sales effected.

(b) *Sales margin variance due to selling prices*. That portion of total margin variance which is due to the difference between the standard price of the quantity of sales effected and the actual price of those sales.

(c) *Sales margin variance due to sales allowances*. That portion of total margin variance which is due to the difference between the budgeted rebates, discounts, etc., on the sales effected and the actual rebates, discounts, etc., allowed on those sales.

(d) *Sales margin variance due to sales quantities (mixture)*. That portion of total margin variance which is due to the difference between the budgeted and actual quantities of each product of which the sales mixture is composed, valuing sales at the standard net selling prices and cost of sales at standard.

THE COST ACCOUNTS

There are a number of ways of recording standard costs in the accounts, but it is proposed to mention only one method in this chapter, *viz.*, all expenses incurred are charged at actual to the accounts concerned, but are recovered in the Work-in-progress Account at standard; work completed is then transferred to Finished Goods Account at standard cost. This has the effect of maintaining the Work-in-progress Account at standard cost, so that any balance of the account at the end of a period will inevitably be valued at standard cost. Finished goods at the end of a period will be similarly valued. Consequently if market prices fall so the standard cost is greater than the actual cost it will be necessary to revalue the stocks so as to conform to the "lowest of cost, net realisable value or replacement price" principle.

DEFINITIONS

At this point it is important to define six of the terms to be used in chapter.

(a) *Actual production (APn)*. The actual quantity produced during the actual hours worked.

(b) *Budgeted production (BPn)*. The budgeted quantity to be produced during the budgeted hours to be worked.

(c) *Standard production* (*SPn*). The quantity which should have been produced during the actual hours worked.

(d) *Actual cost* (*AC*). The actual quantity produced at the actual cost per unit.

(e) *Budgeted cost* (*BC*). The budgeted quantity to be produced at the standard cost per unit.

(f) *Standard cost* (*SC*). The actual quantity produced at the standard cost per unit.

For the convenience of the student the above abbreviations are repeated in tabular form, together with others used in this and the following two chapters.

AC	= Actual cost	BFO	= Budgeted fixed overhead	SC	= Standard cost
ADP	= Actual discounted price	BH	= Budgeted hours	SDP	= Standard discounted price
AFO	= Actual fixed overhead	BP	= Budgeted price	SH	= Standard hours
		BPn	= Budgeted production	SM	= Standard mix
AH	= Actual hours			SP	= Standard price
AM	= Actual mix	BPt	= Budgeted profit	SPn	= Standard production
AP	= Actual price	BQ	= Budgeted quantity		
APn	= Actual production			SPt	= Standard profit
		BS	= Budgeted sales	SQ	= Standard quantity
APt	= Actual profit	PH	= Possible hours		
AQ	= Actual quantity	RBQ	= Revised budgeted quantity	SR	= Standard rate
AR	= Actual rate			SS	= Standard sales
AS	= Actual sales	RSP	= Revised standard profit	ST	= Standard time
AVO	= Actual variable overhead	RSS	= Revised standard sales	SVO	= Standard variable overhead
AY	= Actual yield			SY	= Standard yield
BC	= Budgeted cost				

VARIANCE ANALYSIS

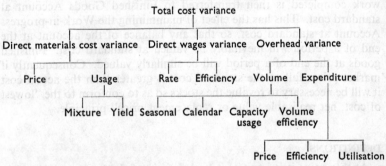

Methods and revision variances can arise under materials, wages or overhead and should normally be isolated before other variances are calculated.

EXAMPLE 1. DIRECT MATERIAL VARIANCES

In an engineering factory one product, Marvid, is manufactured. From every ton of raw material consumed it is estimated that 200 articles will be produced. £120 per ton is to be taken as the standard price of the material. 50 tons of material were issued to production during February. The actual price of the material was £118·50 per ton. Production during the month was 10,100 articles.

(a) Direct Materials Price Variance

	£
Standard price of materials used: 50 tons at £120	6,000
Actual price of materials used: 50 tons at £118·50	5,925
Variance	£75 (F)

$Formula$ = Actual quantity (Actual price — Standard price)
          = AQ (AP — SP)
          = 50 (£118·50 — £120)   =   £75 (F)

NOTES: Quantity relates to quantity of materials used.
       (F) means a favourable variance; (A) means an adverse variance.

Accounting entries

	£	£
Dr. Work in progress	6,000	
Cr. Direct material price variance		75
Stores Ledger control		5,925

It should be observed that work in progress is shown at standard cost.

(b) Direct Materials Usage Variance

In (a) above the variance due to changes in price was eliminated so that in calculating the usage variance only the standard price of materials need be considered.

From every ton of material consumed it is estimated that 200 articles will be produced, therefore as 50 tons of materials were used, 10,000 articles should have been produced.

	£
Standard price of standard quantity: 10,000 at £0·60	6,000
Standard price of actual quantity: 10,100 at £0·60	6,060
	£60 (F)

$Formula$ = Standard price (Actual quantity — Standard quantity)
          = SP (AQ — SQ)
          = 120 (50 — 50½)   =   £60 (F)

NOTES: $SQ = \dfrac{\text{Actual output}}{\text{Standard output per ton}} = \dfrac{10,100}{200}$.

Actual quantity used was less than standard, so a favourable variance results.

Accounting entries

		£	£
Dr.	Work in progress	60	
Cr.	Direct material usage variance		60
Dr.	Finished Goods Ledger	6,060	
Cr.	Work-in-progress Ledger		6,060

It should be observed that as usage variance is favourable it is credited to the Variance Accounts while Work-in-progress Account is debited so as to bring the amount up to standard cost of actual production.

Check 1

(*i*) Finished goods = standard cost of actual production
$$= 10,100 \text{ at } £0·60 \qquad\qquad = £6,060$$

(*ii*) Entries in Finished Goods Ledger (above) = £6,060

Check 2

(*i*) Direct material cost variance = SC − AC
$$= £6,060 - £5,925 \qquad = £135 \text{ (F)}$$

(*ii*) Direct material cost variance = Price variance
$$\qquad\qquad\qquad\qquad\qquad + \text{ Usage variance}$$
$$= £75 \text{ F} + £60 \text{ F} \qquad = £135 \text{ (F)}$$

EXAMPLE 2. DIRECT WAGES VARIANCES

In the manufacture of the product, 200 employees are engaged at a rate of £0·60 per hour. A 42-hour working week is in operation and there are 4 weeks in February. The standard performance is set at 60 articles per hour. During February 182 employees were paid at the standard rate of £0·60 per hour, but 10 employees were paid at £0·62½ per hour, while 8 employees were paid at £0·57½ per hour. The factory stopped production for 2 hours due to a power failure.

(a) Direct Wages Rate Variance

Standard cost of hours worked:

	£	£
200 employees × 42 hours × 4 weeks × £0·60 per hour		20,160·00
Actual cost of hours worked:		
182 employees × 42 hours × 4 weeks × £0·60 per hour	18,345·60	
10 employees × 42 hours × 4 weeks × £0·62½ per hour	1,050·00	
8 employees × 42 hours × 4 weeks × £0·57½ per hour	772·80	20,168·40
		£8·40 (A)

Formula = Actual hours (Actual rate − Standard rate)
= AH (AR − SR)

$$= \begin{cases} 1{,}680\ (£0{\cdot}62\tfrac{1}{2} - £0{\cdot}60) & £ \\ 1{,}344\ (£0{\cdot}57\tfrac{1}{2} - £0{\cdot}60) \end{cases} \quad \begin{matrix} 42{\cdot}00\ (A) \\ 33{\cdot}60\ (F) \end{matrix} = \underline{\underline{£8{\cdot}40\ (A)}}$$

NOTE: A rate variance can only occur where actual rate differs from standard, so only those hours worked at non-standard rates are considered, *e.g.* 10 employees × 42 hours × 4 weeks = 1,680 hours at £0·62½.

(b) Direct Labour Efficiency Variance

Standard labour cost of 1 article:

$$\frac{\text{Employees}}{\text{Articles per hour}} \times \text{Rate per hour}$$

$$= \frac{200}{60} \times £0{\cdot}60 = £2{\cdot}00.$$

		£
Standard cost of production = Actual quantity × Standard cost per unit = 10,100 × £2·00		20,200
Actual hours worked at standard rate = 200 employees × 166 hours × £0·60		19,920
		£280 (F)

NOTE: The standard rate per hour must be used because the actual rate was eliminated in the rate variance. Idle time amounting to 2 hours is considered in the next variance.

Formula = Standard rate (Actual hours − Standard hours)
= SR (AH − SH)
= £0·60 (33,200 − 33,666·66) = £280 (F)

NOTES: Actual hours = 200 employees × 166 hours worked.

$$\text{Standard hours} = \text{Number of men} \times \frac{\text{Quantity produced}}{\text{Standard quantity per hour}}$$

$$= 200 \times \frac{10{,}100}{60}.$$

(c) Direct Labour Idle-time Variance

Cost = Hours idle × Standard hourly rate
= 200 employees × 2 hours × £0·60 per hour = £240 (A)

Accounting entries

	£	£
Dr. Work in progress	20,160·00	
Direct wages rate variance	8·40	
Cr. Wages		20,168·40
Dr. Direct labour idle-time variance	240·00	
Finished goods	20,200·00	
Cr. Direct labour efficiency variance		280·00
Work in progress		20,160·00

Check 1

    (*i*) Finished goods = Standard cost of actual production
                  = 10,100 articles × £2·00 per unit   = £20,200

    (*ii*) Entries in Finished Goods Ledger (above)   £20,200

Check 2

    (*i*) Direct wages variance = SC − AC
                         = £20,200 − £20,168·40   = £31·60 (F)

    (*ii*) Direct wages variance =

$$\frac{\text{Rate}}{\text{variance}} + \frac{\text{Efficiency}}{\text{variance}} + \frac{\text{Idle-time}}{\text{variance}}$$

         = £8·40 A + £280·00 F + £240·00 A = £31·60 (F)

EXAMPLE 3. OVERHEAD EXPENDITURE VARIANCE

This arises from two sources, *viz.*:

    (*a*) variable overhead;
    (*b*) fixed overhead.

It is convenient to consider these separately.

(*a*) Variable Overhead Variance

The term "variable overhead" implies that this element of cost varies directly with production. It is therefore relatively easy to calculate the standard variable overhead, per article produced. Thus, *e.g.* if budgeted output is 2,000 articles and the budgeted variable overheads are £1,000, the rate per article will be £0·50. If 3,000 articles are actually produced the variable overheads incurred will be 3,000 × £0·50 = £1,500. Irrespective of the number of articles produced or the time taken to produce them, the variable overhead cost per unit will not change. If the actual variable overhead is different from the standard rate per unit this will be due to an expenditure variance.

The budgeted variable overhead for the month was £5,000. Budgeted production for the month was 10,000 articles. Actual variable overheads incurred were £5,000. Actual production was 10,100 articles.

Expenditure variance

Standard variable overhead (SVO) per unit is $\dfrac{£5,000}{10,000} = £0·50$

Standard variable overhead 10,100 × £0·50   = 5,050
Actual variable overhead (AVO)   = 5,000

                                              £50 (F)

Formula = SVO − AVO
          = £5,050 − £5,000   = £50 (F)

Accounting entries

	£	£	£
Dr. Work in progress	5,050		
Cr. Variable overhead expenditure variance		50	
Variable overhead		5,000	
Dr. Finished Goods Ledger	5,050		
Cr. Work in progress		5,050	

Check

(*i*) Finished goods = SC of APn
    = 10,100 articles at £0·50   = £5,050

(*ii*) Entries in Finished Goods Account (above)   = £5,050

The *Terminology* suggests that the expenditure variance may be sub-divided into:

(*a*) price;
(*b*) efficiency;
(*c*) utilisation;

whether for variable or fixed overhead. For the moment we will not complicate the example by bringing in these subsidiary variances, but the matter will be referred to again under fixed overhead.

(*b*) Fixed Overhead Variances

Of all the variances considered in this illustration, the fixed overhead variances are the most difficult. The term "fixed overhead" implies that this element of cost does not vary directly with production. In Chapter 11 the recovery of overheads was discussed, from a study of which the student should realise that recovery depends on two factors, *viz.*, production of articles and expenses incurred. It therefore follows that fixed overhead variances occur due to these two factors which are now classified as volume variance and expenditure variance. These variances may be divided into sub-variances which are discussed later.

There are a number of reasons why the volume of production in a factory may be above or below that budgeted; *e.g.* fewer hours worked than expected, inefficient utilisation of machinery. All the variances mentioned above will be calculated in this illustration.

The production budget is 126,000 articles per year. £50,400 was budgeted for fixed overheads for the year. During February the amount of overheads actually incurred was £4,200.

There are 50 working weeks in the year, of which 4 are in February. The production standard was 60 articles per hour. Actual production during February was 10,100 articles. 2 hours were lost due to idle time.

The budgeted fixed overheads (BFO) for the month of February amount to £4,032. This is calculated:

$$\frac{\text{BFO} \times \text{Weeks in month}}{\text{Weeks in year}} = \frac{£50,400}{50} \times 4.$$

or

$$\frac{\text{BFO} \times \text{Budgeted production for month}}{\text{Budgeted production for year}} = \frac{£50,040 \times 10,080}{126,000}.$$

$$\text{Budgeted cost per unit} = \frac{\text{Budgeted cost}}{\text{Budgeted production}} = \frac{£4,032}{10,080} = £0·40$$

The standard fixed overheads for the month:

Actual production at standard cost per unit = 10,100 at £0·40 = £4,040.

(i) Expenditure variance

This variance is in effect a price variance, rather similar to the material price variance, labour rate variance and variable overhead expenditure variance.

$$\begin{array}{ll}
& £ \\
\text{Budgeted fixed overhead} = & 4,032 \\
\text{Actual fixed overhead} = & 4,200 \\
\hline
& = £168 \text{ (A)}
\end{array}$$

$$\begin{aligned}
Formula &= \text{BFO} - \text{AFO} \\
&= £4,032 - £4,200 \qquad\qquad = £168 \text{ (A)}
\end{aligned}$$

Accounting entries

	£	£
Dr. Expenditure variance	168	
Dr. Work in progress	4,032	
Cr. Fixed Overhead Account		4,200

(ii) Volume variance

$$\begin{aligned}
Formula &= \text{Standard cost (Actual quantity} - \text{Budgeted quantity)} \\
&= \text{SC (AQ} - \text{BQ)} \\
&= £0·40 (10,100 - 10,080) \qquad\qquad = £8 \text{ (F)}
\end{aligned}$$

More output was achieved than budgeted, therefore £8 would be over-recovered.

(iii) Volume efficiency variance

$$\begin{aligned}
Formula &= \text{Standard cost (Actual quantity} - \text{Standard quantity)} \\
&= \text{SC (AQ} - \text{SQ)} \\
&= £0·40 (10,100 - 9,960) \qquad\qquad = £56 \text{ (F)}
\end{aligned}$$

NOTE: The standard quantity produced is calculated:

$$\begin{aligned}
& \text{Hours worked} \times \text{Articles produced per hour (standard)} \\
= \quad & \quad 166 \qquad \times \qquad 60 \qquad\qquad = 9,960
\end{aligned}$$

9,960 articles should have been produced in the time available, but as 10,100 were actually produced, a favourable variance results.

(*iv*) **Capacity usage variance**

Formula = Standard cost (Budgeted quantity − Standard quantity)
= SC (BQ − SQ)
= £0·40 (10,080 − 9,960) = £48 (A)

The quantity expected during February was 10,080 units, but in the time available only 9,960 units could be produced; due to idle time, machine capacity was reduced.

Accounting entries

		£	£
Dr.	Capacity usage variance	48	
	Finished goods	4,040	
Cr.	Volume efficiency variance		56
	Work in progress		4,032

NOTE: Volume variance is not shown in the accounting entries because it is composed of volume efficiency variance and capacity usage variance, both of which are shown above.

Check 1

(*i*) Finished goods = Standard cost of actual production
= 10,100 units at £0·40 = £4,040

(*ii*) Entries in Finished Goods Account (above) = £4,040

Check 2

(*i*) Overhead variance = SC − AC
= £4,040 − £4,200 = £160 (A)

(*ii*) $\dfrac{\text{Overhead}}{\text{variance}} = \dfrac{\text{Efficiency}}{\text{variance}} + \dfrac{\text{Capacity}}{\text{variance}} + \dfrac{\text{Expenditure}}{\text{variance}}$

= £56 (F) + £48 (A) + £168 (A) = £160 (A)

Standard cost of production
(Output = 10,100 articles)

Element of cost	Per unit	Total production
	£	£
Direct material	0·60	6,060·00
Direct labour	2·00	20,200·00
Variable overhead	0·50	5,050·00
Fixed overhead	0·40	4,040·00
TOTAL	£3·50	£35,350·00

All production for the month was sold for £40,400. The accounts would appears as follows:

Stores Ledger Control Account

	£		£
Purchases	5,925	Work in progress	6,000
Direct materials price variance	75		
	£6,000		£6,000

Direct Wages Control Account

	£		£
Wages paid	20,168·40	Work in progress	20,160·00
		Direct labour rate variance	8·40
	£20,168·40		£20,168·40

Variable Overhead Control Account

	£		£
Expenses paid	5,000	Work in progress	5,050
Expenditure variance	50		
	£5,050		£5,050

Fixed Overhead Control Account

	£		£
Expenses paid	4,200	Expenditure variance	168
		Work in progress	4,032
	£4,200		£4,200

Work-in-progress Ledger Control

	£		£
Stores Ledger Control A/c	6,000	Direct labour idle-time variance	240
Wages Control A/c	20,160	Fixed overhead capacity variance	48
Variable Overhead Control A/c	5,050	Finished stock	35,350
Fixed Overhead Control A/c	4,032		
Direct labour efficiency variance	280		
Direct material usage variance	60		
Fixed overhead efficiency variance	56		
	£35,638		£35,638

Finished Stock Control Account

Work in progress	£35,350	Cost of sales	£35,350

Cost of Sales

Finished stock	£35,350	Profit and Loss A/c	£35,350

Direct Materials Price Variance Account

Profit and Loss A/c	£75	Stores Ledger Control A/c	£75

Direct Materials Usage Variance Account

Profit and Loss A/c	£60	Work in progress	£60

Direct Wages Rate Variance Account

Wages Control A/c	£8·40	Profit and Loss A/c	£8·40

Direct Labour Efficiency Variance Account

Profit and Loss A/c	£280	Work in progress	£280

Direct Labour Idle-time Variance Account

Work in progress	£240	Profit and Loss A/c	£240

Variable Overhead Expenditure Variance Account

Profit and Loss A/c	£50	Variable Overhead Control A/c	£50

Overhead Efficiency Variance Account

Profit and Loss A/c	£56	Work-in-progress Control A/c	£56

Overhead Capacity Usage Variance Account

Work-in-progress Control A/c	£48	Profit and Loss A/c	£48

Fixed Overhead Expenditure Variance Account

Fixed Overhead Control A/c	£168	Profit and Loss A/c	£168

It will be observed that the "price" variances, *i.e.* direct materials price, direct labour rate, variable overhead expenditure and fixed overhead expenditure variances are calculated in the respective expense accounts, while the "quantity" variances, *i.e.* direct materials usage, direct labour efficiency, direct labour idle time, fixed overhead efficiency, fixed overhead capacity usage variances are calculated in the Work-in-progress Ledger Control Account.

PRESENTATION

It is essential that management are presented with details of standard and actual costs of each product manufactured, together with the appropriate variance. This information must be made available quickly if full benefit is to be obtained from the standard costing system. Quick action is vital if adverse variances are to be investigated and possibly rectified.

If a standard costing system were not in operation, management would be presented with a simple financial account such as the following:

Trading and Profit and Loss Account
for period ending February 19...

	£		£
Direct materials consumed	5,925·00	Sales	40,400·00
Direct wages	20,168·40		
Variable expenses	5,000·00		
Fixed expenses	4,200·00		
Net profit	5,106·60		
	£40,400·00		£40,400·00

This account reveals that a profit of £5,106·60 was made for the month, which represents a profit of 12·6% on turnover. Management may consider this figure satisfactory, but they are unable to know whether this figure could be improved upon; efficiencies or inefficiencies are not revealed.

In a standard costing system, however, the information to be presented to management may be shown in such form as below:

Profit and Loss Statement
for period ending February 19...

	£	£
Sales:		40,400
Less Standard cost of sales:		
Materials	6,060	
Labour	20,200	
Variable overhead	5,050	
Fixed overhead	4,040	
		35,350
STANDARD NET PROFIT		£5,050

Variances	F £	A £	F £	A £
Direct materials: Price	75			
Usage	60			135
Direct labour: Rate		8·40		
Efficiency	280			
Idle time		240		
				31·60
Variable overhead: Expenditure	50			
				50
Fixed Overhead: Volume efficiency	56			
Capacity usage		48		
Expenditure		168		
				160
				56·60
ACTUAL NET PROFIT				£5,106·60

From this statement, management can see quite easily that the net profit expected was £5,050·00, compared with the actual net profit obtained of £5,106·60, a favourable difference of £56·60. It can be ascertained that this increase in profit is mainly due to labour efficiency and expenditure on variable expenses being less than expected, partly offset by abnormal idle time and increased costs of fixed expenses. Management are thus able to take quick action in respect of any inefficiencies thus revealed.

Examination questions on Chapters 25–27 are given at the end of Chapter 27.

CHAPTER 26

STANDARD COSTING

Calculation of Advanced Variances

THE previous illustration showed the normal type of variance which can be easily illustrated in a composite example. There are, however, a number of variances which most students find difficult to understand; it is therefore proposed to illustrate these variances individually.

DIRECT MATERIALS MIXTURE VARIANCE

This is defined in the *Terminology* as follows:

"That portion of the direct materials usage variance which is due to the difference between the standard and actual composition of a mixture."

A material mix variance occurs therefore only when there is a mixture, *e.g.* when cement is added to sand and gravel to make concrete, or when a bakery firm has a standard cake mixture. If the quantities issued to production differ from the standard quantities there is first of all a direct material usage variance, but if part of the usage variance is due to the composition of the mixture having been changed, then that part is segregated as a mixture variance.

The standard mixture of a product determines the combination of raw materials input to obtain a given output. Thus a standard mix may be shown as follows:

Material required	Units	Price per unit
		£
G	40	0·25
P	30	0·50
J	20	0·20
S	10	0·60
	100	

If, during an accounting period, quantities of raw materials of G, P, J and S were used which were in different proportions from those prescribed, a direct materials usage variance would arise, part of which would be due to a change of mix. This situation occurs frequently in a process industry, *e.g.* in the manufacture of sausages, where it may be

518

necessary to consume more pork and less beef than planned, due to a temporary shortage of beef.

EXAMPLE

Let us assume that the standard mix shown above will produce 100 units of product Marart.

Material	Standard mix			Actual mix		
	Units	Price £	Amount £	Units	Price £	Amount £
G	40	0·25	10	36	0·25	9
P	30	0·50	15	24	0·50	12
J	20	0·20	4	30	0·20	6
S	10	0·60	6	10	0·60	6
	100		£35	100		£33

Direct material mixture variance

Formula = SP (SQ — AQ)

G £0·25 (40 — 36)	£1·00 (F)	
P £0·50 (30 — 24)	£3·00 (F)	
J £0·20 (20 — 30)	£2·00 (A)	
S £0·60 (10 — 10)	—	
		£2·00 (F)

This calculation shows that, due to a reduction in the consumption of the high-priced materials, a favourable variance has arisen, even though it was partly offset by an increase in consumption of the low-priced materials.

It will be noted that the formula used for this variance is the same as that used in the calculation of the direct materials usage variance, which was discussed in Chapter 25. This is quite in order, because in this simple example we are ignoring the direct materials yield variance, and, as according to the Institute of Cost and Works Accountants' *Terminology*, yield variance + mixture variance = usage variance, then in this example, because there is no yield variance, mixture variance will be the same as usage variance. An example in which both variances are shown, follows at a later stage.

DIRECT MATERIALS YIELD VARIANCE

"That portion of the direct material usage variance which is due to the difference between the standard yield specified and the actual yield obtained."

In Chapter 20, the problem of normal and abnormal loss was discussed in detail. In most processes a normal loss in process is expected, so it is usually possible to set a standard for the normal yield expected. The standard yield is the output expected from the standard input of raw materials. Quite frequently, the actual yield may differ from the standard yield; the difference is termed the "yield variance" in standard costing, as compared with "abnormal loss" in actual costing systems.

EXAMPLE 1

The standard mix of product Jerart is as follows:

Raw material	Units	Price £
G	60	0·25
P	40	0·50

The standard loss per mix is 30%.

During March one mix was processed.

	Standard mix			Actual mix		
Raw material	Units	Price £	Amount £	Units	Price £	Amount £
G	60	0·25	15	56	0·25	14
P	40	0·50	20	44	0·50	22
	100		35	100		36
	30	Standard loss		26	Actual loss	
	70		£35	74		£36

Direct materials yield variance

Formula = SC (SY − AY)

£0·5 (70 − 74) = £2 (F)

This reveals that an additional four units of output were produced during the month, at a value of £2.

The direct materials mixture variance can be calculated as follows:

Formula = SP (SQ − AQ)

G £0·25 (60 − 56) £1·00 (F)
P £0·50 (40 − 44) £2·00 (A)

= £1·00 (A)

The Work-in-progress Account would appear as follows:

Work-in-progress Account

	£		£
Stores control	36	Direct materials mixture variance	1
Direct materials yield variance	2	Finished goods (standard cost)	37
	£38		£38

EXAMPLE 2

During April, the same standard costs applied as shown in example 1 above, but 1·5 mixes were processed.

Raw material	Units	Standard mix Price	Amount	Units	Actual mix Price	Amount
		£	£		£	£
G	60	0·25	15	80	0·25	20
P	40	0·50	20	70	0·05	35
	100		35	150		55
	30	Standard loss		35	Actual loss	
	70		£35	115		£55

Direct materials yield variance

Formula = SC (SY − AY)
£0·50 (105 − 115) = £5·00 (F)

This reveals that an additional ten units of output were produced during the month, at a value of £5.

NOTE: *The standard yield.*

1·5 mixes were processed.
The standard loss is 1·5 × 30 = 45.
Therefore the standard yield is 150 − 45 = 105.

Direct materials mixture variance

Formula = SP (SQ − AQ)
G £0·25 (90 − 80) £2·50 (F)
P £0·50 (60 − 70) £5·00 (A) = £2·50 (A)

Work-in-progress Account

	£		£
Stores control	55·0	Direct materials mixture	
Direct materials yield variance	5·0	variance	2·5
		Finished goods (standard cost)	57·5
	£60·0		£60·0

EXAMPLE 3

This example is based on a question set at a Part Two examination of the I.C.W.A. In addition to the direct materials yield variance, the other direct materials variances are to be shown, so it is more comprehensive than the two previous examples. The standard mix of product M5 is as follows:

lb	Material	Price per lb £
50	J	0·25
20	D	0·20
30	M	0·45

The standard loss in production is 10% of input. There is no scrap value. Actual production for May was 7,350 lb of M5 from 80 mixes.

Actual purchases and consumption of materials during the month were as follows:

lb	Material	Price per lb £
4,160	J	0·27½
1,680	D	0·17½
2,560	M	0·47½

Calculate the direct material variances. Show also the following accounts in the Cost Ledger:

(a) Work-in-progress Ledger Control.
(b) Stores Ledger Control.
(c) Direct Material Price Variance.
(d) Direct Materials Usage Variance.
(e) Direct Materials Yield Variance.

In this example one is required to calculate the direct materials usage variance, in addition to the direct materials mixture variance and yield variance. According to the Institute of Cost and Works Accountants' *Terminology*, the direct materials usage variance is:

"that portion of the direct materials cost variance which is due to the difference between the standard quantity specified and the actual quantity used."

When calculating this variance (and when it is also required to show the sub-variances mixture and yield), this formula shown below may be applied. It will be noted that in order to allow for the calculation of all the direct material variances, it is necessary to calculate the standard cost of input as well as the standard cost of output.

Raw material	Standard mix (80 mixes) lb	Price £	Amount £	Actual mix lb	Price £	Amount £
J	4,000	0·25	1,000	4,160	0·27½	1,144
D	1,600	0·20	320	1,680	0·17½	294
M	2,400	0·45	1,080	2,560	0·47½	1,216
	8,000		2,400	8,400		2,654
	800 Standard loss			1,050 Actual loss		
	7,200		£2,400	7,350		£2,654

Raw material	Standard cost of input			Standard cost of output		
	lb	Price	Amount	lb	Price	Amount
		£	£		£	£
J	4,160	0·25	1,040	4,083·3	0·25	1,020·84
D	1,680	0·20	336	1,633·3	0·20	326·66
M	2,560	0·45	1,152	2,450·0	0·45	1,102·50
	8,400		2,528	8,166·6		2,450·00
	1,050 Actual loss			816·6 Standard loss		
	7,350		£2,528	7,350·0		£2,450·00

Direct materials cost variance

SC − AC

	£		£	£
J	1,020·84	−	1,144·00	123·16 (A)
D	326·66	−	294·00	32·66 (F)
M	1,102·50	−	1,216·00	113·50 (A)
	£2,450·00	−	£2,654·00	£204·00 (A)

Direct materials price variance

AQ (SP − AP)

J 4,160 (£0·25 − £0·27$\frac{1}{2}$)	£104 (A)	
D 1,680 (£0·20 − £0·17$\frac{1}{2}$)	£42 (F)	
M 2,560 (£0·45 − £0·47$\frac{1}{2}$)	£64 (A)	= £126 (A)

Direct materials usage variance

SC of output − SC of input

	£		£	£
J	1,020·84	−	1,040·00	19·16 (A)
D	326·66	−	336·00	9·34 (A)
M	1,102·50	−	1,152·00	49·50 (A)
	£2,450·00	−	£2,528·00	£78·00 (A)

Direct materials mixture variance

SP (SQ − AQ)

J £0·25 (4,000 − 4,160)	40 (A)	
D £0·20 (1,600 − 1,680)	16 (A)	
M £0·45 (2,400 − 2,560)	72 (A)	= £128 (A)

Direct materials yield variance

SC (SY − AY)

£0·33$\frac{1}{2}$ (7,200 − 7,350)   = £50 (F)

Check

    (*i*) Cost variance = Price variance + Usage variance
        £204 (A) = £126 (A) + £78 (A)
    (*ii*) Usage variance = Mixture variance + Yield variance
        £78 (A) = £128 (A) + £50 (F)

NOTE: Standard cost of output may be expressed as follows:

$$AQ \times SC \text{ per unit, } i.e. \text{ } 7,350 \text{ units} \times £0.33\tfrac{1}{2} = £2,450.$$

It may be expressed as shown in the table above, calculations for which were as follows:

$$J \frac{7,350}{7,200} \times 4,000 = 4,083 \cdot 3$$

$$D \frac{7,350}{7,200} \times 1,600 = 1,633 \cdot 3$$

$$M \frac{7,350}{7,200} \times 2,400 = 2,450 \cdot 0$$

Stores Ledger Control Account

	£		£
Financial Ledger control	2,654	Direct materials price variance	126
		Work-in-progress control	2,528
	£2,654		£2,654

Work-in-progress Ledger Control Account

	£		£
Stores Ledger control	2,528	Direct materials mixture	
Direct materials yield variance	50	variance	128
		Finished goods control	2,450
	£2,578		£2,578

Direct Materials Price Variance Account

Stores Ledger control	£126		

Direct Materials Usage Variance Account

	Nil		

Direct Materials Mixture Variance Account

Work-in-progress control	£128		

Direct Materials Yield Variance Account

	Work-in-progress control	£50

NOTE: The Direct Materials Usage Variance Account shows nil because the sub-variances (mixture variance £128 Dr. and yield variance £50 Cr.), have been shown. In the accounts one can show only the main variance or the sub-variances, but not both.

An alternative method of calculating the direct materials variances from that shown in example 3 is now given. A number of authorities would calculate the direct materials usage variance in the way to be shown, but it is not in accordance with the I.C.W.A. *Terminology*, so the authors would stress the importance of the above method. However, this alternative does have some merit, so it is shown below.

Standard mix, actual mix and standard cost of output are calculated as above, but instead of calculating the standard cost of input, the actual mix in standard proportions is calculated. In other words, this shows what should theoretically have been the correct proportions of the actual quantity of raw materials consumed.

Actual mix in standard proportions at standard prices

Raw materials	lb	Price	Amount
		£	£
J	4,200	0·25	1,050
D	1,680	0·20	336
M	2,520	0·45	1,197
	8,400		2,583
	1,050	Actual loss	
	7,350		£2,583

Direct materials cost variance (as above)	£204 (A)
Direct materials price variance (as above)	£126 (A)

Direct materials usage variance
SC (RSQ − SQ)

J £0·25 (4,200 − 4,000)	£50 (A)	
D £0·20 (1,680 − 1,600)	£16 (A)	
M £0·45 (2,520 − 2,400)	£54 (A)	£120 (A)

Direct materials mixture variance
SP (AQ − RSQ)

J £0·25 (4,160 − 4,200)	£10 (F)	
D £0·20 (1,680 − 1,680)	—	
M £0·45 (2,560 − 2,520)	£18 (A)	£8 (A)

Direct materials yield variance

SC (SY − AY)

£0·33½ (7,200 − 7,350)   £50 (F)

NOTE: RSQ represents the revised standard quantity, or in other words, the standard proportion of the actual mix at standard prices.

Check

Cost V = Price V + Usage V + Mixture V + Yield V

£204 (A) = £126 (A) + £120 (A) +   £8 (A)   + £50 (F)

The main accounts involved would appear as follows:

Stores Ledger Control Account

	£		£
Financial Ledger Control	2,654	Direct materials price	
		variance	126
		Work in progress	2,528
	£2,654		£2,654

Work-in-progress Ledger Control Account

	£		£
Stores Ledger control	2,528	Direct materials usage	
Direct materials yield		variance	120
variance	50	Direct materials mixture	
		variance	8
		Finished Goods Ledger	2,450
	£2,578		£2,578

NOTE: The direct materials usage variance shows £120, because in this method of calculating the variance it is not sub-divided into mixture variance and yield variance. Each of the three variances, together with the price variance, is a sub-variance of the cost variance.

REVISION VARIANCE

During an accounting period, it may be necessary to alter a standard due to unforeseen circumstances. Once a standard has been set for, say, a period of a year, it is undesirable that it should be changed, because this will affect budgets, standard costs, etc. It is often preferable, therefore, to create a revision variance, which segregates the difference due to this new factor. This step, while it obviously cannot rectify the situation, at least helps in the control of costs by explaining how the change occurred and how much was the effect on profit. Possible situations when a revision variance could be used are where there is a sudden, steep rise in the price of a raw material due to an acute shortage of supply caused by a poor harvest, or a change in mix of labour due to a shortage of a certain type of labour.

EXAMPLE

During May, the same standard costs applied as shown in example 1 above. However, at the beginning of the month, it was necessary to change the mix of the product because of a shortage of material G. The mix was changed from a proportion of 3 : 2 to 2 : 3.

Material	Units	Standard mix Price £	Amount £	Units	Revised standard mix Price £	Amount £	Units	Actual mix Price £	Amount £
G	60	0·25	15	40	0·25	10	44	0·30	13·20
P	40	0·50	20	60	0·50	30	62	0·45	27·90
	100		35	100		40	106		41·10
	30	Standard loss		30	Standard loss		36	Actual loss	
	70		£35	70		£40	70		£41·10

Direct materials revision variance

Formula = SP (SQ — RSQ)

G £0·25 (60 — 40)	£5 (F)	
P £0·50 (40 — 60)	£10 (A)	
		£5 (A)

Here the revision variance could be called a mix variance, but as it is a deliberate policy decision to change the mix, the authors consider it preferable to refer to it as a revision variance. Once the revision variance has been calculated, the new revised standard mix would become, in effect, the standard mix of the product, and variations would be calculated therefrom to show the direct material price variance and the direct materials usage variance.

Direct materials price variance

AQ (SP — AP)

G 44 (£0·25 — £0·30)	£2·20 (A)	
P 62 (£0·50 — £0·45)	£3·10 (F)	
		£0·90 (F)

Direct materials usage variance

SP (RSQ — AQ)

G £0·25 (40 — 44)	£1·00 (A)	
P £0·50 (60 — 62)	£1·00 (A)	
		£2·00 (A)

Direct materials cost variance

SC — AC

£35·00 — £41·10		£6·10 (A)

Check

Cost variance = Revision variance + Price variance + Usage variance

£6·10 (A)   =   £5·00 (A)   +   £0·90 (F)   +   £2·00 (A)

It should be noted that due to the introduction of a revision variance, the usage variance is calculated from the revised standard quantity.

DIRECT LABOUR MIX VARIANCE

In theory, this variance is rather similar to the direct materials mixture variance. A variance will arise, if, during a particular period the grades of labour used in production are different from those budgeted.

EXAMPLE 1

The standard labour force for producing product Jerart during one week in July, is as follows:

	£
40 men at £0·60 per hour for 40 hours	960
20 women at £0·40 per hour for 40 hours	320
10 boys at £0·30 per hour for 40 hours	120
	£1,400

The actual labour force employed during the week was as follows:

	£
35 men at £0·60 per hour for 40 hours	840
20 women at £0·40 per hour for 40 hours	320
10 women at £0·50 per hour for 40 hours	200
5 boys at £0·30 per hour for 40 hours	60
	£1,420

Direct labour rate variance

Formula = AH (AR − SR)

400 (£0·50 − £0·40)   £40 (A)

NOTE: Only 10 women have been paid a rate which differs from the standard rate, and as a 40-hour week is in operation, 400 hours is the actual time which has been paid.

Direct labour mix variance

Formula = SC of SM − SC of AM

	£	£	£
Men	960 −	840	120 (F)
Women	320 −	480	160 (A)
Boys	120 −	60	60 (F)
	1,400 −	1,380	£20 (F)

NOTE: Standard cost of actual mix is calculated as follows:

	£
35 men at £0·60 per hour for 40 hours	840
30 women at £0·40 per hour for 40 hours	480
5 boys at £0·30 per hour for 40 hours	60
	£1,380

The accounting entries would be

	£	£
Dr. Work in progress	1,380	
Direct wages rate variance	40	
Cr. Wages control		1,420
Dr. Finished goods control	1,400	
Cr. Direct labour mix variance		20
Work-in-progress control		1,380

EXAMPLE 2

This example is based on a question set at an I.C.W.A. Final Examination. A gang of workers usually consists of 10 men, 5 women and 5 boys, paid at standard hourly rates of £0·62½, £0·40 and £0·35 respectively. In a normal working week of 40 hours, the gang is expected to produce 1,000 units of output.

In a certain week, the gang consisted of 13 men, 4 women and 3 boys; actual wages paid were £0·60, £0·42½ and £0·32½ respectively. Two hours were lost due to abnormal idle time and 960 units of output were produced.

The standard labour mix is as follows:

	£
10 men at £0·62½ for 40 hours	250
5 women at £0·40 for 40 hours	80
5 boys at £0·35 for 40 hours	70
	£400

Standard output is 1,000 units.
The actual labour mix is:

	£
13 men at £0·60 for 40 hours	312
4 women at £0·42½ for 40 hours	68
3 boys at £0·32½ for 40 hours	39
	£419

The actual labour mix at standard rates is:

	£
13 men at £0·62½ for 40 hours	325
4 women at £0·40 for 40 hours	64
3 boys at £0·35 for 40 hours	42
	£431

Actual output is 960 units.

Direct wages variance

SC − AC

£384 − £419 £35 (A)

Direct wages rate variance

AH (AR − SR)

520 (£0·60 − £0·62½)	£13 (F)
160 (£0·42½ − £0·40)	£4 (A)
120 (£0·32½ − £0·35)	£3 (F)

£12 (F)

Direct labour efficiency variance

SR (AH − SH)

£10 (38 − 38·4) £4 (F)

Direct labour mix variance

SC of SM − SC of AM

	£	£	£
Men	250 −	325	75 (A)
Women	80 −	64	16 (F)
Boys	70 −	42	28 (F)
	£400 −	431	£31 (A)

Direct labour idle-time variance

Hours idle × SC per hour

2 × £10 £20 (A)

NOTE 1. SC = AQ × SC per unit

960 × £0·40

2. AH = Actual hours paid − idle time

40 − 2

3. SH = Actual output × $\dfrac{\text{Standard hours}}{\text{Standard output}} = 960 × \dfrac{40}{1,000}$

This represents the actual output expressed in terms of standard hours.

OVERHEAD VARIANCES

In the previous chapter, the basic overhead variances were discussed and illustrated, and it was mentioned that in the new I.C.W.A. *Terminology* a number of additional variances have been introduced. Some of these variances are not shown frequently, but all will be illustrated in this chapter.

EXPENDITURE VARIANCE

This is defined as:

"That portion of the overhead variance which represents the difference between the standard allowance for the output achieved and the actual expenditure incurred."

This variance, together with the volume variance is equal to the overhead variance. It is sub-divided into the following sub-variances:

(a) *Overhead price variance.* "That portion of the overhead. expenditure variance which is due to the difference between the standard price of the service specified and the actual price paid." This variance is similar to the direct material price variance and the labour rate variance.

(b) *Overhead efficiency variance.* "That portion of the overhead expenditure variance which is the difference between the standard allowance for the activity (standard hours achieved) and the standard allowance for the actual hours worked." This variance only arises on costs which vary with time taken rather than with volume of output. This variance measures how efficiently a service has been used in the production process; *e.g.*, how efficiently gas has been used in a bakery. It should be noted that this variance, together with the price variance and the utilisation variance, relates to input costs rather than output values. The volume variance and its sub-variances (discussed later) relate to the efficiency and usage of output facilities.

(c) *Overhead utilisation variance.* "That portion of the overhead expenditure variance which is due to the difference between the standard quantity of the service specified, and the actual quantity of the service used."

EXAMPLE

The production overhead budget for Department 6 shows that for an eight-hour day, 10,000 kilowatts should be consumed at £1 per 200 kilowatts. The output expected is 1,000 units of product.

During Monday of week 10, 12,000 kilowatts were consumed at £1 per 160 kilowatts. Nine hours were worked and an output achieved of 1,100 units of product.

Overhead expenditure variance

$$SC - AC$$
$$£55 - £75 \qquad \underline{£20 \ (A)}$$

Overhead price variance

$$AQ \ (SR - AR)$$
$$12,000 \left(\frac{£1}{200} - \frac{£1}{160} \right) \qquad \underline{£15 \ (A)}$$

Overhead efficiency variance

$$SR (SQ - RBQ)$$
$$\frac{£1}{200} (11,000 - 11,280) \qquad\qquad £1·25 (A)$$

Overhead utilisation variance

$$SR (RBQ - AQ)$$
$$\frac{£1}{200} (11,250 - 12,000) \qquad\qquad £3·75 (A)$$

NOTE 1. Expenditure variance = Price variance + Efficiency variance
$$\qquad\qquad\qquad\qquad\qquad\qquad + \text{ Utilisation variance}$$
$$£20 (A) = £15 (A) + £1·25 (A) + £3·75 (A)$$

2. Under normal conditions, when the overhead expenditure variance is not sub-divided, the formula for fixed overhead expenditure variance is BC − AC, while that for variable overhead expenditure variance is SC − AC (as discussed in the previous chapter). However, when the expenditure variance is sub-divided, and it will be noted in the I.C.W.A. *Terminology* that an overhead efficiency variance arises only when costs vary with time taken rather than with volume of output, the formula is the same as that for a variable overhead expenditure variance, *viz.* SC − AC ("the difference between the standard allowance for the output achieved and the actual expenditure incurred").

3. SC = AQ × SC per unit
$$11,000 \times \frac{£1}{200} = £55$$

SQ: The quantity which should have been produced in the time available. In an eight-hour day, 10,000 kilowatts should be consumed and 1,000 units produced, thus, 1,250 kilowatts per hour and 100 kilowatts per unit. Actual production was 1,100 units so 11,000 kilowatts should have been consumed.

RBQ: Budget is eight hours per day at 1,250 kilowatts per hour. Nine hours were worked, which means that one would now expect 9 × 1,250 kilowatts to be consumed.

VOLUME VARIANCE

This is defined as:

"That portion of the overhead variance which is the difference between the standard cost of overhead absorbed in actual output, and the standard allowance for that output."

This variance, together with the overhead expenditure variance, is equal to the overhead variance. It is sub-divided into the following sub-variances:

(a) *Seasonal variance.* "That portion of the volume variance which is due to the difference between the seasonally budgeted output and the average output on which standards have been calculated. (The sum of the seasonal variances over a complete year would be zero.)" This sub-variance could occur in an industry which varies its production according to seasonal fluctuations.

(b) *Calendar variance.* "That portion of the volume variance which is due to the difference between the number of working days in the budget period and the number of working days in the period to which the budget is applied. (The sum of the calendar variances in a complete year would be zero.)" This variance arises from the convention that fixed costs are the same for each period, whatever the number of working days, and it can be eliminated by apportioning standard allowances and actual fixed costs on a working-day basis.

Many companies which operate a yearly budget divide the year into 13 budget periods of 4 weeks. However, some firms divide the yearly budget into 12 budget periods according to the calendar months. Where a firm adopts the latter system, it is necessary to operate a calendar variance.

Fixed overheads do not vary with production, and they are usually recovered at an hourly rate. The budgeted total fixed overheads for the year will be divided by the 12 budget periods in the year thus giving a fixed rate per budget period. The actual recovery of fixed overheads will depend on how many hours are worked during a budget period, and, because the number of hours worked in each period will frequently differ, a variance from budget will occur.

EXAMPLE

Fixed overheads for the year are budgeted at £17,640. The factory operates an 8-hour day and a 5-day week. The number of days which could be worked in the year are given in the table overleaf:

$$\text{Overhead recovery} = \frac{£17,640}{1,960 \text{ hours}} = £9 \text{ per hour.}$$

$$\text{Accrued} = \frac{£17,640}{12 \text{ months}} = £1,470 \text{ per month.}$$

It should be noted that the calendar variance over a period of one year is self-eliminating.

To find the calendar variance for a month, the following formula can be used:

Formula = Budgeted rate for fixed overhead (Revised budgeted hours − Budgeted hours)

= BFO (RBH − BH)

Consider the month of July:

Revised budgeted hours = 104.

Budgeted hours = $163\frac{1}{3}$ (*i.e.* 1,960 hours ÷ 12 months)

9 $(104 - 163\frac{1}{3})$

9 $(59\frac{1}{3})$ £534 (A).

Consider the month of October:

Revised budgeted hours = 184.

Budgeted hours = $163\frac{1}{3}$ (*i.e.* 1,960 hours ÷ 12 months)

9 $(184 - 163\frac{1}{3})$

9 $(20\frac{2}{3})$ £186 (F).

Month	Days worked	Hours worked	Over-head rate per hour	Over-head re-covered	Over-head accrued	Variance Adverse	Variance Favour-able
			£	£	£	£	£
January	23	184	9	1,656	1,470	—	186
February	20	160	9	1,440	1,470	30	—
March	21	168	9	1,512	1,470	—	42
April	20 (Easter)	160	9	1,440	1,470	30	—
May	21 (Whit.)	168	9	1,512	1,470	—	42
June	21	168	9	1,512	1,470	—	42
July	13 (Annual Hol.)	104	9	936	1,470	534	—
August	20 (Bank. Hol.)	160	9	1,440	1,470	30	—
September	22	176	9	1,584	1,470	—	114
October	23	184	9	1,656	1,470	—	186
November	20	160	9	1,440	1,470	30	—
December	21 (Christmas)	168	9	1,512	1,470	—	42
		1,960	—	£17,640	£17,640	654	654

Hours worked = Number of days × Hours per day.

(*c*) *Capacity usage variance.* "That portion of the volume variance which is due to working at higher or lower capacity usage than standard." This sub-variance measures the utilisation of plant and machinery and has been illustrated already in the previous chapter.

(*d*) *Volume efficiency variance.* "That portion of the volume variance which reflects the increased or reduced output arising from efficiency above or below the standard which is expected." This sub-variance measures the efficiency with which the employees or machines have been working, as distinct from how much time the employees or machines have been working. Thus, it is possible to work for only one hour in a normal eight-hour day (thereby showing an adverse capacity usage variance), but during the hour to work very productively (thereby showing a favourable volume efficiency variance).

EXAMPLE

The production budget of the Mart Engineering Co. Ltd. is 120,000 articles per year, made up as follows:

January–March	33,000 units
April–June	24,000 units
July–September	37,000 units
October–December	36,000 units.

Budgeted fixed overheads for the year are £60,000. The company works 50 weeks in the year, 5 days per week, 8 hours per day. Standard output is 60 units per hour.

During February, there were 4 working weeks. However, due to very severe weather 2 working days were lost. Actual output was 9,500 units. Actual hours worked were 140.

Volume variance

SC (AQ − BQ)
£0·50 (9,500 − 10,000)   £250 (A)

Volume efficiency variance

SC (AQ − SQ)
£0·50 (9,500 − 8,400)   £550 (F)

Capacity usage variance

SC (SQ − RBQ)
£0·50 (8,400 − 9,000)   £300 (A)

Calendar variance

SC (RBQ − SBQ)
£0·50 (9,000 − 11,000)   £1,000 (A)

Seasonal variance

SC (SBQ − BQ)
£0·50 (11,000 − 10,000)   £500 (F)

These variances show that during the month of February, volume of output was lower than that budgeted (adverse volume variance), and there was under-utilisation of plant (due to idle time). These losses were partly offset by a change in seasonal production (favourable seasonal variance) and increased efficiency (favourable volume efficiency variance).

NOTE: BQ = 120,000 articles per year.
             120,000 ÷ 12 = 10,000 per month.

SBQ = During the period January to March the seasonal fluctua-
tions in production allow for 33,000 units to be produced.
This represents 11,000 per month.
(SBQ = Seasonal budgeted quantity.)

RBQ = Budgeted quantity is 10,000 units per month.
During the month, instead of working 20 days, only 18 days
were worked. 18/20 × 10,000 = 9,000.
(RBQ = Revised budgeted quantity.)

SQ = 140 hours were worked.
During this time production should have been 140 × 60.

OVERHEAD VARIANCES CALCULATED BY THE STANDARD HOUR

In this text, overhead variances have been calculated in terms of the
standard cost per unit. However, it is sometimes desirable to calculate
the variances in terms of standard hours. This is particularly important
in examinations, when questions may be asked in which the output is
expressed in standard hours, thus necessitating a different method of
calculation of variances. This method is briefly illustrated because it is
basically the same as the former method, except, of course, that production is expressed in terms of standard hours rather than in units.
It will be recalled that on page 497, an example was given of the conversion of units of output to standard hours of output.

The overhead variances which were discussed on pages 512 to 513
would be calculated as follows:

Overhead expenditure variance
(as before)   £168 (A)

Volume variance
Standard cost (Standard hours − Budgeted hours)
SC (SH − BH)
£24 (168$\frac{1}{3}$ − 168)   £8 (F)

Volume efficiency variance
Standard cost (Standard hours − Actual hours)
SC (SH − AH)
£24 (168$\frac{1}{3}$ − 166)   £56 (F)

Capacity usage variance
Standard cost (Actual hours − Budgeted hours)
SC (AH − BH)
£24 (166 − 168)   £48 (A)

NOTE 1. Standard cost per hour = $\dfrac{\text{Budgeted cost per month}}{\text{Budgeted hours per month}}$

$$= \frac{£4,032}{168}$$

2. Standard hours $= \dfrac{\text{Actual production}}{\text{Standard quantity per hour}}$

$= \dfrac{10,100}{60}$

3. Budgeted hours $= \text{Weeks in month} \times \text{hours per day}$

$ 4 \quad \times \quad 42$

4. Actual hours $= \text{Budgeted hours} - \text{Abnormal idle time}$

$ 168 \quad - \quad 2$

These calculations result in the same variances as were previously shown. It is suggested that readers should calculate the variances which are discussed on pages 559 to 562, using the standard hour method to check the accuracy of the variances shown by using the standard cost per unit method and so become conversant with both methods.

MATERIAL PRICE VARIANCE

There are two popular ways of showing material price variance; the variance may be calculated when:

(a) the material is taken into stock;
(b) the material is issued to production.

If method (a) is adopted, stocks will be kept at standard cost so that stores accounting is relatively easy, with purchases and issues appearing at the same price.

EXAMPLE

Purchase of 1,000 units at standard price of £0·25 each; actual price £0·27½ each. Of the units bought, 600 were issued to production. Under an integral accounting system, show the entries relating to the above transactions.

	£	£
Dr. Stock A/c	250	
Direct Materials Price Variance A/c	25	
Cr. S. Creditors A/c		275
Dr. Work-in-progress A/c	150	
Cr. Stock A/c		150

Readers may care to visualise the entries under a separate cost accounting and financial accounting system.

If method (b) is adopted, purchases will be recorded at actual price, issues at standard price and the resulting variance shown. The above illustration would appear thus:

	£	£
Dr. Stock A/c	275	
Cr. S. Creditors A/c		275
Dr. Work-in-progress A/c	150	
Cr. Stock A/c		150
Dr. Direct Materials Price Variance A/c	15	
Cr. Stock A/c		15

In practice, entries of direct materials price variances would not be made in the accounts on the occasion of every issue. Periodically, totals would be posted to the accounts, in a similar manner to those shown above.

SALES VARIANCES

All of the variances discussed previously have been concerned with costs: the effects on profits due to adverse or favourable variances affecting direct materials, direct labour or overheads. Some companies calculate cost variances only, but to obtain the full advantages of standard costing, many companies also calculate sales variances. Sales variances affect the business in matters of changes in revenue; changes caused by either a variation in sales quantities or selling prices.

There are two distinct systems of calculating sales variances, which show the effect of a change in sales as regards:

1. turnover;
2. profit or sales margin.

The turnover method is probably the easier method to understand so will be discussed first. However, it is suggested that this method is not as informative as the profit method, and in fact, in the I.C.W.A. *Terminology* (1966), the definitions shown are in respect of the profit method (there termed "sales margin").

1. TURNOVER METHOD

SPECIMEN QUESTION

A sales budget has been prepared in respect of four standard products. The budgeted sales for one month and the actual results achieved are as follows:

Product	Budget			Actual		
	Quantity	Price	Value	Quantity	Price	Value
		£	£		£	£
G	1,000	5	5,000	1,200	6	7,200
P	750	10	7,500	700	9	6,300
J	500	15	7,500	600	14	8,400
S	250	20	5,000	200	21	4,200
TOTAL			£25,000			£26,100

Calculate the sales variances.

ANSWER

It is suggested that quantities of products sold are not added together, because frequently products are dissimilar. For example, Products G, P, J and S may be boxes of canned beans, canned soups, bottled sauces and jars of pickles, respectively.

Before computing the variances, two calculations are required, *viz.*:

(*a*) Standard sales. The actual quantities sold valued at standard selling prices.

(*b*) Revised standard sales. Standard sales rearranged in the budgeted ratios.

Product	1. Standard sales			2. Revised standard sales	
	Quantity	Price	Value	Ratio, %	Value
		£	£		£
G	1,200	5	6,000	20	5,200
P	700	10	7,000	30	7,800
J	600	15	9,000	30	7,800
S	200	20	4,000	20	5,200
TOTAL			£26,000		£26,000

Calculation of revised standard sales:

$$G \quad \frac{5,000}{25,000} \times 26,000 = 20\% \times 26,000$$

$$P \quad \frac{7,500}{25,000} \times 26,000 = 30\% \times 26,000$$

$$J \quad \frac{7,500}{25,000} \times 26,000 = 30\% \times 26,000$$

$$S \quad \frac{5,000}{25,000} \times 26,000 = 20\% \times 26,000$$

(*a*) Value Variance

Formula = Budgeted sales − Actual sales
= BS − AS

	£		£		£
G	5,000	−	7,200	=	2,200 (F)
P	7,500	−	6,300	=	1,200 (A)
J	7,500	−	8,400	=	900 (F)
S	5,000	−	4,200	=	800 (A)
TOTAL	£25,000	−	£26,100	=	£1,100 (F)

This variance represents the difference between the value of sales expected and that actually achieved.

(b) Price Variance

Formula = Standard sales — Actual sales
= SS — AS

	£		£		£
G	6,000	—	7,200		1,200 (F)
P	7,000	—	6,300		700 (A)
J	9,000	—	8,400		600 (A)
S	4,000	—	4,200		200 (F)
TOTAL	£26,000	—	£26,100		£100 (F)

The effect of changes in prices on value of sales can be determined by this variance.

(c) Volume Variance

Formula = Budgeted sales — Standard sales
= BS — SS

	£		£		£
G	5,000	—	6,000		1,000 (F)
P	7,500	—	7,000		500 (A)
J	7,500	—	9,000		1,500 (F)
S	5,000	—	4,000		1,000 (A)
TOTAL	£25,000	—	£26,000		£1,000 (F)

This variance shows the effect on sales of actual quantities of sales differing from those budgeted.

(d) Quantity Variance

Formula = Budgeted sales — Revised standard sales
= BS — RSS

	£		£		£
G	5,000	—	5,200		200 (F)
P	7,500	—	7,800		300 (F)
J	7,500	—	7,800		300 (F)
S	5,000	—	5,200		200 (F)
TOTAL	£25,000	—	£26,000		£1,000 (F)

This variance forms part of the volume variance and relates to actual sales being greater or less than those budgeted. Thus, if sales of 100 units were budgeted, composed of 80 A and 20 B, and actual sales achieved were 160 A and 40 B, there would be no mix variance as the ratio of A to B has not changed, only the quantity sold.

(e) Mix Variance

Formula = Revised standard sales − Standard sales
= RSS − SS

	£		£	£
G	5,200	−	6,000	800 (F)
P	7,800	−	7,000	800 (A)
J	7,800	−	9,000	1,200 (F)
S	5,200	−	4,000	1,200 (A)
TOTAL	£26,000	−	£26,000	Nil

This variance also forms part of the volume variance and relates to the change in ratio of quantities of sales. Thus, if the sales budget shows 80 A and 20 B, and actual sales achieved were 75 A and 25 B, this would reveal a change of mix.

NOTES: Many students experience great difficulty in ascertaining whether a sales variance is adverse or favourable. Let us consider, for example, Product S:

(a) *Value variance.* Actual sales were less than budgeted sales, and this is obviously not in the company's interest, therefore adverse.

(b) *Price variance.* Actual sales exceeded standard sales. In other words, actual sales at actual prices were greater than actual sales at standard prices, therefore there was a favourable rise in selling price.

(c) *Volume variance.* Budgeted sales exceeded standard sales. In other words, actual sales at standard prices were less than budgeted sales at standard prices, which would have an adverse effect on the company.

(d) *Quantity variance.* Budgeted sales were less than revised standard sales. In other words, there was an increase in actual sales, and if this increase had occurred according to the budgeted ratios, then this figure would have exceeded the budget. The result is therefore favourable.

(e) *Mix variance.* Revised standard sales exceeded standard sales. In other words, the actual sales at standard price expressed in budgeted ratios were greater than the actual sales at standard prices. If the actual sales achieved had been in accordance with expected ratios this figure would have been above what was actually achieved. Therefore, as actual sales of S were not as good as could be expected from the general increase in sales, the result is an adverse mix of sales.

It should be noticed that when sales variances are calculated on turnover, the sales mixture variance must show a zero total, because it is based on the rearrangement of standard sales in terms of budgeted ratios, and we are comparing standard sales with revised standard sales. This does not invalidate the calculation in any way, because we are concerned to know the effect of a change in mix of each product which makes up the total sales. Later in the text when sales variances based on profits are discussed, it will be noticed that due to the different profit percentages this situation will not arise.

Check

(i)   Value variance = Price variance + Volume variance
       £1,100 (F) = £100 (F) + £1,000 (F)

(ii)   Volume variance = Quantity variance + Mix variance
       £1,000 (F) = £1,000 (F) + Nil

Sales Account

	£		£
Budgeted sales	25,000	Actual sales	26,100
Price variance	100		
Quantity variance	1,000		
	£26,100		£26,100

2. PROFIT OR SALES MARGIN METHOD

This method shows the effect of changes in sales quantities or selling prices on the profit expected by a company. Many non-accountants would probably prefer to know how the profits of the company had changed, rather than how the turnover had been affected. It will be noted that there is a change in terminology as far as the variances are concerned. Calculations are based on a similar technique to that used in the turnover method, and the variances can be interpreted in the same way, but in this profit method the definitions used are as shown in the I.C.W.A. *Terminology*.

EXAMPLE

The sales budget and the actual sales for the month of January of two products "Jay" and "Dee" are as follows:

Product	Budgeted sales			Actual sales		
	Quantity	Price	Value	Quantity	Price	Value
		£	£		£	£
"Jay"	6,000	5·00	30,000	5,000	5·00	25,000
				1,500	4·75	7,125
"Dee"	10,000	2·00	20,000	7,500	2·00	15,000
				1,750	1·90	3,325
TOTAL			£50,000			£50,450

Budgeted costs were "Jay" £4, "Dee" £1·50.
Show the sales variances for the month.

Product	Standard sales			Revised standard sales	
	Quantity	Price	Value	Ratio, %	Value
			£		£
"Jay"	6,500	5	32,500	60	30,600
"Dee"	9,250	2	18,500	40	20,400
			£51,000		£51,000

To calculate sales variances based on profit, it is necessary to know what profits were expected to be and what they actually were. This may be done as follows:

Product	Profit			
	Budgeted	Actual	Standard	Revised standard
	£	£	£	£
"Jay"	6,000	6,125	6,500	6,120
"Dee"	5,000	4,450	4,625	5,100
TOTAL	£11,000	£10,575	£11,125	£11,220

Calculation

Budgeted profit

"Jay" selling price £5, cost £4, therefore profit £1 per unit. This represents 20% on turnover:

20% of budgeted sales

$$20\% \times £30,000 = £6,000.$$

Standard profit

"Jay" 20% of standard sales

$$20\% \times £32,500 = £6,500.$$

Revised standard profit

"Jay" 20% of revised standard sales

$$20\% \times £30,600 = £6,120.$$

Actual profit

Actual sales − Actual cost = Actual profit.
"Jay" £32,125 − £26,000 = £6,125.

NOTE: Actual cost = 6,500 units at £4 = £26,000.

Similar calculations are made for "Dee."

(a) Total Sales Margin Variance

Formula = Budgeted profit − Actual profit
= BP − AP

	£		£	£
"Jay"	6,000	−	6,125	125 (F)
"Dee"	5,000	−	4,450	550 (A)
TOTAL	£11,000	−	£10,575	£425 (A)

(b) Sales Margin Variance due to Selling Prices

Formula = Standard profit − Actual profit
= SP − AP

	£		£	£
"Jay"	6,500	−	6,125	375 (A)
"Dee"	4,625	−	4,450	174 (A)
TOTAL	£11,125	−	£10,575	£550 (A)

(c) Volume Variance

Formula = Budgeted profit − Standard profit
= BP − SP

	£		£	£
"Jay"	6,000	−	6,500	500 (F)
"Dee"	5,000	−	4,625	375 (A)
TOTAL	£11,000	−	£11,125	£125 (F)

(d) Quantity Variance

Formula = Budgeted profit − Revised standard profit
= BP − RSP

	£		£	£
"Jay"	6,000	−	6,120	120 (F)
"Dee"	5,000	−	5,100	100 (F)
TOTAL	£11,000	−	£11,220	£220 (F)

(e) Sales Margin Variance due to Sales Quantities (Mixture)

Formula = Revised standard profit − Standard profit
= RSP − SP

	£		£	£
"Jay"	6,120	−	6,500	380 (F)
"Dee"	5,100	−	4,625	475 (A)
TOTAL	£11,220	−	£11,125	£95 (A)

Check

(i) Total sales margin variance = Price variance + Volume variance
£425 (A) = £550 (A) + £125 (F)

(ii) Volume variance = Quantity variance + Mixture variance
£125 (F) = £220 (F) + £95 (A)

Profit and Loss Statement

	£	£
Budgeted sales		50,000
Less Budgeted cost of sales		39,000
Budgeted profit		11,000
Variances: Sales quantity	220 (F)	
Sales mixture	95 (A)	125 (F)
Standard profit on sales		11,125
Variance: Sales price		550 (A)
Actual profit on sales		£10,575

A simple layout for the calculation of sales variances is shown below. It is a quick method of calculating sales margin variances from turnover variances, and it also shows the relationship between the two methods. The figures used are taken from the previous example.

Product	Budgeted sales			Actual sales			Standard sales	Revised standard sales
	Quantity	Price	Amount	Quantity	Price	Amount	Amount	Amount
		£	£		£	£	£	£
"Jay"	6,000	5	30,000	5,000	5·00	25,000	32,500	30,600
				1,500	4·75	7,125		
"Dee"	10,000	2	20,000	7,500	2·00	15,000	18,500	20,400
				1,750	1·90	3,325		
			£50,000			£50,450	£51,000	£51,000

	Turnover Basis			Sales margin basis
Total sales margin variance				
BS — AS				
	£	£	£	£
"Jay"	30,000 —	32,125	2,125 (F)	125 (F)
"Dee"	20,000 —	18,325	1,675 (A)	550 (A)
Total	£50,000 —	£50,450	£450 (F)	£425 (A)
Sales margin variance due to selling prices				
SS — AS				
"Jay"	32,500 —	32,125	375 (A)	375 (A)
"Dee"	18,500 —	18,325	175 (A)	175 (A)
Total	£51,000 —	£50,450	£550 (A)	£550 (A)
Sales volume variance				Profit %
BS — SS				
"Jay"	30,000 —	32,500	2,500 (F)	20	500 (F)
"Dee"	20,000 —	18,500	1,500 (A)	25	375 (A)
Total	£50,000 —	£51,000	£1,000 (F)		£125 (F)
Sales quantity variance				
BS — RSS				
"Jay"	30,000 —	30,600	600 (F)	20	120 (F)
"Dee"	20,000 —	20,400	400 (F)	25	100 (F)
Total	£50,000 —	£51,000	£1,000 (F)		£220 (F)
Sales margin variance due to sales quantities (mixture)				
RSS — SS				
"Jay"	30,600 —	32,500	1,900 (F)	20	380 (F)
"Dee"	20,400 —	18,500	1,900 (A)	25	475 (A)
Total	£51,000 —	£51,000	£—		£95 (A)

It will be seen that the variances are calculated on the turnover basis, and then in the case of the price variance there is no change, because any alteration in the selling price affects turnover and profits equally, while in the case of volume variance and its two sub-variances, the percentage profit on turnover is applied to those variances. Finally, the total sales margin variance is the addition of the price variance and the volume variance.

Check

		£
Budgeted sales		50,000
Standard cost of sales:		
"Jay" 6,000 at £4·00	24,000	
"Dee" 10,000 at £1·50	15,000	
		39,000
Budgeted profit		11,000
Sales variances:		
Price	550 (A)	
Quantity	220 (F)	
Mixture	95 (A)	
		425 (A)
Actual profit		£10,575

		£
Actual sales		50,450
Standard cost of sales:		
"Jay" 6,500 at £4·00	26,000	
"Dee" 9,250 at £1·50	13,875	
		39,875
Actual profit		£10,575

SALES ALLOWANCES

In the examples of sales variances discussed previously, the problem of sales allowances has been ignored. This variance is not seen as frequently as the other sales variances, but as it may arise in business or in examination questions, it must be discussed. The I.C.W.A. *Terminology* defines it as:

"That portion of total margin variance which is due to the difference between the budgeted rebates, discounts, etc., on the sales effected and the actual rebates, discounts, etc., allowed on those sales."

To illustrate this variance, a comprehensive example is given so as to provide an additional opportunity for the reader to apply his technique in analysing sales variances, in addition to calculating the sales margin variance due to sales allowances.

The method which is being illustrated is the sales margin method, primarily because it is the one which is defined in the I.C.W.A. *Terminology* and also because in the comprehensive illustration which follows this chapter the method shown is the turnover method.

EXAMPLE

The budgeted and actual sales of the Emmess Co. Ltd. for July are as shown below. In an attempt to increase sales of the two products, a quantity discount has been introduced. An estimate has been made of sales expectations at the normal sales price and at the reduced sales price which allows for the 10% quantity discount.

Product	Budgeted sales Quantity	Price	Value	Cost Price	Value	Profit Price	Value
		£	£	£	£	£	£
"Emm"	5,000	50	250,000	40	200,000	10	50,000
	800	45	36,000	40	32,000	5	4,000
"Ess"	21,200	20	424,000	15	318,000	5	106,000
	5,000	18	90,000	15	75,000	3	15,000
			£800,000		£625,000		£175,000

Product	Actual sales Quantity	Price	Value	Cost Price	Value	Profit Price	Value
		£	£	£	£	£	£
"Emm"	4,500	50	225,000	40	180,000	10	45,000
	600	48	28,800	40	24,000	8	4,800
	800	45	36,000	40	32,000	5	4,000
	200	44	8,800	40	8,000	4	800
"Ess"	20,000	20	400,000	15	300,000	5	100,000
	3,600	19	68,400	15	54,000	4	14,400
	5,000	18	90,000	15	75,000	3	15,000
	1,000	17	17,000	15	15,000	2	2,000
			£874,000		£688,000		£186,000

The standard and revised standard sales can now be calculated, before finding the sales variances.

Product	Standard sales			Cost		Profit	
	Quantity	Price	Value	Price	Value	Price	Value
		£	£	£	£	£	£
"Emm"	5,100	50	255,000	40	204,000	10	51,000
	1,000	45	45,000	40	40,000	5	5,000
"Ess"	23,600	20	472,000	15	354,000	5	118,000
	6,000	18	108,000	15	90,000	3	18,000
			£880,000		£688,000		£192,000

Product	Revised standard sales	Profit	
	Value	Percentage	Value
	£		£
"Emm"	275,000	20·00 ($\frac{1}{5}$)	55,000
	39,600	11·11 ($\frac{1}{9}$)	4,400
"Ess"	466,400	25·00 ($\frac{1}{4}$)	116,600
	99,000	16·67 ($\frac{1}{6}$)	16,500
	£880,000		£192,500

NOTES

1. Standard sales = Actual quantity, sold at standard prices.
2. Revised standard sales = Budgeted proportions of standard sales.

"Emm" at standard price $= \dfrac{250,000}{800,000} \times$ £880,000 = £275,000.

„   at standard discount price $= \dfrac{36,000}{800,000} \times$ £880,000 = £39,600.

"Ess" at standard price $= \dfrac{424,000}{800,000} \times$ £880,000 = £466,400.

„   at standard discount price $= \dfrac{90,000}{800,000} \times$ £880,000 = £99,000.

3. *Revised standard profit*

According to the budget, the percentage profit to turnover is as follows:

"Emm" at standard price $= \dfrac{10}{50} \times 100 = 20\%$ ($\frac{1}{5}$).

„   at standard discount price $= \dfrac{5}{45} \times 100 = 11\cdot11\%$ ($\frac{1}{9}$).

"Ess" at standard price $= \dfrac{5}{20} \times 100 = 25\%$ ($\frac{1}{4}$).

„   at standard discount price $= \dfrac{3}{18} \times 100 = 16\cdot67\%$ ($\frac{1}{6}$).

Total sales margin variance
  BP — AP

	£		£	£
"Emm"	54,000	—	54,600	600 (F)
"Ess"	121,000	—	131,400	10,400 (F)
Total	£175,000	—	£186,000	£11,000 (F)

Sales margin variance due to selling prices
  SP — AP

	£		£	£
"Emm"	56,000	—	54,600	1,400 (A)
"Ess"	136,000	—	131,400	4,600 (A)
Total	£192,000		£186,000	£6,000 (A)

This variance shows the change in profit due to a normal change in selling price. However, in this illustration, one is considering also the effect on profit of a change in sales quantity discount, therefore one must sub-divide the above variance to show the price change and the discount change. Thus one can replace the above variance by two variances, which reveal to management the information required. The formula used is similar to the simple price variance for direct materials, which was discussed in the previous chapter.

Sales margin variance due to selling prices
  AQ (SP — AP)

"Emm"	600 (£50 — £48)	£1,200 (A)	
"Ess"	3,600 (£20 — £19)	£3,600 (A)	£4,800 (A)

Sales margin variance due to sales allowances
  AQ (SDP — ADP)

"Emm"	200 (£45 — £44)	£200 (A)	
"Ess"	100 (£18 — £17)	£1,000 (A)	£1,200 (A)

The D in the formula represents Discount.

Sales volume variance
  BP — SP

	£		£	£
"Emm"	54,000	—	56,000	2,000 (F)
"Ess"	121,000	—	136,000	15,000 (F)
	£175,000	—	£192,000	£17,000 (F)

Sales quantity variance
  BP — RSP

	£		£	£
"Emm"	54,000	—	59,400	5,400 (F)
"Ess"	121,000	—	133,100	12,100 (F)
	£175,000	—	£192,500	£17,500 (F)

Sales margin variance due to sales quantities (mixture)
RSP − SP

	£		£		£
"Emm"	59,400	−	56,000		3,400 (A)
"Ess"	133,100	−	136,000		2,900 (F)
	£192,500	−	£192,000		£500 (A)

Examination questions on Chapters 25–27 are given at the end of Chapter 27.

STANDARD COSTING

Comprehensive Illustration of Variance Analysis

IN this chapter an advanced illustration is given which includes the majority of the variances mentioned in the previous chapters. This illustration shows how variances could be calculated in a process factory which had adopted a standard costing technique.

Variances have been calculated in respect of two products, "Exe" and "Wye." It is suggested that the reader should follow through the variances shown for "Exe," then should try to calculate those for "Wye," using exactly the same principles as were used for "Exe." Reference could then be made to the illustration to check whether or not the reader had understood the calculation of variances.

EXAMPLE

The Standard Engineering Co. Ltd. manufactures two products "Exe" and "Wye." Details of the direct material cost of these products are as follows:

"Exe"	"Wye"
Material C: 60% at £20 per ton	Material E: 30% at £15 per ton
Material D: 40% at £15 per ton	Material F: 70% at £5 per ton

Normal loss in production of "Exe" is 10% and that of "Wye" is 20%. Owing to a shortage of Materials D and E, it was not possible to use the standard mix in February. However, normal loss in production is expected to be the same as formerly. Actual results for the month were:

"Exe"	£	"Wye"	£
Material C: 280 tons at £19	5,320	Material E: 100 tons at £17	1,700
Material D: 120 tons at £18	2,160	Material F: 300 tons at £4	1,200
400	7,480	400	2,900
Loss 36		Loss 84	
364	£7,480	316	£2,900

MATERIAL

Show in respect of Products "Exe" and "Wye":

(a) price variance;
(b) mixture variance;
(c) yield variance.

1. "EXE"

Material input	Standard cost			Actual cost			Standard cost of A. mix		
	Tons	Price	Amount	Tons	Price	Amount	Tons	Price	Amount
			£			£			£
C	240	20	4,800	280	19	5,320	280	20	5,600
D	160	15	2,400	120	18	2,160	120	15	1,800
	400		7,200	400		7,480	400		7,400
Loss	40		—	36		—	36		
TOTAL	360		£7,200	364		£7,480	364		£7,400

(a) Direct Materials Price Variance

$$Formula = AQ\,(AP - SP)$$
$$= \begin{matrix} C: 280\,(19 - 20) = 280\,(F) \\ D: 120\,(18 - 15) = 360\,(A) \end{matrix} = \underline{\underline{£80\,(A)}}$$

(b) Direct Materials Mixture Variance

$$Formula = SP\,(SQ - AQ)$$
$$= \begin{matrix} C: 20\,(240 - 280) = 800\,(A) \\ D: 15\,(160 - 120) = 600\,(F) \end{matrix} = \underline{\underline{£200\,(A)}}$$

(c) Direct Materials Yield Variance

$$Formula = SC\,(SY - AY)$$
$$= £20\,(360 - 364) = \underline{\underline{£80\,(F)}}.$$

Check

(i) SC − AC = Direct materials cost variance
$$£7,280 - £7,480 = \underline{\underline{£200\,(A)}}$$

(ii)
$$\frac{Price}{variance} + \frac{Mixture}{variance} + \frac{Yield}{variance} = \frac{Cost}{variance}$$
$$£80\,(A) + £200\,(A) + £80\,(F) = \underline{\underline{£200\,(A)}}$$

Accounting entries

Stores Ledger Control Account

	£		£
Actual cost	7,480	Direct materials price variance	80
		Work in progress	7,400
	£7,480		£7,480

Work-in-progress Ledger Control Account

	£		£
Stores	7,400	Direct materials mixture variance	200
Direct materials yield variance	80	Finished goods (standard cost)	7,280
	£7,480		£7,480

NOTE: Standard cost = Actual production at standard cost per unit
= 364 tons at £20 per ton
= £7,280.

2. "WYE"

Material input	Standard cost			Actual cost			Standard cost of A. mix		
	Tons	Price	Amount	Tons	Price	Amount	Tons	Price	Amount
			£			£			£
E	120	15	1,800	100	17	1,700	100	15	1,500
F	280	5	1,400	300	4	1,200	300	5	1,500
	400		3,200	400		2,900	400		3,000
Loss	80		—	84		—	84		—
TOTAL	320		£3,200	316		£2,900	316		£3,000

(a) Direct Materials Price Variance

Formula = AQ (AP − SP)

$$= \begin{array}{l} \text{E: } 100\,(17-15) = 200\,(A) \\ \text{F: } 300\,(4-5)\ \ = 300\,(F) \end{array} = \underline{\underline{£100\,(F)}}$$

(b) Direct Materials Mixture Variance

Formula = SP (SQ − AQ)

$$= \begin{array}{l} \text{E: } 15\,(120-100) = 300\,(F) \\ \text{F: } 5\,(280-300) = 100\,(A) \end{array} = \underline{\underline{£200\,(F)}}$$

(c) Direct Materials Yield Variance

Formula = SC (SY − AY)
= £10 (320 − 316) = £40 (A)

Check

(*i*) SC − AC = Direct materials cost variance
£3,160 − £2,900 = £260 (F)

(*ii*)

$$\frac{\text{Price}}{\text{variance}} + \frac{\text{Mixture}}{\text{variance}} + \frac{\text{Yield}}{\text{variance}} = \frac{\text{Cost}}{\text{variance}}$$

£100 (F) + £200 (F) | £40 (A) = £260 (F)

Accounting entries

Stores Ledger Control Account

	£		£
Actual cost	2,900	Work in progress	3,000
Direct materials price variance	100		
	£3,000		£3,000

Work-in-progress Ledger Control Account

	£		£
Stores	3,000	Direct materials yield variance	40
Direct materials mixture variance	200	Finished goods (standard cost)	3,160
	£3,200		£3,200

NOTE: Standard cost = Actual production at standard cost per unit
= 316 tons at £10 per ton
= £3,160.

LABOUR

In the factory of the Standard Engineering Co. Ltd. 100 men and 35 women were employed. A 5-day week of 40 hours is worked. There were 4 weeks in the month, so the budgeted number of working hours was 160 hours. 21 days were actually worked.

Standard wages costs were:

"Exe": 60 men at £0·50
15 women at £0·40
"Wye": 40 men at £0·50 } per hour for 160 hours.
20 women at £0·40

There was a temporary shortage of men operatives, which necessitated an increase in the number of women operatives employed.

Actual wages paid during the month were:

"Exe": 50 men at £0·55
25 women at £0·40
"Wye": 30 men at £0·55 } per hour for 168 hours.
30 women at £0·40

Show the labour variances in respect of products "Exe" and "Wye."

1. "EXE"

Operatives	Standard cost			Actual cost			Revised standard cost		
	Hours	Rate	Amount	Hours	Rate	Amount	Hours	Rate	Amount
			£			£			£
Men	9,600	£0·50	4,800	8,400	£0·55	4,620	8,000	£0·50	4,000
Women	2,400	£0·40	960	4,200	£0·40	1,680	4,000	£0·40	1,600
TOTAL	12,000		£5,760	12,600		£6,300	12,000		£5,600

(a) Direct Wages Rate Variance

$Formula$ = AH (AR − SR)

= Men: 8,400 (£0·55 − £0·50) = £420 (A)

(b) Direct Labour Mix Variance

$Formula$ = SC of SM − revised SC

$= \begin{matrix} \text{Men:} & 4,800 - 4,000 = £800 \text{ (F)} \\ \text{Women:} & 960 - 1,600 = £640 \text{ (A)} \end{matrix} = £160 \text{ (F)}$

NOTE: Where there is a specific change in mix of labour, the revised standard cost is compared with the original standard cost to show the mix variance.

(c) Direct Labour Efficiency Variance

$Formula$ = SR (AH − SH)

$= \begin{matrix} \text{Men:} & £0·50 (8,400 - 8,000) = £200 \text{ (A)} \\ \text{Women:} & £0·40 (4,200 - 4,000) = £80 \text{ (A)} \end{matrix} = £280 \text{ (A)}$

NOTE: Owing to the introduction of a mix variance, the revised standard time must be used.

It was pointed out earlier that the many variances described were items generally used in many industries. Of course, there are a number of other variances peculiar to some industries, and one such variance occurs in this illustration.

It will have been noted that this illustration is applicable to a process industry, two products "Exe" and "Wye" being manufactured in a continuous process in which normal losses in production occur; in addition, in the current month there was an abnormal gain of 4 tons of "Exe" and an abnormal loss of 4 tons of "Wye." In many firms losses in production are not related to inefficiency of labour: they may be caused by poor-quality materials, adverse weather conditions, etc. Thus, abnormal gains or abnormal losses may not necessarily be due to efficiency or inefficiency, therefore a separate variance may be shown, viz.: yield variance.

(d) Direct Labour Yield Variance

The direct labour yield variance is analogous to the direct materials yield variance, and reflects the gain or loss to the firm in terms of labour, of an increase or decrease in yield.

Formula = SC (SY − AY)
$$= £16 (360 − 364) = \underline{£64 \text{ (F)}}$$

NOTE: £5,760 ÷ 360 tons = £16 per ton.

Check

(*i*) SC − AC = Direct wages variance
$$£5,824 − £6,300 = \underline{£476 \text{ (A)}}$$

(*ii*) $\dfrac{\text{Rate}}{\text{variance}} + \dfrac{\text{Mix}}{\text{variance}} + \dfrac{\text{Efficiency}}{\text{variance}} + \dfrac{\text{Yield}}{\text{variance}} = \dfrac{\text{Direct wages}}{\text{variance}}$

£420 (A) + £160 (F) + £280 (A) + £64 (F) = £476 (A)

Accounting entries

Direct Wages Control Account

	£		£
Actual wages	6,300	Direct wages rate variance	420
		Work in progress	5,880
	£6,300		£6,300

Work-in-progress Ledger Control Account

	£		£
Direct wages	5,880	Direct labour efficiency variance	280
Direct labour mix variance	160	Finished goods (standard cost)	5,824
Direct labour yield variance	64		
	£6,104		£6,104

NOTE: Standard cost = Actual production at standard cost per unit
= 364 tons at £16 per ton
= £5,824.

2. "WYE"

Operatives	Standard cost			Actual cost			Revised standard cost		
	Hours	Rate	Amount	Hours	Rate	Amount	Hours	Rate	Amount
			£			£			£
Men	6,400	£0·50	3,200	5,040	£0·55	2,772	4,800	£0·50	2,400
Women	3,200	£0·40	1,280	5,040	£0·40	2,016	4,800	£0·40	1,920
TOTAL	9,600		£4,480	10,080		£4,788	9,600		£4,320

(a) Direct Wages Rate Variance

Formula = AH (AR − SR)
$$= \text{Men: } 5,040 (£0·55 − £0·50) = \underline{£252 \text{ (A)}}$$

(b) Direct Labour Mix Variance

$Formula$ = SC of SM — revised SC

$$= \begin{matrix} \text{Men:} & £3,200 - £2,400 = £800 \text{ (F)} \\ \text{Women:} & £1,280 - £1,920 = £640 \text{ (A)} \end{matrix} = £160 \text{ (F)}$$

(c) Direct Labour Efficiency Variance

$Formula$ = SR (AH — SH)

$$= \begin{matrix} \text{Men:} & £0{\cdot}50 \; (5,040 - 4,800) = £120 \text{ (A)} \\ \text{Women:} & £0{\cdot}40 \; (5,040 - 4,800) = \;\; £96 \text{ (A)} \end{matrix} = £216 \text{ (A)}$$

(d) Direct Labour Yield Variance

$Formula$ = SC (SY — AY)

$$= £14 \; (320 - 364) = £56 \text{ (A)}$$

NOTE: £4,480 ÷ 320 tons = £14 per ton.

Check

(i) SC — AC = Direct wages variance

$$£4,424 - £4,788 = £364 \text{ (A)}$$

(ii) $\dfrac{\text{Rate}}{\text{variance}} + \dfrac{\text{Mix}}{\text{variance}} + \dfrac{\text{Efficiency}}{\text{variance}} + \dfrac{\text{Yield}}{\text{variance}} = \dfrac{\text{Direct wages}}{\text{variance}}$

$$£252 \text{ (A)} + £160 \text{ (F)} + £216 \text{ (A)} + £56 \text{ (A)} = £364 \text{ (A)}$$

Accounting entries

Direct Wages Control Account

	£		£
Actual wages	4,788	Direct wages rate variance	252
		Work in progress	4,536
	£4,788		£4,788

Work-in-progress Ledger Control Account

	£		£
Direct wages	4,536	Direct labour efficiency variance	216
Direct labour mix variance	160	Direct labour yield variance	56
		Finished goods (standard cost)	4,424
	£4,696		£4,696

NOTE: Standard cost = Actual production at standard cost per unit
= 316 tons at £14 per ton
= £4,424.

VARIABLE OVERHEAD

The standard variable overhead has been set at £5 per ton in respect of "Exe" and £4 per ton in respect of "Wye." The actual variable overhead incurred during the month was £1,880 and £1,300 in respect of "Exe" and "Wye" respectively.

1. "EXE"

Expenditure Variance

Formula = Actual variable overhead — Standard variable overhead
= AVO — SVO
= £1,880 — £1,820 = £60 (A)

Accounting entries

Variable Overhead Control Account

	£		£
Actual overhead	1,880	Expenditure variance	60
		Work in progress	1,820
	£1,880		£1,880

NOTE: Standard cost = Actual production at standard cost per unit
= 364 tons at £5 per ton
= £1,820.

2. "WYE"

Expenditure Variance

Formula = AVO — SVO
= £1,300 — £1,264 = £36 (A)

Accounting entries

Variable Overhead Control Account

	£		£
Actual overhead	1,300	Expenditure variance	36
		Work in progress	1,264
	£1,300		£1,300

NOTE: Standard cost = Actual production at standard cost per unit
= 316 tons at £4 per ton
= £1,264

FIXED OVERHEAD

The budgeted production for the year is:
"Exe" 4,500 tons, "Wye" 4,000 tons.

The budgeted fixed overheads for the year are:
"Exe" £90,000, "Wye" £60,000.

There are 50 working weeks in the year; 4 weeks in February. One extra day was actually worked during the month.

The actual fixed overheads for February amounted to £7,100 and £4,750 in respect of "Exe" and "Wye" respectively.

Show the overhead variances.

1. "EXE"

> *Actual* production for the month = 364 tons
> *Budgeted*   „   „   „   = 360 „
> *Standard*   „   „   „   = 378 „

(Budgeted production is 18 tons per day, therefore the standard production for 21 days is 378 tons.)

Budgeted fixed overhead = $\frac{4}{50} \times$ £90,000 = £7,200.

Check: Budgeted production at BFO per ton $\left(= \frac{£90,000}{4,500} = £20 \right)$

$$= 360 \text{ tons at £20} = £7,200.$$

Standard fixed overhead = Actual production at standard cost per ton
= 364 tons at £20 = £7,280.

(a) Overhead Expenditure Variance

Formula = AFO − BFO
= £7,100 − £7,200 = £100 (F)

(b) Volume Variance

Formula = SC (AQ − BQ)
= 20 (364 − 360) = £80 (F)

(c) Volume Efficiency Variance

Formula = SC (AQ − SQ)
= 20 (364 − 378) = £280 (A)

NOTE: This variance does not reflect the true volume efficiency variance, because, as in the case of materials and labour, one must consider the effect of the increase in yield, which was an abnormal gain. In effect, the work performed was on 400 tons processed, out of which 360 tons finished production were expected. It is incidental that 364 tons were actually produced; it was not necessarily caused by efficient use of machinery. Therefore this variance can be split to show the effect of increased yield. This would have the effect of showing the actual quantity produced, as being the work commensurate with the actual effort involved.
    The position would then be:

(c) Volume Efficiency Variance

Formula = SC (AQ − SQ)
= 20 (360 − 378) = £360 (A)

(d) Fixed Overhead Yield Variance

$$Formula = SC (SY - AY)$$
$$= £20 (360 - 364) = £80 (F)$$

As can be observed the net total of the last two variances is the same as the previous efficiency variance.

(e) Capacity Usage Variance

$$Formula = SC (RBQ - SQ)$$
$$= 20 (378 - 378) = Nil$$

(f) Calendar Variance

$$Formula = BFO (RBH - BH)$$

This formula was illustrated on page 534 and is convenient when calculating variances on a standard hour basis which is discussed on page 536. However in this illustration we are using the standard cost per unit method, so students might find the following formula more convenient:

$$SC (RBQ - BQ)$$
$$20 (378 - 360) = £360 (F)$$

When a calendar variance occurs it is necessary to revise the formula for the capacity usage variance, because if more hours are available the capacity of the plant is obviously increased; alternatively, less hours available would reduce the capacity of the plant. Thus the budget is revised to allow for the increased/decreased capacity. The revised budgeted quantity is:

$$21 \text{ days worked at 18 tons per day} = 378 \text{ tons.}$$

Check 1

(i) SC − AC = Overhead variance

$$£7,280 - £7,100 = £180 (F)$$

(ii) Expenditure variance + Volume variance = Overhead variance

$$£100 (F) + £80 (F) = £180 (F)$$

Check 2

Volume variance	=	Volume efficiency variance	+	Yield variance	+	Capacity usage variance	+	Calendar variance
£80 (F)	=	£360 (A)	+	£80 (F)	+	Nil	+	£360 (F)

Accounting entries

Fixed Overhead Control Account

	£		£
Actual overhead	7,100	Work in progress	7,200
Overhead expenditure variance	100		
	£7,200		£7,200

Work-in-progress Ledger Control Account

	£		£
Fixed overhead	7,200	Volume efficiency variance	360
Calendar variance	360	Finished goods (standard cost)	7,280
Yield variance	80		
	£7,640		£7,640

NOTE: Standard cost = Actual production at standard cost per unit
= 364 tons at £20 per ton
= £7,280.

2. "WYE"

Actual production for the month = 316 tons
Budgeted „ „ „ = 320 „
Standard „ „ „ = 336 „

Budgeted fixed overhead = $\frac{4}{50} \times$ £60,000 = £4,800.

Check: Budgeted production at BFO per ton $\left(= \frac{£60,000}{4,000} = £15 \right)$
= 320 tons at £15 = £4,800.

Standard fixed overhead = Actual production at standard cost per ton
= 316 tons at £15 = £4,740.

(a) **Overhead Expenditure Variance**

Formula = AFO − BFO
= £4,750 − £4,800 = £50 (F)

(b) **Volume Variance**

Formula = SC (AQ − BQ)
= 15 (316 − 320) = £60 (A)

(c) **Volume Efficiency Variance**

Formula = SC (AQ − SQ)
= 15 (320 − 336) = £240 (A)

(d) Fixed Overhead Yield Variance

$$Formula = SC\,(SY - AY)$$
$$= 15\,(320 - 316) = \underline{\underline{£60\,(A)}}$$

(e) Capacity Usage Variance

$$Formula = SC\,(RBQ - SQ)$$
$$= 15\,(336 - 336) = \underline{\underline{Nil}}$$

(f) Calendar Variance

$$Formula = SC\,(RBQ - BQ)$$
$$= 15\,(336 - 320) = \underline{\underline{£240\,(F)}}$$

Check 1.

  (i) SC − AC = Overhead variance
$$£4,740 - £4,750 = \underline{\underline{£10\,(A)}}$$

  (ii) Expenditure variance + Volume variance = Overhead variance
$$£50\,(F) + £60\,(A) = \underline{\underline{£10\,(A)}}$$

Check 2.

$$\frac{\text{Volume}}{\text{variance}} = \frac{\text{Volume efficiency}}{\text{variance}} + \frac{\text{Yield}}{\text{variance}} + \frac{\text{Capacity usage}}{\text{variance}} + \frac{\text{Calendar}}{\text{variance}}$$

£60 (A) = £240 (A) + £60 (A) + Nil + £240 (F).

Accounting entries

Fixed Overhead Control Account

	£		£
Actual overhead	4,750	Work in progress	4,800
Overhead expenditure variance	50		
	£4,800		£4,800

Work-in-progress Ledger Control Account

	£		£
Fixed overheads	4,800	Volume efficiency variance	240
Calendar variance	240	Fixed overhead yield variance	60
		Finished goods (standard cost)	4,740
	£5,040		£5,040

NOTE: Standard cost = Actual quantity at standard cost per unit
               = 316 tons at £15 per ton
               = <u>£4,740.</u>

SALES

The sales budget and the actual sales achieved for the month of February are as follows:

Product	Budget			Actual		
	Quantity	Price	Value	Quantity	Price	Value
		£	£		£	£
"Exe"	360	80	28,800	364	79	28,756
"Wye"	320	50	16,000	316	51	16,116
TOTAL			£44,800			£44,872

Show the sales variances in respect of products "Exe" and "Wye."

The standard value of the actual mix of sales and the standard value of the standard mix of sales must be calculated.

Product	Standard sales			Revised standard sales	
	Quantity	Price	Value	Ratio	Value
		£	£		£
"Exe"	364	80	29,120	288 : 160	28,877
"Wye"	316	50	15,800	160 : 288	16,043
TOTAL			£44,920		£44,920

1. "EXE"

(a) Value Variance

$Formula = BS - AS$
$= £28,800 - £28,756 = \underline{\underline{£44 \text{ (A)}}}$

(b) Price Variance

$Formula = SS - AS$
$= £29,120 - £28,756 = \underline{\underline{£364 \text{ (A)}}}$

(c) Volume Variance

$Formula = BS - SS$
$= £28,800 - £29,120 = \underline{\underline{£320 \text{ (F)}}}$

(d) **Quantity Variance**

$Formula$ = BS − RSS
= £28,800 − £28,877 = £77 (F)

(e) **Mix Variance**

$Formula$ = RSS − SS
= £28,877 − £29,120 = £243 (F)

Check
1.   Value variance = Price variance + Volume variance
£44 (A) = £364 (A) + £320 (F)

2.   Volume variance = Quantity variance + Mix variance
£320 (F) = £77 (F) + £243 (F)

Accounting entries

Sales Account

	£		£
Mix variance	243	Price variance	364
Quantity variance	77	Actual sales	28,756
Budgeted sales	28,800		
	£29,120		£29,120

2. "WYE"

(a) **Value Variance**

$Formula$ = BS − AS
= £16,000 − £16,116 = £116 (F)

(b) **Price Variance**

$Formula$ = SS − AS
= £15,800 − £16,116 = £316 (F)

(c) **Volume Variance**

$Formula$ = BS − SS
= £16,000 − £15,800 = £200 (A)

(d) **Quantity Variance**

$Formula$ = BS − RSS
= £16,000 − £16,043 = £43 (F)

(e) **Mix Variance**

$Formula$ = RSS − SS
= £16,043 − £15,800 = £243 (A)

Check

1.   Value variance = Price variance + Volume variance

£116 (F) = £316 (F) + £200 (A)

2.   Volume variance = Quantity variance + Mix variance

£200 (A) = £43 (F) + £243 (A)

Accounting entries

Sales Account

	£		£
Price variance	316	Mix variance	243
Quantity variance	43	Actual sales	16,116
Budgeted sales	16,000		
	£16,359		£16,359

Standard cost of "Exe"
(Output = 364 tons)

Item	Per unit	Total production
	£	£
Direct material	20	7,280
Direct labour	16	5,824
Variable overhead	5	1,820
Fixed overhead	20	7,280
TOTAL	61	22,204
Profit	19	6,916
SALES	£80	£29,120

Standard cost of "Wye"
(Output = 316 tons)

Item	Per unit	Total production
	£	£
Direct material	10	3,160
Direct labour	14	4,424
Variable overhead	4	1,264
Fixed overhead	15	4,740
TOTAL	43	13,588
Profit	7	2,212
SALES	£50	£15,800

PRESENTATION TO MANAGEMENT

Simplified Trading and Profit and Loss Account for the month of February

	"Exe"	"Wye"	Total		"Exe"	"Wye"	Total
	£	£	£		£	£	£
Direct material	7,480	2,900	10,380	Sales	28,756	16,116	44,872
Direct labour	6,300	4,788	11,088				
Variable overhead	1,880	1,300	3,180				
Fixed overhead	7,100	4,750	11,850				
Net profit	5,996	2,378	8,374				
	£28,756	£16,116	£44,872		£28,756	£16,116	£44,872

The above account reveals to management that a net profit of £8,374 has been achieved, of which product "Exe" contributed £5,996 and product "Wye" £2,378, but it does not give much more guidance. It does not reveal what profit could have been expected, or whether the actual profit realised was due to efficient or inefficient utilisation of the firm's resources.

Under a standard costing system, information could be presented to management which would reveal the expected profit and clearly illustrate where any efficiency or inefficiency had been experienced. The information could be presented in a form such as the following:

Profit and Loss Statement for the month of February

	"Exe"	"Wye"	Total	"Exe"	"Wye"	Total
Budgeted sales				28,800	16,000	44,800
Sales variances:						
Price	364 (A)	316 (F)	48 (A)			
Quantity	77 (F)	43 (F)	120 (F)			
Mix	243 (F)	243 (A)	Nil			
				44 (A)	116 (F)	72 (F)
Actual sales				28,756	16,116	44,872
Less Standard cost of sales						
Material	7,280	3,160	10,440			
Labour	5,824	4,424	10,248			
Variable overhead	1,820	1,264	3,084			
Fixed overhead	7,280	4,740	12,020			
				22,204	13,588	35,792
STANDARD NET PROFIT				6,552	2,528	9,080
Production variances:						
Direct material—						
Price	80 (A)	100 (F)	20 (F)			
Mixture	200 (A)	200 (F)	—			
Yield	80 (F)	40 (A)	40 (F)			
				200 (A)	260 (F)	60 (F)
Direct labour—						
Rate	420 (A)	252 (A)	672 (A)			
Mix	160 (F)	160 (F)	320 (F)			
Efficiency	280 (A)	216 (A)	496 (A)			
Yield	64 (F)	56 (A)	8 (F)			
Variable overhead:				476 (A)	364 (A)	840 (A)
Expenditure	60 (A)	36 (A)	96 (A)	60 (A)	36 (A)	96 (A)
Fixed overhead:						
Expenditure	100 (F)	50 (F)	150 (F)			
Volume efficiency	360 (A)	240 (A)	600 (A)			
Yield	80 (F)	60 (A)	20 (F)			
Capacity usage	Nil	Nil	Nil			
Calendar	360 (F)	240 (F)	600 (F)			
				180 (F)	10 (A)	170 (F)
TOTAL				556 (A)	150 (F)	706 (A)
ACTUAL NET PROFIT				£5,996	£2,378	£8,374

The above statement reveals that sales of £44,800 were expected, which would yield a profit of £9,008 (£44,800 − £35,792). Due to an increase in sales value, achieved by a better mix of sales, the profit should have been increased to £9,080. However, this figure was not achieved, due to the following main factors:

1. MATERIAL

A favourable mix variance on "Wye" was offset by an adverse variance on "Exe." A favourable yield variance on "Exe" was only partly offset by an adverse variance on "Wye."

2. LABOUR

Due to a shortage of men operatives, there was a high adverse rate variance. This probably affected the efficiency of the labour force, resulting in an adverse efficiency variance. The fact that women operatives were paid less than men operatives resulted in a favourable mix variance, but this was not enough to offset the high adverse rate and efficiency variances.

3. VARIABLE OVERHEAD

There was a small adverse variance because of increased expenditure due to higher prices.

4. FIXED OVERHEAD

The inefficiency already referred to under 2 above resulted in inefficient utilisation of plant and equipment, resulting in a high adverse variance. This variance cancelled out the benefit which should have been obtained by the working of one extra day during the month. There was an adverse expenditure variance due to increased prices.

The actual profit realised was £8,374, which was £634 less than that which should have been achieved. Investigation into the main variances shown should be made immediately.

This investigation of variances, part of "management by exception," concentrates attention on what has gone wrong, thus saving time and effort of management and staff. It must be emphasised that if a standard costing system is to be efficiently operated, action is essential. Variances must be investigated, explained and the necessary action taken.

EXAMINATION QUESTIONS
Also includes questions on Chapters 25 and 26

1. Give the main bases used in building up a standard cost within the divisions of material, labour and overhead costs.

(Comm. A. Final)

2. Explain the meaning of the following terms in relation to standard costing:

    (a) Capacity variance.
    (b) Calendar variance.
    (c) Efficiency variance.

(A.I.A. Final)

3. Define the following terms commonly used in cost accounting: standard hour; labour efficiency variance; yield variance; machine hour rate; accelerated rate of depreciation.

(C.A. Final)

4. State precisely what you understand by the following variances in a standard costing statement: (a) idle time; (b) revision; (c) sales mix; (d) fixed expenditure efficiency; (e) capacity; (f) calendar; and (g) extra allowances.

(I.C.A. Final, May 1963)

5. (a) Explain precisely the meaning of "calendar variance" in relation to standard costing.

(b) Using assumed figures, show how you would calculate a calendar variance.

(I.C.A. Final, May 1962)

6. It sometimes happens that a favourable variance from one standard is directly related to an adverse variance from another, *e.g.* the purchase of processed materials may cause an adverse material price variance but a favourable labour efficiency variance. Give two examples other than the one given above, and explain how you would present and interpret the analysis of variances in such cases.

(I.C.W.A. Final)

7. Material price variance may be accounted for at one of two different stages in the accounting procedure. Set out simple journal entries with suitable figures illustrating the two methods as far as the Work-in-progress Account.

How may the two methods be combined, and what advantage would there be when preparing annual accounts?

(I.C.W.A. Final)

8. Define "cost variance." In practice "total cost variance" would be divided into material cost variance, wages variance, expense variance, etc.

These variances may again be divided. Into what divisions would you separate these variances?

Some variances may either directly or indirectly cause other variances. Give examples, and show how you would bring these facts to the attention of management.

(I.C.W.A. Final)

9. State what you understand by:

    (a) efficiency ratio;
    (b) activity ratio.

Illustrate your answer with a formula and an example of each, calculated from the following figures:

Budgeted production	88 units
Standard hours per unit	10
Actual production	75 units
Actual working hours	600

(I.C.W.A. Inter.)

10. Distinguish between:

(a) an efficiency ratio; and
(b) an overhead efficiency variance.

Illustrate your answer with an example of each calculated from the following figures:

Actual hours worked	12,000
Flexible budget—overhead allowance	£5,750
Standard man-hours per unit	200
Standard overhead rate per standard man-hour	£0·50
Actual units produced	50

(I.C.W.A. Inter.)

11. To assist factory management it is usual to analyse wages cost variances as to cause. Give two instances each of the causes of:

(a) wages rate variance;
(b) labour efficiency variance.

In each case show how the amount of the variance would be obtained and what corrective action factory management might take.

(I.C.W.A. Inter.)

12. Utopians Ltd. commenced business on January 1, and a system of standard costing was installed. The company manufactures one product of a standard type, and the standard cost was fixed:

Standard price of materials	£0·30 per lb
Standard quantity of materials	8 lb per unit
Standard direct labour cost	£10 per unit

Factory overheads were estimated at £60,000 for the year. Normal operating time for the year was estimated at 2,000 hours and standard time for the production of one unit is determined as 12 machine hours. The company has twenty-four machines of a uniform type.

It was found that the actual total operating time for the year was exactly 2,000 hours and all machines were fully employed for the whole of the time. The actual output for the year was 3,600 units.

The actual quantity of materials used was 30,000 lb; and the cost £9,150.

The actual direct wages for the year amounted to £40,000. Rates of pay did not vary from the estimated rate used in fixing the standard cost. The actual factory overheads for the year were £61,800. You are required:

(a) to compute the standard cost per unit and the standard cost of the output;

(b) to set out the variances.

(C.I.S. Final)

13. Doers Ltd. operates a standard costing system. In connection with the weekly cost report for Process 9 you have been informed:

1. that the standard costs per hour of the process, based on a normal week of 40 hours' work, are:

	£
Wages	0·9
Variable expenses	0·25
Fixed expenses	1·25
	£2·40

Standard output in units per hour   20

2. that the following information has been recorded in respect of the process for the week ended November 23, 1962:

Hours worked	36
Non-productive hours (waiting work)	4
Total hours paid for	40
Output	850 units
Actual wages paid	£37
Actual variable expenses	£12
Actual fixed expenses	£50

You are required to compute the variances relating to Process 9 for the week.

(I.C.A. Final, November 1962)

14. Delaware Ltd. has computed the following information for the calendar year:

Budgeted production	10,000 units
Budgeted fixed overhead	£5,000
Budgeted total machine hours	25,000 hours
Budgeted variable overhead	£6,000

It is also found that each unit requires 1 lb of raw material at a standard cost of £0·25 per lb. Labour rates are £0·33½ per hour, and a unit of output requires 1½ standard hours.

Labour rates have been stable, but raw material prices have proved to be 5% above standard.

In the present budget period (March) the following information is obtained:

Fixed expenses	£550
Normal machine hours	2,000 hours
Machine hours paid for (these differ from the standard time because of a strike)	1,600 hours
Idle time (machine)	60 hours
Actual production	450 units
Raw materials	£125
Variable overhead	£280
Direct wages	£210

You are required to set out the variances under their separate heads for the month of March, showing precisely how each is calculated, together with variances summary and analysis.

(C.A.A. Final)

15. A manufacturing company operates a standard costing system and showed the following data in respect of November:

Actual number of working days	22
Actual man-hours worked during the month	4,300
Number of products produced	425
Actual overhead incurred	£1,800

Relevant information from the company's budget and standard cost data is as follows:

Budgeted number of working days per month	20
Budgeted man-hours per month	4,000
Standard man-hours per product	10
Standard overhead rate per man-hour	£0·5

You are required to calculate for the month of November:

(a) the overhead variance;
(b) the calendar variance;
(c) the volume variance.

(I.C.W.A. Inter.)

16. Mass Production Ltd. manufactures one product of a standard type. A system of standard costing is in operation. The standard costs per hour were:

	£
Factory wages	22·50
Factory overhead	10·00
	£32·50

The standard output is 100 articles per hour. The normal working hours for a four-week period are 160. During the four weeks ended November 4, 1967, the actual factory wages paid amounted to £3,750, representing payments for 160 hours, of which 148 were working hours and 12 were idle hours.

The actual factory expenses were £1,600. The output of the factory was 15,600 articles.

You are required to set out and complete a table in the following form:

		Unfavourable	Favourable
Wages variances:	Efficiency		
	Idle time		
	Rate		
	TOTAL	£	£
Overhead variances:	Efficiency		
	Volume		
	TOTAL	£	£

(*C.I.S. Final, December 1967*)

17. The Trading and Profit and Loss Accounts of A.B.C. Ltd. for the year ended March 31 are as follows:

	£		£
Materials	6,800	Sales (14,400 units)	14,400
Labour	4,280		
Direct charges	800		
	11,880		
General works charges	880		
Office charges	600		
Net Profit	1,040		
	£14,400		£14,400

The standard output for the year to March 31 was fixed at 20,000 units. Standard costs per unit were as follows:

	£
Materials	0·45
Labour	0·30
Direct charges	0·10

General works charges are fixed at £600 per annum, the balance of expenditure being variable, with a standard of £0·02½ per unit.

Office charges are fixed at £600 per annum.

You are required to prepare a Profit and Loss Statement, showing the standard cost figures, actual costs and variances, suggesting reasons for the variances shown. Assume there were no opening and closing stocks.

(*C.A.A. Final*)

18. Blues Ltd., paint manufacturers, have a number of production processes. In one of these processes four main items are manufactured which form the base stocks of subsequent processes.

The specifications of the base stock items are:

	Standard cost per lb	A lb	B lb	C lb	D lb
Ingredient p	0·12½	50	45	30	40
q	0·05	5	—	30	—
r	0·10	10	25	30	25
s	0·15	20	15	5	35
t	0·20	15	15	5	20
Standard batch size		100	100	100	120

Spillage allowance, not included above 2%.
During the four-week period ended April 28 the production was:

A	300 batches
B	450 batches
C	99 batches
D	940 batches

The actual quantities of ingredients used were reported as:

		Actual cost per lb
p	78,000 lb	£0·14
q	4,600 lb	£0·05
r	42,000 lb	£0·12½
s	46,000 lb	£0·12½
t	30,500 lb	£0·22½

On a form suitable for presentation to the departmental manager concerned, calculate the value of the material price and material usage variances. Show all workings.

(C.A. Final)

19. A factory manufactures a product which passes through two processes, machining and finishing.
Standard direct costs for the product are:

	Standard cost per unit
Machining	
Materials	£10
Labour	£2
Finishing	
Labour	£1

These standard costs are based on full capacity output of 12,000 units, which would require 120,000 man-hours on machining, and 48,000 man-hours on finishing.

In November actual results were:

Production   10,000 units

Machining
Materials used, at standard cost	£99,000
Materials used, actual cost	£105,000
Labour (104,000 man-hours), actual wages paid	£20,800

Finishing
Labour (46,000 man-hours), actual wages paid	£10,350

You are required to:

(*a*) analyse the direct cost variances for November; and
(*b*) state which of the following explanations of the variances are *not* consistent with the accounting information:

(*i*) pilfering of materials caused above standard material consumption;
(*ii*) labour efficiency in the machining department was higher than the standard set.
(*iii*) some workers were employed in finishing whose skill and pay were lower than was anticipated in setting the standards;
(*iv*) there was a general pay increase to workers in the finishing department.

A discussion is not required; simply give your answer in the form: "The variances provide no evidence for explanations . . . *numbers* . . ."

(A.C.C.S. Final)

20. The following statistics relate to a recent week's working in a machine shop at Biobso Ltd., a company engaged in manufacturing motor car components:

	Process A	Process B	Total
Hours:			
Output expressed in standard hours	440	720	
Normal working hours	400	900	
Actual hours worked on production	360	810	
Idle hours	40	90	
Total hours paid for	400	900	
Wages:			
Standard cost per hour	£2	£1	
Actual wages paid	£800	£880	
Variable expense:			
Standard cost per hour	£0·50	£1	
Actual expense	—	—	£1,210
Fixed expense:			
Standard cost per hour	£1·50	£1	
Actual expense	—	—	£1,350

You are required to prepare a statement showing the capacity, efficiency and activity (or volume) ratios for the two processes, and a full variance analysis of wages, variable and fixed expenses for both processes and the machine shop as a whole.

(*I.C.A. Final, May 1969*)

21. The Alfa Manufacturing Company has, at your instigation, introduced a system of standard costing. The operating statement covering the first three months has just been prepared and is detailed below. Prepare a report for the management of the organisation in non-technical language outlining the meaning and significance of the figures disclosed.

Operating statement for three months ended . . .

		Budget	*Variation from budget increase decrease*	*increase decrease*
	£	£	£	£
Sales		100,000		4,500
Standard cost of sales		75,000		7,500
Standard gross profit		25,000		3,000
Selling expenses	6,500		500	
Administration expenses	4,500		150	
Research expenses	5,000		650	
	——	16,000	——	300
Standard net profit		£9,000		£2,700

Factory variances	*Favourable* £	*Adverse* £
Material price	50	
Material usage	200	
Labour rate		550
Labour mix		210
Labour efficiency	65	
Variable overhead expenditure		10
Fixed overhead expenditure		375
Fixed overhead calendar	125	
Fixed overhead efficiency		140
	£440	£1,285
		845
Total variation from budget profit		£3,545

(*A.C.C.A. Final*)

22. A gang of workers normally consists of 10 men, 5 women and 5 boys, paid at standard hourly rates of £0·4, £0·3 and £0·2 respectively. In a normal

working week of 40 hours, the gang is expected to produce 1,000 units of output.

In a certain week the gang consisted of 13 men, 4 women and 3 boys; 720 hours were worked; actual wages paid amounted to £250; 1,000 units of output were produced.

Present information in respect of the labour cost variances arising during this period.

(I.C.W.A. Final)

23. In standard costing, certain "ratios" are used to illustrate the effective use of the resources of the company. Define these ratios, and illustrate your answer by using the following figures, which are in respect of a four-week period. In this period there was a special one-day holiday due to a national event.

Standard working:	8 hours per day	
	5 days per week	
Maximum capacity	50 employees	
Actually working	40 employees	
Actual hours expected to be worked per four weeks		6,400 hours
Standard hours expected to be earned per four weeks		8,000 hours
Actual hours worked in the four-week period		6,000 hours
Standard hours earned in the four-week period		7,000 hours

(I.C.W.A. Final)

24. A company operating a standard costing system uses standard direct wages rates of:

		Per hour £
Department: A		0·73½
	B	0·70
	C	0·75

During the month of November there was produced:

		Standard hours allowed
Department: A		180 dozen at 270 per gross
	B	30 gross at 26 per dozen
	C	9,600 units at 130 per 100 units

There was worked:

	Actual hours		Actual hourly wage rate £
Department: A	4,080	at	0·75
	B	9,900	at	0·66½
	C	11,000	at	0·80

You are required to calculate and present to works management in summary form for each department and in total the standard value of production and the appropriate variances which arise.

(I.C.W.A. Inter.)

25. The following monthly data relate to a production department in a manufacturing company:

	Budgeted overhead £	Actual overhead £
Fixed:		
Depreciation of machinery	1,300	1,300
Rent and rates	500	500
Insurance	200	235
Supervision	1,600	1,625
	3,600	3,660
Variable:		
Fuel	4,000	3,600
Indirect labour	2,000	1,700
Power, light, heat	1,600	1,500
Maintenance	800	600
	8,400	7,400
Total	£12,000	£11,060

Budgeted hours were 8,000 per month. During January actual hours worked were 6,400 and actual goods produced were valued at 6,800 standard hours.

Calculate:

(*a*) the standard fixed overhead rate per hour;
(*b*) the standard variable overhead rate per hour;
(*c*) the overhead variance in total;
(*d*) the overhead variance sub-divided into:

    (*i*) capacity usage variance;
    (*ii*) volume efficiency variance;
    (*iii*) overhead efficiency variance;
    (*iv*) overhead price variance (assume that this relates to fixed costs only);
    (*v*) overhead utilisation variance (assume that this relates to variable costs only).

(I.C.W.A. Inter.)

26. Caton Ltd. make two qualities of fireclay brick by mixing clay with either bauxite or "grog." The standard price of clay is £2 per ton and of bauxite is £15 per ton.

Bauxite is an imported ore. "Grog" is crushed scrap brick of either quality. Excess scrap can be absorbed by substituting it for ordinary clay, and if scrap is insufficient to supply the need for grog a satisfactory substitute can be purchased for £3 per ton. A loss of weight takes place in the firing process which may be regarded as affecting all materials equally.

The product standards are:

	Quality A	Quality B
Clay	87½%	80%
Bauxite	—	20%
Grog	12½%	—
	100%	100%

Product standard cost	£10 per ton	£14 per ton

In period 1 Quality A was in fact made from a mixture of 83⅓% clay and 16⅔% grog. Other information in respect of period 1 was:

		Quality A	Quality B
Bricks produced (gross)	Budget	2,500 tons	1,000 tons
	Actual	2,400 „	1,500 „
Process loss	Budget	75 „	30 „
Scrapped	Budget	250 „	100 „
	Actual	360 „	75 „
Raw material input	Actual	Clay	3,289 „
		Bauxite	312 „
		Grog	428 „

You are required:

1. to prepare a materials usage statement for period 1 and calculate the materials mixture and yield variances;
2. to calculate the scrap efficiency variance.

(I.C.A. Final)

27. The standard mix of a product is as follows:

Material	% of input	Standard price per lb £
A	10	0·50
B	40	0·25
C	20	0·12½
D	30	0·16½

From each mix of 200 lb of input, a standard output of 180 lb is obtained.

During the month of May, 20 mixes were processed from which the actual output was 3,500 lb. Actual consumption during May was as follows:

Material	Consumption	Price per lb
	lb	£
A	420	0·47½
B	1,540	0·22½
C	880	0·14
D	1,160	0·15

There was no opening or closing work-in-progress stock.
You are required to:

(a) calculate the following variances:

    (i) Direct materials cost;
    (ii)   ,,   ,,   price;
    (iii)   ,,   ,,   mixture;
    (iv)   ,,   ,,   yield;

(b) show the Materials Work-in-progress Account in the Cost Ledger for the month of May with issues at standard prices.

(I.C.W.A. Inter.)

28. A company manufactures two products Stanco and Actco. It budgeted to produce five batches of Stanco and six batches of Actco each month. The standard material details for each product are as follows:

	Stanco			Actco	
		Standard			Standard
	Percentage	price		Percentage	price
Material	used	per ton	Material	used	per ton
S1	70	£6	A1	40	£15·00
S2	30	£10	A2	60	£18·50
	Loss is 10% of input			Loss is 5% of input	

Actual details of production for May were:

	Stanco			Actco	

Consumption:

	Tons	Actual price		Tons	Actual price
Material	used	per ton	Material	used	per ton
S1	300	£7	A1	300	£14
S2	200	£9	A2	300	£19

Output:

    455 tons from 5 batches   568 tons from 6 batches

There were no opening or closing stocks of finished products.
The cost accountant has commenced the compilation of the Profit and Loss Statement for May as given below:

Profit and Loss statement
for month of May

	Stanco	Actco	Total
	£	£	£
Budgeted sales	15,750	34,200	49,950
Sales variances	320 (F)	552 (A)	232 (A)
Less Standard cost of sales:			
Direct materials			
Direct labour	2,275	5,680	7,955
Overheads	7,735	12,496	20,231
Standard profit			
Production variances:			
Materials: Price			
Mix			
Yield			
Labour: Rate	40 (A)	55 (A)	95 (A)
Efficiency	60 (F)	45 (F)	105 (F)
Overhead: Expenditure	45 (A)	40 (A)	85 (A)
Efficiency	200 (F)	100 (F)	300 (F)
Capacity	90 (A)	140 (A)	230 (A)
Total			
Actual profit			

NOTE: Adverse variances are indicated by "A" and favourable variances by "F."

(*a*) Compile the standard product costs for a standard batch of 90 tons output of Stanco and a standard batch of 95 tons output of Actco.

(*b*) Complete the Profit and Loss Statement for May.

(*I.C.W.A. Inter.*)

29. The standard mix of product M.5 is as follows:

lb	Material	Price per lb
		£
50	A	0·25
20	B	0·20
30	C	0·50

The standard loss in production is 10% of input. There is no scrap value. Actual production for May was 7,240 lb of M.5 from 80 mixes. Actual purchases and consumption of materials during the month were:

lb	Material	Price per lb
		£
4,160	A	0·27½
1,680	B	0·19
2,560	C	0·47½

You are required to:

(a) calculate and present the following variances:

(i) material cost;
(ii) material price;
(iii) material usage;
(iv) material mix;
(v) yield.

(b) Show how the following accounts would appear in the Cost Ledger after the transactions relating to product M.5 had been posted:

(i) stores ledger control;
(ii) work-in-progress ledger control;
(iii) material price variance;
(iv) material usage variance;
(v) material mix variance;
(vi) yield variance.

(I.C.W.A. Inter.)

30. (a) Within the context of materials accounting, enumerate the steps which have to be taken to install variance analysis procedure.

(b) In a manufacturing process the following standards apply:

Standard price: raw material A £1 per lb
           ,,   ,, B £5 ,,
Standard mix: 75% A; 25% B (by weight)
Standard yield (weight of product as percentage of weight of raw materials): 90%

In a period, the actual costs, usages and output were as follows:

Used: 4,400 lb A, costing £4,650
     1,600 ,, B,   ,, £7,850
Output: 5,670 lb of products
The budgeted output for the period was 7,200 lb.

Prepare an operating statement, showing how the material cost variance is built up, and give activity and yield percentages.

(*I.C.W.A. Inter.*)

31. A brass foundry, making castings which are transferred to the machine shop of the same company at standard prices, uses a standard costing system. Basic standards in regard to materials, stocks of which are kept at standard prices, are as follows:

Standard mixture:	70% copper	
	30% zinc	
Standard prices:	Copper	£240 per ton
	Zinc	£65 „ „
Standard loss in melt	5% of input	

Figures in respect of a costing period are as follows:

Commencing stocks:	Copper	100 tons
	Zinc	60 „
Finishing stocks:	Copper	110 „
	Zinc	50 „
Purchases: Copper	300 tons, cost £73,250	
Zinc	100 „ „ £6,250	
Metal melted	400 „	
Castings produced	375 „	

Present figures showing:

(a) material price variances;
(b) material mixture variance;
(c) material yield variance.

(*I.C.W.A. Final*)

32. In Department X the following data are submitted for the week ended February 20:

Standard output for 40-hour week	1,400 units
Standard fixed overheads	£140
Actual output	1,200 units
Actual hours worked	32
Actual fixed overheads	£150

Compute the variances.

(*A.C.C.A. Final*)

33. From the following basic data calculate:

(a) efficiency variance;
(b) volume variance;
(c) calendar variance.

Item	Budget	Actual
Number of working days	20	22
Standard man-hours per day	8,000	8,400
Output per man-hour in units	1·0	1·2
Total unit output	160,000	221,760
Standard overhead rate per man-hour	£0·10	

(*I.C.W.A. Final*)

34. For the six months ended June 30 the standard output and costs of three products, A, B and C were as follows:

	A	B	C
Output (units)	10,000	20,000	15,000
Cost: Materials	£1,500	£2,500	£3,375
Labour	£2,500	£3,000	£4,500
Standard labour time	1½ hours	1 hour	2 hours
Overhead: Variable	£500	£500	£750
Fixed	£750	£1,000	£1,875

Each product is made in a separate works department. Production and—except as stated below—production costs accrued evenly throughout the six-months' period. Material prices (for Product A only) were increased by 5% on May 1. As from April 1 a wage award of £0·01 per hour was made as regards A and C only.

Actual output and costs for the six months were:

	A	B	C
Output (units)	9,600	18,400	14,200
Cost: Material	£1,560	£2,415	£3,550
Labour	£2,460	£2,875	£4,591
Overhead: Variable	£440	£460	£769
Fixed	£810	£1,230	£1,875

Prepare a statement showing clearly, in respect of each product standard and actual costs, and the nature and amount of the variances that arise.

(A.C.C.A. Final)

35. 1. Explain:

(a) efficiency variance;
(b) capacity variance;
(c) expenditure variance.

2. In a certain firm the planned overheads for a three-month period are £4,000.

The hours actually worked (adjusted by average piece-work hours) and charged at the standard hourly rate are £4,200. Actual overhead amounted to £4,100, while standard overhead charged to production was £4,300.

Compute the variances shown in 1 above.

(A.C.C.A. Final)

36. The standard cost sheet for producing a job consisting of 100 articles for the Harem Manufacturing Co. showed:

Materials

60 lb of A at £0·50 per lb
50 lb of B at £0·60 per lb

Direct wages

20 hours operation 1 at £0·45 per hour
30   „   „   2 at £0·60   „
40   „   „   3 at £0·80   „

Overheads based on direct wages at £0·70 per hour.

Actual costs of the job were:

Materials

70 lb of A at £0·52½ per lb
48 lb of B at £0·65 per lb

Direct wages

25 hours operation 1 at £0·40 per hour
28   „   „   2 at £0·60   „
40   „   „   3 at £0·82½   „

Prepare a table to show:

(a) the standard and actual cost of the job;
(b) the variances analysed as between quantity and price.

(*I.C.W.A. Final*)

37. The standard cost of a certain chemical mixture is:

40% Material A at £20 per ton
60% Material B at £30 per ton

A standard loss of 10% is expected in production. During a period there is used:

90 tons Material A at a cost of £18 per ton
110   „   „   B   „   „   £34   „

The weight produced is 182 tons of good production.
Calculate and present:

(a) material price variance;
(b) material usage variance;
(c) material mix variance;
(d) material yield variance.

(*I.C.W.A. Inter.*)

38. The standard raw material mix for a ton of finished production is:

Material A 1,200 lb at £0·05 per lb
„   B   500 „   £0·20   „
„   C   500 „   £0·10   „
„   D   100 „   £0·50   „

Materials used during an accounting period were as follows:

Material A 2,900 lb at £0·05½ per lb
„   B 1,300 „   £0·21½   „
„   C 1,350 „   £0·09   „
„   D   260 „   £0·40   „

Production during the period was 5,600 lb. Identify and calculate the material cost variances.

(*I.C.W.A. Inter.*)

39. A company manufacturing a special type of facing tile, 12 inches × 8 inches × ½ inch uses a system of standard costing. The standard mix of the compound used for making the tiles is:

1,200 lb of material A at £0·07 per lb
500 ,, ,, B ,, £0·15 ,,
800 ,, ,, C ,, £0·17½ ,,

This compound should produce 12,000 square feet of tiles of ½ inch thickness. During a period in which 100,000 tiles of the standard size were produced, the material usage was:

7,000 lb of material A at £0·07½ per lb
3,000 ,, ,, B ,, £0·16 ,,
5,000 ,, ,, C ,, £0·18½ ,,

Present the cost figures for the period showing:

    (a) material price variance;
    (b) material mixture variance;
    (c) yield variance.

                                      (I.C.W.A. Final)

40. A foundry producing castings of a standard alloy uses standard costs. The standard mixture is as follows:

40% material A at £300 per ton
30% material B at £100 per ton
10% material C at £420 per ton
20% scrap metal of this alloy

It is expected that from each charge there will be a 5% loss in melt, 35% will be returned to scrap stock (runners, heads, etc.) and 60% will be good castings. Scrap is credited and charged at the standard average cost of the metal mixture.

In a certain period the following materials are purchased and used:

380 tons material A at £310 per ton
330 tons material B at £110 per ton
 90 tons material C at £420 per ton
200 tons scrap metal at standard price

From this material, 608 tons of good castings are produced, and 340 tons of scrap metal are returned to scrap metal stock.

Present information to management, showing standard metal costs, and variances from standard in respect of this period.

                                        (I.C.W.A. Final)

41. A company manufactures a product by passing raw materials through a series of processes.

Materials used consist of three basic materials as follows:

Material		Standard price per ton £
A	50%	30
B	30%	50
C	20%	70

There is an expected (standard) loss of 12% in processing.

Standard costs are in operation, and during one month 90 batches of 10 tons are put into process.

Commencing stocks are:

Material	Tons
A	70
B	20
C	80

Purchases during the period are:

Material	Tons	Cost £
A	400	12,500
B	250	10,400
C	200	14,750

Requisitions show that 900 tons have been issued, but divided as follows:

Material	Tons
A	460
B	260
C	180

Actual production amounts to 788 tons of finished product.

Stock-taking reveals the following stocks at the end of the period:

Material	Tons
A	5
B	15
C	85

Present figures to management, showing actual costs, standard costs and all variances, assuming that there is no work in progress at the beginning and end of the period.

(I.C.W.A. Final)

42. A sales budget has been formulated using standard volumes and prices of five standard products. Since the preparation of the budget sales prices have increased and the sales manager has requested a monthly return which will show him to what extent each product sale has fluctuated from the budget due to volume or price. You are required to:

(a) Calculate the respective sales variances for each product from the following information for the month of May:

Product	Budget Sales price £	Volume	Actual Volume	Actual Value £
A	10	1,000	1,500	16,000
B	3	700	900	3,000
C	8	800	850	7,000
D	2	300	200	500
E	5	200	100	600

(b) Design a form to meet the sales manager's request and insert the figures for May.

(I.C.W.A. Inter.)

43. The sales and product cost budget for an engineering company for November is as follows:

	Units	Sales value £	Product cost £
Product A	1,000	10,000	9,000
B	500	8,000	6,000
C	1,000	12,000	10,800
D	500	18,000	14,200
		£48,000	£40,000

When the analysis of sales for November has been completed, the following statement of actual sales is compiled:

	Units	Sales value £
Product A	920	9,200
B	700	11,000
C	1,200	14,600
D	200	7,800
		£42,600

Calculate the variation in profit from that budgeted, and show how much is due to the factors of sales price, volume and mix.

(I.C.W.A. Final)

CHAPTER 28

PROFITABILITY

THE concept of profitability is very important in considering many problems in management and cost accounting. It is frequently considered when, for example, policy decisions are to be made on the following:

(a) A change in product design.
(b) The introduction of a new pack.
(c) The increasing or decreasing volume of production.
(d) The introduction of a new product.
(e) The quantity of various products to be manufactured.
(f) A change in selling price.
(g) The introduction of new machinery to replace old machinery.
(h) The replacement of labour by machinery.

The cost accountant will frequently be expected to produce statements of anticipated costs and profits relating to such problems as those listed above. Profitability measurement is thus a guide to effective management.

Profitability can be measured in a number of ways, seven measurements being as follows:

(a) Comparison of total or unit-profits.
(b) Percentage profit related to sales.
(c) Percentage profit related to capital employed.
(d) Profit related to the time factor.
(e) Contribution related to the key factor.
(f) Discounted cash flow.
(g) Pay-back period.

These measurements will be discussed in this chapter.

THE KEY FACTOR

In budgeting for production or sales it is very important to consider the key factor, sometimes termed the limiting or principal budget factor. This factor limits the production and/or sales potential, and is to be found in most industries.

Typical examples of key factors are as follows:

(a) *Materials* (i) Availability of supply.
 (ii) Restrictions imposed by licences, quotas, etc.

(b) *Labour*   (i) General shortage.
               (ii) Shortage in certain grades.

(c) *Plant*   (i) Insufficient capacity due to shortage in supply.
               (ii)   „   „   „   lack of capital.
               (iii)   „   „   „   „   space.

(d) *Management* (i) Insufficient capital, restricting policy.
               (ii) Policy decisions, *e.g.* maintaining sales prices by limiting production.
               (iii) Shortage of efficient executives.

(c) *Sales*   (i) Consumer demand.
               (ii) Inefficient or insufficient advertising.
               (iii) Shortage of good salesmen.

Any of these factors may influence budgets.

It is common practice to measure net profit of commodities produced in terms of percentage net profit to turnover, or the rate of profit per article. Two products, X and Y, may be sold at the same price and produce the same percentage profit, but, owing to a key factor, may yield a different periodic contribution to profit. The key factor may be a shortage of materials needed in the manufacture of Product Y, as a result of which it may be possible to produce twice as many of Product X as compared with Product Y. Assuming that all production can be sold, then Product X will yield profits twice as large as those from Product Y.

EXAMPLE

X.Y.Z. Ltd. is a manufacturing company engaged in the production of three products: X, Y and Z. The budgeted output per day of the three products is 140, 100 or 50 respectively. The cost of production is as follows:

Element of cost	Cost per product		
	X	Y	Z
	£	£	£
Direct material	11	8	11
Direct labour	4	8	10
PRIME COST	15	16	21
Production overhead	2	4	5
PRODUCTION COST	17	20	26
Administration overhead	1	2	3
Selling and distribution overhead	1	1	2
TOTAL COST	£19	£23	£31

The selling prices are: X £21; Y £26; Z £36.
The production limiting factor is a shortage of machine capacity.
Profitability statements of X, Y and Z are:

Details	Product		
	X	Y	Z
	£	£	£
Selling price	21	26	36
Total cost	19	23	31
Net profit per product	2	3	5
Net profit % to sales	9·5	11·5	13·9
Net profit per day	£280	£300	£250

The following points emerge:

(a) Maximum net profit per product is obtained by Product Z.
(b) Maximum net profit to sales is obtained by Product Z.
(c) Maximum net profit per day is obtained by Product Y.

Assuming that the demand for Y is enough to absorb the total potential production of the product, X.Y.Z. Ltd. should concentrate their production resources on Product Y. If eventually the market cannot absorb all of Product Y at £26 each, it may be necessary to reduce the selling price so as to stimulate fresh sales by appealing to a wider group of consumers.

Let us assume that the selling price of Y would be reduced to £25 per article. The position may be:

Details	Product		
	X	Y	Z
	£	£	£
Selling price	21	25	36
Total cost	19	23	31
Net profit per product	2	2	5
Net profit % to sales	9·5	8·0	13·9
Net profit per day	£280	£200	£250

It can now be seen that Product X reflects the greatest relative profitability per product, so the production budget should allow for additional production of Product X. In brief, X.Y.Z. Ltd. will produce and sell as many of Product

Y at £26 as possible; however, when the market demand at that price is absorbed the price will not be lowered to £25, but instead Product X will be produced and sold at £21 each. This process of evaluating the relative profitability per product will continue until maximum plant capacity is utilised.

LEVEL OF ACTIVITY PLANNING

Profitability is important when budgeting the level of activity at which the manufacturing unit is to be operated. The ratio of profit to the amount of capital employed should be ascertained.

EXAMPLE

The M.S. Co. Ltd. is a company which specialises in the manufacture of Product M. The present production capacity of the company is 10,000 units per year. There is a potential sales market for 8,000 units at £16 each or 10,000 units at £15 each. The marginal cost of manufacturing Product M is:

	£
Direct material	5
Direct labour	3
PRIME COST	8
Variable production overhead	2
TOTAL	£10

The fixed overheads amount to £25,000 per year. It is estimated that if the production capacity of the factory were increased to 15,000 units, sales could be achieved of 12,000 units at £14·50 each, or 15,000 units at £14 each.

The cost of installing the additional plant and machinery required to achieve the extra production capacity was estimated at £50,000. Due to this additional capital expenditure, the fixed overheads would be increased by £5,000 per year (additional depreciation of plant, etc.).

In addition to the overheads already mentioned, selling overheads are estimated as follows:

Capacity	£
8,000 units	4,000
10,000 „	5,000
12,000 „	6,000
15,000 „	8,000

The present capital of the company is £300,000. The additional capital required to finance the new plant and machinery required will be obtained by a new issue of shares.

The budgeted position of the company at the four levels of activity specified will be:

Details	Level of activity			
Units produced	8,000	10,000	12,000	15,000
Capital employed	£300,000	£300,000	£350,000	£350,000
Element of cost	£	£	£	£
Direct material	40,000	50,000	60,000	75,000
Direct labour	24,000	30,000	36,000	45,000
PRIME COST	64,000	80,000	96,000	120,000
Variable production overhead	16,000	20,000	24,000	30,000
Variable selling overhead	4,000	5,000	6,000	8,000
MARGINAL COST	84,000	105,000	126,000	158,000
Fixed overhead	25,000	25,000	30,000	30,000
TOTAL COST	109,000	130,000	156,000	188,000
PROFIT	19,000	20,000	18,000	22,000
SALES	£128,000	£150,000	£174,000	£210,000
Net profit per product	£2·375	£2·000	£1·500	£1·466
% net profit to sales	14·8	13·3	10·3	10·5
% net profit to capital	6·3	6·7	5·1	6·3

The following points emerge:

(*a*) At 8,000 units the maximum percentage profit to sales is achieved, and also the maximum amount of net profit per product.

(*b*) At 10,000 units the maximum percentage profit to capital is obtained.

(*c*) At 12,000 units the lowest percentage profit to both sales and capital is realised.

(*d*) At 15,000 units the maximum amount of net profit is earned.

It is obvious that to increase the capital of the business, install new plant and machinery, and to increase production to 12,000 units is not profitable: the increase in sales revenue is not enough to absorb the sharp rise in fixed overhead expenditure. If production is increased to 15,000 units, then the resulting profit is high, but owing to the increased selling overheads incurred to attract the greater amount of sales, the burden of fixed overheads, and the effects of reduced selling prices, the percentage profit to capital is less than would be achieved if no additional production capacity had been installed.

At 8,000 units the maximum percentage to sales is achieved, but at this level of activity the full potential of plant and machinery utilisation is not achieved, with the resulting higher cost per article than that which results at 10,000 units (£13·62½ as compared with £13). The decreased selling price obtained at 10,000 units level has affected the profit to some extent, but the amount of £20,000 profit obtained from an investment of £300,000 gives a yield of 6·7% which is the maximum percentage profit to capital.

The management of M.S. Co. Ltd. would be recommended to utilise their present plant and machinery at a level of activity of 10,000 units per year.

CAPITAL AND THE SHAREHOLDER

A shareholder in a company or the owner of a business can reasonably expect a return on his capital invested, for two basic reasons:

(a) Payment for the use of his capital.
(b) Payment for the risk he takes in investing his resources.

He may be interested either in obtaining an actual return by way of dividend, or in the growth of the business. In either case the profit has to be there, whether or not it is paid out in cash, and if this is so then it would seem reasonable that the success of a business may be measured in terms of profitability: the percentage profit realised related to capital employed. This concept and measurement of profitability is very important. The board of a company may consider that their products are providing a satisfactory rate of profit, but to achieve this position the value of investment may be so high that the return on investment is much too low.

EXAMPLE

Typit Ltd. is a manufacturing company specialising in the manufacture of typewriters. The investment in operating assets is £500,000. The budgeted production for the year is 4,000 units. The standard cost of production is as follows:

Element of cost	Per unit
	£
Direct material	8
Direct labour	5
Variable overhead	3
MARGINAL COST	£16

Fixed overheads for the year are budgeted at £16,000. It is company policy to add 25% to the total cost of the product; this is considered to be a satisfactory figure, having regard to the rate of turnover.

The budgeted position of Typit Ltd. is analysed:

Budget	Total production
Output in units	4,000
Investment	£500,000
Element of cost	£
Direct material	32,000
Direct labour	20,000
Variable overhead	12,000
MARGINAL COST	64,000
Fixed overhead	16,000
TOTAL COST	80,000
Profit—25% on cost	20,000
SALES	£100,000

The following points emerge:

    (a) Profit for the year is £20,000.
    (b) Percentage profit to sales is 20%.
    (c) Percentage profit to capital employed is 4%.

It will be appreciated that even though there is a profit expected for the year, and the percentage profit to sales appears quite satisfactory, the return on investment is ludicrous. It is obvious that the shareholders of the business are not obtaining a return on investment which is sufficient to cover both use of capital and risk of losing it. If all the profits of the company were distributed to shareholders the return could be a maximum of only 4%. The situation is even worse than this if one considers that:

    (a) only operating assets were considered; the actual capital of the company may be greater than £500,000;
    (b) there has been no reference to taxation, which in practice could not be ignored;
    (c) there was no provision for "ploughing-back" profits into the firm, which is often a very necessary step.

The position is far from satisfactory, especially when one compares this dividend with a tax-free dividend paid by a building society.

There are many channels of investigation which management may pursue, some or all of which may prove profitable; possible improvements are discussed later in this chapter. If the company does not consider the profitability of its production or ignores the warning signals given by this device it may leave the company open to the possibility of take-over bids. Other people may realise that the company has some useful assets which they think could be used advantageously. Investors will probably take over the company and initiate improvements which the old management failed to do.

CONTRIBUTION AND THE KEY FACTOR

Marginal costing has been discussed in a previous chapter, in which the aspect of contribution was illustrated; key factors were discussed earlier in this chapter. It is possible to measure profitability in terms of the key factor, the formula for which is as follows:

$$\% \text{ Profitability} = \frac{\text{Contribution}}{\text{Key factor}} \times 100.$$

EXAMPLE

Keyfact Ltd. is a manufacturing company which specialises in the manufacture of electrical equipment. Three products are manufactured: X, Y and Z. The production budget for the year reveals the following information:

Details	Product		
	X	Y	Z
Output in units	5,560	2,000	4,000
Machine hours per unit	2	3	1
Element of cost	£	£	£
Direct materials	20	30	15
Direct labour	15	17	12
Direct expense	3	3	1
PRIME COST	38	50	28
Variable overhead	7	9	3
MARGINAL COST	£45	£59	£31

Fixed overhead is budgeted at £105,600 for the year, and for illustration purposes only are allocated to total production of the three products on a basis of machine-hour rates. The key factor is a temporary shortage of raw materials required in this industry; delivery of increased supplies is not possible for at least three years. Owing to the shortage of materials, the factory is operating at 80% activity level. Selling prices of the products are as follows: X £60; Y £80; Z £40.

The profitability statement would appear as below:

Profitability Statement

Details	Product		
	X	*Y*	*Z*
Output (units)	5,560	2,000	4,000
Machine hours per unit	2	3	1
Element of cost	£	£	£
Direct materials	111,200	60,000	60,000
Direct labour	83,400	34,000	48,000
Direct expense	16,680	6,000	4,000
PRIME COST	211,280	100,000	112,000
Variable overhead	38,920	18,000	12,000
MARGINAL COST	250,200	118,000	124,000
Fixed overhead	55,600	30,000	20,000
TOTAL COST	305,800	148,000	144,000
PROFIT	27,800	12,000	16,000
SALES	£333,600	£160,000	£160,000
Profit per article	£5	£6	£4
% Profit to sales	8·3	7·5	10·0
% Profitability	75	70	60

The following points emerge:

    (*a*) Maximum profit per article is obtained by Y.
    (*b*) Maximum % profit to sales is obtained by Z.
    (*c*) Maximum % profitability is obtained by X.
    (*d*) Minimum amount of key factor per units is required by Z.

NOTES

1. Fixed overheads are calculated:

    Budgeted fixed overhead for year = £105,600
    Budgeted machine hours = X: 5,560 at 2 = 11,120
                              Y: 2,000 at 3 = 6,000
                              Z: 4,000 at 1 = 4,000
                                    —————
                                       £21,120.

    Therefore machine hour rate:

$$\frac{£105,600}{21,120} = £5.$$

Budgeted fixed overhead = X: 11,120 at £5 = 55,600
                          Y: 6,000 at £5 = 30,000
                          Z: 4,000 at £5 = 20,000
                                              ——— £105,600.

2. Maximum percentage profitability is calculated:

$$\frac{\text{X: Fixed overhead} + \text{Profit}}{\text{Key factor}} \times 100$$

$$\frac{55,600 + 27,800}{111,200} \times 100 = 75\%.$$

A similar calculation is made for Y and Z.

Maximum profitability is realised by Product X, so management would be advised to concentrate production resources on this product. This can be explained as follows:

It was mentioned earlier in the illustration that production of all three products cannot be expanded. One or two products could be produced in greater quantity, but only at the expense of another product. If the market can absorb more units of X, then if possible the company should discourage sales of one or both of the remaining products, preferably of Z, which realises the lowest relative profitability. If production is carried out as budgeted, then the following should be the contribution of the products to fixed overhead and profit:

Budgeted contribution

Details	Product			
	X	Y	Z	Total
	£	£	£	£
Fixed overhead	55,600	30,000	20,000	105,600
Profit	27,800	12,000	16,000	55,800
TOTAL CONTRIBUTION	£83,400	£42,000	£36,000	£161,400

It is now possible to consider the effect on contribution if management decided to adopt the recommendation outlined above, *viz.* to concentrate production on one product only.

Under the current budget, the cost of materials to be purchased is:

		£
Material cost—X:		111,200
Y:		60,000
Z:		60,000
TOTAL		£231,200

If production resources are to be concentrated on one product only, the position would be:

Details	Product		
	X	or Y	or Z
Direct materials	231,200	231,200	231,200
% Profitability	75	70	60
	£173,400	£161,840	£138,720

The position can be summarised:

	£
Total contribution at present	161,400
Total contribution if only X produced	173,400
	£12,000

Thus if only Product X is produced, the contribution will be £12,000 greater than that originally expected. This can be checked as follows:

If total purchases of £231,200 were used in the production of X only, then 11,560 units could be produced (£231,200 ÷ £20). The position would then be:

	£
Sales 11,560 at £60	693,600
Marginal cost 11,560 at £45	520,200
Contribution of X	173,400
Original budgeted contribution	161,400
Increased contribution	£12,000

It is a policy decision of management whether to produce as originally budgeted or to manufacture only Product X.

THE INTRODUCTION OF NEW MACHINERY

Management are often confronted with the problem of whether or not they should introduce new machinery either to replace old machinery, to replace labour or to increase machine capacity. Good decisions are vital when one considers that:

(a) future company operations may be determined by these decisions;

(b) large amounts of capital may be locked up.

It is therefore essential that capital projects should be undertaken which will utilise resources to the best possible advantage. Normally the projects are measured in terms of profitability; in other words, which project is the most profitable? There may, occasionally, be projects which cannot be measured in this way; e.g.:

(a) where there is no alternative machinery;

(b) where new or better safety devices are introduced;

(c) where there is urgent replacement of a damaged section of a production line.

However, in this chapter only the profitability aspect will be considered. Profitability of new projects is usually measured in at least one of four ways:

1. The pay-back period.
2. The percentage return on investment.
3. Discounted cash flow—excess present value.
4. Net terminal value.

1. THE PAY-BACK PERIOD

This is the period required for the net incremental cash flows to recover the investment. The real profitability of an investment depends on the number of years it will continue to operate after the pay-back period.

Formula

$$\text{Pay-back period in years} = \frac{\text{Cost of asset}}{\text{Average net incremental cash flows}}.$$

The term "average net incremental cash flow" means:

"the increase in revenue plus the savings, if any, in marginal costs."

Depreciation is not taken into account in the calculation.

EXAMPLE

It is proposed to introduce a new machine to increase the production capacity of Department X. Two machines are available, Type A and Type B. The following information is available in respect of A and B respectively:

Details	A	B
Cost of machine	£30,000	£63,000
Estimated life (years)	5	10
Increase in revenue	£3,000	£4,000
Number of operatives not required if project introduced	9	11
Average earnings of operatives per year	£500	£500
Additional cost of maintenance men, supervisors, etc., required if project introduced	£1,000	£1,500
Expected savings in indirect materials	£500	£200
Expected savings in scrap losses due to greater efficiency	£500	£800

Profitability Statement

Details	Machine	
	A	B
Estimated working life (years)	5	10
Cost	£30,000	£63,000
	£	£
Increase in revenue	3,000	4,000
Savings in marginal costs per year:		
Direct labour	4,500	5,500
Indirect labour	(1,000)	(1,500)
Indirect material	500	200
Scrap	500	800
	£7,500	£9,000
Pay-back period in years: $\dfrac{\text{Cost of machine}}{\text{Incremental cash flows}}$	4	7

It is the weakness of this method that profitability is not calculated. A decision is reached simply on the basis that A has the shorter pay-back period. The profitability accrues in the period beyond the pay-back period, and would be calculated as follows:

Cash flows per year (Working life — Pay-back period)

Thus: A £7,500 (5 — 4)   £7,500
          B £9,000 (10 — 7)   £27,000

It will be observed that, under this method of calculating profitability, Machine B is the more profitable investment.

2. THE PERCENTAGE RETURN ON INVESTMENT

This measures the relationship between the amount invested and the amount of expected additional profits which will be earned yearly arising from the use of the machine.

Formula

$$\frac{\text{Average yearly additional profit}}{\text{Average amount invested}} \times 100.$$

EXAMPLE

It is proposed to introduce a new machine, D, to replace an old machine, C. The following information is available in respect of C and D respectively:

Details	C	D
Cost of machine	£10,000	£100,000
Estimated life of machine (years)	10	10
Number of operatives required at £1,000 p.a.	20	15
Cost of maintenance men, supervisors, etc., required if project adopted	£2,000	£4,500
Disposal value now	£2,000	
Disposal value next year	£1,000	
Direct material cost per article £2 at present level of output, but if new project is introduced a discount of £0·05 per article will be obtained		
Indirect material cost	£1,000	£2,000
Output (units)	20,000	30,000
Sales value per unit	£5	£5
Estimated scrap value	Nil	Nil

Profitability Statement

Details	Machine	
	C	D
Output (units)	20,000	30,000
Selling price per unit	£5	£5
Investment	£10,000	£100,000
Disposal value now	£2,000	—
Disposal value next year	£1,000	—
	£	£
Sales	100,000	150,000
Less Marginal costs:		
Direct material	40,000	58,500
Direct labour	20,000	15,000
Indirect material	1,000	2,000
Indirect labour	2,000	4,500
	63,000	80,000
Marginal Income	37,000	70,000
Depreciation	1,000	10,000
	£36,000	£60,000
Profitability	48%	

Profitability is calculated as follows:

$$\frac{£24,000}{£50,000} \times 100 = \underline{\underline{48\%}}.$$

NOTE: Administration expenses, etc., have been ignored.

There has been considerable controversy concerning the calculation of average amount invested. There are two main schools of thought:

(a) The purchase price of the new asset less the disposal value (not the book value) of the old asset should be regarded as the amount invested. The profitability calculation would then be:

$$£100,000 - £2,000 = \underline{\underline{£98,000}}.$$

£98,000 to be written off over the economic life of the asset results in an average amount of capital locked up per year of £49,000.

Depreciation costs would be £9,800, thus increasing the profit to £60,200.

$$\frac{£24,200}{£49,000} \times 100 = \underline{\underline{49\%}}.$$

(b) The purchase price of the new asset should be regarded as the amount invested. The profitability calculation would be as shown in the illustration.

In general we may say that the return on amount invested is obtained thus:

$$\frac{\text{Average net earnings (after depreciation)}}{\frac{1}{2}(\text{Net cost of asset} + \text{Estimated terminal value})} \times 100.$$

Thus, for example:

Average net earnings, after depreciation		£8,250
	£	
Cost of asset	80,000	
Less Disposal value of old asset	5,000	
	75,000	
Add Estimated terminal value of new asset	7,500	
	£82,500	

Therefore:

$$\frac{8,250}{\frac{1}{2}(82,500)} \times 100 = \underline{\underline{20\%}}.$$

3. DISCOUNTED CASH FLOW

This method deduces the present cash value of net incremental future earnings, calculated before deduction of depreciation but after taxation and thus enables an estimate to be made of how much should be invested *now*. Thus, £3,846 invested now at 4% interest will amount to £4,000 at the end of one year.

EXAMPLE

A piece of plant is offered for £10,000. Its estimated life (shortened for the sake of simplicity) is three years. During that period it is estimated that the net incremental earnings of the plant will be at the rate of £4,000 per annum, and the rate of interest to be taken is 4%.

Note that the net incremental earnings exclude depreciation, because it is not a cash flow, but only a book entry. On the other hand the incidence of taxation *is* taken into account.

We have, using the compound interest formula:

$$A = PR^n$$

where

A = net incremental earnings

$R = 1 + r/100$; r = rate %; P = present value.

(a) Year	(b) *Net incremental earnings or cash flow* *	(c) R^n	(d) $1/R^n$	(e) $= (b) \times (d)$ P
1	£4,000	1·04	0·9615	£3,846
2	£4,000	1·04²	0·9245	£3,698
3	£4,000	1·04³	0·8889	£3,556
				£11,100

* Before depreciation, but after taxation.

We should be justified in paying up to £11,100 for the piece of plant, to produce £4,000 earnings per annum over its life of three years assuming that 4% on capital invested is the acceptable rate of return, after tax.

It is desirable to consider this discounted cash flow method in greater detail.

There are a number of preliminary considerations to be made:

1. What is the aim of the exercise?

(*a*) Sometimes the rate of interest is given—that is to say, we know the rate of interest on capital employed which the project has to sustain in order to satisfy the predetermined requirements of management—and the aim is to find out whether or not sufficient margin over cost will be achieved. This is known as the present value method.

(*b*) Sometimes the rate of interest is not given, and the aim is to find out what rate of interest the project returns—that is to say, what rate of interest must be used in order that the discounted cash flows, when totalled, equal the original capital cost. The usual method of doing this is by trial and error, usually referred to as the internal rate of return method, but another method by which the calculation can be made more directly is explained later.

2. The projected cash flows

(a) Obviously, the quality of the results achieved depends on the accuracy of the forecasted cash flows, and this should be done with proper care and judgment. Always the incremental cash flows should be considered: that is, additional turnover less additional costs.

(b) The cash flows in the near future may be foreseen with some degree of accuracy, but to see the likely position further into the future, becomes a series of "guesstimates". Fortunately, however, the discount factors obtained beyond twenty years become so small that it becomes rather pointless to pursue investigations beyond that period.

3. The incidence of taxation

(a) It is important to consider exactly when taxation is paid and becomes a cash flow outwards.

(b) Conversely, close attention has to be paid to the timing of any taxation allowances, and the cash flows inwards.

4. What method of compounding interest is to be employed?

(a) Assume that each year's cash flow is received continuously throughout the year, and use continuous compounding. This is considered to be too complicated for general acceptance.

(b) Assume that each year's income is received at the end of each year, and compound annually.

(c) Assume that each year's income is received at the mid-point of the year, and compound interest in half-yearly periods.

The method is familiar, since it is often used in hire purchase transactions. In effect, the rate of interest is halved, and the half years are treated as years. However, as noted above, we shall reach very low discount factors by the twentieth half-year (the tenth year) and our investigation will not proceed far enough.

(d) Assume that each year's cash flow is received at the mid-point of the year, but compound annually.

By this method tables are prepared for various interest rates, by dividing 1 by 1 plus half the interest rate for the first year, the rate being expressed as a decimal. The discount factors for subsequent years are then obtained by dividing the factor for the previous year by 1 plus the annual interest rate, expressed as a decimal. This method was suggested by David McElvain in an article "Keying the Short-run Capital Flow to Return on Investment Objectives," *Management Accounting*

(December 1967), The National Association of Accountants, New York.

Thus for a 5% table:

Year			Discount factor
1	1/1·025 log 1	= 0·0000	
	Less log 1·025	= 0·0107	
		$\overline{1}$·9893	Antil. = 0·9760
2	0·9760/1·05		0·9292
3	0·9292/1·05		0·8850

and so on.

This is the method which has been adopted in the following example.

In the first place, therefore, we begin by forming our discount factors for an 8% table. This percentage is taken as a likely rate of after tax rate of return.

Year					Discount factor	
1	log 1·04	0·0170	Deduct from 0	$\overline{1}$·9830	0·9620	0·9620
2	1·08	0·0334	Deduct from log above	$\overline{1}$·9496	0·8902	1·8522
3		0·0334		$\overline{1}$·9162	0·8245	2·6767
4		0·0334		$\overline{1}$·8828	0·7635	3·4402
5		0·0334		$\overline{1}$·8494	0·7070	4·1472
6		0·0334		$\overline{1}$·8160	0·6546	4·8018
7		0·0334		$\overline{1}$·7826	0·6061	5·4079
8		0·0334		$\overline{1}$·7492	0·5612	5·9691
9		0·0334		$\overline{1}$·7158	0·5197	6·4888
10		0·0334		$\overline{1}$·6824	0·4813	6·9701
11		0·0334		$\overline{1}$·6490	0·4456	7·4157

and so on.

Note that the last column on the right is a cumulative total of the discount factors, and is useful in the following way:

Suppose the cash flow is £3,000 for each of years 8, 9 and 10.
One can use an average discount factor (6·9701 − 5·4079)/3 = 1·5622/3 = 0·5207, and multiply this by 3 × 3,000.

Let us now suppose the following expenditure is contemplated, and that we have to evaluate the present value of the forecasted cash flows, using an 8% discount rate.

	£
Plant and equipment	50,000
Working capital	28,000
	£78,000

We may set out the work thus:

Year	Operating income	Operating expenses	Depreciation 20%	Net taxable income	Taxation, say 40%	Cash flows	Discount factor	Present value
	£	£	£	£	£	£	£	£
1	40,000	20,000	10,000	10,000	4,000	16,000	0·9620	15,400
2	30,000	30,000	0,000	12,000	4,800	15,200	0·8902	13,530
3	50,000	30,000	6,400	13,600	5,440	14,560	0·8245	12,000
4	50,000	30,000	5,120	14,820	5,952	14,048	0·7635	10,700
5	50,000	30,000	4,096	15,904	6,362	13,638	0·7070	9,640
6	40,000	30,000	3,277	6,723	2,689	7,311	0·6546	4,775
7	40,000	30,000	2,622	7,378	2,951	7,049	0·6061	4,275
8	40,000	32,000	2,098	5,902	2,361	5,639	0·5612	3,100
9	30,000	15,000	1,678	13,322	5,329	9,671	0·5197	5,030
10	20,000	15,000	1,342	3,658	1,463	3,537	0·4813	1,700
	£410,000	£262,000	£44,633	£103,367	£41,347	106,653	0·7533	80,150
Scrap value, say (£50,000 − £44,633)						5,367	0·4625	490
Working capital						28,000	0·4625	12,910
						£140,020		£95,550

NOTE: The method of obtaining the discount factor for the scrap and working capital is to take the discount factor for year 10, viz., 0·4813, and to divide it by 1·04 (1 plus half the interest rate).

Tax allowances at this stage have been ignored; they will be discussed later.

The pay-back period (using incremental cash flows) is $4\frac{3}{4}$ years.

The rate of return on investment would normally be calculated on a trial and error basis. It is clear that it is much higher than 8% and we may assume that the operating income has been much overstated in this fictitious example.

We now come to a method of calculation of the rate of return directly, and we take a simple illustration for the purpose.

EXAMPLE 1

Suppose the following cash flows occur:

Year	Cash flows £	Discount factor
$\frac{1}{2}$	800	$1/(1 + i)^{\frac{1}{2}}$
$1\frac{1}{2}$	3,600	$1/(1 + i)^{1\frac{1}{2}}$
$2\frac{1}{2}$	3,600	$1/(1 + i)^{2\frac{1}{2}}$

Let us also suppose that the cost of the asset is £6,000.
The following steps are necessary:

(i) Make $x = 1/(1 + i)$ and change the periods to half years.
Then $800x + 3,600x^3 + 3,600x^5 = 6,000$.

(ii) Assume that $x = 0·9$ (close to the discount factor for year 1).
Then $800(0·9) + 3,600(0·729) + 3,600(0·59049) = 5,470$.

The difference between 6,000 and 5,470 is 530. Now, if we take the expression shown in (i) and say $y = 800x + 3,600x^3 + 3,600x^5$ then using the method of differentiation, we have:

$$\frac{dy}{dx} = 800 + 3(3,600)x^2 + 5(3,600)x^4$$

$$= 800 + 10,800x^2 + 18,000x^4.$$

Hence:

We have $\Delta x(800 + 10,800x^2 + 18,000x^4) = 530.$

(*iii*) And $\Delta x = 530 \div (800 + 10{,}800(0{\cdot}81) + 18{,}000(0{\cdot}6561))$.
Therefore $\Delta x = 0{\cdot}024815$.

(*iv*) Add the assumed value of x to the Δx, and solve for i.

Assumed value of $x = 0{\cdot}9$.
$\Delta x \qquad\qquad = 0{\cdot}024815$

Hence corrected $x \; = 0{\cdot}924815$

Now $x = 1/(1 + i)$, and $i = (1/x) - 1$
$\qquad = 1/0{\cdot}924815 - 1 = \; 8{\cdot}13\%$ half year

Add Interest $8{\cdot}13\%$ $\qquad\qquad 0{\cdot}66$
$\qquad\qquad\qquad\qquad\qquad\;\; 8{\cdot}13\%$ second half year

$\qquad\qquad\qquad\qquad\qquad 16{\cdot}92\%$ per annum

Therefore rate of return is approximately 17%.

Let us now check this, using the method of compounding already used.

Year			Discount factor	Cash flow	Present value £
1	$\log 1$	$= 0$			
	$\log 1{\cdot}085$	$= 0{\cdot}0354$			
		$\overline{1}{\cdot}9646$	$0{\cdot}9220$	800	738
2	$\log 1{\cdot}17$	$0{\cdot}0682$			
		$\overline{1}{\cdot}8964$	$0{\cdot}7878$	3,600	2,836
3	$\log 1{\cdot}17$	$0{\cdot}0682$			
		$\overline{1}{\cdot}8282$	$0{\cdot}6733$	3,600	2,424
					£5,998

EXAMPLE 2

Cost of asset = £8,000.

Year	Cash flows £	Discount factor
$\frac{1}{2}$	1,000	$1/(1 + i)^{\frac{1}{2}}$
$1\frac{1}{2}$	4,000	$1/(1 + i)^{1\frac{1}{2}}$
$2\frac{1}{2}$	3,000	$1/(1 + i)^{2\frac{1}{2}}$
$3\frac{1}{2}$	2,000	$1/(1 + i)^{3\frac{1}{2}}$

Making $x = 1(1 + i)$ and changing periods to half years we have:
$$1{,}000x + 4{,}000x^3 + 3{,}000x^5 + 2{,}000x^7 = 8{,}000.$$

Assume that $x = 0{\cdot}90$ and substitute in the left-hand side, then:
$$1{,}000(0{\cdot}90) + 4{,}000(0{\cdot}729) + 3{,}000(0{\cdot}59049) + 2{,}000(0{\cdot}4783)$$
$$= 900 + 2{,}916 + 1{,}771 + 957 = 6{,}544.$$

The difference between 8,000 and 6,544 = 1,456.

$$\Delta x\{1,000 + 3(4,000)x^2 + 5(3,000)x^4 + 7(2,000)x^6\} = 1,456.$$

$$\begin{aligned}
\Delta x &= 1,456/(1,000 + 12,000x^2 + 15,000x^4 + 14,000x^6) \\
&= 1,456/\{1,000 + 12,000(0\cdot81) + 15,000(0\cdot6561) + 14,000(0\cdot5314)\} \\
&= 1,456/(1,000 + 9,720 + 9,840 + 7,440) \\
&= 1,456/28,000 \\
&= 0\cdot04842.
\end{aligned}$$

Corrected $x = 0\cdot90 + 0\cdot04842 = \underline{0\cdot94842}.$

Then since $x = 1/(1 + i)$, $i = (1/x) - 1$.
Substituting $1/0\cdot94842 - 1$

$$\begin{aligned}
1\cdot054 - 1 & \\
= 0\cdot054 \quad &\text{or} \quad 5\cdot40\% \text{ for } \tfrac{1}{2} \text{ year}
\end{aligned}$$

Add interest at 5·4% 0·292

$$\underline{5\cdot40} \quad \text{second } \tfrac{1}{2} \text{ year}$$

$$\underline{11\cdot092}$$

Therefore rate of return is approximately $\underline{11\%}$.

Check

Year			Discount factor	Cash flow £	Present value £
1	log 1 = 0				
	log 1·055 = 0·0232				
		$\overline{1}$·9768	0·9479	1,000	948
2	1·11	0·0453			
		$\overline{1}$·9315	0·8543	4,000	3,417
3	1·11	0·0453			
		$\overline{1}$·8862	0·7695	3,000	2,309
4	1·11	0·0453			
		$\overline{1}$·8409	0·6933	2,000	1,387
					£8,061

This is as close a result as one can reasonably expect.

NET TERMINAL VALUE METHOD

This method was suggested by R. Skinner, of Liverpool University, ("Terminal Values in Capital Budgeting": *The Cost Accountant*, December 1964), but it does not seem to have been developed as much as it deserves. Instead of compounding backwards to find present values of future cash flows, it works forwards, and asks the question, to what sum will the cash flows amount at the end of the useful life of the asset if they are left in the business to accumulate at compound interest?

This method has the merit of enabling us to compare projects of different capital costs and different lengths of life, which is not possible by the discounted cash flow method, and also it is claimed that it is far easier to explain to the average managing director!

To explain the method, let us assume that there are two projects available, A and B, one costing £10,000 and the other £20,000. The full £20,000 is available, if necessary. The life of the investment is the same in each case, viz., 3 years.

	Project A	Project B
Capital cost	£10,000	£20,000
Life of investment	3 years	3 years

Rate of compound interest, say 5% in each case

End of year	Cash flows				
1	5,000	$1 \cdot 05^2 = 1 \cdot 1025$	5,513	9,000	9,923
2	5,000	$1 \cdot 05^1 = 1 \cdot 05$	5,250	9,000	9,450
3	5,000	$1 \cdot 05^0 = 1 \cdot 00$	5,000	9,000	9,000
			15,763		28,373
Less Cost			10,000		20,000
Net terminal value			5,763		8,373

The cash flows are arrived at on the same basis as for the previous example.

In order to make comparison we assume that the other £10,000 (cost of B less cost of A) is available for investment at 5%. Then:

$$10,000 \quad 1 \cdot 05^3 \quad 1 \cdot 158 = 11,580$$

Less	10,000
	1,580
	7,343

Therefore Project B is better, having the greater net terminal value.

Suppose now that we want to compare Project B with Project C, the particulars of which are:

Capital cost = £20,000
Life of investment = 2 years.

It is considered that one should compare over the life of the longest lived project, in this case 3 years, and make the assumption that C will be renewed at the end of its life.

End of year	Cash flows			Capital	Interest
	£		£	£	£
1	15,000	$1 \cdot 05^1$	15,750	15,000	750
2	9,000	$1 \cdot 05^0$	9,000	9,000	—
				£24,000	750
		Less Cost		20,000	

Net terminal value, apart from interest, at the end of first life	4,000
Net terminal value at the end of 4 years (second life)	8,000
Hence, the net terminal value at 3 years, by averaging	6,000

Further interest has to be taken into account:

On £750 for 1 year	38
On £4,000 for 1 year, that is, on first 2 years' income *less* cost of renewal (£24,000 − £20,000)	200
Actual interest over 3 years	988

Therefore, the net terminal value of this project at the end of 3 years is £6,000 + £988 = £6,988.

This is considerably lower than for Project B, and therefore Project B is to be recommended.

Incidentally, Skinner claims that net terminal value calculations always lead in the same direction as discounted cash flow calculations. The results will be different, obviously, but the same conclusions and decisions would be taken.

TAX ALLOWANCES

The treatment of tax allowances has been ignored in this chapter, but because of its importance it cannot be excluded. It will be discussed now, but before doing so, it is important to point out that only a very general situation can be illustrated, because tax allowances and rates change very frequently so it would be impossible to cover every specific point regarding each change in tax legislation. For convenience, it will be assumed that corporation tax is 40%, that annual allowances are 20% and that the company which is being considered is in a non-development area. In addition to taking a general view of tax allowances, to keep the illustration reasonably simple, it will be assumed that cash flows occur at the end of the year (*see* comments on page 604), so that one can use the present value discount tables which are shown in the Appendix.

EXAMPLE

The cost of a new asset is £5,000.
The estimated scrap value at the end of its life of 3 years is £750.
The estimated incremental cash flows are £2,000 p.a.
Corporation tax at 40% is assumed to be payable 18 months after the end of the accounting year.
Capital allowances are 20% p.a.
Capital grant 20%, payable 18 months after purchase of the machine.

Cash Flow Statement

Year	0	1	2	3	4	5
Cash outflow						
Investment	£5,000					
Corporation tax			£480	£544	£595	(£519)
TOTAL	£5,000	—	£480	£544	£595	(£519)
Cash inflow						
Capital grant			£1,000			
Trade in allowance					£750	
Profit		£2,000	2,000	£2,000		
TOTAL	—	2,000	3,000	2,000	750	—
Net cash flow	£(5,000)	£2,000	£2,520	£1,456	£155	£519

NOTES

1. Capital allowance calculations

Year		£
1	Purchases	5,000
	Capital grant	1,000
		4,000
	Capital allowance	800
		3,200
2	Capital allowance	640
		2,560
3	Capital allowance	512
		2,048
4	Sale of asset	750
		£1,298

Balancing allowance = (£1,298).

2. *Corporation tax calculations*

Year	1	2	3	4
Profit before tax and depreciation	£2,000	£2,000	£2,000	—
Capital allowance	800	640	512	(£1,298)
	1,200	1,360	1,488	(1,298)
Corporation tax at 40%	480	544	595	519

Profitability Statement

Year	Cash flow	Trial No. 1		Trial No. 2		Trial No. 3	
		Discount factor	Present value	Discount factor	Present value	Discount factor	Present value
	£	20%	£	10%	£	14%	£
0	(5,000)	1·000	(5,000)	1·000	(5,000)	1·000	(5,000)
1	2,000	0·833	1,666	0·909	1,818	0·877	1,754
2	2,520	0·694	1,749	0·826	2,082	0·769	1,938
3	1,456	0·579	843	0·751	1,093	0·675	983
4	155	0·482	75	0·683	106	0·592	92
5	519	0·402	209	0·621	323	0·519	269
TOTAL	£1,650		(£458)		£422		£36

It will be noted that in the trial and error method, the first trial was at 20%, when cash outflows exceeded cash inflows. The next trial was at 10%, when cash inflows exceeded cash outflows. The discount factor at which cash inflows are equated with cash outflows is clearly between these two limits. The solution is marginally closer to 10% than to 20%, so for trial number three, 14% was used. The result is sufficiently accurate for the purpose, so it has been established that the present value factor expected is at least 14%.

In the above example, one should observe the importance of the tax allowance. If one had ignored tax, the position would not have appeared to be very profitable (invest £5,000 now to earn £2,000 p.a. before depreciation over a life of three years). This is particularly pertinent when one thinks of discounting these earnings over a three-year span.

It may have been observed that the year 0 was used for the cash outflow. It was mentioned earlier in this section that it was assumed that cash flows occurred at the end of each year; therefore if the machine is to be installed and in operation, it must be completed before the cash inflow can be considered. Thus, if the first year inflow is in year 1, the outflow must be regarded as being in the previous year, *viz.* year 0. If an asset takes three years to install, the cash outflow would be shown as years 3, 2 and 1, while the cash inflow would be shown as years 1, 2, 3 and so on.

HOW PROFITABILITY CAN BE IMPROVED

In this chapter a number of measurements of profitability have been illustrated, all of which may be useful to management. However, in addition to calculating profitability the cost accountant should be able to suggest ways of improving profitability where necessary.

Possible suggestions are as follows:

1. Increased rate of profit

This could be effected by the following:

(a) *Reduced costs.* Perhaps a system of budgetary control and/or standard costing could be introduced. If such a system is in existence perhaps standard costs could be reduced and quick action initiated to correct adverse variances where possible.

(b) *Increased selling prices.* Research could be undertaken into possible market reaction to higher prices.

(c) *Reduced selling prices.* The possibility of greater sales due to a lower selling price should be investigated. Greater sales mean greater production which may lead to reduced costs.

(d) *Improved planning of production and sales.* Review of techniques should be undertaken.

2. Reduced investment

There are three possible ways in which this could be effected:

(a) *Reduced stocks.* Capital is often locked up unnecessarily in stocks.

(b) *Reduced amounts owing by debtors.* Better credit control may be instituted.

(c) *Better utilisation of plant and equipment.* Capacities could be investigated; over- and under-loading could be corrected; idle plant disposed of.

The subject of profitability is an interesting and fascinating one, and there is wide scope for research. It is expected that there will be many developments in techniques, uses and measurements in the future.

EXAMINATION QUESTIONS

1. An expanding business, making modest profits, finds its bank overdraft to be increasing. The managing director states that this indicates a need for the introduction of further capital, but a study of the figures indicates to you that with more efficient management, ample capital exists in the business. Using suitable figures, prepare a report to the managing director, indicating how the necessary capital can be found within the business.

(*I.C.W.A. Final*)

2. An item of plant costing £200,000 is estimated to have a life of 25 years. After about 15 years a substantial portion of the plant (original cost £100,000) is due for replacement in order to prolong the life of the plant to 25 years. Assume the annual production of the plant is 300,000 units and the estimated cost of replacement £120,000. Explain clearly how you would absorb the

original and replacement costs of the rebuildable portion of the plant. Give reasons.

(I.C.W.A. Final)

3. Your directors are considering introducing additional capital into a business to:

    (*a*) replace old machinery with modern equipment;

    (*b*) build and equip a new department to manufacture a part of the final product which has hitherto been bought from outside.

Discuss the various factors you would consider to ascertain the additional profits which will result from this new capital expenditure.

(I.C.W.A. Final)

4. Your management is considering the purchase of an expensive unit of plant which will do the work at present being done on three relatively cheap machines, assisted by a number of workers using hand tools.

The new unit of plant will need four operators, but in a normal working week will produce 50% more output than was previously produced by the three machines, each with one operator, together with five workers using hand tools.

You have an efficient costing system in operation and management requires you to prepare figures which will enable a decision to be made regarding the purchase of the plant.

Explain how you would proceed to present the information using any figures you consider necessary by way of illustration.

(I.C.W.A. Final)

5. Your directors are contemplating the purchase of a new machine to replace a machine which has been in the factory for 5 years.

From the following information prepare a statement for submission to the board showing the effect of the installation on costs and profits and comment on the results shown. Ignore interest.

	Old machine	*New machine*
Purchase price	£4,000	£6,000
Estimated life of machine	10 years	10 years
Machine running hours p.a.	2,000	2,000
Units produced per hour	24	36
Wages per running hour	£0·3	£0·52½
Power p.a.	£200	£450
Consumable stores p.a	£600	£750
All other charges p.a.	£800	£900
Material cost per unit	£0·05	£0·05
Selling price per unit	£0·12½	£0·12½

(I.C.W.A. Final)

6. To increase productivity in Department X the works management are considering the complete replacement of the plant used. Present output is approximately 12,000 units p.a. selling at £2 per unit, and there is an unsatisfied demand at that price. Output after the replacement is estimated at

about 50% more, retaining all existing labour but using no more labour. Selling prices will remain unaltered, for the time being at least. Present production costs p.a. (excluding depreciation) are:

	£
Raw material	12,000
Direct labour	3,000
Indirect charges (mainly fixed)	1,500

The plant in use cost £3,000 and has a scrap value of £1,400. The cost of new plant is £20,000, and depreciation would be provided at 10% p.a.
Draft a statement showing:

(a) present and prospective profit;
(b) the average yield (using simple interest) on the new capital outlay.

You are expected to point out any factors that may qualify your figures.

(A.C.C.A. Final)

7. During a trade recession, production in a certain factory has fallen from an average of 8,000 to 7,000 units per week. In spite of this fall in production, the productivity of direct labour has increased.

Using suitable figures, present a report to management showing the effects of the increase in productivity and the fall in production. The following figures for a normal average week may be used as a basis for your answer:

Production (units)	8,000
Labour hours	4,000
Production costs:	£
Direct materials	6,000
Direct labour	1,000
Factory overheads (variable)	2,000
„ „ (fixed)	1,000
Total production cost	£10,000

(I.C.W.A. Final)

8. To increase productivity the works management are considering the complete replacement of the plant used in a particular department.

Present output is approximately 6,000 units per annum, selling at £2 per unit, and there is an unsatisfied demand at that price.

Output after the replacement is estimated at 50% more, retaining all existing labour but using no more.

Selling prices will remain unaltered, for the time being at least.

Present production costs per annum (excluding depreciation) are:

	£
Raw material	6,000
Direct labour	1,500
Indirect charges (mainly fixed)	750

The plant in use cost £1,500 and has a scrap value of £200. The cost of the new plant is £10,000, and depreciation would be provided at the rate of 10% per annum.

Draft a statement showing present and prospective profit and mention any factors that may qualify your figures.

(Comm. A. Final)

9. The plant and machinery in a works department produces 2,400 units p.a., all of which are sold at the fixed price of £5 per unit.

Average annual costs incurred are £6,000 for direct materials, £200 for direct labour and £500 for fixed overhead.

The plant and machinery cost £2,000, and its estimated scrap value is £400.

Management propose to replace it by new plant costing £12,000. If this step is taken output and sales (at £5 per unit) are expected to increase by 50%, without alteration in direct labour costs or fixed overhead.

Assuming that the new plant and machinery has an effective working life of ten years and that, on average, over the life of a fixed asset only half the capital remains invested, calculate:

    (*a*) the increased annual profit; and
    (*b*) the yield per cent on the new investment.

(A.C.C.A. Inter.)

10. A warehousing concern proposes to purchase electric high-lift trucks and auxiliary equipment to replace hand trucks now used. The new trucks would necessitate additional capital expenditure being made on buildings and fittings. The following appeared in last year's Profit and Loss Account:

	£		£
Management and clerical costs	32,000	Space rentals	250,000
Warehouse wages cost	104,000		
Rates and licences cost	18,000		
Power, light and water cost	15,000		
Insurance cost	7,000		
Maintenance cost	3,000		
Depreciation:			
Buildings	10,000		
Hand trucks (final)	2,000		
	£191,000		£250,000

Proposed new expenditure:

    Trucks, etc., £60,000, life 10 years, residual value £10,000.
    Buildings and fittings, £50,000, to be written off over 20 years.

Estimated increased operating costs:

Management and clerical—estimated increase 10%		
Warehouse wages	,, ,,	25%
Power, etc.	£3,000	
Insurance	£2,000	
Maintenance	£500	

Rental income: increase of space available for renting 50%.

It is estimated that an overall reduction of charges of 10% will be possible.

From the above information present a forecast comparing the present Profit and Loss Account with the projected Profit and Loss Account when the scheme is in full working.

(*I.C.W.A. Inter.*)

11. Report to management on the relative profitability of the two products A and B.

	Production cost per unit	
	Product A	Product B
	(*output 200 per week*)	(*output 100 per week*)
Materials	20	15
Wages	10	20
Fixed overhead	35	10
Variable overhead	15	20
	80	65
Gross profit	20	35
	£100	£100

Explain the variations disclosed by your statement.

(*I.C.W.A. Inter.*)

12. A certain factory producing packaging material has a 10-year-old plant, depreciated by the straight-line method, to which the following details apply:

Purchase price, including installation	£60,000
Estimated total life	20 years
Residual value after 20 years	£10,000
Output per minute	200 units

An offer is received to supply new plant to the value of £95,000. The offer also proposes a part-exchange provision of £20,000 in respect of the existing plant. The output of the new plant is 400 units per minute. It has an estimated life of 15 years, and residual value of £10,000.

The annual costs, etc., are to be taken as follows:

	Existing plant	New plant
Repairs and maintenance	£2,000	£2,500
Sundry indirect materials	£12,000	£15,000
Power and steam service	£6,000	£7,000
Proportion of general fixed cost	£1,500	£2,000
Wages of attendants	£2,500	£3,500
Running hours	2,500	2,500

The installation cost of the new plant will be £5,000.

No change in the method of charging depreciation is proposed.

Disregarding direct materials cost, which is constant to both, prepare a comparative cost schedule to show total and marginal costs per 1,000 units of product produced by the new, and the existing plant.

(I.C.W.A. Final)

13. Most businesses are today faced with alternative uses for available funds. What criteria would you, as an accountant, recommend should be used to decide which use should be satisfied? What problems would the application of your criteria bring?

Give a formula for the evaluation of a capital expenditure project by the discounted cash-flow method, explaining clearly how each term in the formula is obtained.

(A.C.C.A. Final)

14. In a manufacturing company, where the main aim is to maximise return on investment and achieve a satisfactory growth rate, decisions are necessary from time to time whether to buy outside, or expand facilities and make, to obtain the required output.

The setting up of a make-or-buy committee is proposed. Compile a procedure, using brief numbered paragraphs, which the committee should follow and supervise from design to final recommendation. Specify desirable features of the accounting system in operation.

(I.C.W.A. Final)

15. (a) In connection with proposals for capital expenditure, write a brief explanatory note on, and illustrate, each of the following:

(i) pay-back period;
(ii) return on investment.

(b) Design a form of application for authority to incur capital expenditure. Provide for the insertion of figures which you consider necessary, summarised reasons for the application, the purpose to be achieved by the expenditure and any other descriptive or supporting data appropriate.

(I.C.W.A. Final)

16. A small manufacturing company has a capital of £100,000 employed in the business, and is making a profit of approximately £12,000 per annum. Business is expanding, and management is considering the installation of a new machine which will cost £15,000. It is estimated that the installation of the machine will increase profits by £1,500 per annum as soon as it commences to work. The company already has an overdraft on which interest is being paid at the rate of 6% per annum, and the bank is prepared to increase overdraft facilities by £10,000.

Using suitable figures, present a case to management, and make recommendations regarding the installation. As an appendix to the report, give your reasons for considering interest (or for omitting it) in your calculations.

(I.C.W.A. Final)

17. A decision has to be taken relating to the possible introduction of a new product. There are three basic design versions of this product, aimed at

different sections of the consumer market. The relevant figures are as follows:

	Model I £	Model II £	Model III £
Variable cost (per unit):			
Materials	1·54	1·21½	0·86
Labour	1·06	0·95	0·58
Variable overheads	0·40	0·33½	0·31
	3·00	2·50	1·75
Selling price per unit	4·25	3·50	2·50
Expected sales volume per month (units)	800	2,000	4,000
Capital expenditure necessary before production can commence (financed by bank overdraft at 6% per annum)	£8,000	£30,000	£40,000
Fixed overheads per month attributable to new models, including depreciation on capital expenditure, but excluding interest	£280	£850	£1,100

You are required to prepare:

(a) a schedule of relative profitability showing, for each model, the figures making up expected total cost per unit, the expected net profit per unit and the percentage of net profit to selling price at the expected sales volume;

(b) a graph of net profit (or loss) against sales, for Model II only, showing the effect on net profit (or loss) as sales rise from nil to the expected level of 2,000 units per month.

Ignore taxation.

(I.C.A. Final November 1965)

18. The financial director of a holding company calls for budgets of capital expenditure for the forthcoming year from each subsidiary company. At the same time he points out that expenditure on approved projects will be rationed in proportion to the profits made by the various subsidiaries in the current year.

The managing director of a subsidiary which has incurred a loss objects. This he considers is tantamount to saying that because a company has not made a profit in the past, it shall not be given the opportunity to do so in the future. He suggests that it is probably the unprofitable company which requires the biggest infusion of new finance.

Do you agree?

(I.C.W.A. Final)

19. As chief accountant you are asked to approve capital expenditure of £12,500 on the purchase of a crankshaft grinding machine. The proposal states that this machine will replace an existing machine which is badly worn and obsolete.

The new machine would give a superior micro finish and would save twenty minutes on each crankshaft ground (a reduction from 35 minutes to 15 minutes). As 5,000 shafts are at present ground in a year, the annual saving claimed in support of the proposal is 5,000 × 20/60 hours at £1·50 per hour (direct labour cost £0·50 plus absorption of works overhead at 200%): a total of £2,500 per annum, giving a five-year pay-off.

(a) Do you consider so far as its financial implications are concerned that this proposal is fully and correctly justified? If not, explain why and state what other information you would require before coming to a decision.

(b) What courses of action could you suggest as alternatives to the immediate purchase of the machine specified?

(*I.C.W.A. Final*)

20. In the materials handling department of a company, a task is done manually by operators who can move 1,500 pallets per week each and whose wages are £13 per week each. The cost of expendable supplies in this task is £2 per 1,000 pallets.

As a result of a work-study investigation it is found that the task can be undertaken by a piece of equipment costing £1,000, with a capacity of up to 6,000 pallets per week. This equipment involves the following costs:

Operator's pay	£16 per week
Maintenance	£3 ,, ,,
Operating costs	£1 per 1,000 pallets
Expendable supplies	£2 ,, ,, ,,

Company policy will be to depreciate this equipment on a 5-year straight-line basis of 50 weeks per annum.

You are required to calculate in pallets the weekly level of activity beyond which there is a cost saving to the company by having the task done by use of the equipment instead of manually. Show your workings.

(*I.C.W.A. Inter.*)

21. P.Q. Limited produces two products, A and B in Departments X and Y. With each completed product sold is included one stand of a type common to both A and B. Stands are produced in the Stand department and are included in the selling prices given.

The standard prime costs and selling prices for these items per unit are:

	A £	B £	Stand £
Direct materials cost	10·00	15·00	1·08½
Direct wages:			
Department X (£0·3 per hour)	7·50	9·00	
Department Y (£0·5 per hour)	5·00	10·00	
Stand department (£0·5 per hour)			3·33½
	12·50	19·00	3·33½
Prime cost	22·50	34·00	4·42
Selling price	67·00	105·00	—

The budget information for the coming year includes the following:

Production:
Product A	1,000
Product B	2,000
with one stand for each product	

Direct labour hours: Stand department 20,000

Overhead:

Variable: for all three departments is 20% of direct wages

	£
Fixed:	
Department X	85,000
Department Y	37,500
Stand department	23,750
Total	£146,250

NOTE: The fixed overhead of Departments X and Y are charged to the products on the basis of the direct labour involved.

P.Q. Limited could sell substantially more of both products if it could produce them. While Department X labour can easily be obtained, the type of labour used in the Stand department is scarce and in terms of skill is the same as that used in Department Y. The productive equipment used in the Stand department is also similar to that in Department Y.

The company is considering buying these stands from an outside supplier and making the Stand department part of Department Y. If it were to do so, it estimates that it would not alter its total fixed costs but it would pay £20 per stand to the outside supplier.

P.Q. Limited wants to know whether it should make this change and, if so, whether it should concentrate the stand capacity released on Product A or Product B.

Using the information supplied, you are required to:

(a) prepare a statement to show the total profit or loss that would be made by each product and by the whole company under the present system in which P.Q. Limited makes its own stands;

(b) prepare a statement to show the total profit or loss that would be made by the company under the proposed system of buying stands from outside and turning its present Stand department into part of Department Y by using the labour from the Stand department entirely on:

(i) Product A; or
(ii) Product B;

(c) state which of the above three courses would show the greatest profit;
(d) examine the unit revenue and cost situation of each of Product A,

Product B and the stands and give figures to show how you could have arrived at the decision required in (c) above without having to prepare the statements in (a) and (b) above.

(I.C.W.A. Inter.)

22. The Alpha Company Ltd. are considering the purchase of a new machine which will cost £40,000. It is estimated that the machine will have a life of seven years at the end of which it will have a scrap value of £1,000. This will also involve an investment in working capital of £10,000. The net pre-tax cash flows which this will produce are as follows:

Year	£
1	10,000
2	10,000
3	14,000
4	13,000
5	11,000
6	12,000
7	10,000

The company has a target return on capital of 15% and on this basis you are required to prepare a statement evaluating the above project.

Assume the following about taxation:

1. Income tax £0·40 in the £ (ignore profits tax).
2. Investment allowance 30%. Initial allowance 10%.
3. Annual allowances 25%.

The company carries on other trading activities from which it derives taxable profits.

(A.C.C.A. Final)

23. "In assessing the financial profitability of business projects before they begin . . . the larger companies employ the technique known as discounted cash flow (D.C.F.) whereby, for comparison with current investments in—e.g. plant, future cash flow receipts are discounted to present day values."

In this connection, statistical tables of discount factors give the undernoted indices required to be applied to future sums to give the present values of these sums at an interest rate of 7% per annum:

Year end	Discount factor
0	1·00
1	0·94
2	0·87
3	0·82
4	0·76
5	0·71
6	0·67

Two alternative schemes of investment are envisaged in which the estimated cash flows would be as follows:

Year	Cash outflow	Scheme A	Scheme B
0	Initial outlay	£1,000	£1,000
	Cash inflow	£	£
1	Net receipts	100	600
2	,,	100	400
3	,,	200	200
4	,,	200	100
5	,,	500	100
6	,,	500	100
		£1,600	£1,500

NOTE: No further receipts are anticipated.

You are required:

(a) by using the table of discount factors to determine the comparative values at year 0 of the cash inflow for each of the alternative schemes;
(b) to state which scheme is the more attractive investment; and
(c) to write a brief note on the benefit to be derived from D.C.F. in appraising investment proposals.

(C.A. Final)

24. The M.N. Company Ltd. has decided to increase its productive capacity to meet an anticipated increase in demand for its products. The extent of this increase in capacity has still to be determined and a management meeting has been called to decide which of the following two mutually exclusive proposals —I and II—should be undertaken. On the basis of the information given below you are required to:

1. evaluate the profitability (ignoring taxation and investment grants) of each of the proposals, and
2. on the assumption of a cost of capital of 8% advise management of the matters to be taken into consideration when deciding between Proposal I and Proposal II.

Capital expenditure	I	II
	£	£
Buildings	50,000	100,000
Plant	200,000	300,000
Installation	10,000	15,000
Working capital	50,000	65,000
Net income		
Annual pre-depreciation profits (Note (*i*))	70,000	95,000
Other relevant income/expenditure		
Sales promotion (Note (*ii*))	—	15,000
Plant scrap value	10,000	15,000
Buildings disposable value (Note (*iii*))	30,000	60,000

NOTES

(*i*) The investment life is 10 years.

(*ii*) An exceptional amount of expenditure on sales promotion of £15,000 will require to be spent in year 2 on Proposal II. This has not been taken into account in calculating pre-depreciation profits.

(*iii*) It is not the intention to dispose of the buildings in 10 years' time; however, it is company policy to take a notional figure into account for project evaluation purposes.

(*A.C.C.A. Final*)

CHAPTER 29

AUDITING OF COST ACCOUNTS

INTERNAL auditing is a recognised feature of modern business life, and there is every reason for applying it to the activities of the cost office, just as much as in the other departments.

The intention behind the appointment of an internal auditor is to protect management against errors of principle and against neglect of duty, and it is therefore essential that he should be responsible direct to management as a whole and not be dependent on any one department or sectional interest.

In the broad scope of his activities the internal auditor is in a position to sit back and survey the accounting, financial, costing and other operations, subjecting them to a critical appraisal as to their effectiveness, and giving constructive advice to management on any changes in system which seem to be called for.

No doubt each departmental head has methods of checking postings, records and so on for his own purposes, but the internal auditor is not concerned with them, and pursues his task in his own way and in his own time.

In the first place, an audit programme is drawn up for the year ahead, but it is made flexible enough to admit of a change of sequence, if thought desirable. It is therefore arranged in sections, and for each section there will be specified:

(a) which books, accounts and records are to be checked;
(b) against which original sources the check is to be made.

Space is left at the end of each section of the audit programme to allow for notes to be made during the course of the audit, and for the initials of those clerks who have completed it.

The checking referred to is usually termed *vouching*, and this is more than merely ticking one figure to another in order to check the arithmetical accuracy: it is rather the careful scrutiny of the vouchers constituting the basis of the original entries, and ensuring that errors of principle have not crept in. In fact, carried out intelligently and purposefully, vouching lies at the heart of every well-conducted audit.

TYPICAL COST AUDIT PROGRAMME

In a typical cost audit programme the following action would be taken.

(*a*) Comparison of actual production and sales with budget estimates.

(*b*) An analysis of standard variances to confirm that they are being correctly interpreted to management.

For example, in the illustration given on page 556 it will be seen that a yield variance occurs for the labour element due to the fact that an additional 4 tons of product "Exe" were obtained over and above the standard rate of production. This, however, may not be attributable to any greater efficiency of labour. Indeed the efficiency variance is adverse.

(*c*) An examination with a critical eye of all statements put forward for management attention.

(*d*) A discussion of queries with the officers concerned, and a follow up to ensure that action agreed upon is actually taken.

Questionnaire forms. These are useful to "break down" the information required, and to find out if satisfactory procedures are in operation. A specimen of such a form is shown in Fig. 89.

INTERNAL CHECK

As has been pointed out, this proceeds side by side with, but independently of, the work of the internal auditor. It is initiated by the head of the department concerned, and the aim is to make the procedure followed by the department as self-checking as possible. It is not done blatantly, however, thus calling attention to the security aspect: one clerk is not set the specific task of checking the work of another colleague. Instead, the work is so organised that while one clerk automatically and inevitably checks the work of another, this arises quite naturally and in the ordinary course of routine, and no ill feeling or atmosphere of tension is created. As an example of this, consider the case of stores control. The production control department manages the balances of stores; the Stores Ledger is kept by the Stores Ledger clerk; and the stores and bin cards are in the charge of the storekeeper. In addition, there are frequent physical checks carried out as part of the stores control system, and the various records have to agree or be reconciled. Discrepancies must be dealt with according to a specified procedure.

This internal checking helps to make the work of the internal auditor easier, but he does not entirely rely on it, for he has to be personally satisfied on behalf of management on all matters which he deems necessary to investigate.

Although security measures are kept in the background, they cannot be totally ignored. Thus, every clerk should be required to take at least one holiday per annum, the reason being that any cash or stocks for which he is responsible have then to be handed over to someone else. Again, it is usually possible to arrange a daily check on the entries made in the books, by means of total accounts. It is important, too, that clerks should not be given responsibility which exceeds the status which is accorded to them. Employers are not free from fault when they expect large sums of money to be handled by those who are not paid adequately, and in such circumstances the temptation to misappropriate may become too strong.

INTERNAL AUDIT 19.../19...

QUESTIONNAIRE—STORES DEPARTMENT

Question	Reply	Initial
1. Are goods received notes obtained for all incoming goods?		
2. Are bin cards entered daily from goods received notes?		
3. Are stores requisitions checked as to authorisation?		
4. Are stores taken from bin recorded daily on bin cards?		
5. Have stores debit notes been received for all materials returned to store?		
6. Have they been recorded at once on bin cards?		
7. Have the works' rules been observed at all times as to admission to the stores?		
8. Have all known losses, from whatever cause, been reported at once?		
9. Have fire appliances been checked regularly?		
10. Have weighing machines been regularly maintained?		
11. Has the inspector's attention been called to all cases of damage to goods?		
12. Have you any suggestions to put forward to management re the work of your department?		
For use by internal auditor		
Form sent		
Reply received		
Initialled		

FIG. 89.—*Internal audit questionnaire*

These forms are used to obtain confirmation that acceptable procedures are in force in the various departments, and they have some moral effect in ensuring that they are not neglected.

INTERNAL AUDITING IN RELATION TO MECHANISED ACCOUNTING

In accountancy systems which have been mechanised, either by use of keyboard machines or by the use of punched cards, a change of emphasis is required in regard to internal audit:

(*a*) Greater reliance can be placed on the arithmetical accuracy of the figures.

(*b*) Greater care is necessary in checking the original sources from which the entries and calculations have been made.

(*c*) Greater care is required in the control of the issue of new ledger sheets and the transfer of completed sheets.

VERIFICATION OF ASSETS

This is an important duty laid on the shoulders of the external auditor, but nevertheless the internal auditor, too, is vitally interested.

Stocks. Are the stocks of raw materials, stores and finished goods as stated? On what basis have they been valued for costing purposes? Has this basis been consistently followed? Is it different from that used for balance sheet purposes? If so, a check must be made on the reconciliation between the two.

Work in progress. On what basis is work in progress valued? What methods are used to determine the state of completion? Are they adequate?

Incomplete contracts. Have measurements of work been regularly obtained? Are there any particular hazards to be provided for? Is a conservative policy being followed in regard to profit to be taken? Are materials on site excessive, or left there too long before being incorporated into the work?

Plant and machinery. Is the method of depreciation used suitable and sufficient for the type of plant? Is the basis used for costing purposes different from that used in the financial accounts? If so, which has the greater merit? What provision has been made for replacement costs? What are the risks of obsolescence?

Capital expenditure. Has the distinction between capital and revenue expenditure been scrupulously observed?

These questions indicate some of the points on which the internal auditor will want to be satisfied, and on which he will frame his report to management.

EFFICIENCY AUDIT

In taking a broad view of the business as a whole, the internal auditor will consider the organisation chart (*see*, for example, Fig. 90), and assess the functional efficiency of its detailed parts.

Job evaluation. Although this would be done in the first place by time-and-motion-study personnel, or by an organisation-and-methods department, the internal auditor would be expected to cast a critical eye on the results, and to note any anomalies which had arisen.

Merit rating. In the same way the internal auditor would make sure that the general pattern of the agreed wages and salaries structure was being adhered to, and that adequate reasons were being advanced for abnormal pay increases.

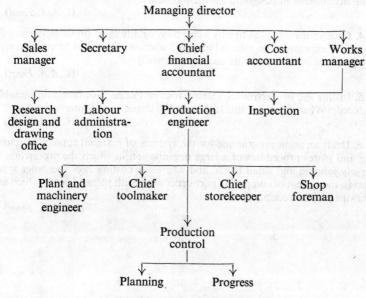

Fig. 90.—*Organisation chart*

This shows the usual type of management organisation of a business. The internal auditor would consider the chart for his own concern, and advise on whether it was in conformity with what was really needed.

It will be seen that the internal auditor's task is to act as the watch-dog for the directors, just as the external auditor acts on behalf of the shareholders and creditors. To some extent their duties are similar, but that is purely coincidental, and the internal auditor goes into his investigations much more closely and continuously, and with a different motive. He is less concerned with adherence to law than with adherence to policy; less concerned with giving sufficient information than with giving maximum information in the most assimilable form.

EXAMINATION QUESTIONS

1. In which direction are the costing records of value to the auditors of the financial accounts? To what extent do you consider an independent audit of the cost accounts is necessary?

(*I.C.W.A. Final*)

2. As cost auditor to a group of factories, describe the procedure you would adopt with regard to labour and material costs.

(*I.C.W.A. Final*)

3. What are your views on the suggestion that an internal auditor of an organisation with various branch offices should act in conjunction with the chief accountant in designing any new system?

(*C.A.A. Final*)

4. Give your reasons as to why a company or any large organisation should incur the expense of an internal auditor, when in fact it has to employ professional auditors to audit its accounts annually.

(*C.A.A. Final*)

5. In this age of electronics, clerical routine duties have been considerably reduced. What effect has this laid upon the duties of the internal auditor?

(*C.A.A. Final*)

6. Draft an audit programme for the systems of material control, purchasing and stores procedures of a large organisation in which the production is largely jobbing and small batch, and where the costing is of the order type, that is, the system of comparing part-order costs with planned costs, which are drawn up upon receipt of order.

(*I.C.W.A. Final*)

CHAPTER 30

MECHANISED COST ACCOUNTING

INTRODUCTION

ONE of the main functions of the cost and management accountant is to use the facts of a business in order to present meaningful information to management as a basis for action: an accountant is therefore a data processor. He is concerned with the following processes:

(*a*) The recording of data.
(*b*) Their communication.
(*c*) Their storage and retrieval.
(*d*) Their calculation.
(*e*) Their printing and display.

The data processed are essentially of two kinds: source or fresh data, *e.g.* the quantity of a product required by a customer; and file data, that is to say, data permanently available, *e.g.* the customer's name and address, the discount terms, etc.

Source data are then combined with file data, and the two are processed in order to provide:

(*a*) orders for action;
(*b*) status reports for credit control;
(*c*) answers to enquiries.

When it has been decided what information the management-accounting system has to provide, and when, it becomes pertinent to consider the best means of achieving it. The range of equipment available is very wide, and although emphasis will be placed on computers and the many functions which they can tackle, it is as well to bear in mind that some tasks do not require such complicated machines.

For the sake of convenience, we shall classify our enquiry into mechanisation under the following headings:

1. Filing, duplicating and copying.
2. Manually operated clerical aids.
3. Power operated clerical aids.
4. Punched cards.
5. Computers.

FILING, DUPLICATING AND COPYING

The essence of filing is to be able to put away, and find again. Such simple devices as spikes, bulldog clips, box files and lever arch files, all have their uses and should not be overlooked. Then there are vertical filing systems in wooden or steel filing cabinets, the necessary files and pockets often costing more than the cabinet itself; or, as an alternative, there are lateral filing systems which are effective and often cheaper. The method of indexing is all important, and there are a number of pre-sorting systems designed to arrange the data in suitable order for filing. Filing trolleys and filing shelves to hook on to the drawers while filing is in progress both usefully assist the filing operation. Large-sized documents may require special cabinets or drawers, and there are many to choose from.

The techniques available for duplicating and copying are often not adequately understood by accountants. They include the following:

(a) Embossed plates for names and addresses.
(b) Carbons of various kinds and colours.
(c) Stencil duplicating.
(d) Spirit duplicating.
(e) Electrostatic methods.
(f) Dye-transfer methods.
(g) Photographic methods.
(h) Infra-red methods.
(i) Dyeline copying.
(j) Offset litho.

Each of these techniques has special applications, but of particular interest to the cost accountant is the spirit duplicator. It is flexible, and, with its blocking and multi-line facility, is used very frequently in costing and production-control applications.

It should be borne in mind that a number of these methods may be combined with computer processes, sometimes using the computer printer, for example, to prepare masters automatically.

MANUALLY OPERATED CLERICAL AIDS

Under this heading we may distinguish the following groups:

1. Recording and calculating.
2. Arranging.
3. Analysing and charting.

Before any choice of equipment is made, certain criteria should be satisfied:

(a) It should be easy and comfortable to use.

(b) It must be able to cope with future expansion.

(c) It must take peak loading problems in its stride.

(d) Its operating costs, as well as its capital cost, must be satisfactory.

1. RECORDING SYSTEMS

Many recording systems depend on the use of cards or slips of various sizes, shapes and colours, these being the *pro-formas* for the regular processing of data. The cost of the documentation is itself often significant, and may require specialised equipment for its housing, such as visible indexes, vertical and horizontal cardwheels, and the more normal post binder.

Other recording devices include desk registers using continuous stationery; three-in-one writing boards for the speedy production of the payroll, employee's record sheet and pay advice sheet; peg boards, etc. Peg boards can be extremely useful in summarising job costs, orders by product lines, cross casting stock summaries, and so on.

In the day-to-day recording activities, there is often a need for some kind of calculation to be made. A simple, but under-rated aid is the ready reckoner. These can be of the sheet variety, or a circular or slide type, and they are very effective if tailored to the special needs of the organisation. The general-purpose slide-rule, which can now also be obtained in circular form, is useful if a wider variety of calculation is required. Manually operated calculating machines are also being increasingly used, and should be considered.

2. ARRANGING EQUIPMENT

The arranging of data often requires equipment to assist the collating and sorting of information. Flap-type sorters, pigeon holes, racks and boxes may be investigated in this connection.

3. ANALYSING MATERIAL

Analysis of data may be done by peg boards, as referred to above, but of very material assistance is the development of edge-punched cards. By coding and punching information round the edge of the card, it is readily available when required. Needles are inserted through the pack of cards in any desired position, and the cards in which that hole has been punched will fall out. Information may thus be sorted in a surprisingly speedy manner. Figure 39 shows how this is done.

Charts may take the form of graphs, bar charts, pie charts, coloured patterns, strip indexes, etc., and provide visual aids which have considerable impact. They provide a simple means of showing the up-to-date position of sales, production, machine loading, stocks, labour, materials, progress of orders, targets, budgets, etc. A wide choice of display techniques is available from many suppliers, but often all that is needed is a little ingenuity to make one's own.

There is one important point to note in regard to charts: they are very useful so long as they are kept up to date. If they cannot be looked after, they will certainly not be consulted.

POWER OPERATED CLERICAL AIDS

Three main types of machine should be noted:

1. Add-listing machines.
2. Accounting machines.
3. Calculating machines.

1. ADD-LISTING MACHINES

These are primarily used for summarising and control total work. The printed record which usually appears on a tally roll is very convenient for checking and batch totalling. The machines have a variety of capabilities, but most can add, subtract and list. They usually have a full keyboard, perhaps ten vertical rows of keys numbered 0 to 9, or a smaller and simplified keyboard of either ten keys if it is a decimal model, or twelve keys numbered 0 to 11 if it is a sterling model. The machines can be manually, but are more often electrically, operated, and have facilities such as total and sub-total, repeat, non-add, correction, etc.

2. ACCOUNTING MACHINES

These are used to classify and to summarise information. They may have standard typewriter keys, twelve numeral keys and some register selection keys; but other more restricted versions provide the notations by means of abbreviations, such as GDS for "goods." Yet another type has a large number of registers for analysis work, and has been developed from the cash register, having no moving carriage.

A variety of sizes and thicknesses of documents can be used with the machines, including continuous stationery. The operation is controlled from the keyboard, but considerable assistance in such matters as spacing, duplicating and totalling can be predetermined for standard applications by means of a "programme bar" which is set up in advance, and kept as an interchangeable unit. This allows for a change-over from, say, a costing routine to a sales routine to take place in a matter of minutes.

3. CALCULATING MACHINES

Calculating machines are used in connection with such matters as pricing material requisitions, making the calculations for time sheets and payroll and working out the details on cost sheets. There are two basic types of calculators:

(a) Key-driven machines, designed mainly to deal with additions and subtractions, but which can also be used for multiplication and division.

(b) Rotary calculators, which are primarily designed to deal with multiplication and division, but which can also be used for addition and subtraction.

Substantial progress is being made in the field of calculators, with the introduction of electronic calculators, which can perform all the basic arithmetical functions at electronic speeds.

Many of the machines mentioned above can have punched paper tape or punched-card attachments, producing tape or card media as a by-product of the operation being carried out. For example, add-listing tally rolls can be produced on paper tape and subsequently read by a computer. Similarly, card-a-type machines may make use of such devices as a card or tape-reading mechanism, a calculator, a typewriter and a card punch, to produce such documents as an invoice, using the static data fed in from the card, and combining them with the variable data which are entered by the typewriter. A summary card for the invoice total is produced at the same time for subsequent ledger work.

PUNCHED CARDS

The essential feature of a punched-card system is that there is one manual operation which records an accounting event by means of perforations in a card, after which the data can be automatically arranged and processed accurately with associated data at high speed. The process begins with the punch-sort-tabulate technique. The size of the card is dictated by the amount of information, and the degree of analysis required. The card is divided into "fields," and punching information into the card is done from an original source document, arranged to correspond with the fields of the card. Figure 91 shows a typical punch. By scanning the document, one may punch from left to right of the card without hesitation. However, errors may occur in picking up the data, and so it is necessary to follow the punching operation with verification. The verifier is a machine similar to the punch, which reads the holes already punched and compares them with the data entered, signalling any discrepancies which may be present (*see* Fig. 91).

FIG. 91.—*A punched-card installation*

An 80-column punched-card installation, showing automatic card punches, a tabulator and an automatic verifier.

After preparation, the cards must be arranged into significant groups or sequences, *e.g.* account number, stores number or inventory number within the stores number. This "sorting of cards," as it is called, is achieved by means of passing the cards a number of times through a machine known as a *sorter*. The machine operates at high speed, but the length of time taken is of course dependent on the volumes involved, and the complexity of the code, since only one column of the card can be read and sorted at a time. The holes in the cards may represent numbers or alphabetical characters, but the machine selects and sorts simply by sensing the holes which have been punched. A sorter is illustrated in Fig. 92.

The tabulating process takes the cards, usually after they have been sorted, and, reading the information, prints out the results. These results include not only detailed information from the cards, but additions and subtractions for each card, and summaries of different categories of cards. There is considerable flexibility in the format of these machines, with the option, for instance, of printing alphabetical and numerical data over any or all of the print positions on each line, usually at speeds of the order of 100 to 150 lines per minute. The program of the machine is normally determined by a plugboard or mechanical connection box together with switches set for each job by the operator.

A summary card punch can also be attached to the tabulator to record, for example, the carry-forward balance in a card for next month's ledger. Figure 91 shows a typical tabulating machine.

Courtesy: International Computers Ltd.

FIG. 92.—*Sorter*

The sorter senses the appropriate perforations, and automatically groups together all cards of the same number or description and arranges the groups into a sequential order.

There are a number of supporting machines in the punched-card range:

(*a*) Gang punches used for the setting-up or replenishing of pre-punched stocks of cards.

(*b*) Collators used to merge groups of cards together.

(*c*) Interpreters used to translate the holes of the card into readable characters on the card itself, which is helpful if the cards have to be inspected by someone outside the punched-card department.

(*d*) Calculating punches, which take cards or groups of cards and carry out fairly intricate calculations, punching the results on to the same cards, or summary cards, or both. They often have a useful measure of internal storage, of, say, 1,000 digits, and have powerful programming facilities by means of plugboards.

Punched cards have been applied to a wide variety of accounting problems, and are particularly valuable when there is the need to make use of the source data in a number of different ways. These applications may be summarised as follows:

(a) *Materials*. Ordering control—stock control—pricing—usage figures—analyses—costs—variance analysis.

(b) *Labour*. Calculation of earnings—preparation of earnings records—payroll—payslips—cost charging—variance analysis, etc.

(c) *Overhead*. Analysis—costs—variance analysis.

(d) *Personnel records*.

(e) *Bought and Sales Ledgers*.

Punched-card procedures provide a very useful introduction to the types of techniques and disciplines that are required in a computer environment, and, indeed, even when a computer has been installed and has begun to operate, it is often found desirable to carry out a number of computer-support operations on punched-card machines. It is interesting to note that many of the current items of computer peripheral equipment had their origins in an earlier version of a punched-card machine. We may therefore conclude that punched cards are likely to be in use for a long time to come, but with gradually diminishing importance.

COMPUTERS

WHAT IS A COMPUTER?

The United States of America Institute (USASI) defines a computer as follows:

"A device capable of solving problems by accepting data, performing described operations on the data, and supplying the results of these operations. Various types of computers are calculators, digital computers and analog computers."

The USASI definition is rather broad for our purposes, and one rather closer to our needs is that given by the International Standards Organisation (ISO):

"A data processor that can perform substantial computation, including numerous arithmetic and logic operations, without intervention by a human operator during the run."

At this stage, then, we are left with three major families:

(a) Analogue computers, which obtain answers by measuring.
(b) Digital computers, which obtain answers by counting.
(c) Hybrid computers, which use a combination of both techniques.

In our everyday life we are in contact with many types of analogue computers, e.g., speedometers, thermometers and slide-rules. The rate at which the needle of the speedometer moves is analogous to—that is to say, bears some correspondence to—the speed of the automobile; the height of the mercury in the thermometer is analogous to the temperature; and the length of the slide on the slide-rule is analogous to some actual quantity. In mechnical analogue computers, numbers are represented on a dial actuated by the rotation of a shaft; but in electronic analogue computers, numbers are represented by the deviation of an electric current or voltage from a standard value.

Unlike digital computers, which represent information in a discrete form, analogue computers represent it in a continuous form. By using analogue computers, engineers are able to simulate mechanical and basic computer functions much more easily and more cheaply than by digital means, provided that not too high a degree of accuracy is required. Analogue computers are often designed for specific jobs, which limits their usefulness; and they require a knowledge of advanced mathematics in order to carry out the programming necessary.

For all these reasons the tendency is to use digital computers, which can be used for almost any data-processing job. Even flight simulation is an example where earlier and less sophisticated types of simulator, supported by analogue devices, are tending to give way to more sophisticated types, which are then supported by hybrid or digital computers.

Commercial data processing has to be extremely accurate, and so, in common business language, the term computer means an "electronic digital computer." It is, therefore, this type of computer with which we shall henceforth concern ourselves in this text.

HOW THE COMPUTER WORKS

The fundamental units of a computer are shown in diagrammatic form in Fig. 93 and have been numbered from 1 to 7 for easy reference. Computer operations begin when the operator presses a button on the console (1). This action brings the control unit (2) into a state of readiness to initiate and control computer actions from that point onwards. At once, then, the control unit brings in a program to be carried out, either from input (3) or from backing storage (6). Input may, for example, be represented by a card reader, and backing storage by a tape or disc unit (see Fig. 94). The program is read into the immediate access store (4) and held there to help the control unit to process the

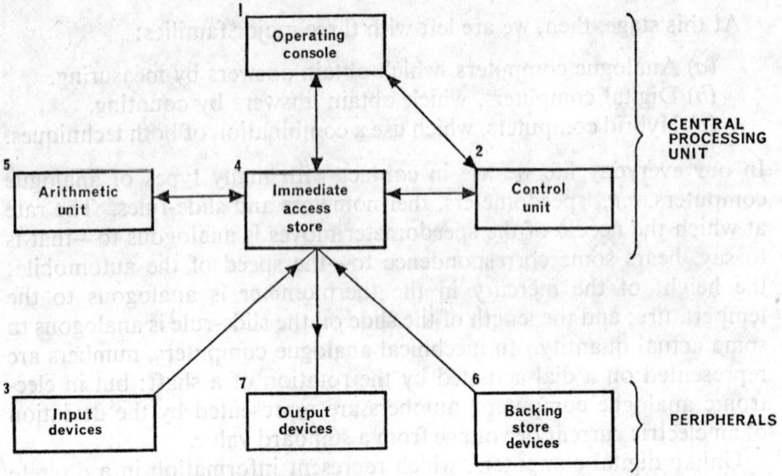

FIG. 93.—*Fundamental units of a computer*
The arrows indicate the main communication paths.

data until the program has been performed for all the available data. Once the program is ready in internal storage the computer can really carry out the job it is designed to do, *i.e.* to process data. Calculations and logical operations are carried out by using the arithmetic and logic unit (5); and after rearrangement in internal storage the results will be seen via the output device (7) which is usually a line printer. The cycle is complete when the operator tells the computer that the day's work is complete, or instructs it, through the console, to go on to the next program.

This description is, perhaps, already a little old-fashioned, for often the transition from one program to another can be automatic, and some machines have the option which allows the computer to run a number of programs simultaneously in a mode known as "multi-programming."

The devices which make up the computer system are known as "hardware." ISO defines hardware as:

"physical equipment, as opposed to the program or method of use: for example, mechanical, magnetic, electrical or electronic devices."

The contrast to "hardware" is "software," which ISO defines as:

"a set of programs, procedures, rules and possibly associated documentation concerned with the operation of a data-processing system."

The console consists of a series of lights and switches, by means of which the operator or maintenance engineer can tell what is happening

Courtesy: I.B.M. United Kingdom Ltd.

FIG. 94.—*A computer system*

An installation showing a card read punch (*left*), a disc storage drive (*background*) and magnetic tape units.

in the various components of the system, and can also interrogate and instruct the machine. The central processor combines in itself the control unit, the internal storage unit (immediate access store) and the arithmetic unit. The card reader and card punch enable card data or programs to be read and to provide ouput in the form of punched cards with the newly calculated data. Backing storage is represented by disc drive devices, and also by magnetic tape drives. Both are capable of storing and retrieving millions of characters of data at high speed, and both have virtually unlimited storage since the discs or tapes are inter-changeable. The disc units operate rather like the conventional record-player, and the tape units like a tape-recorder. Finally, the high-speed line printer produces reports, documents and a whole range of other printing at speeds in the order of 1,000 lines per minute.

DATA REPRESENTATION

Means have to be found to present data to the computer. The ap-proach is to reduce the data to a set of symbols that can be read and interpreted by data-processing machines. The range of devices and media is increasing all the time. The more common forms in use at the present time are punched cards, paper tape, magnetic tape, magnetic-ink characters, optically recognisable characters, microfilm and display film images, communication network signals, etc. Data on punched cards are, as we have already seen, represented by holes cut in specified positions of the card. Similarly holes are cut in paper tape. Data on magnetic tape are represented by small magnetised spots, and magnetic-ink characters are encoded on documents such as cheques with special encoders. Optical reading can now be done on characters produced by an ordinary typewriter, or in some cases by stylised handwriting. Of all these methods, punched cards and paper tape are most common, but the use of magnetic tape encoders is increasing rapidly.

THE FUNCTIONS AND ATTRIBUTES OF THE COMPUTER

The computer can carry out almost all the processing of information required by any organisation—classification, sorting, calculating, decision making, summarising, storing, retrieving, reproducing, recording and communicating. Its ability to perform these functions well is increasing all the time, and the art of computer usage lies in choosing the best areas of activity, and in fixing priorities.

The computer is very fast, very accurate, is tireless, and can store vast amounts of data. It can carry out its arithmetical calculations, perform its logic and reach its decisions at incredible speeds. It can be comprehensive and painstaking, and present its results very clearly and in an orderly manner. The larger machines, for instance, can perform the co-ordinated work of half a million mathematicians, and it is confidently expected that within this generation the contents of the three largest libraries in the world, comprising some twenty-four million volumes will be stored in a cube of very small size.

There are, of course, some difficulties and disadvantages to be considered. Although, for the processing power available, the operating costs are low, the capital cost of the equipment, and the costs involved in setting up systems, are high. This inevitably leads to some inflexibility, although the computer itself is very flexible. There are problems associated with the preparation of programs, of staff recruitment and training, of reorganising existing staff, and of setting up, controlling and timing the whole data-processing operation.

The computer is particularly useful for performing tasks which involve much mental drudgery: those, for example, which require much sorting and numerous repetitive calculations. It also excels where large files of records have to be searched to find answers to queries, where there is a complex relationship between the query and the solution, and where there is a necessity for a quick-response system, involving large file scanning or speedy calculations, or both. The computer is very good at digesting run-of-the-mill data, and drawing attention to results outside acceptable limits, as, for example, throwing out standard cost variances. It can assist in more efficient work, more complete work, new solutions to old problems, staff saving, the elimination of duplicate records, the earlier production of information and, very significantly, the earlier completion of projects of all kinds.

THE APPLICATION OF COMPUTERS TO SPECIFIC PROBLEMS

Provided that requirements are fairly specific and quantifiable, the computer works efficiently in the technical field. Scientific and engineering solutions can be provided for the control of physical operations, for the problems of mathematical numerical analysis, for the numerical control of machine tools and for immediate interactive control of processes (sometimes known as "real-time process control").

The field of business is more complex, and requires more managerial participation. Most companies are concerned with the flow of goods, with finance and with personnel; and each of these involves much data handling. Computer systems are therefore most fruitfully employed in material control, finished stock control, production planning and control, scheduling and transportation; in budgetary control and capital investment appraisal; and to a lesser extent, in the storage and retrieval of information regarding personnel.

The main computer systems thus jointly contribute to the building up of an organisation's vital data, referred to as either the "data base" or the "data bank." This data bank is drawn upon extensively for other requirements such as marketing, research and development, and corporate planning, where historical data are the basis for analysis, and the simulation of possible situations and strategies.

HOW A COMPUTER IS PUT TO WORK

A STANDARD APPLICATION

In order that the reader may acquire some appreciation of a working computer system, this section sets out an outline of a typical system using magnetic tape, which is to cater for the following procedures:

(*a*) Invoice preparation.
(*b*) Sales Ledger and Stock Account posting.
(*c*) Sales analysis.

The invoicing and associated programs will provide all the necessary information to post the accounts and to undertake the analysis.

Two types of input are required:

(a) *Fixed*

    Customer record:

        Name and address
        Code number
        Credit limit
        Discounts allowed

    Product record:

        List price
        Product number
        Minimum stock level
        Re-order level
        Re-order quantity
        Unit of issue

(b) *Variable, or transaction data record:*

        Invoice and docket number
        Date
        Number of units received or ordered
        Debit or credit notation
        Value of cash received or of financial adjustment

NOTE: Each field (*see* the Glossary at the end of this chapter) must be precisely defined; *e.g.* the cash field may be limited to three digits for the pound and there may be only three digits for the decimal places of the pound.

In order to save time, the fixed information is stored on the magnetic-tape backing store at the initiation of the system, and changed only rarely, for instance, with a change of credit limit or product price.

In addition to routine book-keeping operations the system undertakes the following tasks:

(a) Checking stock availability.
(b) Checking credit control.
(c) Controlling orders when stock is not available.
(d) Re-ordering when stock is low.

The system requires four magnetic-tape storage files designed as follows:

Stock file

Product no.	Description	Stock balance	Unit of issue	Re-order level	Minimum stock	Re-order quantity	List price	⟶

Customer's file

Account no.	Name	Address	Credit limit	Discounts	Address to which goods are consigned	Sales representative	--→

Sales Ledger

Account no.	Opening monthly balance	Current balance	Transactions 1	2	3	etc. --→

Transaction file

A record of each invoice is as follows:

Account no.	Invoice no.	Date	Sales representative	Total value	Product no.	No. of units	Value	--→

The student must realise that, the tape being continuous, the patterns shown above repeat endlessly along the tape in the direction of the arrows. In the transaction file, the next account no. will not be recorded until all the items for the current invoice have been stored on the file.

The daily operations are illustrated in the flow charts illustrated on the following two pages. At the end of the month, the Sales Ledger file is read to produce the monthly customer statements, and the transaction file is read to produce the analysis reports required by management.

A further routine will be required to deal with credit rejects, but it has not been thought of sufficient interest to show the flow chart in this case.

SYSTEMS ANALYSIS AND DESIGN

The decision to introduce a computer system into an organisation is a very serious one, and the process on which such a decision is based is often referred to as "systems analysis, design and implementation." The person entrusted with overall responsibility for the function is known as "the systems analyst."

The stages of a project may be listed as follows:

1. Feasibility study.
2. System prototype design.
3. Machine selection.
4. Working system design.
5. Programming and operation.
6. Implementation and control.
7. Evaluation, maintenance and development.

It will be seen that the range of activities is a complex sequence, in which there is bound to be some overlapping.

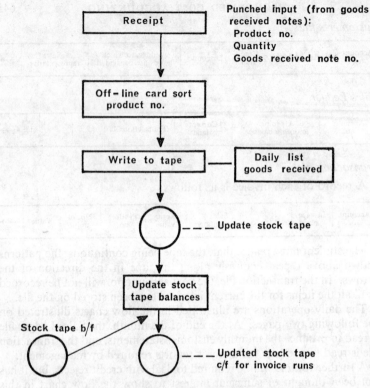

Punched input (from goods received notes):
Product no.
Quantity
Goods received note no.

Receipt

Off-line card sort product no.

Write to tape — Daily list goods received

Update stock tape

Update stock tape balances

Stock tape b/f

Updated stock tape c/f for invoice runs

CASH POSTINGS AND FINANCIAL ADJUSTMENTS

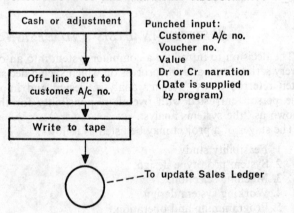

Cash or adjustment

Punched input:
Customer A/c no.
Voucher no.
Value
Dr or Cr narration
(Date is supplied by program)

Off-line sort to customer A/c no.

Write to tape

To update Sales Ledger

Flow chart (1)

This chart illustrates the processes for updating stock tape for receipts.

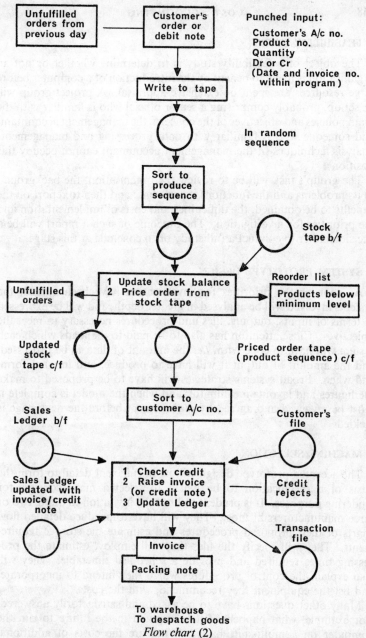

Punched input:

Customer's A/c no.
Product no.
Quantity
Dr or Cr
(Date and invoice no.
within program)

Flow chart (2)

This chart shows the processes for the preparation of invoices (and credit notes for returned goods). Except for the Dr. and Cr. aspect, both are identical functions which need to be recorded in the stock file.

NOTE: The customer's file will supply "fixed" information.

1. FEASIBILITY STUDY

The object of a feasibility study is to determine whether or not an organisation is likely to benefit by the introduction of a computer before large resources are spent on extensive appraisal. A project group will be set up, probably comprising a senior official who is familiar with the main policies and objectives of the concern, the management accountant, and someone who is familiar with data processing and management-analysis techniques (if the management accountant cannot occupy this position).

The group's task will be to review the organisation, the background to its problems and the functions it performs; and then to report on the benefits to be obtained, the difficulties and costs of implementation and the priorities for investigation. The outcome of such a report will be a decision either to conduct a full study or to conclude at this stage.

2. SYSTEM PROTOTYPE DESIGN

As soon as the priorities for investigation have been agreed, the systems involved will be analysed in greater depth, and will be expressed in terms of inputs, outputs, files and procedures necessary to meet the objectives. Close attention has also to be paid to the loads which each system will have to cope with, *i.e.* the amount of data to be processed, and the amount of output it will have to produce, and in what form, and when. Broad systems strategies will have to be proposed to make the figures and layouts meaningful, and when the model is complete it must be reviewed and agreed by management before the next stage is tackled.

3. MACHINE SELECTION

The accepted prototype design will be in sufficient detail to form the basis of a specification to be issued to selected manufacturers for tendering purposes. It is prudent to limit the invitation to quote two or three manufacturers at most. They will have to produce detailed flow charts of their proposed procedures and estimate the storage requirements. They will specify the files they will employ, estimate the processing times required and provide a scheduled timetable. They will also explain the control procedures which they intend to incorporate, and list the equipment they recommend, with the costs.

Many other questions have to be asked and satisfactorily answered. For example, what happens if it is required in the future to run the computer on a multi-shift basis? What are the costs of additional testing time? Who pays for equipment transportation? How much are additional storage media going to cost? What trade-in-terms are available?

Once a decision is made to proceed, there is inevitably a substantial commitment to the project, and to the manufacturer. It is therefore of the utmost importance that the decision be fully justified from every angle.

4. WORKING SYSTEM DESIGN

With the critical decisions now made, it is possible to plan for the most important activites such as:

(a) preparing the computer site;

(b) starting general training schemes;

(c) programming;

(d) preparing to convert manual files into computer media, which is usually a difficult and lengthy process;

(e) making provision for the new functions.

Details of the systems and procedures should be finalised and agreed, so that programming can start as soon as the system has been reduced to a number of computer runs. Once the specifications have been agreed, describing in detail the documents, layouts and procedures, further changes should only be allowed with the authorisation of the data-processing manager. This stage is known as "system freeze." Changes may be appropriate, for instance, if caused by external reasons beyond the control of the organisation; if due to policy changes; or if there is a significant error or gap in the specification. If changes are to be made, it is important that the implications are apparent to all concerned, because of their effects on costs and on scheduled completion dates.

A programming strategy may now be evolved. Standards of procedure will be framed to monitor and harmonise progress. Programming languages will be recommended, which will take into account such factors as:

(a) the speed of program completion;

(b) the skill of the programmer;

(c) the compatibility of machines;

(d) the amount of internal storage used.

As programs are developed, new facts will come to light, and these must be documented, and when the programs are working satisfactorily, operating instructions have to be framed and documented, so that the programs can be run on a regular basis.

Groups of programs are often split into individual programs for allocation to different programmers, and individual programs may often be subdivided still further. Each module has to be programmed and tested both separately and as combined in a group.

5. PROGRAMMING AND OPERATION

The first stage of programming is to design a set of instructions for the machine and its operator to follow. This means that the programmer must first become fully acquainted with the problem he has to solve. When he has decided on his course of action, he sets out his strategy in a diagram known as a *flow chart*, such as we have already considered. He then codes the flow-chart procedures into a language and form which the computer can understand, for the computer only responds to numerical codes. Programming the earlier computers involved the coding of instructions in these terms, together with such tasks as the allocation and registration of storage use. This was based on the binary system of notation, but writing out whole strings of numbers such as 01000010, which might stand for "read" was error prone and time consuming, and the idea was conceived of using mnemonics, say, "rd." These mnemonics replaced the number codes, and the computer was designed to carry out the clerical function of translating them. This was a major breakthrough, for once it was seen that the computer could carry out one clerical job, it was obvious that the principle might be extended. The next function to be automated was that of allocation of storage.

Two other developments improved the programming throughput. Firstly, it was observed that there are a number of "command sets" common to most programs, involving a set of instructions such as, *e.g.* "read a card," "write to disc," etc. A technique was devised whereby a single instruction by a programmer would create a series of machine instructions which would then be inserted automatically into the program, and such a single instruction became known as a "macro," implying a series of instructions as opposed to one-for-one instructions. At this stage, a program would thus be made up of a number of one-for-one instructions, together with a number of macros.

Then, secondly, as speeds of computer operation were increasing all the time, it became possible for the machine to read, write and compute simultaneously, instead of sequentially. At the same time the facility was developed for programmers to write a program in sequential mode, which is easier, but for the computer to operate in a simultaneous mode. Other standard programs known as "utilities," such as routines for sorting and merging records, creating record labels, etc., were also developed.

The next development was that of "high-level languages." These enable the more generally found types of business calculations and mathematical statements to be translated and combined with the features already developed. The most common business language is COBOL (short for the "common business orientated language") which was developed by the United States Department of Defence as a computer language to be used for business purposes on almost any type of computer. FORTRAN was developed by I.B.M. for the solution of scientific problems, and was subsequently taken up by other manufacturers. There are many other languages with similar objectives, of which the most common is the I.B.M. language known as PL/1 which seeks to combine the advantages of COBOL and FORTRAN. Since then, the facilities have been extended even further by the provision of standardised systems and program packages for some of the more common requirements such as the payroll, stock control, etc., which can be applied either *in toto* or used to provide modules for incorporation into other programs.

After the programmer has coded his program, it is fed to the computer, which it vets for acceptibility, and produces a machine code. Data are now constructed to see if the program will meet the specification in all respects. This stage is known, in the jargon of the computer world, as "debugging," and it usually involves the amendment and insertion of a number of instructions, which can be a lengthy and frustrating process.

The operator takes over where the programmer leaves off. He has the duty of feeding in data to the computer, monitoring its activities and the output it produces, logging all activities of operating personnel and the machine, referring faults to control and effecting re-runs as they arise. He needs to be well trained, quick, tidy, conscientious and responsible.

Just as some of the programmer's activities have been taken over by the computer, so now are some of the operator's. The techniques which include this facility are known as "operating systems." Such systems allow the machine to exercise overall control of user programs and input/output operations; to select the input/output devices; to supervise the loading of program packages or modules; to schedule jobs; to make the transition from one job to another; and to keep the operator informed of what it is doing. With certain reservations, of course, the operator may override its control.

It should be noted that there are often facilities for running more than one job at a time; *e.g.* the payroll may be calculated at the same time as enquiries on the stock position are being answered.

6. IMPLEMENTATION AND CONTROL

After the programmer has completed his task, and before the system becomes fully operational, the stage of implementation is necessary, in which the greatest degree of co-operation between all departments is vital.

A detailed plan for the change-over from the old system to the new computerised system will have been drawn up. During this period of conversion, the existing system has to be maintained while additional staff and resources from all departments are busy testing the new procedures, and converting the existing data into computer media. The computer files must be loaded on to the backing store, and additional equipment, staff and accommodation may well be necessary. This must be foreseen.

Training schemes must be organised for management and operational staff, so that everyone knows and accepts the new system. The precise timing of the conversion is also important. One should aim to avoid peak periods when work loads are heavy, or holiday periods when staff are not available.

Control systems must also be established to ensure that no records of cash or goods are mislaid in the data-processing department. There should also be input controls, run-to-run controls, file controls and the control of rejects. What procedures are to be adopted for the retention and protection of files and programs? Will they be kept on or off the premises? What back-up procedures will be available in the event of computer-system failure? What file re-creation procedures are available?

It will readily be seen that the secret of successful implementation lies in initial comprehensive and thorough planning. Failures occur—and the fact must be faced that they are far too common—and they are due to allowing insufficient time to elapse after each stage of conversion takes place. It is imperative to allow the new system to be assimilated, and the strain imposed by it to wear off before the next stage is attempted. Often, too, there is inadequate training, and there are insufficient and badly conceived controls.

7. EVALUATION, MAINTENANCE AND DEVELOPMENT

When the new system has had a chance to settle, it is necessary to review it, in order to determine how successful it has been in meeting its objectives. Deficiencies have to be remedied, and improvements made. Often new computer applications are seen to be possible which had never been considered under the old methods of operation.

Throughout its life, the computer system will require a measure of maintenance. New equipment or software features may possibly be added, and at all times the ever-changing demands of statutory, market and operational conditions have to be satisfied.

GLOSSARY OF TERMS USED IN AUTOMATIC DATA PROCESSING

Access time. The time required to locate a particular store and either write data into it or read data from it.

Accumulator. The register in the arithmetic unit used for temporary storage and for the formation of sums and other arithmetical and logical results.

Address. A label that identifies for the computer a specific location in its memory unit.

Alphameric or alphanumeric. Letters of the alphabet, special characters and numerals.

Analogue computer. A computer operating on the principle of creating a physical analogy of the mathematical problem to be solved.

Arithmetic unit. The section of the central processor hardware in which arithmetical and logical operations are performed.

Automatic programming language. A programming language in which the written instructions are like English. A compiler program converts this language into machine language.

Binary. Pertaining to the concept of "two" (*cf.* denary). The basic form of character representation in most computers.

Binary coded decimal. A representation of a maximum of sixty-four characters (numbers, alphabet and symbols) in six binary digits.

Bit. The abbreviation for binary digit.

Blocking. The storage of more than one item in a record.

Buffer. A temporary store between the input/output equipment and the computer.

Central processor. The computing centre of the machine. It includes the control unit, memory and the arithmetic unit.

Character. A digit, a letter or a special symbol, *e.g.* +, %, etc.

Compiler. A programming system supplied by the manufacturer to convert a program written in an automatic language into machine language.

Console. The computer control panel of manual switches, etc.

Debug. To seek and correct program errors.

Digital. The use of discrete symbols to represent data.

Dump. To write out the partial or complete contents of internal or external storage devices, usually for checking purposes.

Exit. The point in a program where the control sequence is changed so that the computer jumps to another part of the program.

Field. A group of characters comprising one descriptive unit, *e.g.* the bits used to encode a person's name.

File. A collection of records, punched cards, magnetic tape, etc.

Hardware. Electro-mechanical and electronic equipment (*cf.* software).

Instruction. The basic step in a computer program.

Library. An ordered collection of standard or checked routines and sub-routines by which problems and parts of problems may be solved.

Load. To move data from external storage into the proper locations in internal storage.

Location. A storage position in memory capable of storing one word. An address.

Loop. The cyclic repetition of a sequence of instructions.

Machine language. The set of signs, characters or symbols and the rules for combining these which are used to represent instructions and information within the computer.

Magnetic tape unit. A peripheral device which transports magnetic tape for the purpose of storing information on the tape or detecting previously stored information.

Microsecond. One-millionth of a second.

Millisecond. One-thousandth of a second.

Mnemonic language. A non-machine language more easily remembered by humans than machine language.

Modification. The alteration of data by performing arithmetic upon it.

Object language. Machine language.

Off line. Peripheral equipment working independent of the computer.

On line. Operating under computer control.

Operand. The data specified in an instruction which are required to be operated on by the instruction.

Parity check. A means of checking that information is not lost or garbled.

Peripheral equipment. Input/output devices, referred to as peripheral because they are exterior to the main frame (*i.e.* central processor) of the computer.

Program. A logical sequence of step by step operations which are performed by the computer in order to solve a problem.

Random access. Access to storage where the access time is independent of the location of the word obtained.

Read. To take or accept data for use elsewhere.

Register. A device within the central processor which is used for storing a piece of information while or until it is used. A register usually stores no more than one word at a time.

Routine. Part of a program.

Run. One performance of a program on a computer.

Software. A program (*cf.* hardware) designed to assist installations on routine work, *e.g.* input/output.

Storage. A device which can receive information and hold it indefinitely.

Storage external. Storage facilities external to the central processor which hold information before and after it has been processed within the computer. Information in external storage is in a form suitable for entering into the computer.

Storage internal. The memory unit which is an integral physical part of the central processor and directly controlled by it.

Storage temporary. Storage facilities within the central processor reserved for intermediate and partial results (*e.g.* the accumulator).

Sub-routine. A section of a program which is stored once in memory and can be used over and over again during the course of the program to accomplish a certain routine.

Update. To change information in a file by bringing it up to date.

Word. A set of characters which occupies one memory location and is treated by the computer circuits as a unit and transported as such.

Write. To record data (*e.g.* by writing data into a store or on to tape, etc.).

EXAMINATION QUESTIONS

1. Your company is planning to acquire a computer. You are required to submit a report to the chairman in which the various stages of a feasibility study are defined and the main considerations which determine the configuration of a computer system are detailed.

(*A.C.C.A. Final*)

2. You are chief financial executive of an organisation which has recently appointed a computer manager, who will be directly responsible to you for a new computer installation. You are required to write a letter confirming his conditions of service and to enclose a schedule of his responsibilities.

(*A.C.C.A. Final*)

3. Outline the investigations which a company should require to be undertaken before a decision is made whether to purchase a computer for commercial work within the company.

(*A.C.C.A. Final*)

4. What type of controls do you consider necessary to ensure accuracy in the preparation of commercial data where a computer is used?

(*A.C.C.A. Final*)

5. A company is considering installing a computer to replace its mechnical accounting department which can no longer maintain up-to-date records. What enquiries should the company make before it finally decides to purchase a computer?

(*A.C.C.A. Final*)

6. State briefly what, in your opinion, comes within the sphere of automatic data processing.

(*A.C.C.A. Final*)

7. It has been suggested that one of the dangers of the mechanisation of accounting records is to increase the possibility of fraud. Discuss this contention.

(*I.C.W.A. Final*)

8. Detail the difficulties which might be met by the auditor of a large company which maintains its records on punched cards, and state what steps you think might be taken in practice to overcome these difficulties.

(A.C.C.A. Final)

9. Prepare a brief report on the main features of an electronic computer and on its possible applications as an aid to management.

(I.C.W.A. Final)

10. A client has requested your advice regarding the installation of a computer to deal initially with purchases and sales, and also a newly introduced system of perpetual inventory. Draft a reply to the client outlining the main problems which will arise on the change-over from manual records, and provide the solutions to these problems. Also state in your reply the effects on the conduct of subsequent audits, the information you will require and the controls that should be built into the system.

(A.C.C.A. Final)

APPENDIX I

TERMINOLOGY OF COST ACCOUNTANCY

*(Reprinted, by permission, from the official terminology issued by
the Institute of Cost and Works Accountants)*

THIS terminology, issued with the authority of the Council of the Institute, represents the second major revision of the original costing terminology since it was first published in March, 1937, in the Institute's *Journal*.

The revised work is intended to contribute still further to the improvement of communication and understanding in the field of cost and management accounting. In preparing this edition, the Terminology Sub-committee sought at every stage to satisfy itself that the terms and definitions included could reasonably be expected to achieve this end. Wherever it was apparent that differing points of view would need to be recognised additional comment was introduced, stating an alternative usage or indicating a preference.

The publication of this terminology should not restrict the development of new and informative forms of expression which may in the future prove to be more acceptable than those now in use. For the present, however, it is believed that the terminology, like its forerunners, will be widely adopted.

The student, in particular, should note that the examiners are aware of this revision and should make himself familiar with it.

COST ACCOUNTANCY

The application of costing and cost accounting principles, methods and techniques to the science, art and practice of cost control and the ascertainment of profitability. It includes the presentation of information derived therefrom for the purpose of managerial decision making.

COSTING

The techniques and processes of ascertaining costs.

TYPES OF COSTING

Historical costing. The ascertainment of costs after they have been incurred.

Standard costing. The preparation and use of standard costs, their comparison with actual costs and the analysis of variances to their causes and points of incidence.

Marginal costing. The ascertainment of marginal costs and of the effect on profit of changes in volume or type of output by differentiating between fixed costs and variable costs.

NOTE: In this method of costing only variable costs are charged to operations, processes or products while fixed costs are written-off against profits in the period in which they arise.

Direct costing. The practice of charging all direct costs to operations, processes or products, leaving all indirect costs to be written-off against profits in the period in which they arise.

NOTE: This differs from marginal costing in that some fixed costs could be considered to be direct costs in appropriate circumstances.

Absorption costing. The practice of charging all costs, both variable and fixed, to operations, processes or products.

Uniform costing. The use by several undertakings of the same costing principles and/or practices.

COSTING PROCEDURES

Cost classification. (a) The process of grouping costs according to their common characteristics.

(b) A series of specified groups according to which costs are classified.

Cost allocation. The allotment of whole items of cost to cost centres or cost units.

Cost apportionment. The allotment of proportions of items of cost to cost centres or cost units.

NOTE: The words "allocation," "apportionment" and "allotment" will be found in some textbooks to have exactly the same meaning. The distinction made in the above two definitions implies a greater degree of precision to "allocation." Thus one allocates direct expenditure which can be directly identified with a cost centre or cost unit, but one apportions indirect expenditure.

Overhead absorption. The allotment of overhead to cost units.

NOTE: Overhead absorption is usually achieved by the use of one or a combination of overhead rates. Such rates are often referred to as "recovery" rates. The use of this term is somewhat confusing since it may be understood to imply recovery in selling price which is not necessarily achieved, and for this reason "absorption" is recommended.

COST

(a) The amount of expenditure (actual or notional) incurred on, or attributable to, a given thing.

(b) To ascertain the cost of a given thing.

NOTE: The word "cost" can rarely stand on its own and should be qualified as to its nature or limitations (*e.g.* historical, variable, etc.) and related to a particular thing or "object of thought" (*e.g.* a given quantity or unit of goods made or services performed).

ELEMENTS OF COST

The primary classification of costs according to the factors upon which expenditure is incurred, *viz.*, materials cost, wages (labour cost) and expenses.

Materials cost. The cost of commodities supplied to an undertaking.

Wages (labour cost). The cost of remuneration (wages, salaries, commissions, bonuses, etc.) of the employees of an undertaking.

Expenses. The cost of services provided to an undertaking and the notional cost of the use of owned assets.

PRIME COST

The aggregate of direct materials cost, direct wages (direct labour cost) and variable direct expenses.

Direct materials cost. Materials cost which can be identified with, and allocated to, cost centres or cost units.

Direct wages (direct labour cost). Wages (labour cost) which can be identified with, and allocated to, cost centres or cost units.

Direct expenses. Expenses which can be identified with, and allocated to, cost centres or cost units.

OVERHEAD

The aggregate or indirect materials cost, indirect wages (indirect labour cost) and indirect expenses.

NOTE: "Oncost" and "burden" are synonymous terms which are not recommended.

Indirect materials cost. Materials cost which cannot be allocated but which can be apportioned to, or absorbed by, cost centres or cost units.

Indirect wages (indirect labour cost). Wages (labour cost) which cannot be allocated but which can be apportioned to, or absorbed by, cost centres or cost units.

Indirect expenses. Expenses which cannot be allocated but which can be apportioned to, or absorbed by, cost centres or cost units.

Absorbed overhead. The overhead which, by means of rates of overhead absorption, is allotted to cost units.

Under- or over-absorbed overhead. The difference between the amount of overhead absorbed and the amount of overhead incurred.

NATURE OF COST

Fixed cost. A cost which tends to be unaffected by variations in volume of output. Fixed costs depend mainly on the effluxion of time and do not vary directly with volume or rate of output. Fixed costs are sometimes referred to as period costs in systems of direct costing.

NOTE: There may be different levels of fixed costs at different levels of output, for example where extra output is only obtainable by extra capital equipment or extra services. At the other extreme, when a whole department may be shut down, many of these costs will, in fact, disappear.

Variable cost. A cost which tends to vary directly with volume of output. Variable costs are sometimes referred to as direct costs in systems of direct costing.

Semi-fixed cost. A cost which is partly fixed and partly variable.

Semi-variable cost. *See* semi-fixed cost.

Controllable cost. A cost which can be influenced by the action of a specified member of an undertaking.

Uncontrollable cost. A cost which cannot be influenced by the action of a specified member of an undertaking.

Normal cost. A cost at a given level of output in the conditions in which that level of output is normally attained.

Obsolescence. The loss in the value of an asset due to its supersession at an earlier date than was foreseen.

NOTE: Loss of value which can be foreseen should be covered by the depreciation provision.

Depreciation. The diminution in the value of a fixed asset due to use and/ or the lapse of time.

NOTE: Conventional methods of calculating depreciation, which usually take into account the assumed life of the asset and any residual value, are given on page 670 (Methods of Calculating Depreciation). *See also* Obsolescence.

CLASSIFICATION OF COST

Production cost. The cost of the sequence of operations which begins with supplying materials, labour and services and ends with primary packing of the product.

Selling cost. The cost of seeking to create and stimulate demand (sometimes termed "marketing") and of securing orders.

Distribution cost. The cost of the sequence of operations which begins with making the packed product available for despatch and ends with making the reconditioned returned empty package, if any, available for re-use.

NOTE: As well as including expenditure incurred in transporting articles to central or local storage, distribution cost includes expenditure incurred in moving articles to and from prospective customers as in the case of goods on sale or return basis. In the gas, electricity and water industries "distribution" means pipes, mains and services which may be regarded as the equivalent of packing and transportation.

Administration cost. The cost of formulating the policy, directing the organisation and controlling the operations of an undertaking, which is not related directly to a production, selling, distribution, research or development activity or function.

Research cost. The cost of searching for new or improved products, new applications of materials, or new or improved methods.

Development cost. The cost of the process which begins with the implementation of the decision to produce a new or improved product or to employ a new or improved method and ends with the commencement of formal production of that product or by that method.

Pre-production cost. That part of development cost incurred in making a trial production run preliminary to formal production.

NOTE: This term is sometimes used to cover all activities prior to production, including research and development, but in such cases the usage should be made clear in the context.

Conversion cost. The sum of direct wages, direct expenses and overhead costs of converting raw material to the finished state or converting a material from one stage of production to the next.

NOTE: In some circumstances this phrase is used to include any excess materials costs or loss of materials incurred at the particular stage of production. Whichever meaning is used should be made clear.

Policy cost. Cost which is additional to normal requirements, incurred in accordance with the policy of an undertaking.

Idle facilities cost. The cost of abnormal idleness of fixed assets or available services.

TYPES OF COST

Predetermined cost. A cost which is computed in advance of production on the basis of a specification of all the factors affecting cost.

Standard cost. A predetermined cost which is calculated from management's standards of efficient operation and the relevant necessary expenditure. It may be used as a basis for price fixing and for cost control through variance analysis.

Marginal cost. The amount at any given volume of output by which aggregate costs are changed if the volume of output is increased or decreased by one unit. In practice this is measured by the total variable cost attributable to one unit.

NOTE: In this context a unit may be a single article, a batch of articles, an order, a stage of production capacity, a process or a department. It relates to the change in output in the particular circumstances under consideration.

Cost of sales. The cost which is attributable to the sales made.

NOTE: It is not uncommon to use this in a restricted sense as the production cost of goods sold.

Total cost. The sum of all costs attributable to the unit under consideration.

NOTE: This term should always be qualified, as it can mean the total cost of an undertaking or it can mean the total cost attributed to a process or to a product or to a service.

COST CENTRE

A location, person or item of equipment (or group of these) for which costs may be ascertained and used for the purposes of cost control.

Impersonal cost centre. A cost centre which consists of a location or item of equipment (or group of these).

Personal cost centre. A cost centre which consists of a person or group of persons.

Operation cost centre. A cost centre which consists of those machines and/or persons carrying out similar operations.

Process cost centre. A cost centre which consists of a specific process or a continuous sequence of operations.

COST UNIT

A unit or quantity of product, service or time (or a combination of these) in relation to which costs may be ascertained or expressed.

Job. A cost unit which consists of a single order (or contract).

Batch. A cost unit which consists of a group of identical items which maintains its identity throughout one or more stages of production.

Product group. A cost unit which consists of a group of similar products.

COST ACCOUNTING

The process of accounting for cost from the point at which expenditure is incurred or committed to the establishment of its ultimate relationship with cost centres and cost units. In its widest usage it embraces the preparation of statistical data, the application of cost control methods and the ascertainment of the profitability of activities carried out or planned.

BASIC DOCUMENTS

Materials requisition. A document which authorises and records the issue of materials for use.

Materials return note. A document which records the return of unused materials.

Materials transfer note. A document which records the transfer of materials from one store to another, from one cost centre to another or from one cost unit to another.

Materials issue analysis sheet. A document which is a classified record of materials issues, returns and transfers.

Labour time record. A document which records the amount of time spent by an employee, showing the analysis between a number of activities during a payment period. It may record the wages (labour cost) of the time spent.

Wages (labour cost) analysis sheet. A document which is a classified record or time and/or wages compiled from labour time records.

Expenses analysis sheet. A document which is a classified record of expenses.

Cost journal voucher. A document which provides the details necessary to support an entry in the cost accounts.

Machine time record. A document which records the amount of time an item of equipment is operated or remains idle, and the work done by the machine and which may record the cost of the time so recorded.

BOOKS AND ACCOUNTS

Integrated accounts. A system in which the financial and cost accounts are interlocked to ensure that all relevant expenditure is absorbed into the cost accounts.

Cost Ledger. A subsidiary ledger whose accounts record those transactions which are included in costs.

Cost Ledger Control Account. An account which is maintained in the principal ledger (and sometimes in the Cost Ledger) which records the totals of the transactions recorded in detail in the Cost Ledger and provides a check on the accuracy of the latter.

Cost account. An account in the Cost Ledger.

STATEMENTS

Cost estimate sheet. A document which provides for the assembly of the estimated detailed cost in respect of a cost centre or a cost unit.

Cost sheet. A document which provides for the assembly of the detailed cost of a cost centre or a cost unit.

Operating statement. A summary of the operating costs (and where appropriate of the income and margins) of the whole or part of the activities of an undertaking for a given period.

NOTE: In budgetary control and standard costing systems operating statements will usually provide information regarding the units produced in the period, the comparison of actual and standard or budgeted costs, income and margins and an analysis of the variances.

"Break-even" chart. A chart which shows profit or loss at various levels of activity, the level at which neither profit nor loss is shown being termed the break-even point. This may take the form of a chart on which is plotted the relationship either of total cost of sales to sales or of fixed costs to contribution.

MISCELLANEOUS

Cost manual. A document which sets out the responsibilities of the persons engaged in, the routine of, and the forms and records required for, costing and cost accounting.

Cost code. A series of alphabetical and/or numerical symbols, each of which represents a descriptive title in a cost classification.

STANDARD COSTING

STANDARD

Basic standard. A standard which is established for use unaltered for an indefinite period which may be a long period of time.

Current standard. A standard which is established for use over a short period of time, and is related to current conditions.

Expected standard. The standard which it is anticipated can be attained during a future specified budget period.

Normal standard. The average standard which it is anticipated can be attained over a future period of time, preferably long enough to cover one trade cycle.

Ideal standard. The standard which can be attained under the most favourable conditions possible.

Standard hour. A hypothetical hour which represents the amount of work which should be performed in one hour under standard conditions.

NOTE: In certain businesses the standard hour may represent the amount of work which should be performed in forty-five minutes, or even thirty minutes, under standard conditions. This usually is due to the use for standard costing of a standard hour which has already been established for purposes of wage payment by results whereby it is frequently the convention to allow one standard hour for a lesser period of time of work, the difference representing the incentive to the worker.

In this terminology where the term standard hour is used it is assumed that it represents the amount of work to be done in sixty minutes.

Standard allowance. The amount of expenditure which should normally be incurred at the particular level of activity achieved in any given period.

NOTE: This normally comprises fixed costs in full, variable costs in direct proportion to activity and semi-variable costs at the figures calculated for that activity.

Standard margin. The difference between the standard cost of a product and its standard selling price. This includes any charges which may not have been included in standard product costs (*e.g.* administration, selling and distribution costs) as well as profit.

RATIOS

Efficiency ratio. The standard hours equivalent to the work produced, expressed as a percentage of the actual hours spent in producing that work.

Activity ratio. The number of standard hours equivalent to the work produced, expressed as a percentage of the budgeted standard hours.

Calendar ratio. The relationship between the actual number of working days in a period and the number of working days in the relative budget period.

Standard capacity usage ratio. The relationship between the budgeted number of working hours and the maximum possible number of working hours in a budget period.

Actual capacity usage ratio. The relationship between the actual number of working hours and the maximum possible number of working hours in a period.

Actual usage of budgeted capacity ratio. The relationship between the actual number of working hours and the budgeted number.

VARIANCE ANALYSIS

The resolution into constituent parts and the explanation of variances.

NOTE: The following section gives brief definitions of some of the forms of variance analysis commonly used, the order of precedence being the order in which variances are normally identified and computed. The actual order will be settled according to the particular needs of the user. For example, a price variance on materials, if measured on the standard quantity, will leave the materials usage variance valued at actual price, but on the other hand, if measured on actual quantities used, will leave the materials usage variance valued at standard price. The variances ascertained in any business should be designed to provide the particular information which is apposite in the circumstances of that business.

It is not practicable in this terminology to describe the forms and formulae necessary to calculate each variance. This needs a textbook of its own.

The inter-relationship of the variances which are defined below can easily be followed from the chart (page 666). A small section on sales margin variances is included. Although not part of cost variances these are useful in investigating the relationship between costs, volume and profit.

COST VARIANCE

The difference between a standard cost and the comparable actual cost incurred during a period.

Controllable cost variance. A cost variance which can be identified as the primary responsibility of a specified person.

Methods variance. The difference between the standard cost of a product or operation produced or performed by the normal method and the standard cost of the product or operation produced or performed by the alternative method actually employed.

Revision variance. The variance between the basic standard cost and the revised standard cost.

Total cost variance. The difference between the total standard cost value of the output achieved in a period and the total actual cost incurred.

Direct materials cost variance. The difference between the standard cost of direct materials specified for the output achieved and the actual cost of direct materials used.

Direct materials price variance. That portion of the direct materials cost variance which is due to the difference between the standard price specified and the actual price paid.

Direct materials usage variance. That portion of the direct materials cost variance which is due to the difference between the standard quantity specified and the actual quantity used.

Direct materials mixture variance. That portion of the direct materials usage variance which is due to the difference between the standard and actual composition of a mixture. (Applicable only when direct materials are physically mixed.)

Direct materials yield variance. That portion of the direct materials usage variance which is due to the difference between the standard yield specified and the actual yield obtained.

Direct wages variance. The difference between the standard direct wages specified for the activity achieved and the actual direct wages paid.

Direct wages rate variance. That portion of the direct wages variance which is due to the difference between the standard rate of pay specified and the actual rate paid.

Direct labour efficiency variance. That portion of the direct wages variance which is due to the difference between the standard labour hours specified for the activity achieved and the actual labour hours expended.

NOTE: Where efficiency is measured by a line speed or cost centre output as distinct from the output of an individual worker it may be possible to subanalyse this variance between efficiency and amount of direct labour usage.

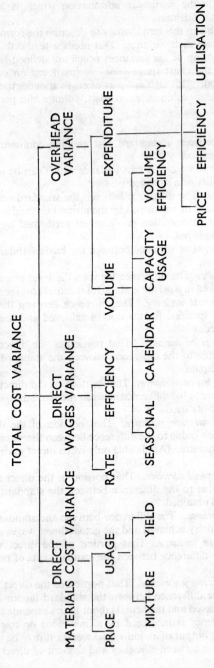

VARIANCE ANALYSIS

METHODS AND REVISION VARIANCES CAN ARISE UNDER MATERIALS, WAGES OR OVERHEAD
AND SHOULD NORMALLY BE ISOLATED BEFORE OTHER VARIANCES ARE CALCULATED.

TOTAL COST VARIANCE

DIRECT MATERIALS COST VARIANCE — DIRECT WAGES VARIANCE — OVERHEAD VARIANCE

PRICE — USAGE

RATE — EFFICIENCY

EXPENDITURE — VOLUME

MIXTURE — YIELD

SEASONAL — CALENDAR — CAPACITY USAGE — VOLUME EFFICIENCY

PRICE EFFICIENCY UTILISATION

Overhead variance. The difference between the standard cost of overhead absorbed in the output achieved and the actual overhead cost.

Volume variance. That portion of the overhead variance which is the difference between the standard cost of overhead absorbed in actual output and the standard allowance for that output. (This represents the over- or under-absorption of fixed costs in the period concerned.)

Seasonal variance. That portion of the volume variance which is due to the difference between the seasonally budgeted output and the average output on which standards have been calculated. (The sum of the seasonal variations over a complete year would be zero.)

Calendar variance. That portion of the volume variance which is due to the difference between the number of working days in the budget period and the number of working days in the period to which the budget is applied. (The sum of the calendar variances in a complete year would be zero.) NOTE: This variance arises from the convention that fixed costs are the same for each period, whatever the number of working days, and it can be eliminated by apportioning standard allowances and actual fixed costs on a working-day basis.

Capacity usage variance. That portion of the volume variance which is due to working at higher or lower capacity usage than standard.

Volume efficiency variance. That portion of the volume variance which reflects the increased or reduced output arising from efficiency above or below the standard which is expected.

Overhead expenditure variance. That portion of the overhead variance which represents the difference between the standard allowance for the output achieved and the actual expenditure incurred.

Overhead price variance. That portion of the overhead expenditure variance which is due to the difference between the standard price of the service specified and the actual price paid.

Overhead efficiency variance. That portion of the overhead expenditure variance which is the difference between the standard allowance for the activity (standard hour achieved) and the standard allowance for the actual hours worked. NOTE: This variance only arises on costs which vary with time taken rather than with volume of output.

Overhead utilisation variance. That portion of the overhead expenditure variance which is due to the difference between the standard quantity of the service specified and the actual quantity of the service used.

SALES VARIANCE

The difference between budgeted value of sales and the actual value of sales achieved in a given period. NOTE: Sales variance can be analysed in many ways to suit a particular business, *e.g.* to isolate the effects of price changes, discounts and allowances from the effect of differing quantities of sales. A distinction is sometimes drawn between quantity and mixture variances. A mixture variance which is based on sales values only may be misleading because the effect of selling a different product mix than was budgeted is not only the difference in sales values but also the difference in standard cost of the mixture. In other words it is a difference in sales margins. The following definitions of sales margin variances are offered in preference to simple sales variances.

SALES MARGIN VARIANCES

Total sales margin variance. The difference between the standard margin appropriate to the quantity of sales budgeted for a period and the margin between standard cost and the actual selling price of the sales effected.

Sales margin variance due to selling prices. That portion of total margin variance which is due to the difference between the standard price of the quantity of sales effected and the actual price of those sales.

Sales margin variance due to sales allowances. That portion of total margin variance which is due to the difference between the budgeted rebates, discounts, etc., on the sales effected and the actual rebates, discounts, etc., allowed on those sales.

Sales margin variance due to sales quantities (mixture). That portion of total margin variance which is due to the difference between the budgeted and actual quantities of each product of which the sales mixture is composed, valuing sales at the standard net selling prices and cost of sales at standard.

PROFIT (OR LOSS) VARIANCE

The difference between the budgeted profit (or loss) and the actual profit (or loss). This will comprise the sum of variances appropriate to standard cost of sales, the sales margin variances and variances on any charges which have not been included in the standard cost of production.

BUDGETARY CONTROL

The establishment of budgets relating the responsibilities of executives to the requirements of a policy, and the continuous comparison of actual with budgeted results either to secure by individual action the objective of that policy or to provide a basis for its revision.

BUDGET

A financial and/or quantitative statement, prepared and approved prior to a defined period of time, of the policy to be pursued during that period for the purpose of attaining a given objective. It may include income, expenditure and the employment of capital.

Fixed budget. A budget which is designed to remain unchanged irrespective of the level of activity actually attained.

Flexible budget. A budget which, by recognising the difference between fixed, semi-fixed and variable costs, is designed to change in relation to the level of activity attained.

Basic budget. A budget which is established for use unaltered over a long period of time.

Current budget. A budget which is established for use over a short period of time and is related to current conditions.

Functional budget. A budget of income or expenditure appropriate to, or the responsibility of, a particular function.

Summary budget. A budget which is prepared from, and summarises, all of the functional budgets.

Master budget. The summary budget incorporating its component functional budgets.

MISCELLANEOUS

Principal budget factor. The factor the extent of whose influence must first be assessed in order to ensure that the functional budgets are reasonably capable of fulfilment.

Budget period. The period for which a budget is prepared and employed.

Budget manual. A document which sets out the responsibilities of the persons, engaged in, the routine of, and the forms and records required for, budgetary control.

Budget centre. A section of the organisation of an undertaking defined for the purposes of budgetary control.

Budget cost allowance. The cost which a budget centre is expected to incur during a given period of time in relation to the level of activity attained by the budget centre.

Budget overhead allowance. The overhead which a budget centre is expected to incur during a given period of time in relation to the level of activity attained by the budget centre.

Budget control basis. The nature of a cost, *i.e.* fixed, semi-fixed, or variable, which determines the manner in which the budget cost allowance is calculated.

RATES

COST RATE

A rate of cost apportionment or overhead absorption.

Market cost rate. A rate of cost apportionment or overhead absorption which is the current market rate payable for a comparable service.

Standard cost rate. A predetermined rate of cost apportionment or overhead absorption calculated by dividing the predetermined cost to be apportioned or absorbed by the predetermined quantity of the base to which the rate is to be applied.

Direct materials cost percentage rate. An actual or predetermined rate of cost apportionment or overhead absorption which is calculated by dividing the cost to be apportioned or absorbed by the materials cost incurred or expected to be incurred, and expressing the result as a percentage.

Direct wages percentage rate. An actual or predetermined rate of cost apportionment or overhead absorption which is calculated by dividing the cost to be apportioned or absorbed by the wages expended or expected to be expended, and expressing the result as a percentage.

Prime cost percentage rate. An actual or predetermined rate of cost apportionment or overhead absorption which is calculated by dividing the cost to be apportioned or absorbed by the prime cost incurred or expected to be incurred, and expressing the result as a percentage.

Labour hour rate. An actual or predetermined rate of cost apportionment or overhead absorption which is calculated by dividing the cost to be apportioned or absorbed by the labour hours expended or expected to be expended.

Machine hour rate. An actual or predetermined rate of cost apportionment or overhead absorption which is calculated by dividing the cost to be apportioned or absorbed by the number of hours for which a machine or machines are operated or expected to be operated.

Cost unit rate. An actual or predetermined rate of cost apportionment or overhead absorption which is calculated by dividing the cost to be apportioned or absorbed by the number of cost units produced or expected to be produced.

OVERHEAD RATE

The expression of overhead in relation to some specific characteristic of a cost centre as a means of providing a convenient basis for its apportionment or absorption.

NOTE: Such rates may include—percentage rates based upon direct wages, direct materials cost, prime cost—rates per machine hour, per labour hour—rates per cost unit, etc.

DEPRECIATION RATES

Single rate of depreciation. A depreciation rate which is calculated by reference to the estimated life of a single asset.

Composite rate of depreciation. A depreciation rate which is calculated by dividing the aggregate of the individual depreciation charges (however calculated) in any one period of all the assets concerned, by the aggregate of the costs of those assets.

Accelerated rate of depreciation. A depreciation rate which consists of a normal depreciation rate augmented to provide for additional depreciation sustained by the asset depreciated.

METHODS OF CALCULATING DEPRECIATION

Straight line method. The method of providing for depreciation by means of equal periodic charges over the assumed life of the asset.

Reducing balance method. The method of providing for depreciation by means of periodic charges calculated as a constant proportion of the balance of the value of the asset after deducting the amounts previously provided.

Production unit method. The method of providing for depreciation by means of a fixed rate per unit of production calculated by dividing the value of the asset by the estimated number of units to be produced during its life.

Production hour method. The method of providing for depreciation by means of a fixed rate per hour of production calculated by dividing the value of the asset by the estimated number of working hours of its life.

Repair provision method. The method of providing for the aggregate of depreciation and maintenance cost by means of periodic charges, each of which is a constant proportion of the aggregate of the cost of the asset depreciated and the expected maintenance cost during its life.

Annuity method. The method of providing for depreciation by means of periodic charges, each of which is a constant proportion of the aggregate of the cost of the asset depreciated and interest at a given rate per period on the written down values of the asset at the beginning of each period.

Sinking fund method. The method of providing for depreciation by means of fixed periodic charges which, aggregated with compound interest over the life of the asset, would equal the cost of that asset. Simultaneously with each periodic charge an investment of the same amount would be made in fixed interest securities which would accumulate at compound interest to provide, at the end of the life of the asset, a sum equal to its cost.

Endowment policy method. The method of providing for depreciation by means of fixed periodic charges equivalent to the premiums on an endowment policy for the amount required to provide, at the end of the life of the asset, a sum equal to its cost.

Revaluation method. The method of providing for depreciation by means of periodic charges, each of which is equivalent to the difference between the values assigned to the asset at the beginning and the end of the period.

Sum of the digits method. The method of providing for depreciation by means of differing periodic rates computed according to the following formula:

> If n is the estimated life of the asset, the rate is calculated each period as a fraction in which the denominator is always the sum of the series 1, 2, 3, ... n and the numerator for the first period is n, for the second $n-1$ and so on.

PRICE

(*a*) The cost to a purchaser of any article or service expressed in money terms.

(*b*) A money rate used to calculate a cost.

(*c*) To record a money rate in order to calculate a cost.

Standard price. A predetermined price fixed on the basis of a specification of all the factors affecting that price.

"First in, first out" price (FIFO). The price paid for the material first taken into the stock from which the material to be priced could have been drawn.

"Last in, first out" price (LIFO). The price paid for the material last taken into the stock from which the material to be priced could have been drawn.

Replacement price. The price at which there could be purchased an asset identical to that which is being replaced or revalued.

Simple average price. A price which is calculated by dividing the total of the prices of the materials in the stock from which the material to be priced could be drawn by the number of prices used in that total.

Weighted average price. A price which is calculated by dividing the total cost of materials in the stock from which the material to be priced could be drawn by the total quantity of materials in that stock.

UNCLASSIFIED TERMS

Management accounting. The presentation of accounting information in such a way as to assist management in the creation of policy and in the day-to-day operation of an undertaking.

Management accounting services. The application of accounting knowledge for the purpose of organising, selecting, compiling and presenting accounting, quantitative and statistical information derived from all the relevant records of a business to assist those responsible for management in controlling the business and in the making of day-to-day decisions and in the formulation of policy, together with the application of knowledge and experience of:

(*a*) techniques for the organisation, control and measurement of production and ancillary services and for the control, measurement and remuneration of human effort;

(*b*) commercial and management practices; and

(*c*) office organisation, methods and equipment.

Cost control. The regulation by executive action of the costs of operating an undertaking, particularly where such action is guided by cost accounting.

Cash flow. The funds generated during an accounting period and their application. Net profit rather than total income is usually the starting point of a cash flow statement.

NOTE: The phrase is used by financial journalists to denote the figure obtained by adding the depreciation charge of the period to retained profit as a measure of the amount made available for additional investment in fixed assets and working capital.

Inventory. A schedule of items held at a particular point in time.

NOTE: The American usage of the term is synonymous with our use of "stocks," including consumable materials, work in progress and finished goods.

Perpetual inventory. A system of records maintained by the controlling department, which reflects the physical movement of stocks and their current balance.

NOTE: A perpetual inventory is usually checked by a programme of continuous stock-taking and the two terms are sometimes loosely considered synonymous. This is not recommended. Perpetual inventory means the system of records, whereas continuous stock-taking means the physical checking of those records with actual stocks.

Forecast. An assessment of probable future events.

NOTE: Forecasting precedes the preparation of a budget; it relates to probable events, whereas a budget is based on the implications of a forecast and relates to planned events.

Cost audit. The verification of cost accounts and a check on the adherence to the cost accounting plan.

Added value. The change in market value resulting from an alteration in the form, location or availability of a product or service, excluding the cost of bought-out materials or services.

NOTE: Unlike conversion cost it includes profit.

Opportunity cost. The net selling price, rental value or transfer value which could be obtained at a point in time if a particular asset or group of assets were to be sold, hired or put to some alternative use available to the owner at that time.

Contribution. The difference between sales value and the marginal cost of sales.

Employment of capital. The way in which capital employed is disposed in assets less liabilities.

CAPITAL EMPLOYED

Total capital employed. The sum of issued share capital, reserves and loans.

Total shareholders capital employed. The sum of issued share capital and reserves.

Total equity capital employed. The sum of issued ordinary share capital and reserves.

APPENDIX II

LOGARITHM TABLES

	0	1	2	3	4	5	6	7	8	9	1	2	3	4	5	6	7	8	9
10	0000	0043	0086	0128	0170						5	9	13	17	21	26	30	34	38
						0212	0253	0294	0334	0374	4	8	12	16	20	24	28	32	36
11	0414	0453	0492	0531	0569						4	8	12	16	20	23	27	31	35
						0607	0645	0682	0719	0755	4	7	11	15	18	22	26	29	33
12	0792	0828	0864	0899	0934						3	7	11	14	18	21	25	28	32
						0969	1004	1038	1072	1106	3	7	10	14	17	20	24	27	31
13	1139	1173	1206	1239	1271						3	6	10	13	16	19	23	26	29
						1303	1335	1367	1399	1430	3	7	10	13	16	19	22	25	29
14	1461	1492	1523	1553	1584						3	6	9	12	15	19	22	25	28
						1614	1644	1673	1703	1732	3	6	9	12	14	17	20	23	26
15	1761	1790	1818	1847	1875						3	6	9	11	14	17	20	23	26
						1903	1931	1959	1987	2014	3	6	8	11	14	17	19	22	25
16	2041	2068	2095	2122	2148						3	6	8	11	14	16	19	22	24
						2175	2201	2227	2253	2279	3	5	8	10	13	16	18	21	23
17	2304	2330	2355	2380	2405						3	5	8	10	13	15	18	20	23
						2430	2455	2480	2504	2529	3	5	8	10	12	15	17	20	22
18	2553	2577	2601	2625	2648						2	5	7	9	12	14	17	19	21
						2672	2695	2718	2742	2765	2	4	7	9	11	14	16	18	21
19	2788	2810	2833	2856	2878						2	4	7	9	11	13	16	18	20
						2900	2923	2945	2967	2989	2	4	6	8	11	13	15	17	19
20	3010	3032	3054	3075	3096	3118	3139	3160	3181	3201	2	4	6	8	11	13	15	17	19
21	3222	3243	3263	3284	3304	3324	3345	3365	3385	3404	2	4	6	8	10	12	14	16	18
22	3424	3444	3464	3483	3502	3522	3541	3560	3579	3598	2	4	6	8	10	12	14	15	17
23	3617	3636	3655	3674	3692	3711	3729	3747	3766	3784	2	4	6	7	9	11	13	15	17
24	3802	3820	3838	3856	3874	3892	3909	3927	3945	3962	2	4	5	7	9	11	12	14	16
25	3979	3997	4014	4031	4048	4065	4082	4099	4116	4133	2	3	5	7	9	10	12	14	15
26	4150	4166	4183	4200	4216	4232	4249	4265	4281	4298	2	3	5	7	8	10	11	13	15
27	4314	4330	4346	4362	4378	4393	4409	4425	4440	4456	2	3	5	6	8	9	11	13	14
28	4472	4487	4502	4518	4533	4548	4564	4579	4594	4609	2	3	5	6	8	9	11	12	14
29	4624	4639	4654	4669	4683	4698	4713	4728	4742	4757	1	3	4	6	7	9	10	12	13
30	4771	4786	4800	4814	4829	4843	4857	4871	4886	4900	1	3	4	6	7	9	10	11	13
31	4914	4928	4942	4955	4969	4983	4997	5011	5024	5038	1	3	4	6	7	8	10	11	12
32	5051	5065	5079	5092	5105	5119	5132	5145	5159	5172	1	3	4	5	7	8	9	11	15
33	5185	5198	5211	5224	5237	5250	5263	5276	5289	5302	1	3	4	5	6	8	9	10	15
34	5315	5328	5340	5353	5366	5378	5391	5403	5416	5428	1	3	4	5	6	8	9	10	11
35	5441	5453	5465	5478	5490	5502	5514	5527	5539	5551	1	2	4	5	6	7	9	10	11
36	5563	5575	5587	5599	5611	5623	5635	5647	5658	5670	1	2	4	5	6	7	8	10	11
37	5682	5694	5705	5717	5729	5740	5752	5763	5775	5786	1	2	3	5	6	7	8	9	10
38	5798	5809	5821	5832	5843	5855	5866	5877	5888	5899	1	2	3	5	6	7	8	9	10
39	5911	5922	5933	5944	5955	5966	5977	5988	5999	6010	1	2	3	4	5	7	8	9	10
40	6021	6031	6042	6053	6064	6075	6085	6096	6107	6117	1	2	3	4	5	6	8	9	10
41	6128	6138	6149	6160	6170	6180	6191	6201	6212	6222	1	2	3	4	5	6	7	8	9
42	6232	6243	6253	6263	6274	6284	6294	6304	6314	6325	1	2	3	4	5	6	7	8	9
43	6335	6345	6355	6365	6375	6385	6395	6405	6415	6425	1	2	3	4	5	6	7	8	9
44	6435	6444	6454	6464	6474	6484	6493	6503	6513	6522	1	2	3	4	5	6	7	8	9
45	6532	6542	6551	6561	6571	6580	6590	6599	6609	6618	1	2	3	4	5	6	7	8	9
46	6628	6637	6646	6656	6665	6675	6684	6693	6702	6712	1	2	3	4	5	6	7	7	8
47	6721	6730	6739	6749	6758	6767	6776	6785	6794	6803	1	2	3	4	5	5	6	7	8
48	6812	6821	6830	6839	6848	6857	6866	6875	6884	6893	1	2	3	4	4	5	6	7	8
49	6902	6911	6920	6928	6937	6946	6955	6964	6972	6981	1	2	3	4	4	5	6	7	8

	0	1	2	3	4	5	6	7	8	9	1	2	3	4	5	6	7	8	9
50	6990	6998	7007	7016	7024	7033	7042	7050	7059	7067	1	2	3	3	4	5	6	7	8
51	7076	7084	7093	7101	7110	7118	7126	7135	7143	7152	1	2	3	3	4	5	6	7	8
52	7160	7168	7177	7185	7193	7202	7210	7218	7226	7235	1	2	2	3	4	5	6	7	7
53	7243	7251	7259	7267	7275	7284	7292	7300	7308	7316	1	2	2	3	4	5	6	6	7
54	7324	7332	7340	7348	7356	7364	7372	7380	7388	7396	1	2	2	3	4	5	6	6	7
55	7404	7412	7419	7427	7435	7443	7451	7459	7466	7474	1	2	2	3	4	5	5	6	7
56	7482	7490	7497	7505	7513	7520	7528	7536	7543	7551	1	2	2	3	4	5	5	6	7
57	7559	7566	7574	7582	7589	7597	7604	7612	7619	7627	1	2	2	3	4	5	5	6	7
58	7634	7642	7649	7657	7664	7672	7679	7686	7694	7701	1	1	2	3	4	4	5	6	7
59	7709	7716	7723	7731	7738	7745	7752	7760	7767	7774	1	1	2	3	4	4	5	6	7
60	7782	7789	7796	7803	7810	7818	7825	7832	7839	7846	1	1	2	3	4	4	5	6	6
61	7853	7860	7868	7875	7882	7889	7896	7903	7910	7917	1	1	2	3	4	4	5	6	6
62	7924	7931	7938	7945	7952	7959	7966	7973	7980	7987	1	1	2	3	4	4	5	6	6
63	7993	8000	8007	8014	8021	8028	8035	8041	8048	8055	1	1	2	3	3	4	5	5	6
64	8062	8069	8075	8082	8089	8096	8102	8109	8116	8122	1	1	2	3	3	4	5	5	6
65	8129	8136	8142	8149	8156	8162	8169	8176	8182	8189	1	1	2	3	3	4	5	5	6
66	8195	8202	8209	8215	8222	8228	8235	8241	8248	8254	1	1	2	3	3	4	5	5	6
67	8261	8267	8274	8280	8287	8293	8299	8306	8312	8319	1	1	2	3	3	4	5	5	6
68	8325	8331	8338	8344	8351	8357	8363	8370	8376	8382	1	1	2	3	3	4	4	5	6
69	8388	8395	8401	8407	8414	8420	8426	8432	8439	8445	1	1	2	2	3	4	4	5	6
70	8451	8457	8463	8470	8476	8482	8488	8494	8500	8506	1	1	2	2	3	4	4	5	6
71	8513	8519	8525	8531	8537	8543	8549	8555	8561	8567	1	1	2	2	3	4	4	5	5
72	8573	8579	8585	8591	8597	8603	8609	8615	8621	8627	1	1	2	2	3	4	4	5	5
73	8633	8639	8645	8651	8657	8663	8669	8675	8681	8686	1	1	2	2	3	4	4	5	5
74	8692	8698	8704	8710	8716	8722	8727	8733	8739	8745	1	1	2	2	3	4	4	5	5
75	8751	8756	8762	8768	8774	8779	8785	8791	8797	8802	1	1	2	2	3	3	4	5	5
76	8808	8814	8820	8825	8831	8837	8842	8848	8854	8859	1	1	2	2	3	3	4	5	5
77	8865	8871	8876	8882	8887	8893	8899	8904	8910	8915	1	1	2	2	3	3	4	4	5
78	8921	8927	8932	8938	8943	8949	8954	8960	8965	8971	1	1	2	2	3	3	4	4	5
79	8976	8982	8987	8993	8998	9004	9009	9015	9020	9025	1	1	2	2	3	3	4	4	5
80	9031	9036	9042	9047	9053	9058	9063	9069	9074	9079	1	1	2	2	3	3	4	4	5
81	9085	9090	9096	9101	9106	9112	9117	9122	9128	9133	1	1	2	2	3	3	4	4	5
82	9138	9143	9149	9154	9159	9165	9170	9175	9180	9186	1	1	2	2	3	3	4	4	5
83	9191	9196	9201	9206	9212	9217	9222	9227	9232	9238	1	1	2	2	3	3	4	4	5
84	9243	9248	9253	9258	9263	9269	9274	9279	9284	9289	1	1	2	2	3	3	4	4	5
85	9294	9299	9304	9309	9315	9320	9325	9330	9335	9340	1	1	2	2	3	3	4	4	5
86	9345	9350	9355	9360	9365	9370	9375	9380	9385	9390	1	1	2	2	3	3	4	4	5
87	9395	9400	9405	9410	9415	9420	9425	9430	9435	9440	0	1	1	2	2	3	3	4	4
88	9445	9450	9455	9460	9465	9469	9474	9479	9484	9489	0	1	1	2	2	3	3	4	4
89	9494	9499	9504	9509	9513	9518	9523	9528	9533	9538	0	1	1	2	2	3	3	4	4
90	9542	9547	9552	9557	9562	9566	9571	9576	9581	9586	0	1	1	2	2	3	3	4	4
91	9590	9595	9600	9605	9609	9614	9619	9624	9628	9633	0	1	1	2	2	3	3	4	4
92	9638	9643	9647	9652	9657	9661	9666	9671	9675	9680	0	1	1	2	2	3	3	4	4
93	9685	9689	9694	9699	9703	9708	9713	9717	9722	9727	0	1	1	2	2	3	3	4	4
94	9731	9736	9741	9745	9750	9754	9759	9763	9768	9773	0	1	1	2	2	3	3	4	4
95	9777	9782	9786	9791	9795	9800	9805	9809	9814	9818	0	1	1	2	2	3	3	4	4
96	9823	9827	9832	9836	9841	9845	9850	9854	9859	9863	0	1	1	2	2	3	3	4	4
97	9868	9872	9877	9881	9886	9890	9894	9899	9903	9908	0	1	1	2	2	3	3	4	4
98	9912	9917	9921	9926	9930	9934	9939	9943	9948	9952	0	1	1	2	2	3	3	4	4
99	9956	9961	9965	9969	9974	9978	9983	9987	9991	9996	0	1	1	2	2	3	3	3	4

Given the logarithm to find the number: The logarithm must be looked for in the body of the table (the *mantissa* part only).

APPENDIX III

PRESENT VALUE FACTORS

Present value of £1 to be received in one payment at the end of a given number of years $(1 + r)^{-n}$

Discount rates of 1% to 9%

Future years	Percentage rate of Discount								
	1	2	3	4	5	6	7	8	9
1	0·990	0·980	0·971	0·962	0·952	0·943	0·935	0·926	0·917
2	0·980	0·961	0·943	0·925	0·907	0·890	0·873	0·857	0·842
3	0·971	0·942	0·915	0·889	0·864	0·840	0·816	0·794	0·772
4	0·961	0·924	0·888	0·855	0·823	0·792	0·763	0·735	0·708
5	0·951	0·906	0·863	0·822	0·784	0·747	0·713	0·681	0·650
6	0·942	0·888	0·837	0·790	0·746	0·705	0·666	0·630	0·596
7	0·933	0·871	0·813	0·760	0·711	0·665	0·623	0·583	0·547
8	0·923	0·853	0·789	0·731	0·677	0·627	0·582	0·540	0·502
9	0·914	0·837	0·766	0·703	0·645	0·592	0·544	0·500	0·460
10	0·905	0·820	0·744	0·676	0·614	0·558	0·508	0·463	0·422
11	0·896	0·804	0·722	0·650	0·585	0·527	0·475	0·429	0·388
12	0·887	0·788	0·701	0·625	0·557	0·497	0·444	0·397	0·356
13	0·879	0·773	0·681	0·601	0·530	0·469	0·415	0·368	0·326
14	0·870	0·758	0·661	0·577	0·505	0·442	0·388	0·340	0·299
15	0·861	0·743	0·642	0·555	0·481	0·417	0·362	0·315	0·275
16	0·953	0·728	0·623	0·534	0·458	0·394	0·339	0·292	0·252
17	0·844	0·714	0·605	0·513	0·436	0·371	0·317	0·270	0·231
18	0·836	0·700	0·587	0·494	0·416	0·350	0·296	0·250	0·212
19	0·828	0·686	0·570	0·475	0·396	0·331	0·277	0·232	0·194
20	0·820	0·673	0·554	0·456	0·377	0·312	0·258	0·215	0·178
21	0·811	0·660	0·538	0·439	0·359	0·294	0·242	0·199	0·164
22	0·803	0·647	0·522	0·422	0·342	0·278	0·226	0·184	0·150
23	0·795	0·634	0·507	0·406	0·326	0·262	0·211	0·170	0·138
24	0·788	0·622	0·492	0·390	0·310	0·247	0·197	0·158	0·126
25	0·780	0·610	0·478	0·375	0·295	0·233	0·184	0·146	0·116
30	0·742	0·552	0·412	0·308	0·231	0·174	0·131	0·098	0·075
35	0·706	0·500	0·355	0·253	0·181	0·130	0·094	0·068	0·049
40	0·672	0·453	0·307	0·208	0·142	0·097	0·067	0·046	0·032
50	0·608	0·372	0·228	0·141	0·087	0·054	0·034	0·021	0·013

PRESENT VALUE FACTORS

Present value of £1 to be received in one payment at the end of a
given number of years $(1 + r)^{-n}$

Discount rates of 10% to 18%

Future years	Percentage rate of Discount								
	10	11	12	13	14	15	16	17	18
1	0·909	0·901	0·893	0·885	0·877	0·870	0·862	0·855	0·847
2	0·826	0·812	0·797	0·783	0·769	0·756	0·743	0·731	0·718
3	0·751	0·731	0·712	0·693	0·675	0·658	0·641	0·624	0·609
4	0·683	0·659	0·636	0·613	0·592	0·572	0·552	0·534	0·516
5	0·621	0·593	0·567	0·543	0·519	0·497	0·476	0·456	0·437
6	0·564	0·535	0·507	0·480	0·456	0·432	0·410	0·390	0·370
7	0·513	0·482	0·452	0·425	0·400	0·376	0·354	0·333	0·314
8	0·467	0·434	0·404	0·376	0·351	0·327	0·305	0·285	0·266
9	0·424	0·391	0·361	0·333	0·308	0·284	0·263	0·243	0·225
10	0·386	0·352	0·322	0·295	0·270	0·247	0·227	0·208	0·191
11	0·350	0·317	0·287	0·261	0·237	0·215	0·195	0·178	0·162
12	0·319	0·286	0·257	0·231	0·208	0·187	0·168	0·152	0·137
13	0·290	0·258	0·229	0·204	0·182	0·163	0·145	0·130	0·116
14	0·263	0·232	0·205	0·181	0·160	0·141	0·125	0·111	0·099
15	0·239	0·209	0·183	0·160	0·140	0·123	0·108	0·095	0·084
16	0·218	0·188	0·163	0·141	0·123	0·107	0·093	0·081	0·071
17	0·198	0·170	0·146	0·125	0·108	0·093	0·080	0·069	0·060
18	0·180	0·153	0·130	0·111	0·095	0·081	0·069	0·059	0·051
19	0·164	0·138	0·116	0·098	0·083	0·070	0·060	0·051	0·043
20	0·149	0·124	0·104	0·087	0·073	0·061	0·051	0·043	0·037
21	0·135	0·112	0·093	0·077	0·064	0·053	0·044	0·037	0·031
22	0·123	0·101	0·083	0·068	0·056	0·046	0·038	0·032	0·026
23	0·112	0·091	0·074	0·060	0·049	0·040	0·033	0·027	0·022
24	0·102	0·082	0·066	0·053	0·043	0·035	0·028	0·023	0·019
25	0·092	0·074	0·059	0·047	0·038	0·030	0·024	0·020	0·016
30	0·057	0·044	0·033	0·026	0·020	0·015	0·012	0·009	0·007
35	0·036	0·026	0·019	0·014	0·010	0·008	0·006	0·004	0·003
40	0·022	0·015	0·011	0·008	0·005	0·004	0·003	0·002	0·001
50	0·009	0·005	0·003	0·002	0·001	0·001	0·001	0·001	

PRESENT VALUE FACTORS

Present value of £1 to be received in one payment at the end of a given number of years $(1 + r)^{-n}$

Discount rates of 19% to 26%

Future years	Percentage rate of Discount							
	19	20	21	22	23	24	25	26
1	0·840	0·833	0·826	0·820	0·813	0·806	0·800	0·794
2	0·706	0·694	0·683	0·672	0·661	0·650	0·640	0·630
3	0·593	0·579	0·564	0·551	0·537	0·524	0·512	0·500
4	0·499	0·482	0·467	0·451	0·437	0·423	0·410	0·397
5	0·419	0·402	0·386	0·370	0·355	0·341	0·328	0·315
6	0·352	0·335	0·319	0·303	0·289	0·275	0·262	0·250
7	0·296	0·279	0·263	0·249	0·235	0·222	0·210	0·198
8	0·249	0·233	0·218	0·204	0·191	0·179	0·168	0·157
9	0·209	0·194	0·180	0·167	0·155	0·144	0·134	0·125
10	0·176	0·162	0·149	0·137	0·126	0·116	0·107	0·099
11	0·148	0·135	0·123	0·112	0·103	0·094	0·086	0·079
12	0·124	0·112	0·102	0·092	0·083	0·076	0·069	0·062
13	0·104	0·093	0·084	0·075	0·068	0·061	0·055	0·050
14	0·088	0·078	0·069	0·062	0·055	0·049	0·044	0·039
15	0·074	0·065	0·057	0·051	0·045	0·040	0·035	0·031
16	0·062	0·054	0·047	0·042	0·036	0·032	0·028	0·025
17	0·052	0·045	0·039	0·034	0·030	0·026	0·023	0·020
18	0·044	0·038	0·032	0·028	0·024	0·021	0·018	0·016
19	0·037	0·031	0·027	0·023	0·020	0·017	0·014	0·012
20	0·031	0·026	0·022	0·019	0·016	0·014	0·012	0·010
21	0·026	0·022	0·018	0·015	0·013	0·011	0·009	0·008
22	0·022	0·018	0·015	0·013	0·011	0·009	0·007	0·006
23	0·018	0·015	0·012	0·010	0·009	0·007	0·006	0·005
24	0·015	0·013	0·010	0·008	0·007	0·006	0·005	0·004
25	0·013	0·010	0·009	0·007	0·006	0·005	0·004	0·003
30	0·005	0·004	0·003	0·003	0·002	0·002	0·002	0·001
35	0·002	0·002	0·001					
40	0·001	0·001						

PRESENT VALUE FACTORS

Present value of £1 to be received in one payment at the end of a given number of years $(1 + r)^{-n}$

Selected discount rates from 28% to 60%

Future years	Percentage rate of Discount							
	28	30	35	40	45	50	55	60
1	0·781	0·769	0·741	0·714	0·690	0·667	0·645	0·625
2	0·610	0·592	0·549	0·510	0·476	0·444	0·416	0·391
3	0·477	0·455	0·406	0·364	0·328	0·296	0·269	0·244
4	0·373	0·350	0·301	0·260	0·226	0·198	0·173	0·153
5	0·291	0·269	0·223	0·186	0·156	0·132	0·112	0·095
6	0·227	0·207	0·165	0·133	0·108	0·088	0·072	0·060
7	0·170	0·159	0·122	0·095	0·074	0·059	0·047	0·037
8	0·139	0·123	0·091	0·068	0·051	0·039	0·030	0·023
9	0·108	0·094	0·067	0·048	0·035	0·026	0·019	0·015
10	0·085	0·073	0·050	0·035	0·024	0·017	0·012	0·009
11	0·066	0·056	0·037	0·025	0·017	0·012	0·008	0·006
12	0·052	0·043	0·027	0·018	0·012	0·008	0·005	0·004
13	0·040	0·033	0·020	0·013	0·008	0·005	0·003	0·002
14	0·032	0·025	0·015	0·009	0·006	0·003	0·002	0·001
15	0·025	0·020	0·011	0·006	0·004	0·002	0·001	0·001
16	0·019	0·015	0·008	0·005	0·003	0·002	0·001	0·001
17	0·015	0·012	0·006	0·003	0·002	0·001	0·001	
18	0·012	0·009	0·005	0·002	0·001	0·001		
19	0·009	0·007	0·003	0·002	0·001			
20	0·007	0·005	0·002	0·001	0·001			
21	0·006	0·004	0·002	0·001				
22	0·004	0·003	0·001	0·001				
23	0·003	0·002	0·001					
24	0·003	0·002	0·001					
25	0·002	0·001	0·001					
30	0·001	0·001						

INDEX

A

B